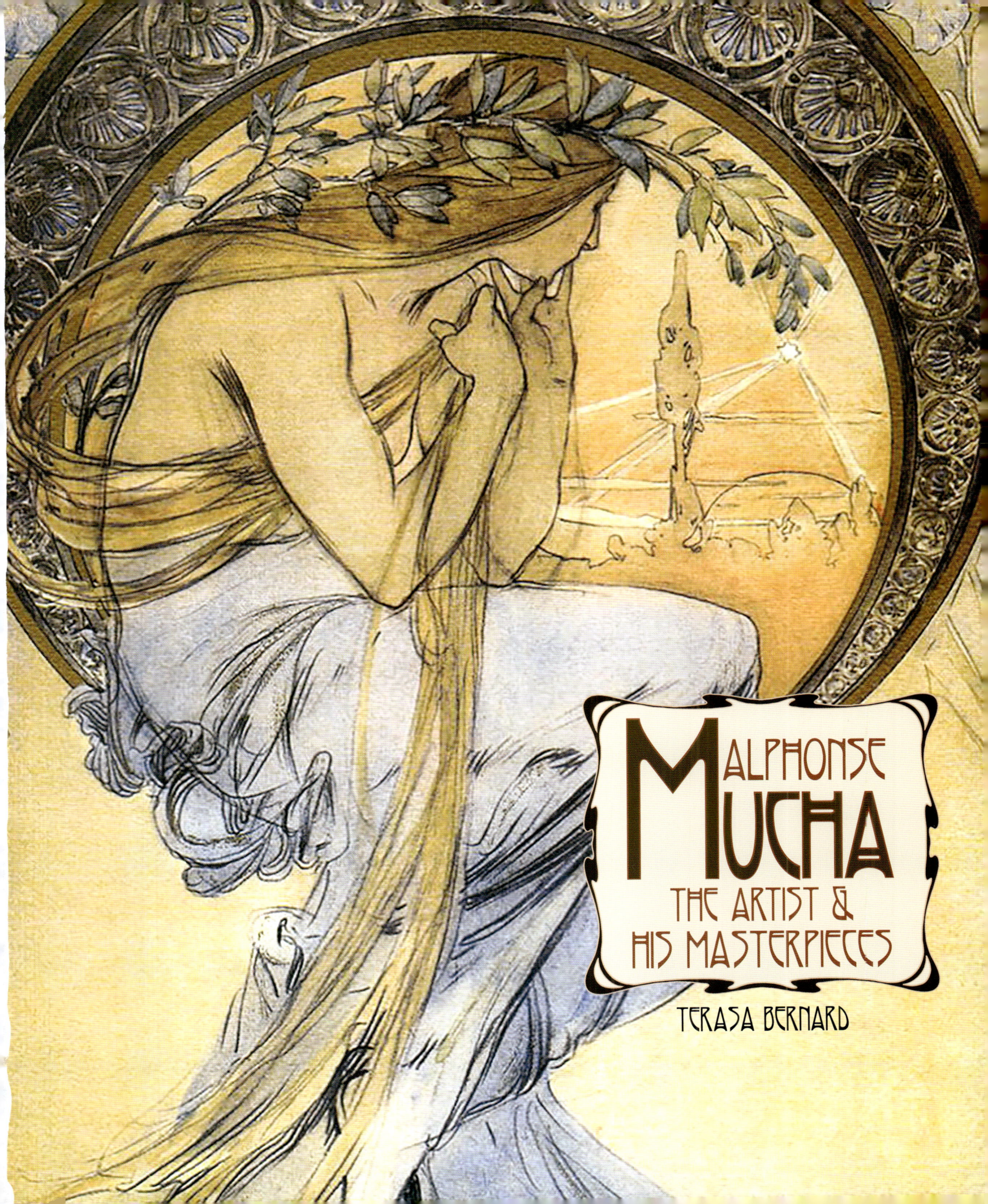

Malphonse Mucha

The Artist & His Masterpieces

Terasa Bernard

CONTENTS

Hinkler Pty Ltd 2025
45–55 Fairchild Street
Heatherton Victoria 3202 Australia
www.hinkler.com

ISBN: 978-1-4889-7508-0

Printed in China

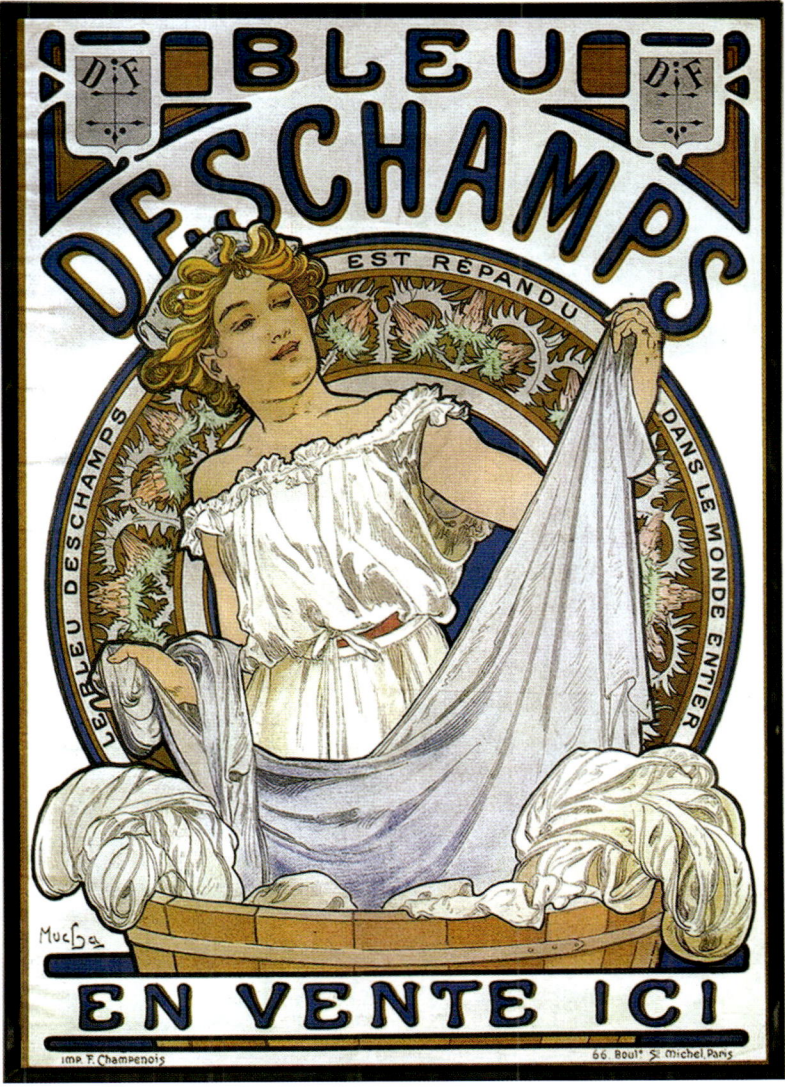

Advertising poster for **Bleu Deschamps** (July 1890).

[TITLE PAGE] Study for **The Arts: Poetry** (1898).

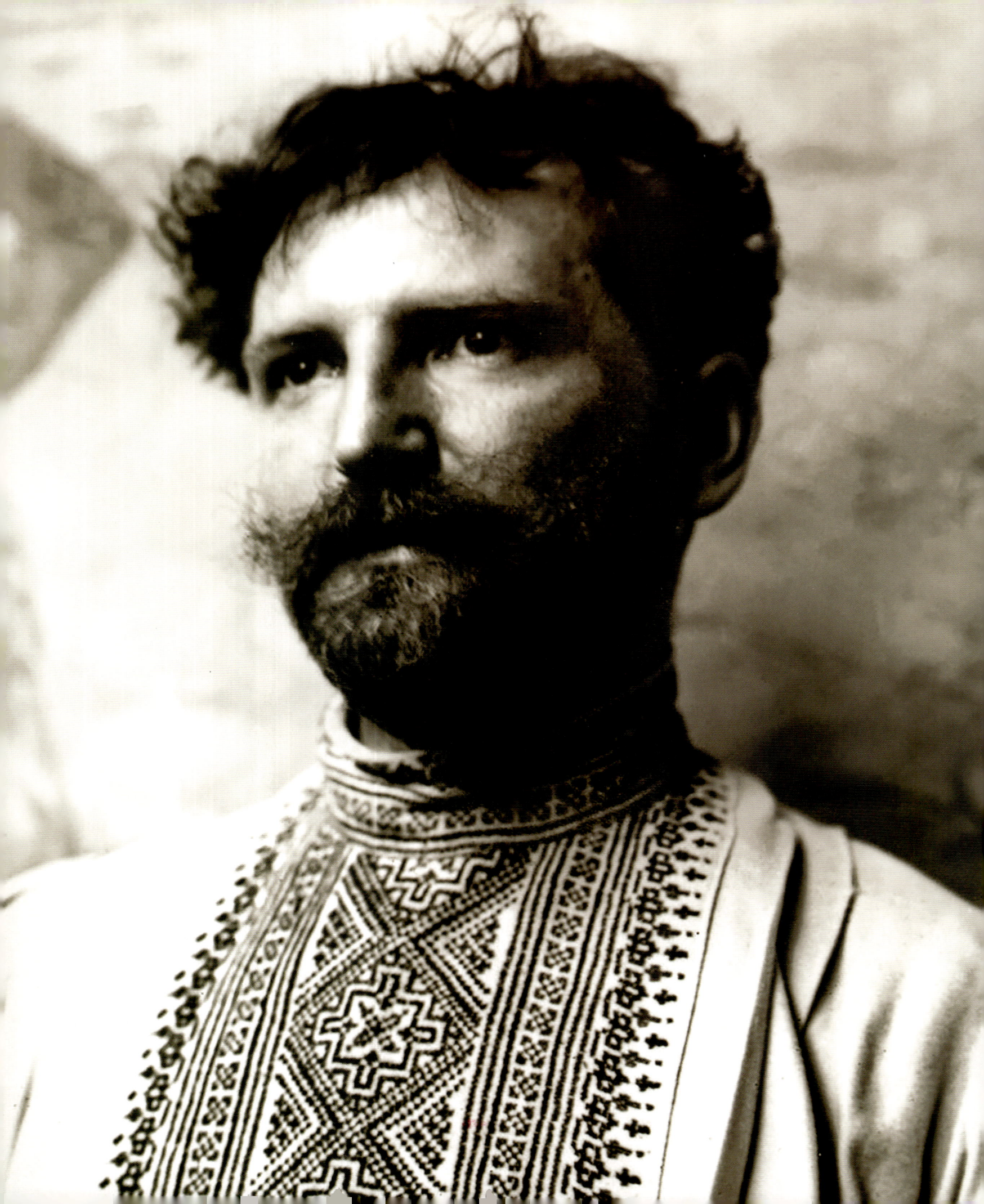

INTRODUCTION
WHO WAS ALPHONSE MUCHA?

ALPHONSE MUCHA WAS A CELEBRATED Czech illustrator, painter, and graphic artist, born on July 24, 1860, in Ivančice, a small town in the South Moravian region of the Czech Republic. He is best known for his pivotal role in shaping the aesthetics of the Art Nouveau movement at the turn of the 20th century. His work is renowned for its distinctive style, characterized by elaborate patterns, ornamental elements, and the evocative use of color. His artistic portfolio spanned a diverse array of mediums, from advertising posters and decorative panels to jewelry, murals, and theatrical sets. In his early teens, he showed an innate affinity for art, producing church decorations and portraits for local patrons. He pursued music for a time, performing as a chorister at the Cathedral of St. Peter and Paul, but his true passion was for art. Despite his undeniable talent, however, he faced financial constraints that impeded his formal art education. His first breakthrough came when he started working for Count Karl Khuen Belasi of Mikulov, who, recognizing Mucha's potential, sponsored his studies at the Munich Academy of Fine Arts. Belasi was a painter and a supporter of the arts, and he took Mucha on several excursions around Europe to see art and meet contemporary artists.

Mucha's life took a transformative turn in 1888 when he moved to Paris, then the epicenter of the world's art scene. Here, he studied at the Académie Julian and later at the Académie Colarossi, immersing himself in the city's vibrant artistic culture. His career skyrocketed in 1894 when he created a lithographed poster for the play Gismonda, starring the legendary actress Sarah Bernhardt. The poster, characterized by its innovative style and exquisite detail, epitomized the Art Nouveau aesthetic; it was a resounding success, leading to a long-term collaboration with Bernhardt and bringing Mucha to fame almost overnight.

His distinctive style, known as *le style Mucha,* became synonymous with the Art Nouveau movement. His art was distinguished by its sensuous lines, complex detail, and the recurring use of beautiful women surrounded by halos and intricate floral motifs. This style was not just confined to paintings and posters but permeated every art form he engaged in, marking him as an artist of remarkable versatility.

Throughout the 1890s and the early 1900s, Mucha's fame soared. His work on various projects, including stage designs for Sarah Bernhardt's theatre productions, illustrations for books, and designs for jewelry, furniture, and interior decoration, showcased his adaptability and creativity.

Despite his success in France, he remained deeply attached to his Czech roots. He believed in the power of art as a vehicle for national expression and was dedicated to the cause of Czech independence from the Austro-Hungarian Empire. His magnum opus, The Slav Epic, a series of 20 large-scale paintings depicting the history of the Slavic people, was a testament to his love for his homeland. He dedicated a significant part of his life to this project, which was completed in 1928 and donated to the city of Prague. Later in his life, however, his nationalist art and beliefs made him a target during the Nazi occupation of Czechoslovakia during World War II. He was arrested and interrogated by the Gestapo in 1939. The ordeal severely affected his health, and he died on July 14, 1939, mere months after his arrest.

Alphonse Mucha's artistic legacy lives on, influencing and inspiring generations of artists and designers. His vision of art as a tool for upliftment, inspiration, and joy remains as relevant today as it was over a century ago.

[OPPOSITE PAGE] *Self-portrait wearing a Russian shirt (rubashka) at the studio in rue de la Grande Chaumière, Paris* (c. 1892). Mucha Trust Collection.

“*The purpose of my work was never to destroy but always to create . . .*”

~ ALPHONSE MUCHA

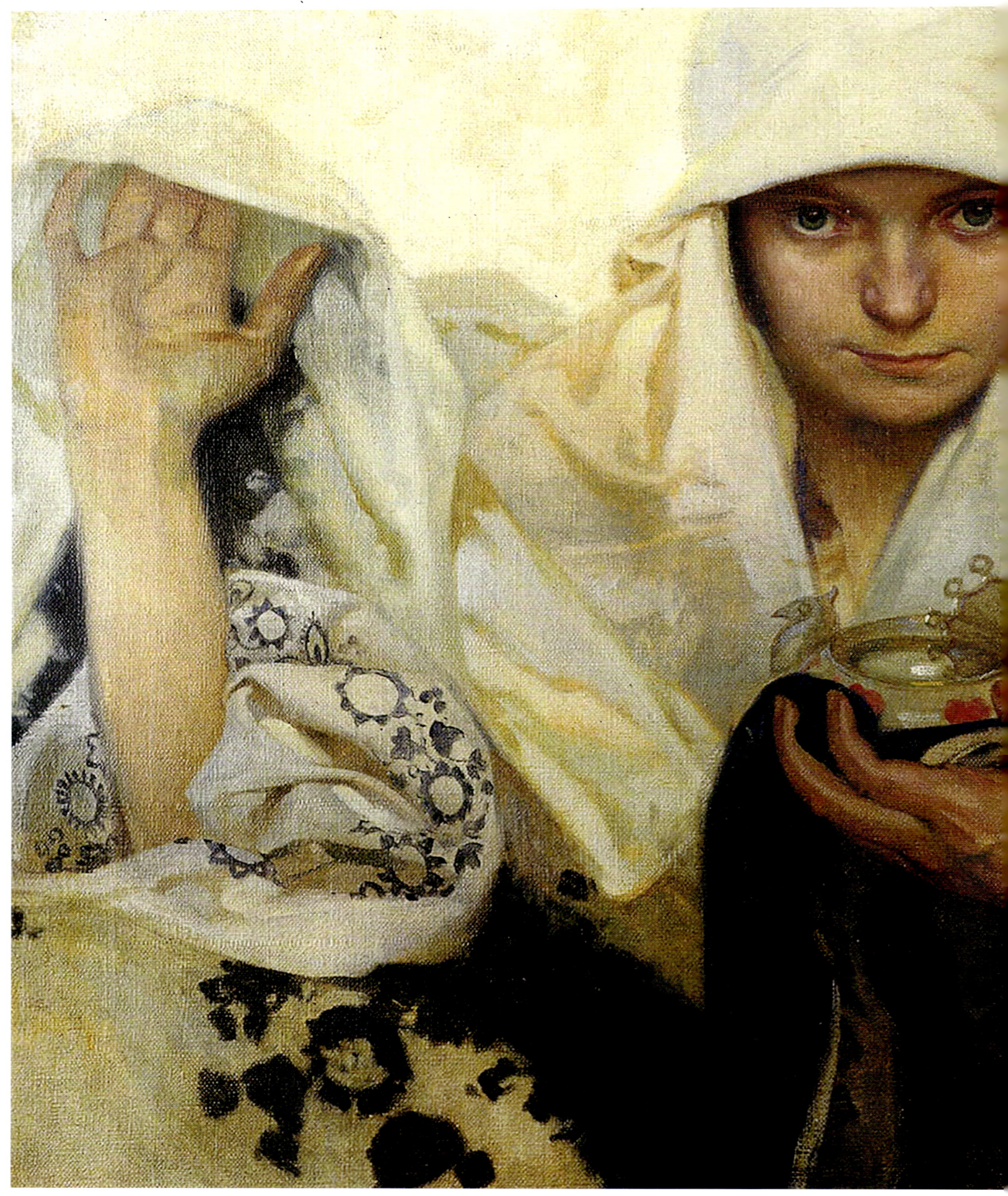

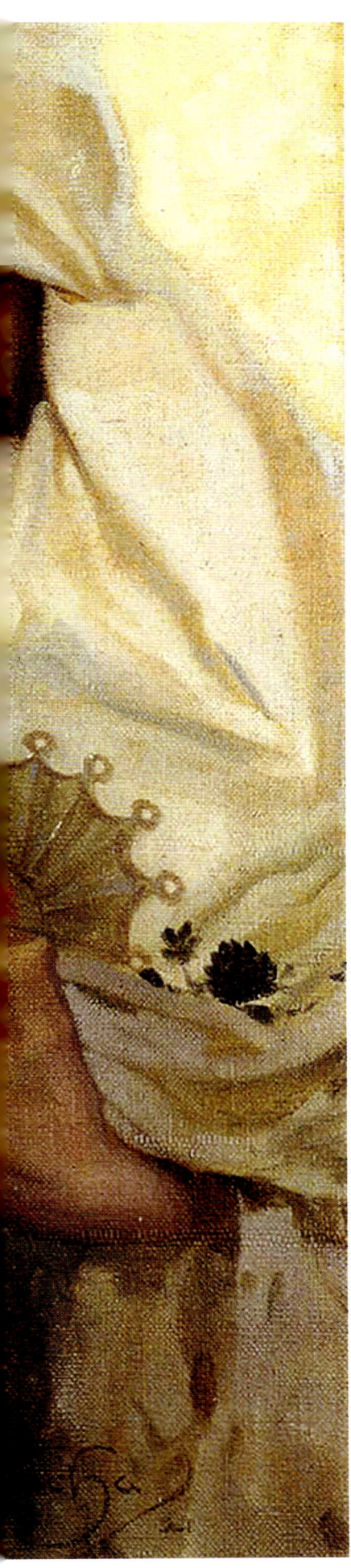

THE PIONEER OF ART NOUVEAU

Alphonse Mucha took his remarkable skills as painter, graphic designer, illustrator, and craftsman and applied them to a wide range of advertising images, theater posters, and decorative works, as well as ventures in a host of other media and methods. His work became so linked with the° ia Belle Époque–period movement of Art Nouveau, that in Paris it was simply called *le style Mucha*.

> "*What is it, Art Nouveau? . . . Art can never be new.*"

~ ALPHONSE MUCHA

[RIGHT] **Fate** (1920). Oil on canvas. Mucha Museum, Prague.

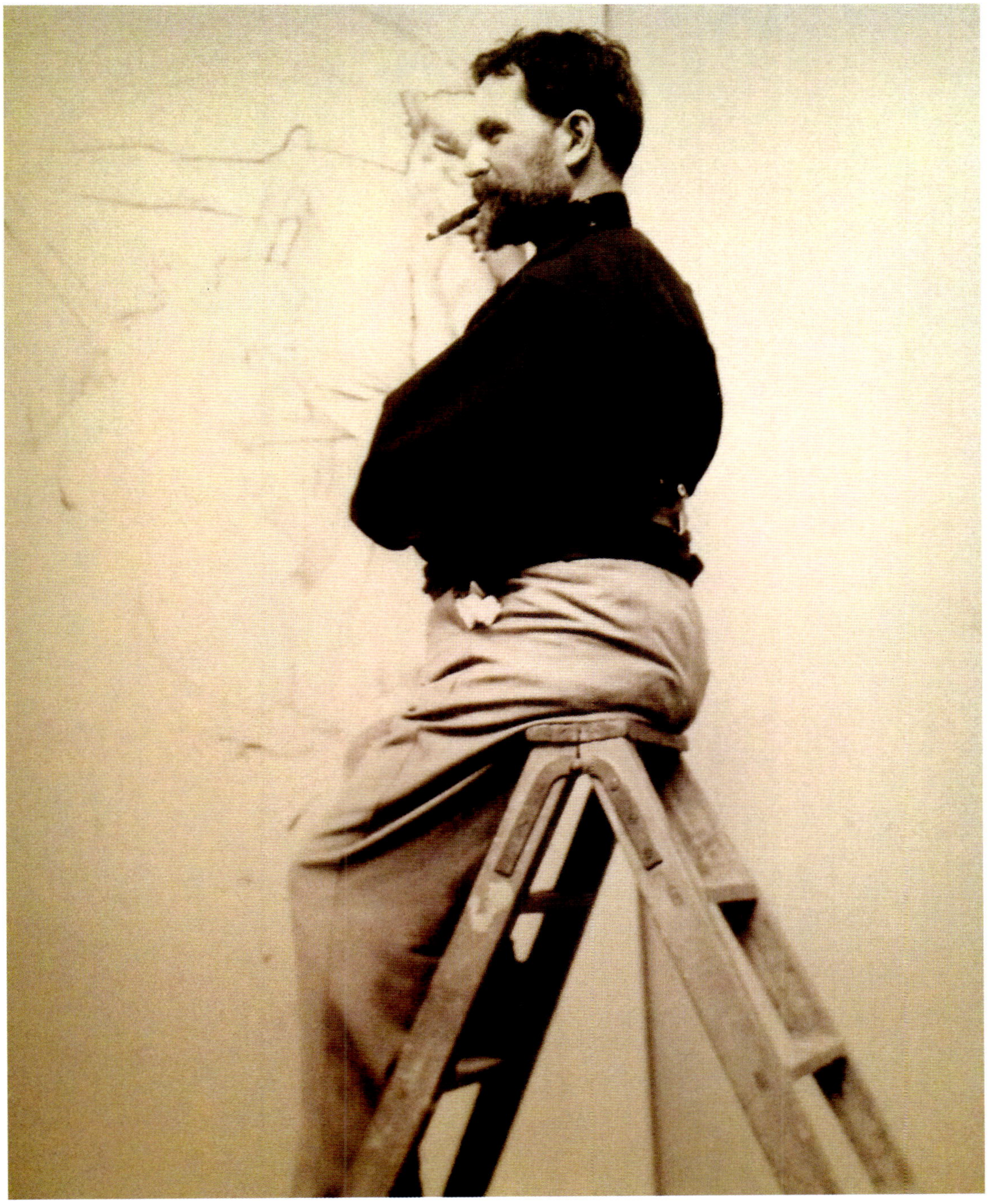

Self-Portrait, working on the cartoon of the poster Imprimerie Cassan Fils (1896).

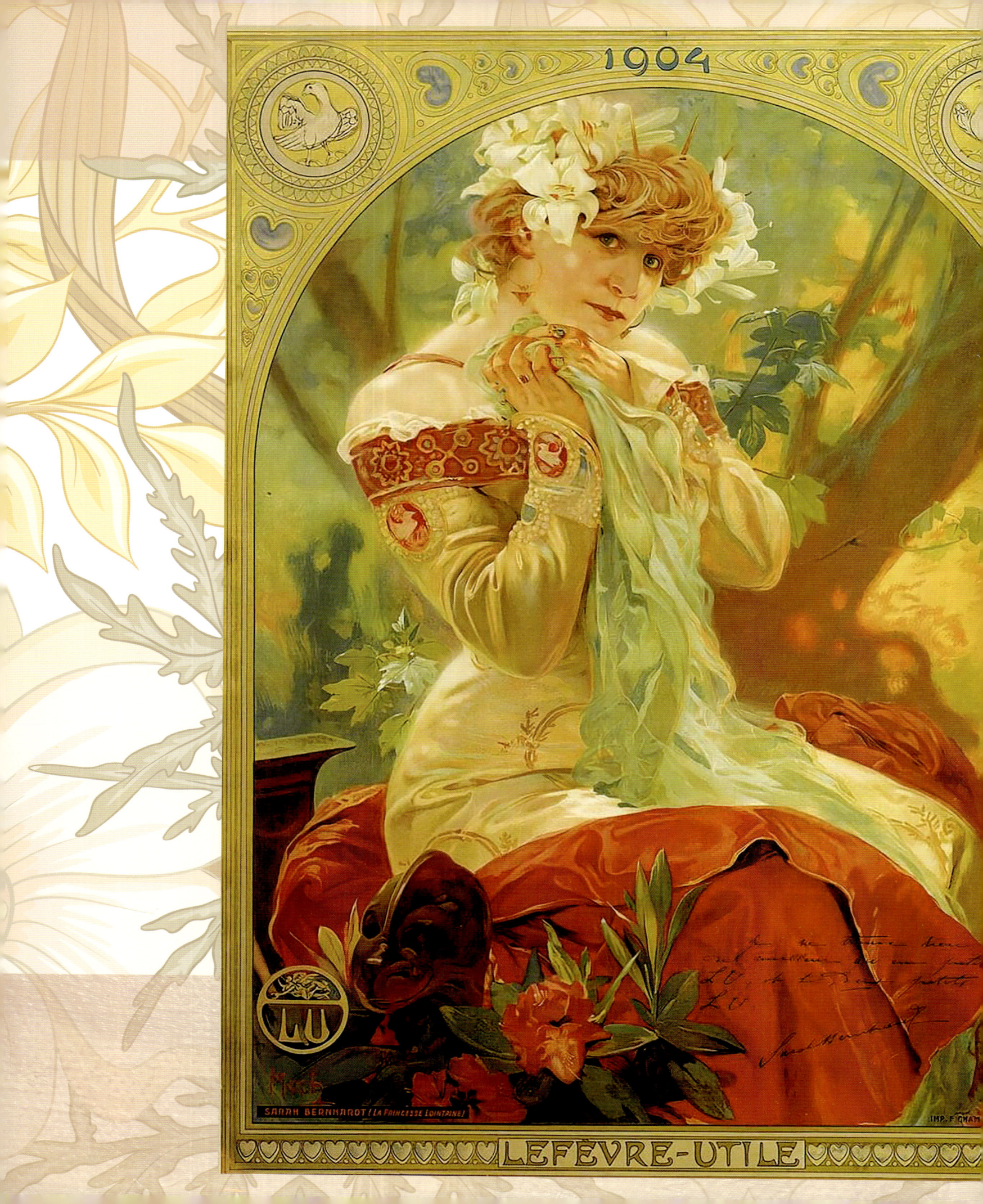

POSTERS & PRINTS

BETWEEN 1895 AND 1900, Mucha's career soared as he produced a series of remarkable posters that would become emblematic of the Art Nouveau movement. During this prolific period, he created iconic posters for various events and products, such as Sarah Bernhardt's plays and JOB cigarette papers. They gained immense popularity for their distinctive style, which combined ornate, intricate details with soft, flowing lines. His stunning use of color, delicate patterns, and depictions of elegant women, often surrounded by natural elements like flowers and leaves, define these works. They not only captured the essence of Art Nouveau, but also revolutionized the world of advertising.

Sarah Bernhardt – La Princesse Lointaine – Lefèvre-Utile (1903). **Color lithograph.**

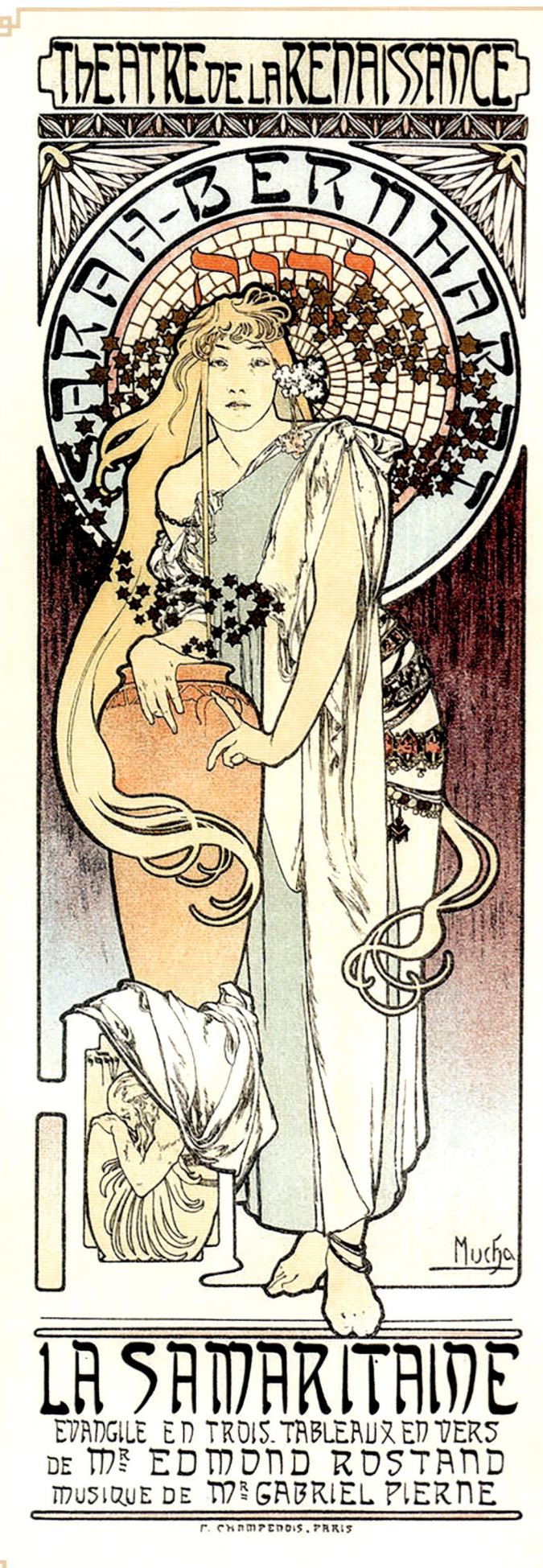

MUCHA & BERNHARDT

It was Mucha's collaboration with the famed French actress Sarah Bernhardt that propelled the artist—and his innovative new style—into the public eye. In 1895, he was commissioned to create a poster for *Gismonda*, Bernhardt's new play opening at the Théâtre de la Renaissance. She loved the result, and these two talented people went on to work together on several other poster projects. Their collaboration helped enhance the careers of both. Mucha essentially crafted an elegant persona for the actress, and his success with her paved the way for his future commercial work. In his creation of Bernhardt's *Gismonda*, Mucha changed how the people of Paris viewed the posters slapped on walls about the city. As the Mucha Foundation notes, "The effect created was astonishing and the poster so popular with the Parisian public that collectors bribed bill stickers to obtain them or simply went out at night and, using razors, cut them down from the hoardings."

"*Gismonda, the poster which Mucha created, was to revolutionize poster design. The long narrow shape, the subtle pastel colors and the 'halo' effect around the subject's head were to remain features of Mucha's posters throughout his life. Most importantly, these elements combined with the stillness of the near life-size figure to introduce a note of dignity and sobriety to what had been up to then garish street-art, qualities which were quite startling in their novelty.*"

~ THE MUCHA FOUNDATION

Poster for **La Samaritaine** (1898). Color lithograph.

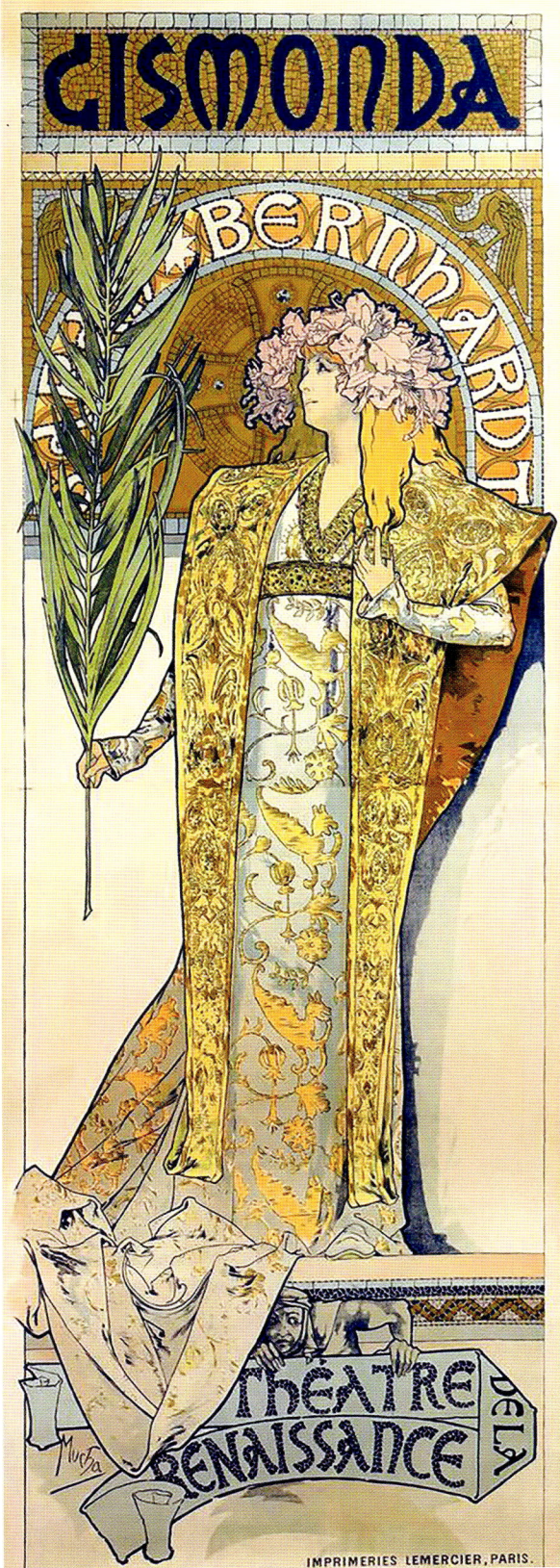

Poster for *Gismonda* (1894). Color lithograph.

In this groundbreaking poster, Bernhardt is shown in the costume of an exotic Byzantine woman that she wore in the last act of the play. So pleased with it, she used the same image for a poster for her 1896 tour in America.

[RIGHT] Poster for Bernhardt's *American Tour* (1896). Color lithograph.

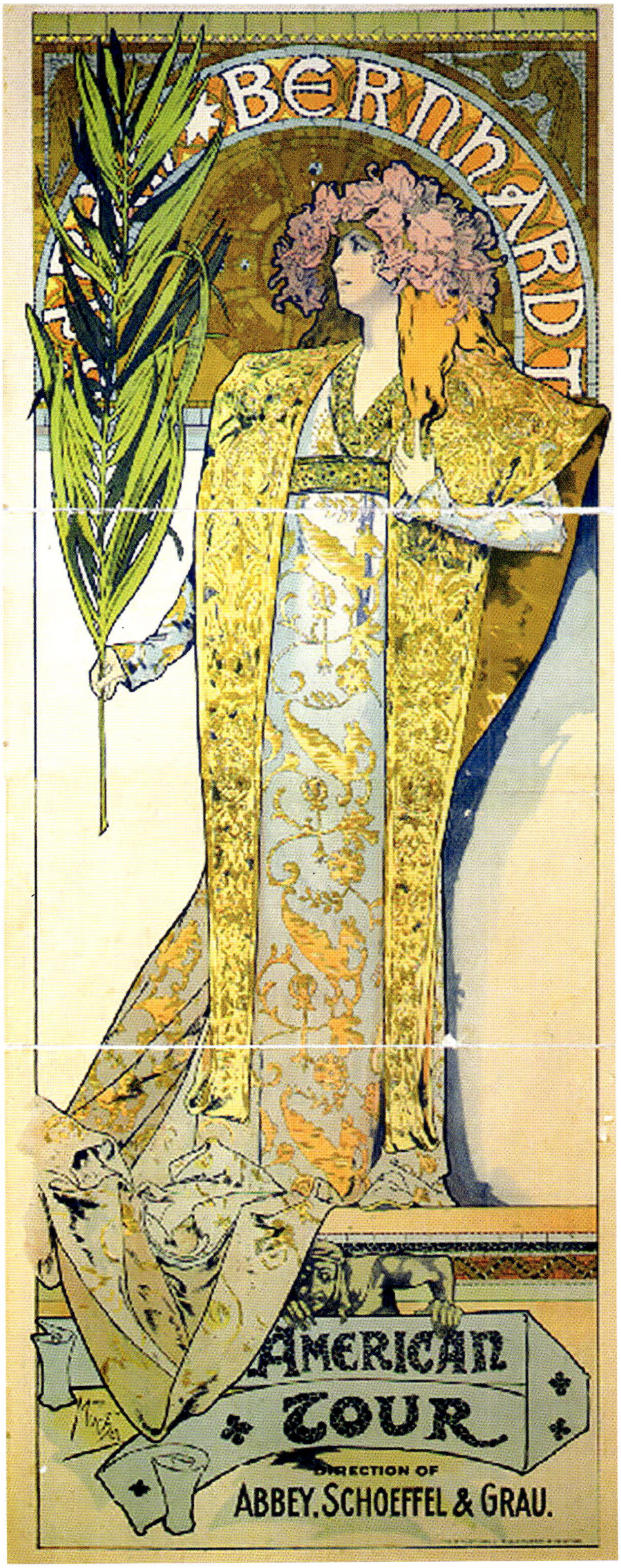

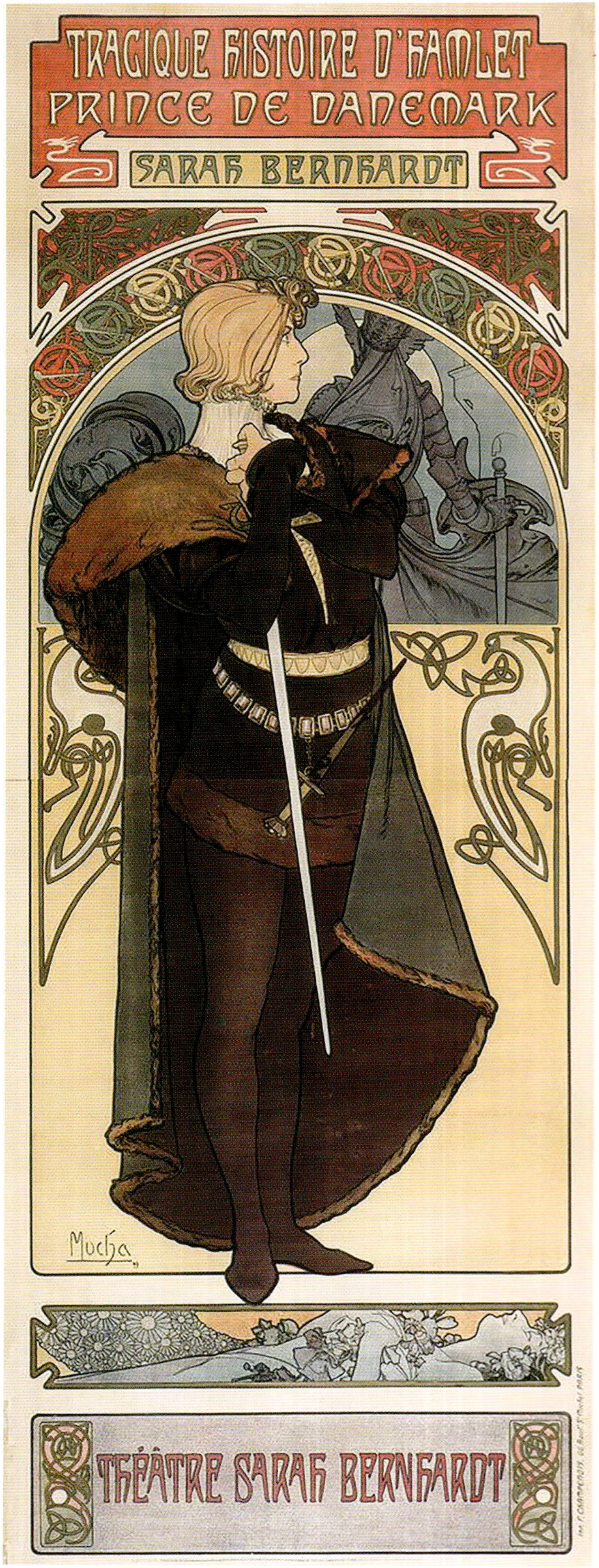

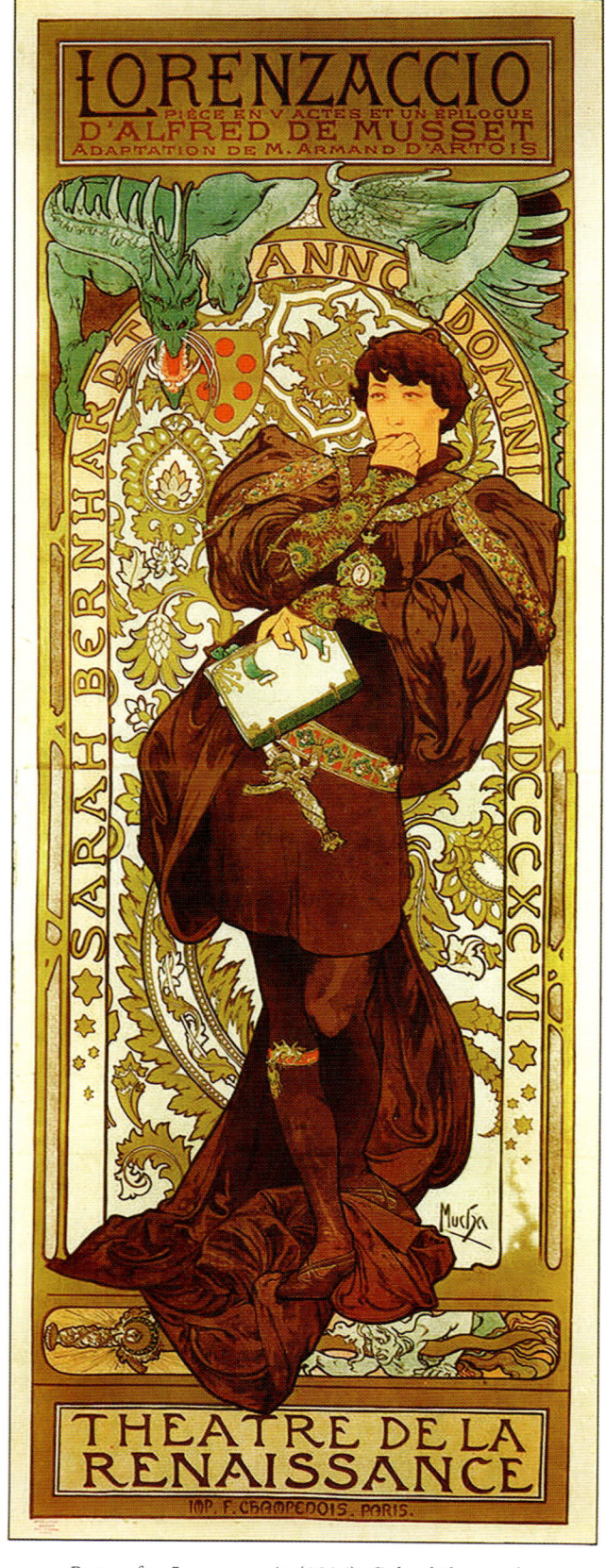

[LEFT]
*Sarah Bernhardt
in* **Hamlet** (1899).
Color lithograph.

[OPPOSITE PAGE]
*Sarah Bernhardt as La Princesse
Lointaine* for *La Plume* magazine:
(1897). Color lithograph.

Poster for **Lorenzaccio** (1896). Color lithograph.

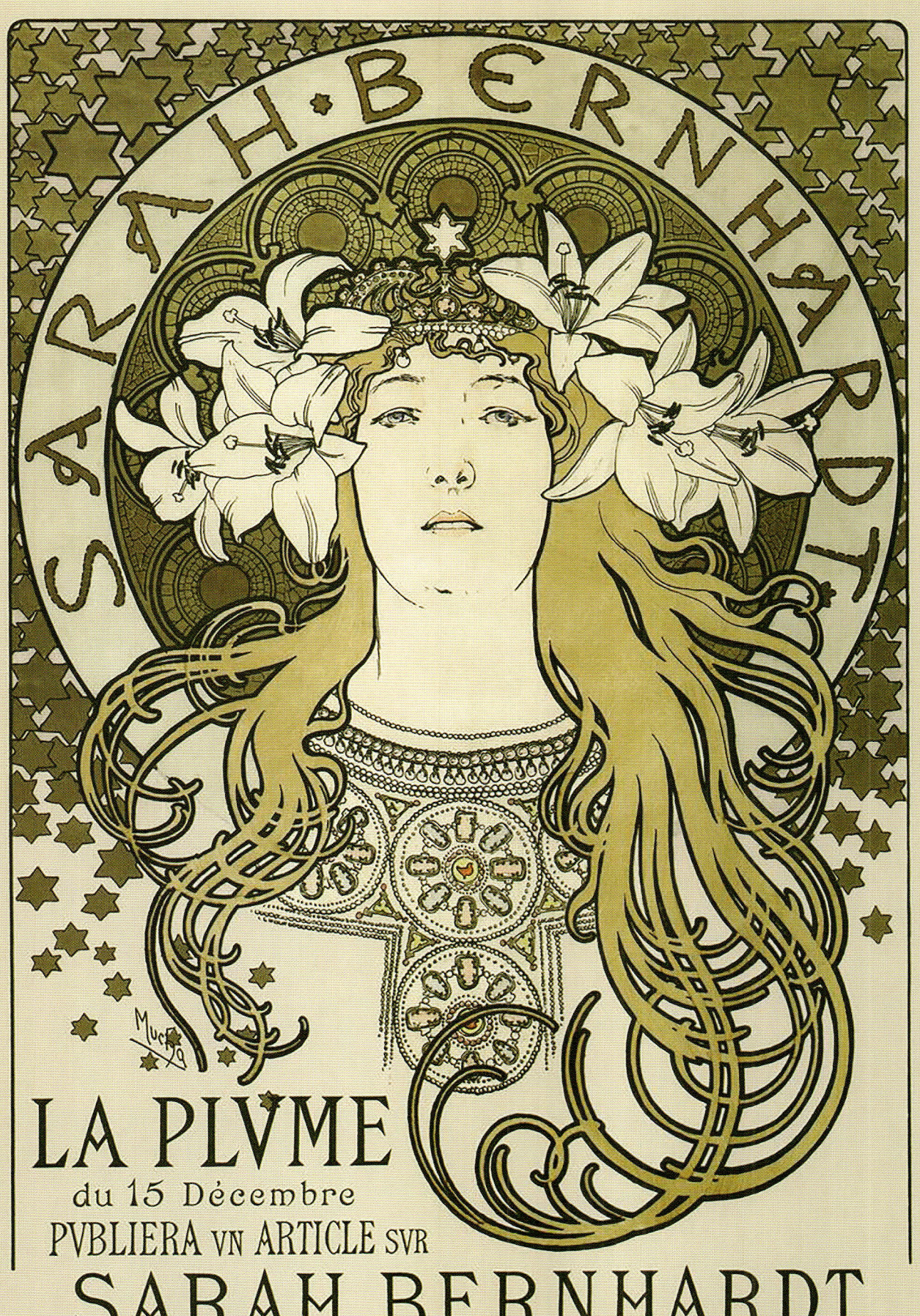

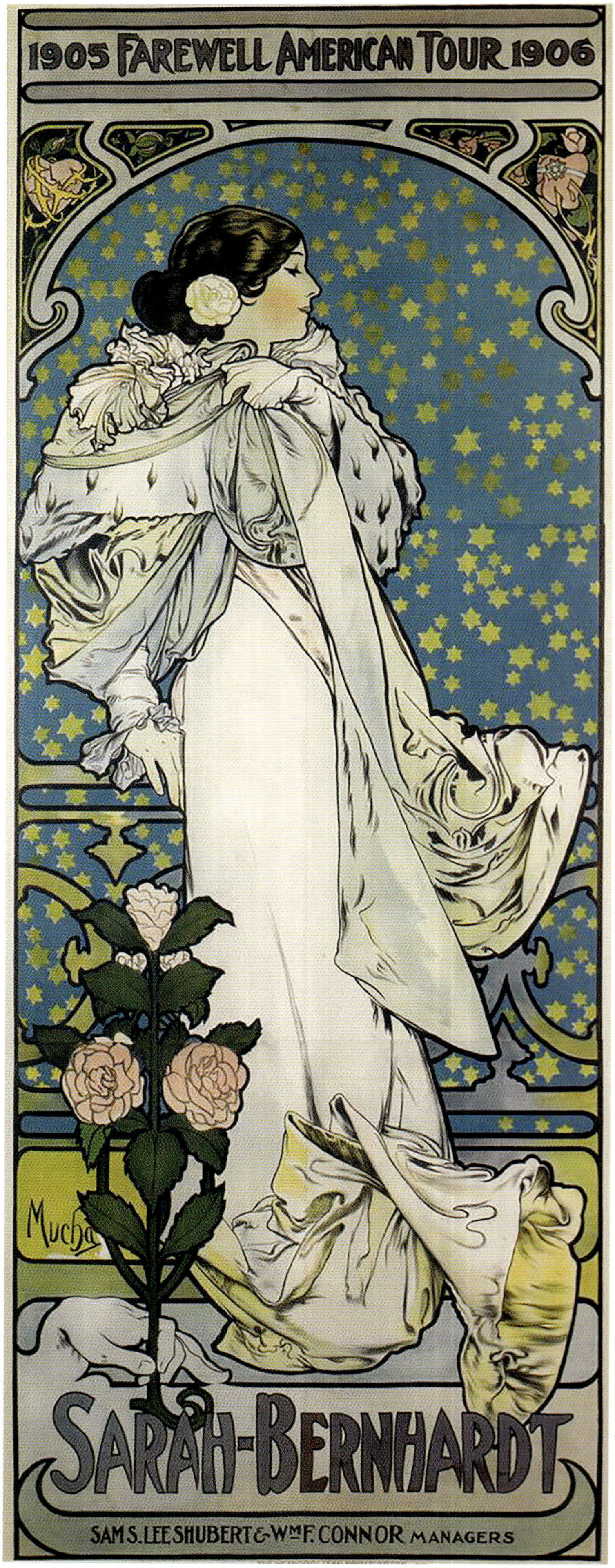

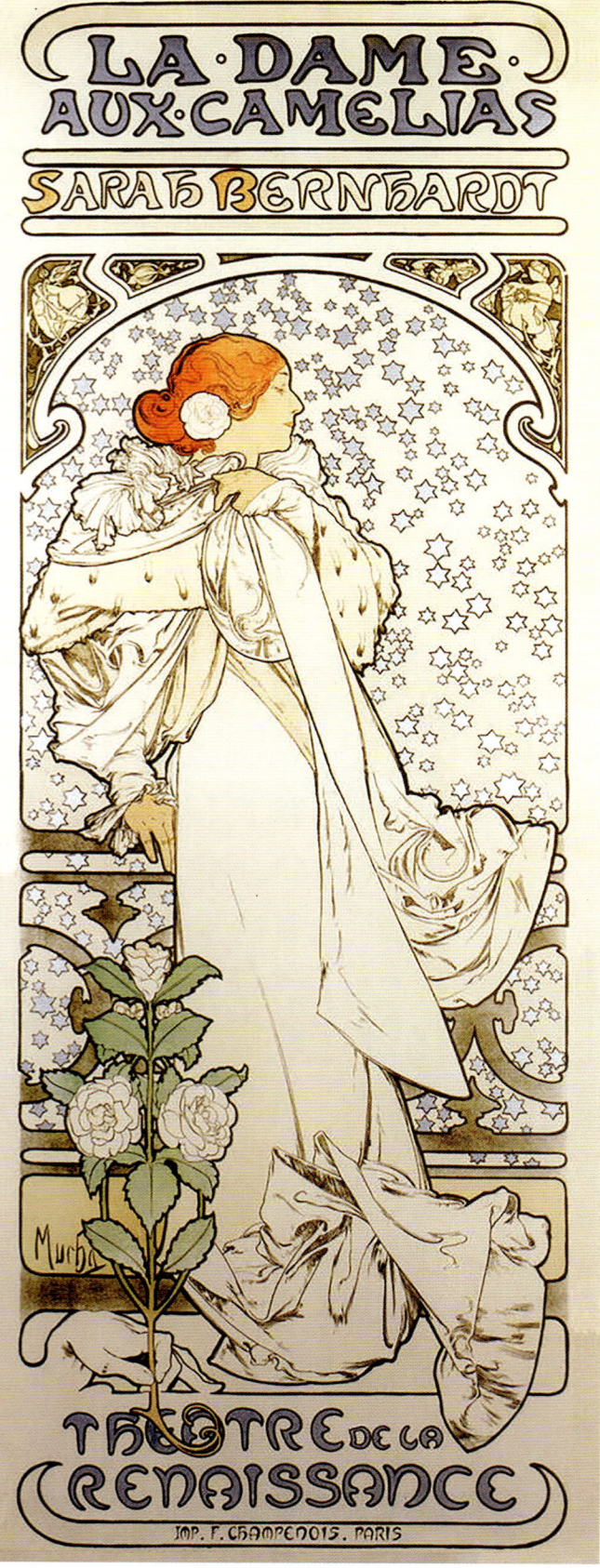

La Dame aux Camélias (1896). Color lithograph.

*One of Bernhardt's favorites, this poster was reused
for her American tours in 1905–1906 and 1910–1911,
with a changed color palette.*

[LEFT] *La Dame aux Camélias* (c. 1905–10) Color lithograph.

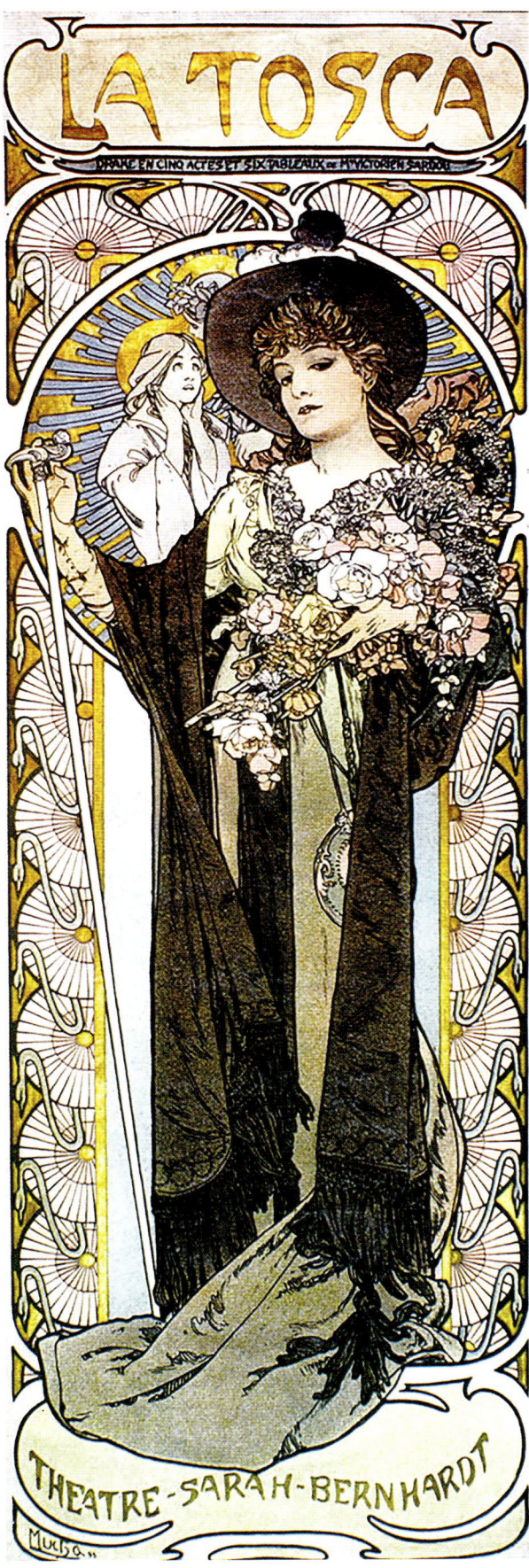

Poster for **La Tosca** (1899). Color lithograph.

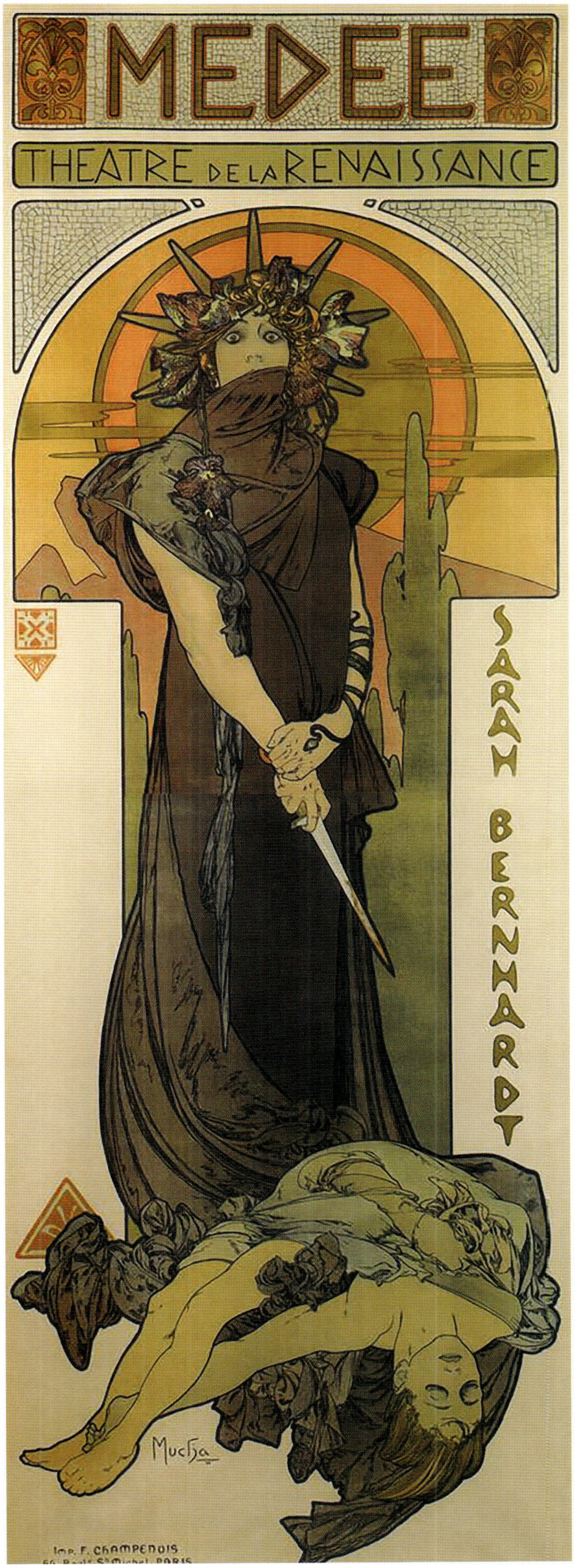

[RIGHT] Poster for **Médée** (1898). Color lithograph.

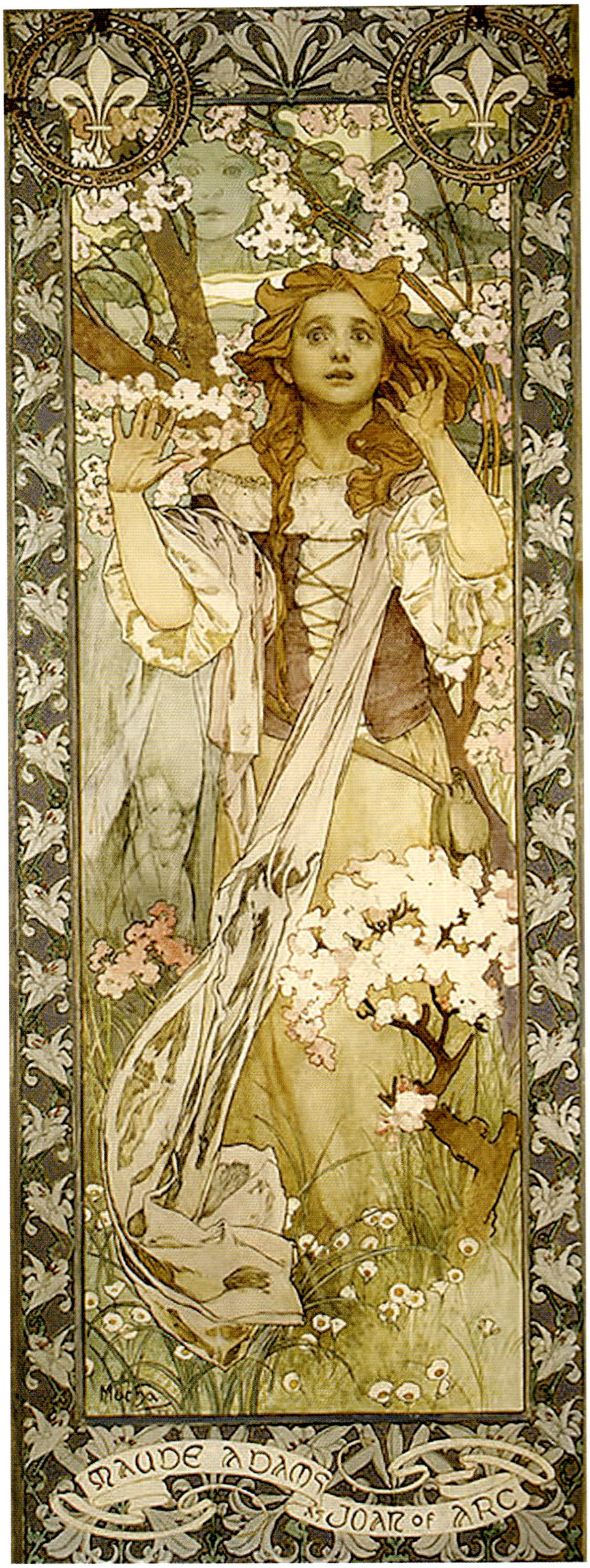

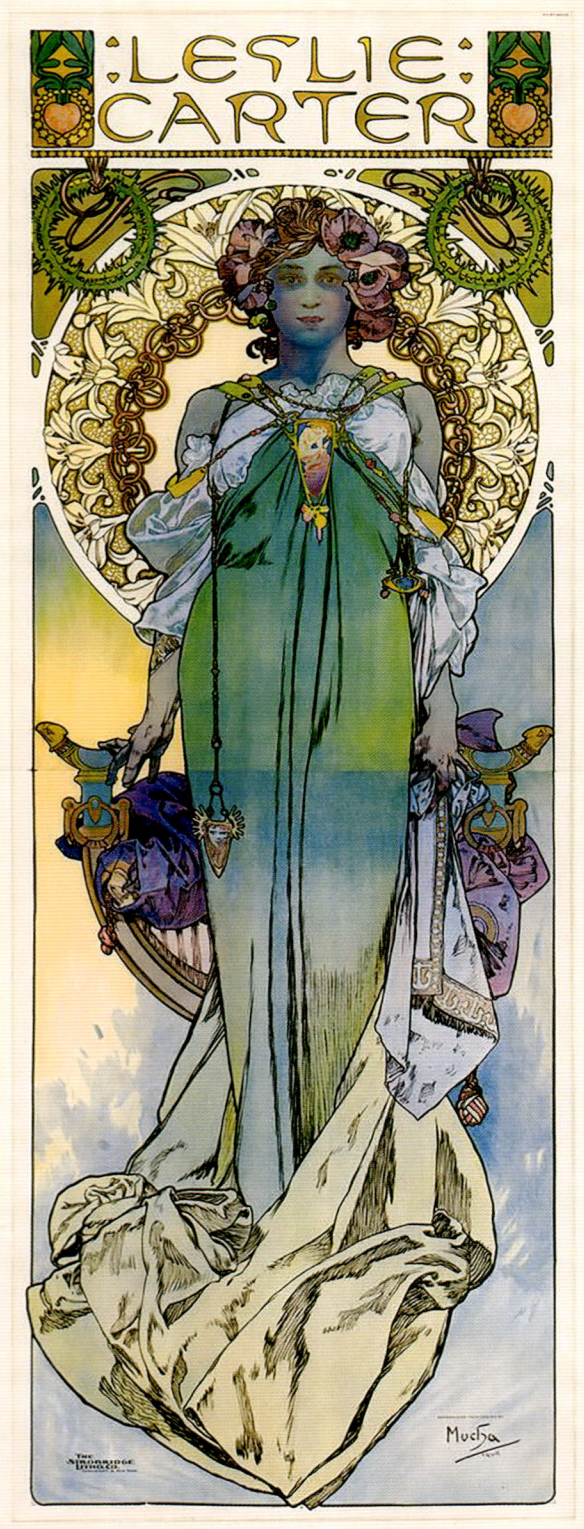

Poster for **Leslie Carter** (1908). Color lithograph.

[LEFT] Poster for **Maude Adams** (1908). Color lithograph.

[OPPOSITE PAGE]
Poster for **Princess Hyacinth** (1911). Color lithograph.

Mucha created promotional works for actresses other than Sarah Bernhardt, including Maude Adams, a star of the fin de siècle *theater, American actress Mrs. Leslie Carter, and Andula Sedláčková in the title role of Oskar Nedbal's ballet-pantomime* Princess Hyacinth.

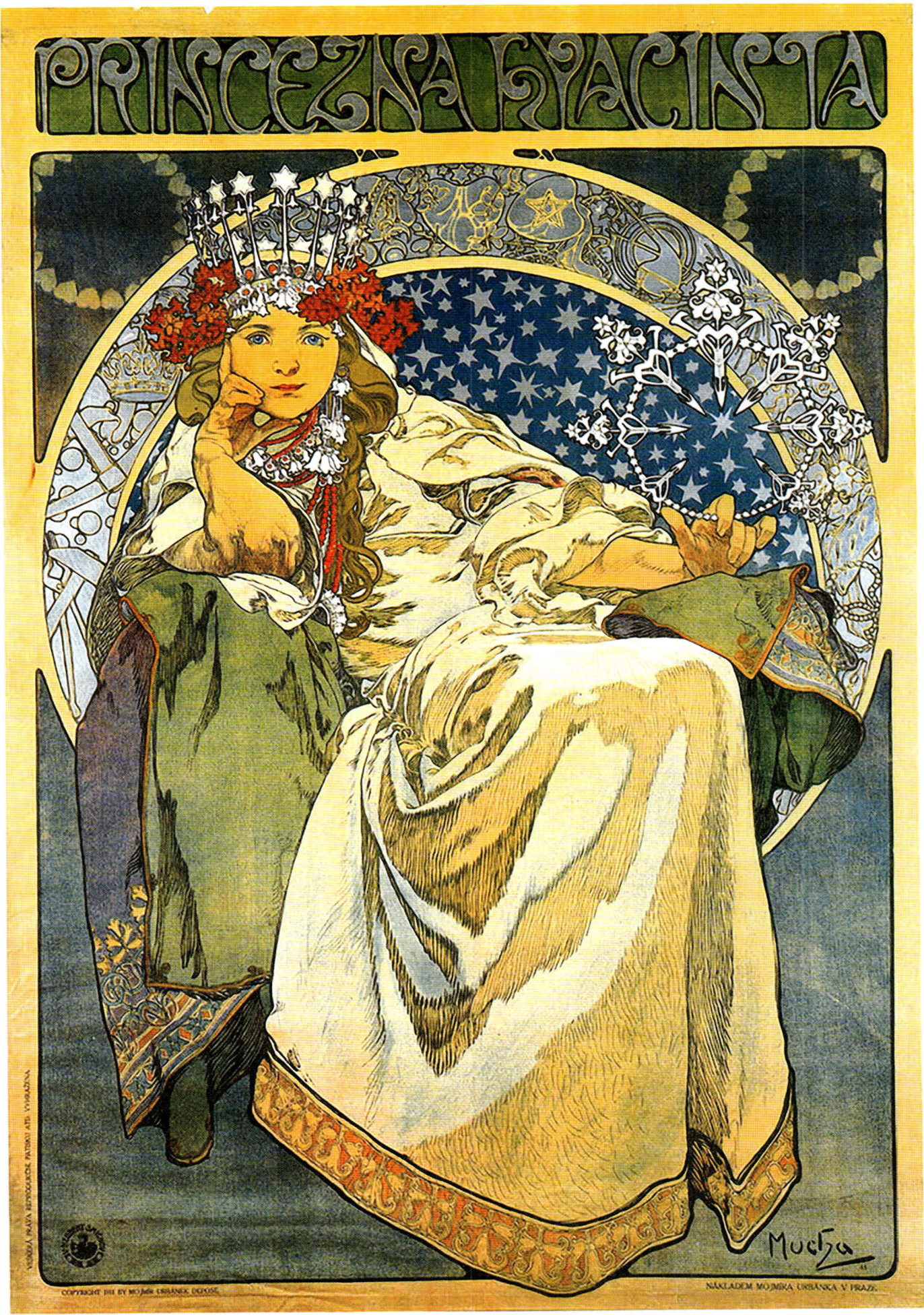

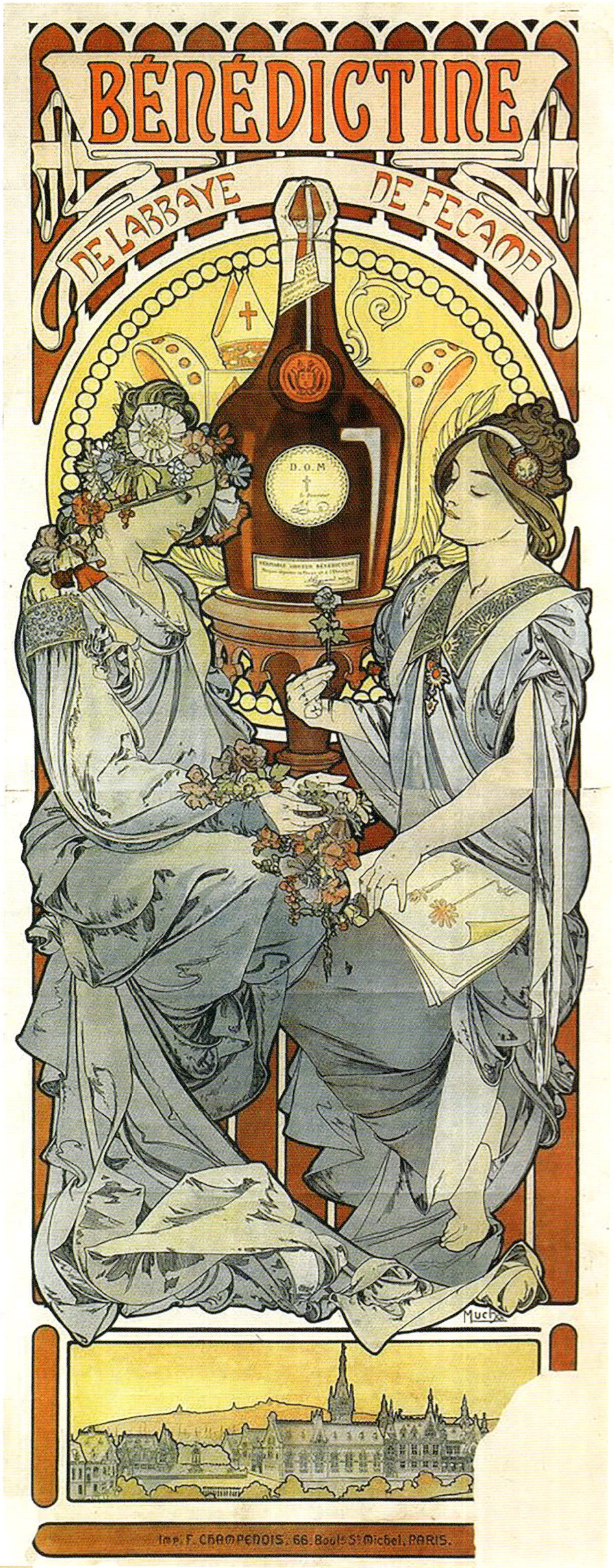
BÉNÉDICTINE
DE L'ABBAYE DE FECAMP
D.O.M
Mucha
IMP. F. CHAMPENOIS, 66, Boul. St Michel, PARIS.

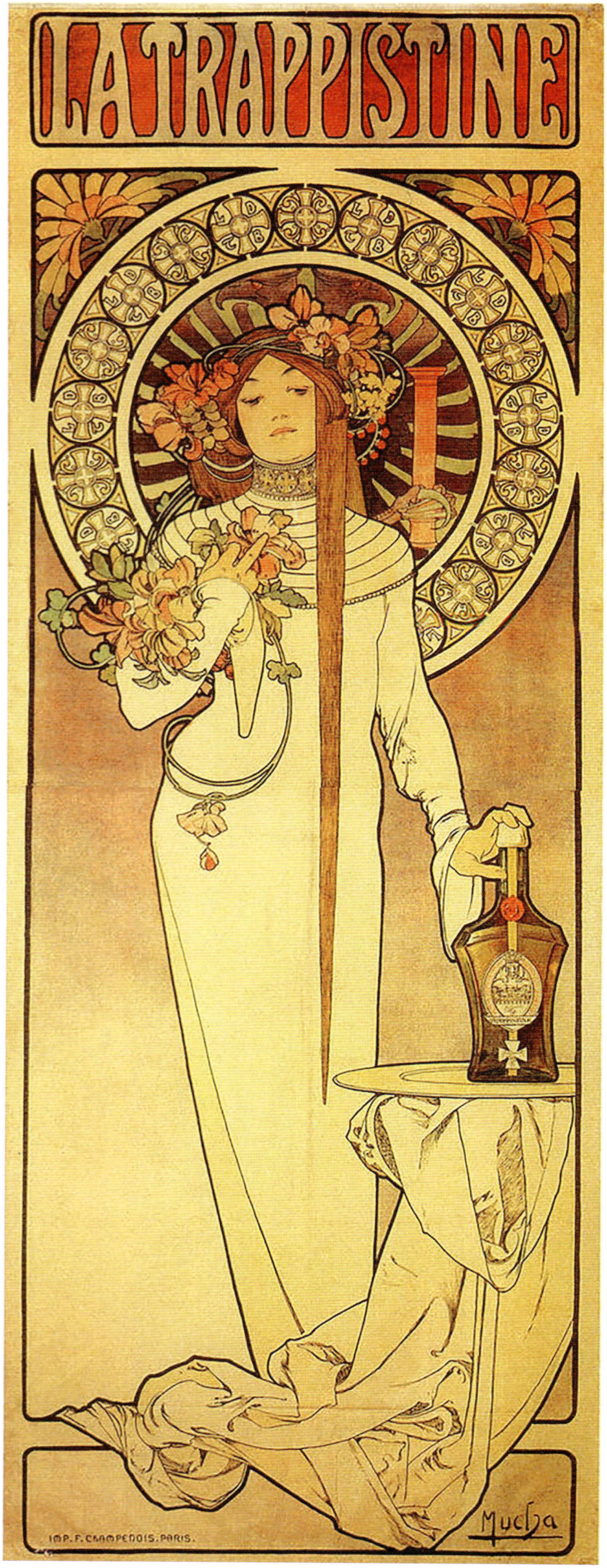
LA TRAPPISTINE
Mucha
IMP. F. CHAMPENOIS, PARIS.

THE ART OF ADVERTISING ALCOHOL

The success of the Bernhardt theater posters brought Mucha commissions for advertising posters, including posters for several companies that produced and sold alcoholic beverages, including Champagne Ruinart, Bières de la Meuse, and Moët-Chandon champagne.

[RIGHT]
Advertising poster for
Champagne Heidsieck
(1901). Color lithograph.

[OPPOSITE PAGE RIGHT]
Advertising poster for
La Trappistine (1897).
Color lithograph.

[OPPOSITE PAGE LEFT]
Advertising poster for
Bénédictine (c. 1898).
Color lithograph.

[BELOW]
Vin des Incas (1897). Color lithograph.

This poster, an advertisement for coca-fortified wine, shows an Inca man gesturing to a goddess of the Incas to hand him the coca, but she refuses, cradling a bottle of coca wine to herself.

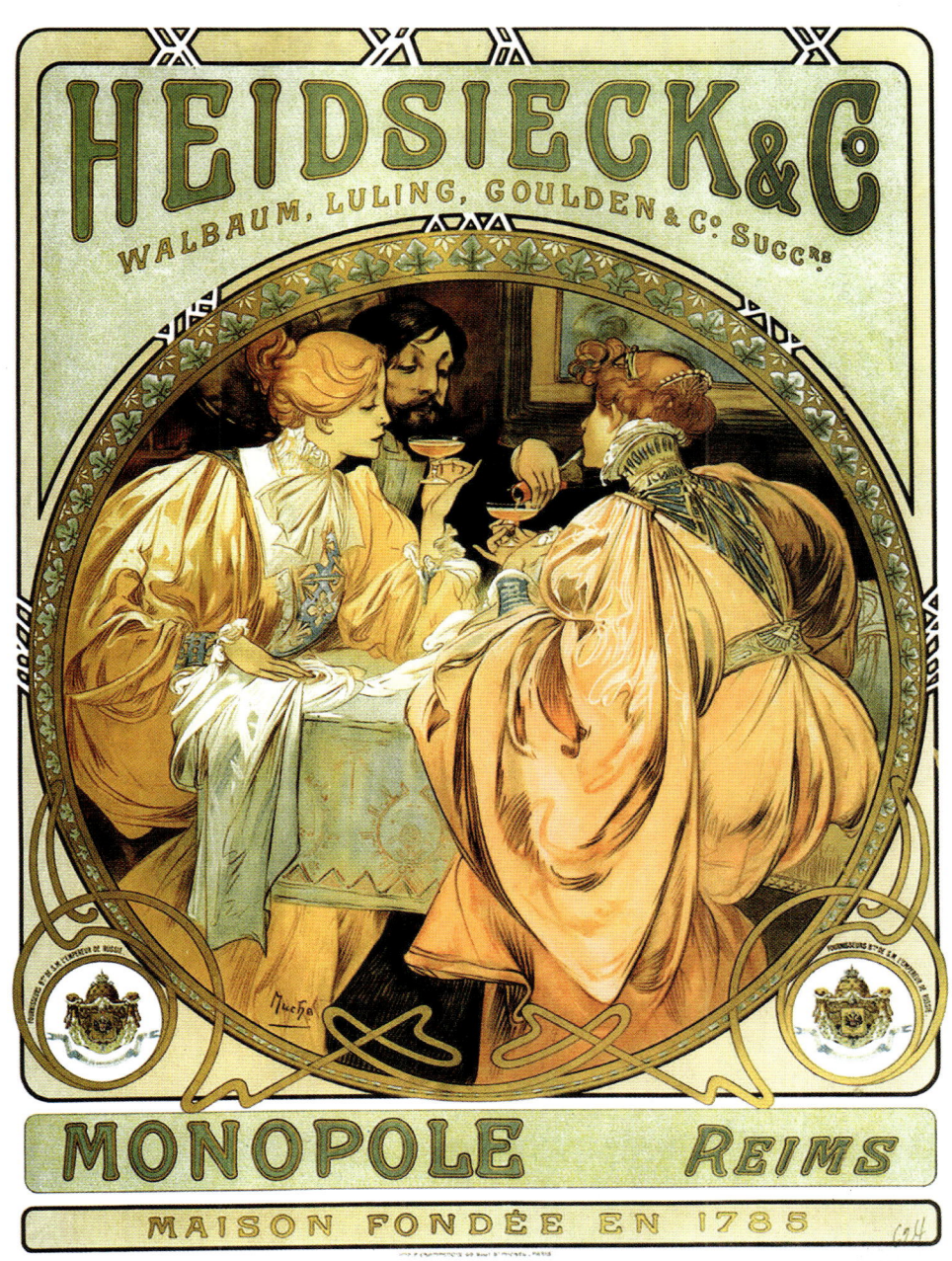

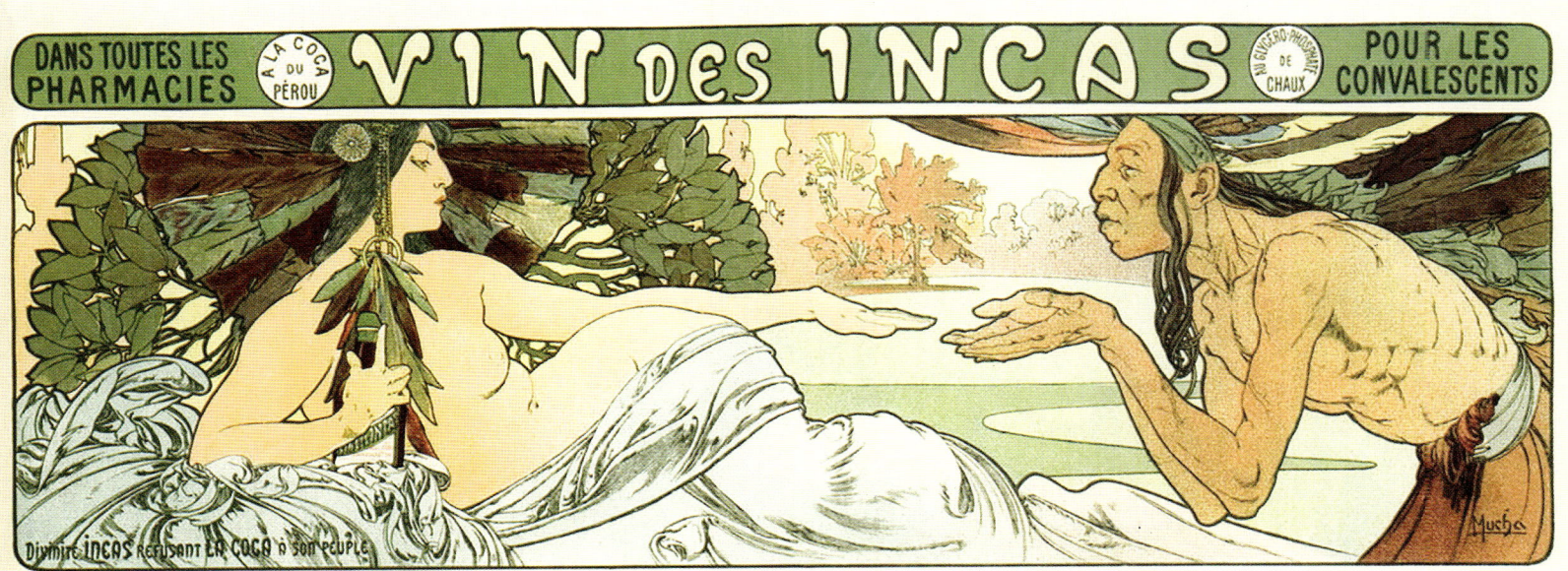

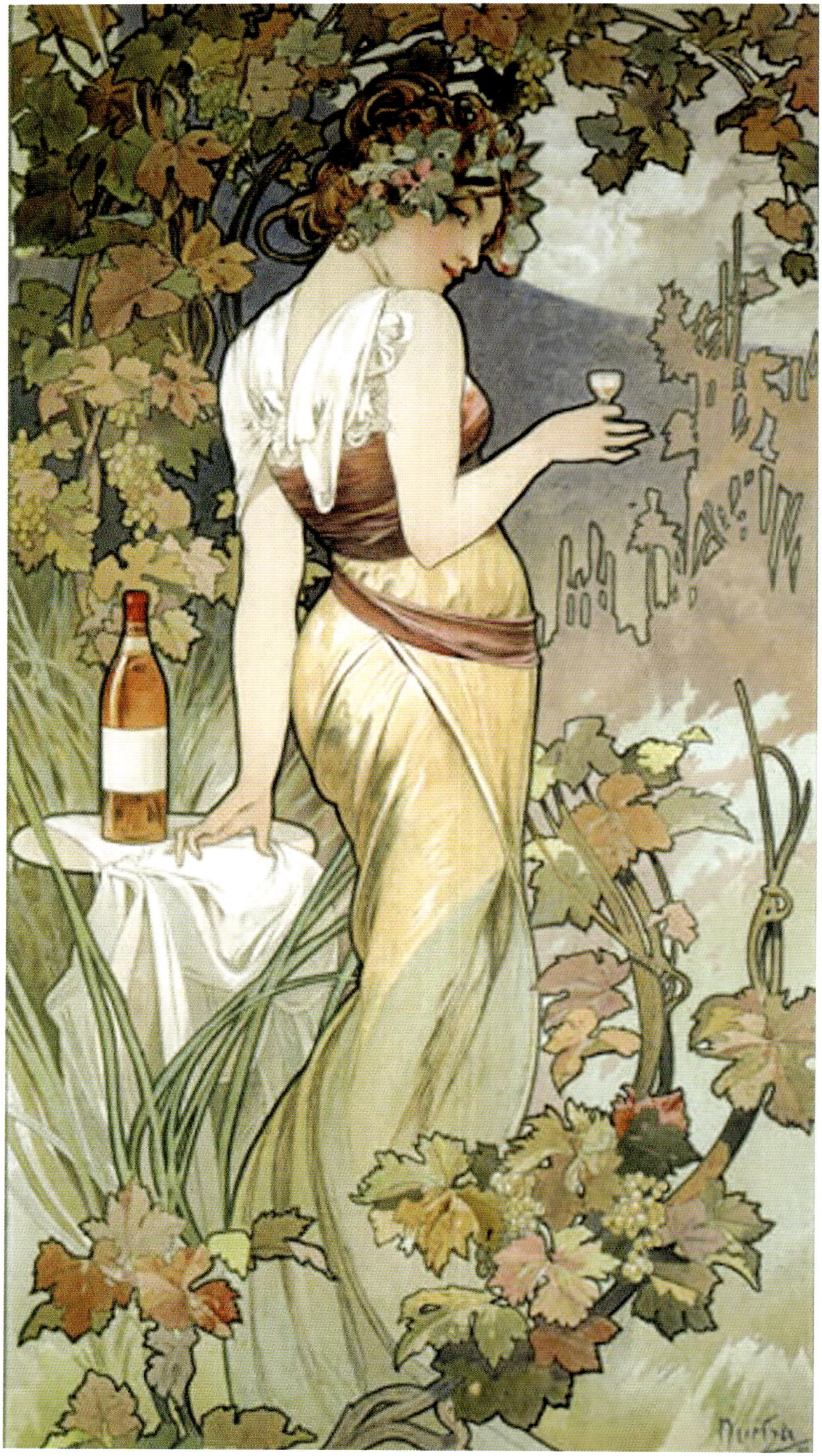

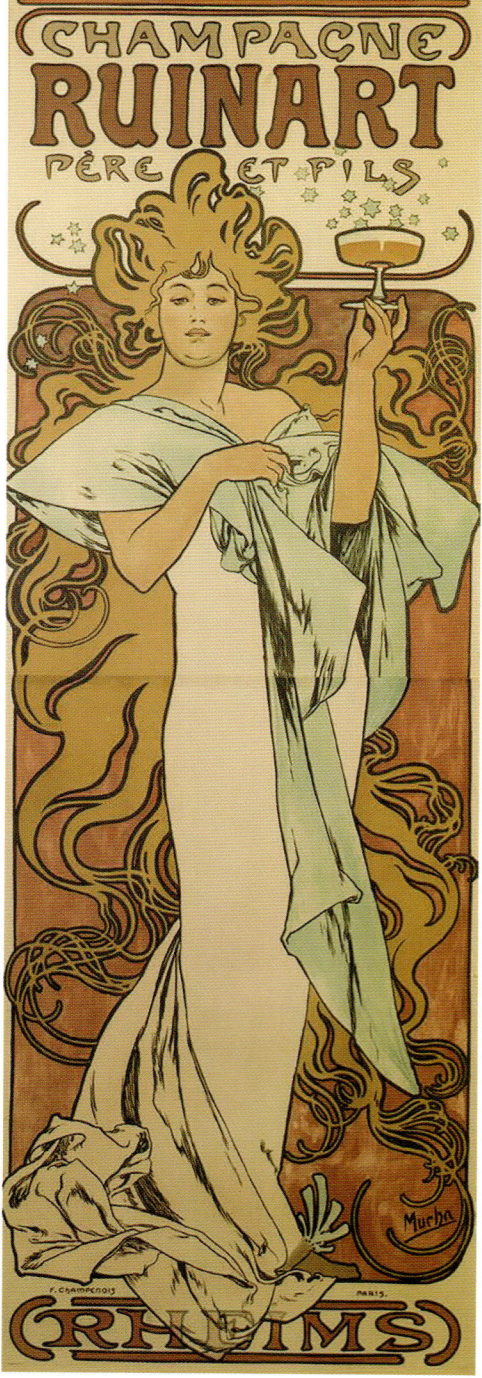

[LEFT]
Advertising poster for
Cognac Bisquit (1897).
Color lithograph.

[OPPOSITE PAGE]
Advertising poster for
**Fox-Land Jamaica
Rum** (1897).
Color lithograph.

[BELOW]
Advertising poster for
Ruinart Champagne (1896).
Color lithograph.

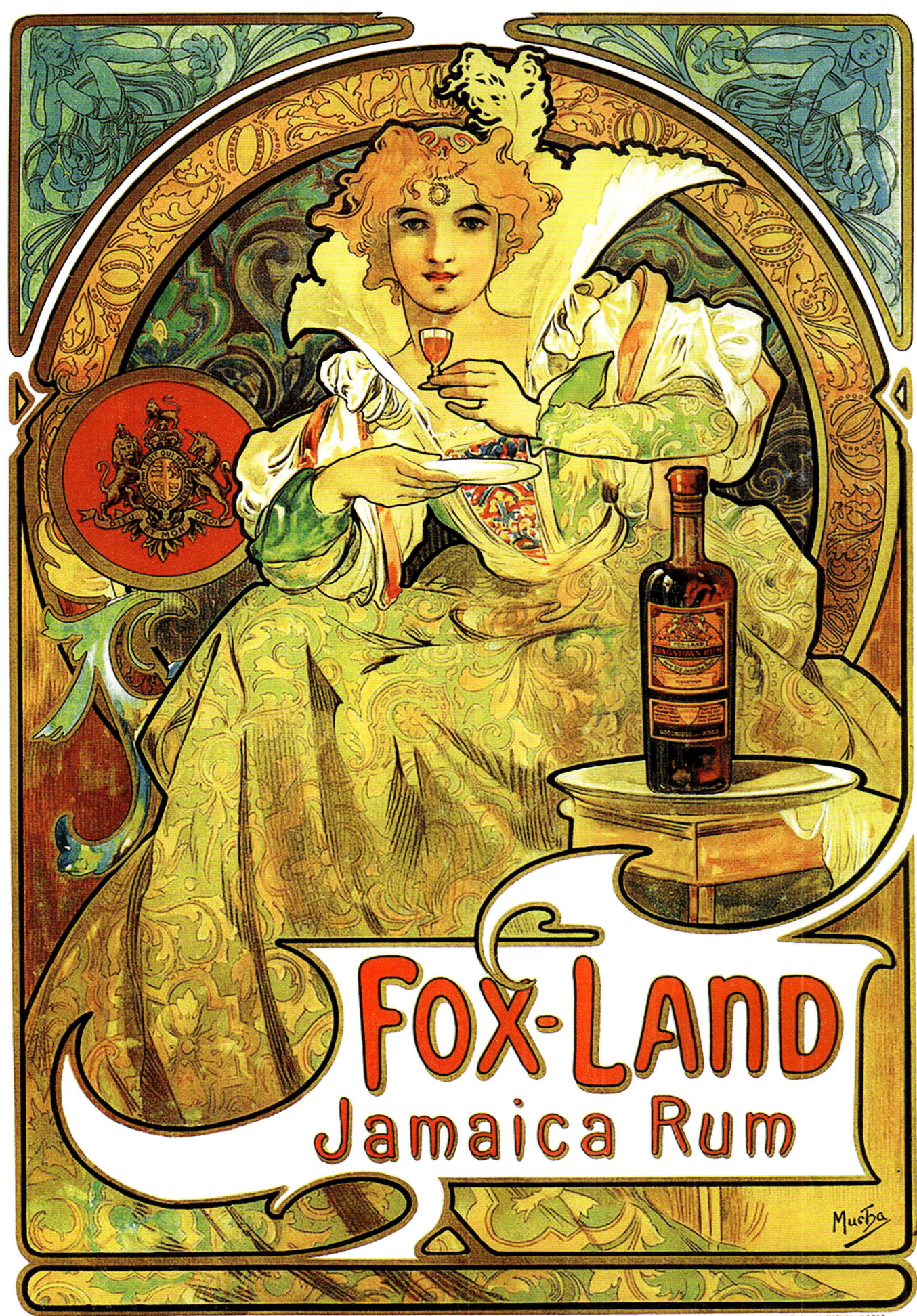

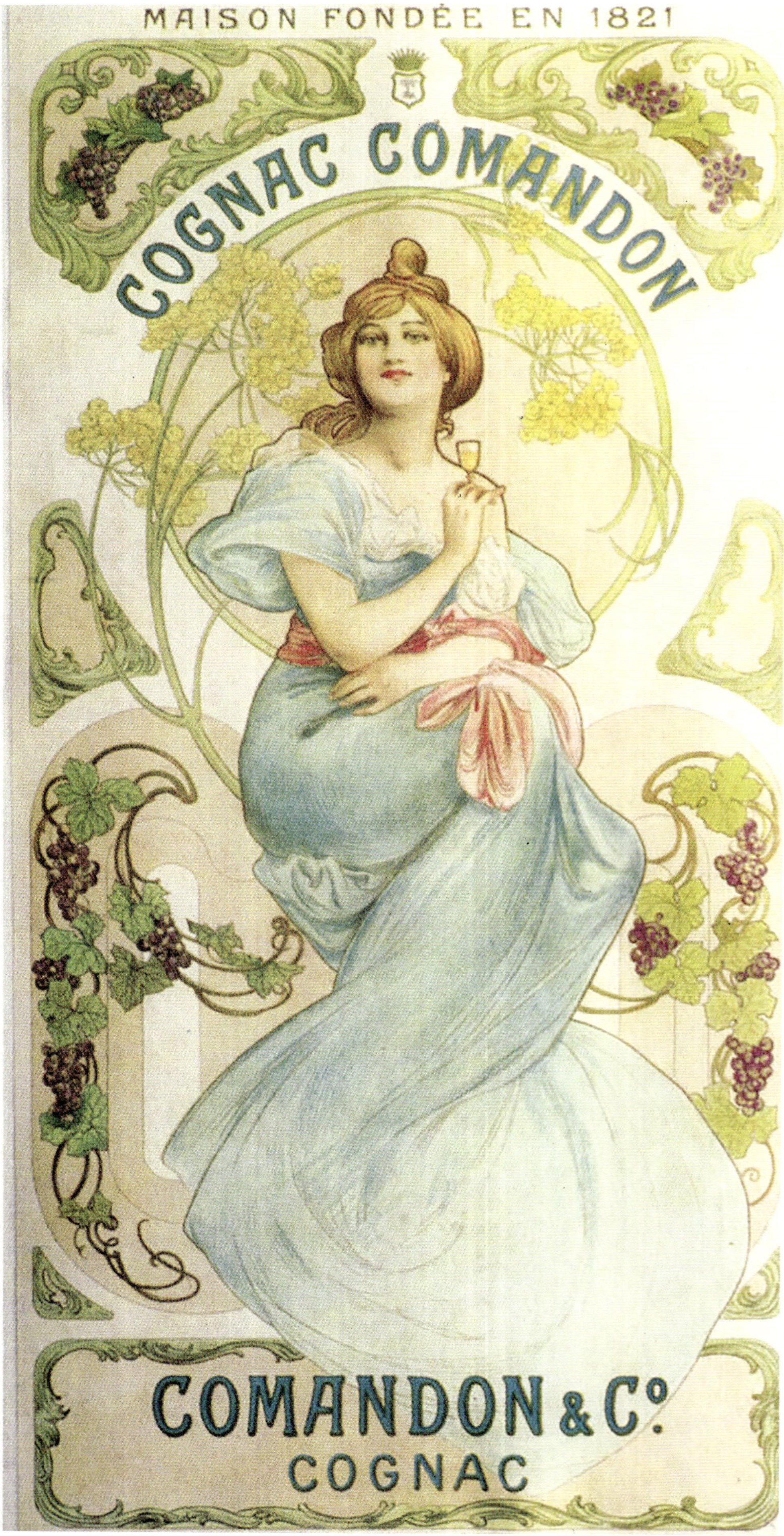

MAISON FONDÉE EN 1821

COGNAC COMANDON

COMANDON & C°.

COGNAC

[LEFT]
Advertising poster for
Cognac Comandon (1897).
Color lithograph.

[OPPOSITE PAGE]
Advertising poster for
Bières de la Meuse
(1897). Color lithograph.

*Beneath Mucha's figure of the
woman, the poster shows two
images drawn by another artist:
the goddess of the river Meuse
and a bird's eye view of the
Bières de la Meuse brewery.*

[BELOW] Advertising poster for
Nectar Liqueur Superfine
(1898). Color lithograph.

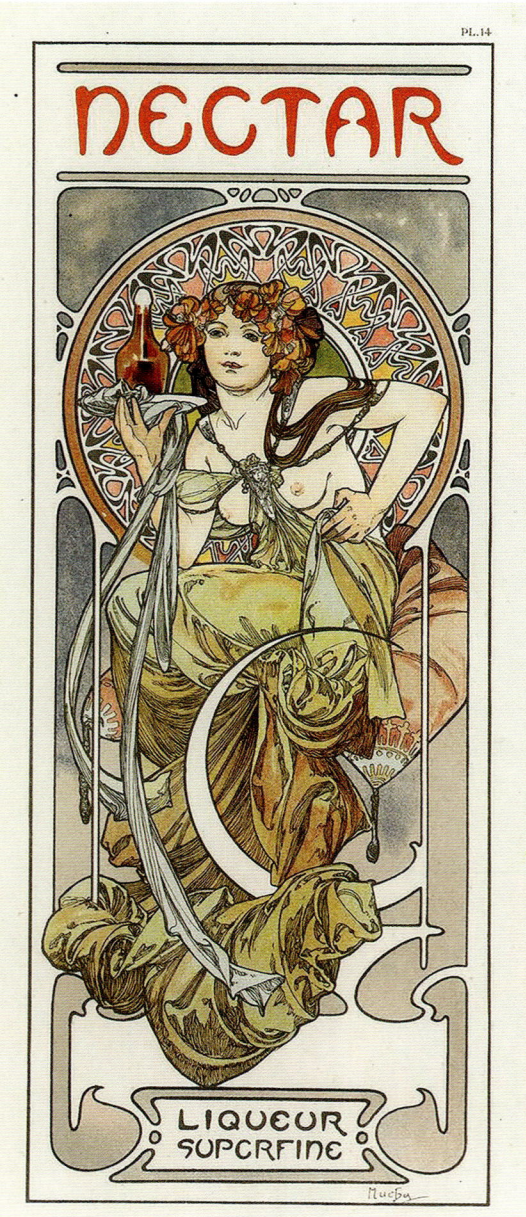

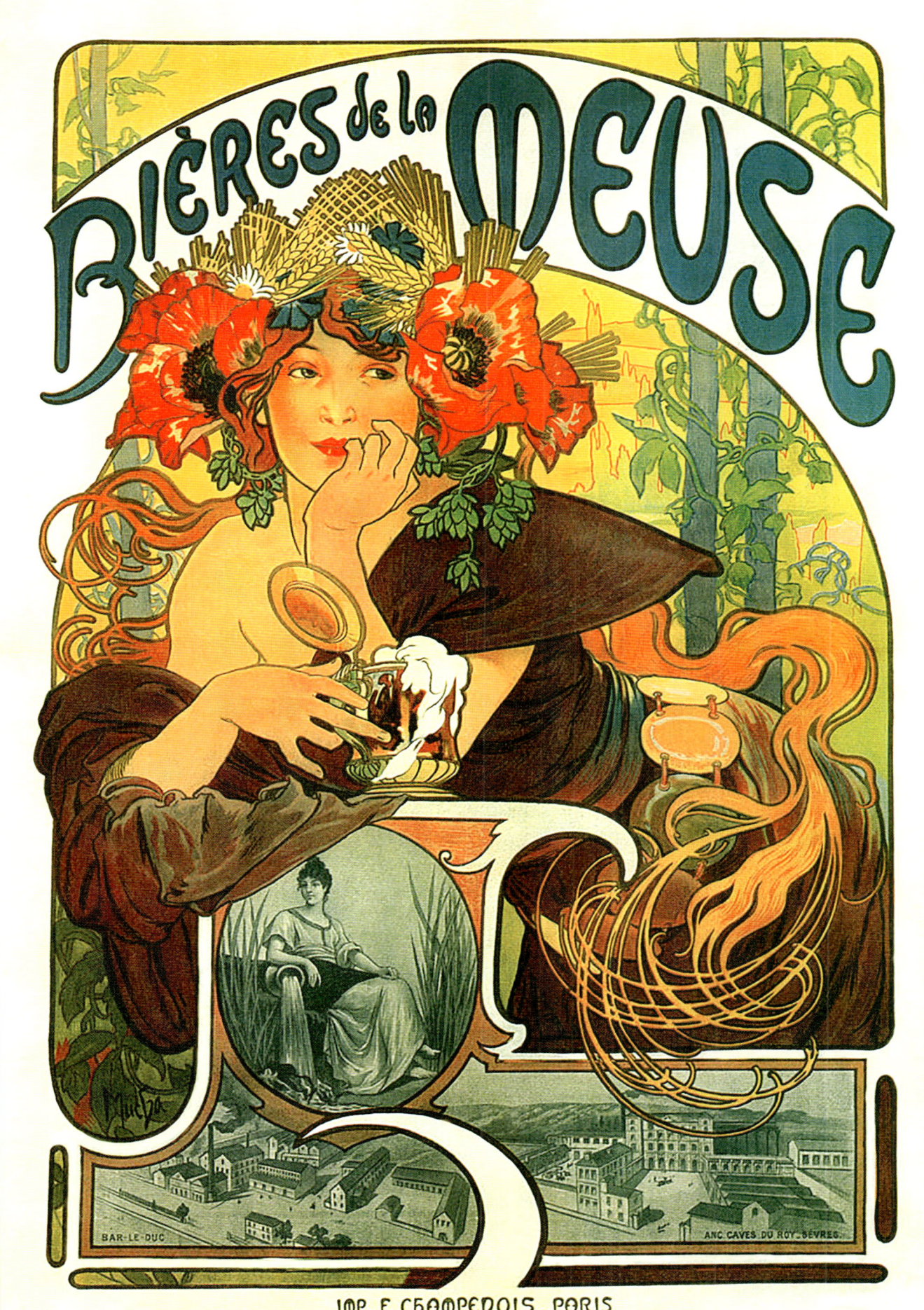

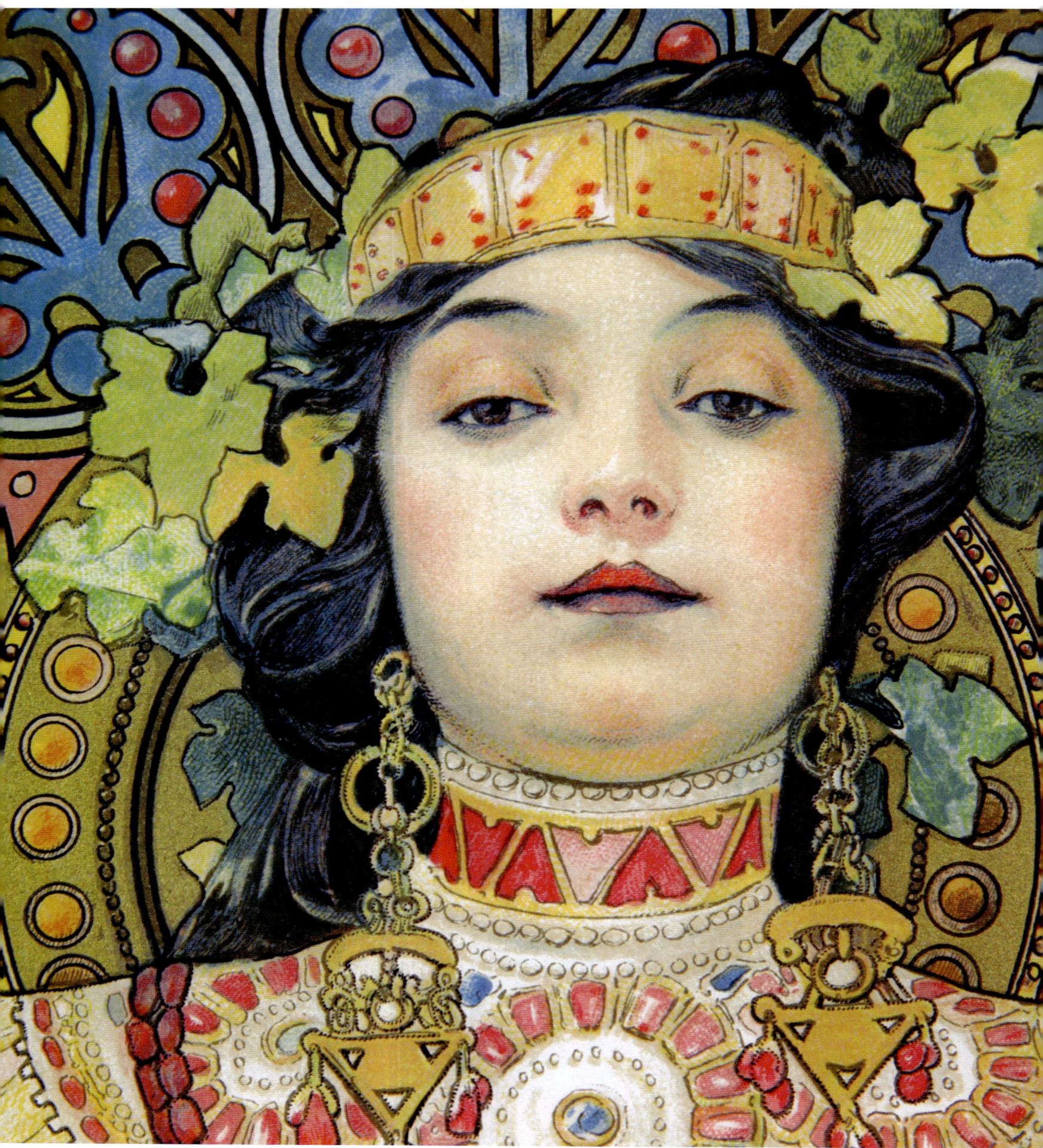

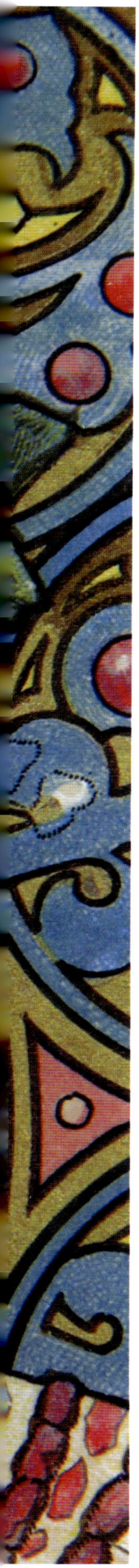

MUCHA & MOËT

Arguably some of the most recognizable of Mucha's advertising works are posters for Moët et Chandon. In these, he depicts women of stunning beauty set against intricate floral and geometric motifs. He also designed postcards and other advertising materials for the French champagne producer.

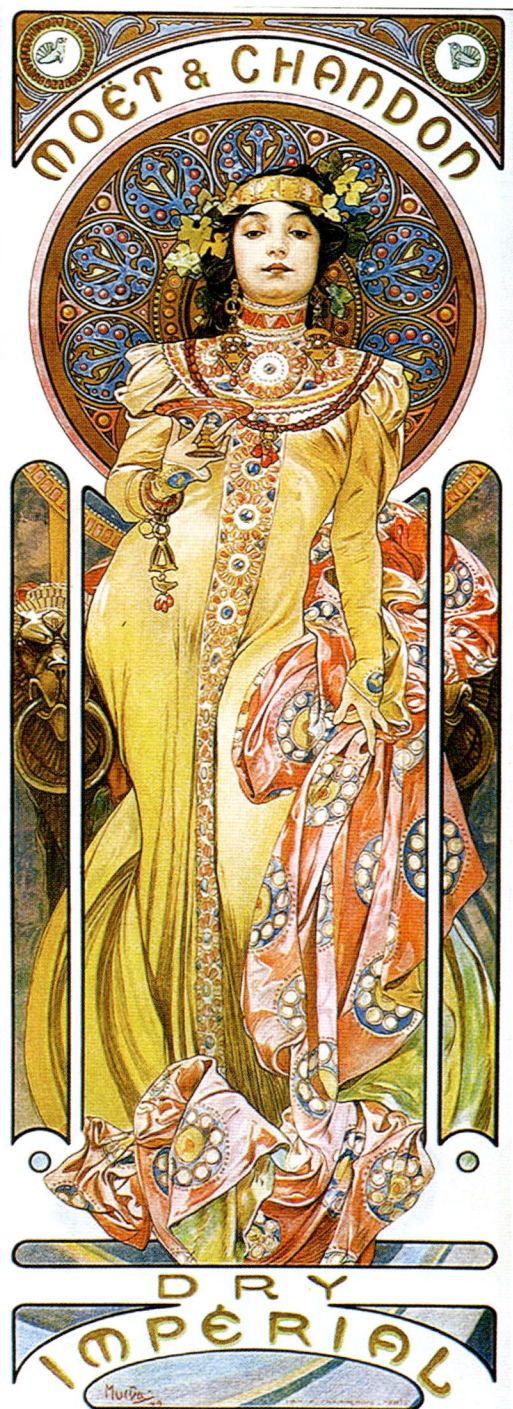

[ABOVE AND LEFT] Advertising poster with detail at left for *Moët & Chandon Crémant Impérial* (1899). Color lithograph.

[RIGHT] Detail for advertising poster for *Moët & Chandon Champagne White Star* (1899). Color lithograph.

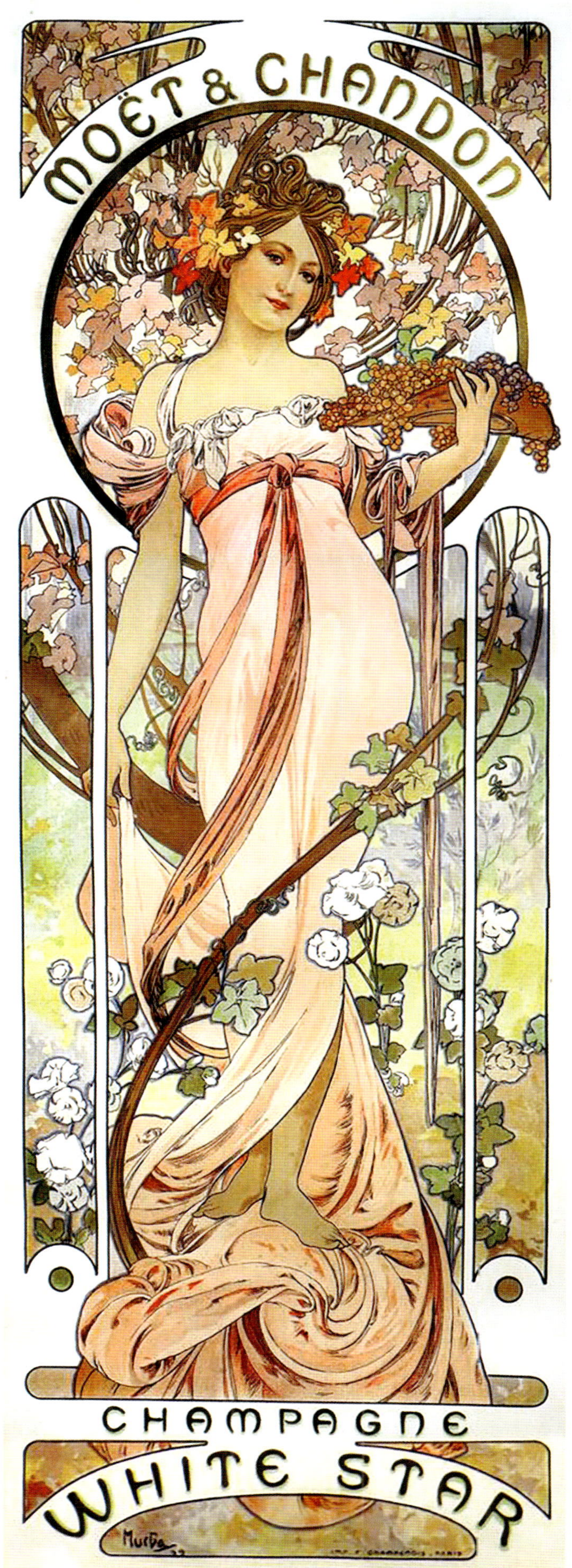

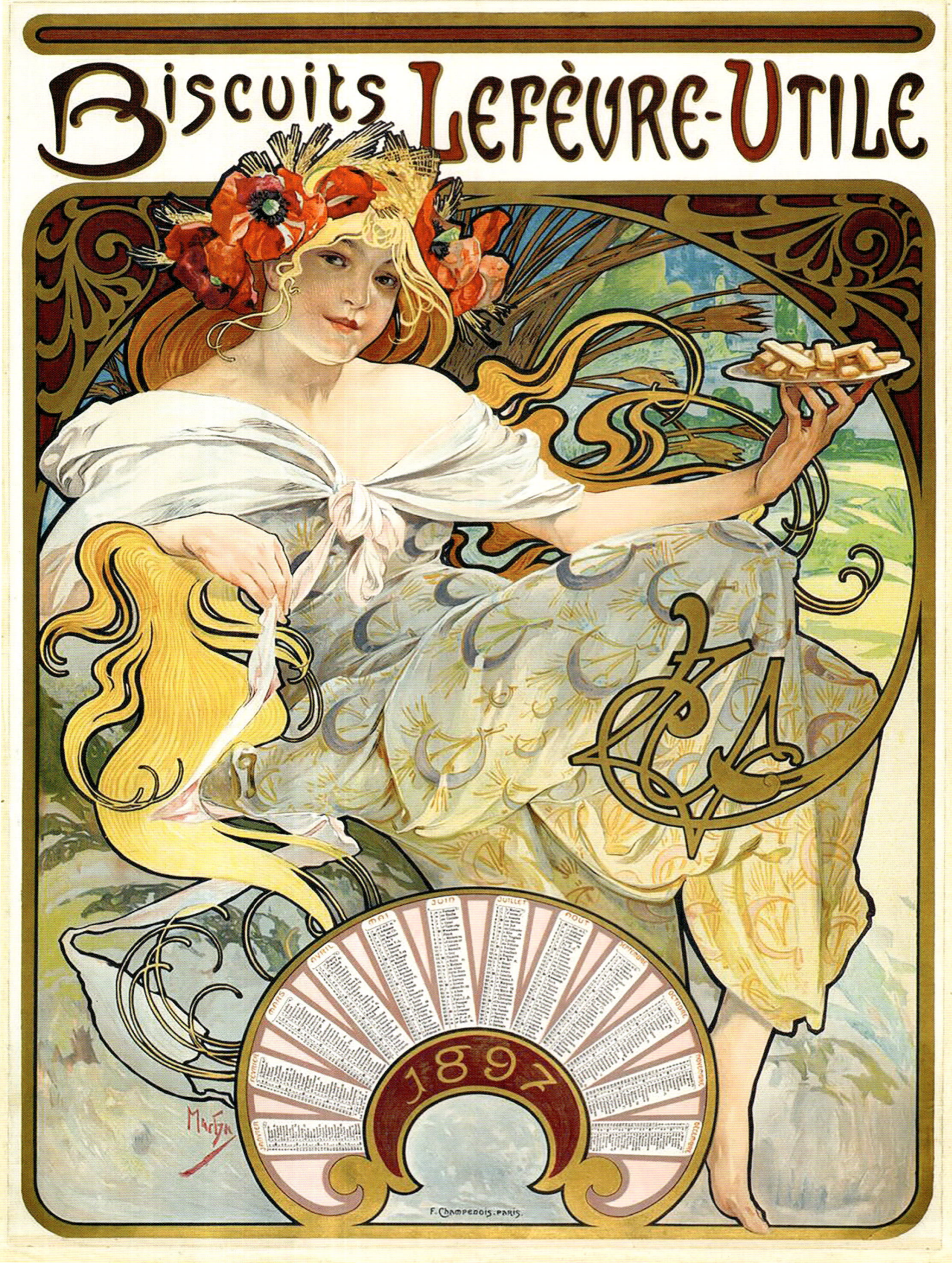

BEAUTY IN BISCUITS

Mucha's biscuit advertisements showcased his talent for elevating everyday products into objects of desire through his distinctive Art Nouveau style. Working with companies like Lefèvre-Utile, a French biscuit manufacturer, Mucha created captivating ads that featured alluring women, intricate patterns, and lush decorative elements. These designs not only promoted the biscuits but also reflected the era's penchant for beauty, sophistication, and indulgence in advertising.

[OPPOSITE PAGE]
Advertising poster/calendar for **Biscuits Lefèvre-Utile** (1897). Color lithograph. Museu Nacional d'Art de Catalunya, Barcelona.

[BELOW]
Packaging for **Gaufrettes Pralinées** by Lefèvre-Utile (c. 1898). Color lithograph.

As well as creating promotional posters, Mucha also designed the packaging for Lefèvre-Utile biscuits.

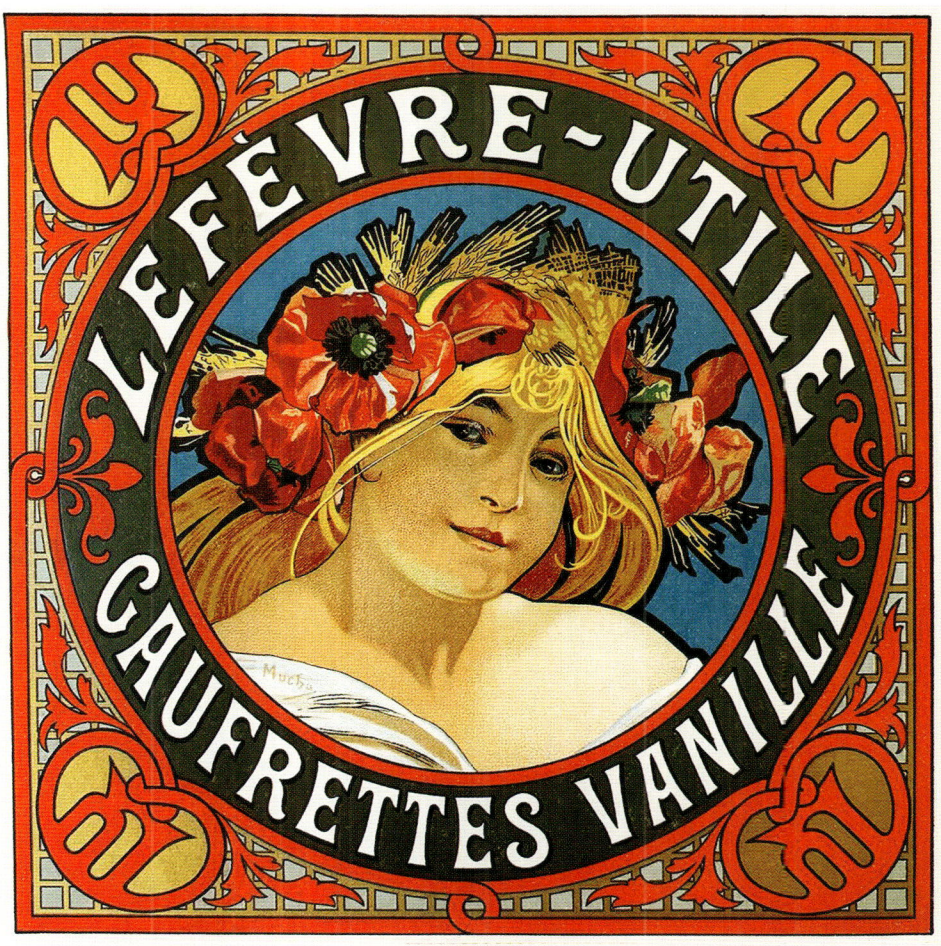

Front label for box of **Gaufrettes Vanille** by Lefèvre-Utile (c. 1900). Color lithograph.

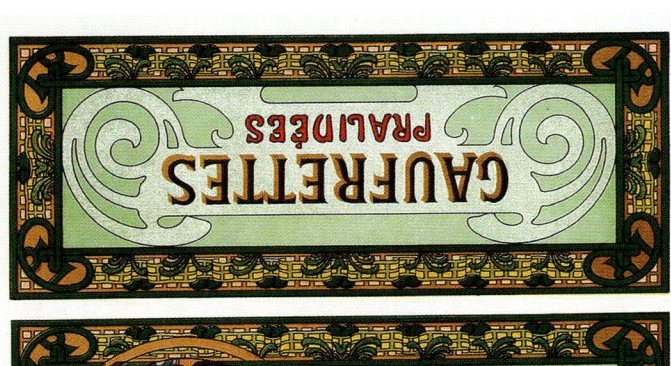
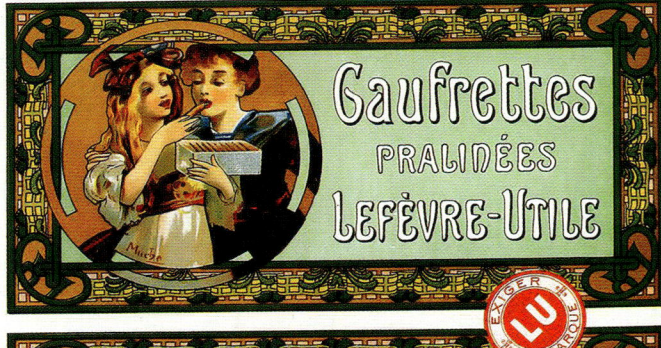
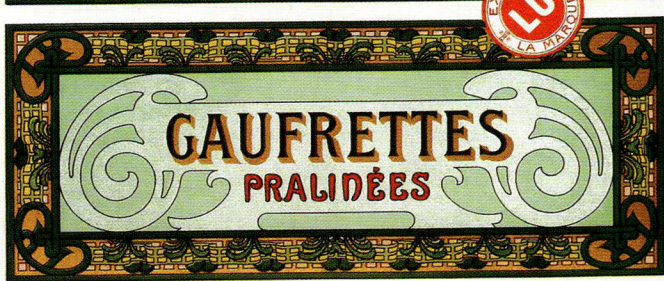

"His art is a sumptuous art, floral, astral, feminine; it reflects with tender nonchalance the fluid beauty of form and the delicately veiled secrets of the soul."

~ CHRISTIAN BRINTON

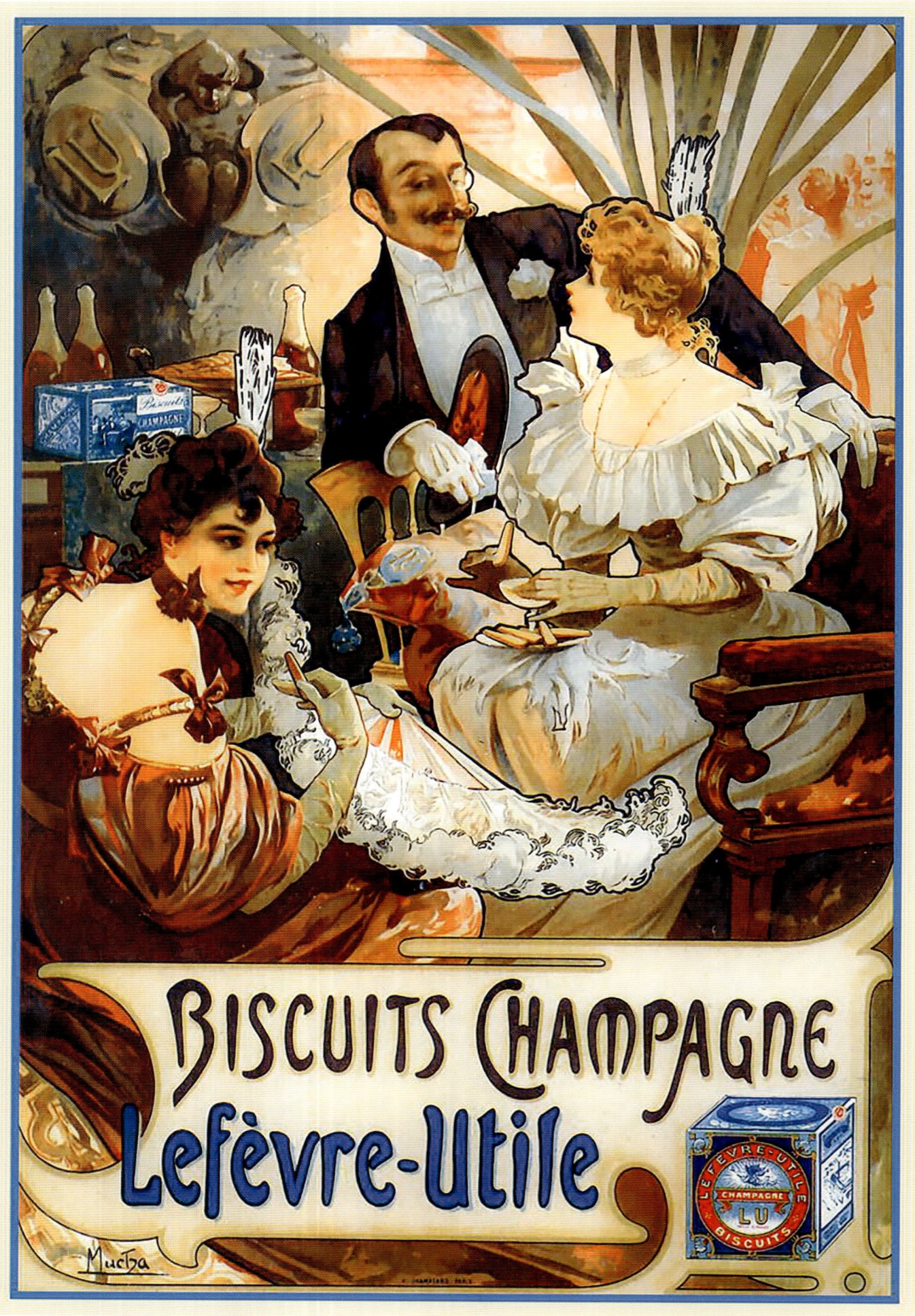

[OPPOSITE PAGE]
Advertising poster for **Biscuits Champagne**
by Lefèvre-Utile (1897). Color lithograph.

[RIGHT] Advertising poster for
**Ed. de Beukelaer & Co.
Biscuits Anvers**
(c. 1900). Color lithograph.

[BELOW]
Flirt, an advertising poster
for Lefèvre-Utile (1890).
Color lithograph.

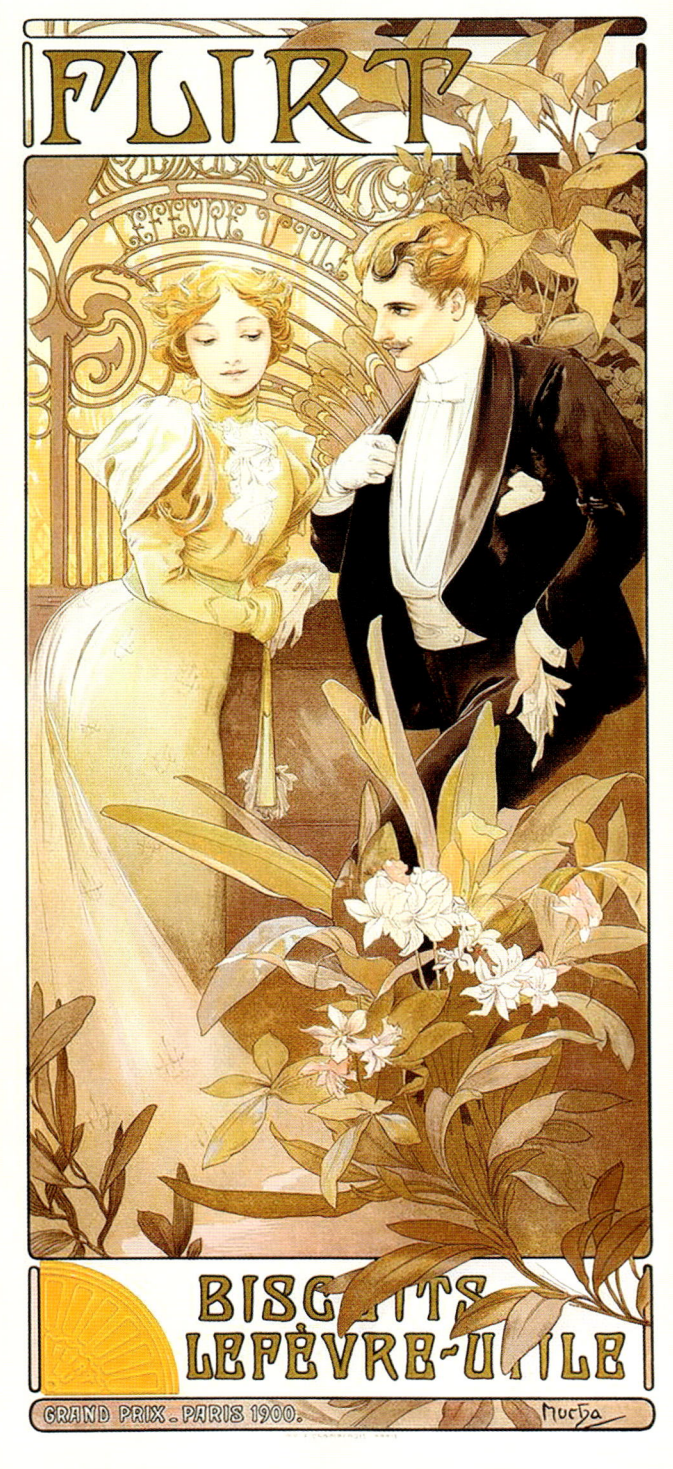

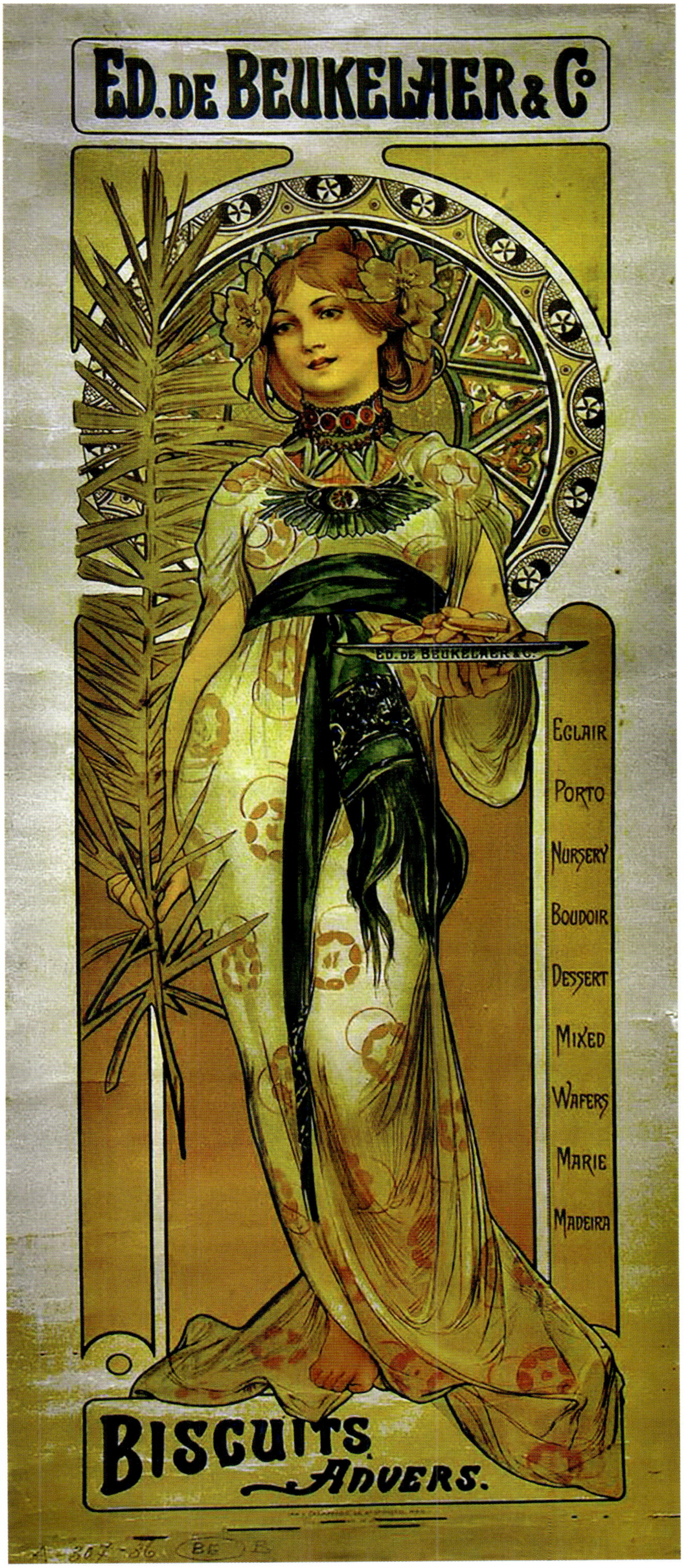

BICYCLES & FREEDOM

In the late 19th century, there was a surge of popularity in the usage of bicycles, and Mucha designed advertisements for bicycle manufacturers. In his works, bicycles were portrayed as symbols of freedom, progress, and modernity. Mucha's illustrations showcased elegant, fashionable women riding bicycles, emphasizing the newfound independence and mobility experienced by women in the late 19th and early 20th centuries. His bicycle advertisements, characterized by vivid colors and intricate details, played a crucial role in popularizing the bicycle as a cultural phenomenon.

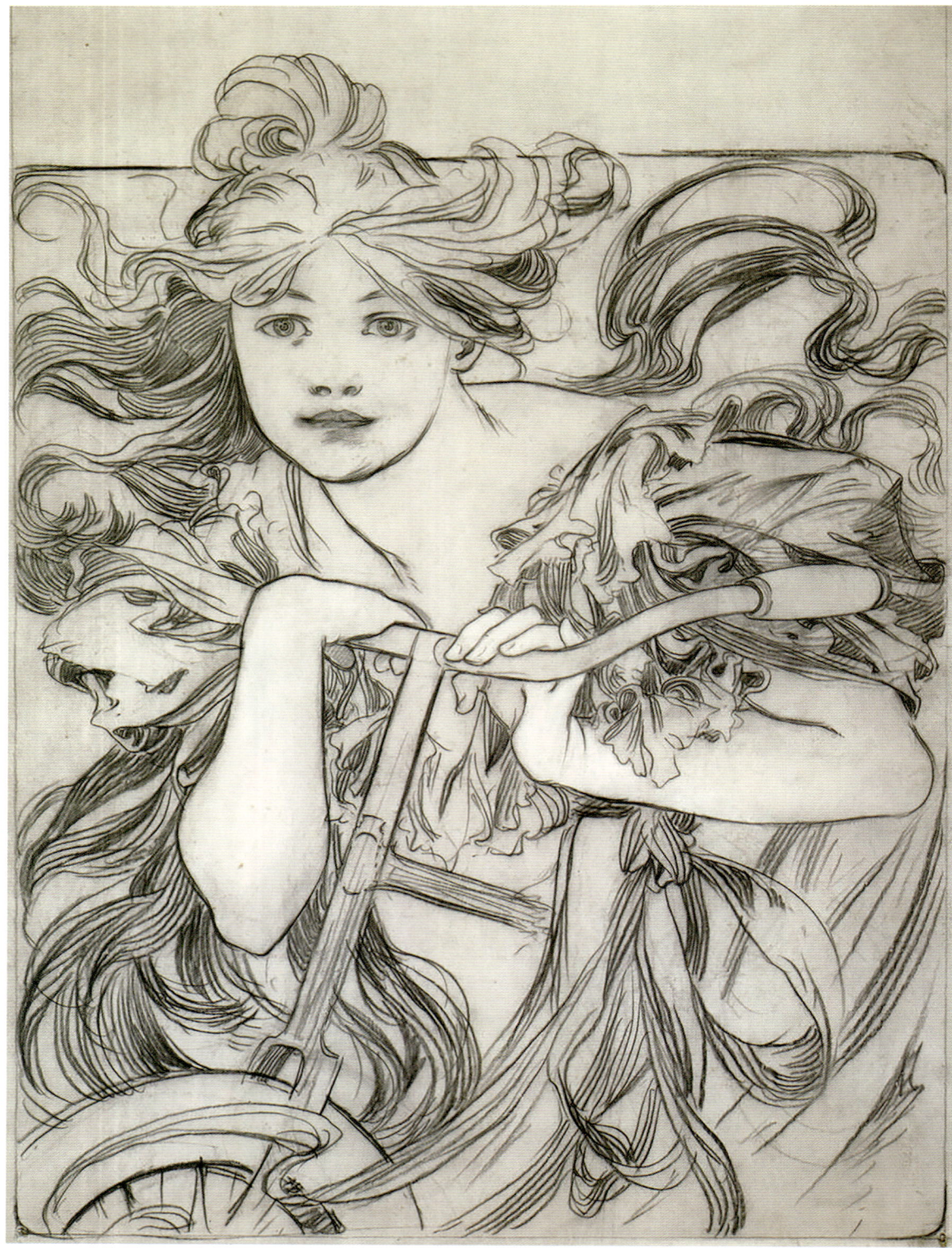

[LEFT]
Preliminary sketch for
Cycles Perfecta poster
(1902). Pencil on paper.

[OPPOSITE PAGE]
Advertising poster for
Cycles Perfecta
(1902). Color lithograph.

"*If we wish to emphasize its character as a straight line we have to augment equally its expression of direction and its width. We can arrive at this result in several ways. First, by parallel lines harmoniously disposed, or by curved lines which are at different intervals touch or come near to it.*"

~ ALPHONSE MUCHA

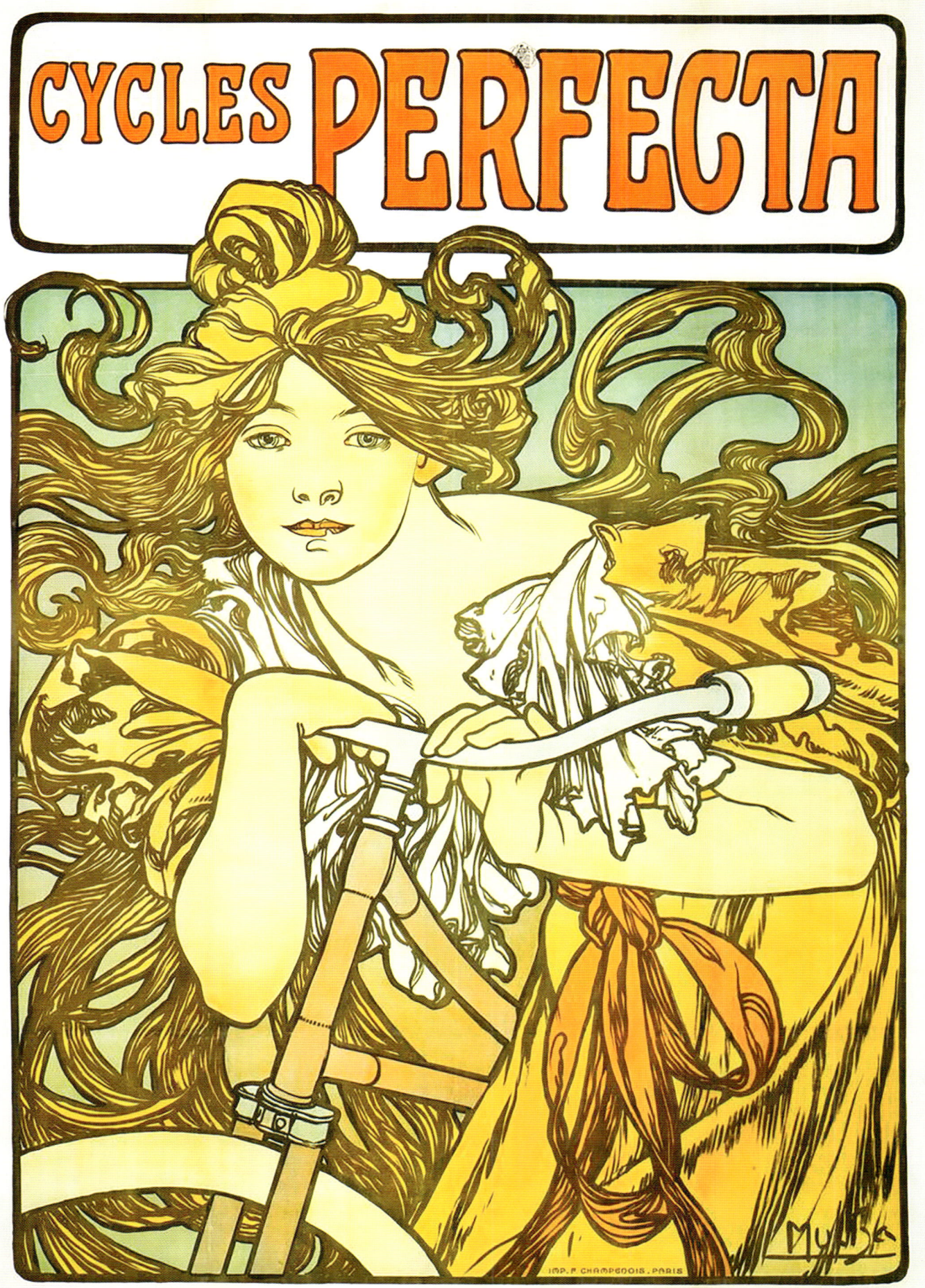

> "*Mucha did not bother to try and show it . . . but expressed it symbolically by having the rather resolute young lady leaning on an anvil. She is holding in her hand a branch of laurel leaves, probably to indicate the prizes won by the product.*"

~ JACK RENNERT AND ALAIN WEILL
IN *ALPHONSE MUCHA*, DESCRIBING
THE WAVERLEY CYCLES ADVERTISEMENT

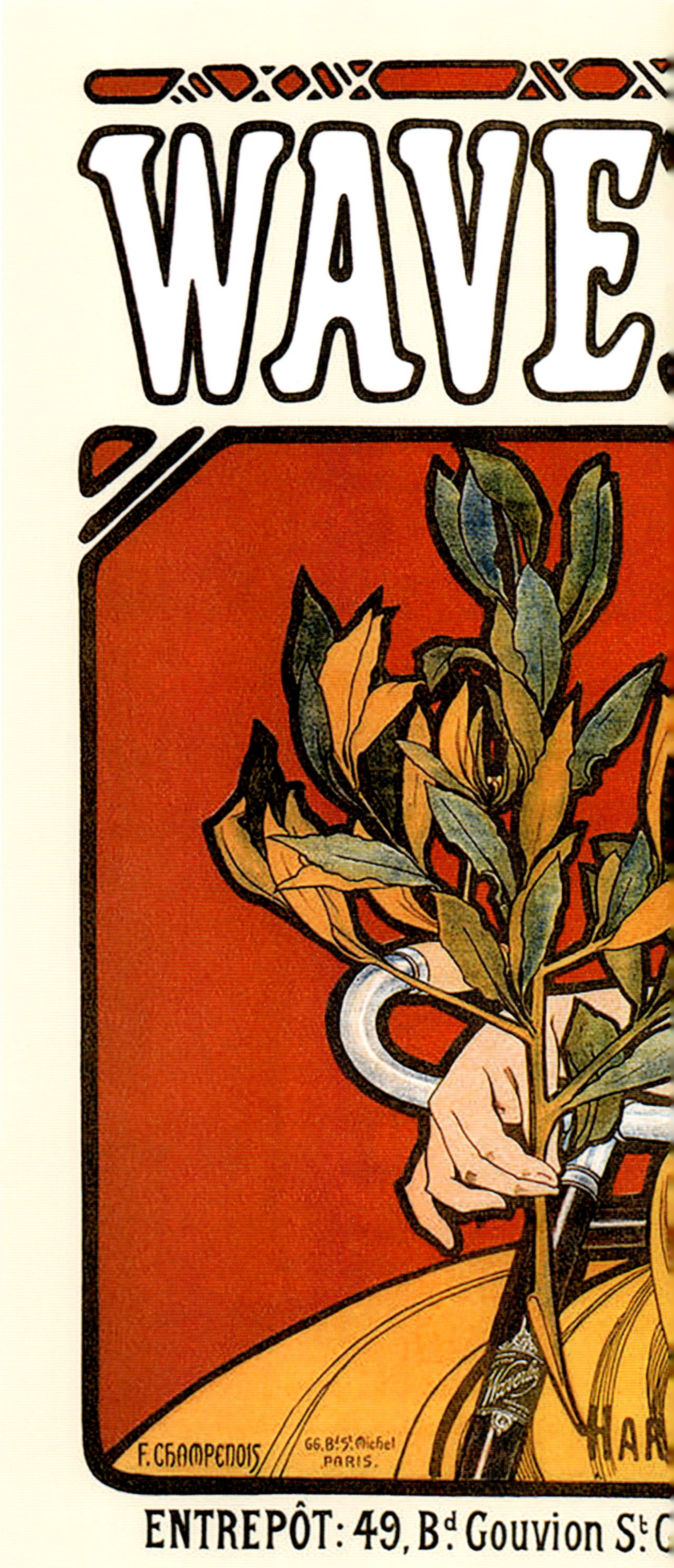

[RIGHT AND BELOW]
Advertising poster for
Waverley Cycles (1898).
Color lithograph.

Because of the nature of a lithograph, variant-color versions can be made of a single image. This poster, created for the American-manufactured bicycles of Waverley Cycles was on display in the streets of Paris at the same time as the poster of its competitor, Cycles Perfecta (shown on previous page).

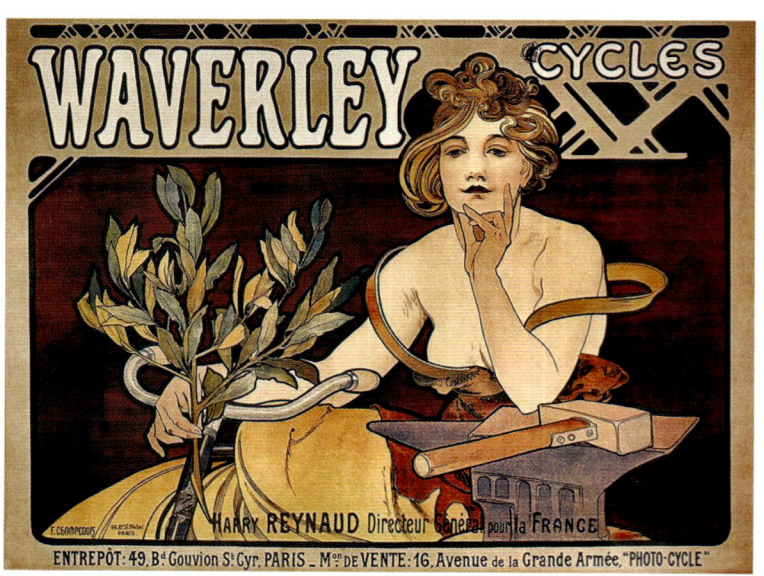

WAVE

F. CHAMPENOIS   66, B⁹ S⁹ Michel
PARIS.

ENTREPÔT: 49, Bᵈ Gouvion Stᵗ C

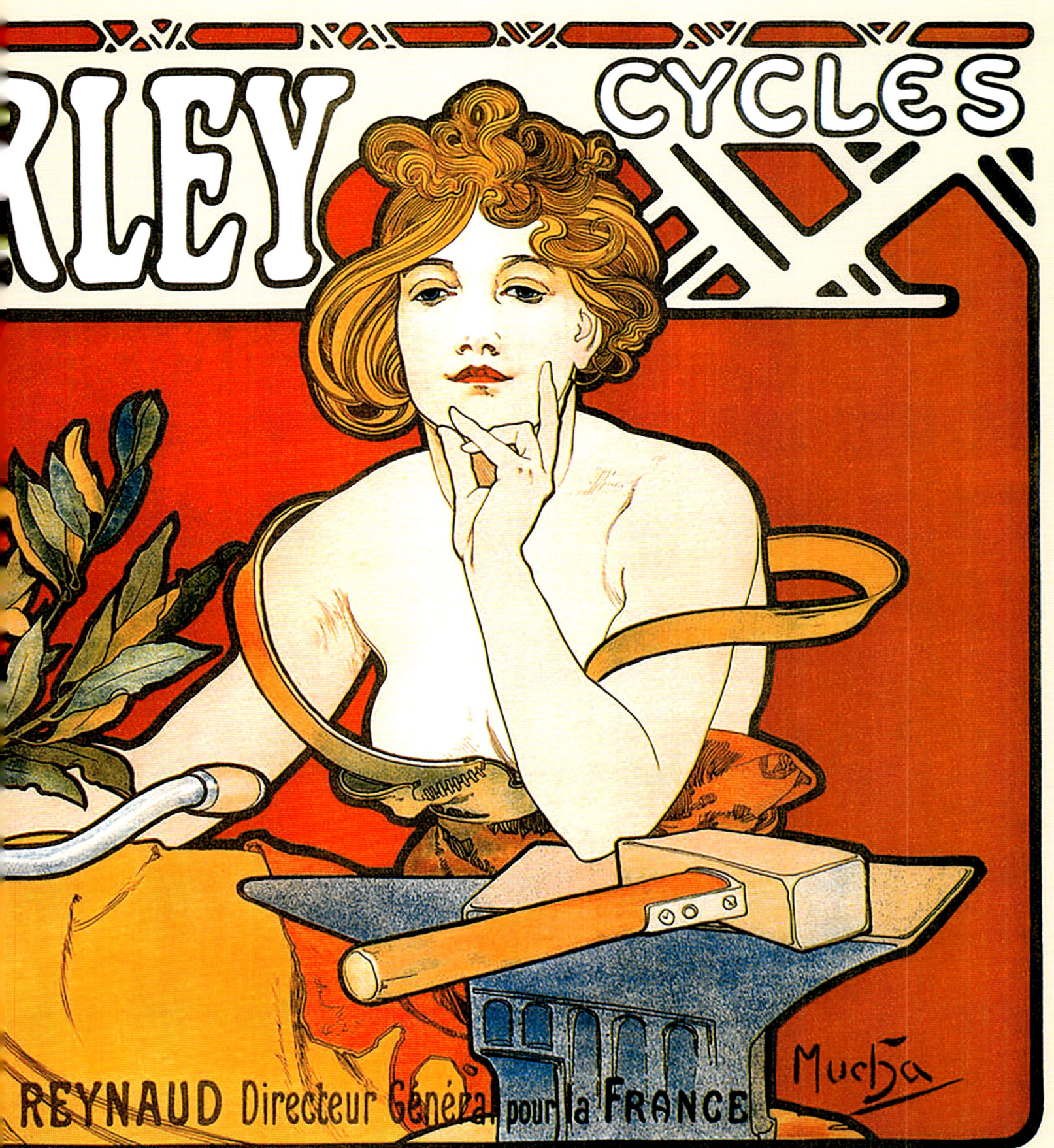

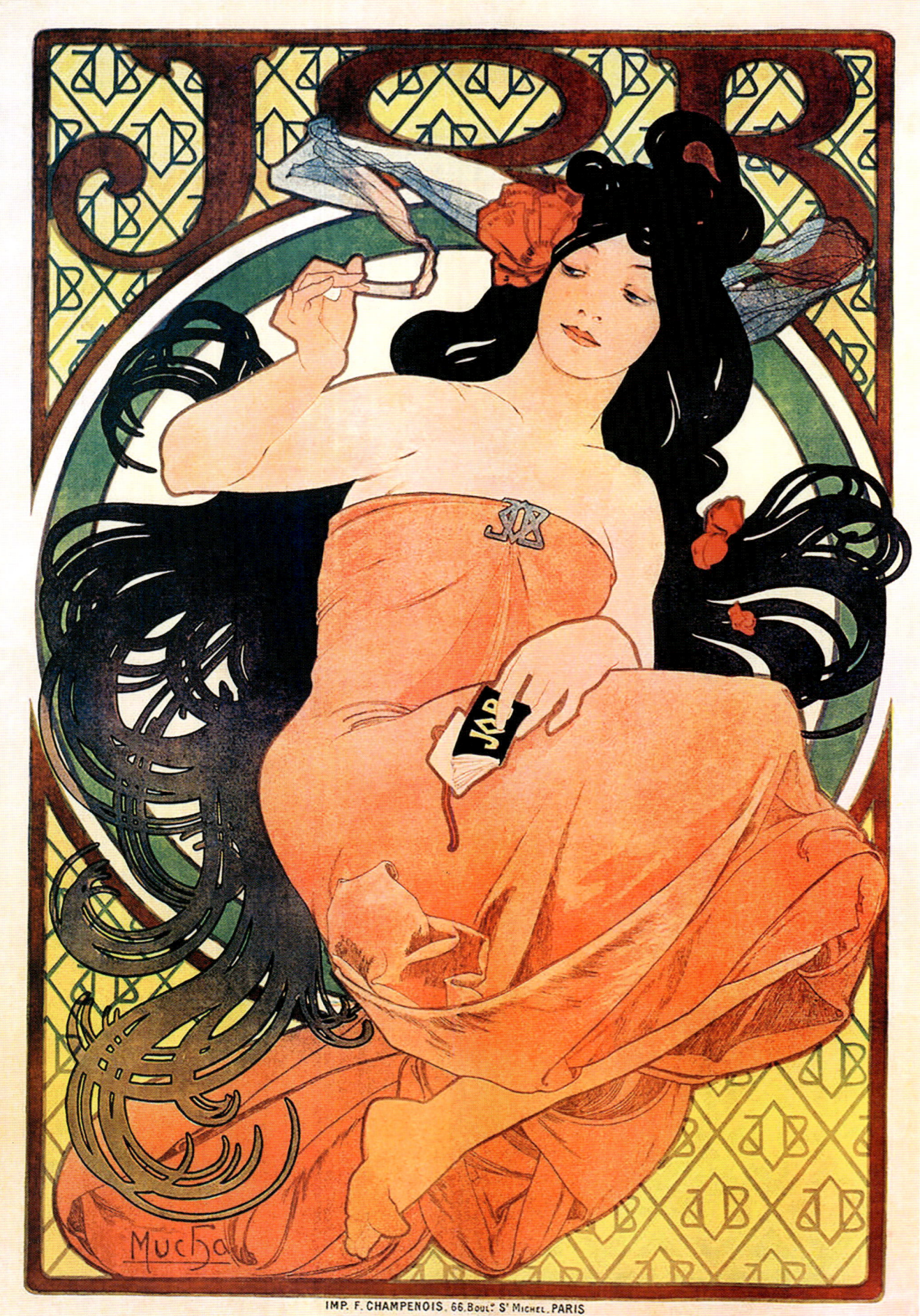

IMP. F. CHAMPENOIS, 66, Boul. St Michel, PARIS

SENSUOUS CIGARETTES

Mucha designed for several tobacco companies during his career, creating visually striking advertisements that showcased his unique style. One notable example is his work for JOB, a French company that produced cigarette papers founded by Jean Bardou. Mucha's designs for JOB succeeded in capturing the sophistication and allure associated with tobacco consumption during that time. Mucha's hugely successful advertisements contributed to this allure, going on to influence other artists in the commercial art world.

[OPPOSITE PAGE]
Advertising poster for
JOB cigarette papers
(1897). Color lithograph.

[BELOW]
Advertising poster for
Los Cicarrillos Paris
(1897). Color lithograph.

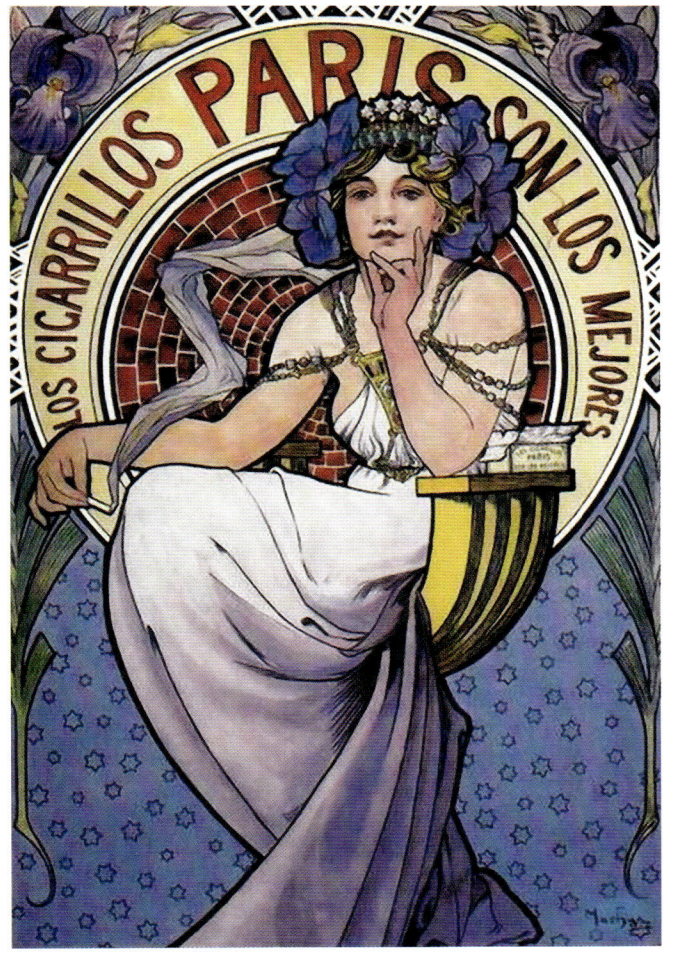

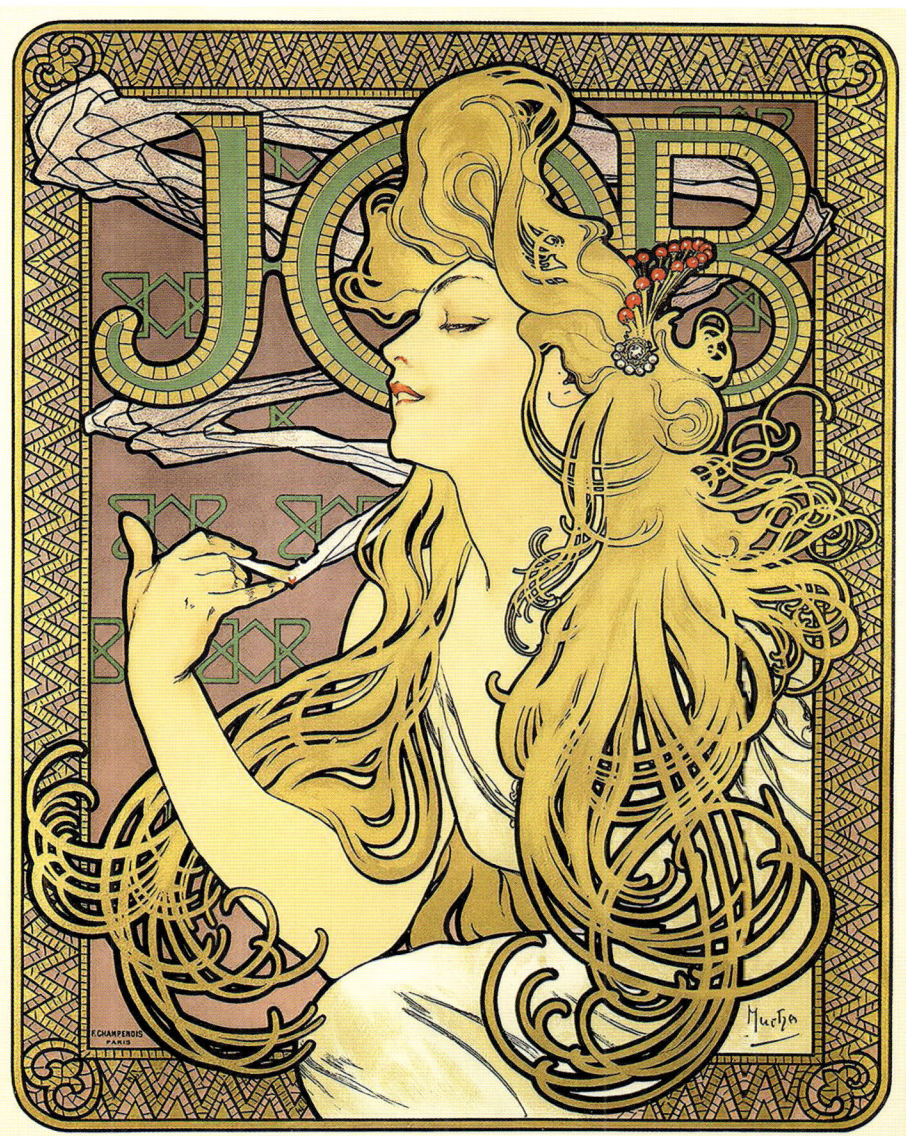

Advertising poster for *JOB cigarette papers* (1896). Color lithograph.

" *His art is a sumptuous art, floral, astral, feminine; it reflects with tender nonchalance the fluid beauty of form and the delicately veiled secrets of the soul.*"

~ CHRISTIAN BRINTON ON ALPHONSE MUCHA

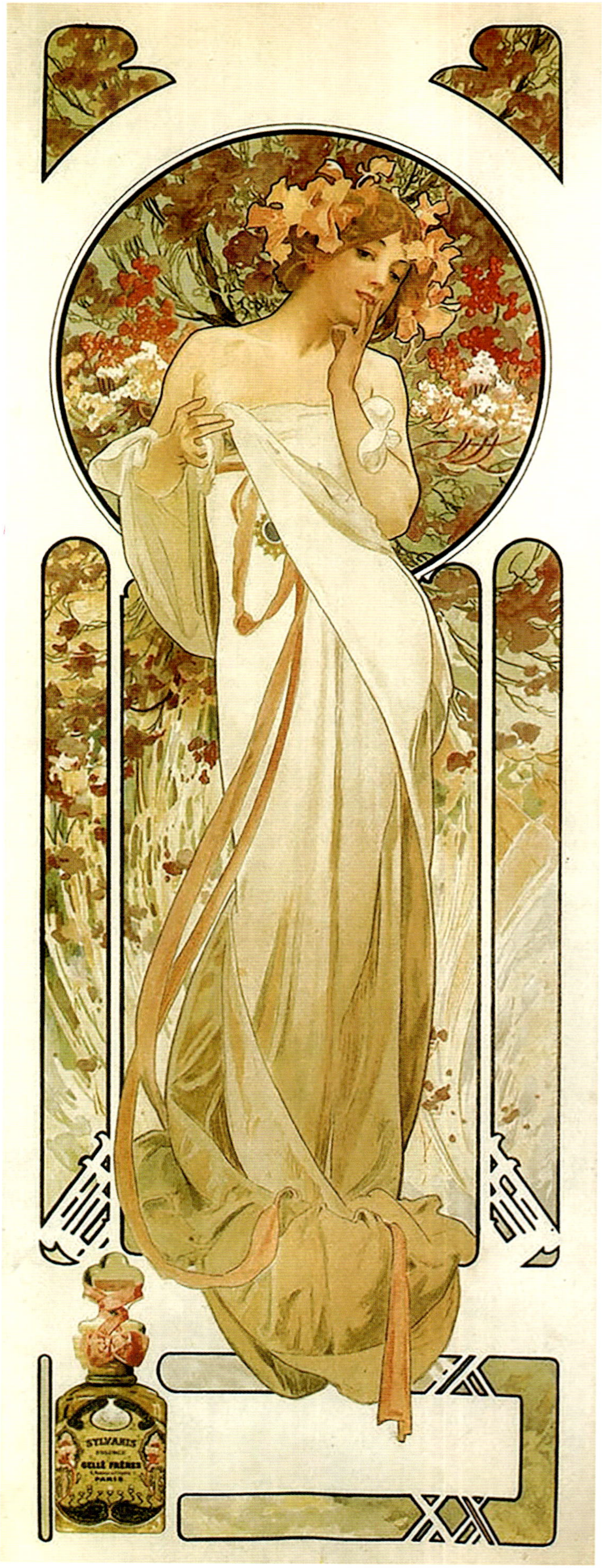

ADVERTS & PROMOTIONS

Mucha's artistic prowess extended to various industries, including perfume and chocolate makers, as well as assorted manufacturers, travel companies, and even the 1900 Paris Exposition. His work for perfume companies, such as the French brand Rodo, showcased his ability to create enticing advertisements and packaging that brought to life the essence of the fragrances being promoted. All of his captivating advertisements, examples of the elevation of the mundane into the luxurious, further solidified his reputation as a highly sought-after commercial artist.

[LEFT]
Advertising calendar for **Sylvanis Perfume** (1896). Color lithograph.

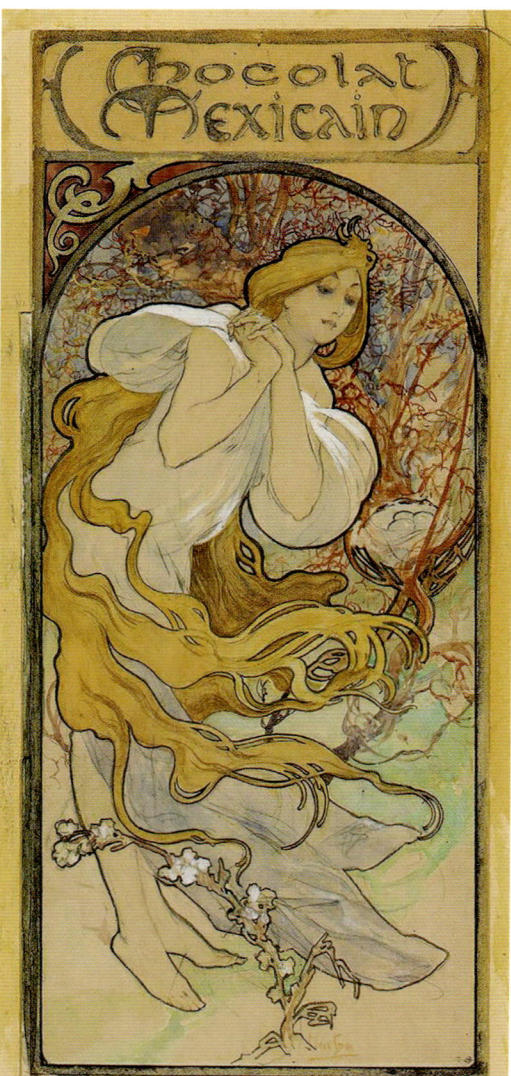

[LEFT]
Detail of promotional calendar for **Chocolat Mexicain** (1896). Color lithograph.

[OPPOSITE PAGE]
Advertising poster for **Lance Parfum Rodo,** a perfume produced by the Société des Usines Chimiques du Rhône in Lyon. (1896). Color lithograph.

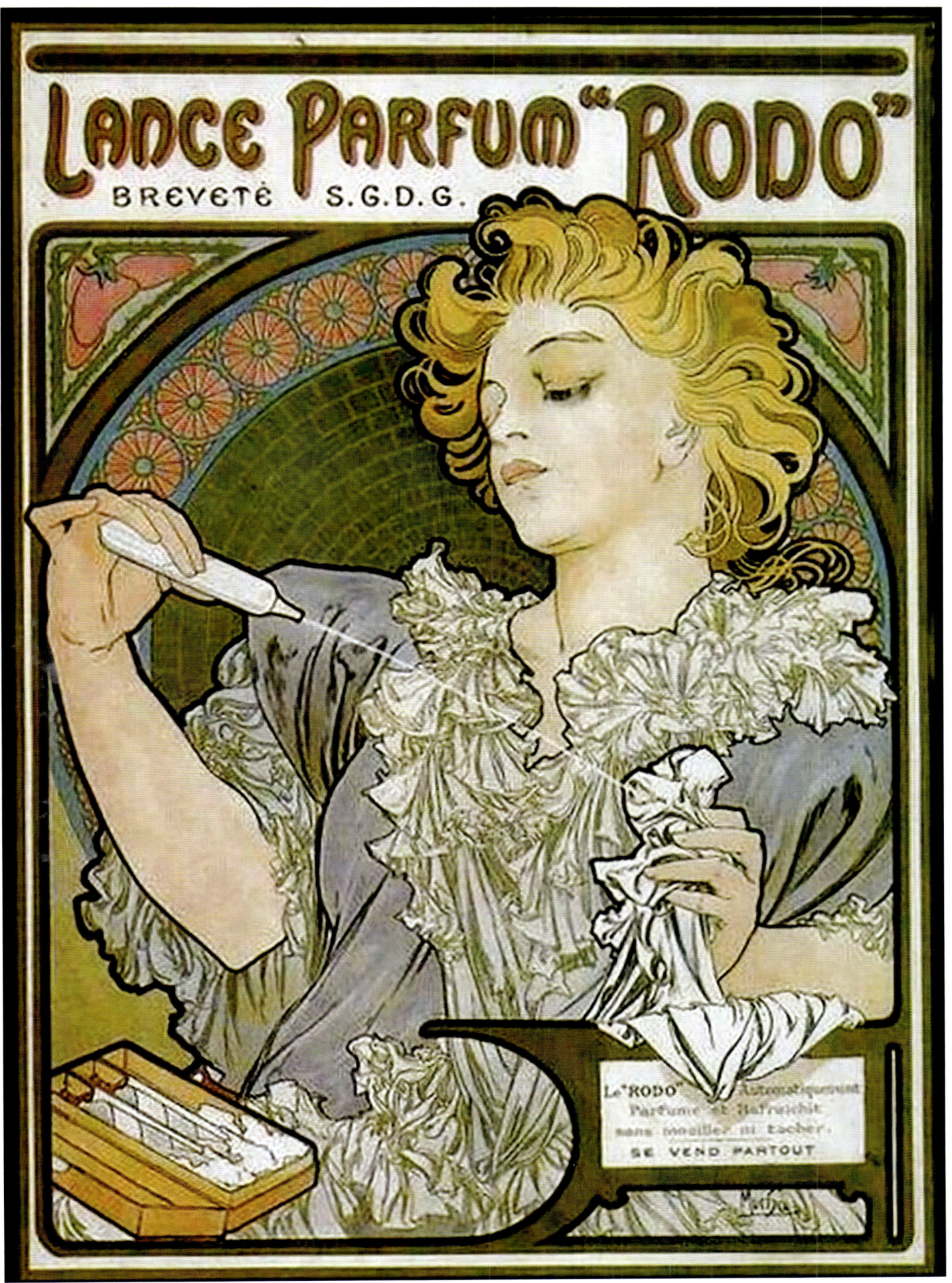

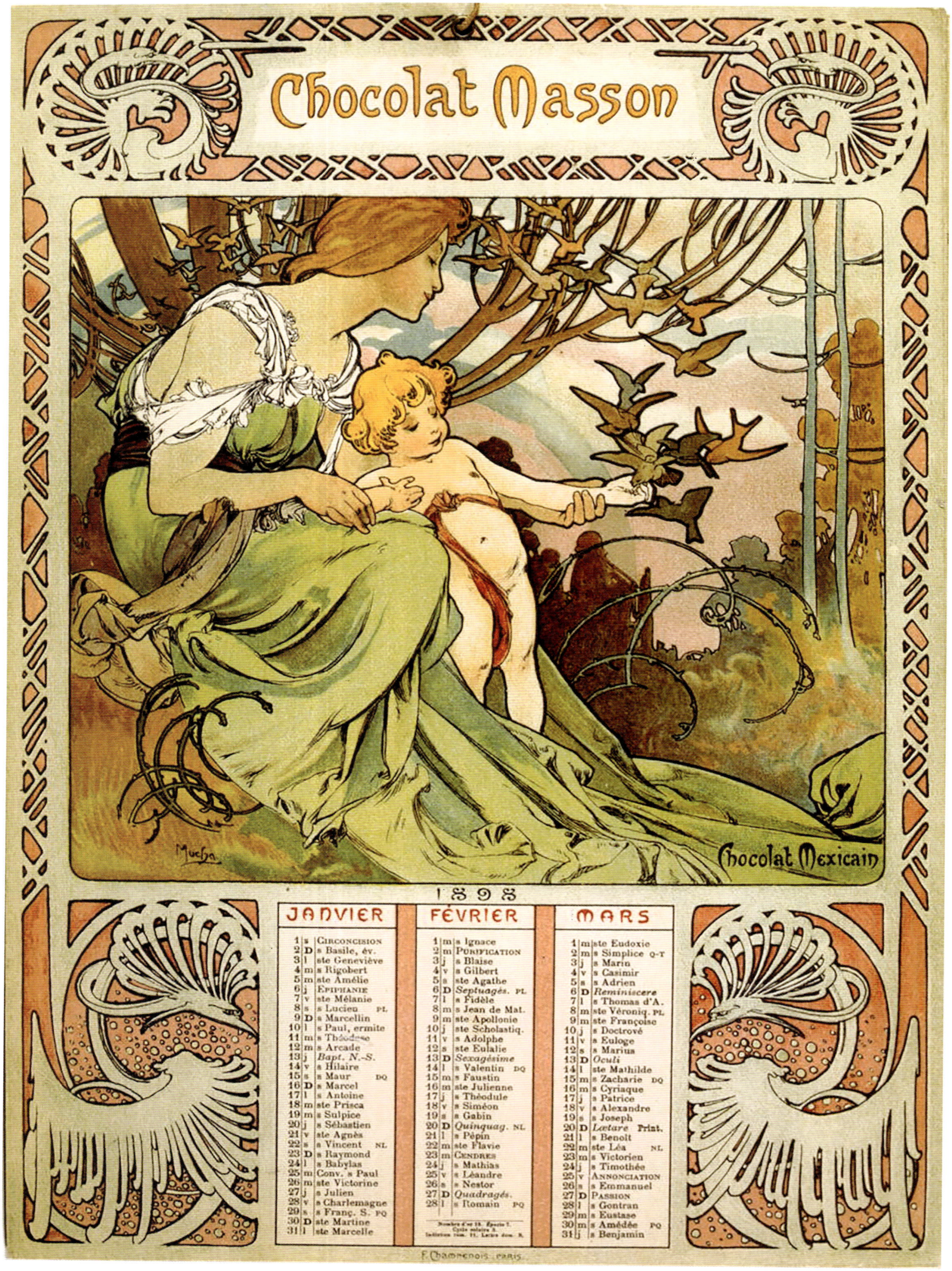

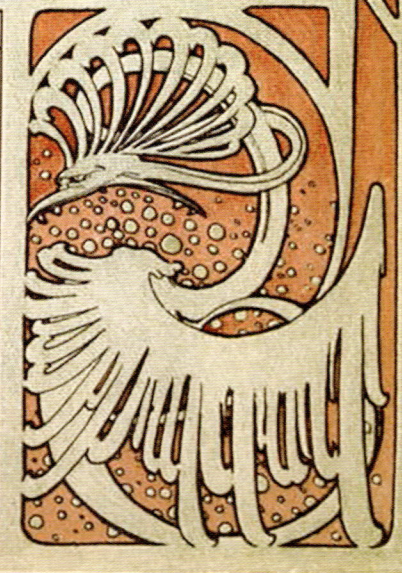

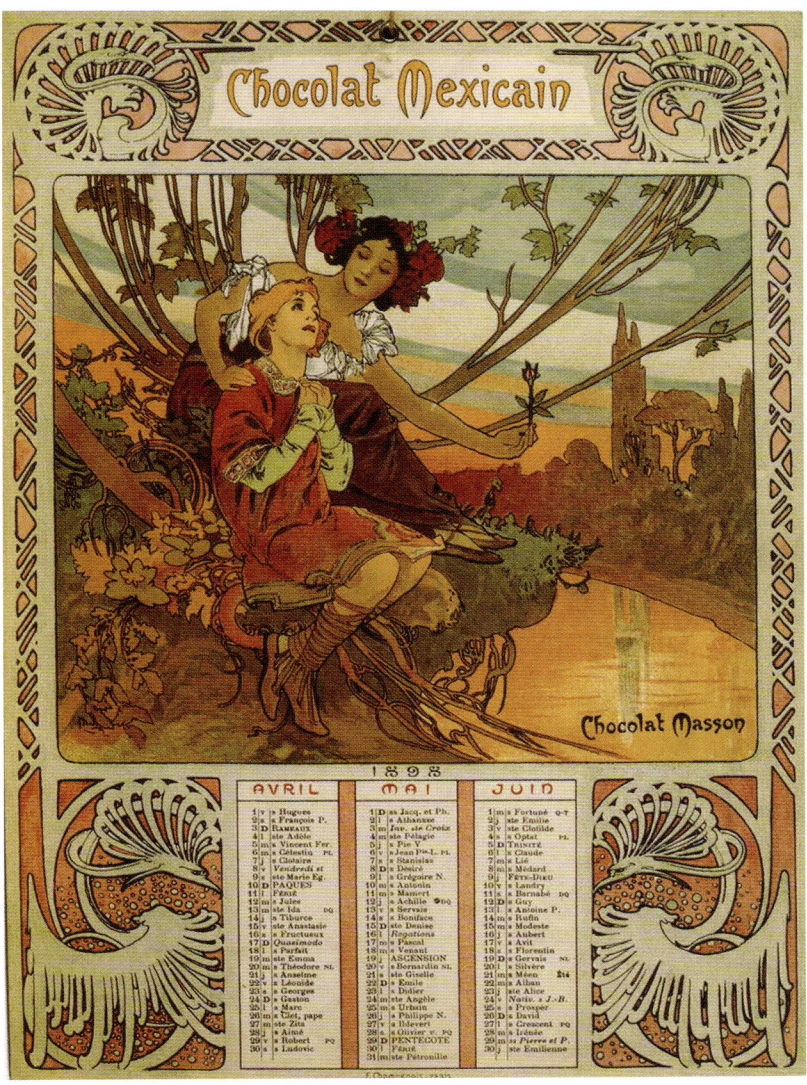

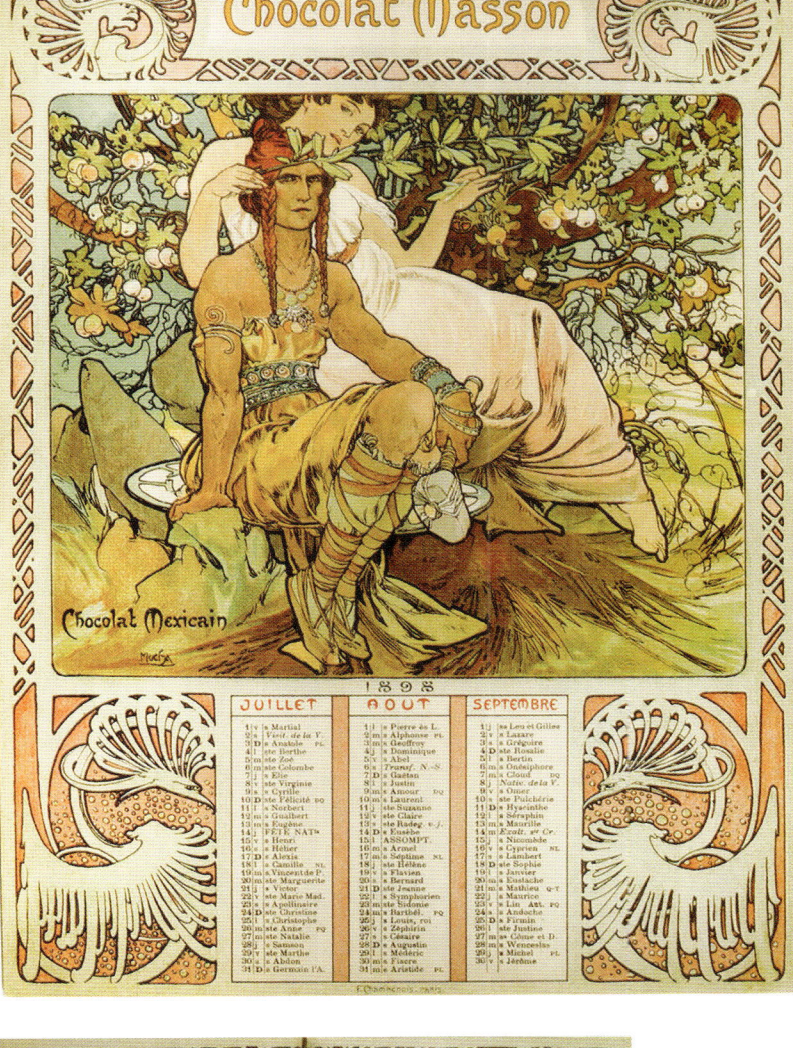

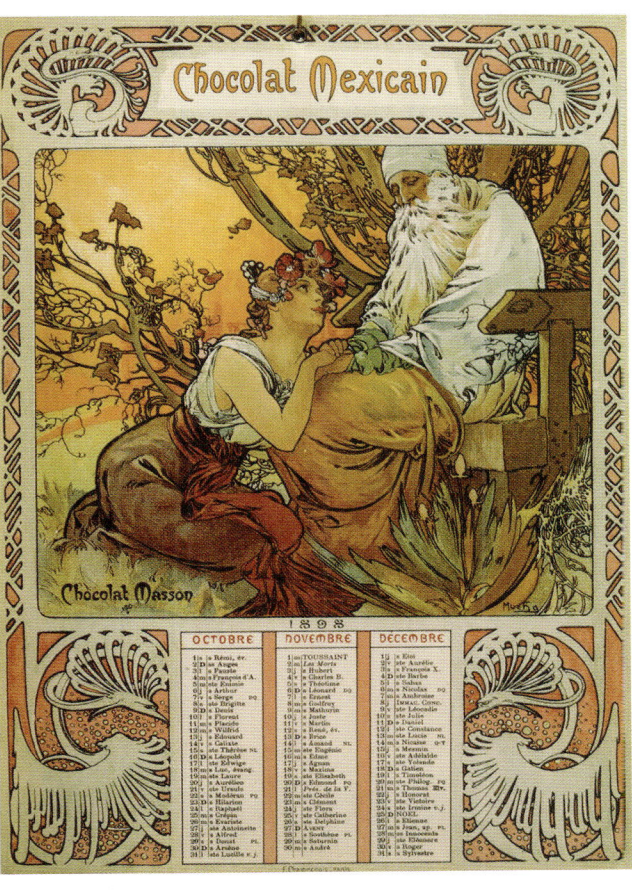

[ABOVE LEFT]
Calendar for **Chocolat Masson/ Chocolat Mexicain** for April, May, and June (1897). Color lithograph.

[ABOVE RIGHT]
Calendar for **Chocolat Masson/ Chocolat Mexicain** for July, August, and September (1897). Color lithograph.

[RIGHT]
Calendar for **Chocolat Masson/Chocolat Mexicain** for October, November, and December (1897). Color lithograph.

[OPPOSITE PAGE]
Calendar for **Chocolat Masson/Chocolat Mexicain** for Januaray, February, and March (1897). Color lithograph.

In 1897, Mucha produced a series of four posters calendars for Chocolat Masson/Chocolat Mexicain, each capturing three months of a calendar. The four together depict the Ages of Man, represented chronologically as the year progresses.

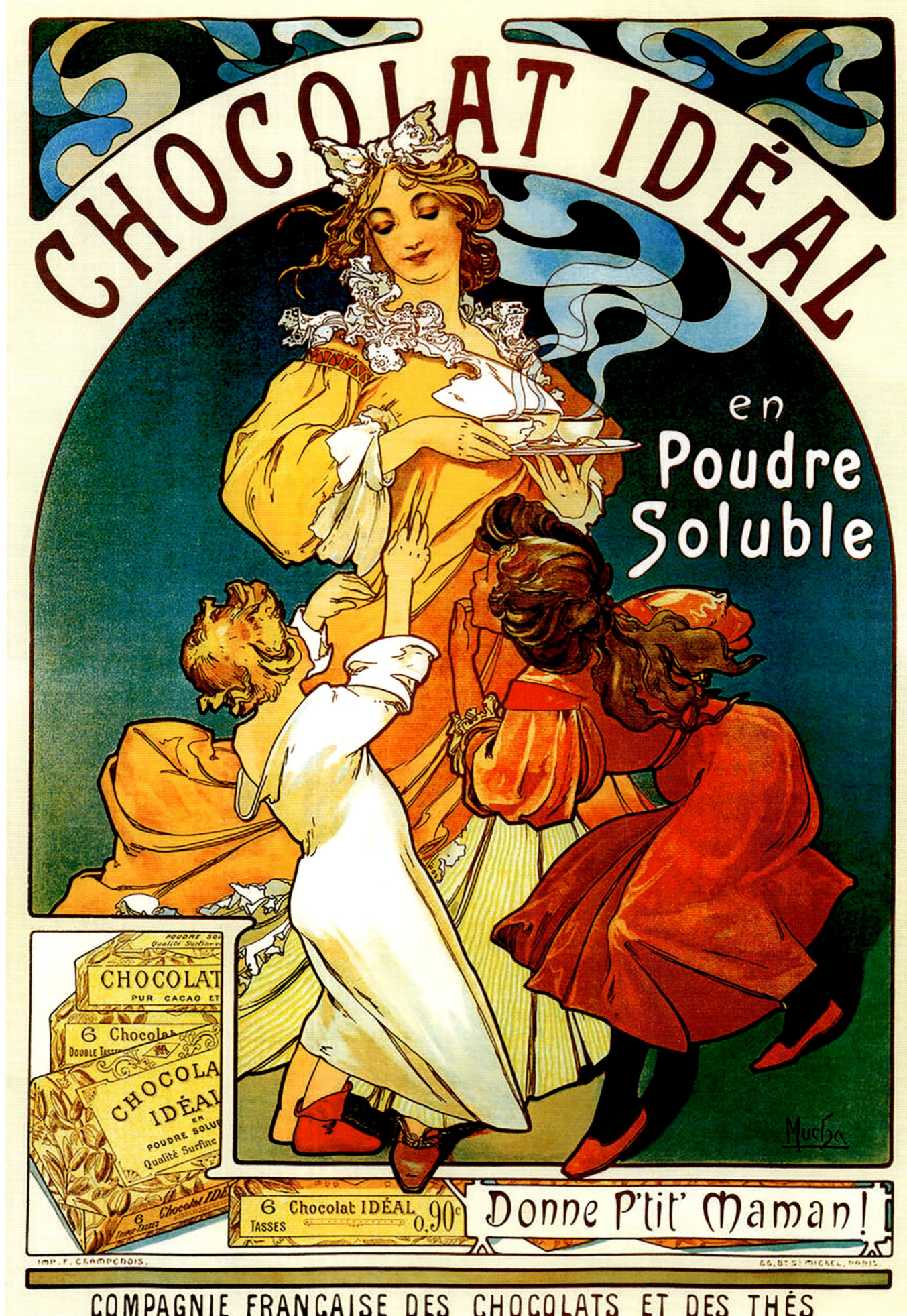

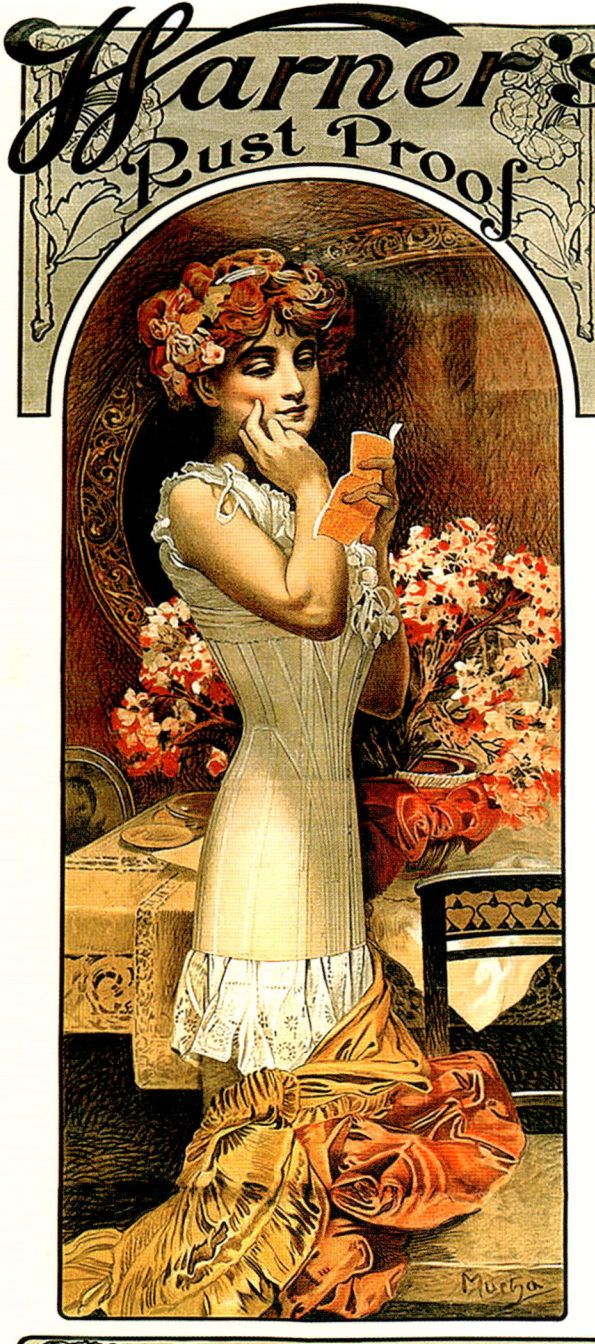

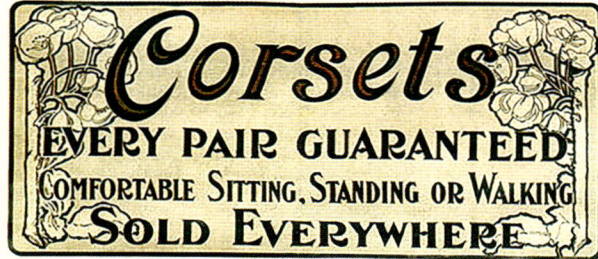

Advertising poster for **Warner's Rust Proof Corsets** (1909). Color lithograph.

[OPPOSITE PAGE]
Advertising poster for Compagnie Française des Chocolats et des Thés **Chocolat Idéal** (1898). Color lithograph.

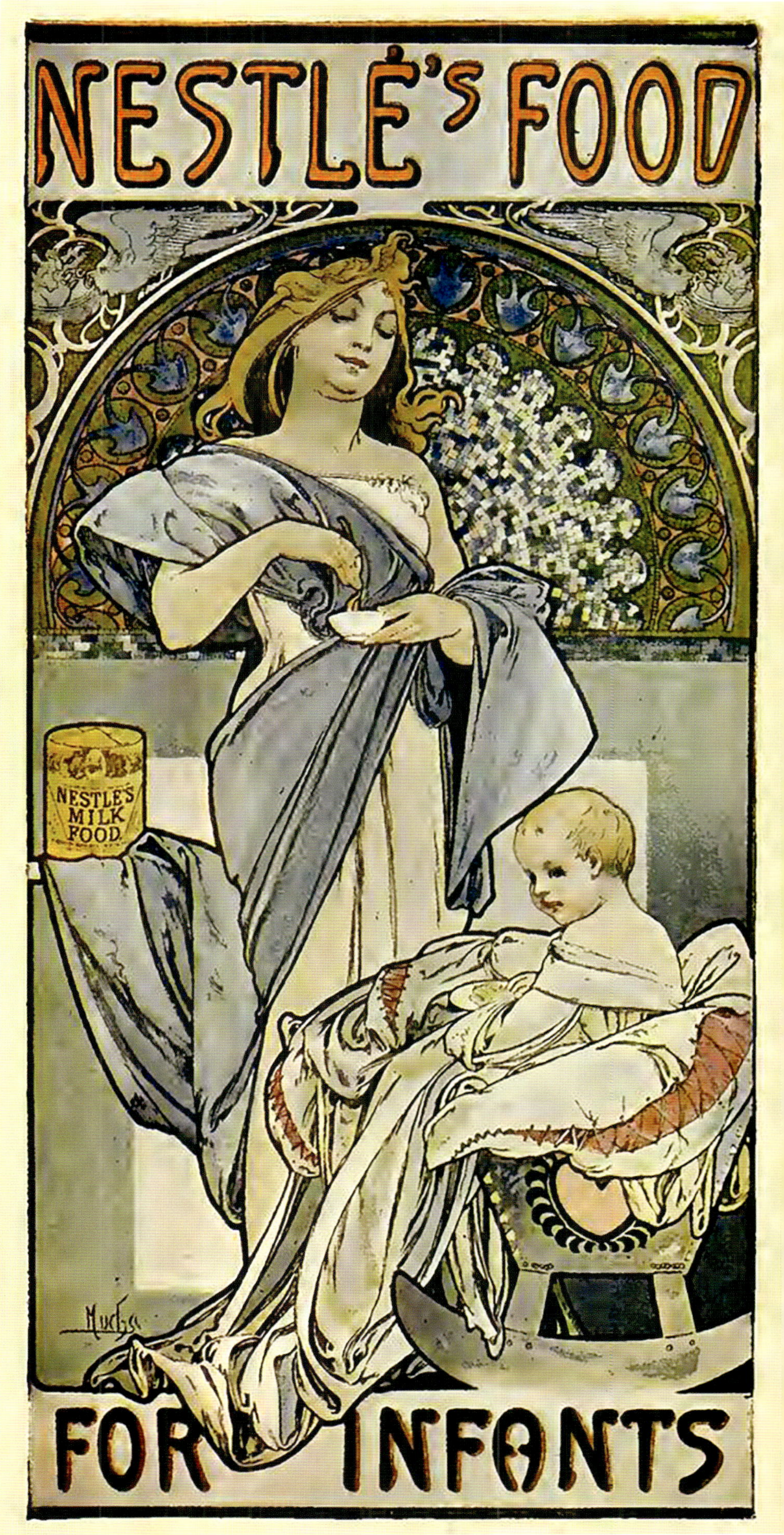

[RIGHT]
Nestlé's Food for Infants (1897). Color lithograph.

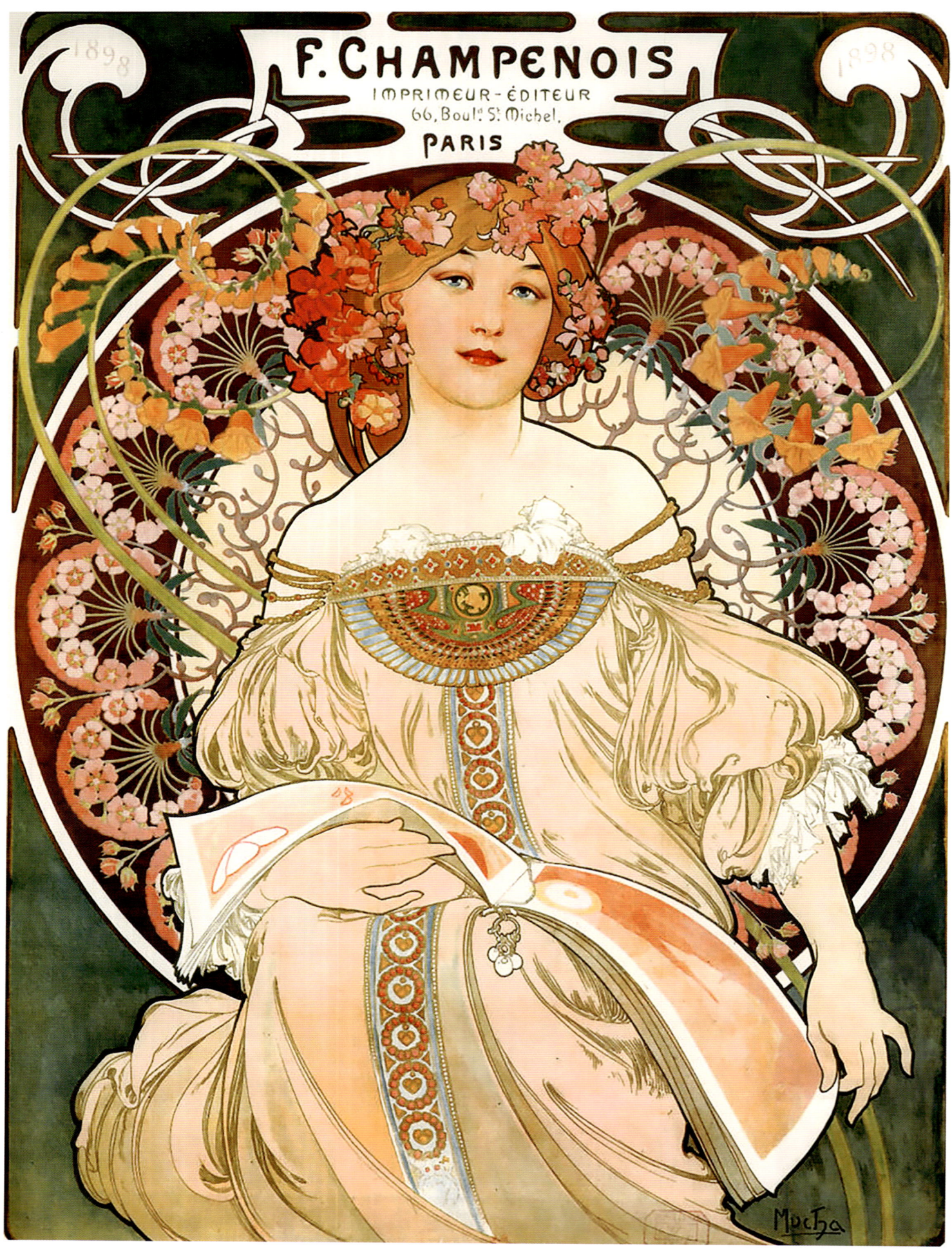

ICONIC POSTERS

Between 1895 and 1900, Mucha's career soared as he produced a series of remarkable posters that would become emblematic of the Art Nouveau movement. During this prolific period, Mucha created posters for various events and products, as well as stand-alone series sold just for their beauty. These works further established his reputation for blending captivating female figures, lush decorative elements, and intricate typography into a harmonious composition. Mucha's distinct aesthetic, which evoked a sense of luxury and refinement, had a profound impact on poster design, elevating the medium from mere advertising to an art form in its own right.

[OPPOSITE PAGE]
F. Champenois Imprimeur–Éditeur (1898). Color lithograph.

In the printing industry, Mucha collaborated with F. Champenois Imprimeur-Éditeur, a prestigious French printing firm that produced high-quality posters and other promotional materials. He designed several pieces for the company, such as the well-known poster that promoted the firm itself. F. Champenois also worked with Mucha to design many of Sarah Bernhardt's posters during their six-year contract.

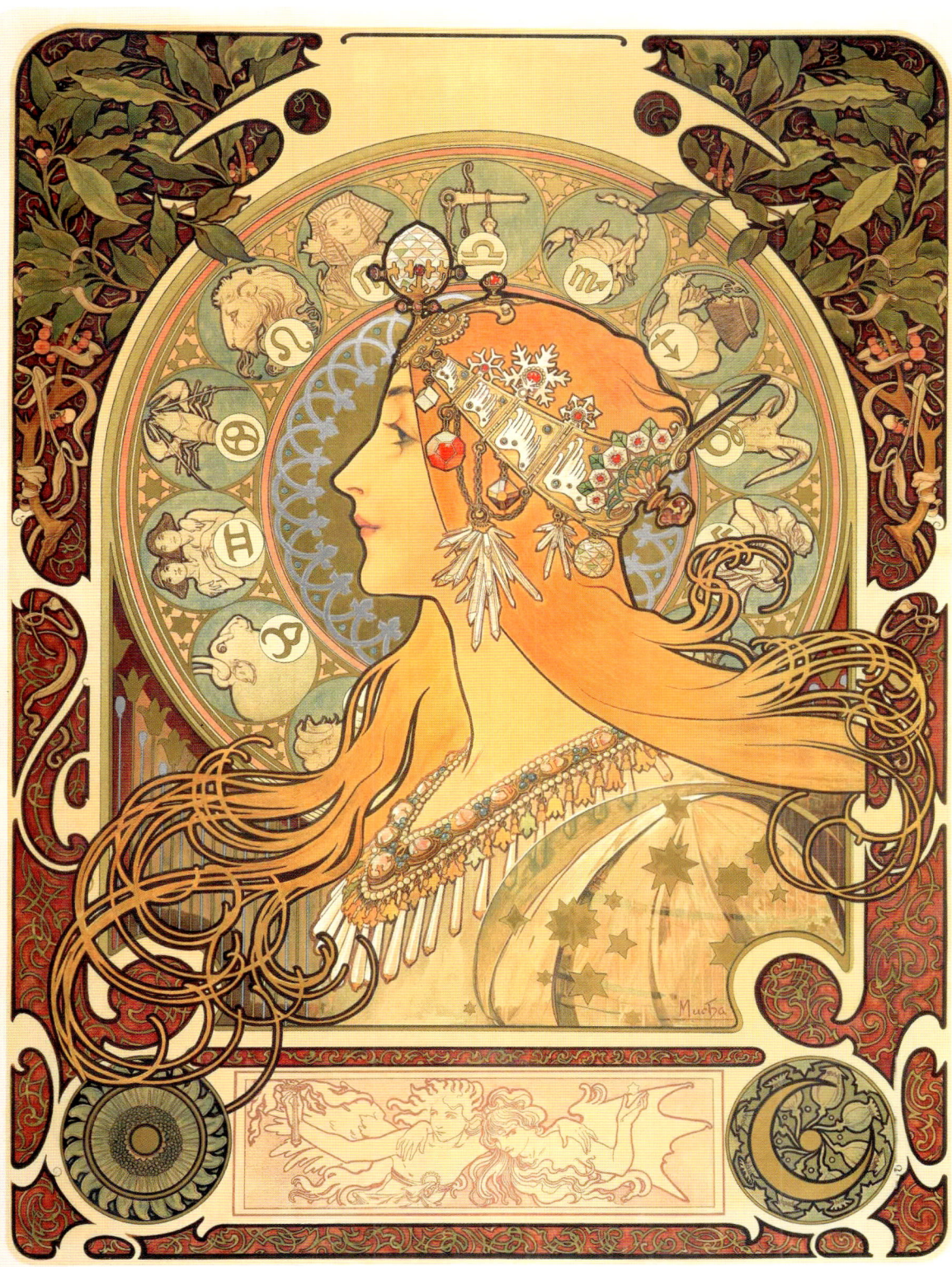

[RIGHT]
Zodiac (1896). Color lithograph.

Created for an in-house calendar, this was Mucha's first work under his contract with F. Champenois .

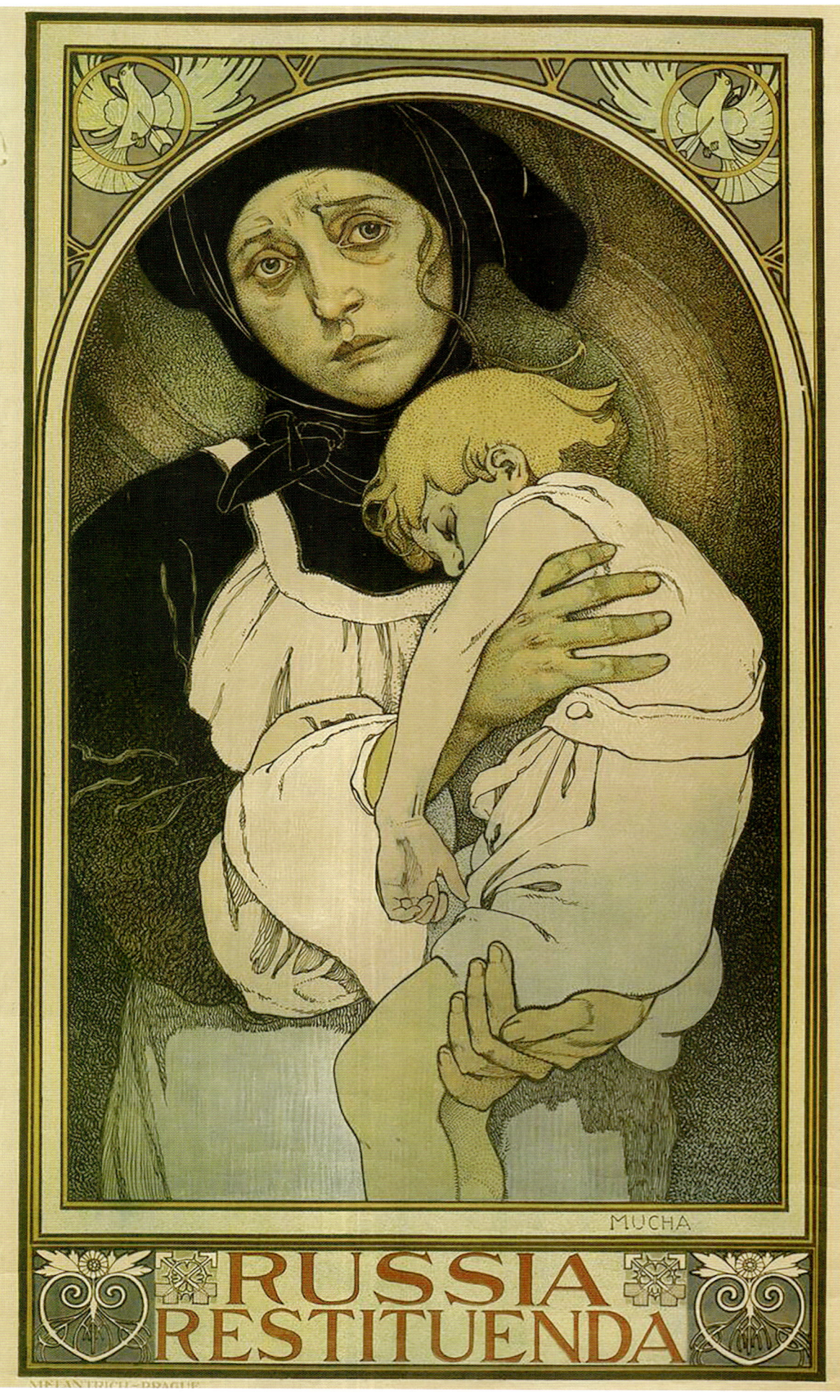

RUSSIA
RESTITUENDA

MUCHA

[LEFT]
Russia Restituenda
("Russia Must Recover")
(1922). Color lithograph.

This poignant poster of Mother Russia with a frail child in her arms was created as a plea for help for starving Russian children, after the collapse of the Russian provisional government to the Soviets.

[OPPOSITE PAGE] *Slavia*
(1896). Color lithograph.

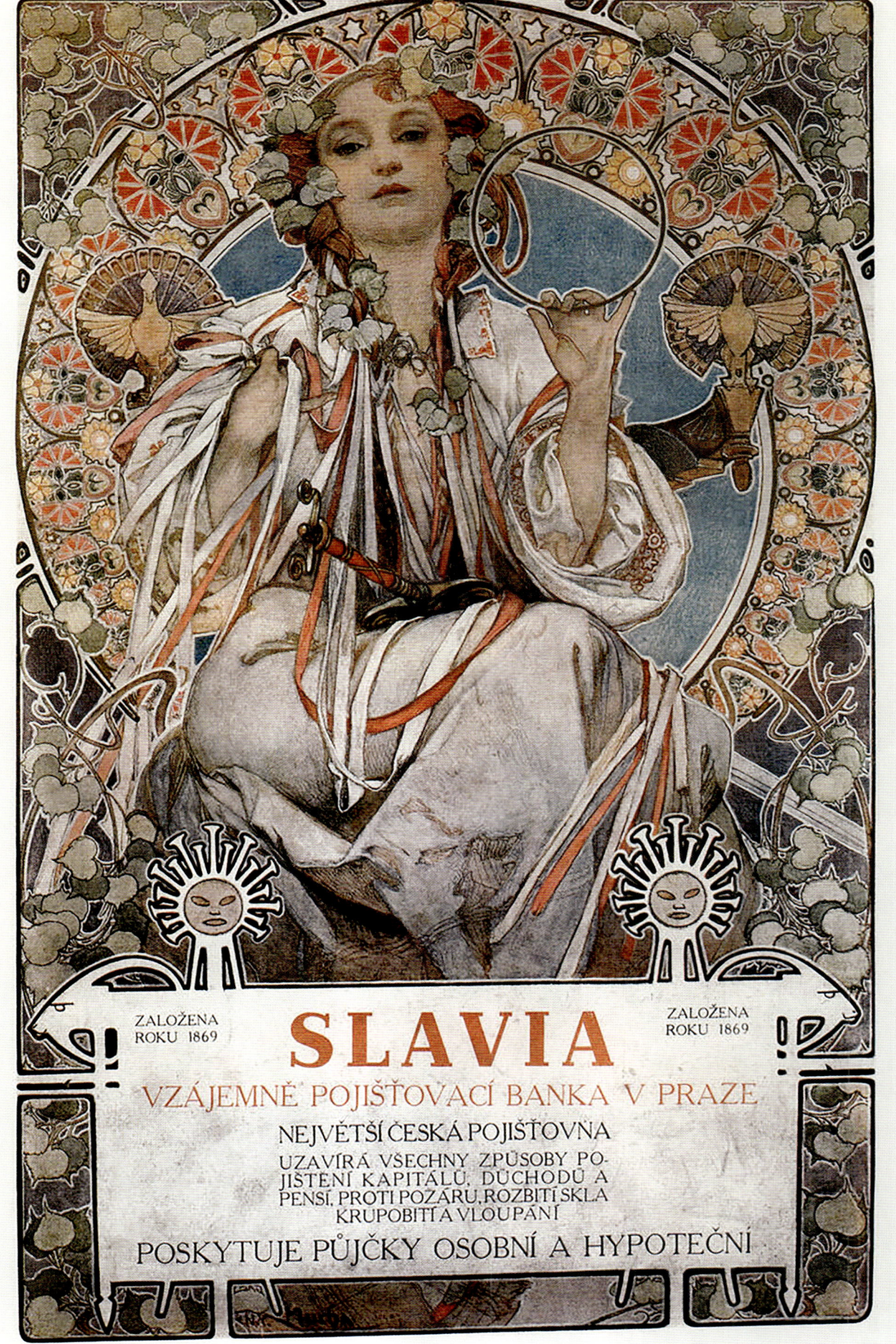

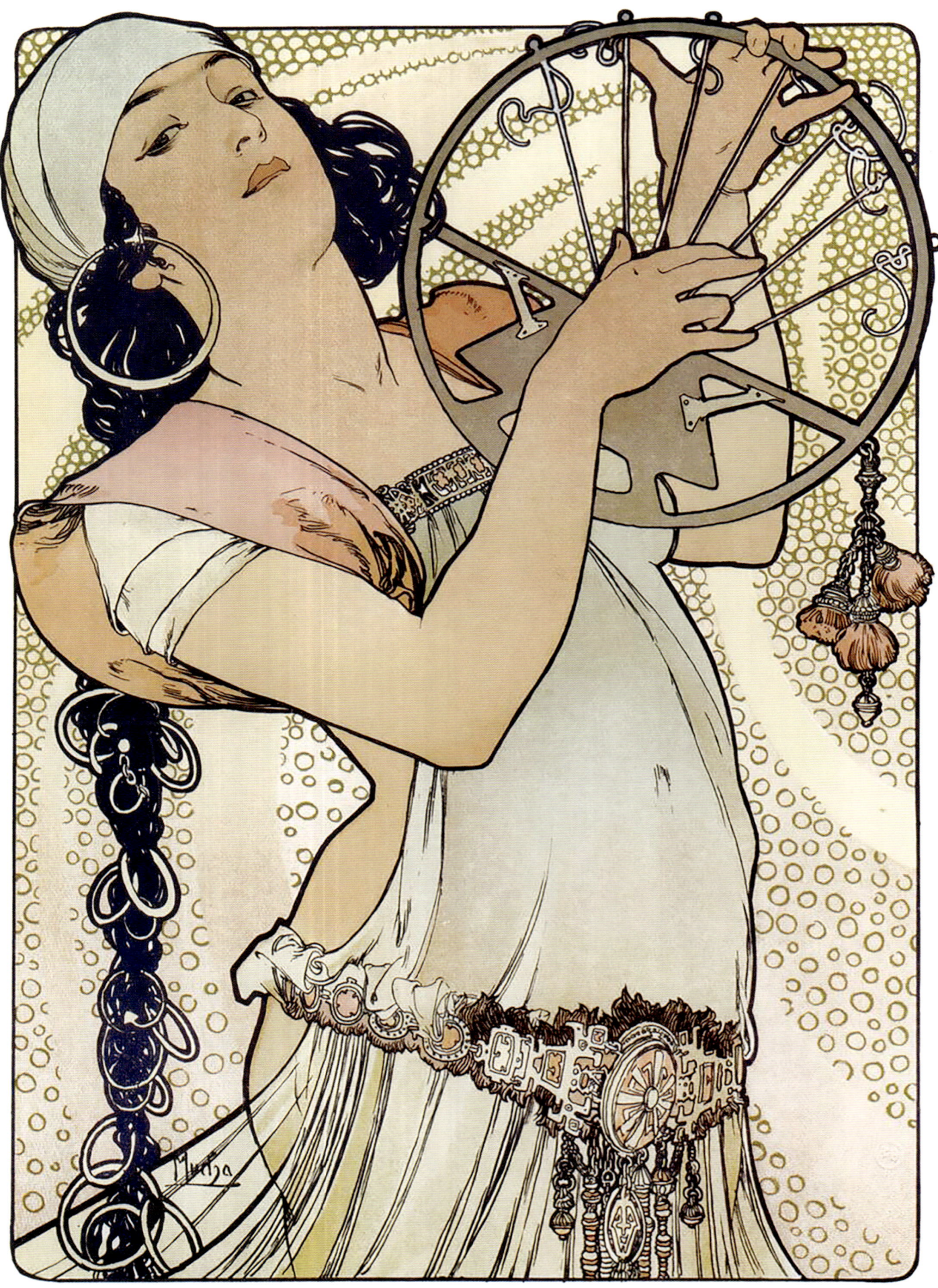

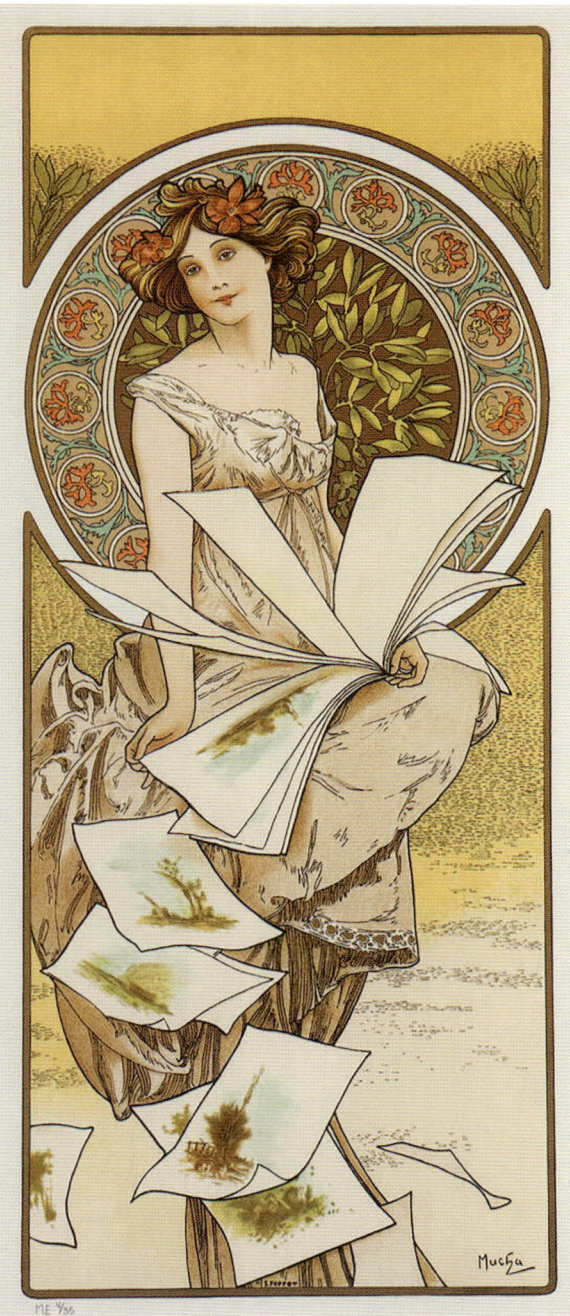

F. Champenois Calendar
(c. 1897). Color lithograph.

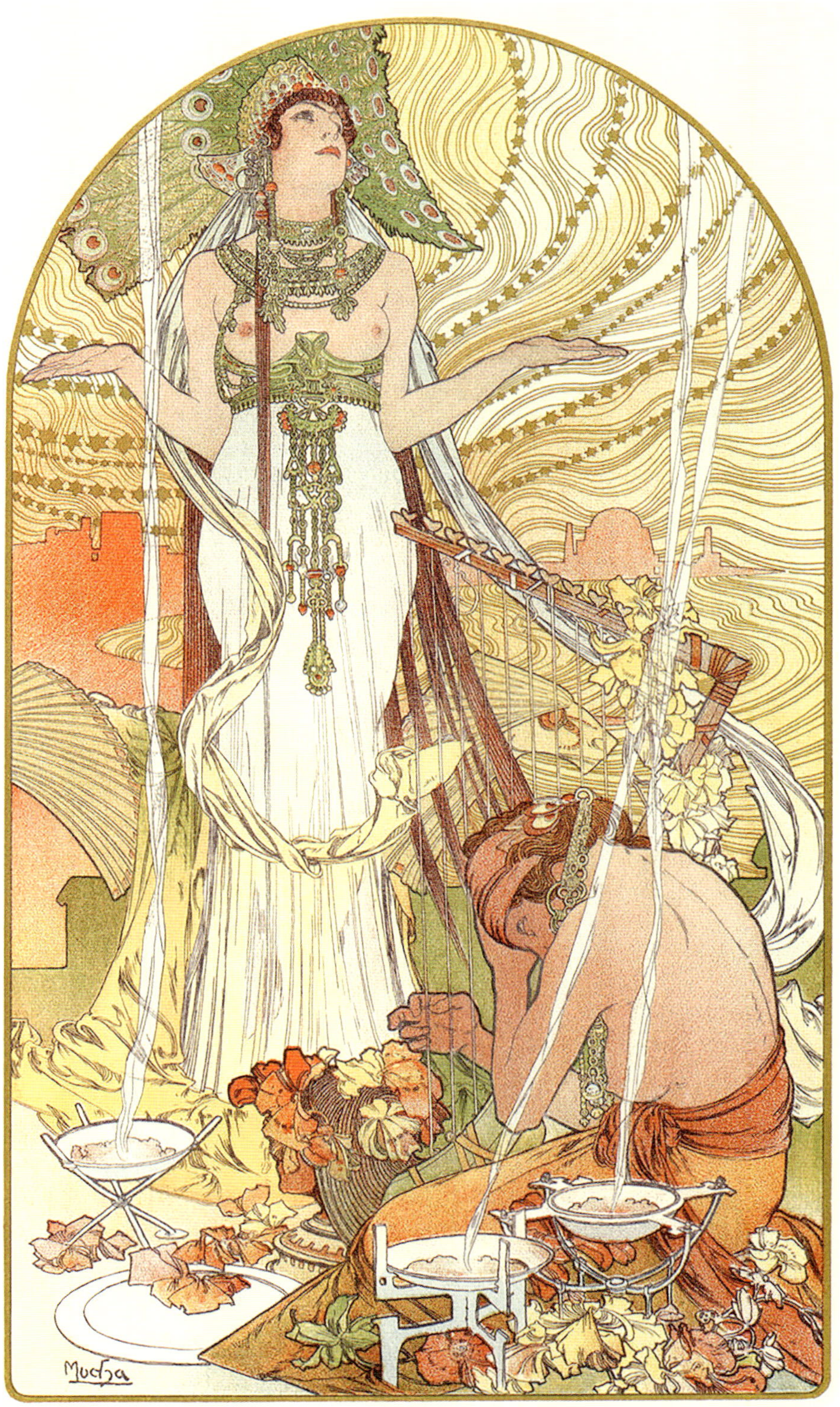

[RIGHT]
Incantation (Salammbo) (c. 1897).
Color lithograph on wove paper.

[OPPOSITE PAGE]
Salomé from *L'Estampe Moderne No. 2*
(1897). Color lithograph.

One from a set of four lithographs from L'Estampe
Moderne, *which appeared in 1897–1899 as a series
of monthly fascicles printed by F. Champenois.
Its aim was to promote the art of printmaking by
commissioning images from noted Art Nouveau artists,
such as Mucha, Henri Fantin-Latour, and Louis Rhead.*

" *I was happy to be involved in an art for the people and
not for private drawing rooms. It was inexpensive,
accessible to the general public, and it found a home in
poor families as well as in more affluent circles.*"

~ ALPHONSE MUCHA

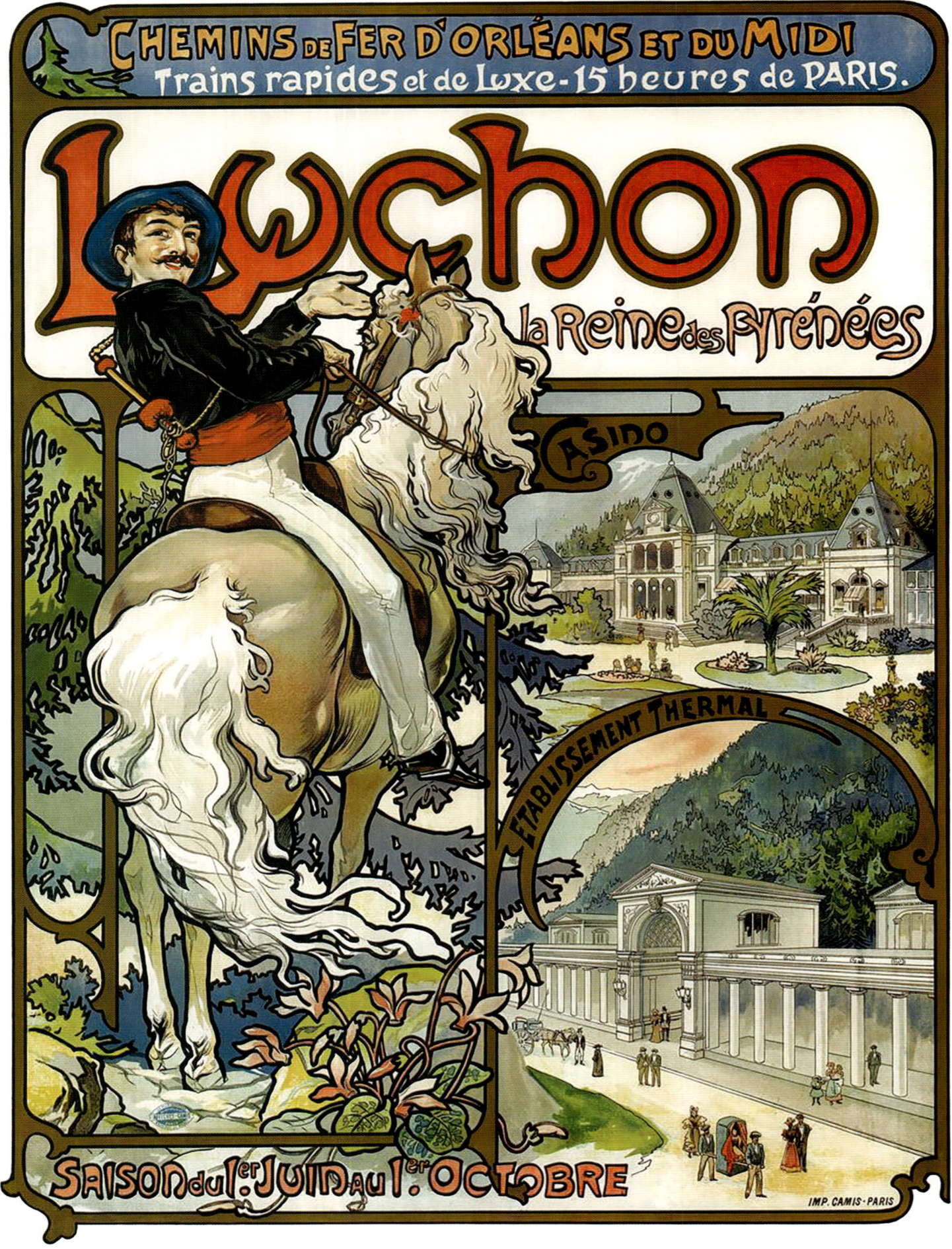

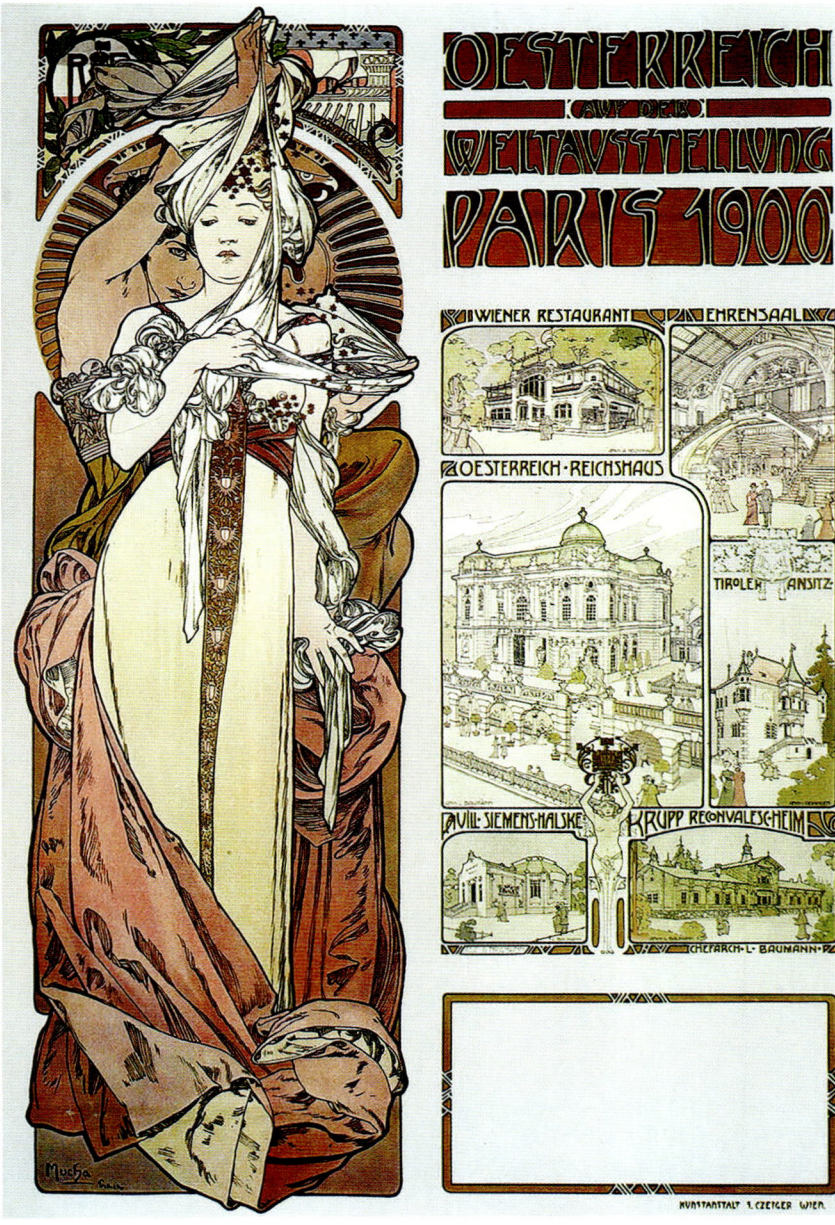

Promotional poster for **Austria at the World Exposition, Paris** (1900). Color lithograph.

[OPPOSITE PAGE]
Railway travel advertisement for **Luchon** (1895). Color lithograph.

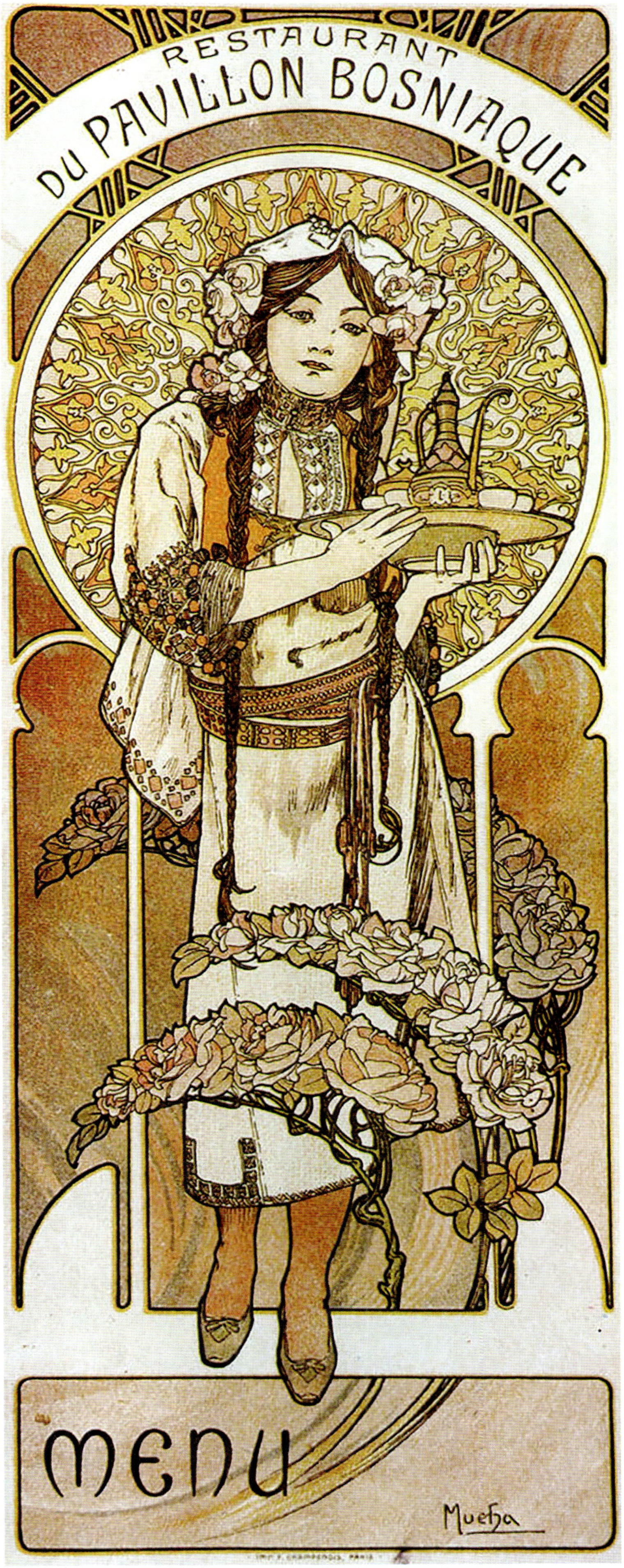

[RIGHT]
Menu du Pavillon Bosniaque (1897). Color lithograph.

Mucha was associated with a number of projects related to the Universal Exhibition in Paris in 1900, the "greatest event of the century," including the Bosnia-Herzegovina pavilion.

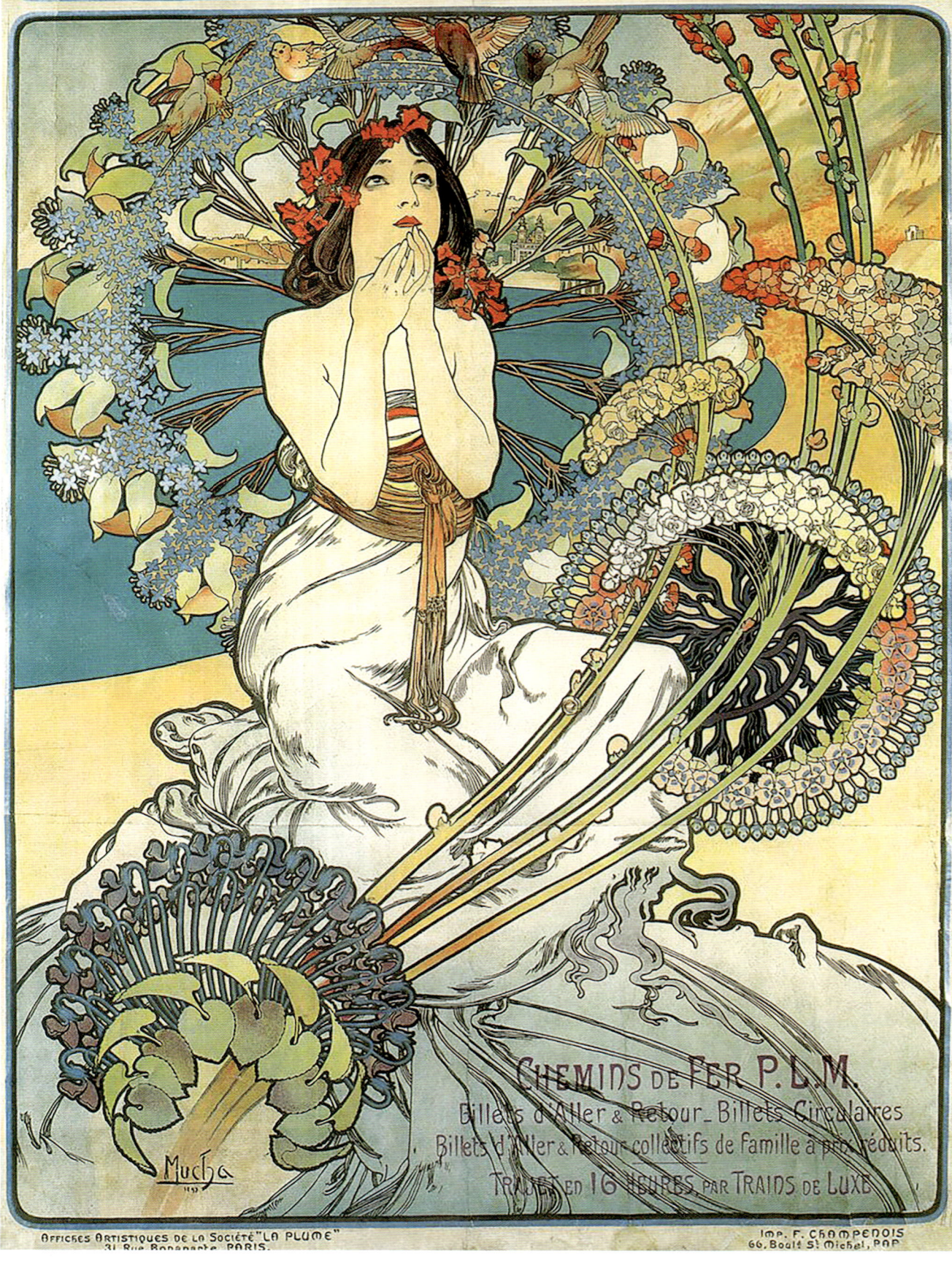

THREE SEASONS

In this series, unusual for the horizontal format of the frames, Mucha evokes the embodiments of the summer and autumn seasons, with languid women draped under the same tree, as it shifts from the leafy greens of summertime to the muted tones of the dying season. Winter huddles instead beneath a snow-draped evergreen. This is a rather obscure set, presumably first printed by F. Champenois, and no one knows why spring is left out.

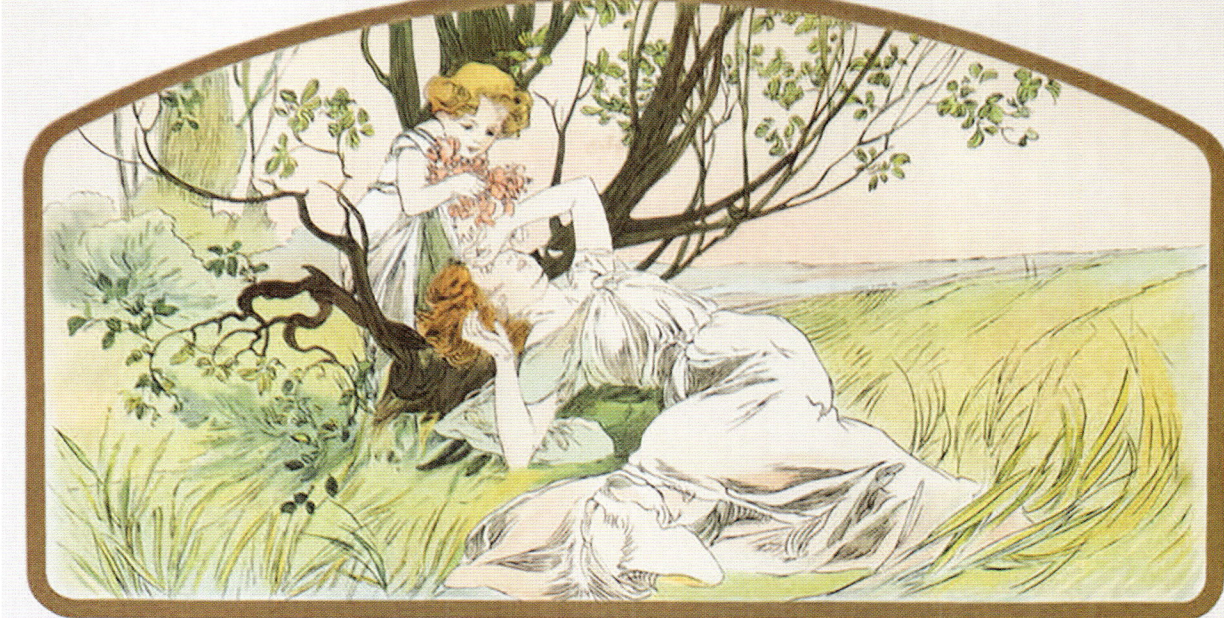

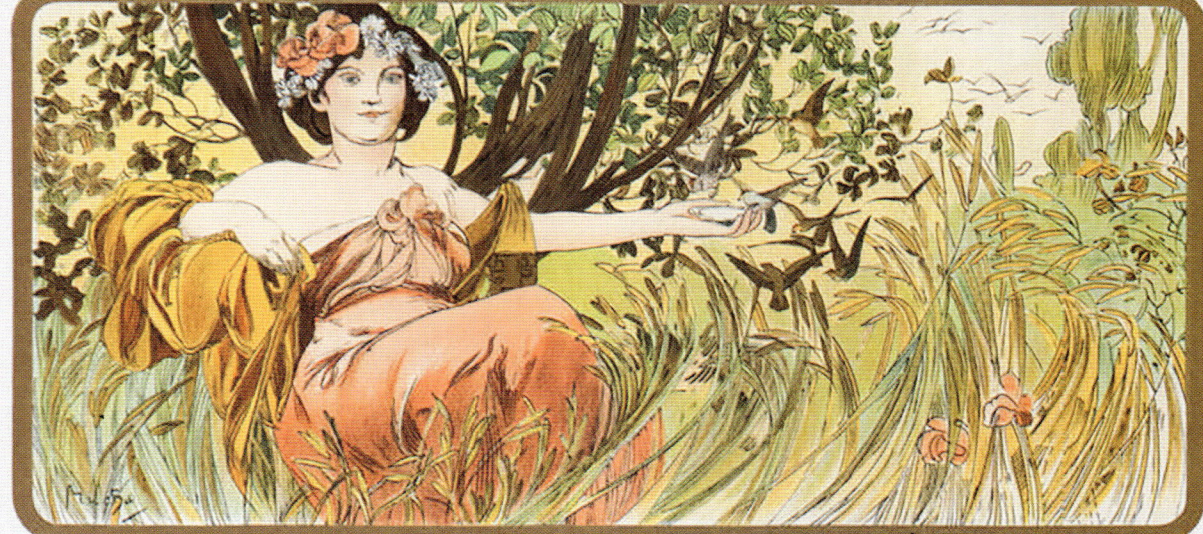

[TOP RIGHT]
Three Seasons: Summer (c. 1898). Color lithograph.

[CENTER RIGHT]
Three Seasons: Autumn (c. 1898). Color lithograph.

[BOTTOM RIGHT]
Three Seasons: Winter (c. 1898). Color lithograph.

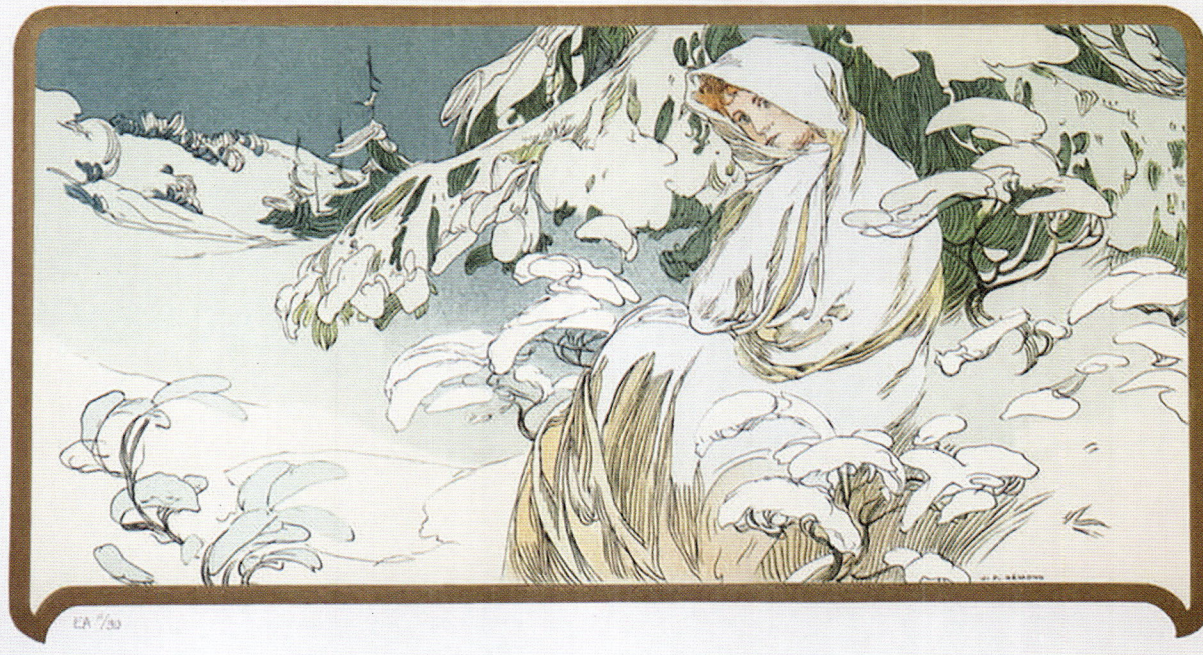

[OPPOSITE PAGE]
Poster for *Monaco – Monte Carlo, P.L.M. railway services* (1897). Color lithograph.

DECORATIVE PANELS

Mucha's decorative panels exemplify his mastery of the Art Nouveau style. These panels, often referred to as *panneaux décoratifs*, were noncommissioned decorative artworks that showcased Mucha's personal vision and artistic ideals. They typically featured allegorical themes, such as the passage of time, seasons, or personifications of abstract concepts. The panels were characterized by elegant female figures, intricate patterns, and rich, harmonious color schemes. His decorative panels gained immense popularity, adorning the walls of countless homes and influencing interior design trends of the time. Today, these works remain an essential part of his artistic legacy, capturing the spirit and beauty of the Art Nouveau movement.

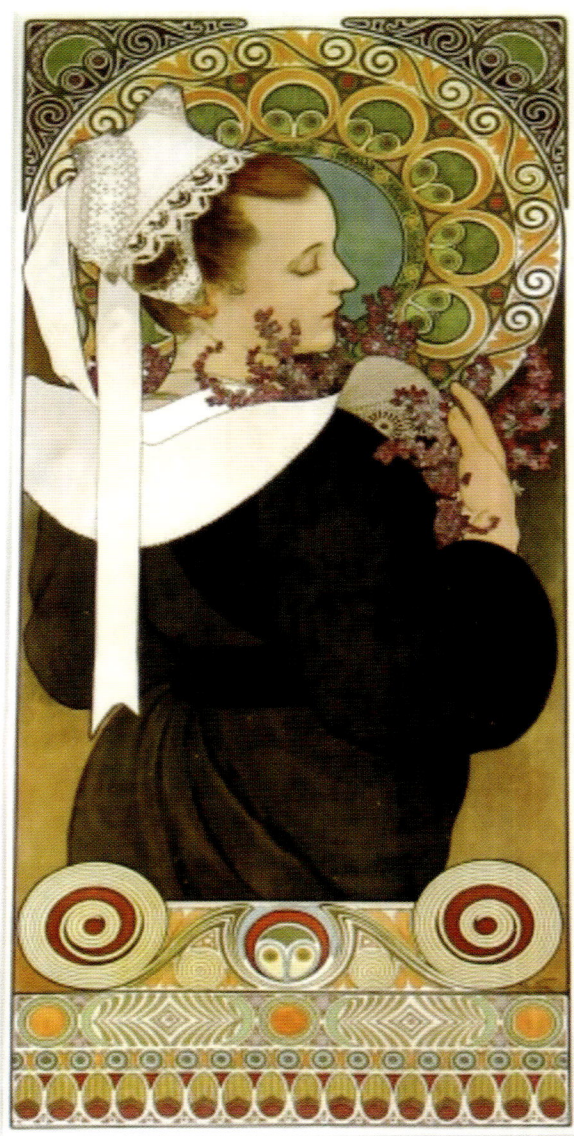

Heather from Coastal Cliffs (1902). Color lithograph.

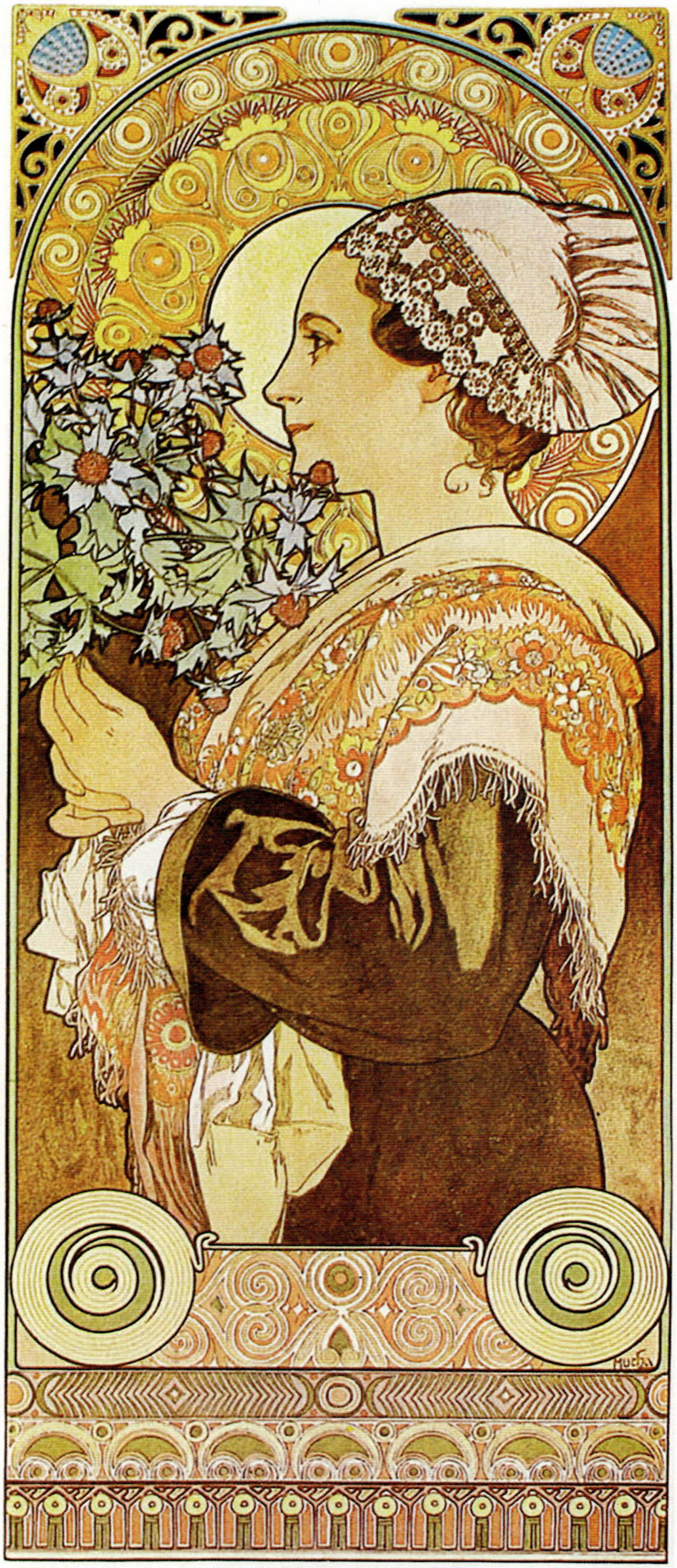

[RIGHT]
Thistle from the Sands (1902). Color lithograph.

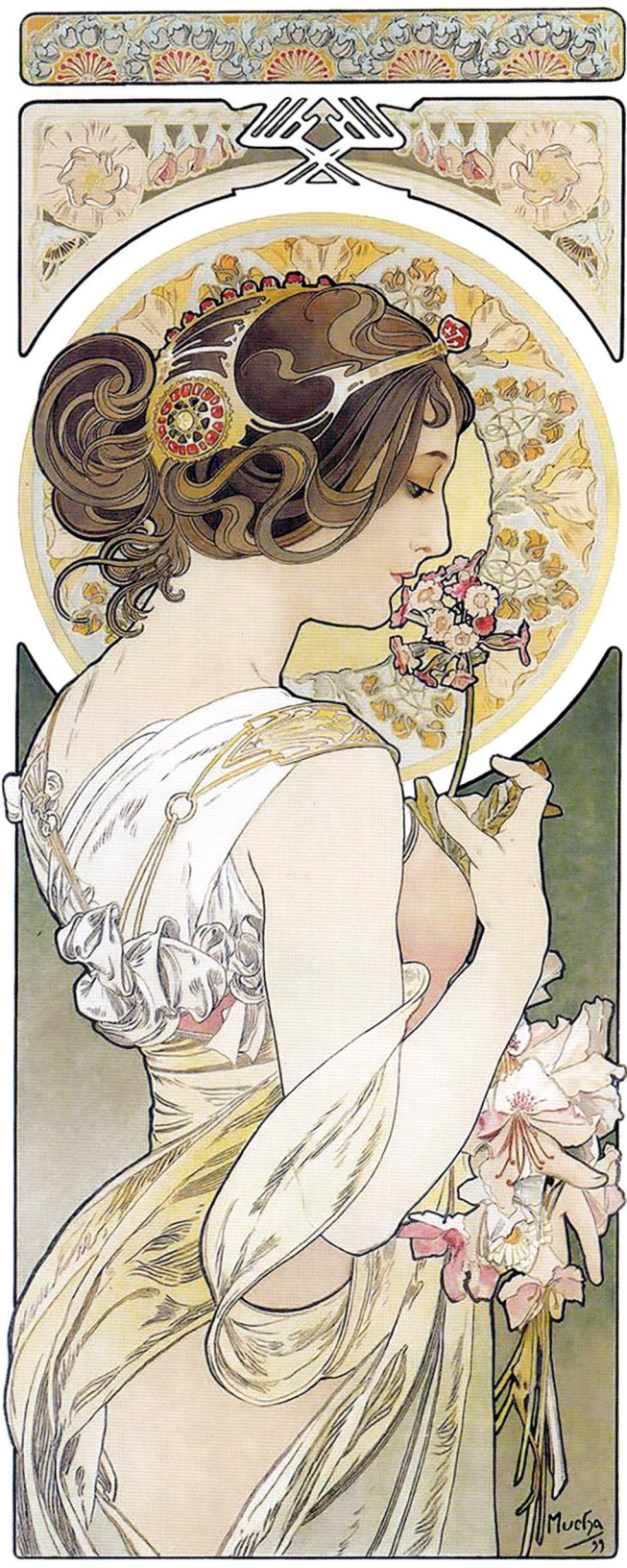

Primrose (1899). Color lithograph.

Created for posters advertising the J Royer printing company, the Primrose *and* Feather *pair of panels was inspired by the title of an 1807 Brothers Grimm story.*

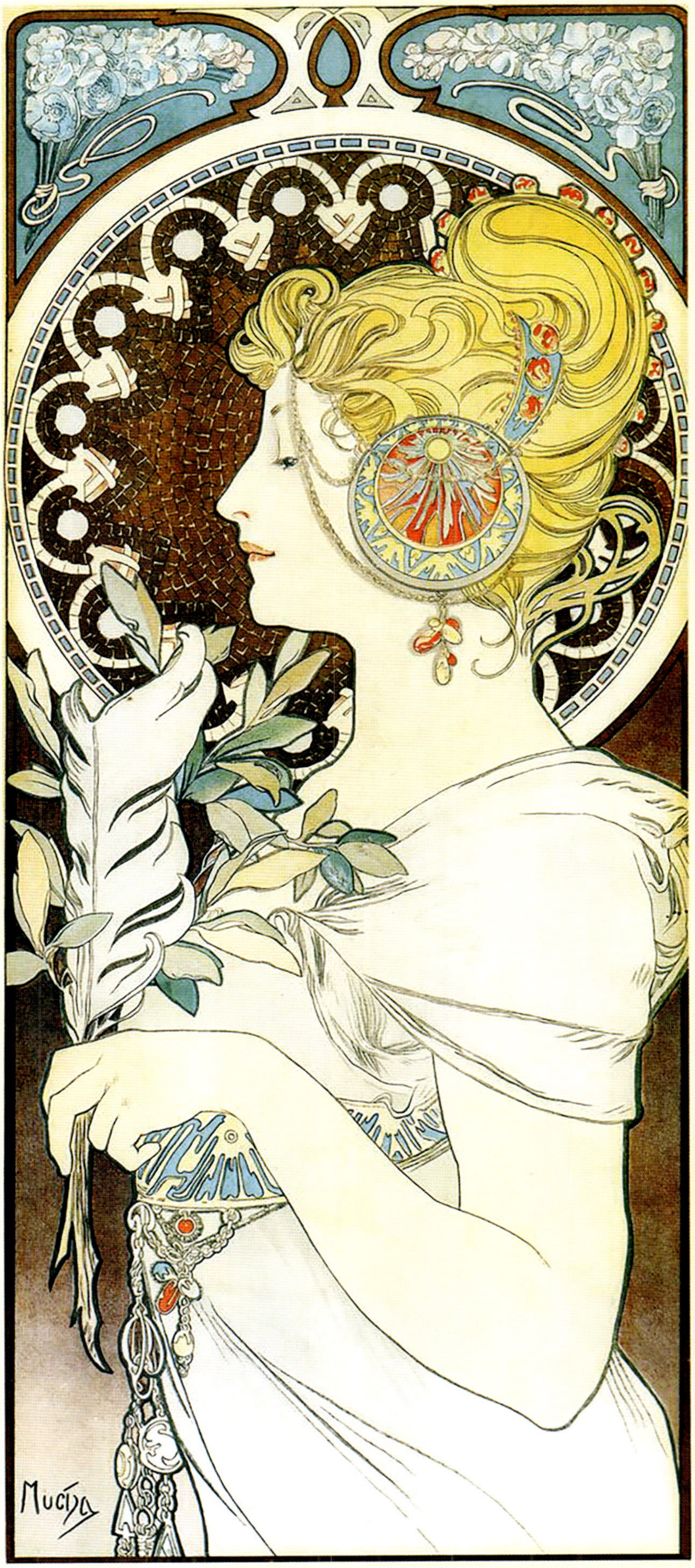

[RIGHT]
Feather (1899). Color lithograph.

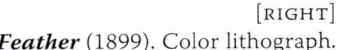

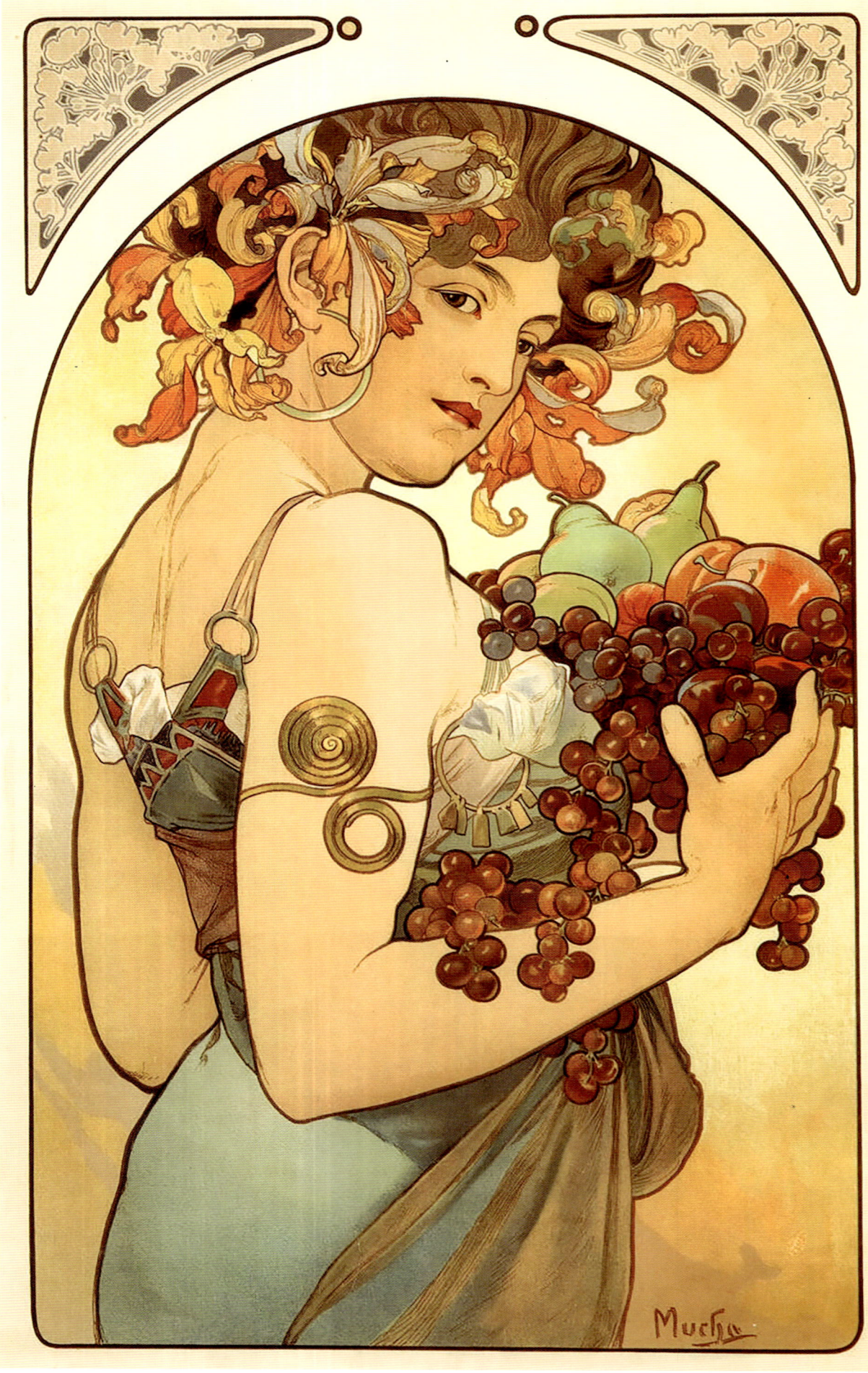

Fruit
(1902).
Color
lithograph.

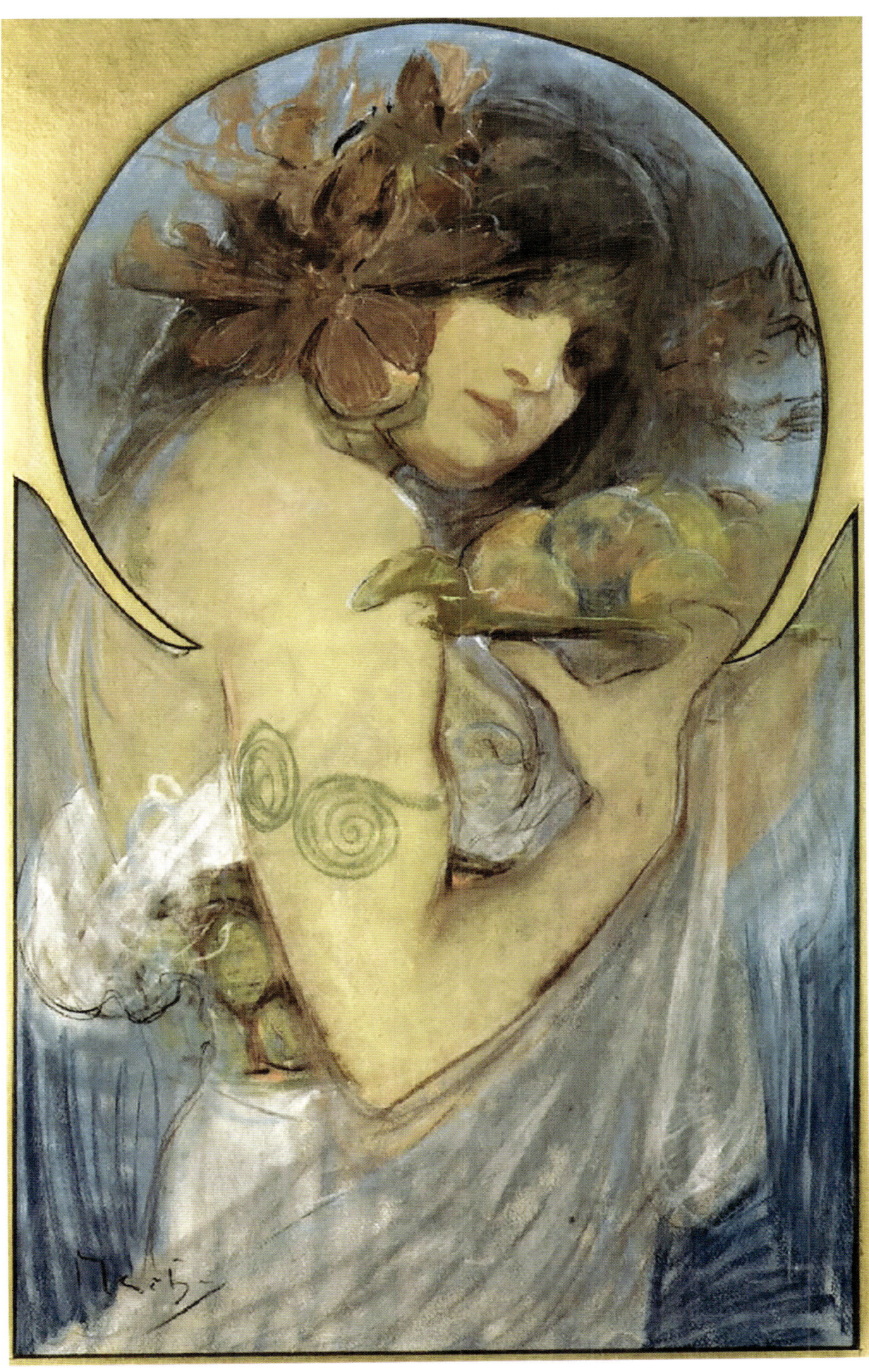

Study for the
poster *Fruit*
(1902).
Cclor
lithograph.

THE SEASONS

The first series of decorative panels that Mucha completed for F. Champenois relies on the venerable trope of personifying the four seasons. Mucha stamped his own Art Nouveau style upon this grouping of ethereal women, which made them highly popular—so much so that he would return to this same theme in 1897 and 1900. There is also evidence that he made at least two other season-themed series.

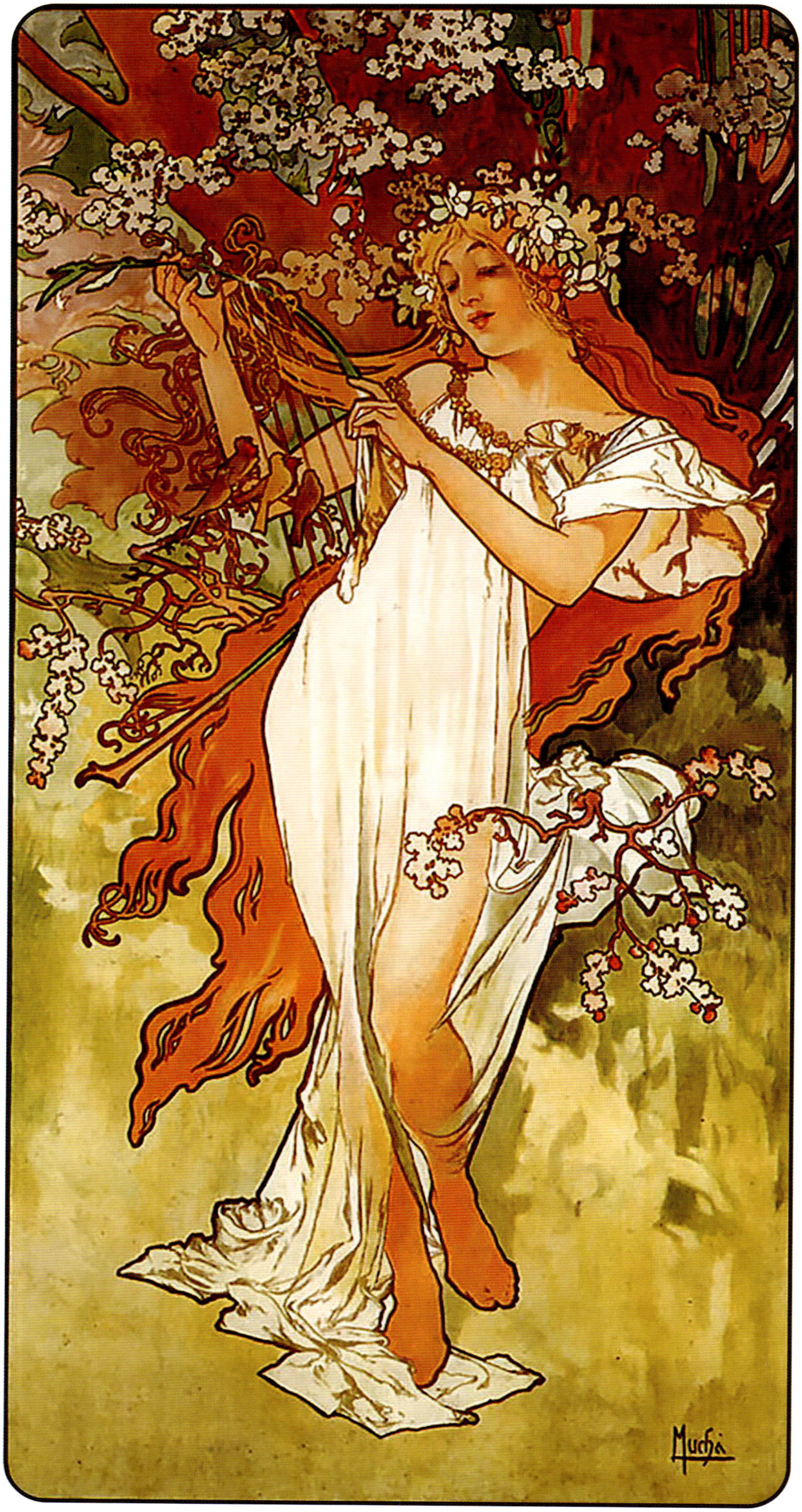

[RIGHT]
The Seasons: Spring
(1896). Color lithograph.

[BELOW]
The Seasons; Winter
(1896). Color lithograph.

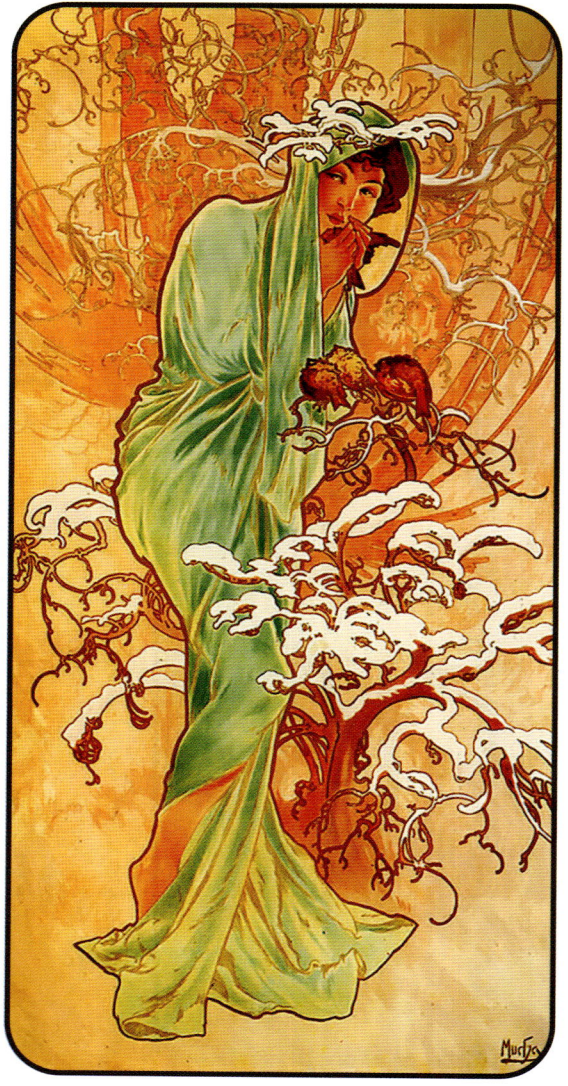

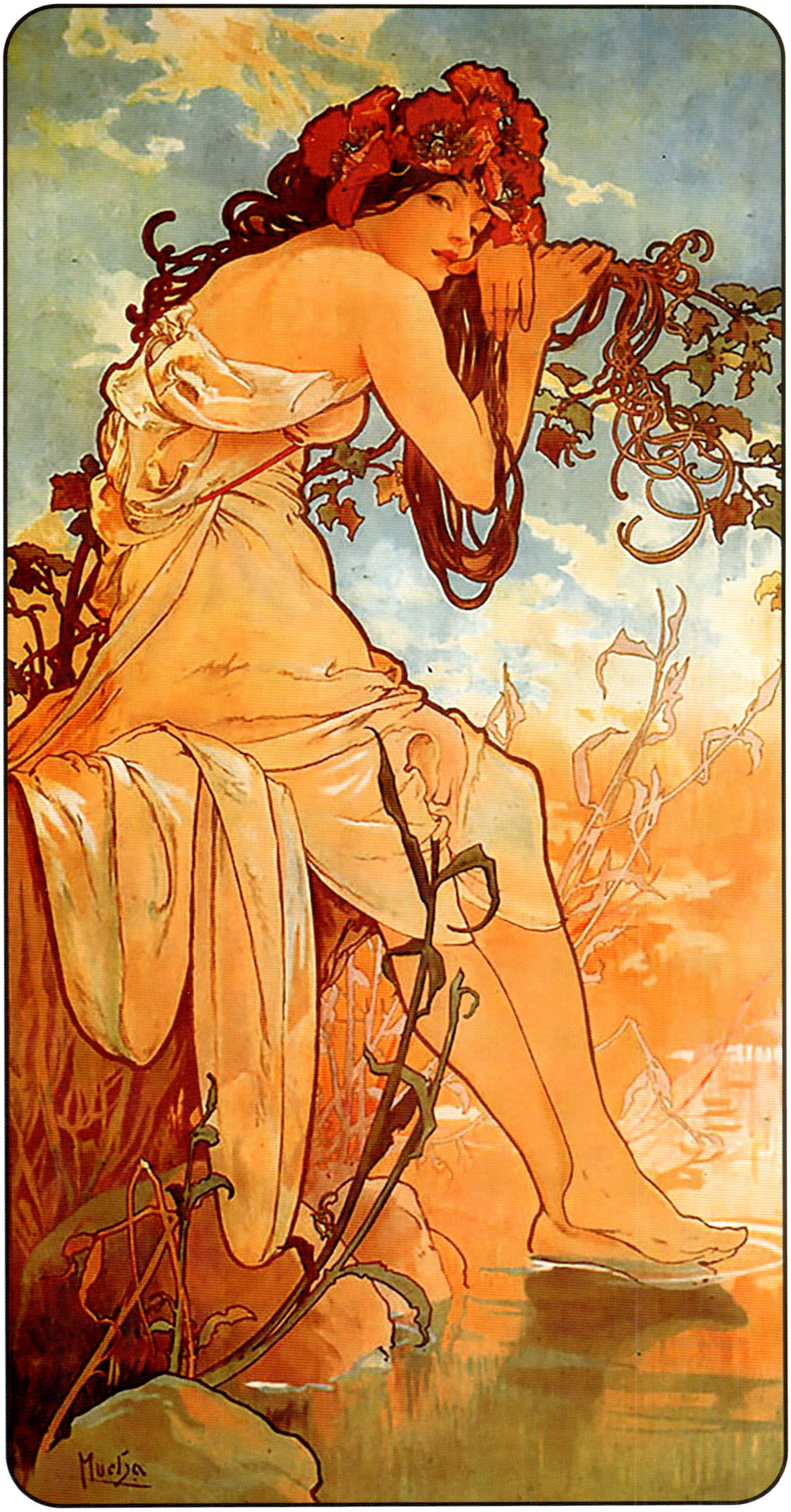

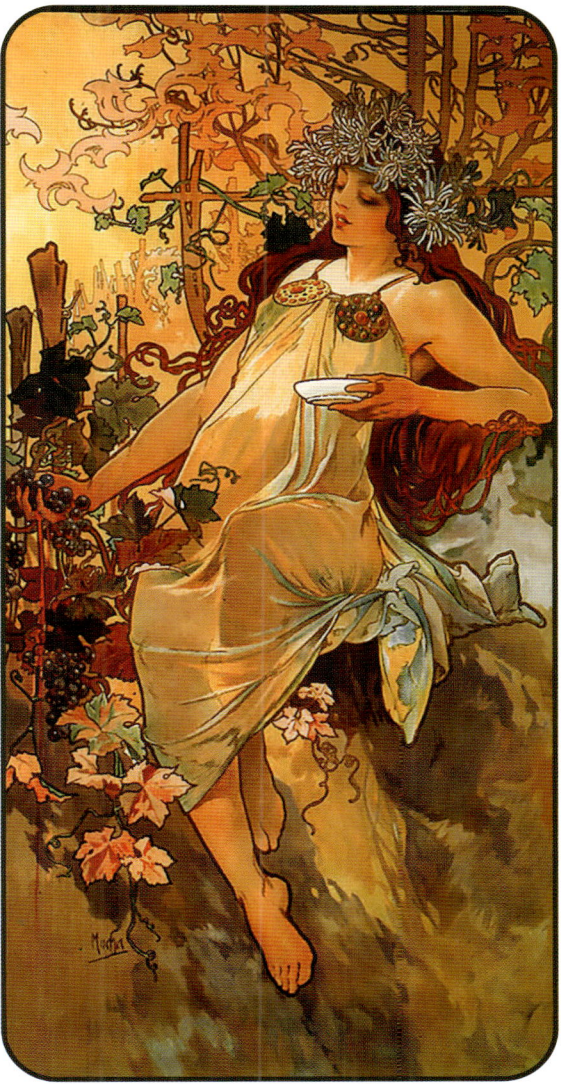

The Seasons: Autumn
(1896). Color lithograph.

[LEFT]
The Seasons: Summer
(1896). Color lithograph.

[OVERLEAF]
The Seasons series (1897). From left to right, ***Spring, Summer, Autumn, Winter***
(1896). Color lithograph.

Mucha's 1897 series of The Seasons is somewhat darker and more ornate than that of 1896, with architectural shapes framing the figures of the women, as well as banners of seasonal flowers above their heads.

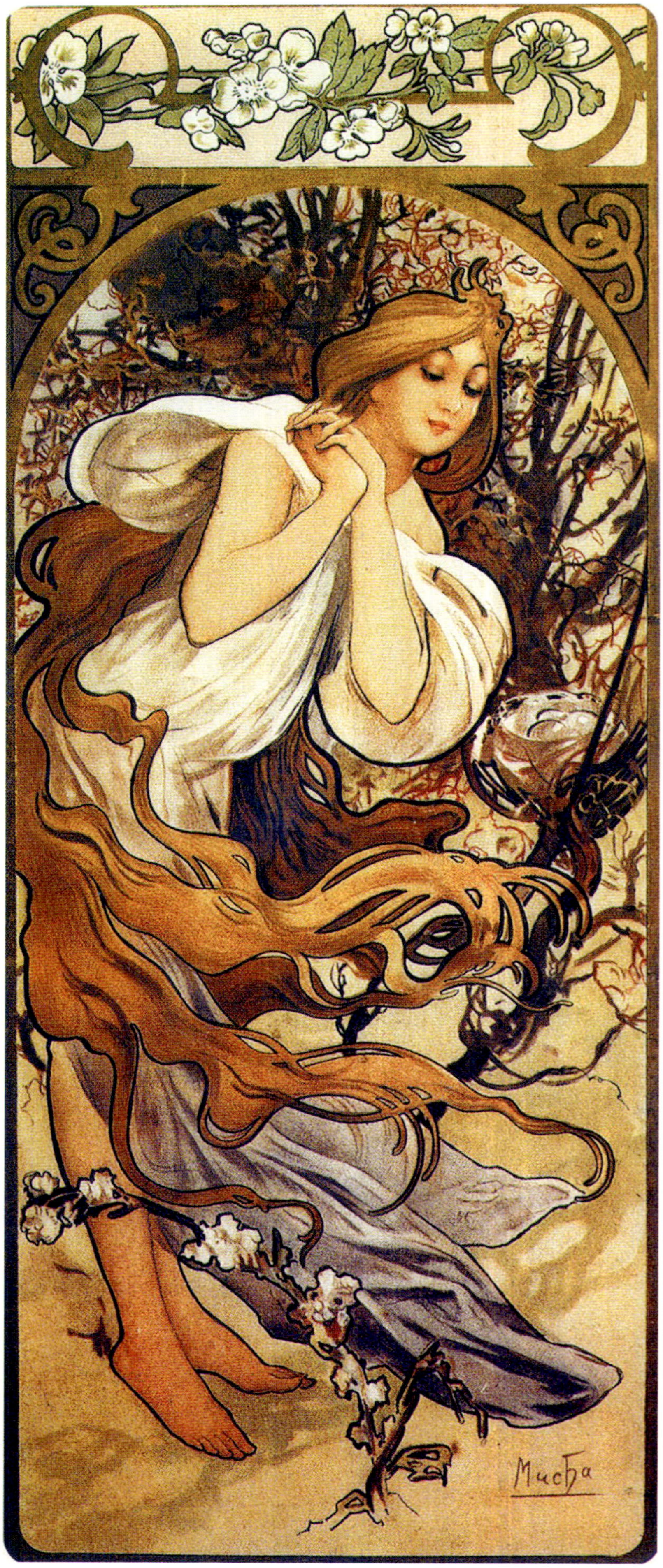
Mucha

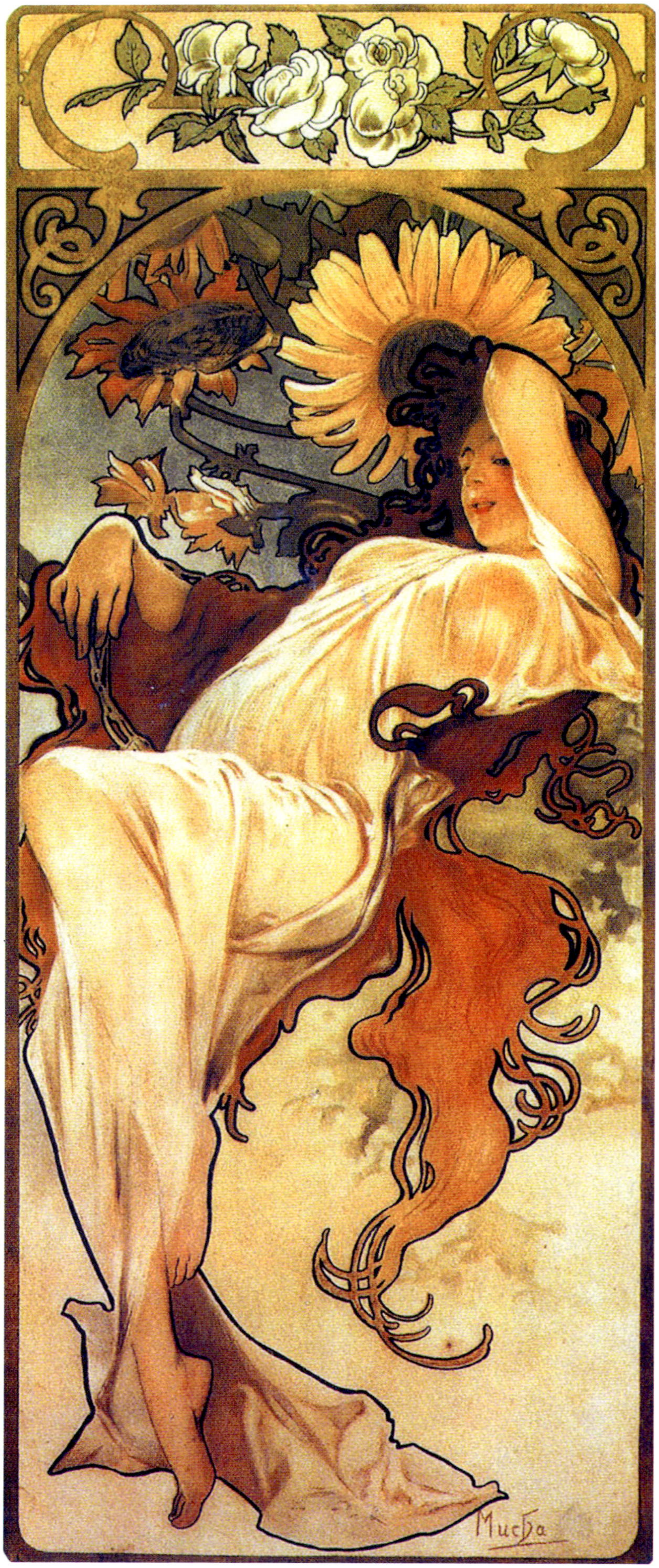
Mucha

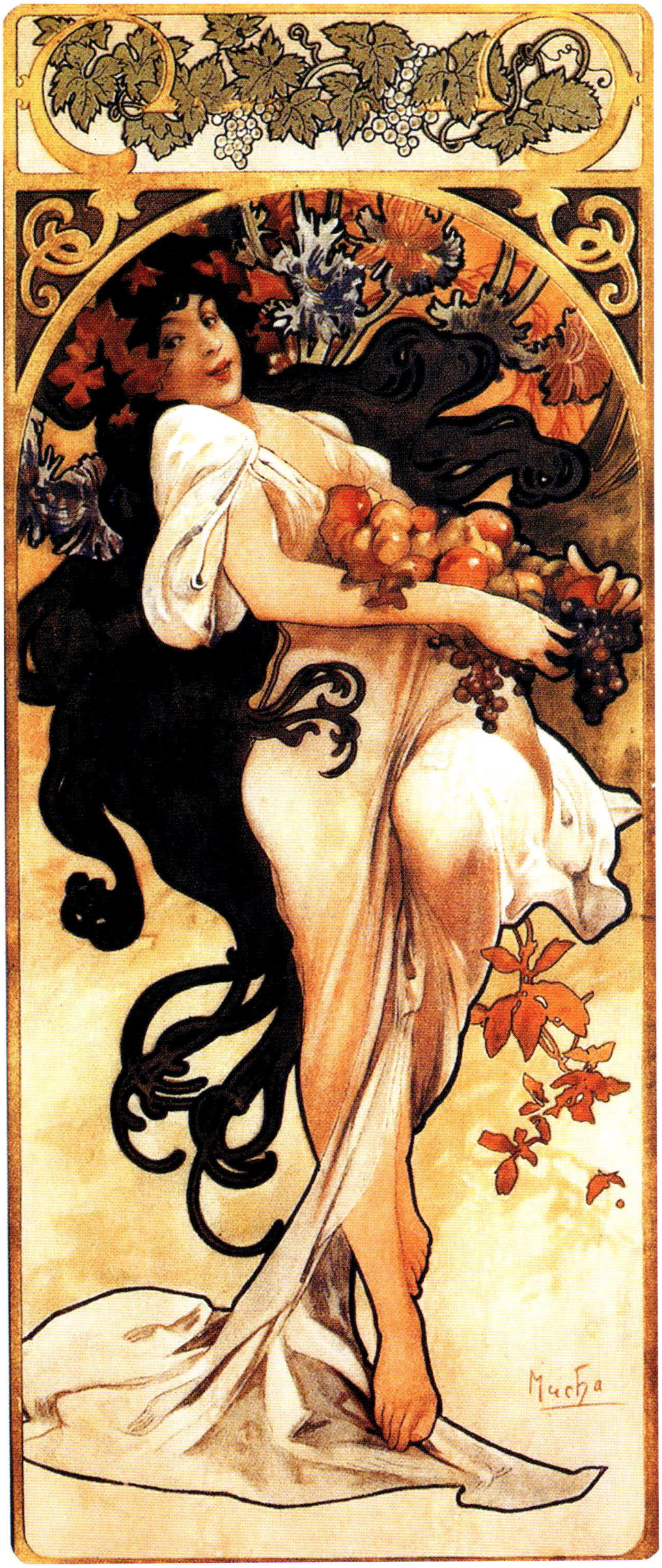
Mucha

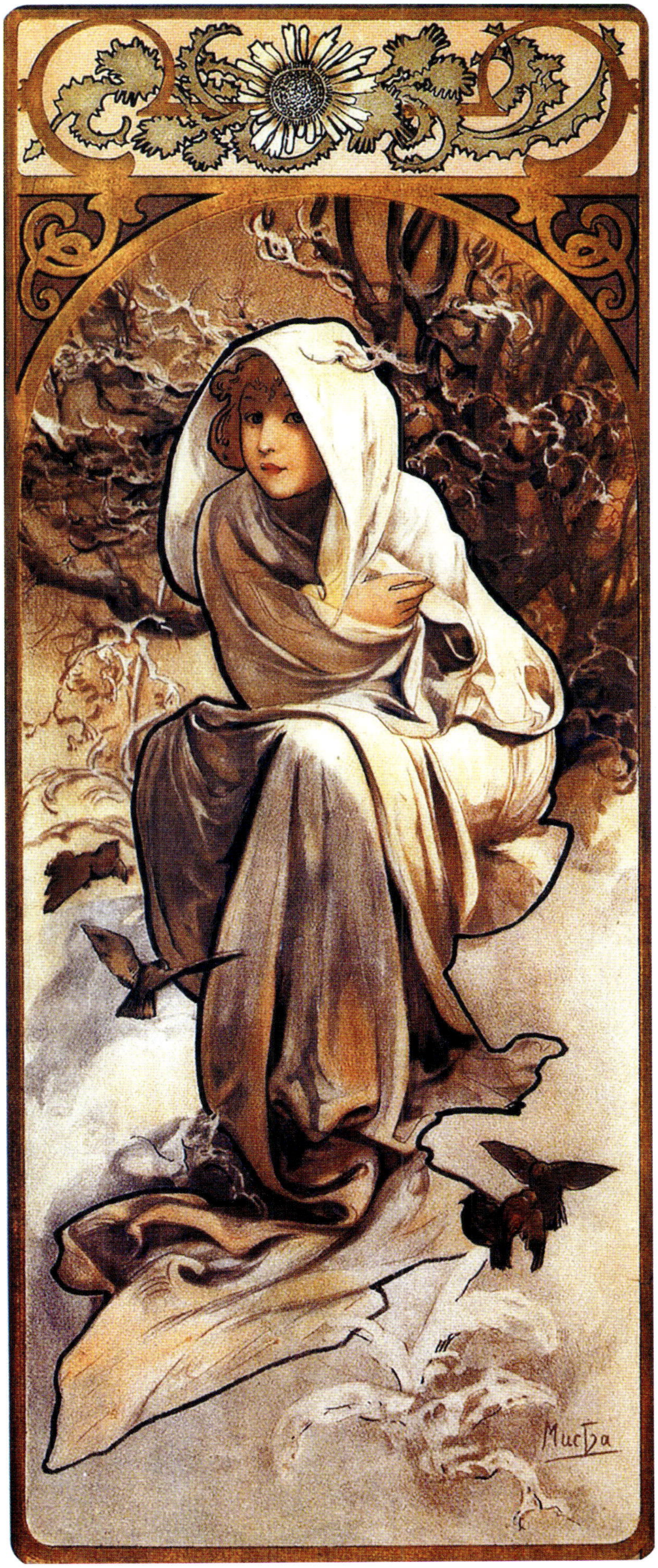
Mucha

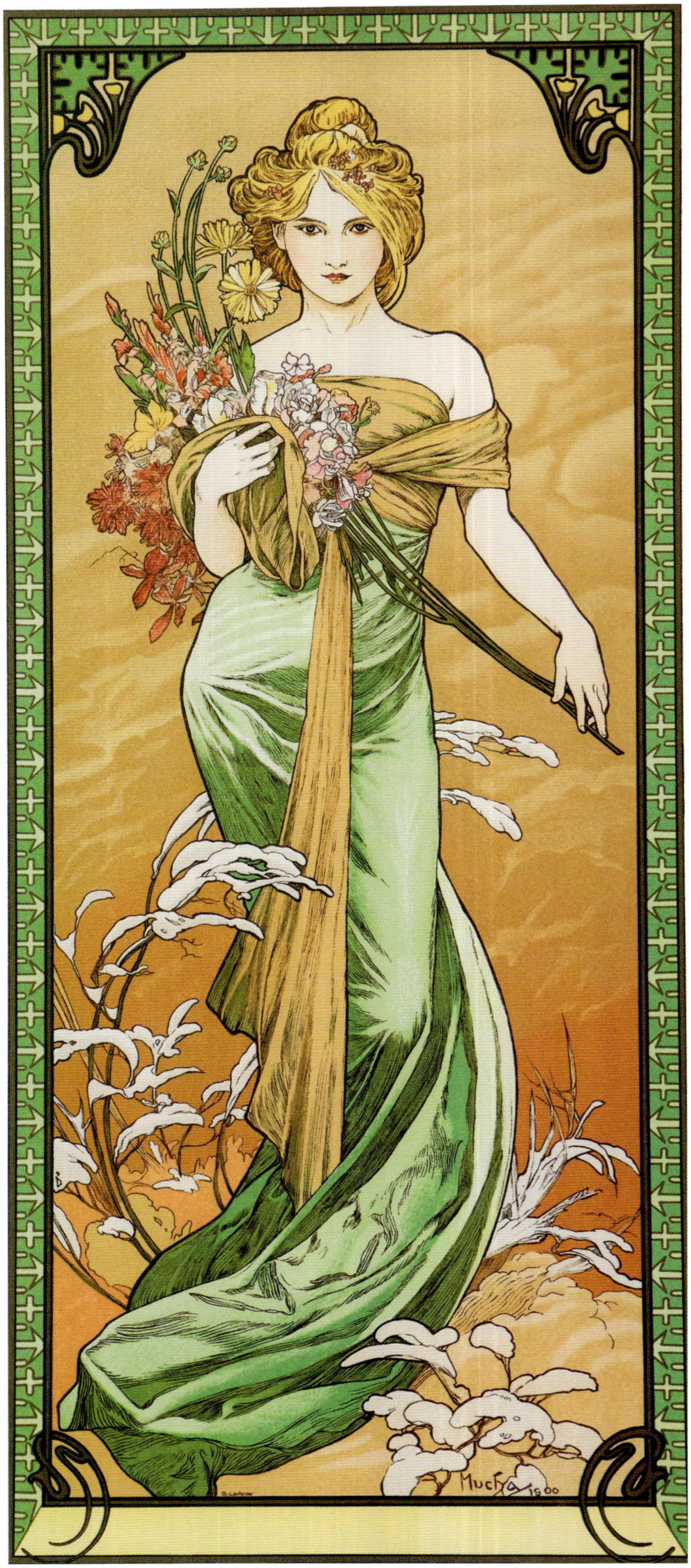

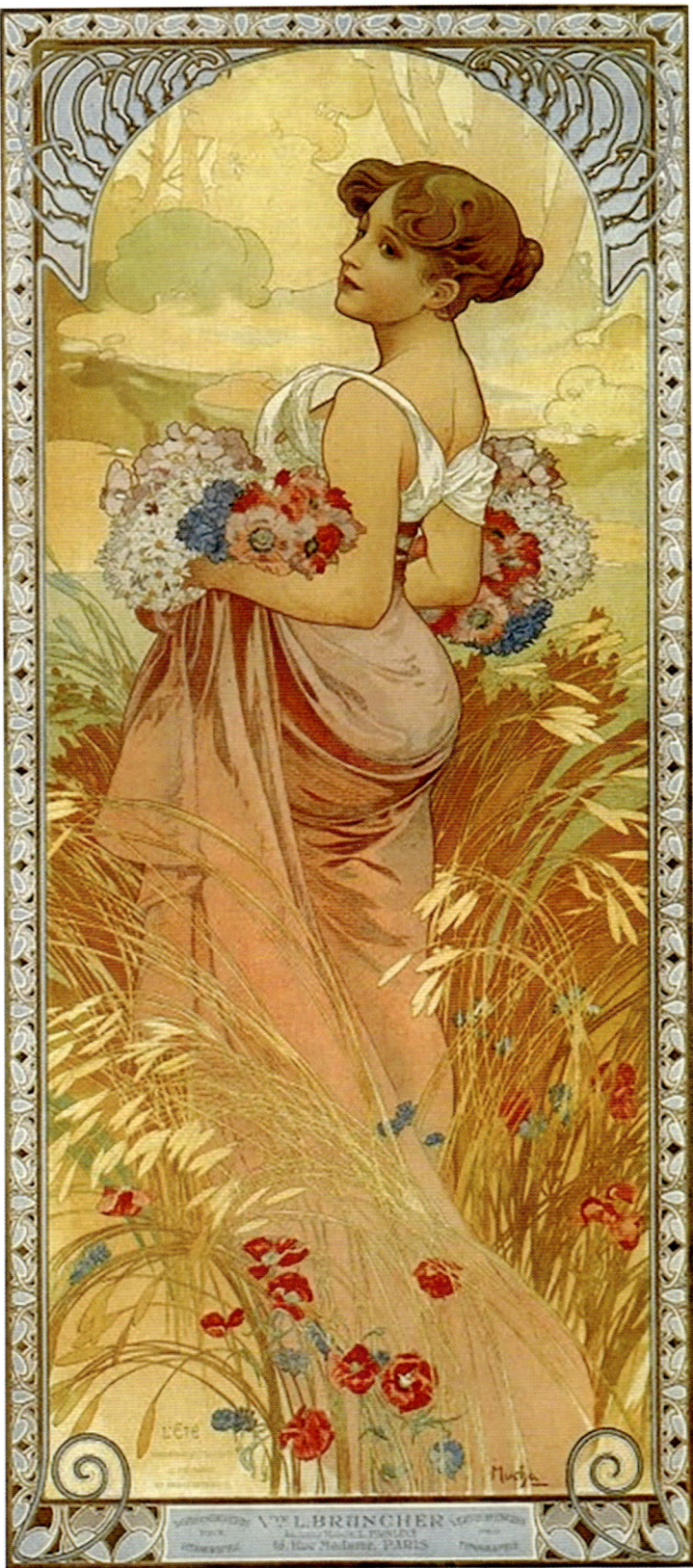

The Seasons: Summer (1900). Color lithograph.

[LEFT]
The Seasons: Spring
(1900). Color lithograph.

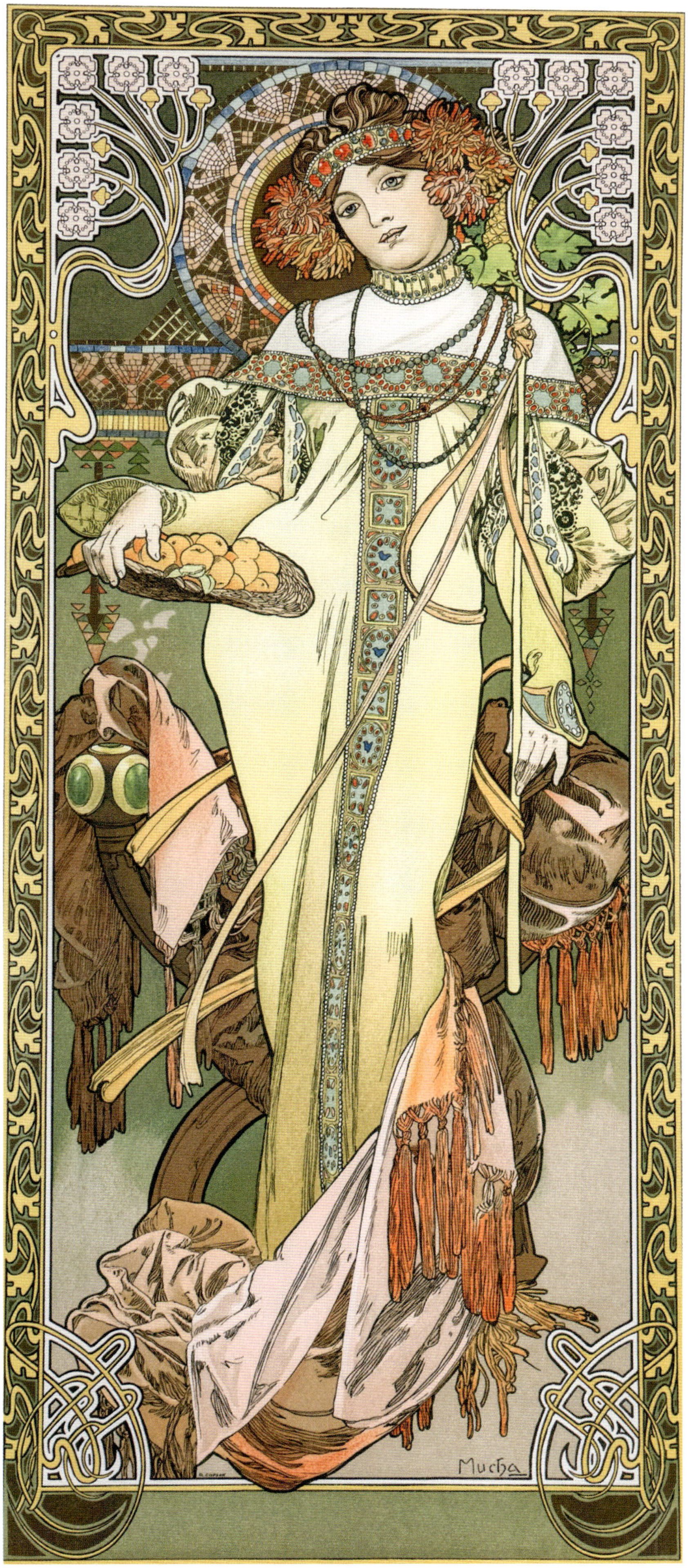

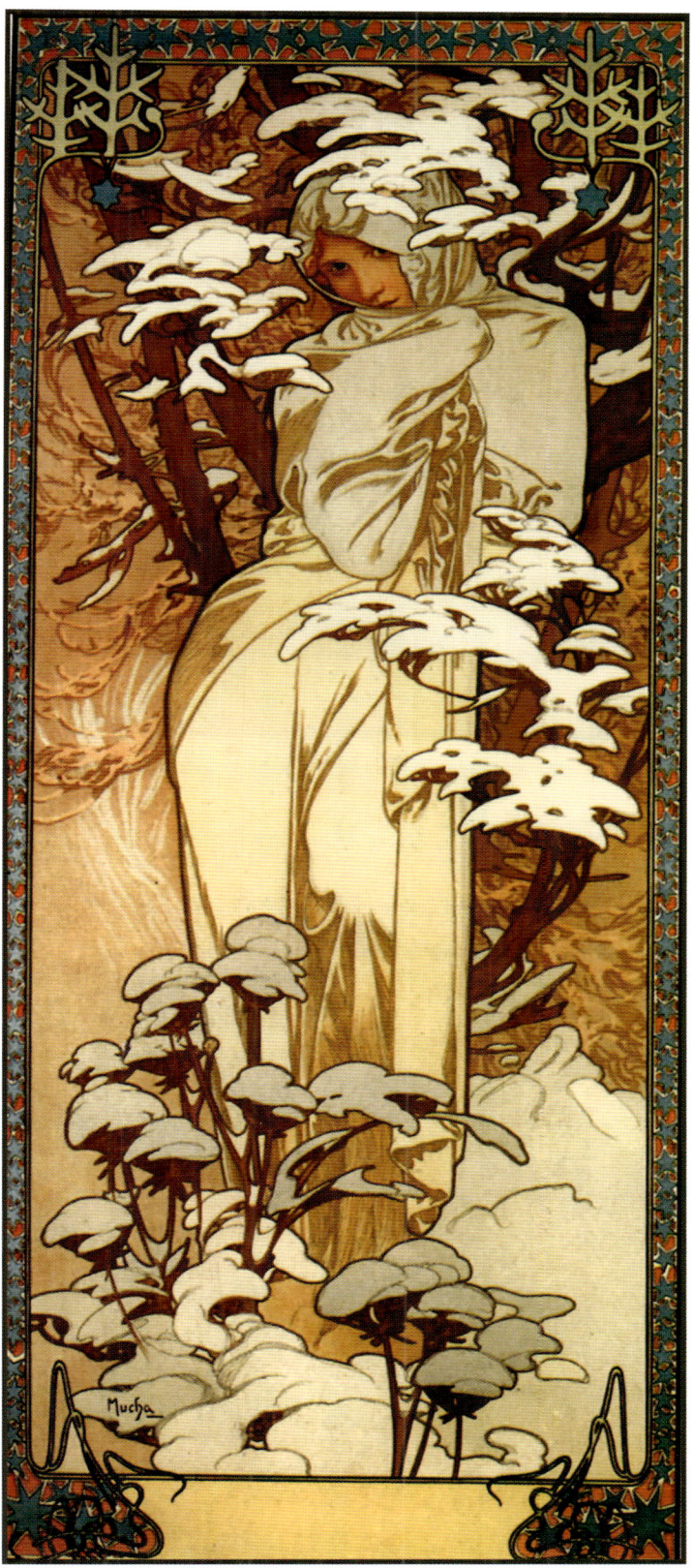

The Seasons: Winter (1900). Color lithograph.

The Seasons: Autumn
(1900). Color lithograph.

THE ARTS

The Arts is a captivating series of four decorative panels that pay homage to various creative disciplines. Created in 1898, this series showcases Mucha's mastery of symbolism. Each panel represents one of four artistic pursuits that he valued: painting, dance, music, and poetry. In each panel, a graceful female figure personifies the respective art form, surrounded by floral patterns, ornate details, and symbolic elements that evoke the essence of these artistic disciplines.

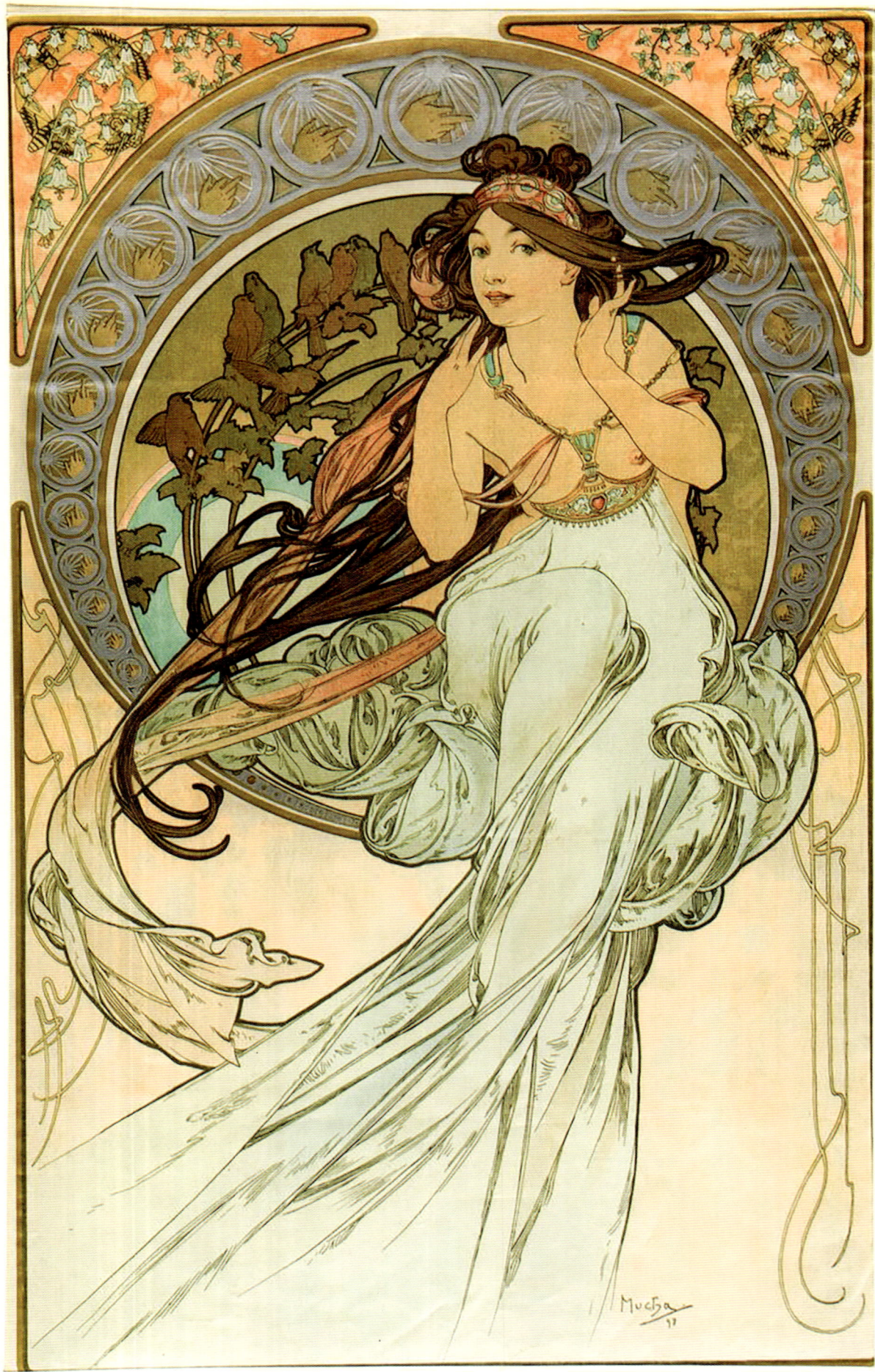

The Arts: Music
(1898). Color lithograph.

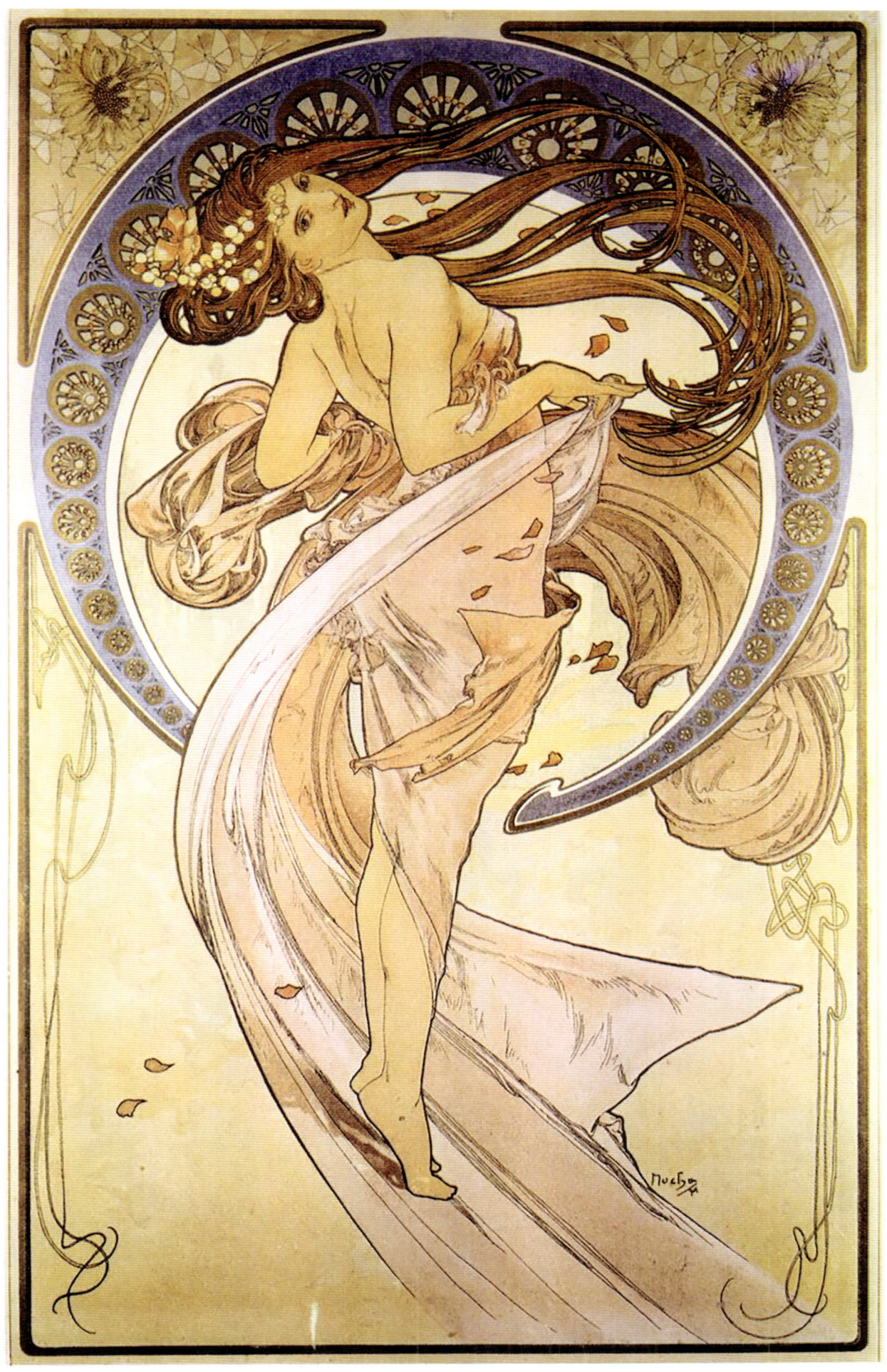

The Arts: Dance
(1898). Color
lithograph.

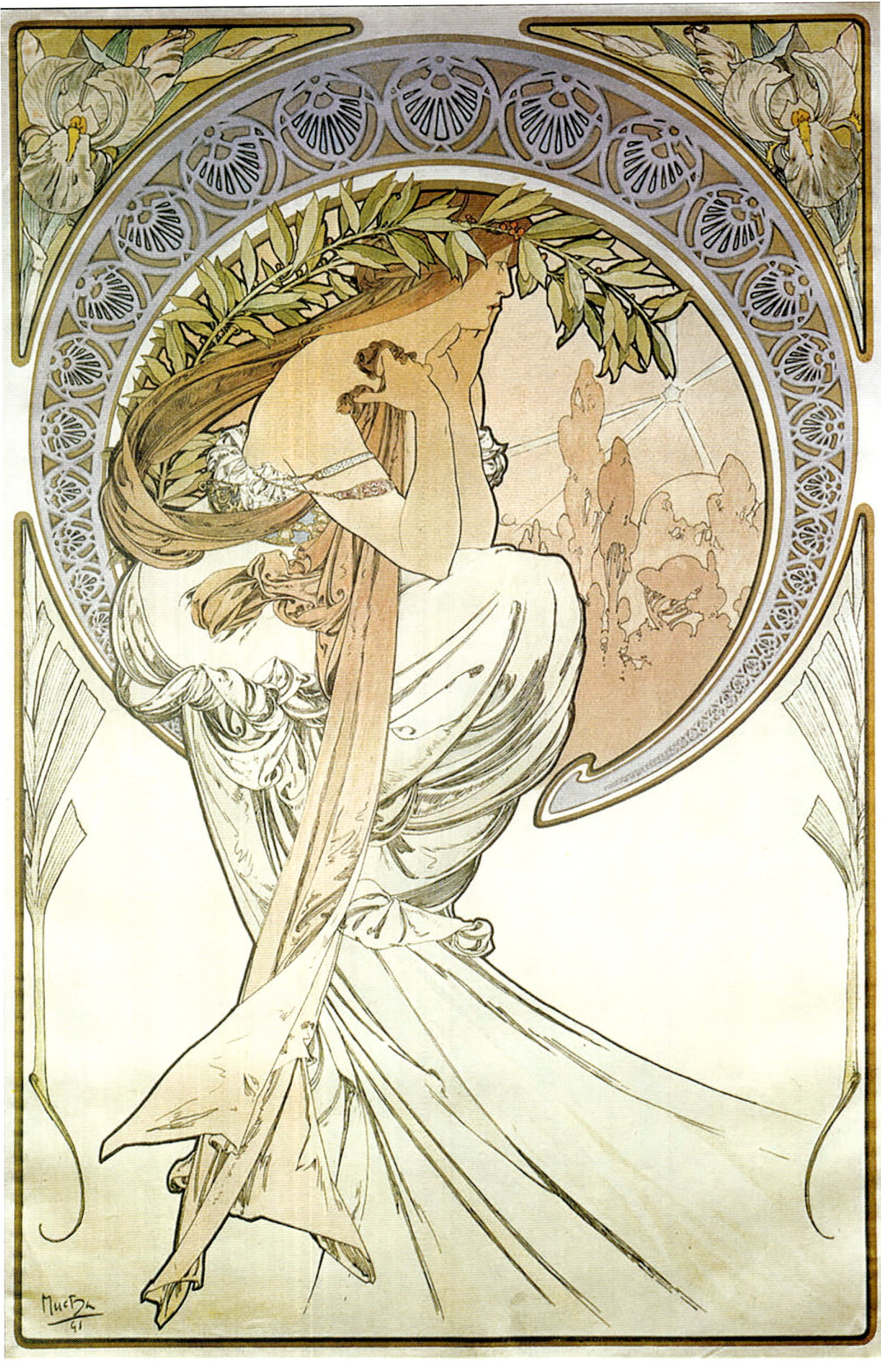

***The Arts:
Poetry***
(1898). Color
lithograph.

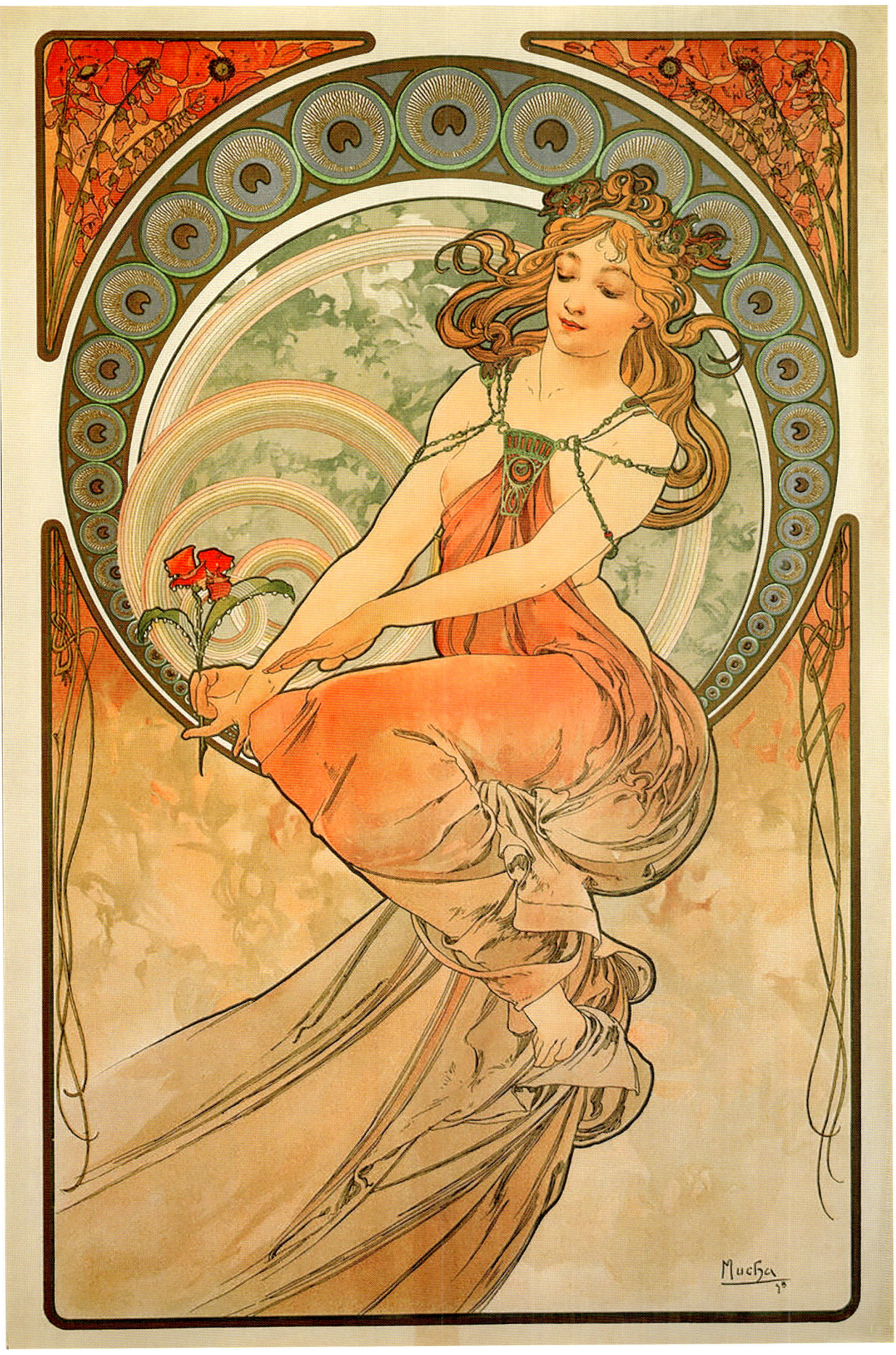

The Arts:
Painting
(1898). Color
lithograph.

THE MOON AND STARS

The Moon and Stars series is a collection of four decorative panels that embody the celestial beauty of the night sky. Each panel features a stunning female figure personifying the moon and the stars. Mucha uses ornate halos, floral motifs, and flowing garments to create a sense of harmony and visual unity across the panels, blending allegory with decorative elements.

[BOTH PAGES]
The Moon and Stars series (1896). Color lithographs.
From left to right: *The Evening Star, The Moon,*
The Morning Star, The Pole Star

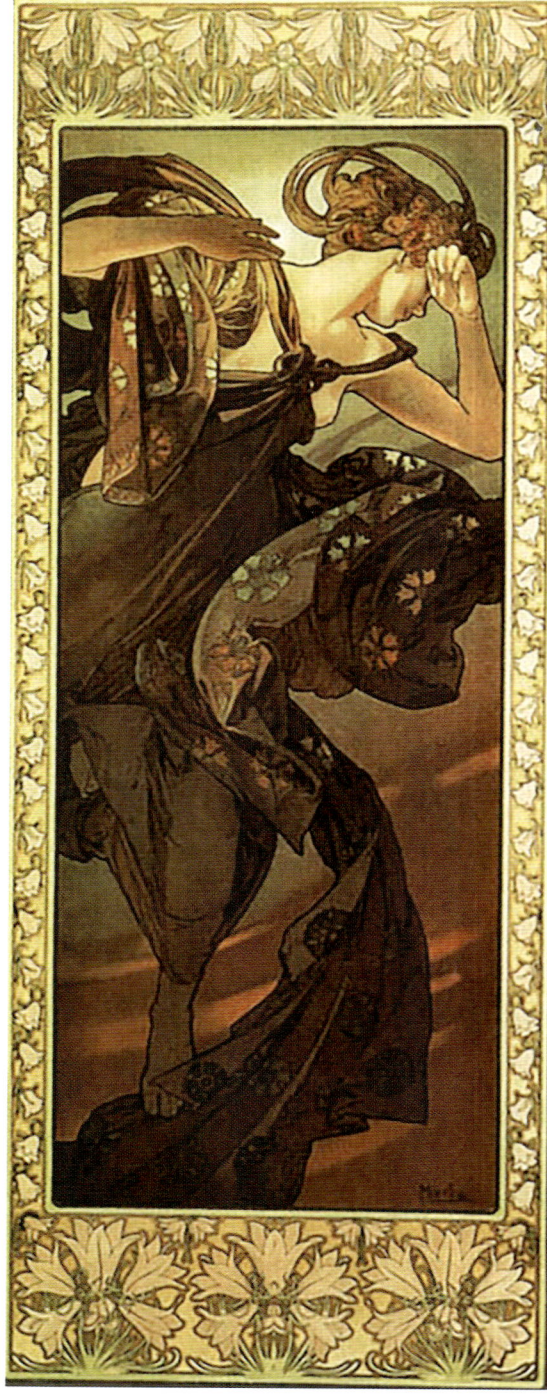

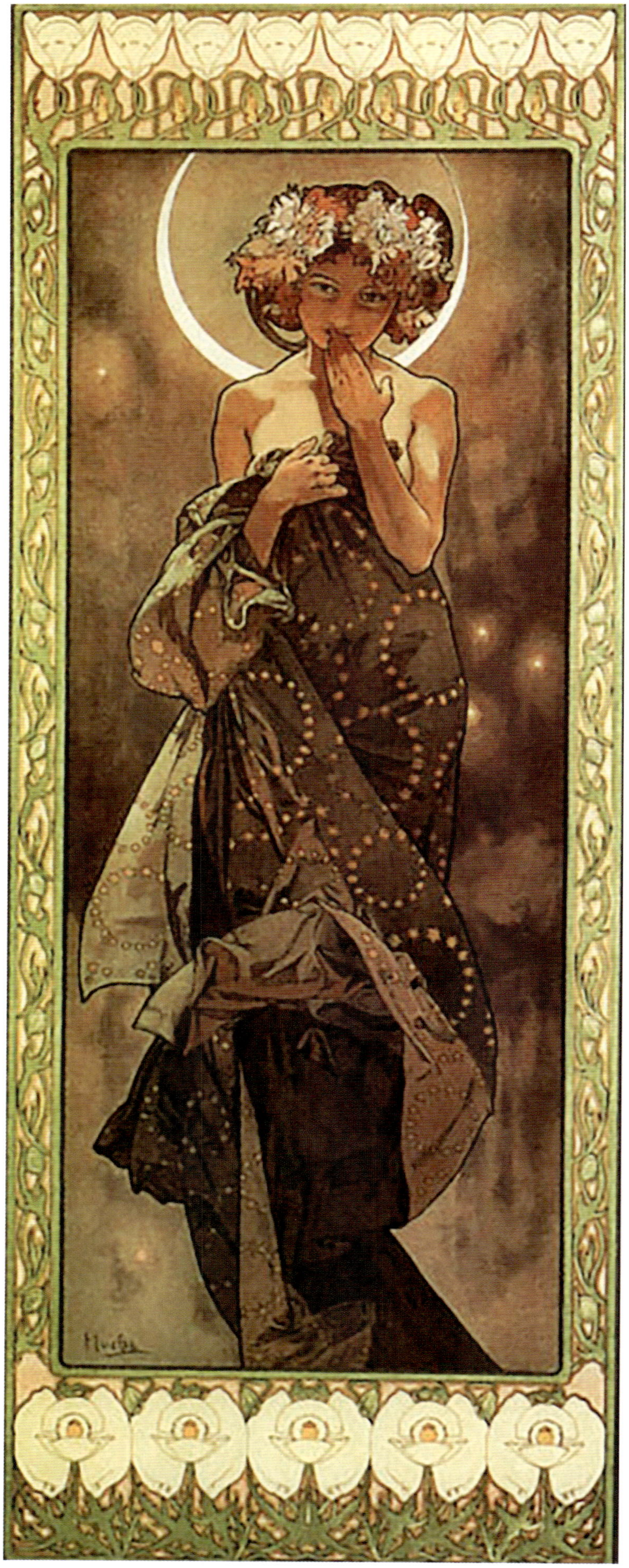

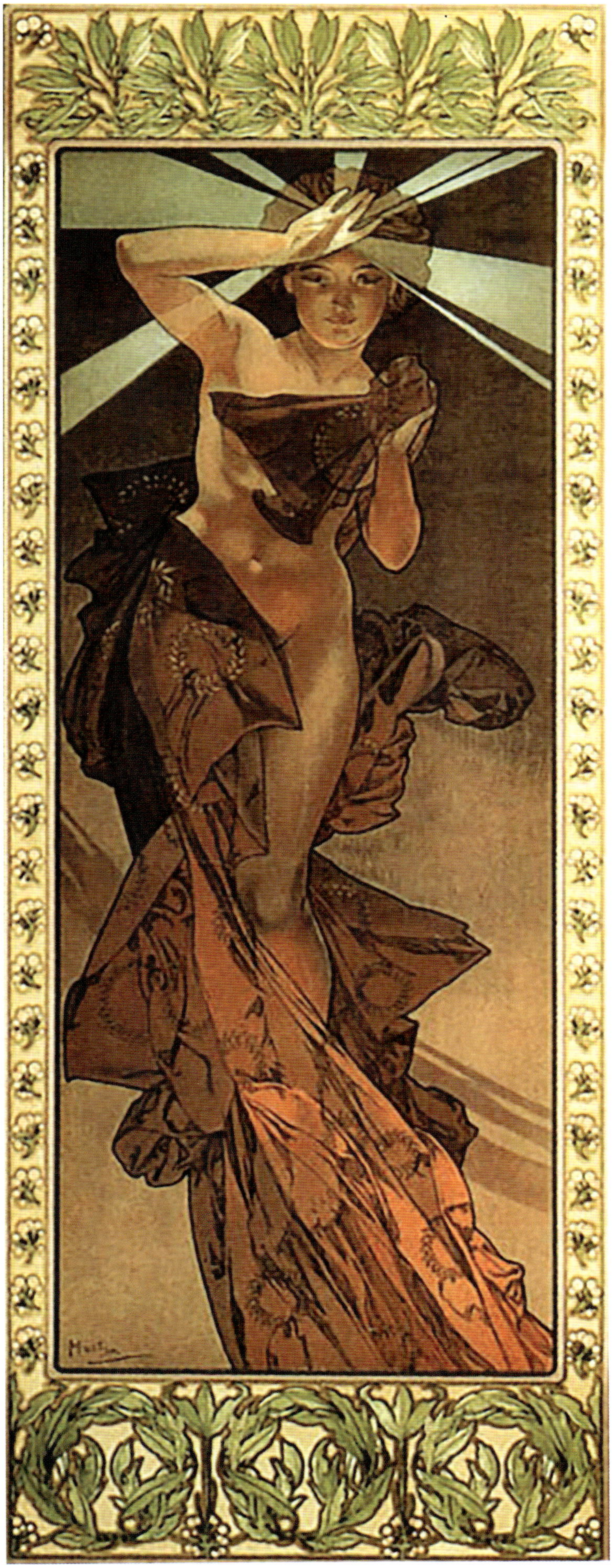

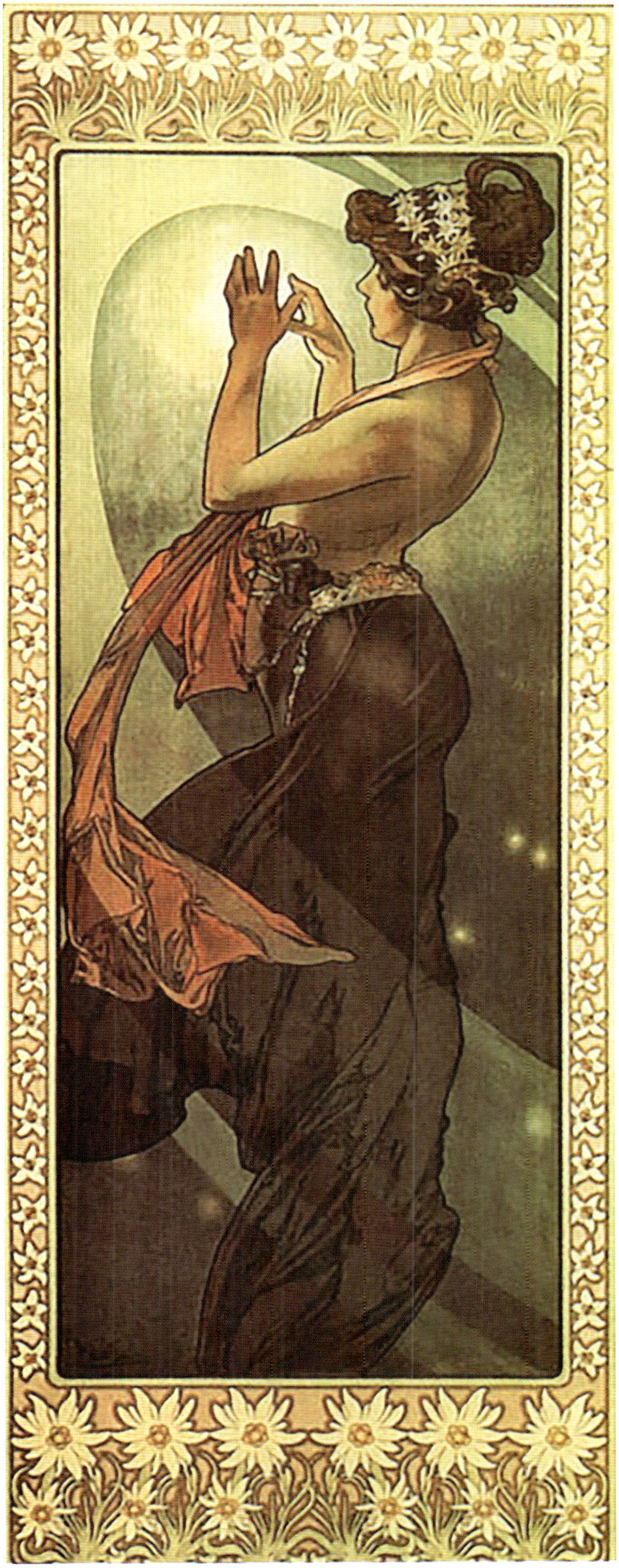

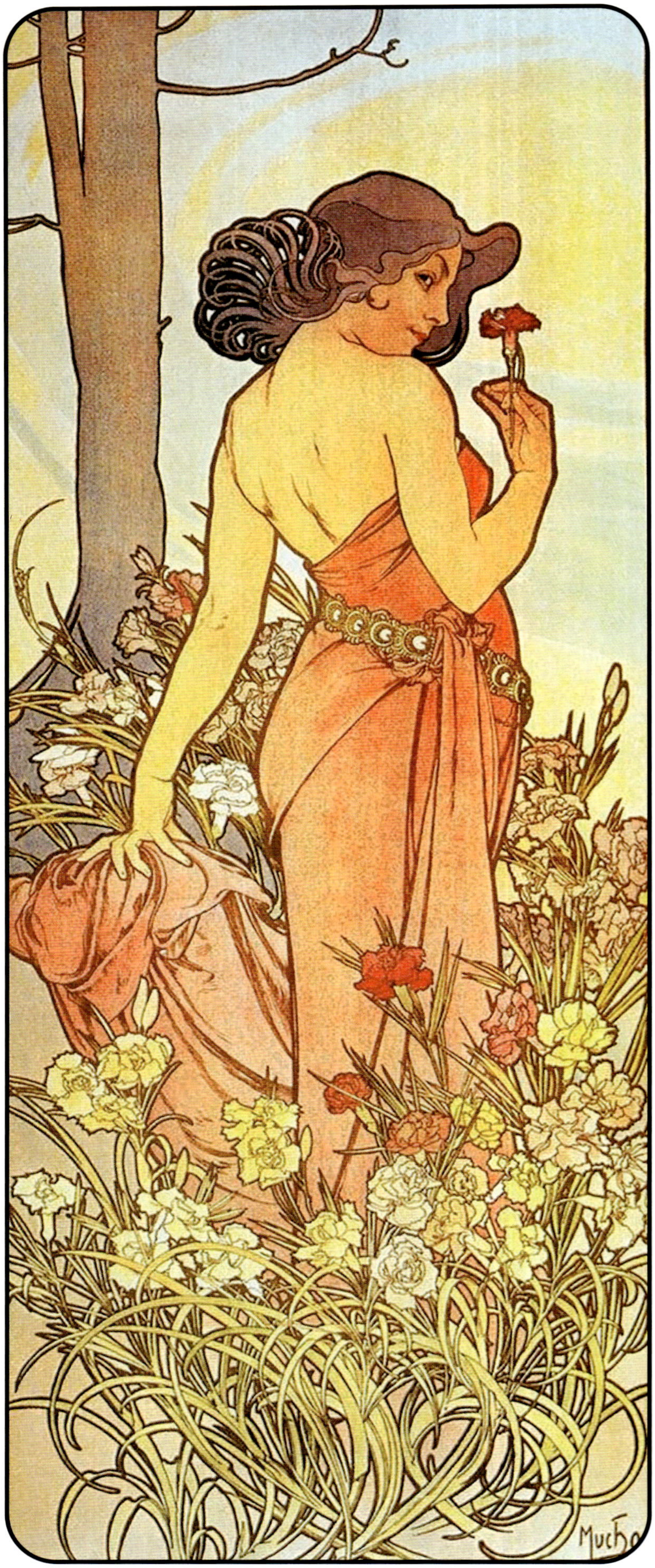
Mucha

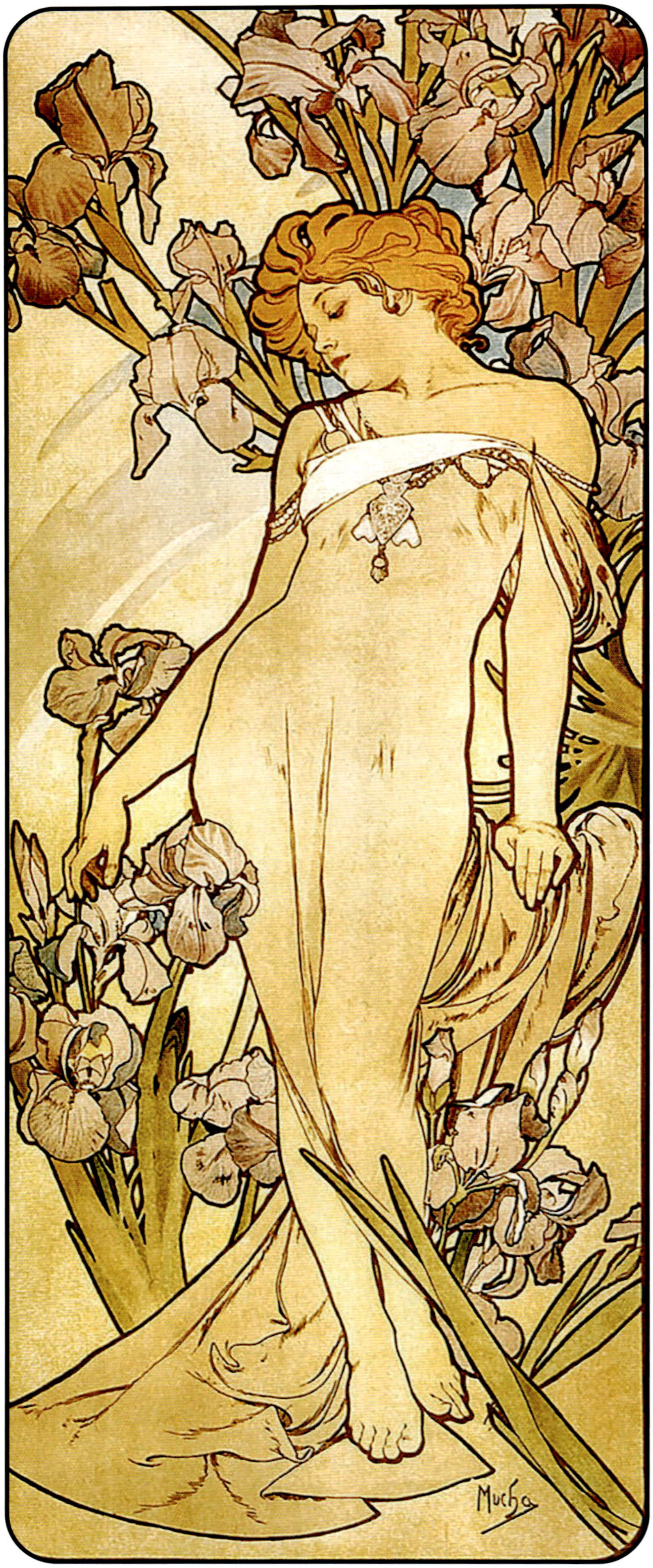
Mucha

FLOWERS & GEMS

Created in 1898, the Flower series for F. Champenois personifies four flowers and was created in a somewhat minimalistic style. Once made into posters, the series sold out in no time; Champenois then printed a smaller version with all four panels presented in a single image. The success of this series led Mucha to create the Precious Stones series.

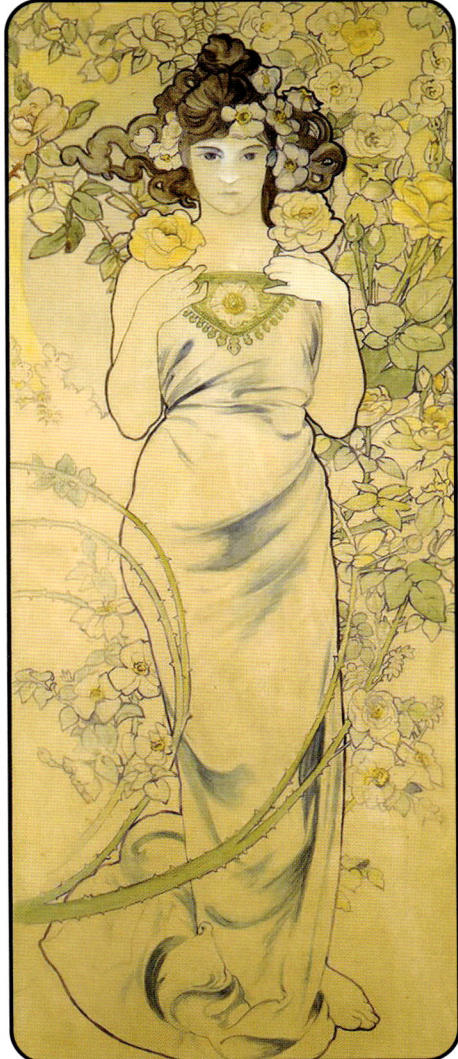

[RIGHT]
***The Flowers:
Lily*** (1898).
Color lithograph.

[LEFT]
The Flowers: Rose
(1898).
Color lithograph.

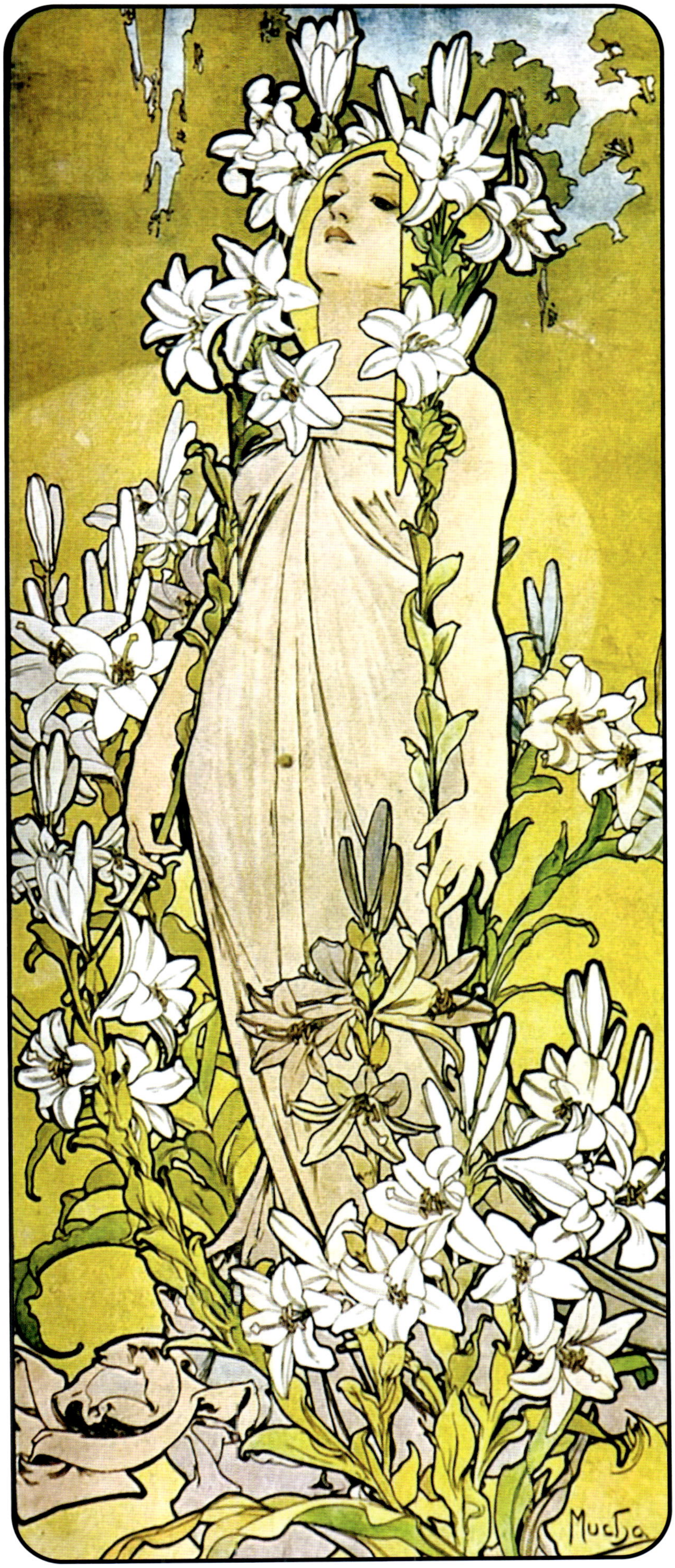

[OPPOSITE PAGE LEFT]
The Flowers: Carnation (1898). Color lithograph.

[OPPOSITE PAGE RIGHT]
The Flowers: Iris (1898). Color lithograph.

[OVERLEAF] ***The Precious Stones*** series (1900).
Color lithographs. From left to right: ***Topaz, Ruby, Amethyst, Emerald***

Despite the name of the series, Mucha chose to use flowers and colors to represent the gems, rather than illustrating the stones themselves. The color palette of each panel, including the women's coloring and clothes and the mosaic encircling their heads, along with the flower beneath them, is the color of a gem.

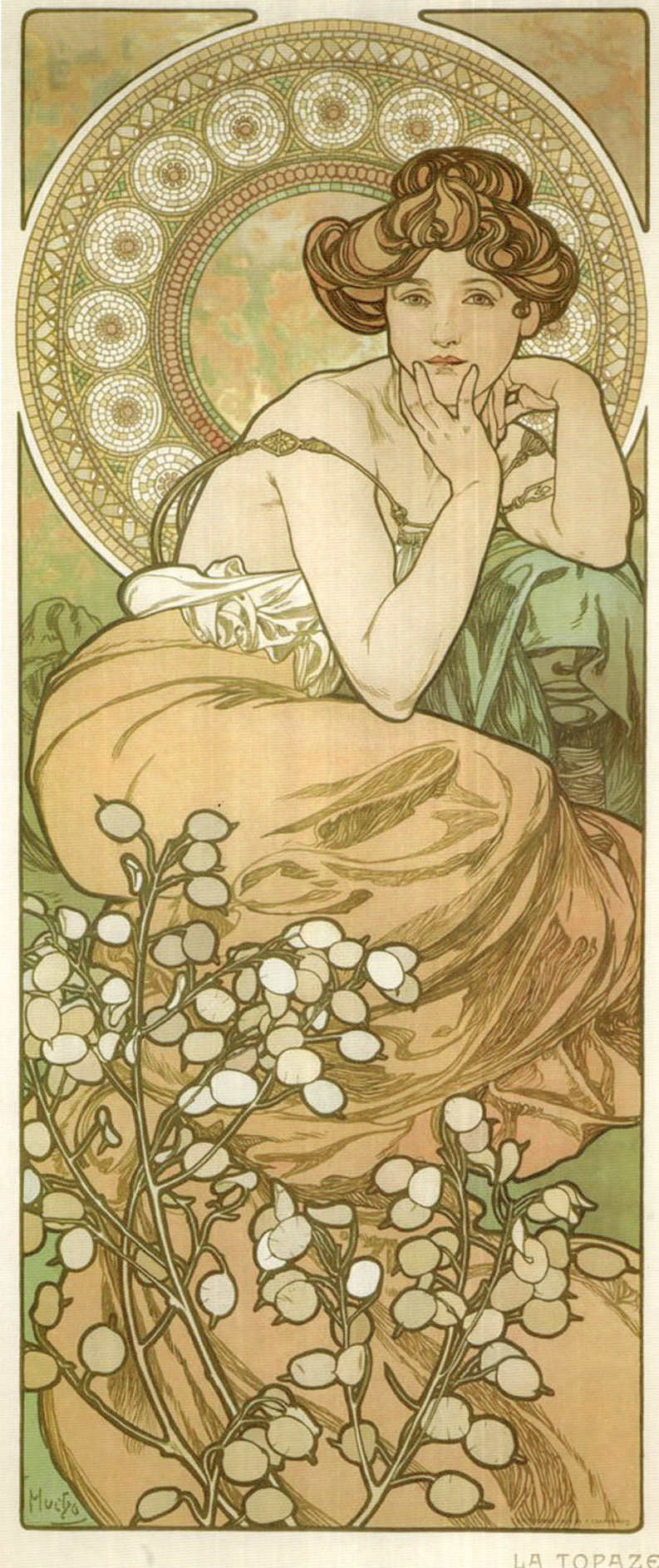

LA TOPAZE

LE RUBIS

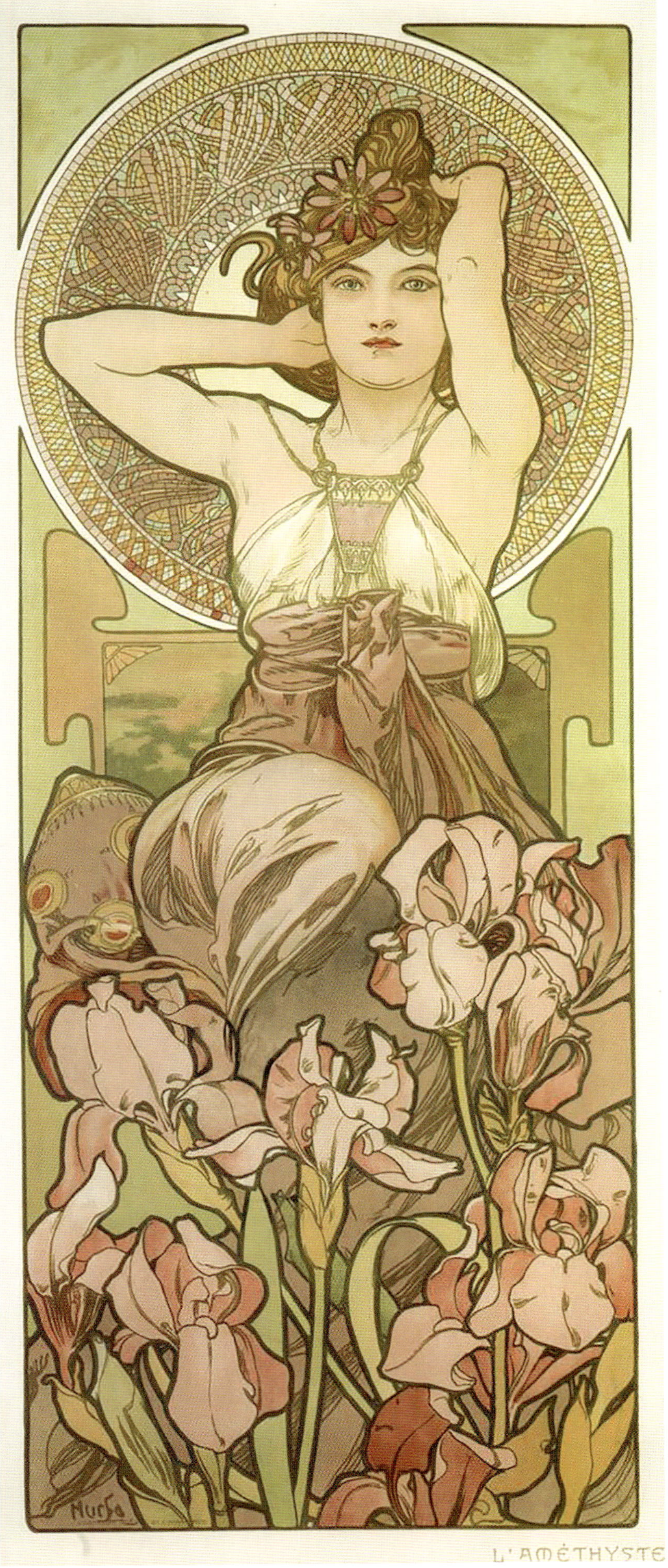

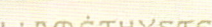

L'AMÉTHYSTE

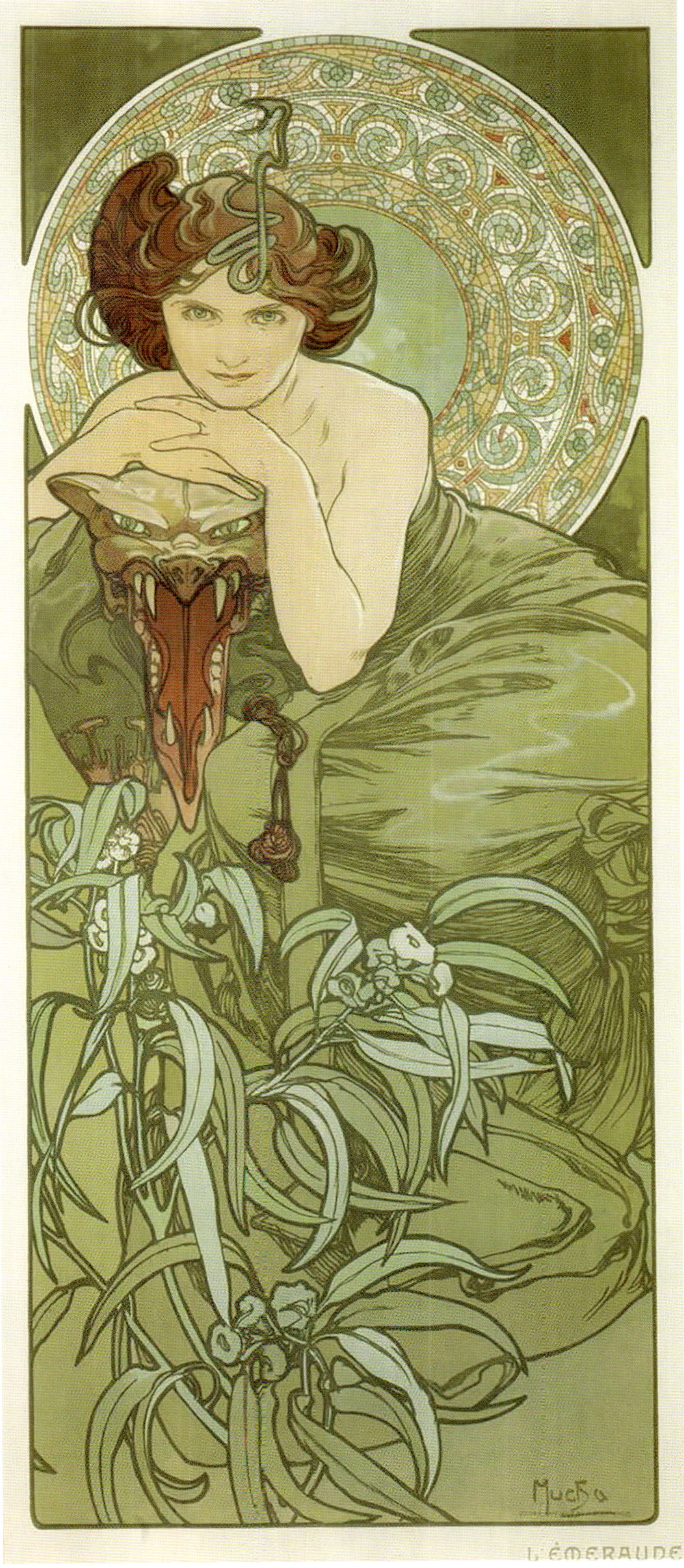

L'ÉMERAUDE

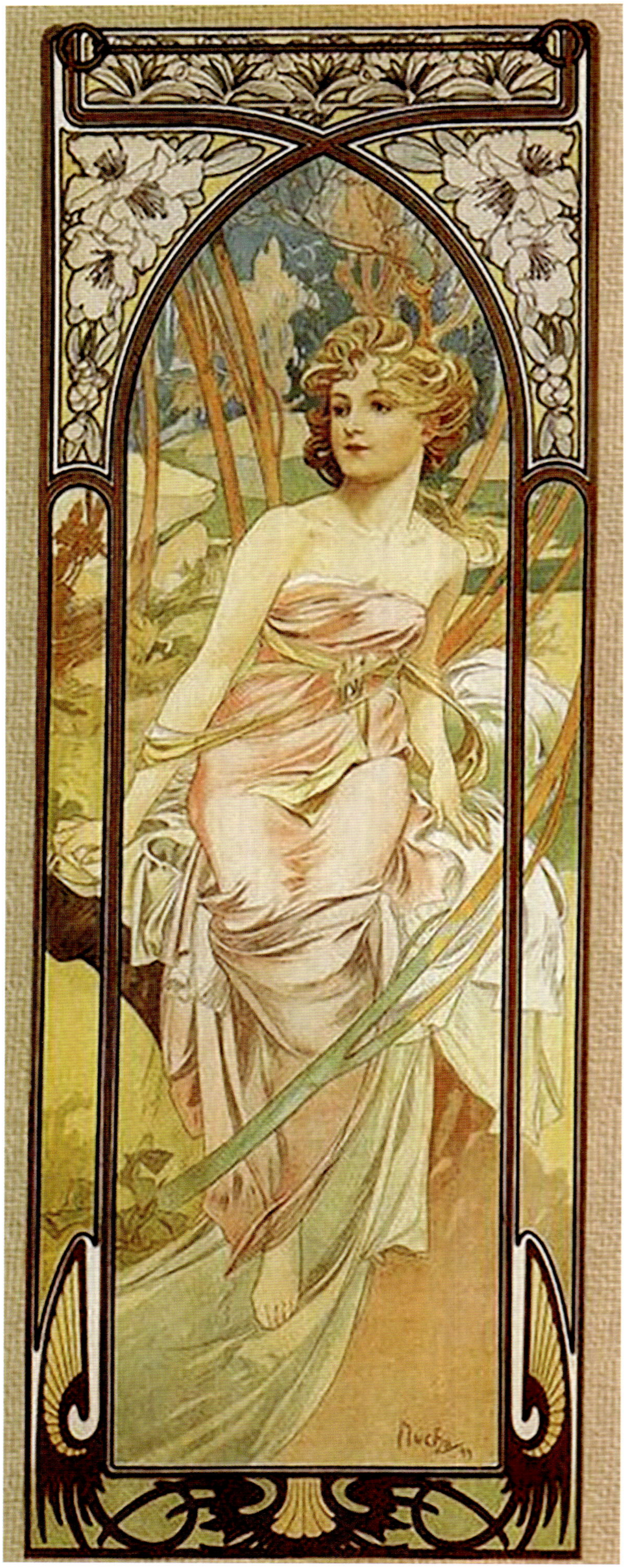

THE TIMES OF THE DAY

This ornate series features elegant floral motifs set in curving shapes that resemble Gothic window frames. Each woman is posed in such a way as to evoke the mood of that hour. A second time-themed set features horizontal panels of *Dusk* and *Dawn*.

[LEFT]
Morning Awakening (1899). Color lithograph.

[BELOW]
Brightness of Day (1899). Color lithograph.

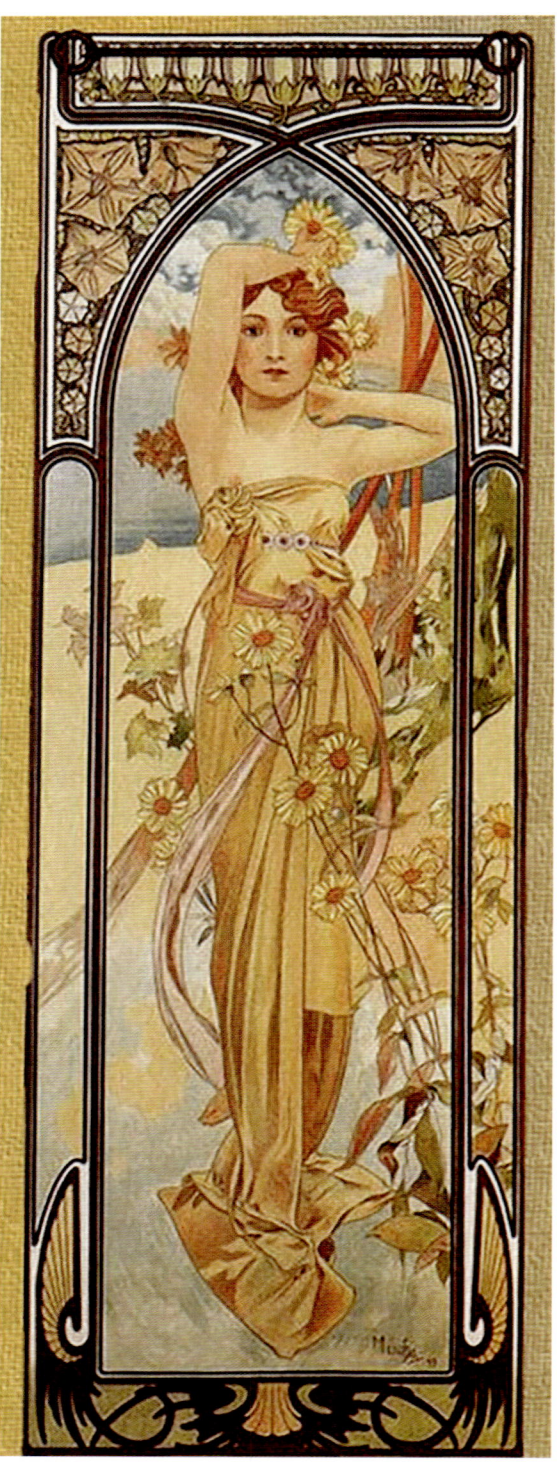

[OPPOSITE PAGE LEFT]
Evening Reverie (1899). Color lithograph.

[OPPOSITE PAGE RIGHT]
Nightly Rest (1899). Color lithograph.

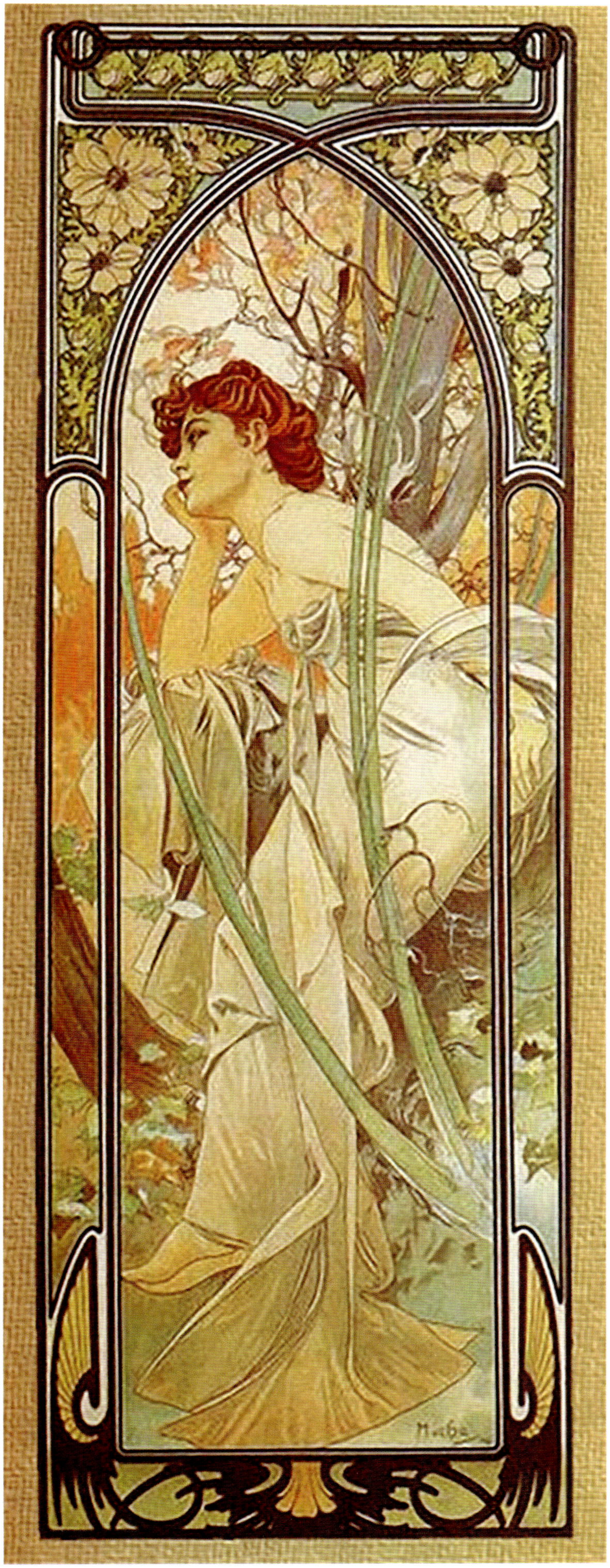

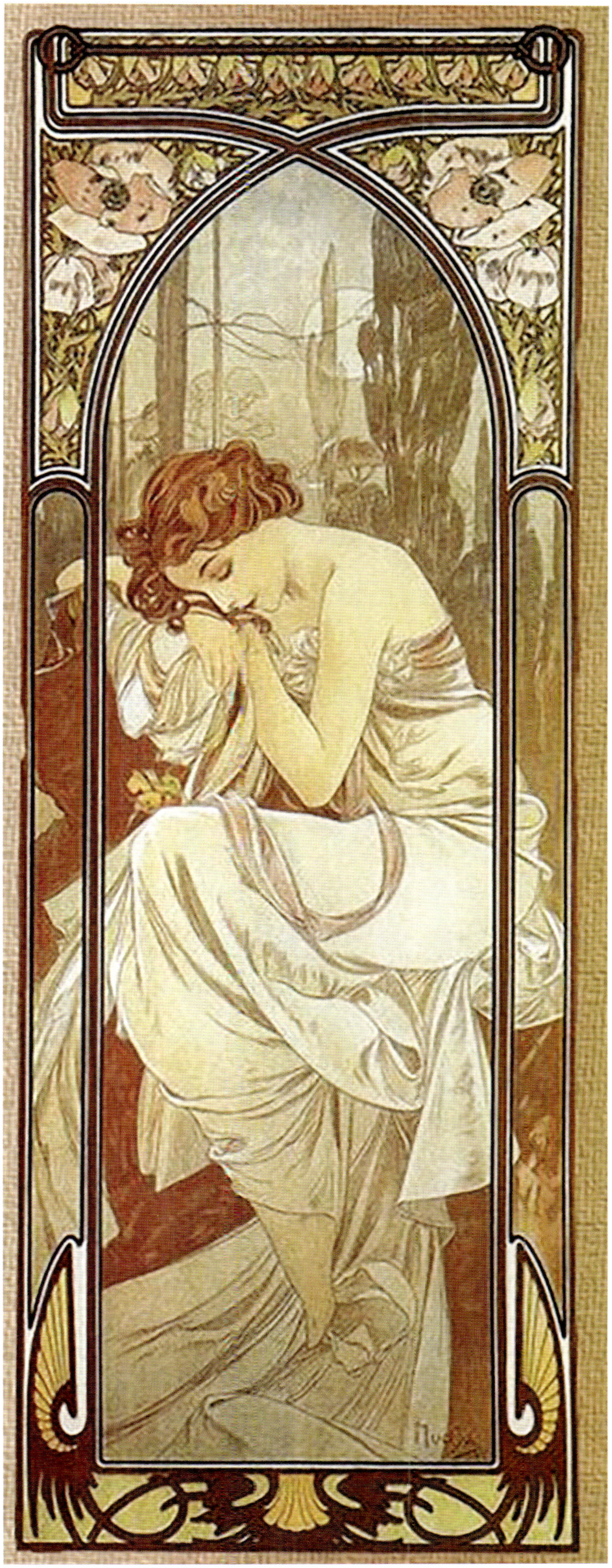

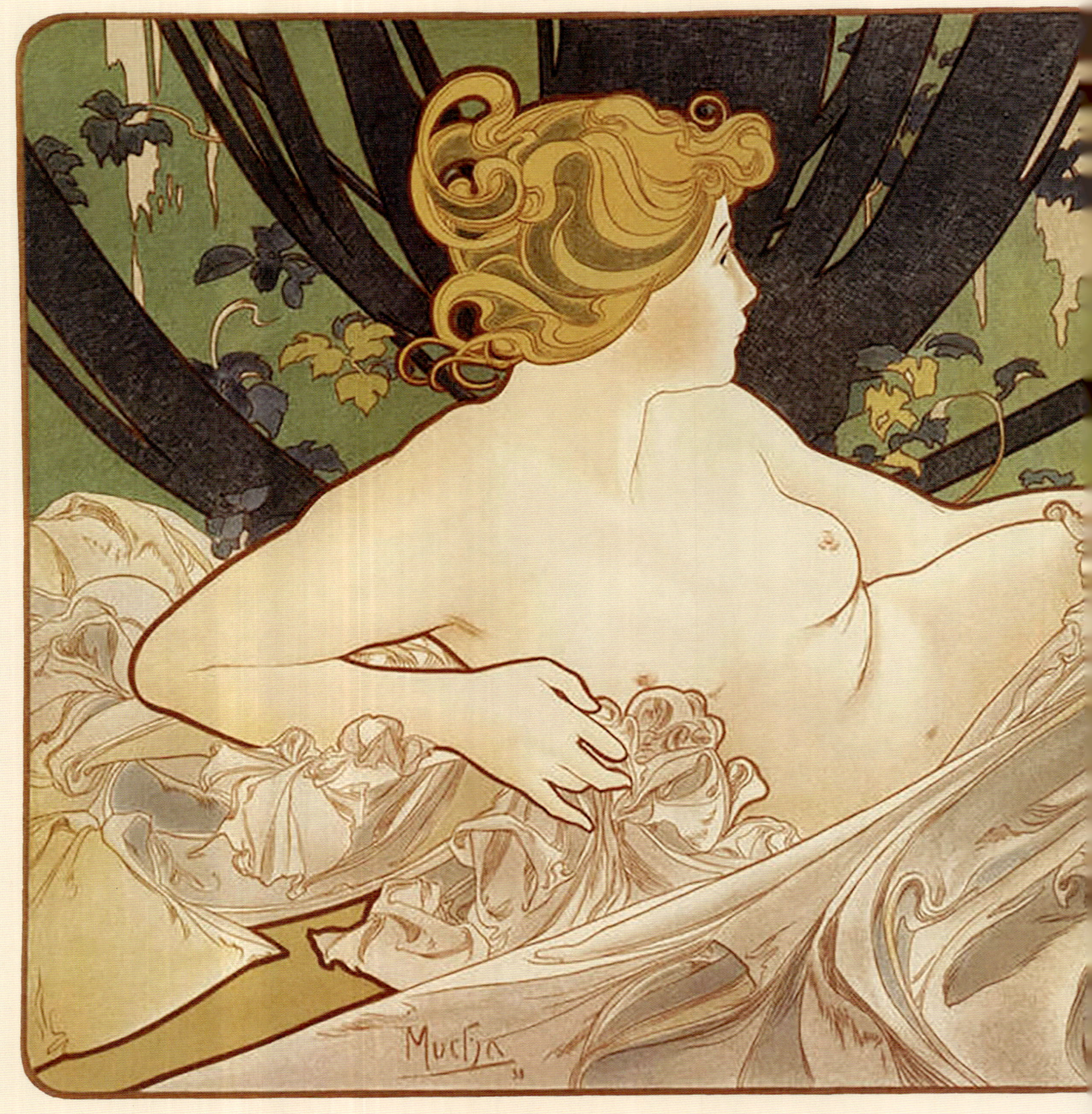

Dawn (1899). Color lithograph.

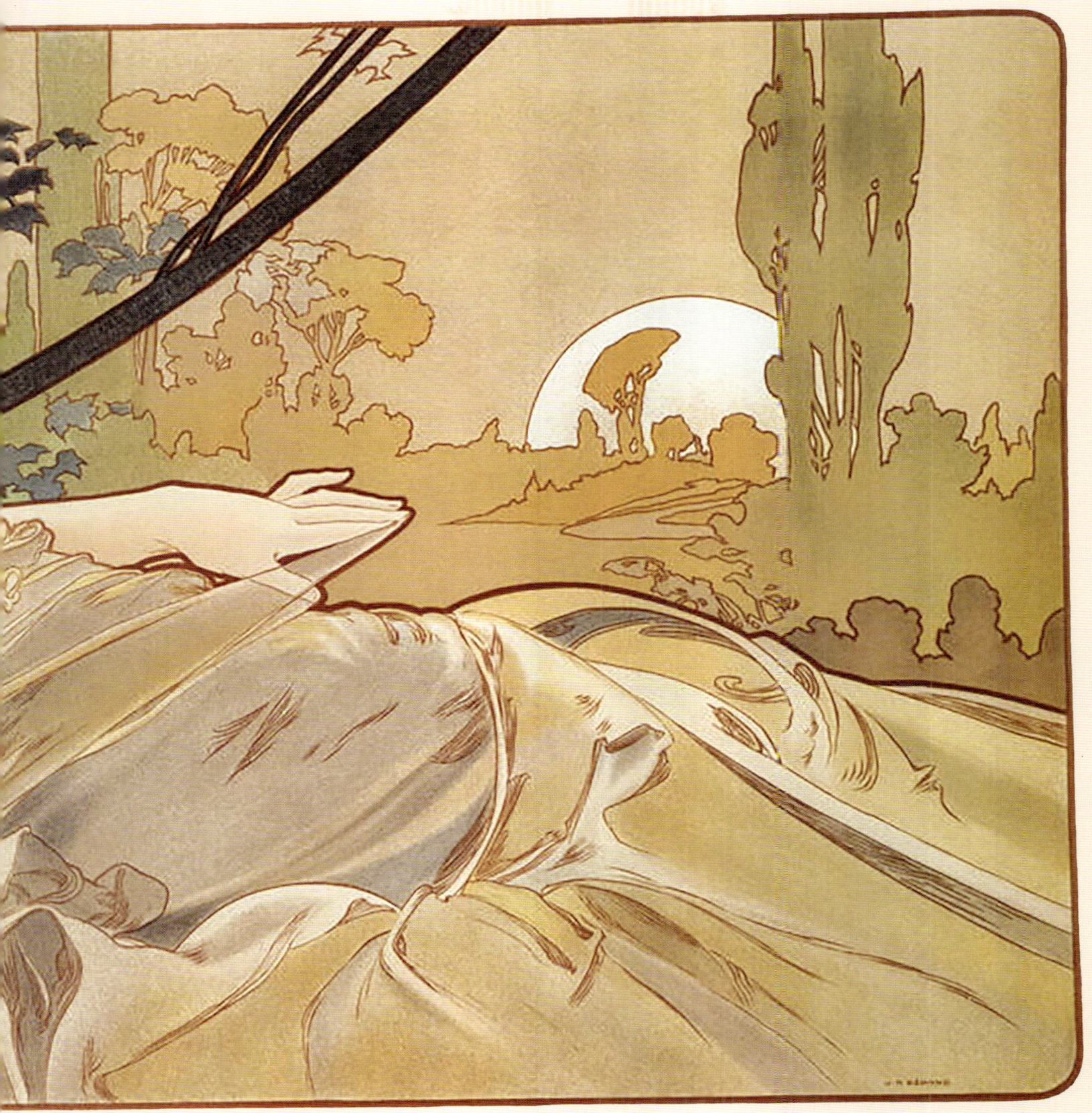

In 1899, Mucha created a pair of allegorical decorative panels, Dawn *and* Dusk. *In* Dawn, *a young woman gazes out at the rising sun.*

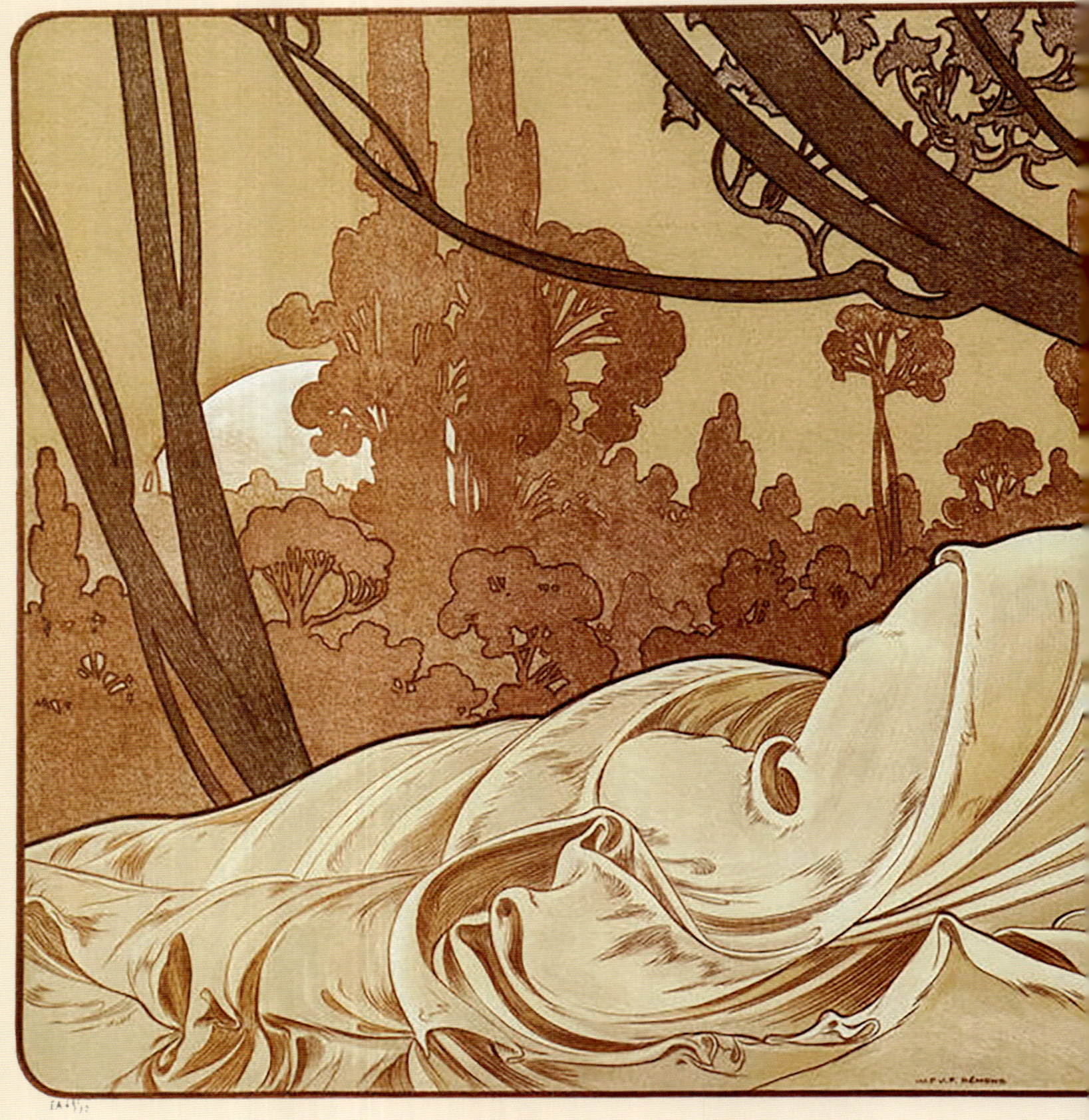

Dusk (1899). Color lithograph.

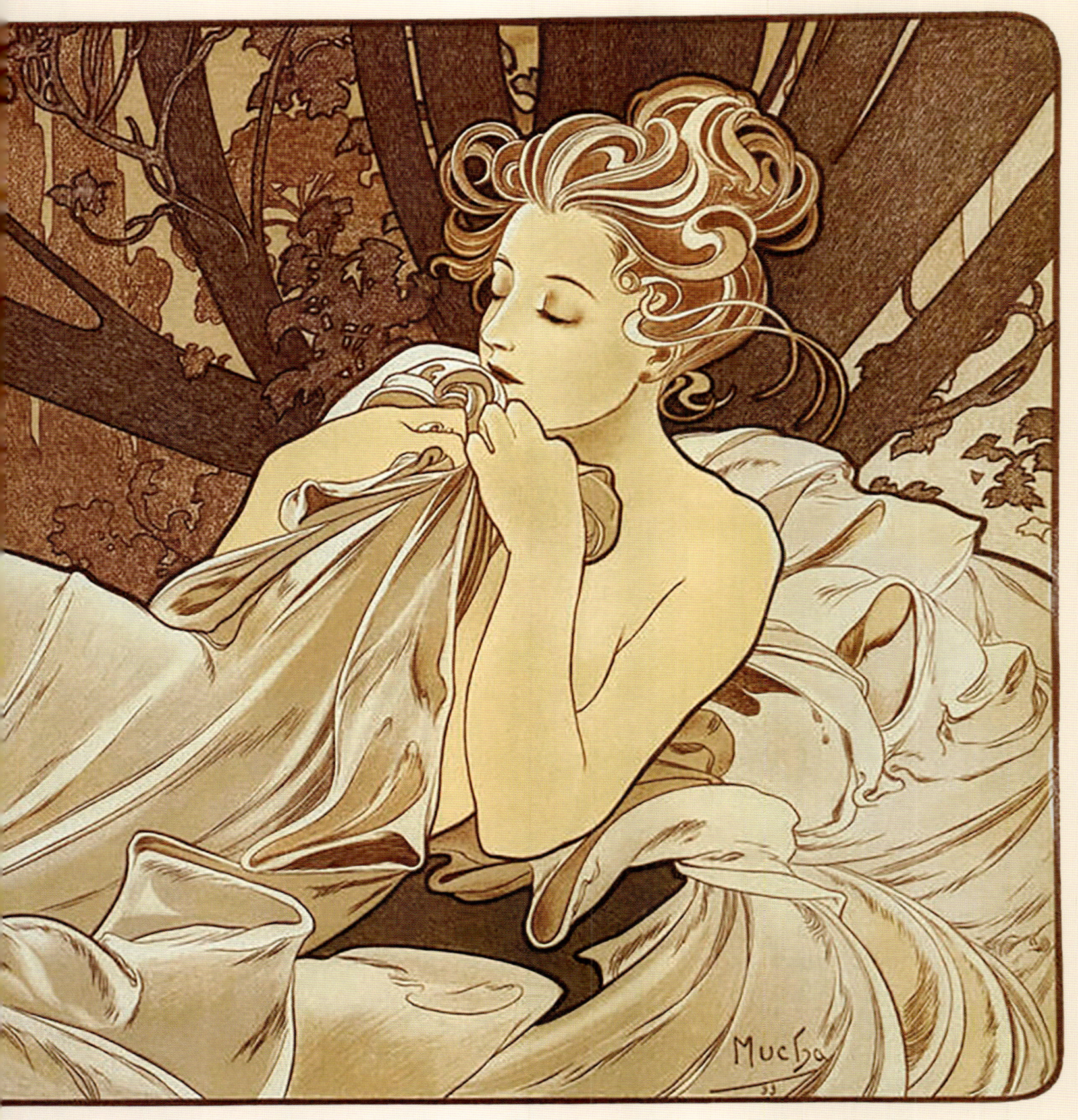

In the Dusk *panel, a young woman prepares for bed as the sun sets.*

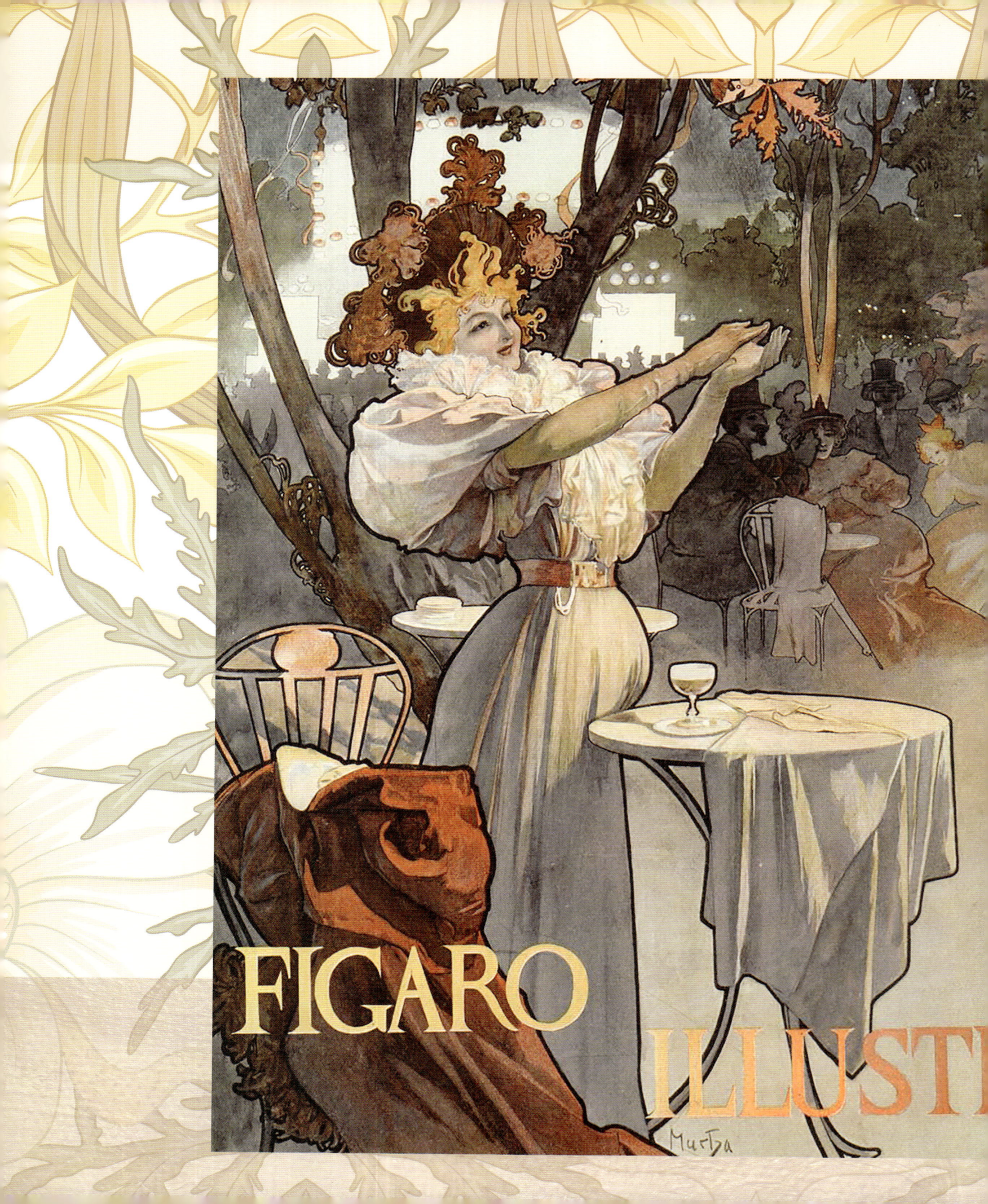

GRAPHIC DESIGN

MUCHA'S SKILL as a superb draughtsperson led him to explore multiple aspects of graphic design. From magazine and journal covers to interior book illustrations, he displayed his talent for turning the mundane into the extraordinary. His artistic mind saw the potential for beauty in all things, and, in 1902, he even published a compendium of quintessential Art Nouveau designs in *Documents Décoratifs,* which applies his unique "le style Mucha" to arts and crafts, as well as numerous everyday objects, from drinking glasses to wallpaper.

Cover of **Figaro Illustré** (Issue No. 75. June 1896).

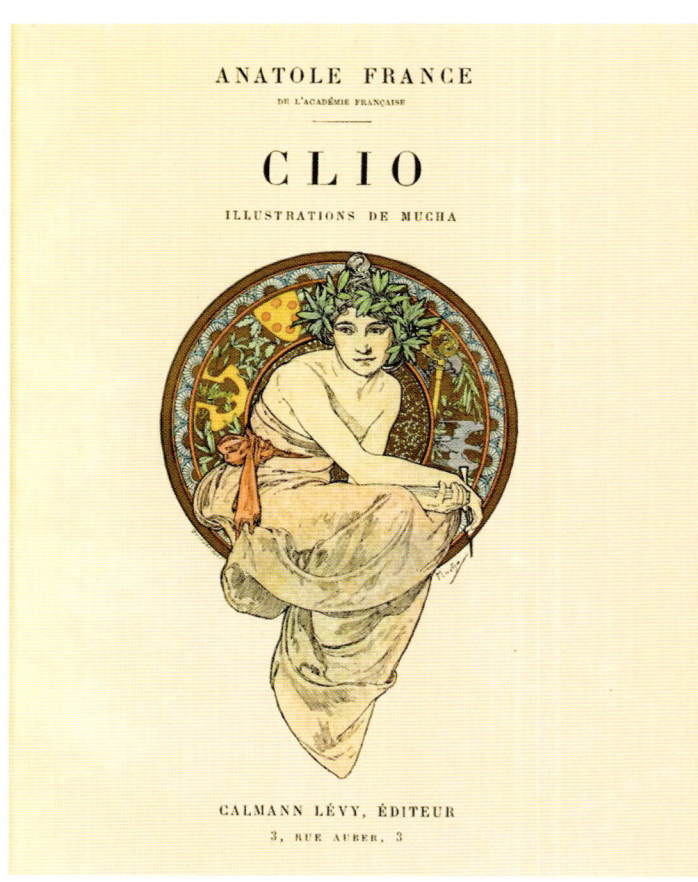

ANATOLE FRANCE
DE L'ACADÉMIE FRANÇAISE

CLIO

ILLUSTRATIONS DE MUCHA

CALMANN LÉVY, ÉDITEUR
3, RUE AUBER, 3

BOOK ILLUSTRATIONS

Mucha's illustration work spanned a range of books and publications. His illustrations were not mere accompaniments to the text but rather integral components of the narrative, enhancing the storytelling experience. One of the most notable examples is Mucha's *Le Pater,* a mystical interpretation of the Lord's Prayer, which he considered his printed masterpiece. He also illustrated a number of Parisian novels and magazines, including *Clio* and *lIlsée, Princess of Tripoli.*

[LEFT]
Frontispiece for **Clio**
by Anatole France (1897).
Color lithograph.

[BELOW AND OPPOSITE PAGE]
Illustrations from the book

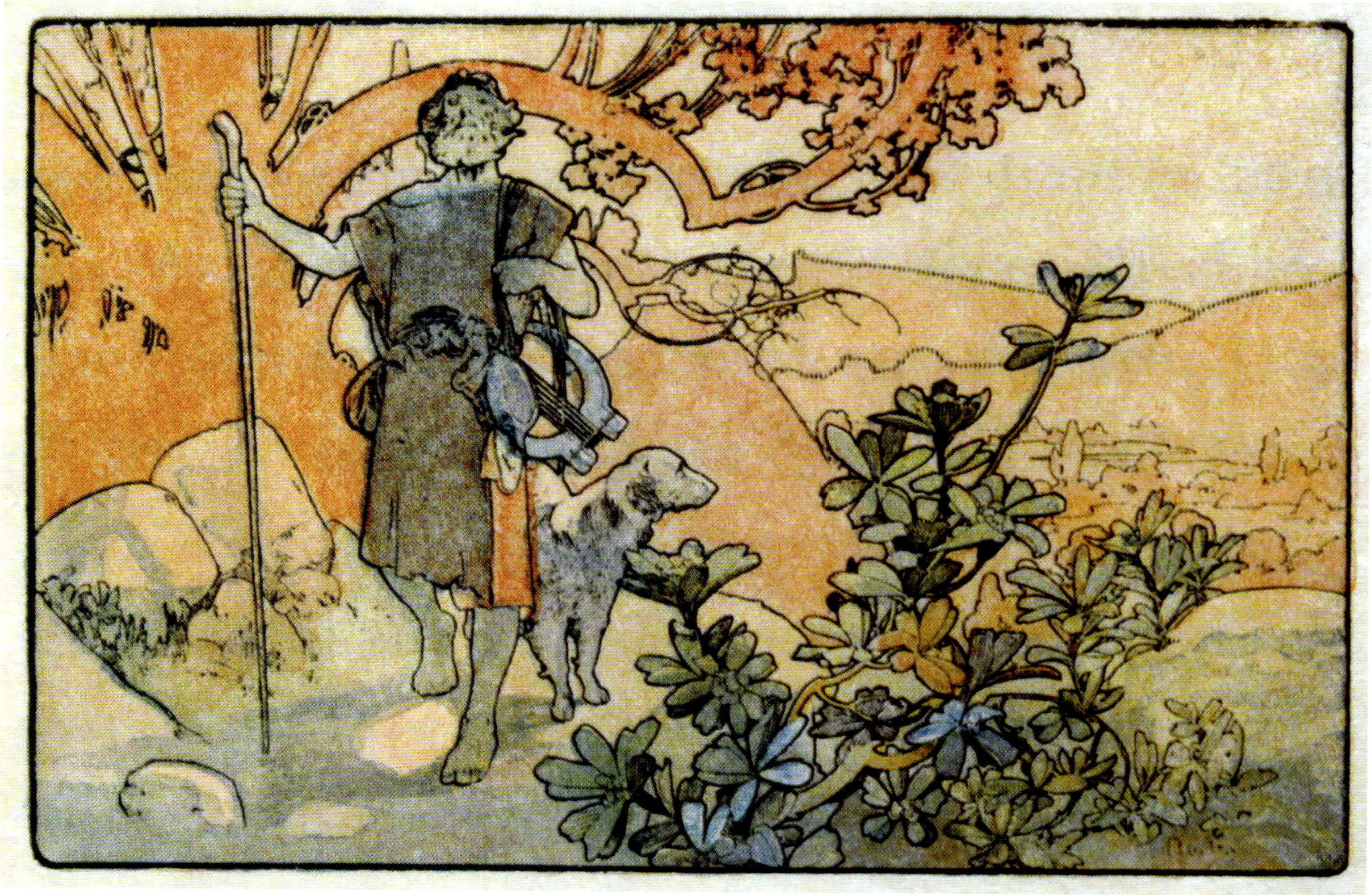

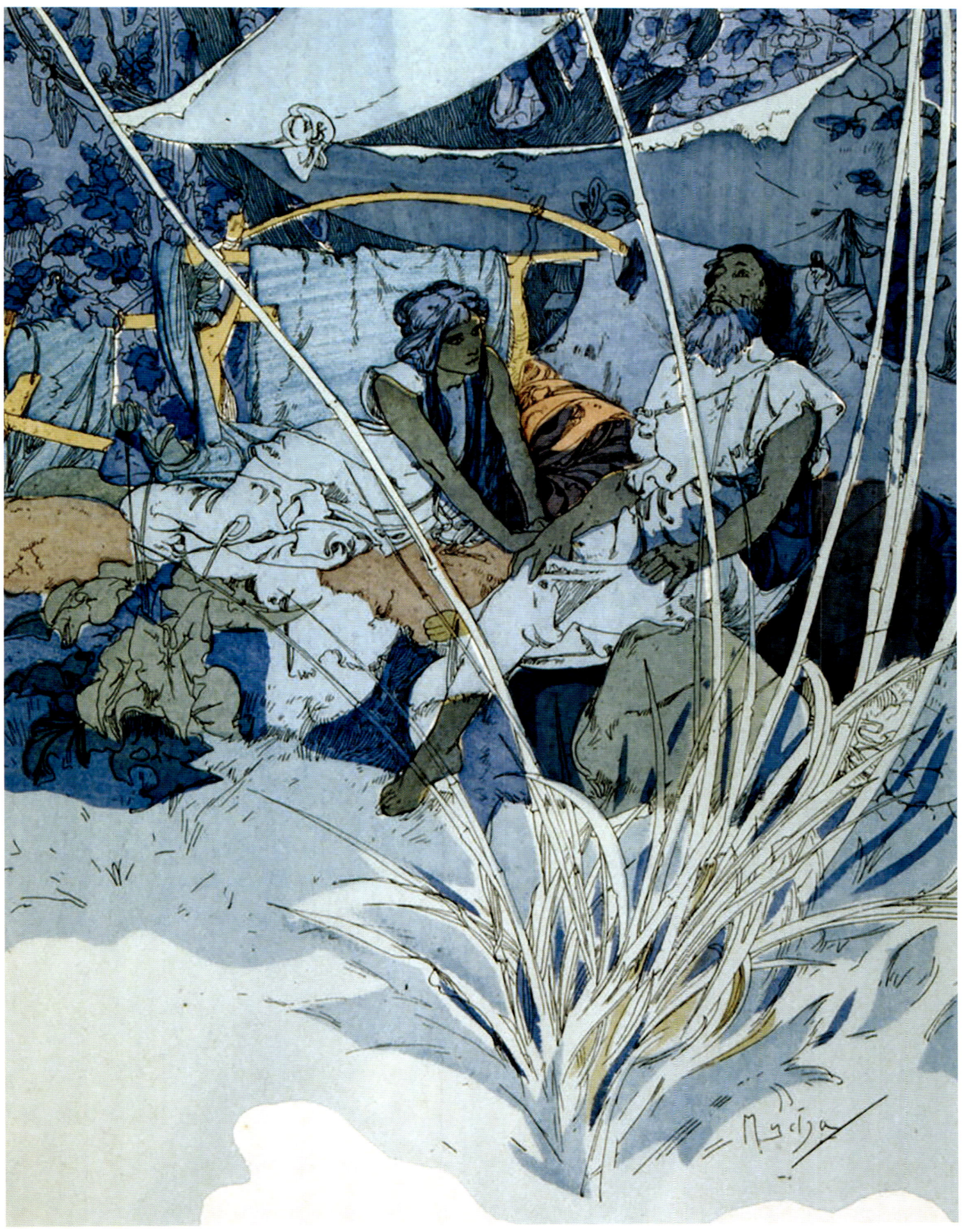

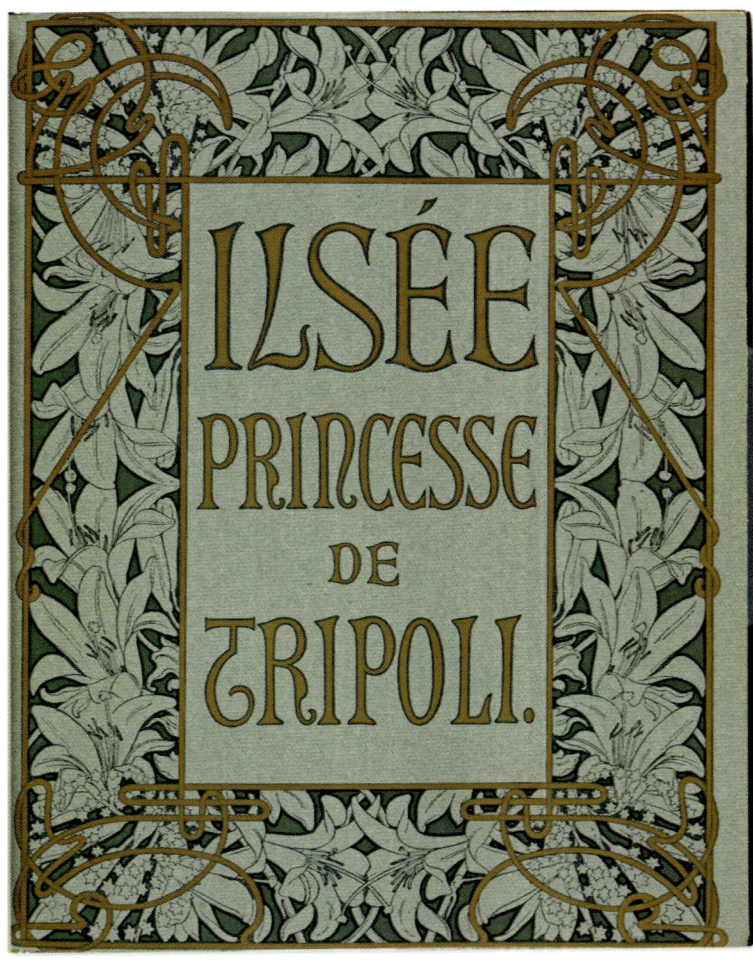

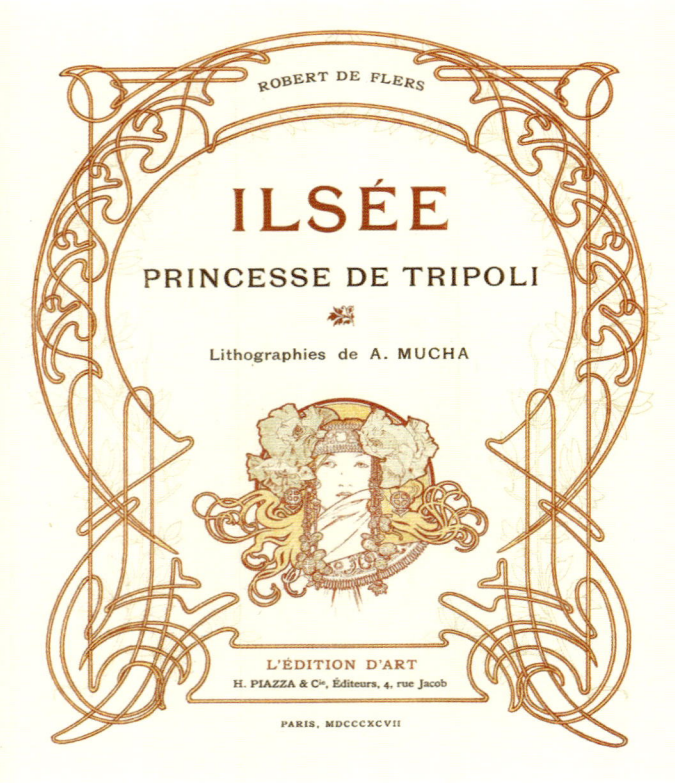

[ABOVE]
Cover of **Ilsée, Princess of Tripoli** (1897).

This is an adaption of Edmond Rostand's La Princesse Lointaine, *written for Sarah Bernhardt in 1895.*

[ABOVE LEFT]
Cover of **Ilsée, Princess of Tripoli** (1897).

[LEFT AND OPPOSITE PAGE]
Illustrations from the book

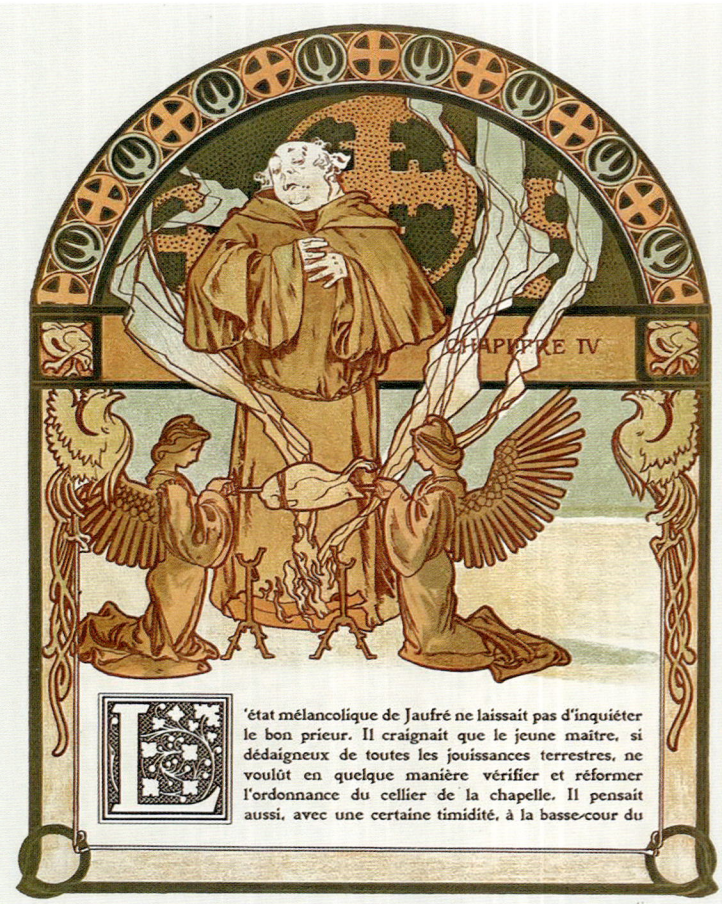

" *We worked on four stones simultaneously. I did some of the drawings straight onto the stone. Other things, particularly the decorative edgings, I drew on tracing paper which was then passed on to the draughtsmen who continued the work with the colors I specified. I hardly had time to sketch out the motif for an ornament when they came and took it from my hands and got down to work on it.*"

~ ALPHONSE MUCHA, ON THE RUSH TO COMPLETE
ILLUSTRATIONS FOR *ILSÉE, PRINCESSE DE TRIPOLI*

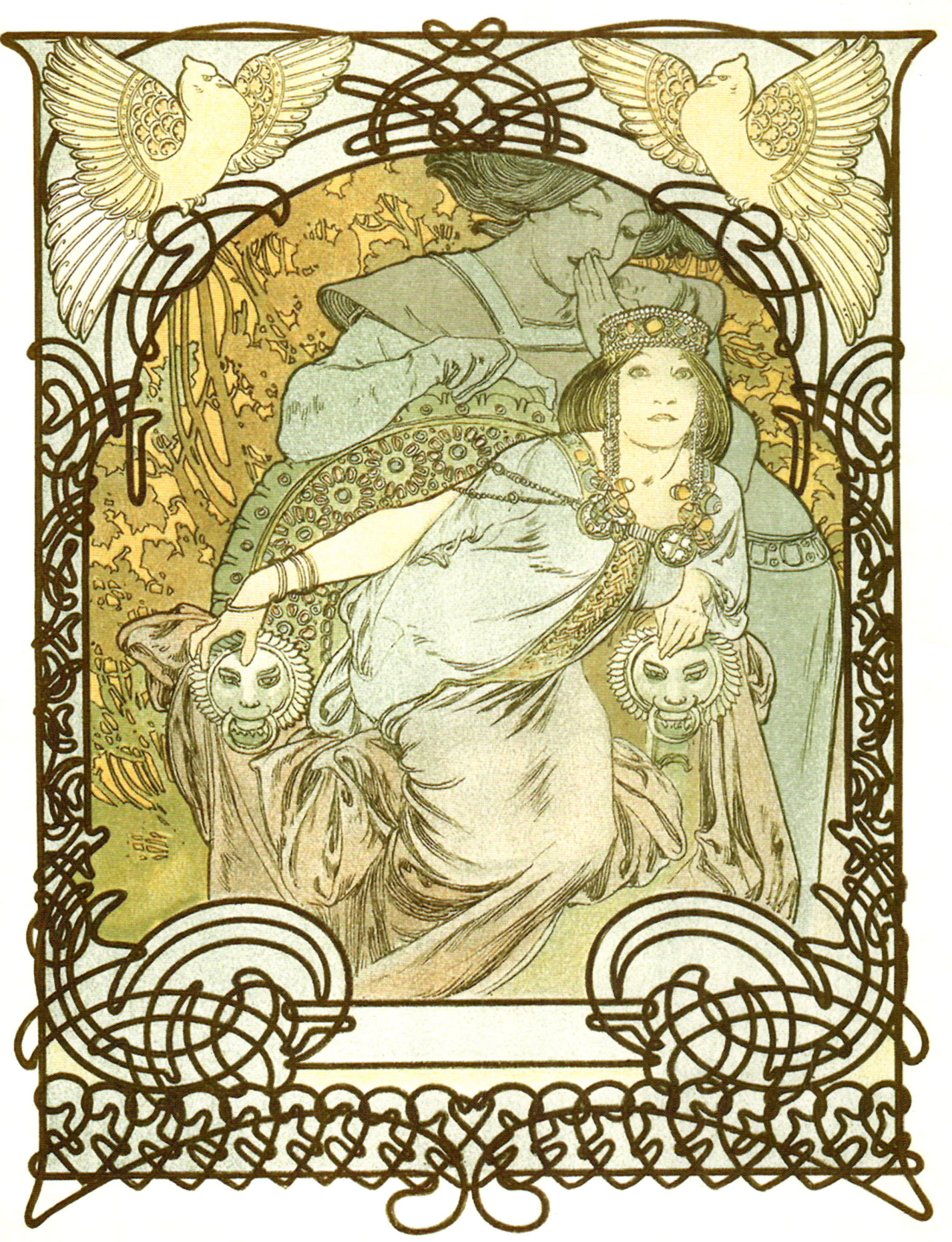

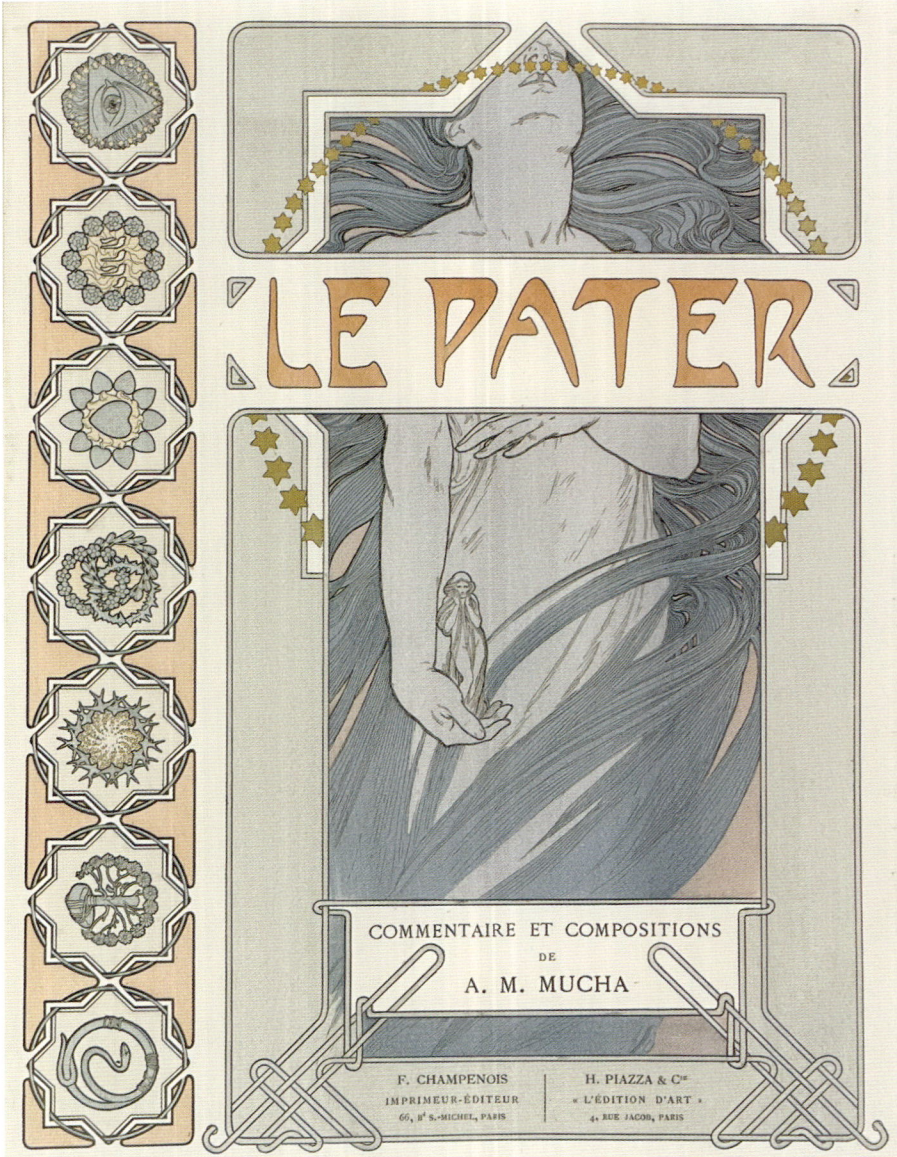

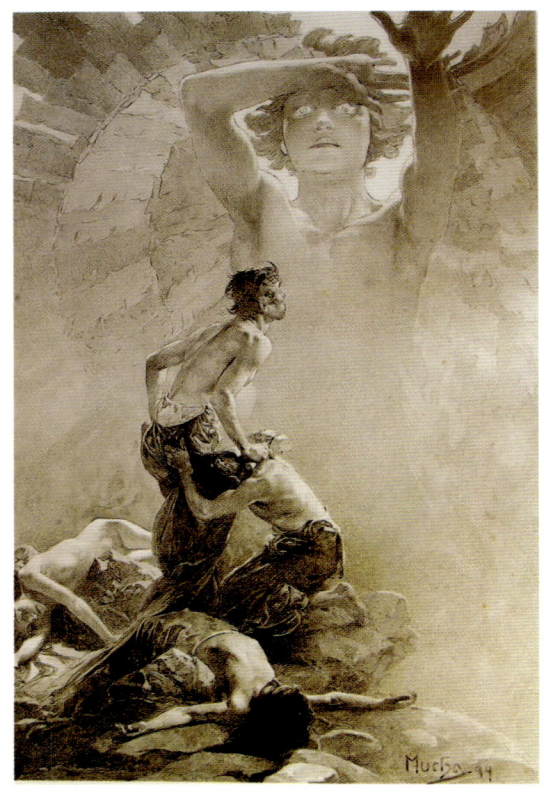

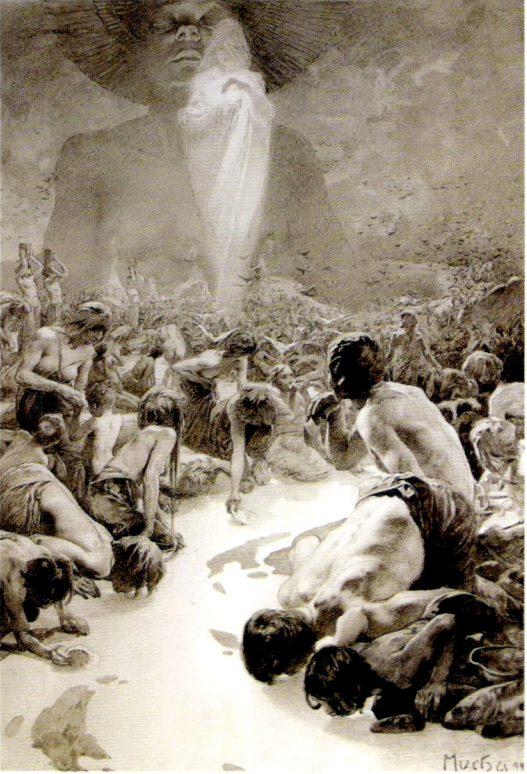

[ABOVE]
Cover of **Le Pater** (1899).

Le Pater *is an illustrated edition of The Lord's Prayer. Mucha created this book at a time in his life when he had become increasingly dissatisfied with solely commercial work.*

[ABOVE RIGHT]
Illustration for **"Forgive us our trespasses as we forgive those who trespass against us."**

[BELOW RIGHT]
Illustration for **"They Kingdom come."**

[OPPOSITE PAGE]
Illustration for **"Lead us not into temptation."**

"*I had not found any real satisfaction in my old kind of work. I saw that my way was to be found elsewhere, little bit higher. I sought a way to spread the light which reached further into even the darkest corners. I didn't have to look for very long. The Pater Noster: why not give the words a pictorial expression?*"

~ ALPHONSE MUCHA

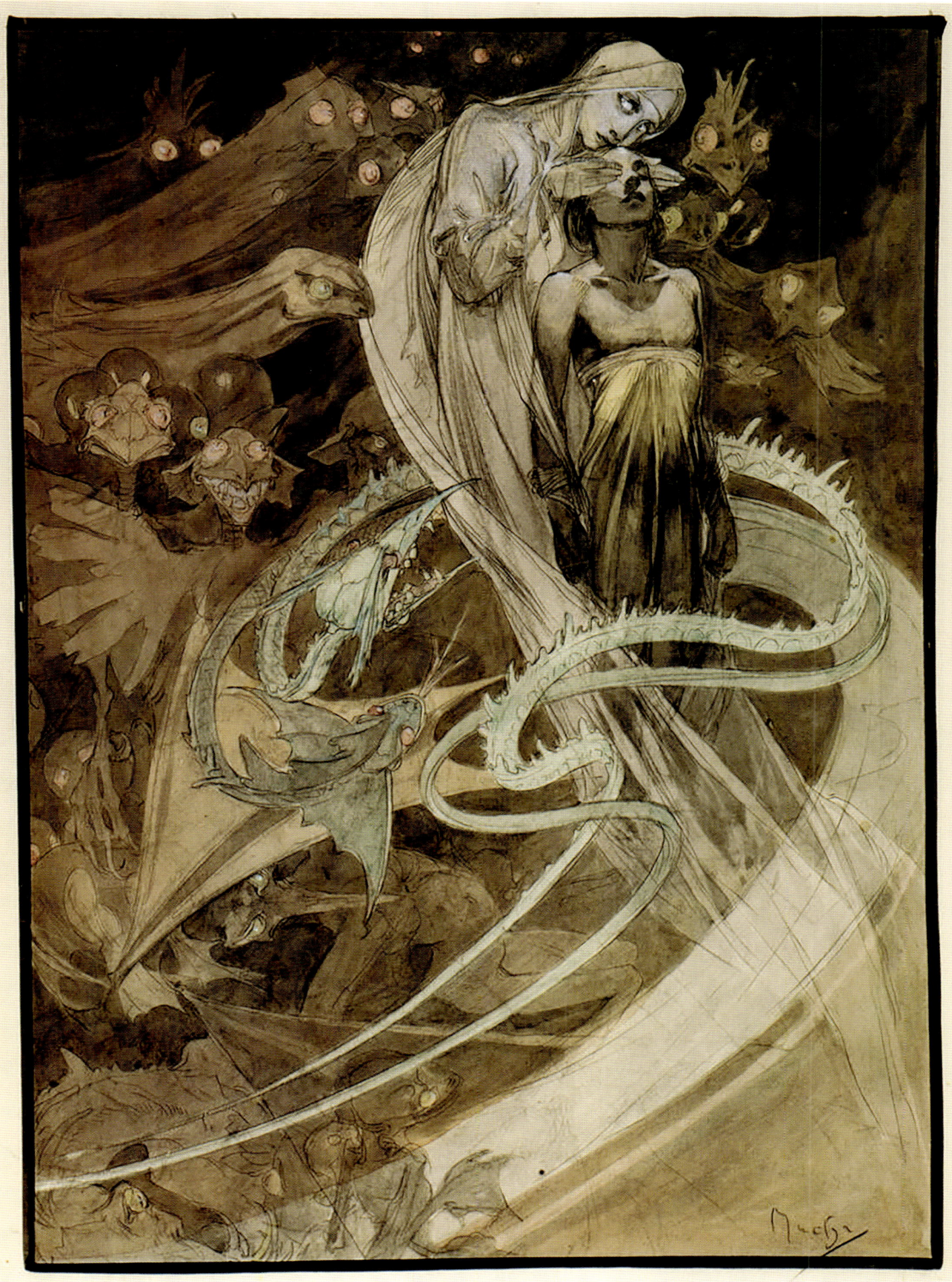

MAGAZINE & PERIODICAL COVERS

While Mucha worked as an illustrator in Paris, he contributed to various magazines and periodicals. His talent for creating eye-catching and elegant illustrations gained recognition, leading to commissions for prominent publications such as *Figaro Illustré, La Plume,* and *The Studio.* Mucha's magazine covers featured his signature style, enhancing the publications' visual appeal and popularizing the Art Nouveau aesthetic. As his reputation grew, he transitioned to designing posters and commercial art, but his early work in magazines and periodicals laid the foundation for his later success.

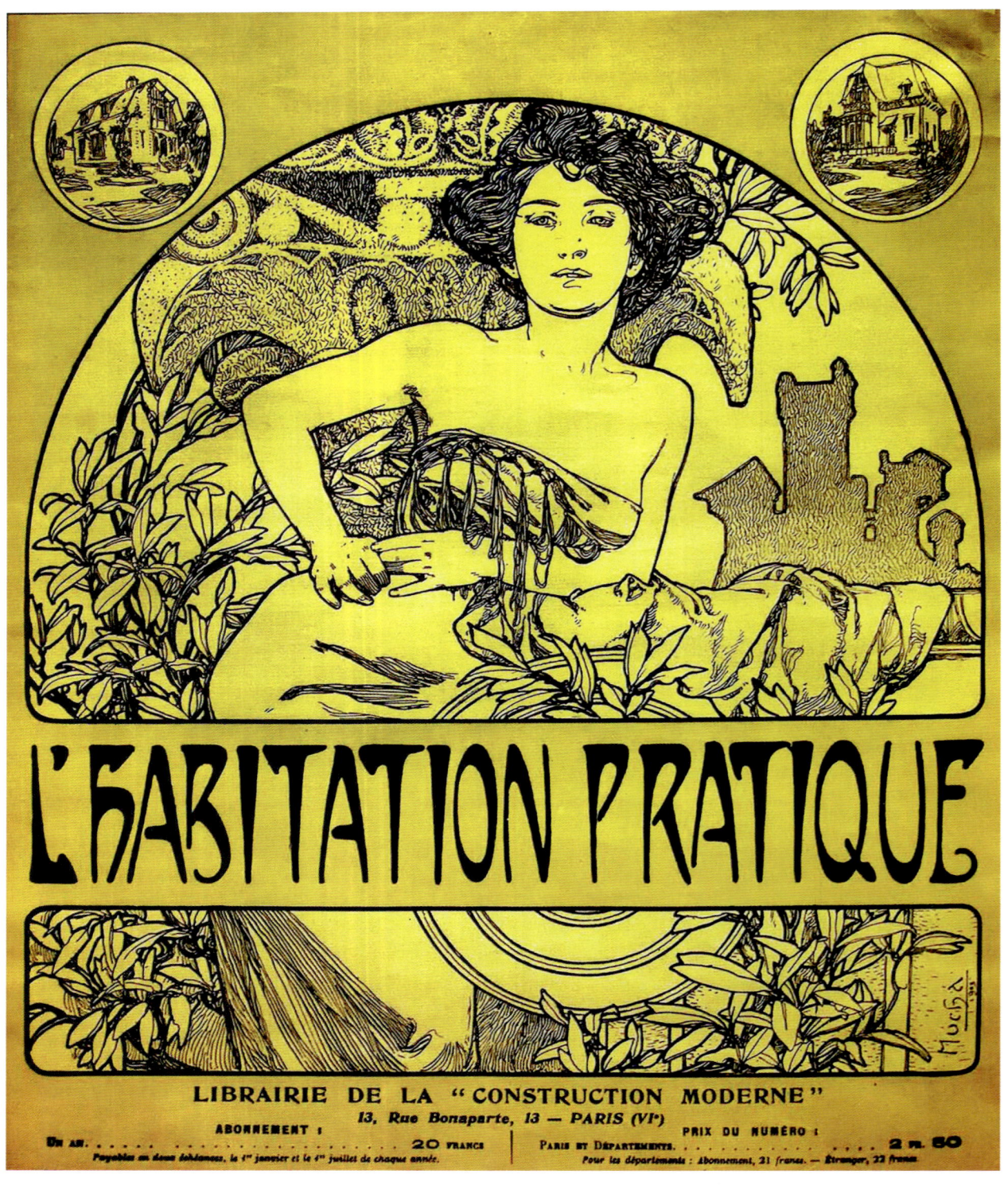

Cover of **L'habitation pratique** (1908). Color lithograph.

L'habitation pratique *was a decoration magazine issued from 1903 to 1912.*

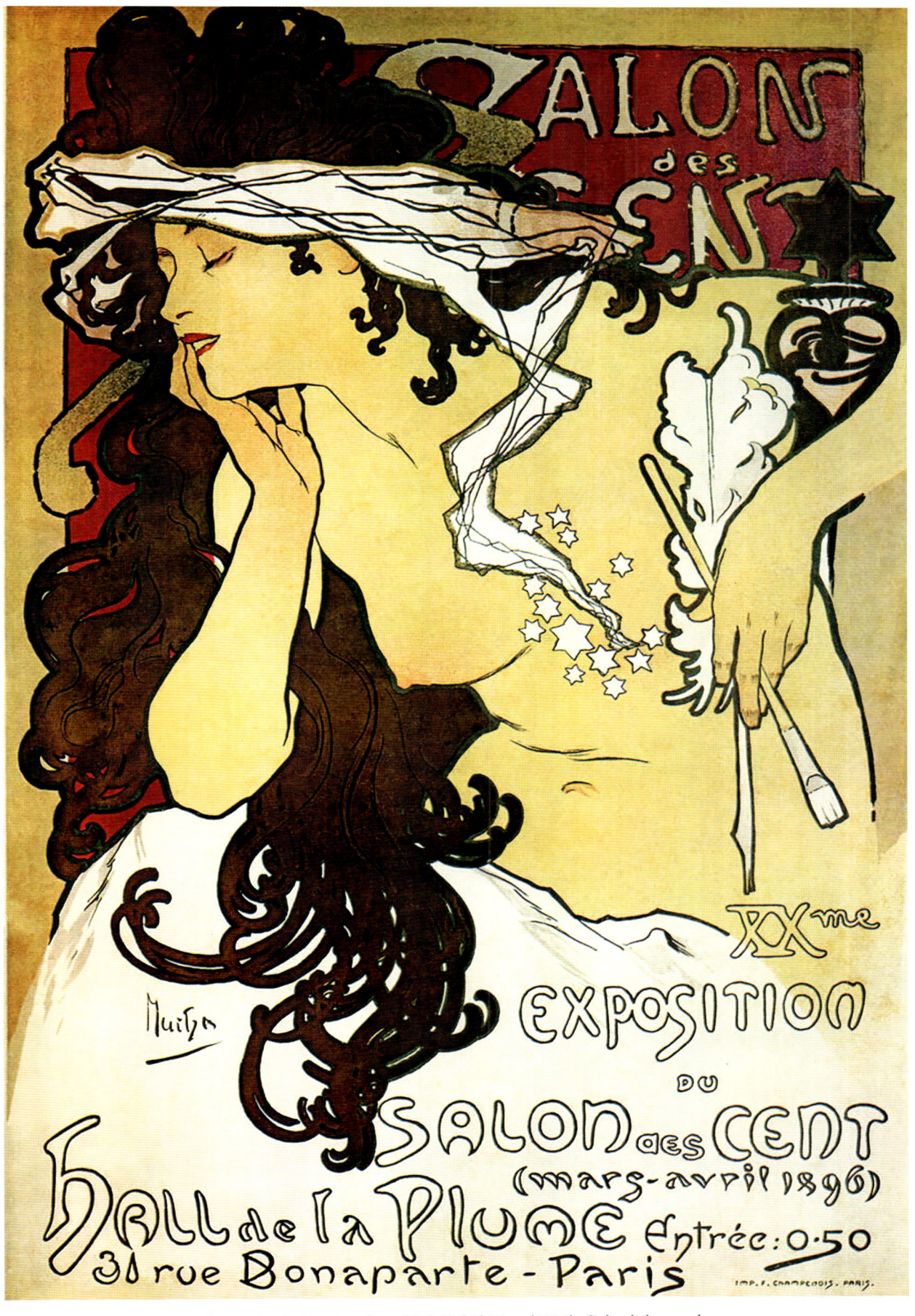

Poster for *Salon des Cent 20th Exhibition* (1896). Color lithograph.

*This exhibition offered for sale lithographic works by artists associated with
the magazine* La Plume, *including Toulouse-Lautrec, Bonnard, Ensor, and Grasset.*

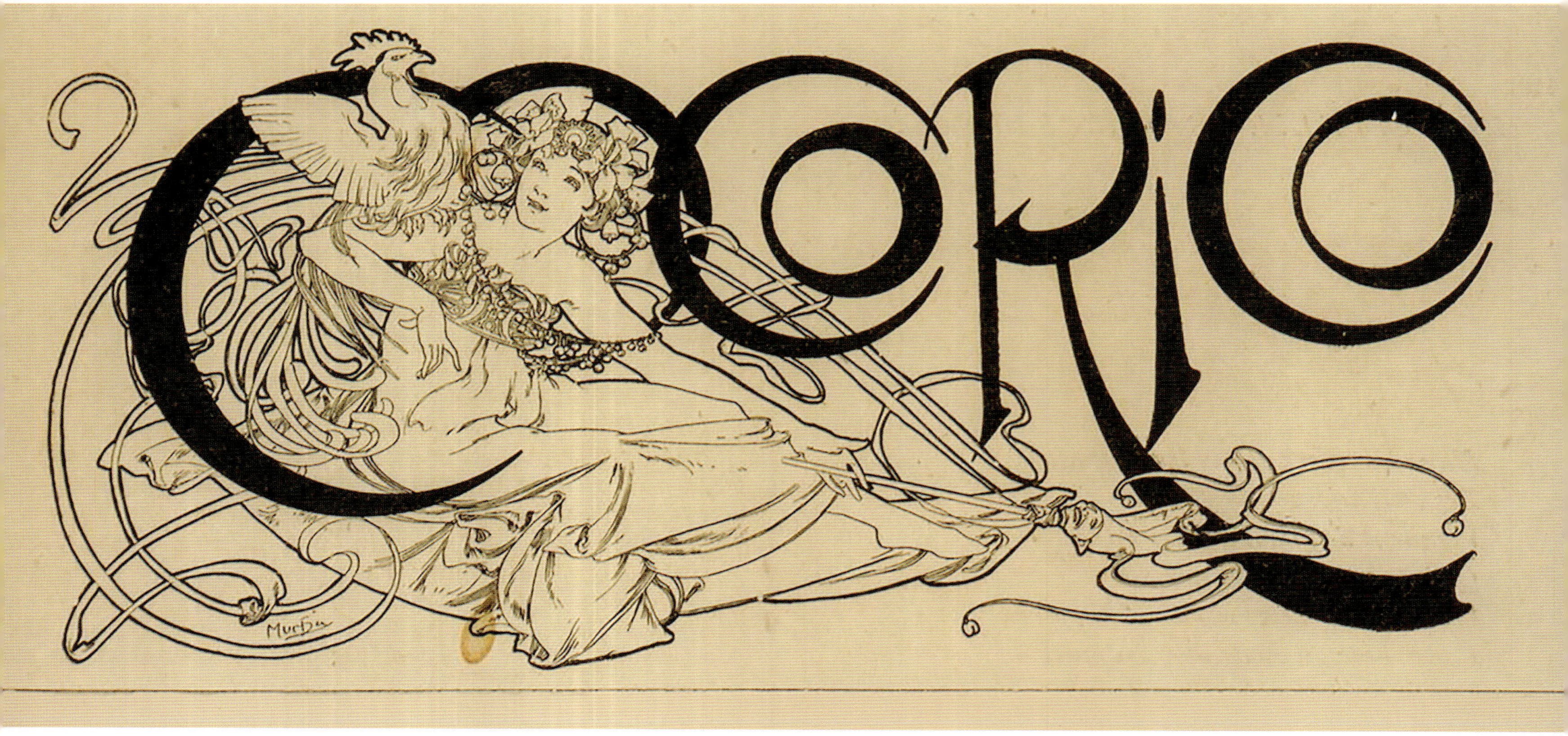

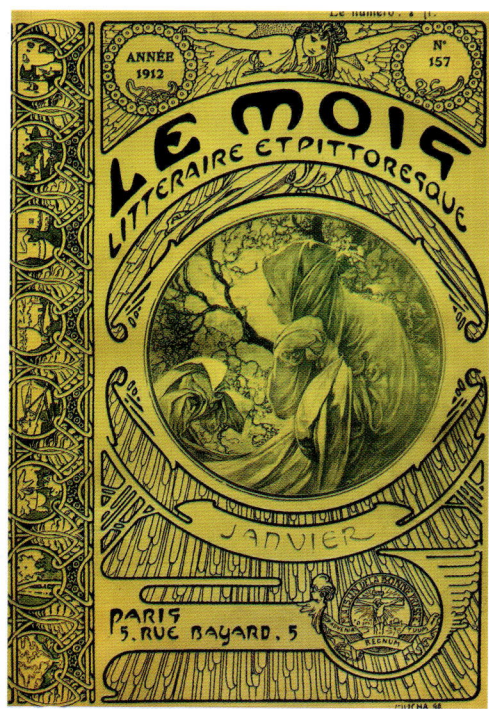

Cocorico magazine title (1898).

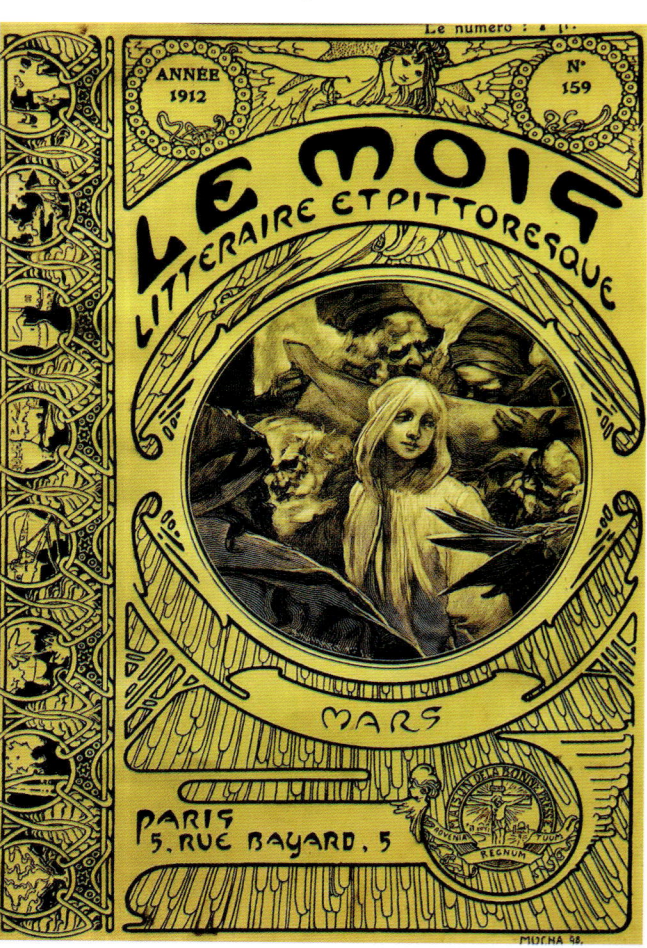

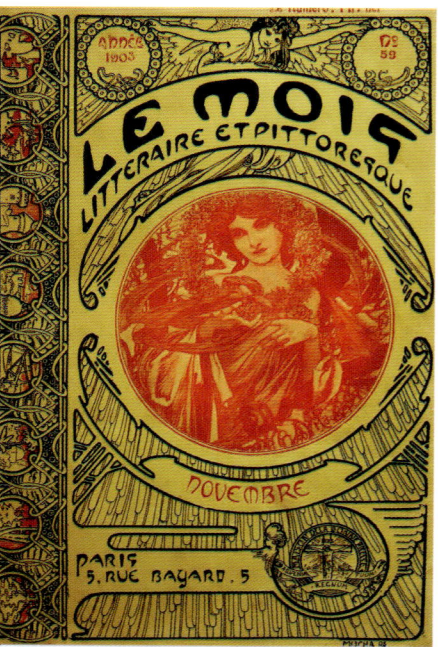

Covers of **Le Mois** *(*1902).
From left to right: January edition,
March edition, November edition

A. MUCHA

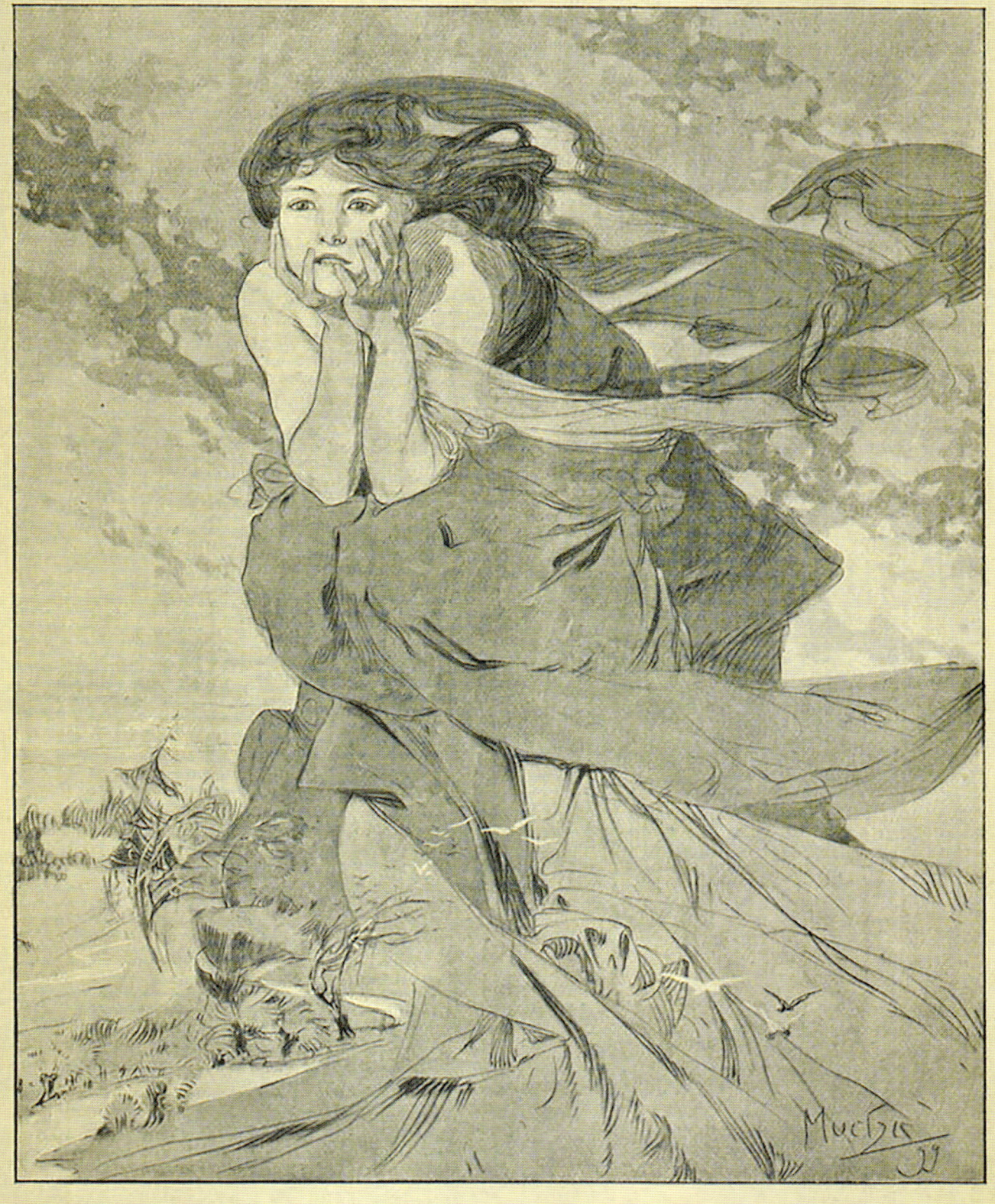

MARS

Les Giboulées.

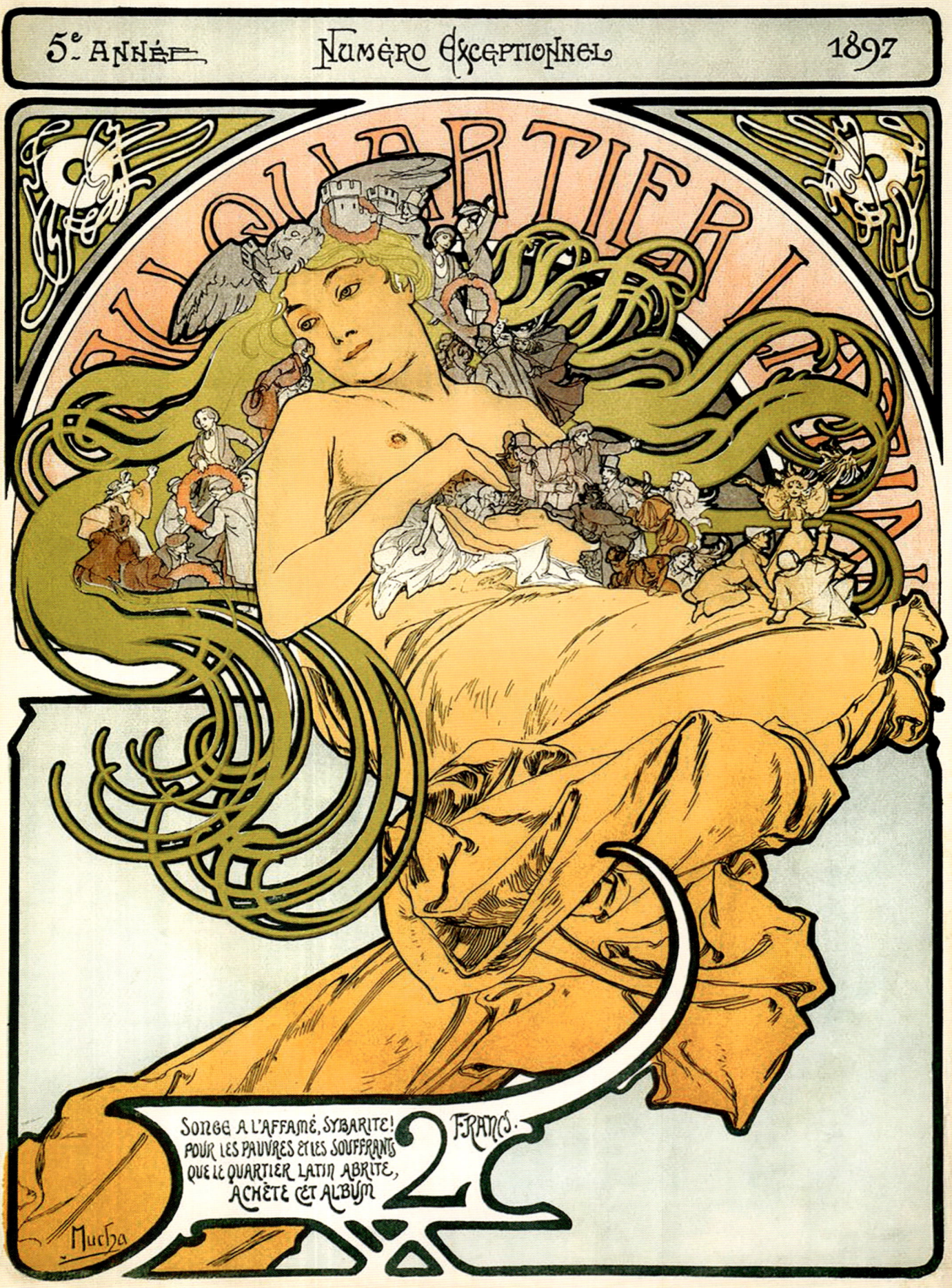

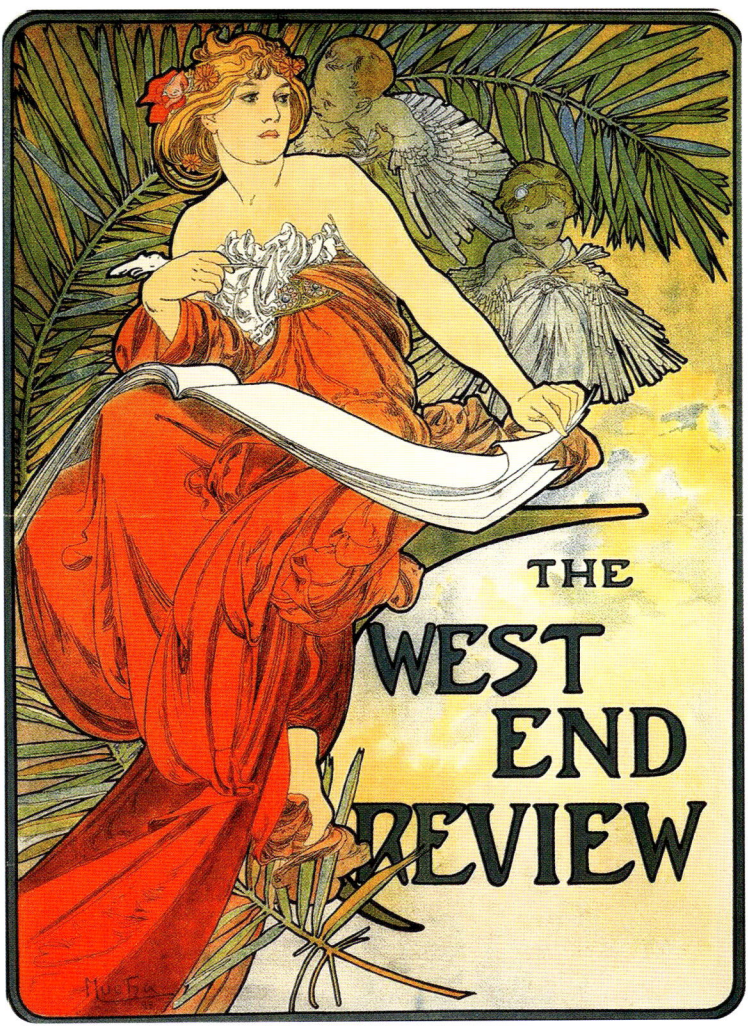

Cover for literary magazine **West End Review** (1898).

[OPPOSITE PAGE]
Cover of a brochure promoting
Au Quartier Latin of Paris,
sold in aid of the poor (1897).

[LEFT]
Cover for the
French literary
and artistic
review **La Plume**
(15 January 1898).

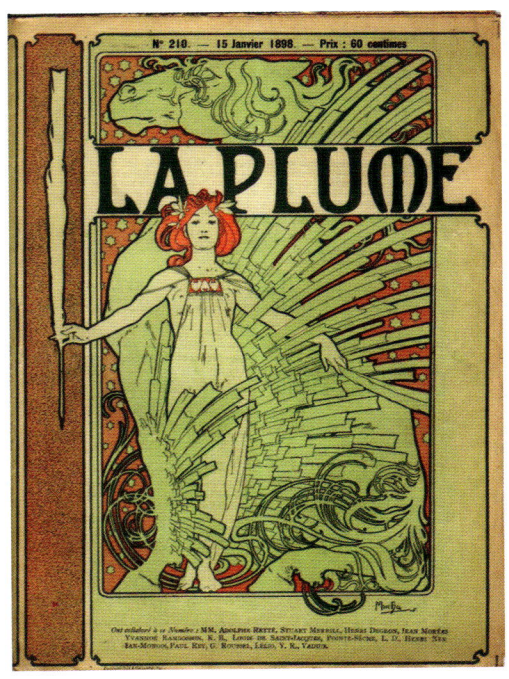

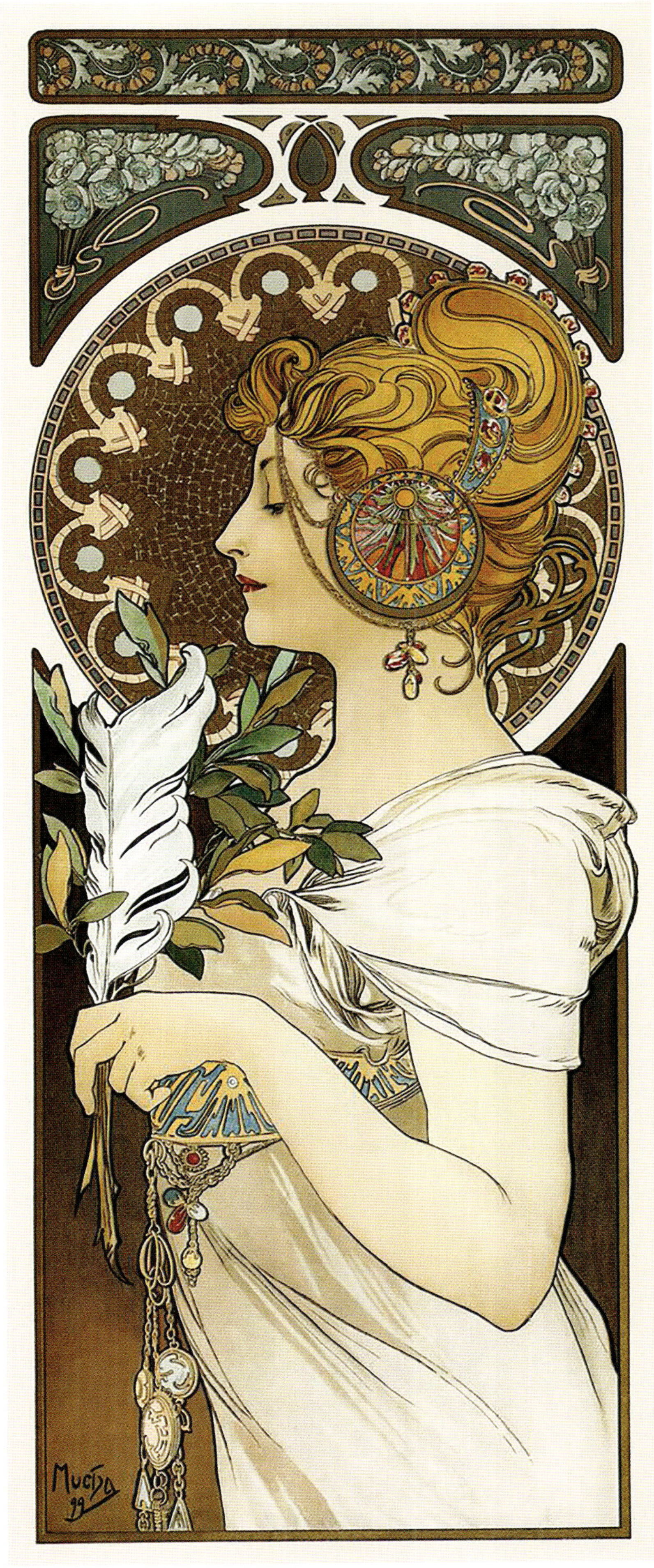

[RIGHT]
Poster for
La Plume
(1899).

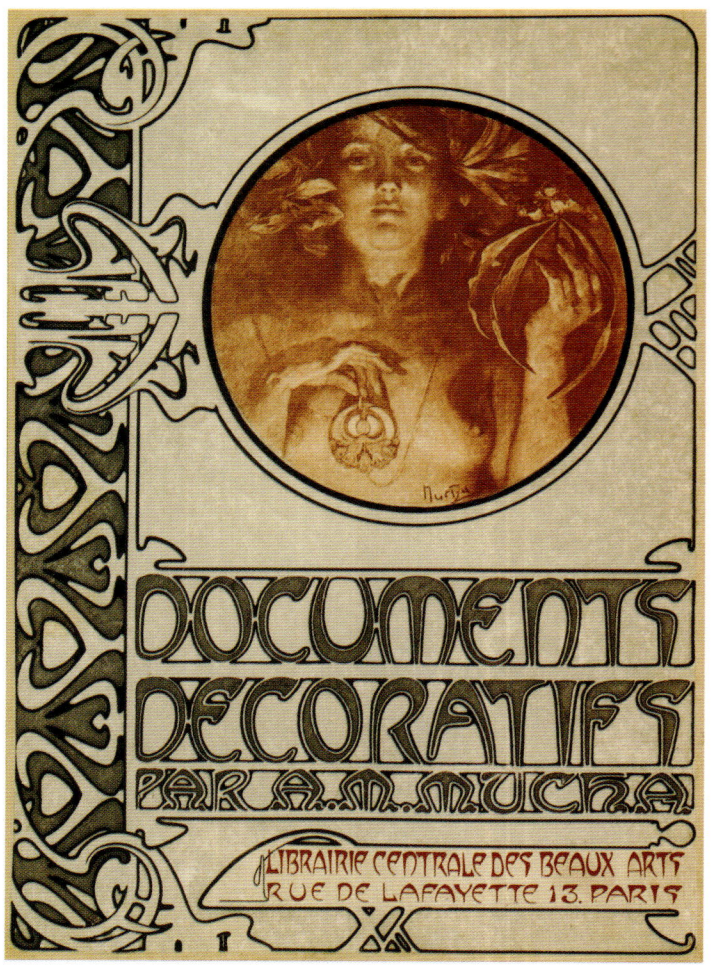

DOCUMENTS DÉCORATIFS

Mucha's *Documents Décoratifs* is an influential work published in 1901. It was designed as a teaching tool and style guide for aspiring artists, decorators, and craftsmen. The encyclopedia encompasses a broad range of designs, including furniture, jewelry, ceramics, textiles, and ornamental frames. *Documents Décoratifs* is emblematic of the Art Nouveau style, characterized by its organic forms, intricate details, and feminine figures.

[RIGHT]
Cover of ***Documents décoratifs: panneaux décoratifs, études des applications de fleurs, papier peints, frises, vitraux, orfévrerie etc.*** Paris: Librairie centrale des beaux-arts (c. 1901).

[OPPOSITE PAGE]
Documents Décoratifs Plate 2

[BELOW LEFT] ***Documents Décoratifs*** Plate 21

[BELOW RIGHT] ***Documents Décoratifs*** Plate 22

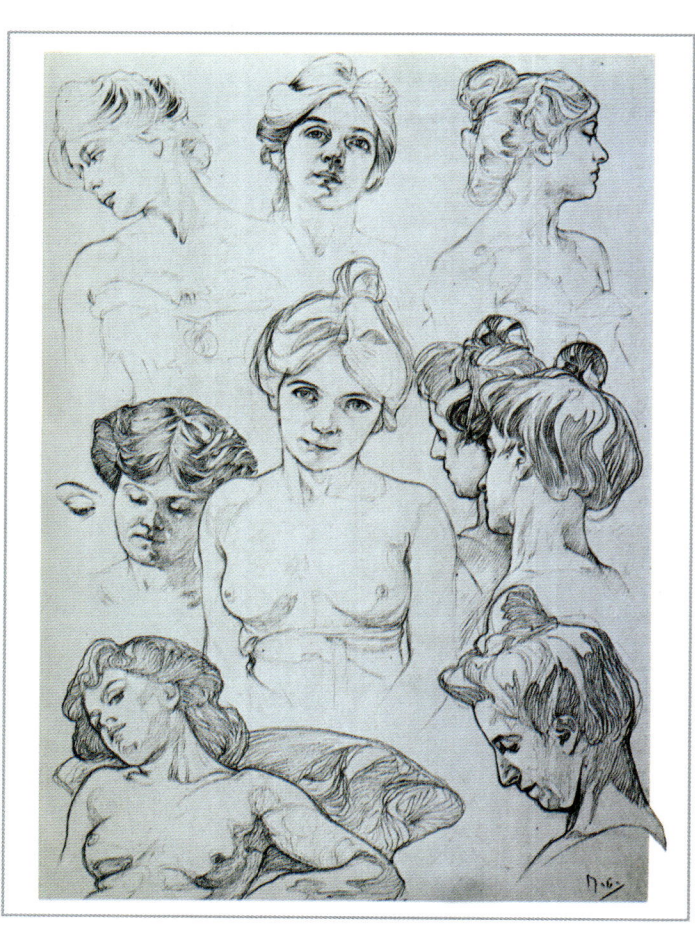

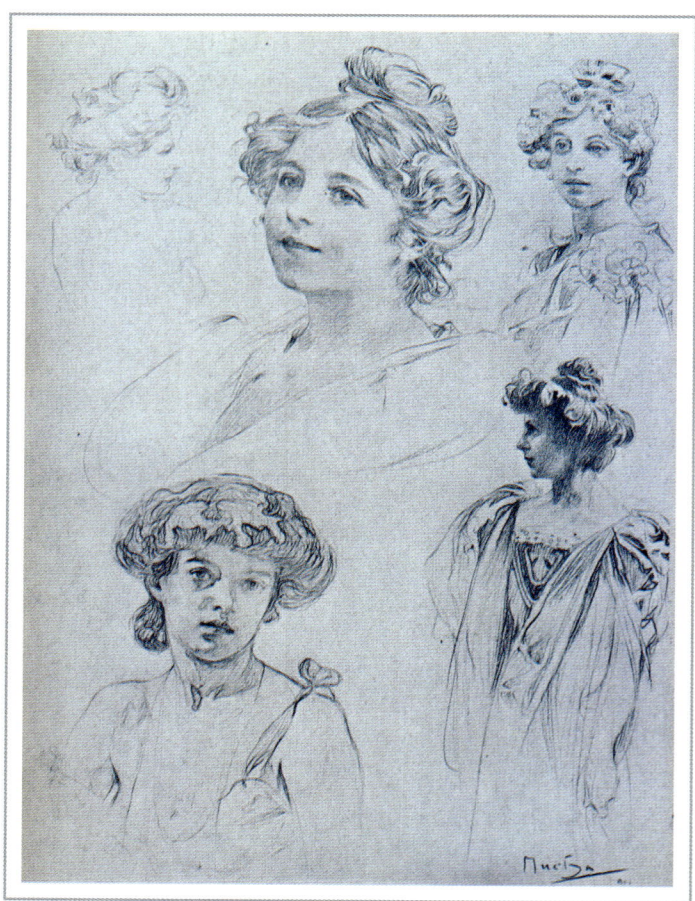

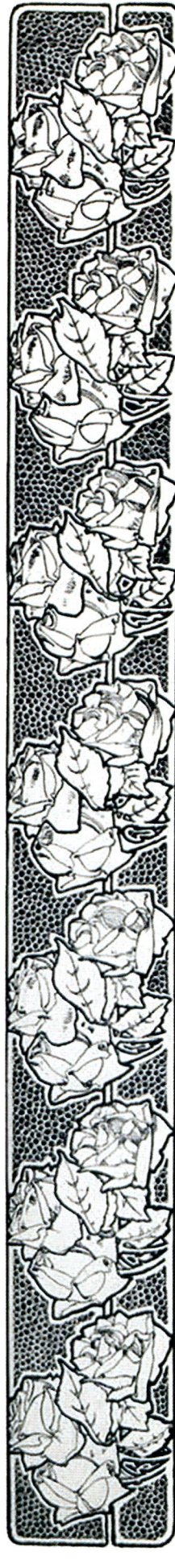

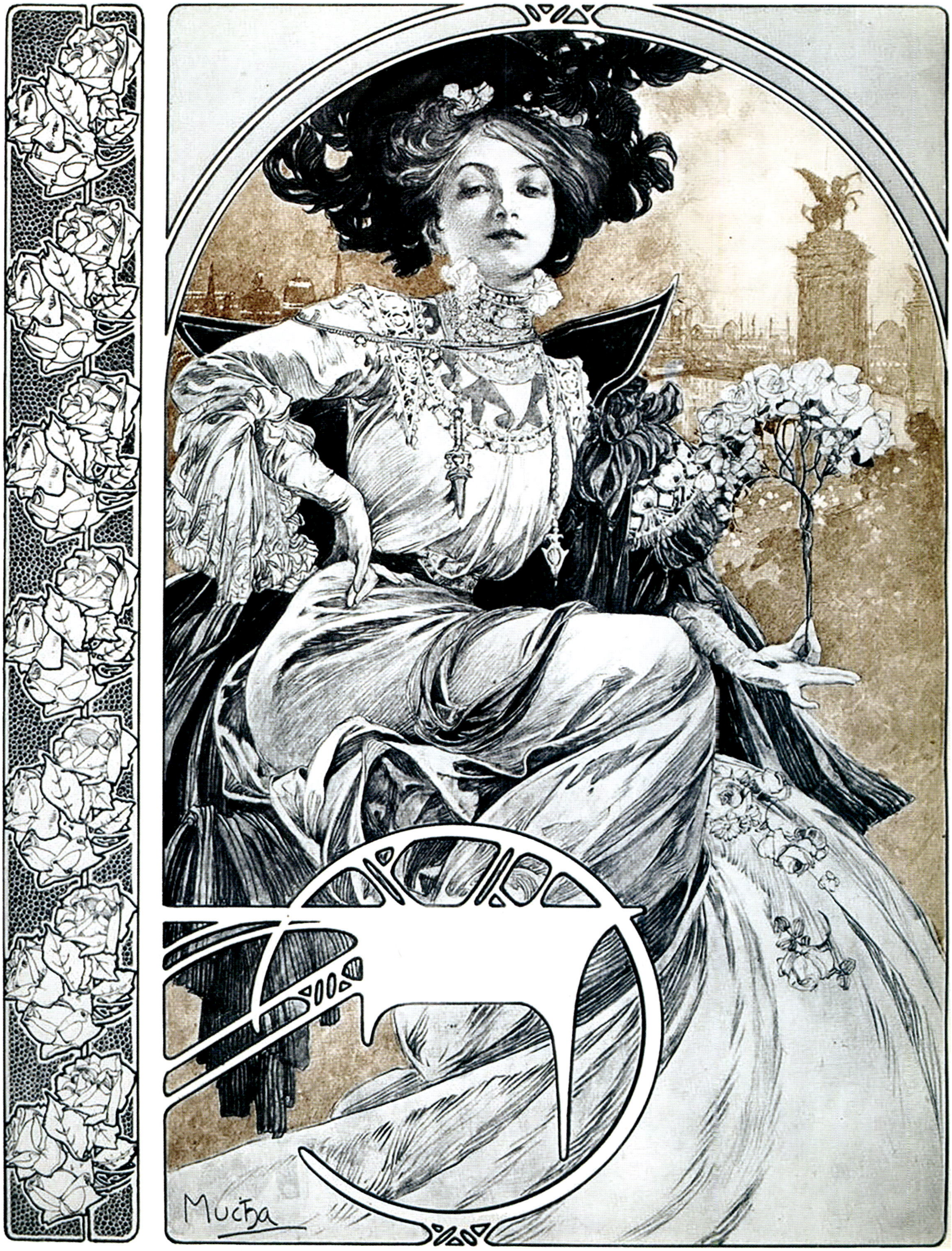

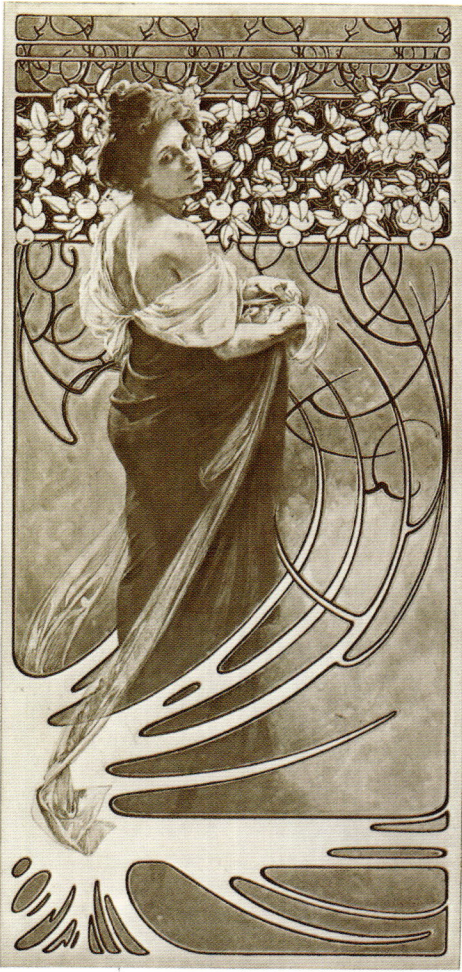

Documents Décoratifs Plate 9

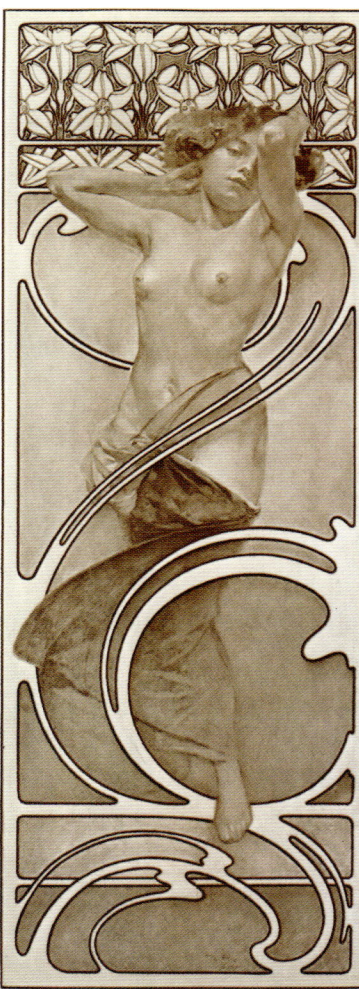

Documents Décoratifs Plate 11

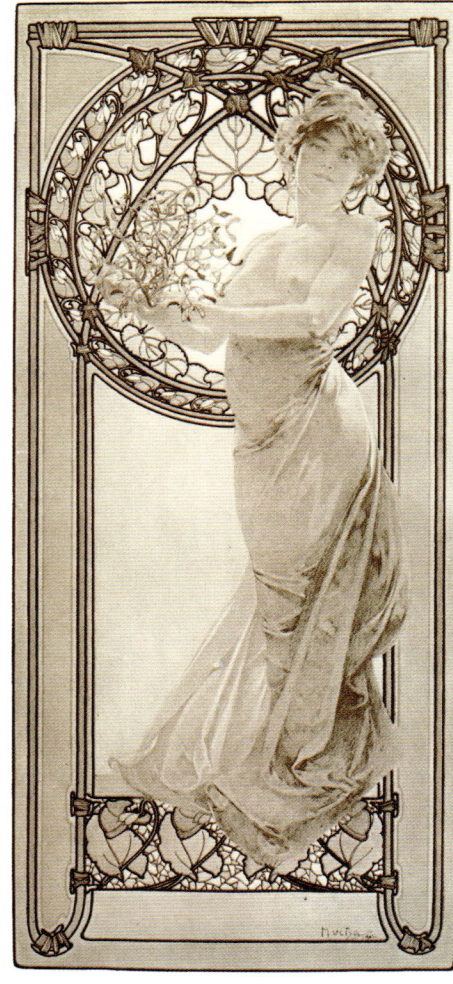

Documents Décoratifs Plate 12

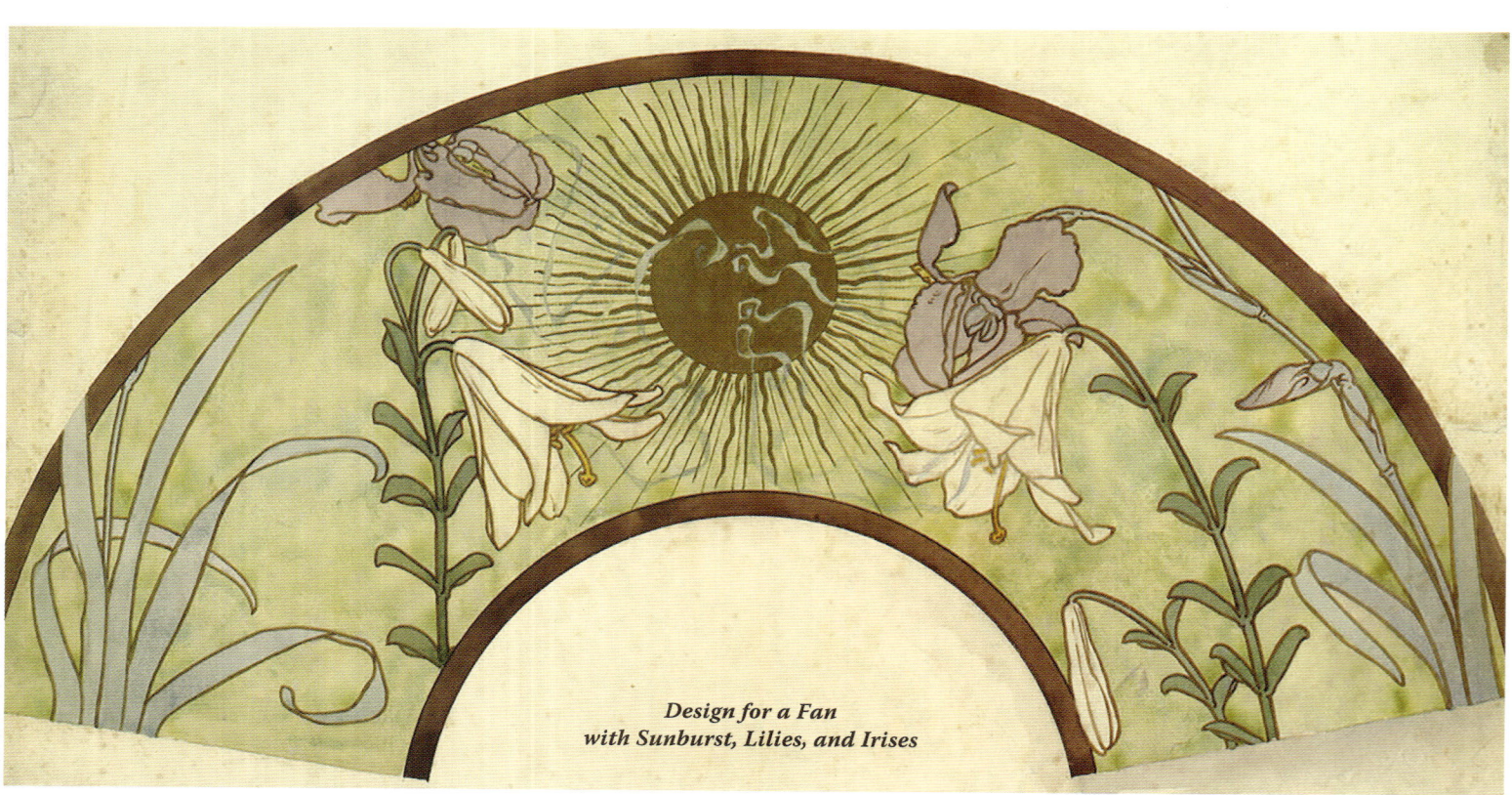

Design for a Fan
with Sunburst, Lilies, and Irises

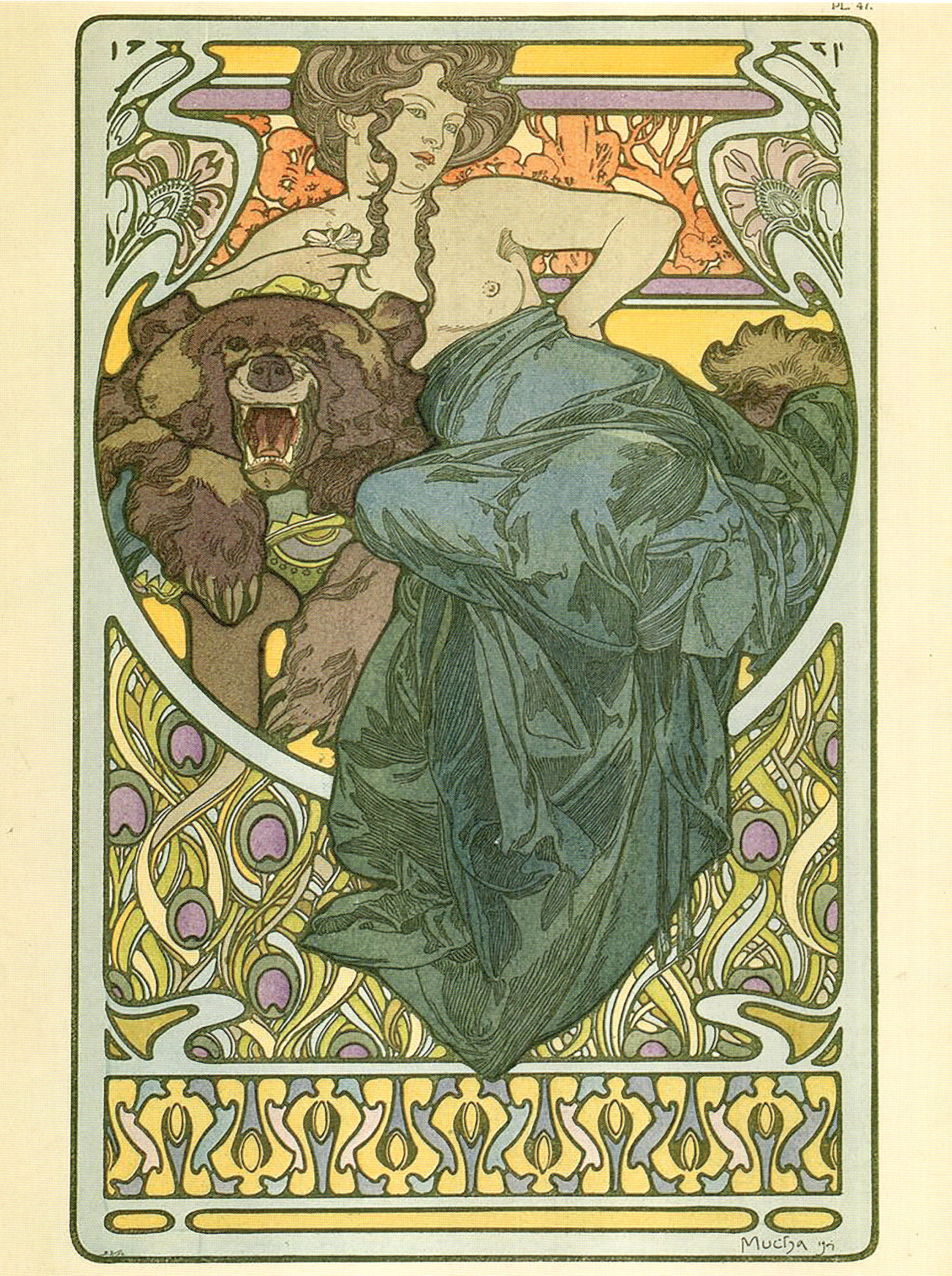

Documents Décoratifs Plate 47

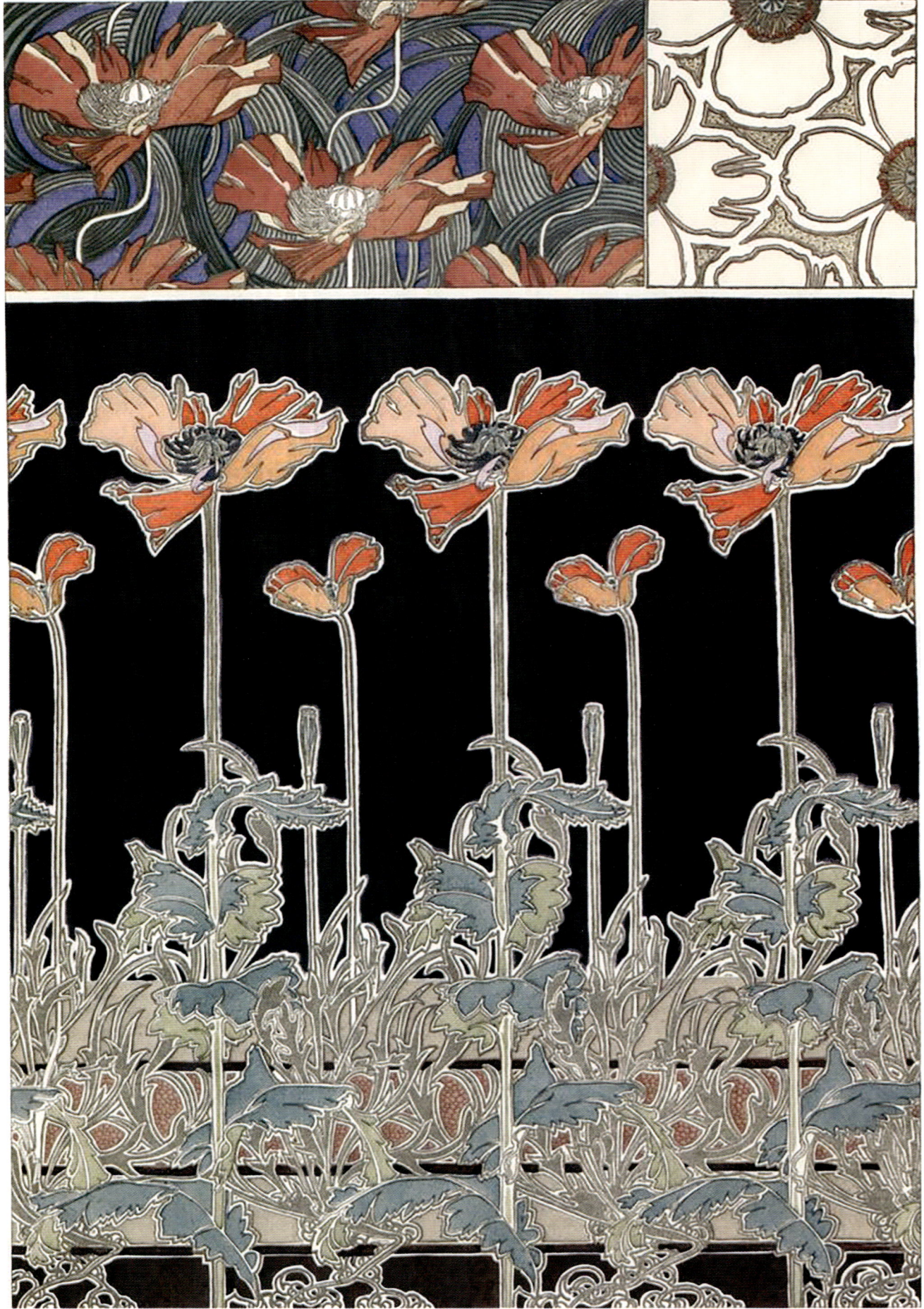

Documents Décoratifs Plate 38

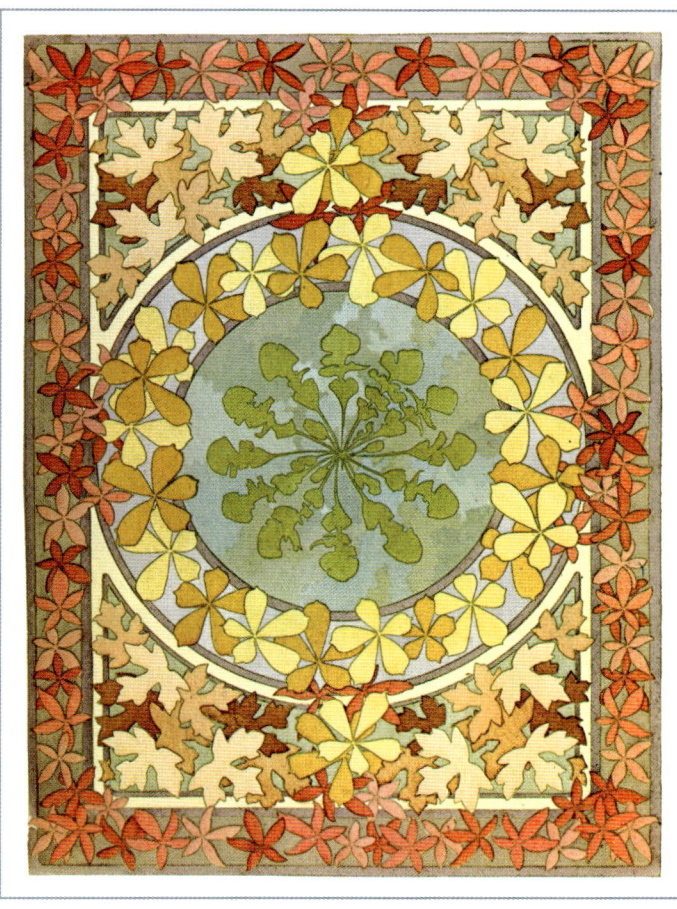

Documents Décoratifs Plate 28

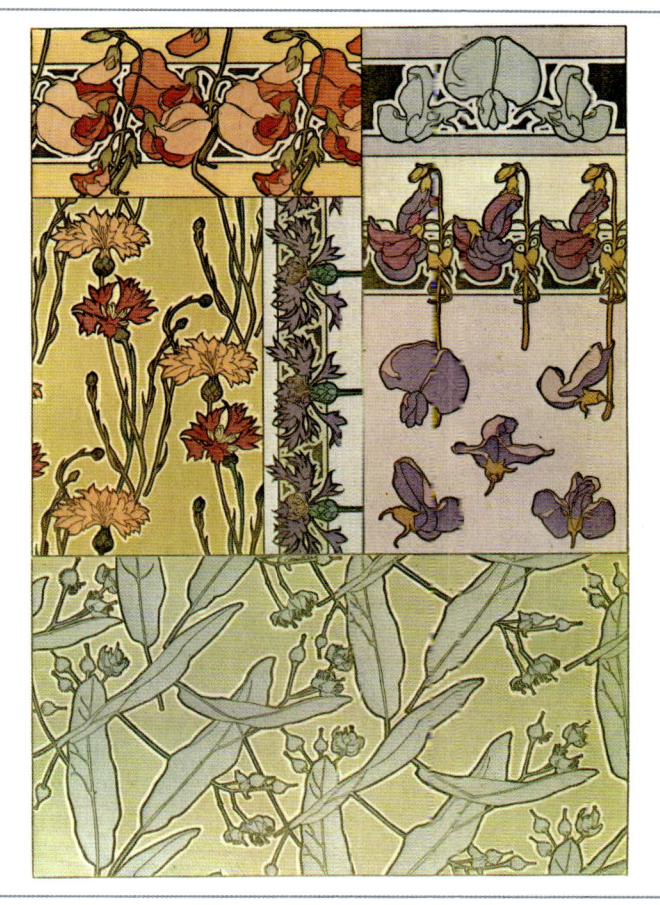

Documents Décoratifs Plate 29

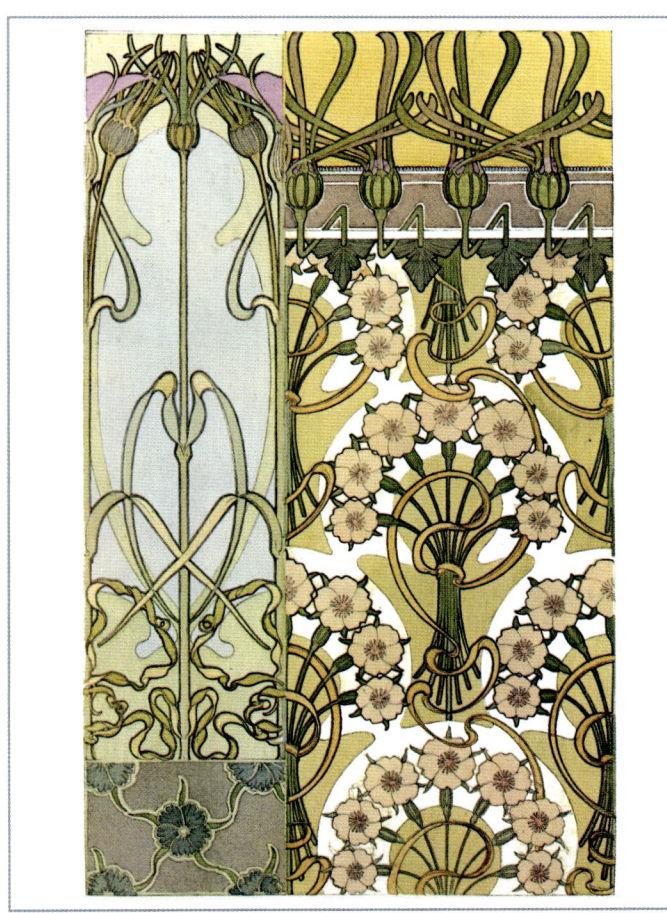

Documents Décoratifs Plate 30

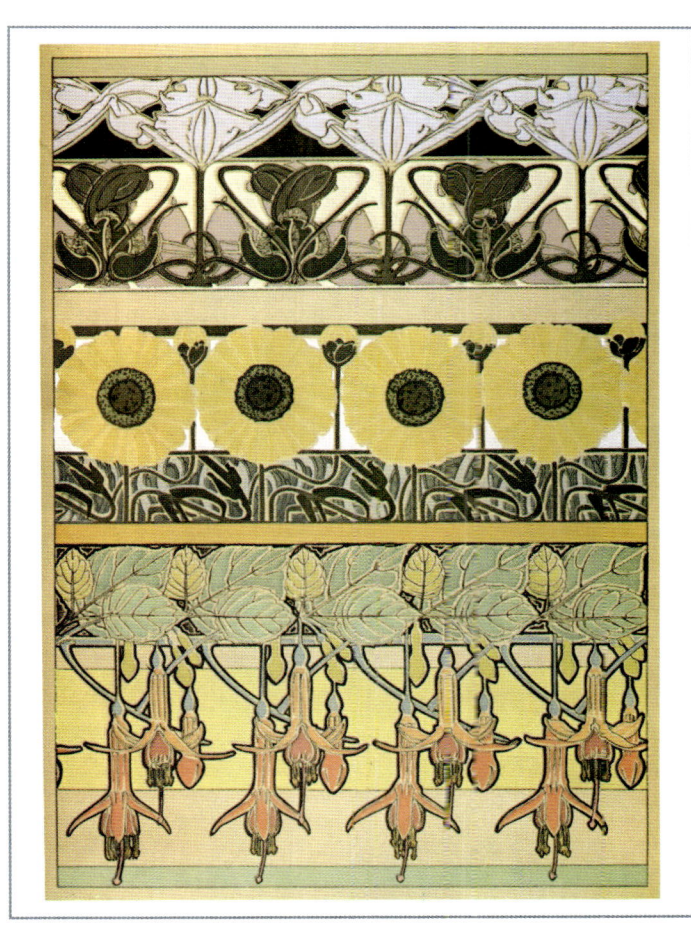

Documents Décoratifs Plate 40

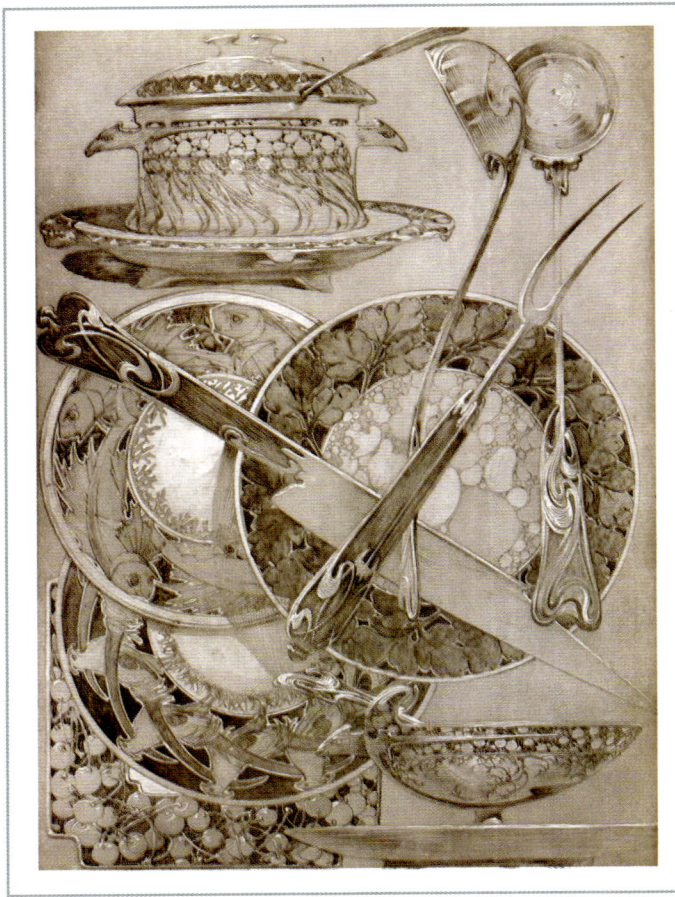

Documents Décoratifs Plate 59

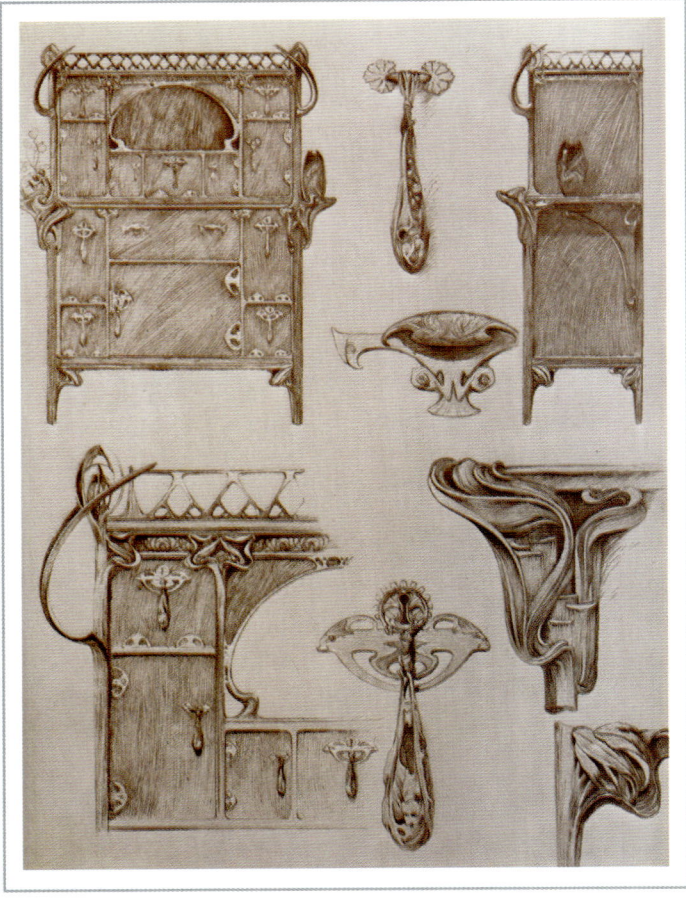

Documents Décoratifs Plate 64

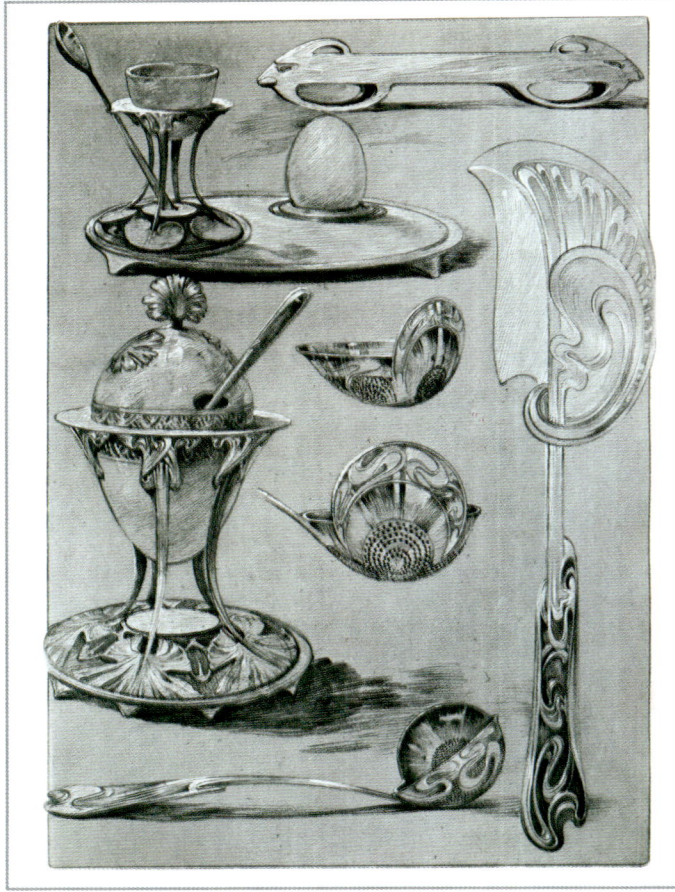

Documents Décoratifs Plate 65

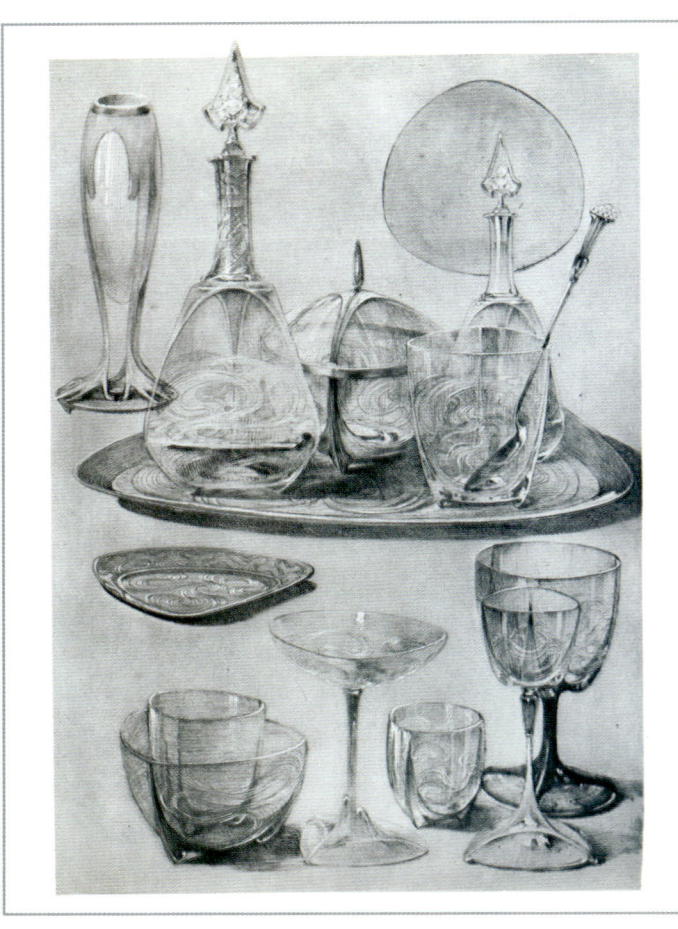

Documents Décoratifs Plate 66

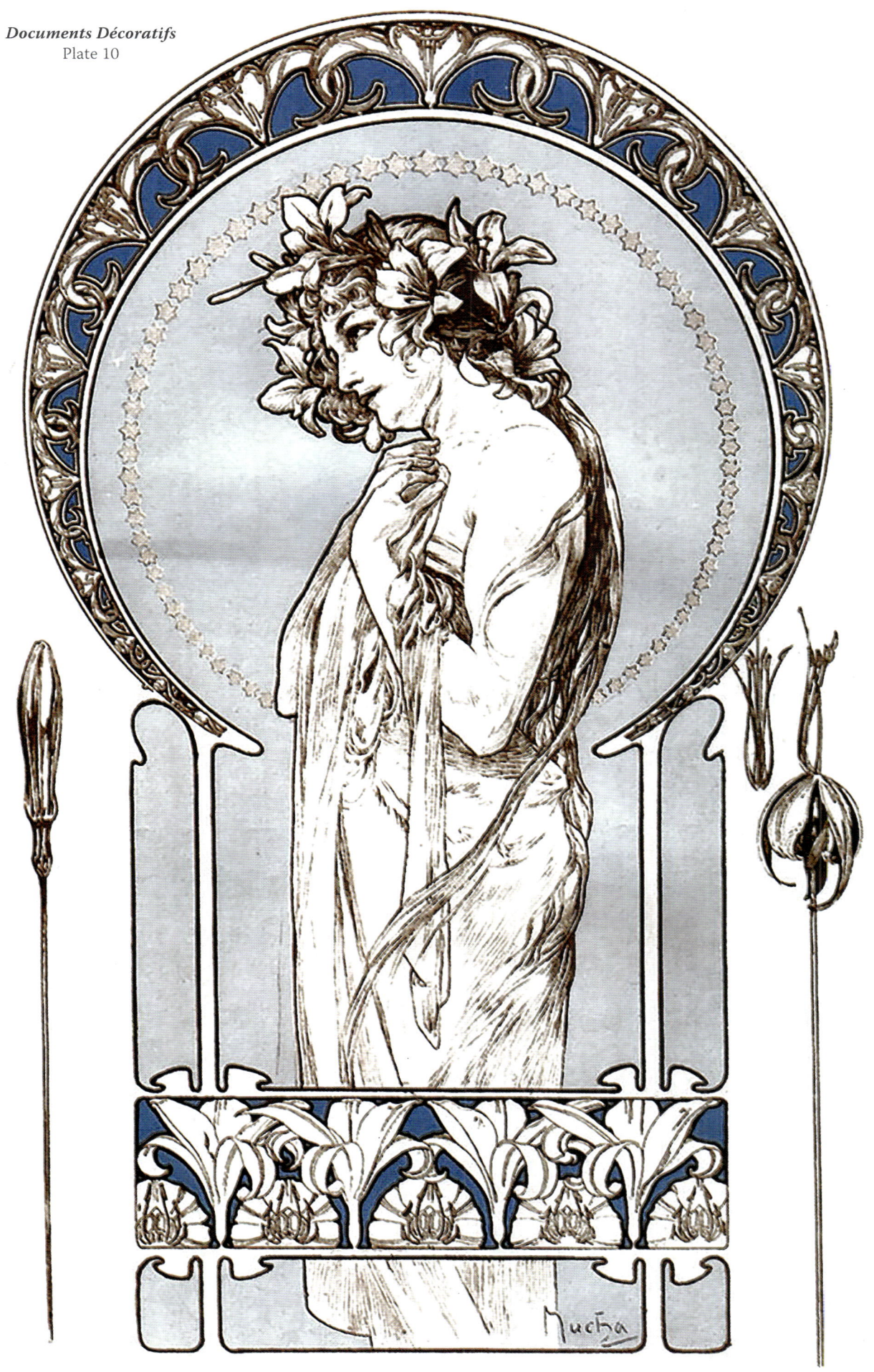

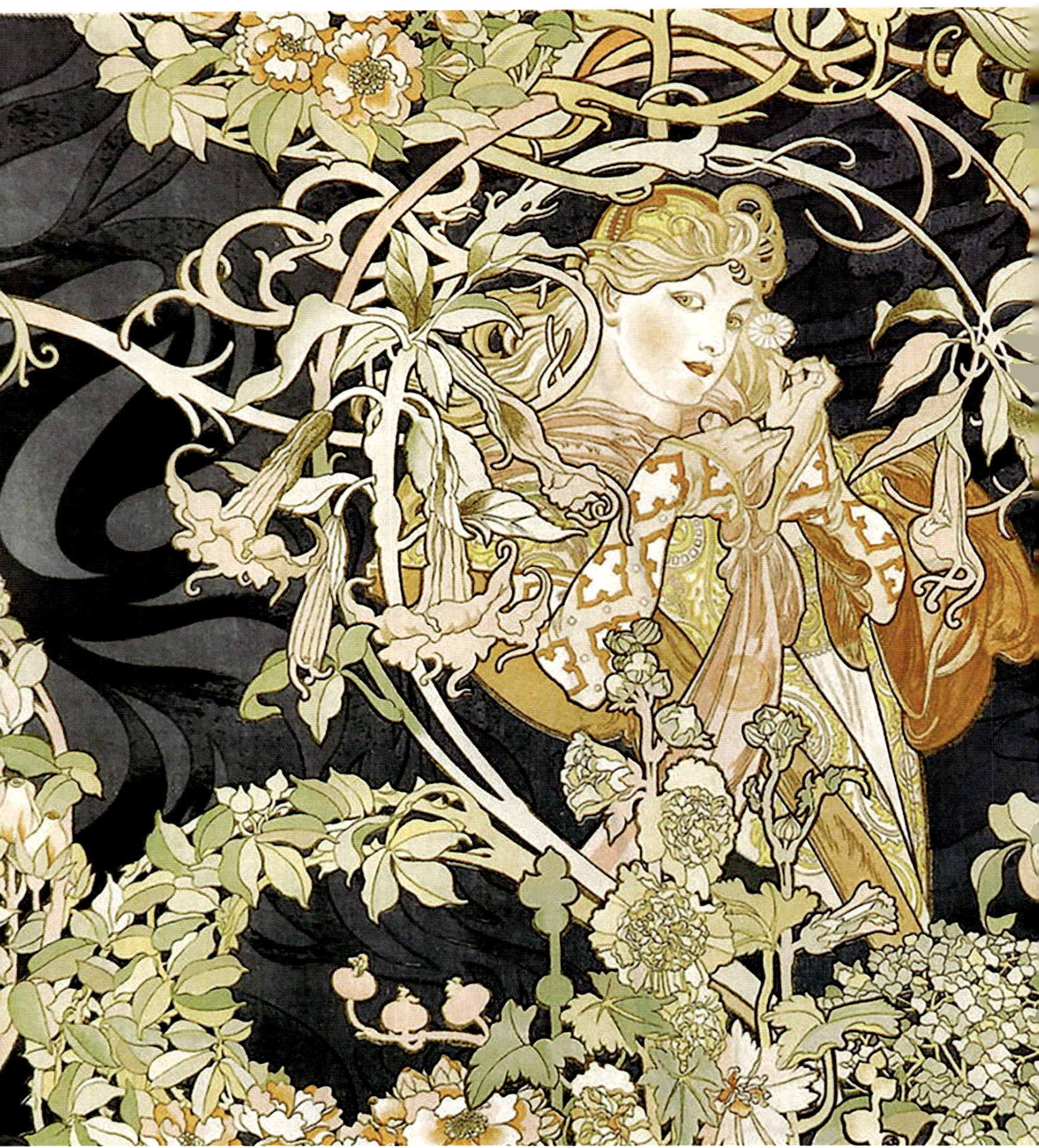

TEXTILES

Multifaceted Mucha, although best-known for his poster work and paintings, did turn his hand to designs on textiles. In these, his love of incorporating floral motifs and graceful women combine to create mesmerizing patterns. Extant examples of this kind of work are assumed to be samples of furnishing fabrics intended to complement an Art Nouveau interior.

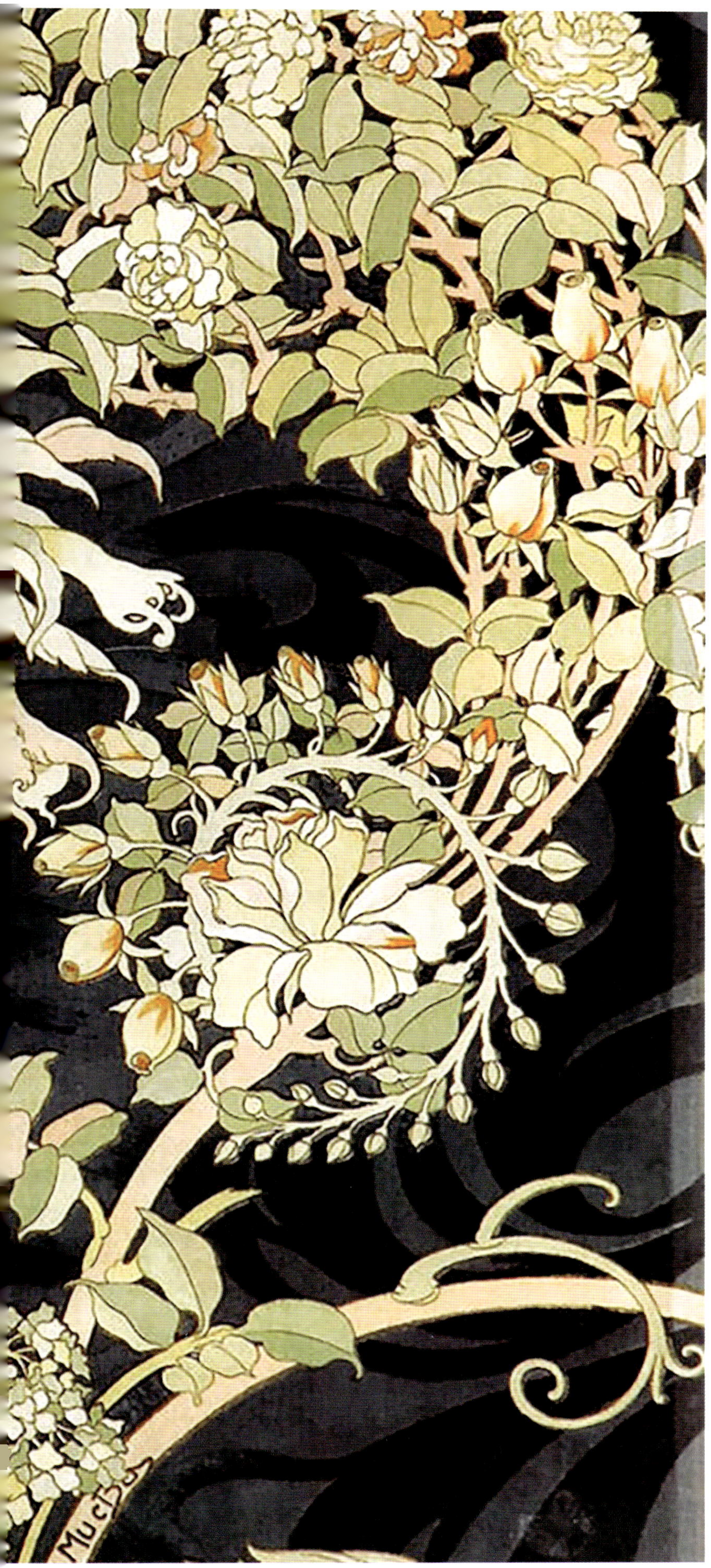

[LEFT]
Femme à Marguerite (Lady with a Daisy)
(c. 1898). Cotton velveteen panel. Baltimore Museum of Art
(The Jane and Worth B. Daniels, Jr. Fund).

This design was printed on velveteen and satin in various colorways. It is uncertain if Mucha intended this pattern to be used as a decorative panel or as a textile sample for furnishings.

[BELOW]
Preparatory art for **Femme à Marguerite** (c. 1898). Watercolor.

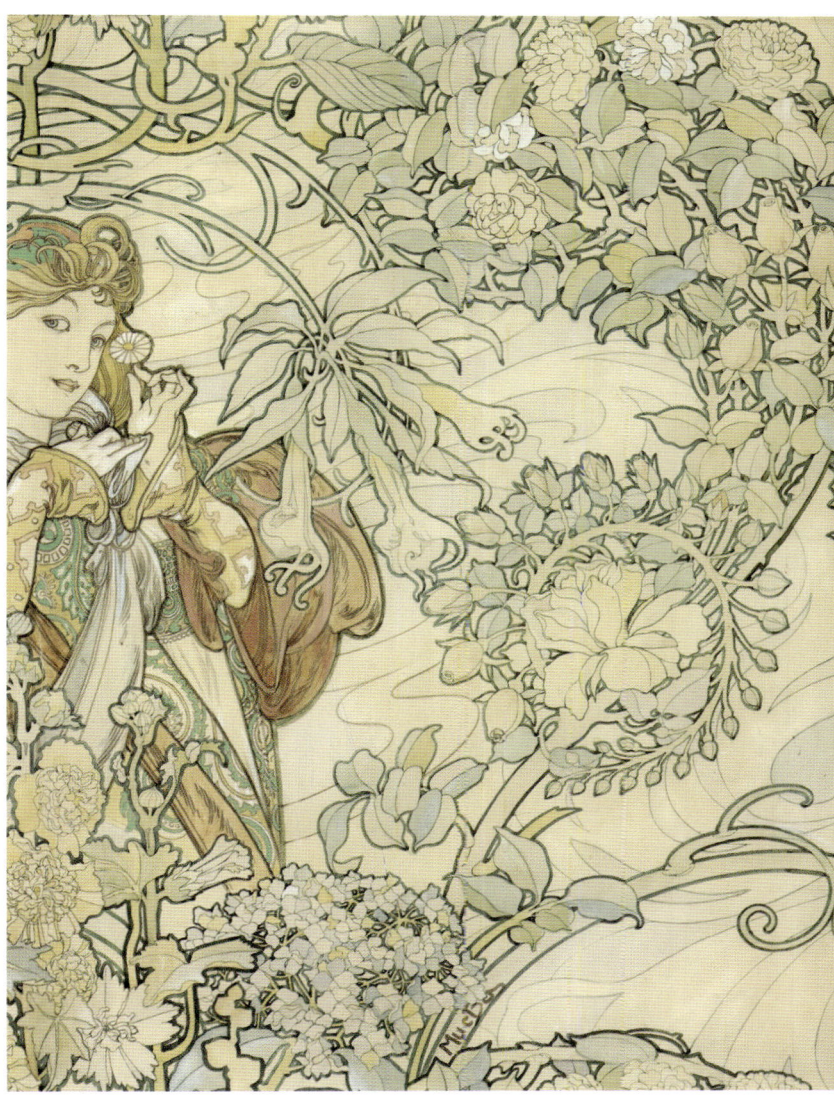

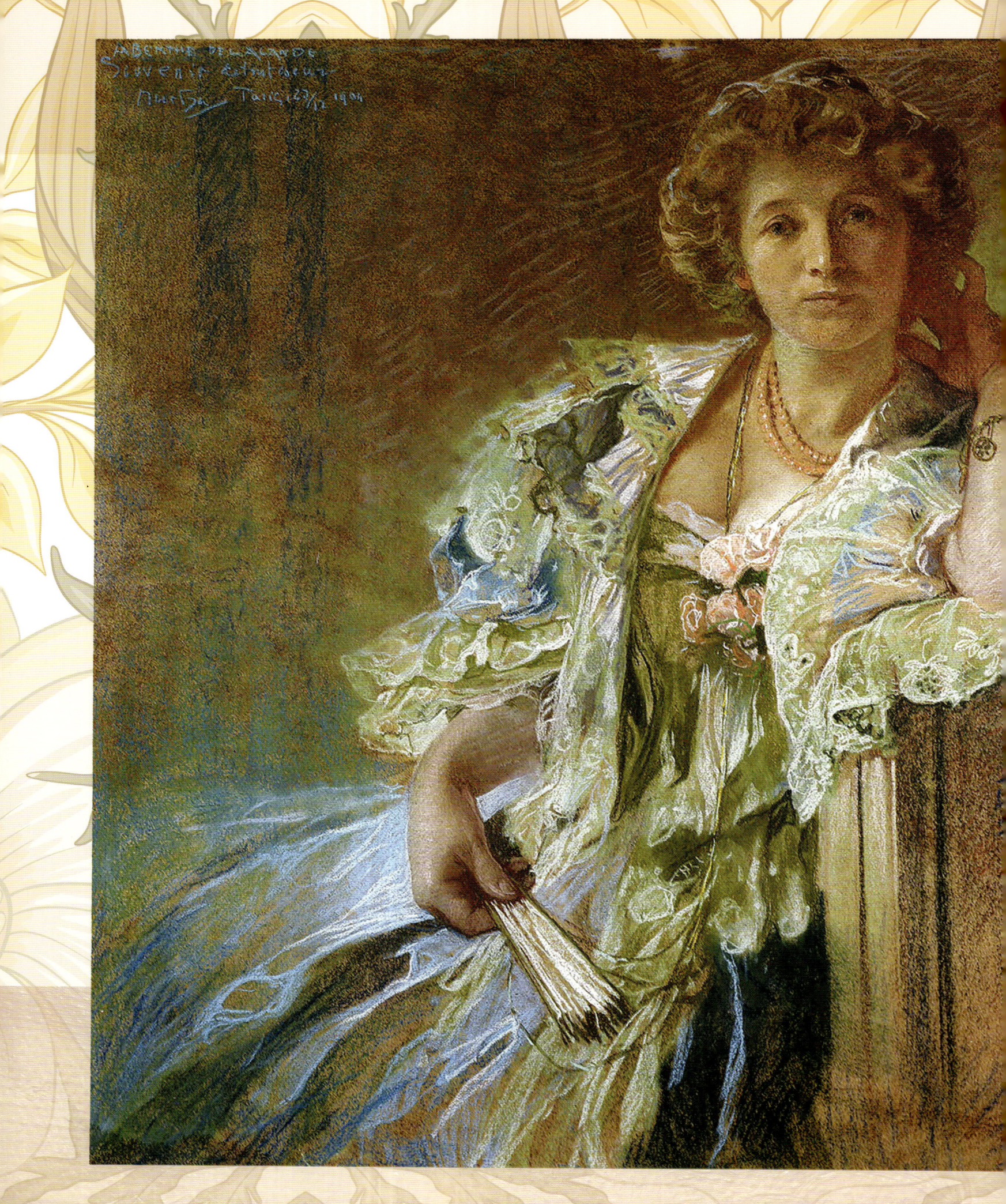

FINE ART

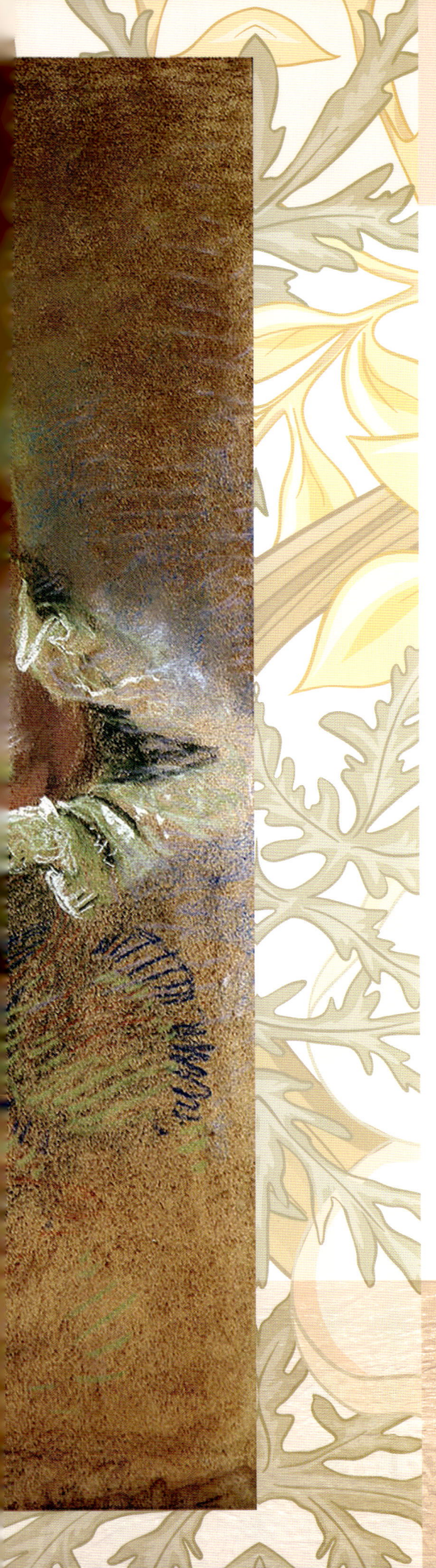

AFTER GAINING FAME as a commercial designer, Mucha's artistic journey evolved toward more personal, classical works. His paintings reveal a profound exploration of Slavic history and mythology. This was most notably captured in his magnum opus, the Slav Epic, a series of 20 large-scale paintings that celebrated the historical narrative of the Slavic people. Mucha's style retained its decorative elegance, but these later works also displayed a deepened emotional intensity. His commitment to his cultural heritage, combined with his unique artistic language, distinguished this phase as a vital chapter in his creative evolution.

Portrait of Berthe Lalande (1897).
Oil on canvas. Private collection.

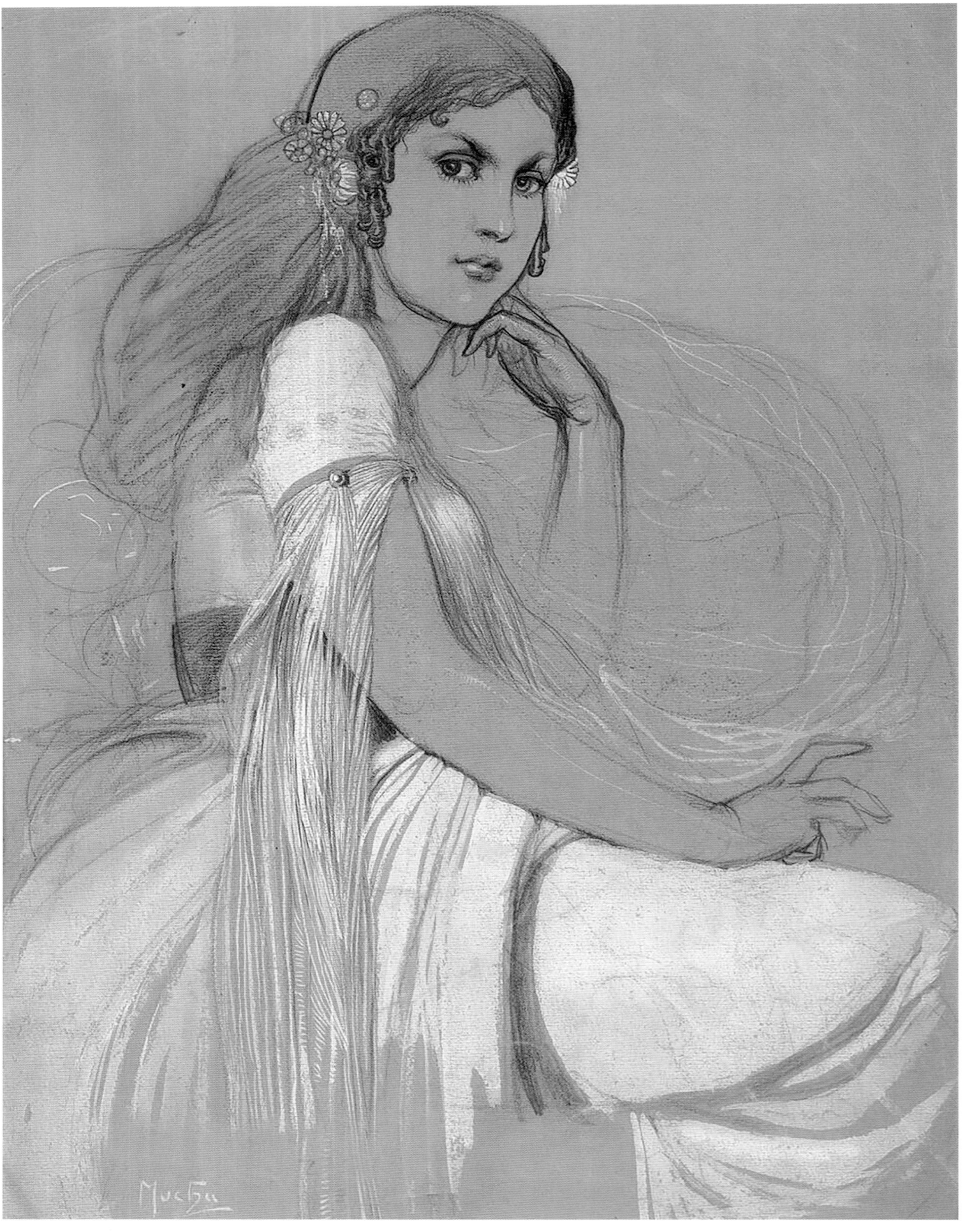

SKETCHES & DRAWINGS

His sketches and drawings provide a critical historical lens into the evolution of Mucha's artistic approach, revealing the progression and experimentation that shaped his contribution to the art world. These sketches serve as a road map to his artistic thought process, often highlighting the initial conceptualization of his later commercial and monumental works.

[OPPOSITE PAGE]
Jaroslava Mucha (c. 1920).
White paint over pencil on beige paper.

[RIGHT]
Sarah Bernhardt
(c. 1898). Pencil on paper.

[BELOW]
One of the works in a collection of Mucha's drawings and prints linked to his *Le Pater* book illustrations reflecting the Christian prayer. Museum of Decorative Arts, Prague.

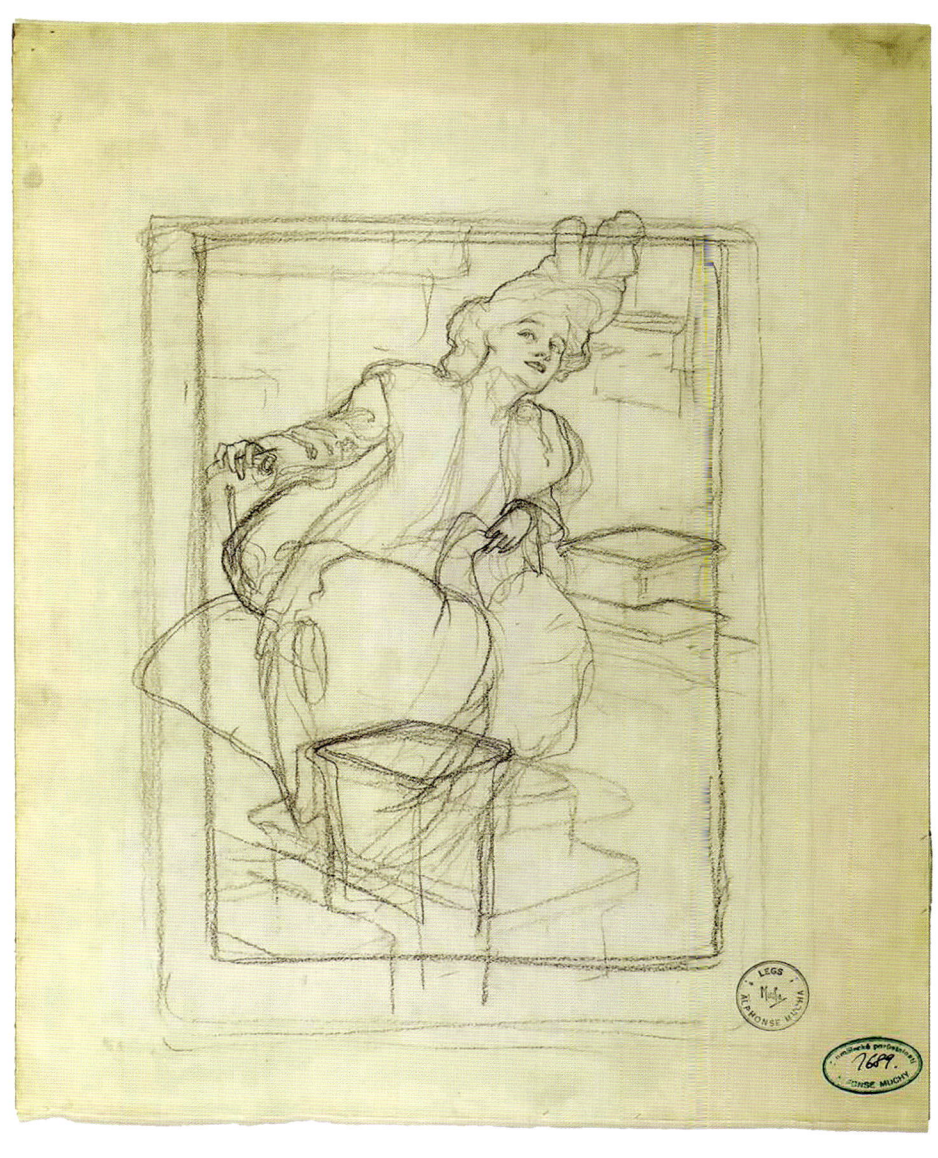

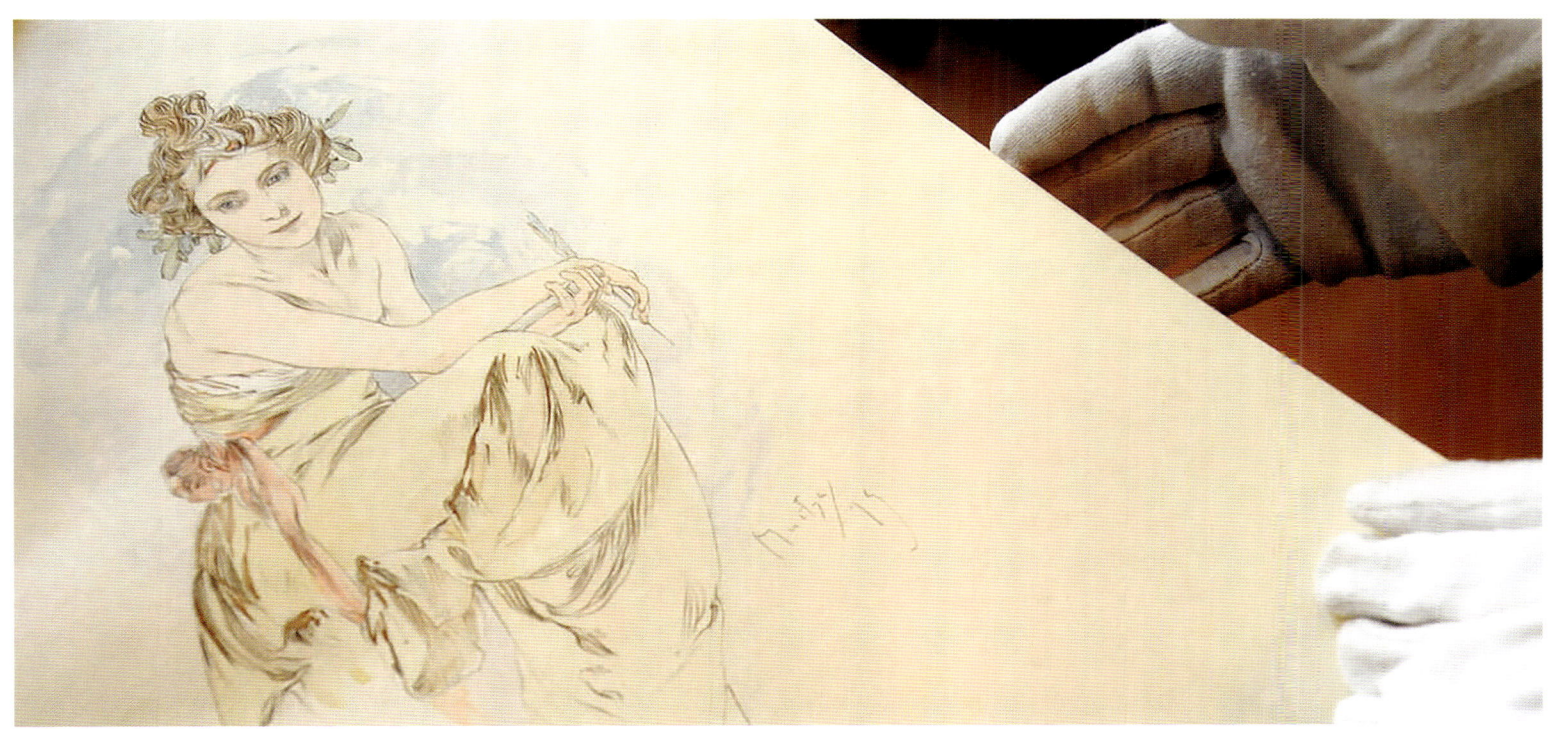

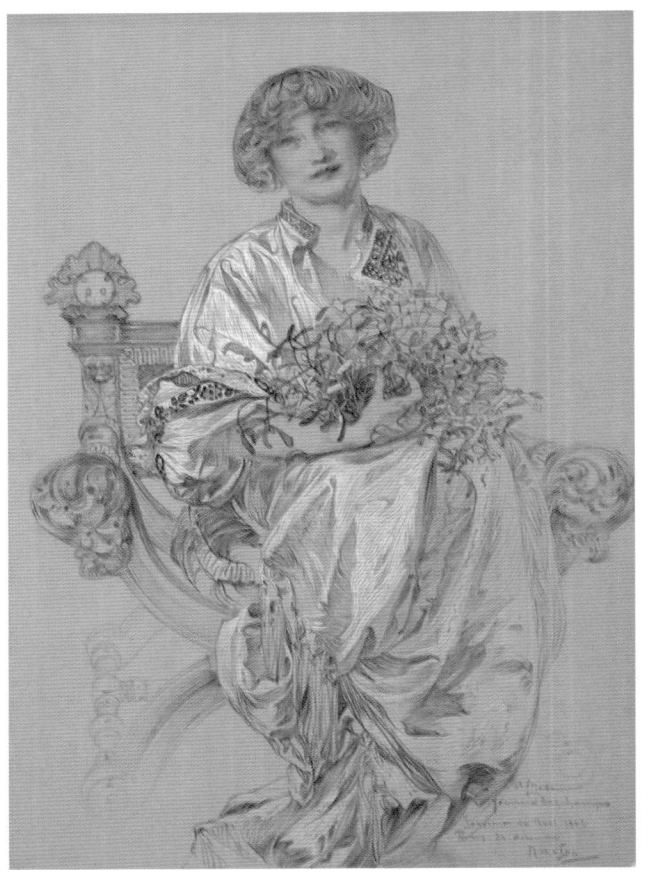

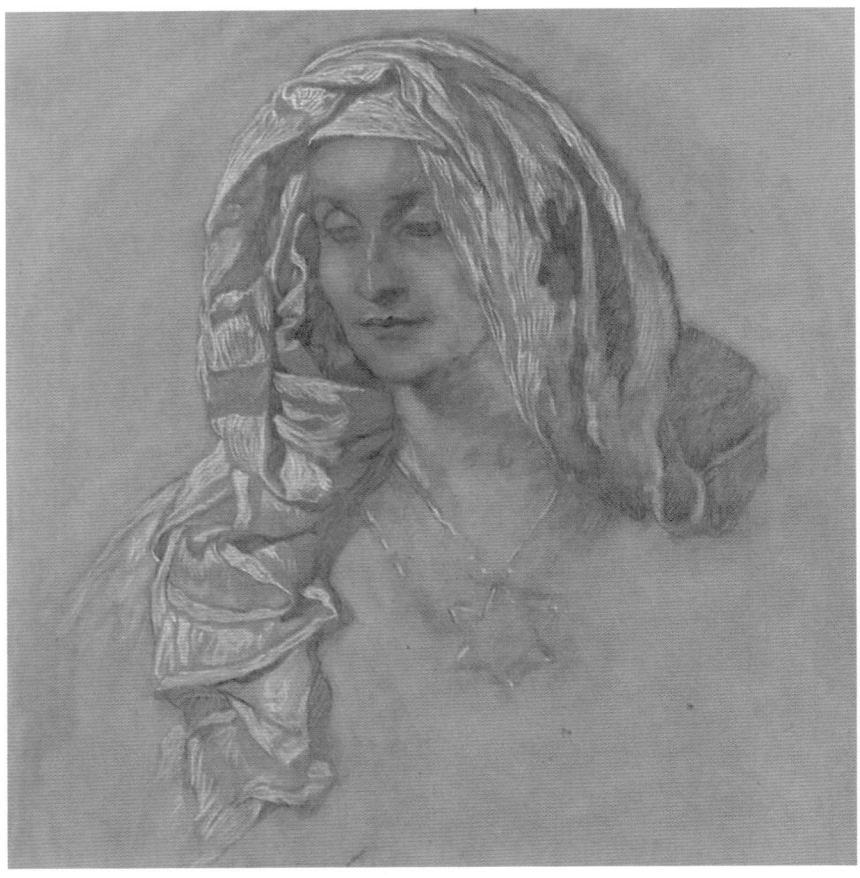

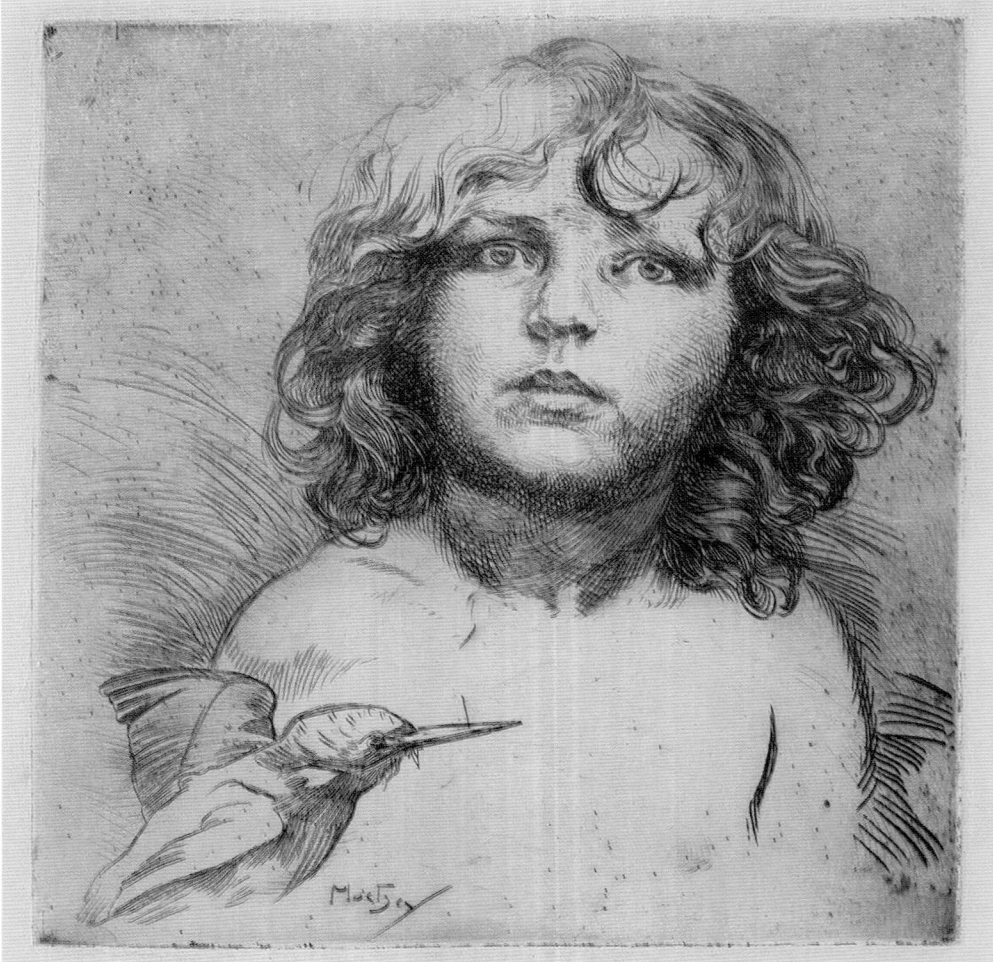

[ABOVE]
Woman with Headscarf and Star Medallion
(n.d.). Pencil and white chalk on paper. Private collection.

[ABOVE LEFT]
Portrait of Madame Deschamps (1903).
Pencil and white chalk on paper. Private collection.

[LEFT]
Portrait of Jiří Mucha
(c. 1920). Etching.
Private collection.

[OPPOSITE PAGE]
Self-Portrait
(c. 1900s–1910s).
Charcoal on paper.
Private collection.

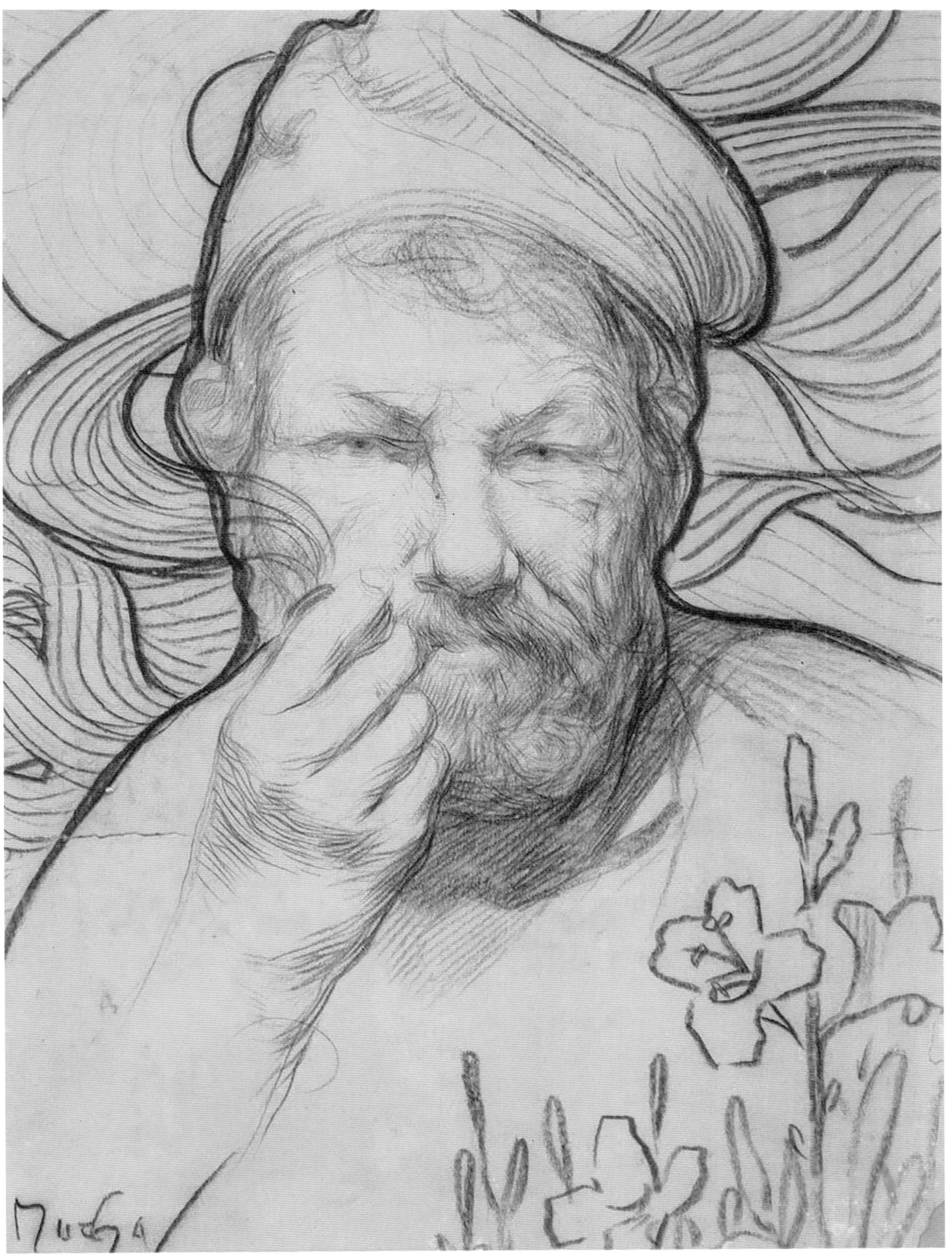

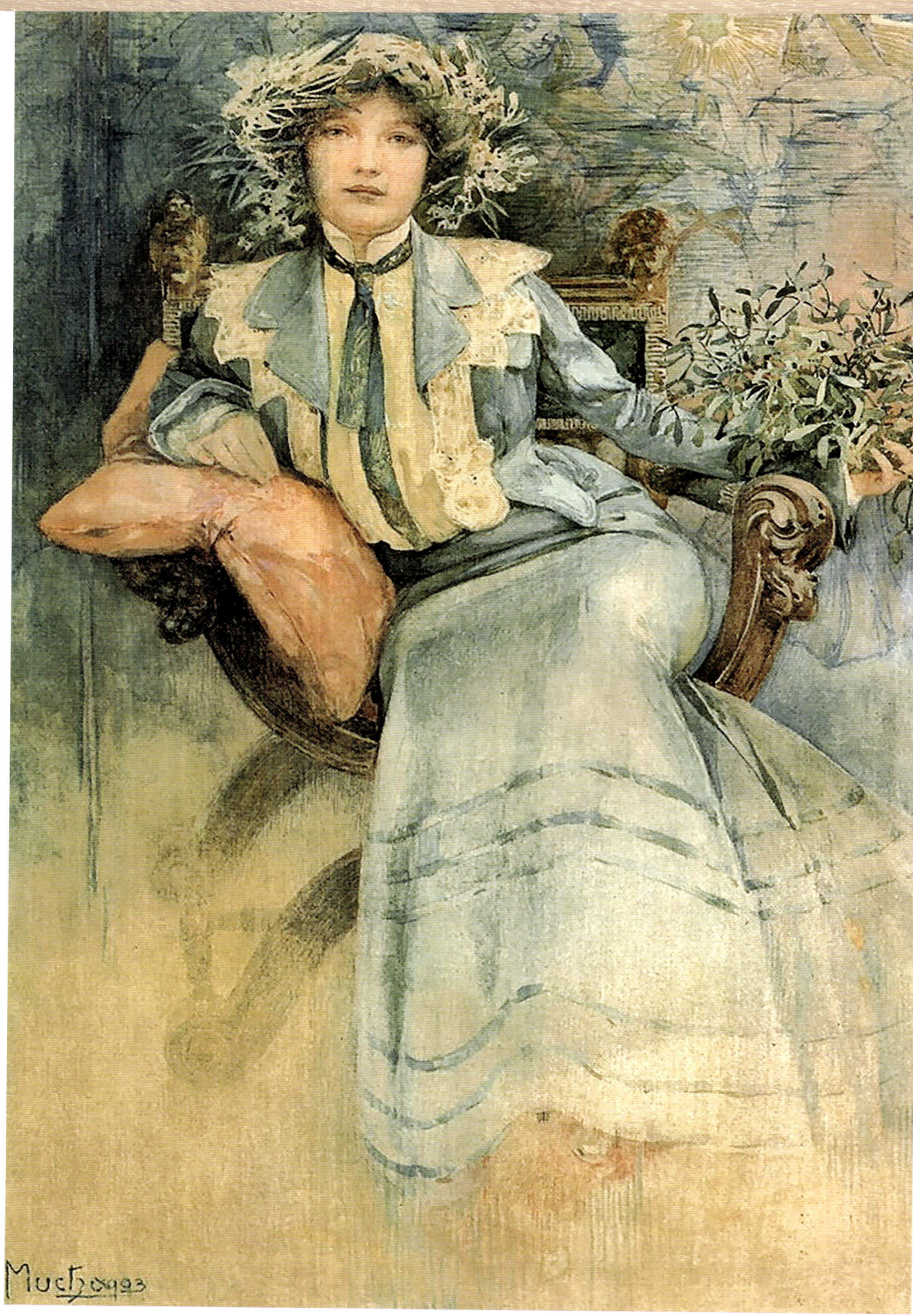

PAINTINGS

Mucha's success as a graphic artist allowed him to take a break from commercial work, and he turned his focus and energy to passion projects. Although the Slav Epic was the masterpiece that he spent nearly 20 years creating, he also produced numerous other paintings throughout his career, including portraits of his family and other people, as well as self-portraits. Mucha often celebrated his Czech identity through his paintings, and they took on a more classical style, while still retaining his characteristic use of ornamentation and rich color.

[OPPOSITE PAGE]
Portrait of Mme Mucha (1897). Watercolor heightened with gouache on linen. Private collection.

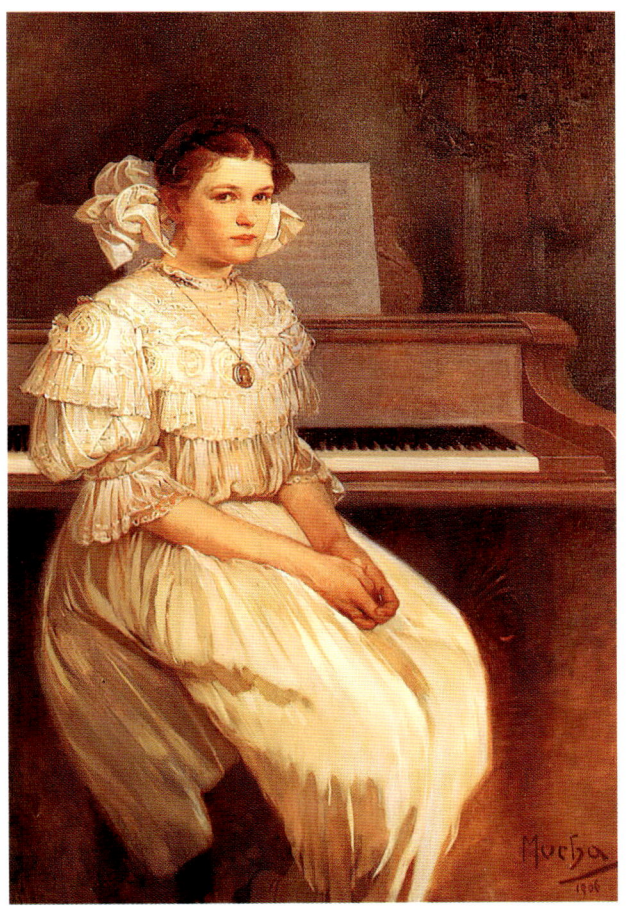

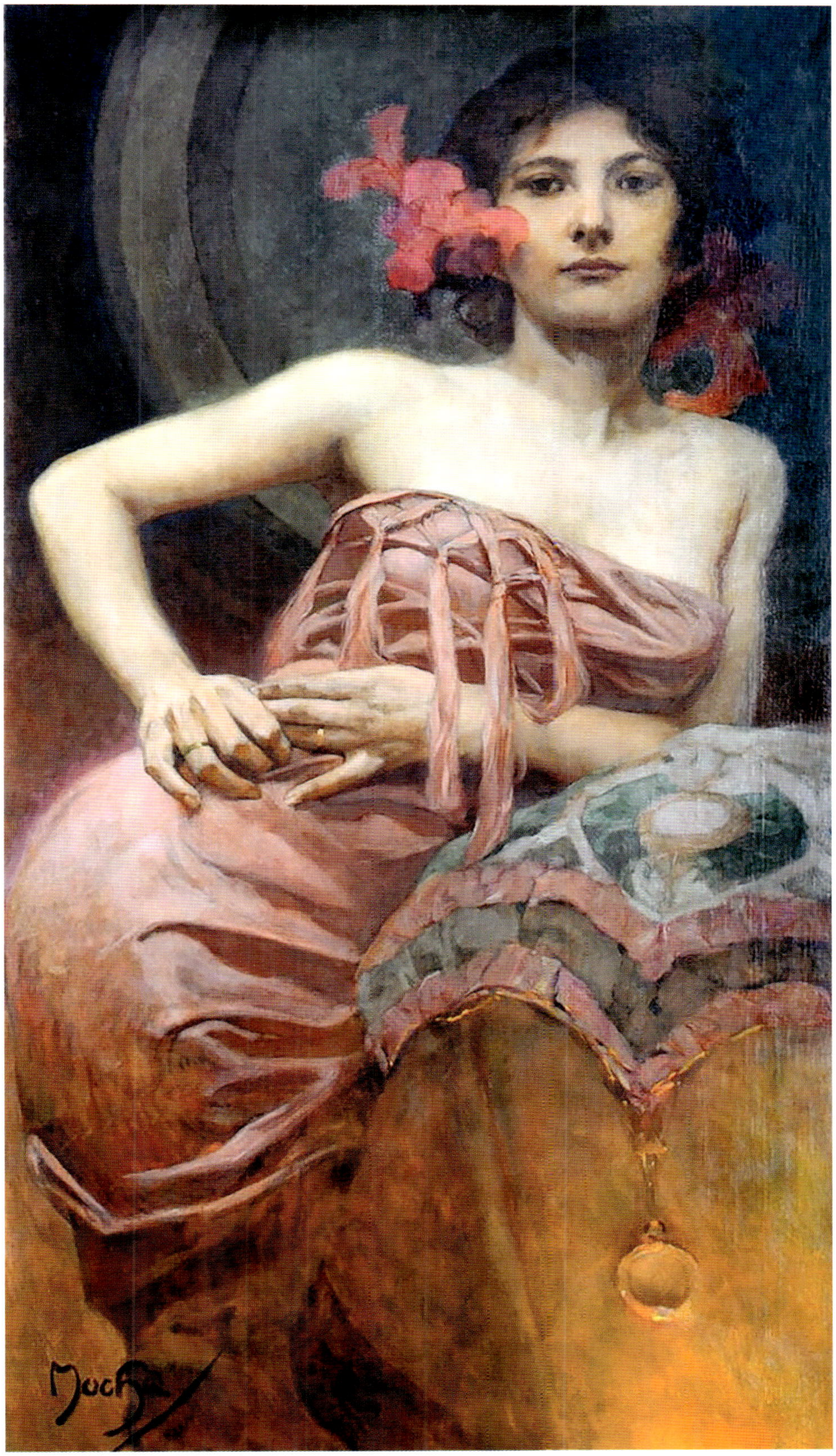

[RIGHT]
Portrait of Milad Cerny (1906), Oil on canvas. Private collection.

[ABOVE]
Portrait of a Woman (c. 1910). Oil on canvas.

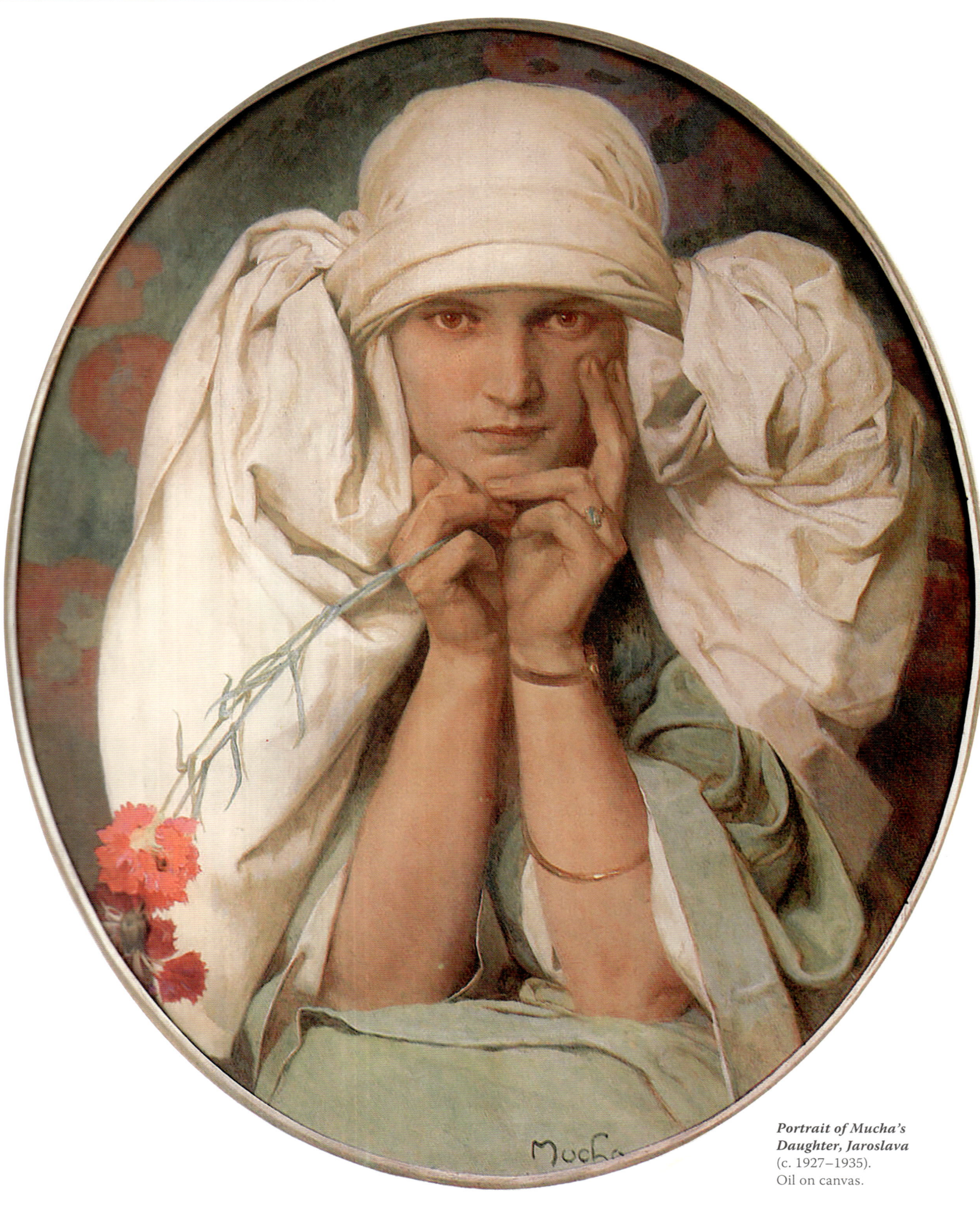

Portrait of Mucha's Daughter, Jaroslava (c. 1927–1935).
Oil on canvas.

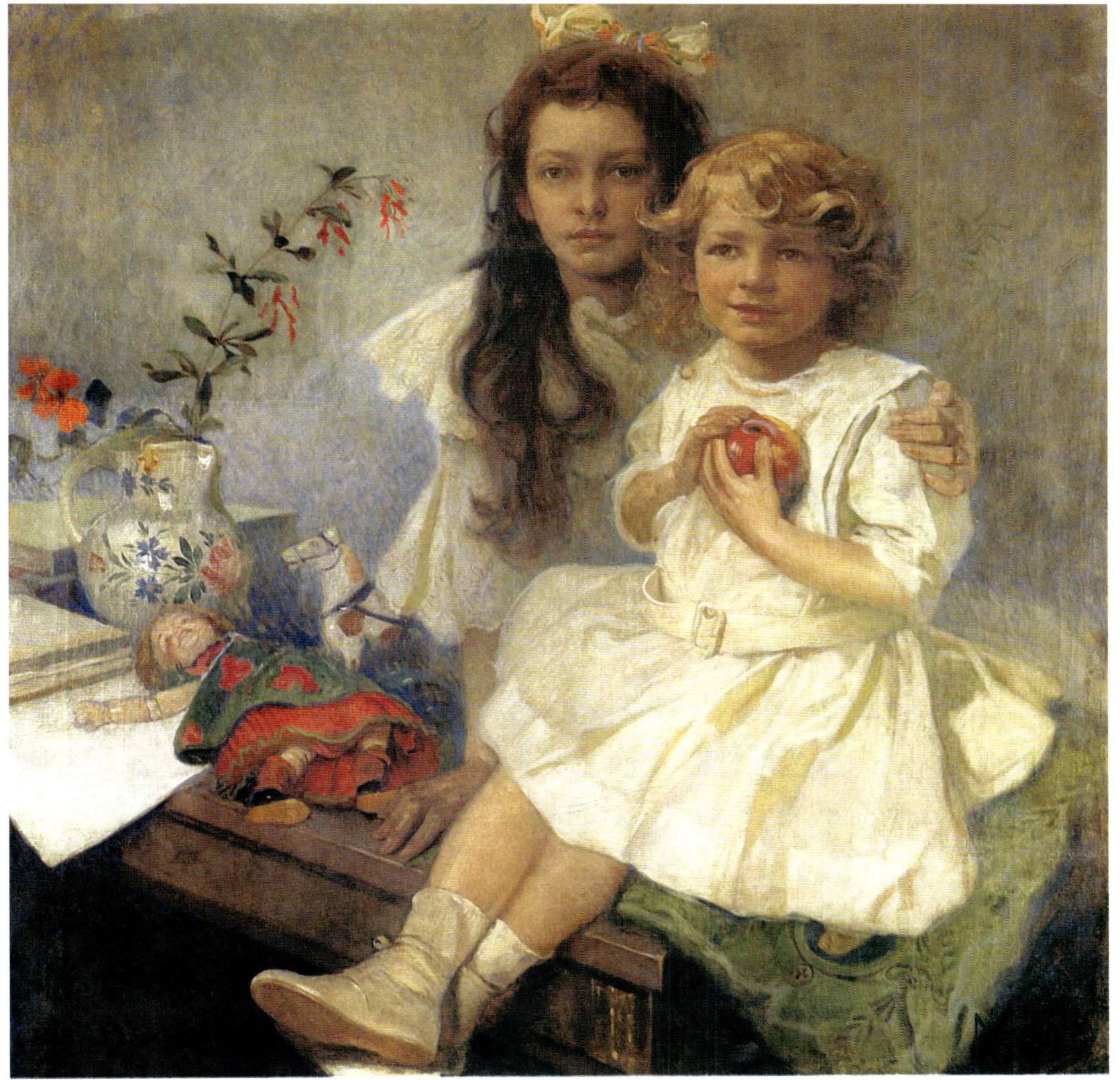

Jaroslava and Jiří (1919). Oil on canvas. Private collection.

*In this portrait of his daughter and son, Mucha paints in a
Romantic style, rather than his signature Art Nouveau technique.
Jaroslava, Mucha's first child, posed as a model for numerous works
of her father, including Czechoslovak banknotes, and also worked as
his technical assistant. She later became a conservator of fine art.*

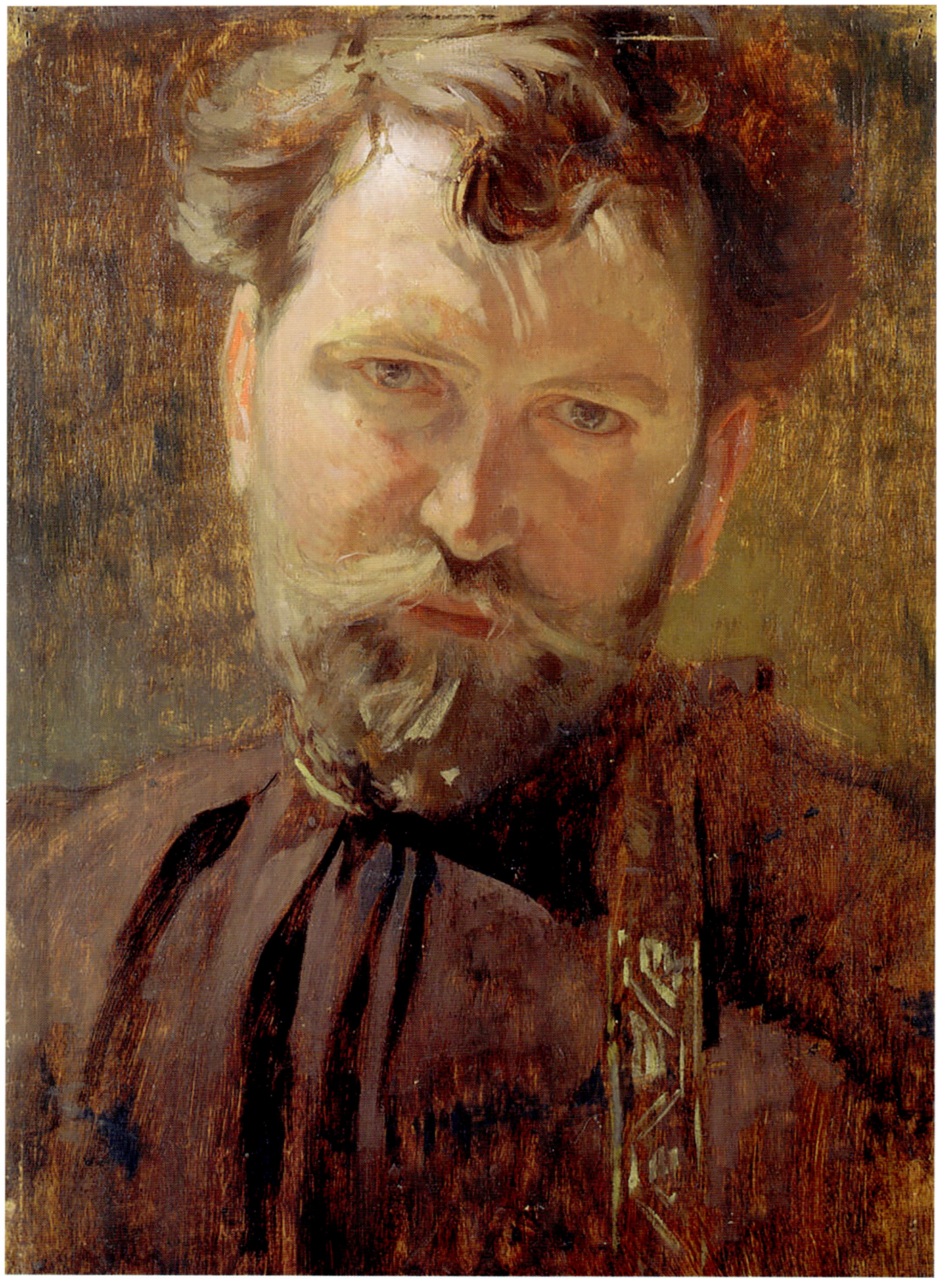

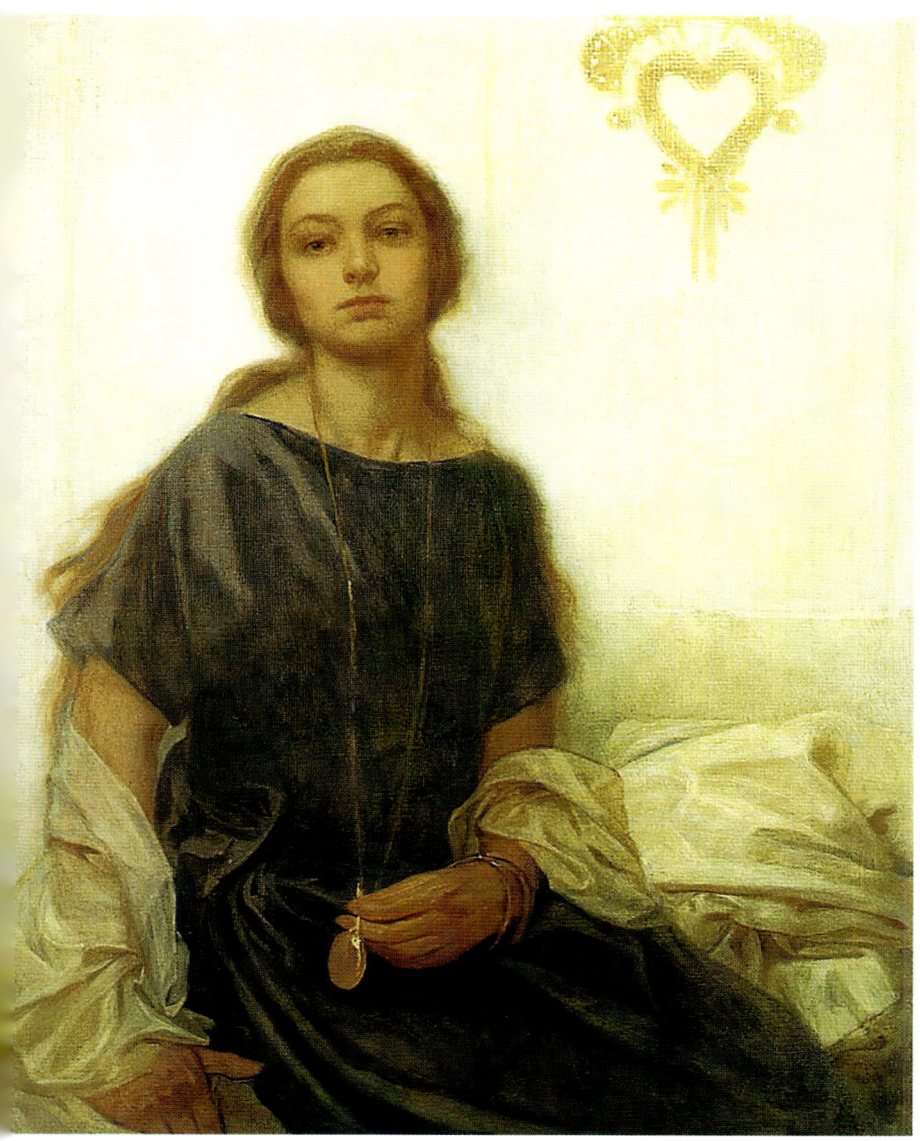

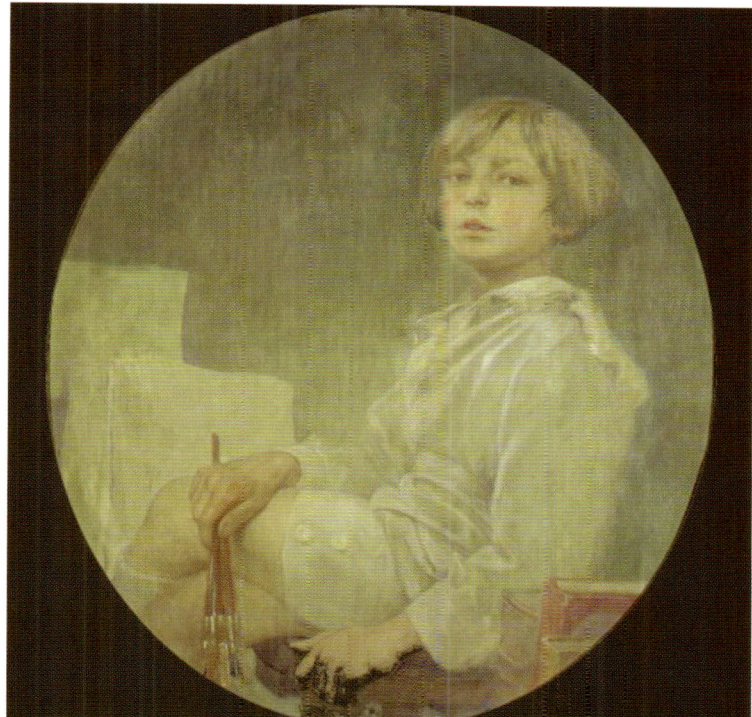

Portrait of Jaroslava (c. 1930). Oil on canvas. Mucha Museum, Prague.

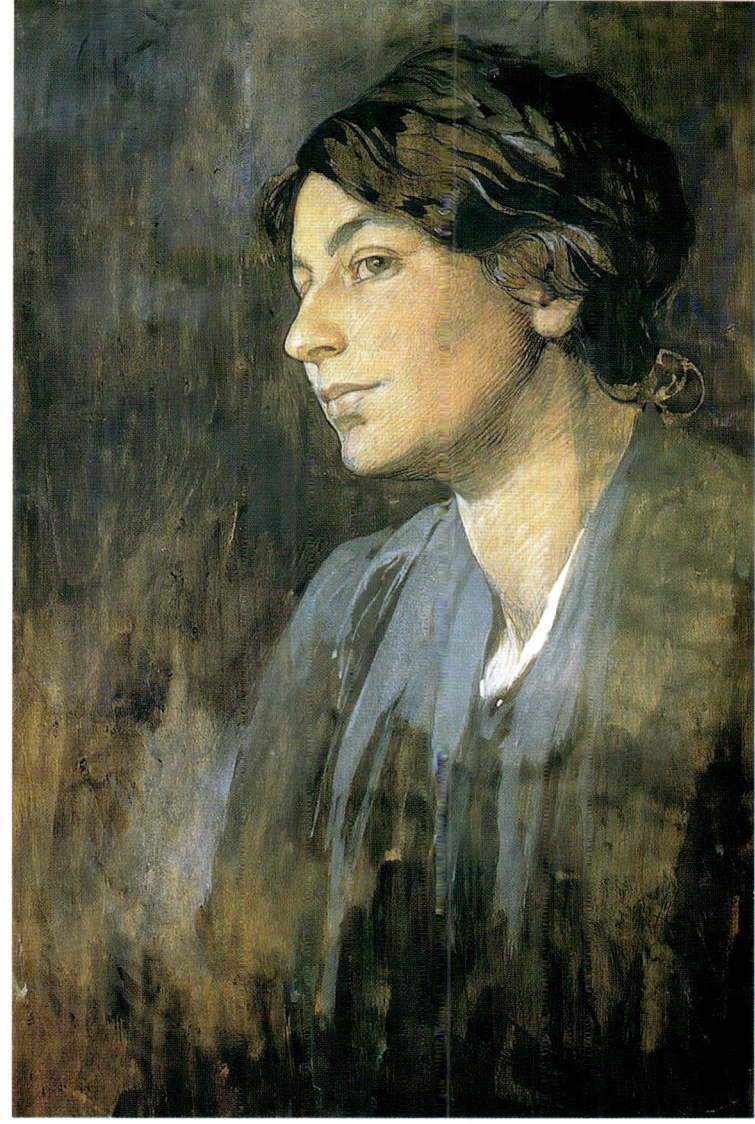

[TOP RIGHT]
Portrait of Mucha's Son, Jiří
(1925). Oil on canvas.
Mucha Foundation/Trust.

[OPPOSITE PAGE]
Self-Portrait (1899).
Oil on board. Mucha
Museum, Prague.

[RIGHT]
*Portrait of Marushka,
the Artist's Wife*
(1905). Oil on canvas.
Mucha Museum, Prague.

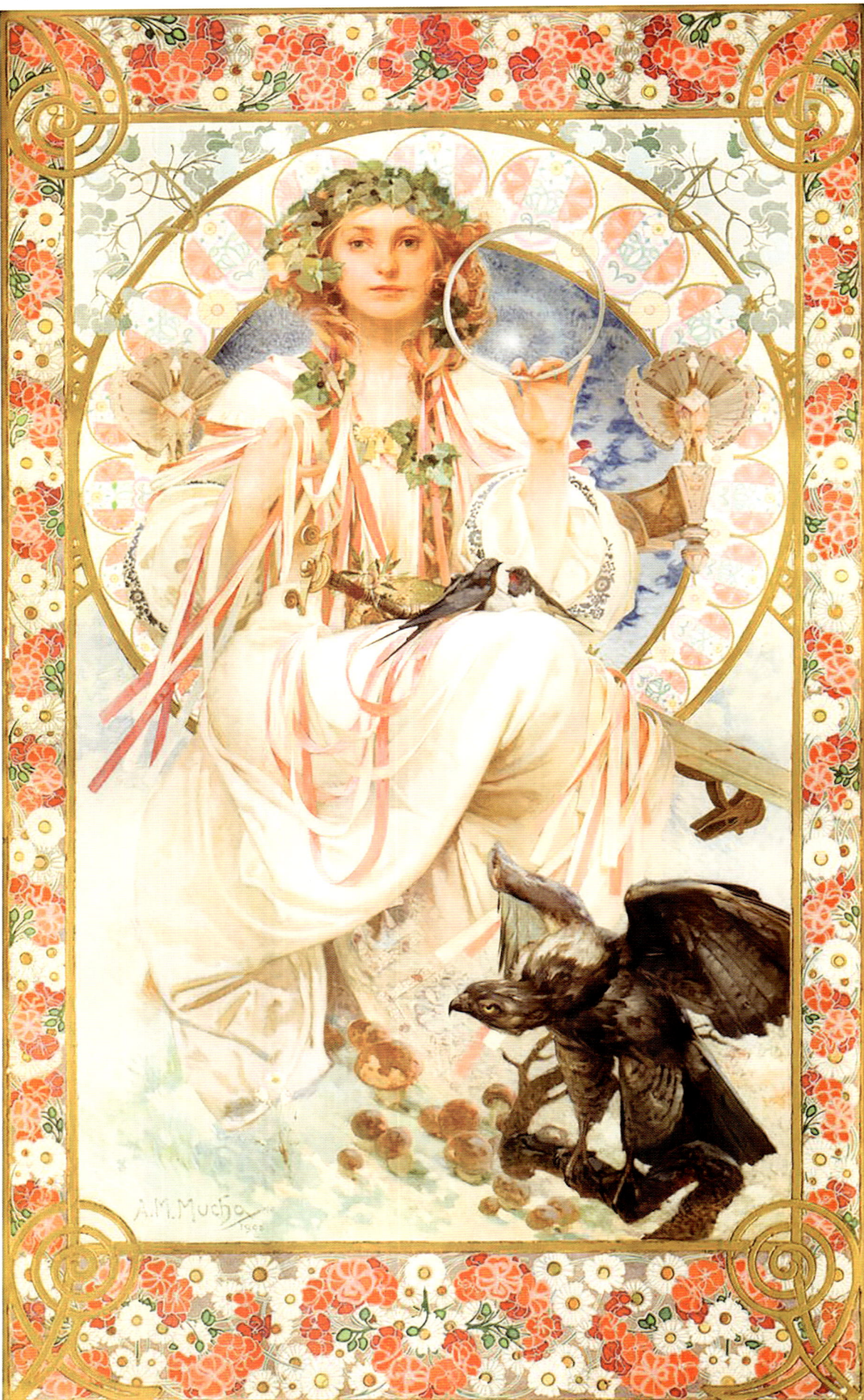

[LEFT]
Portrait of Josephine Crane-Bradley as Slavia (1908). Oil and tempera on canvas. National Gallery Prague.

[RIGHT]
Christmas in America (1919). Oil on canvas. Mucha Trust Collection.

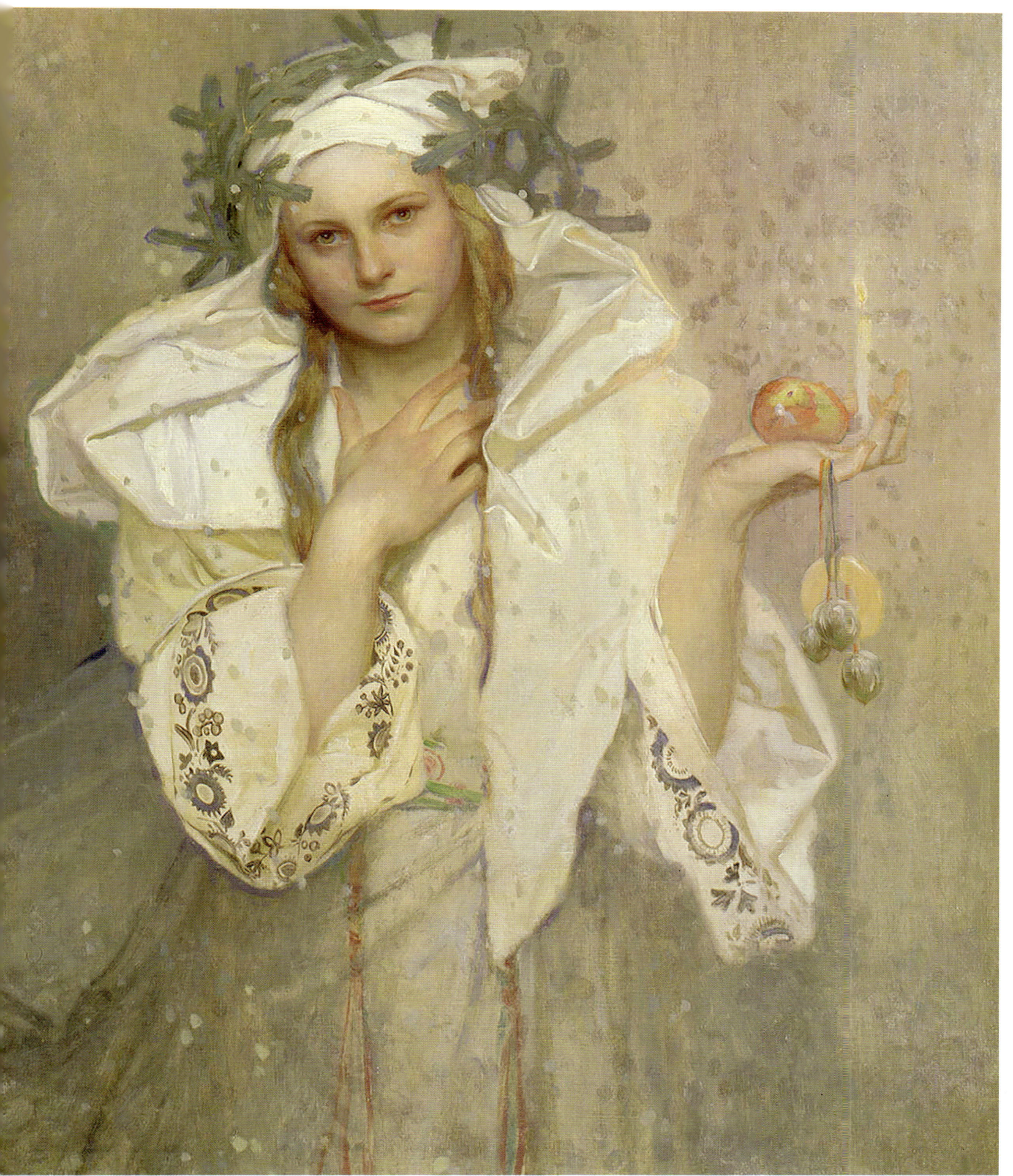

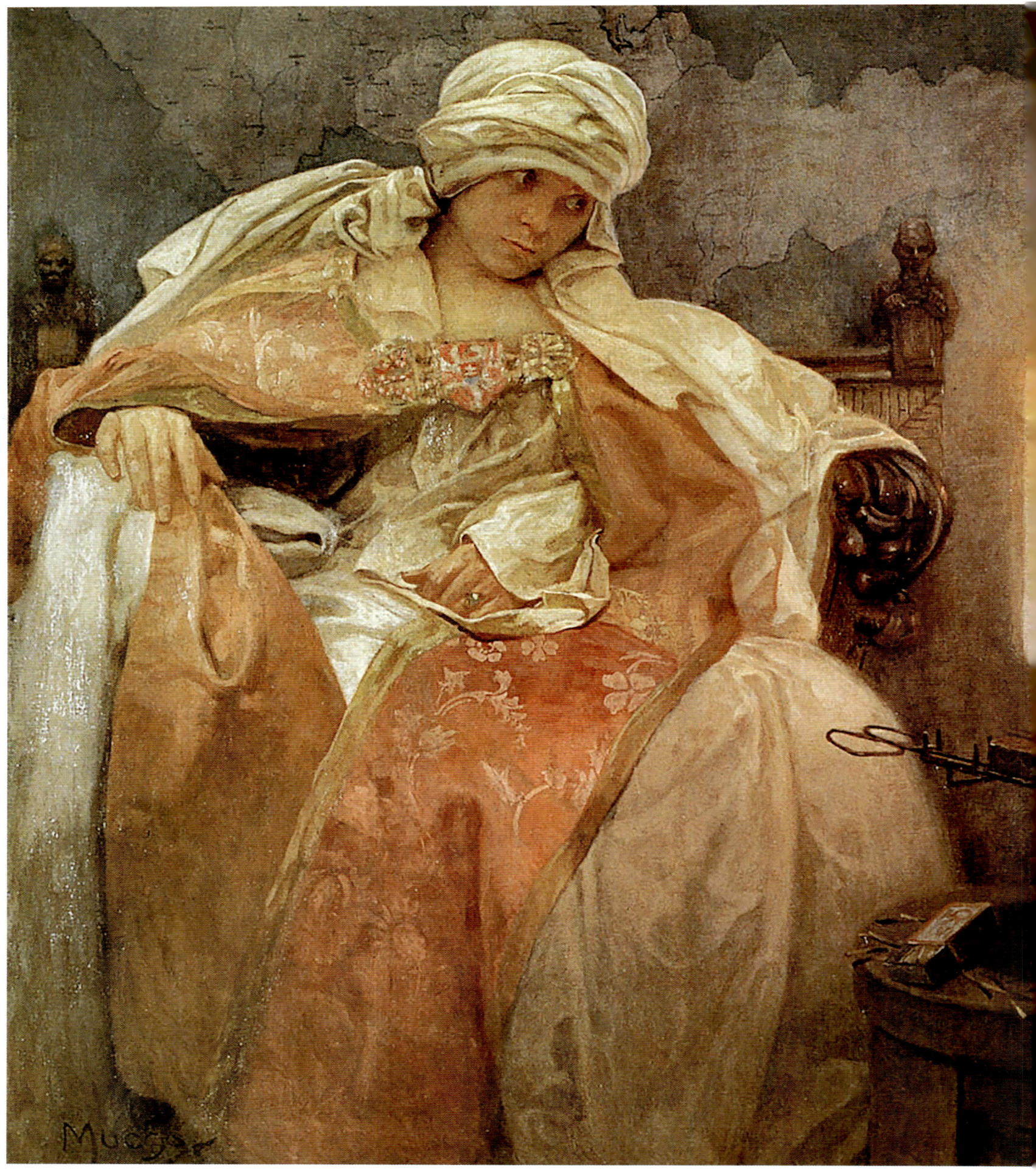

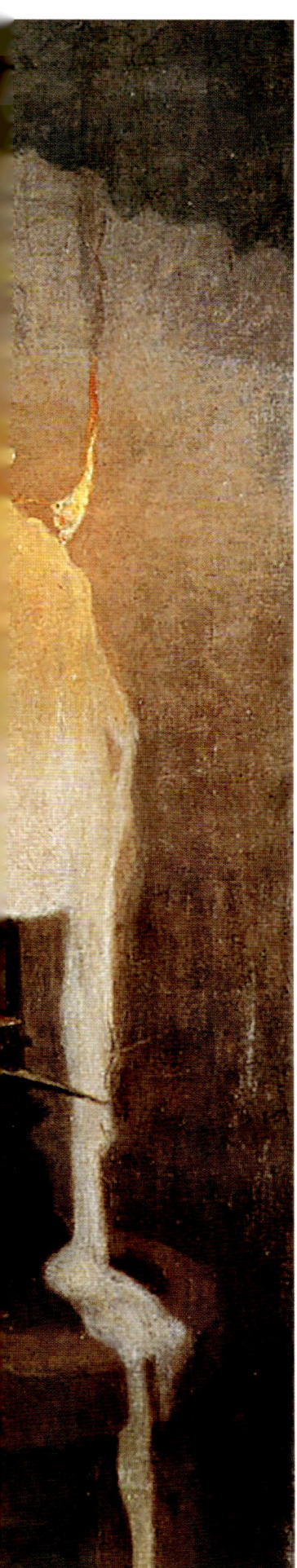

[LEFT]
Woman with Burning Candle (1933).
Oil on canvas. Mucha Museum, Prague.

[BELOW]
Czech Heart (1917).
Oil on canvas. National Gallery Prague.

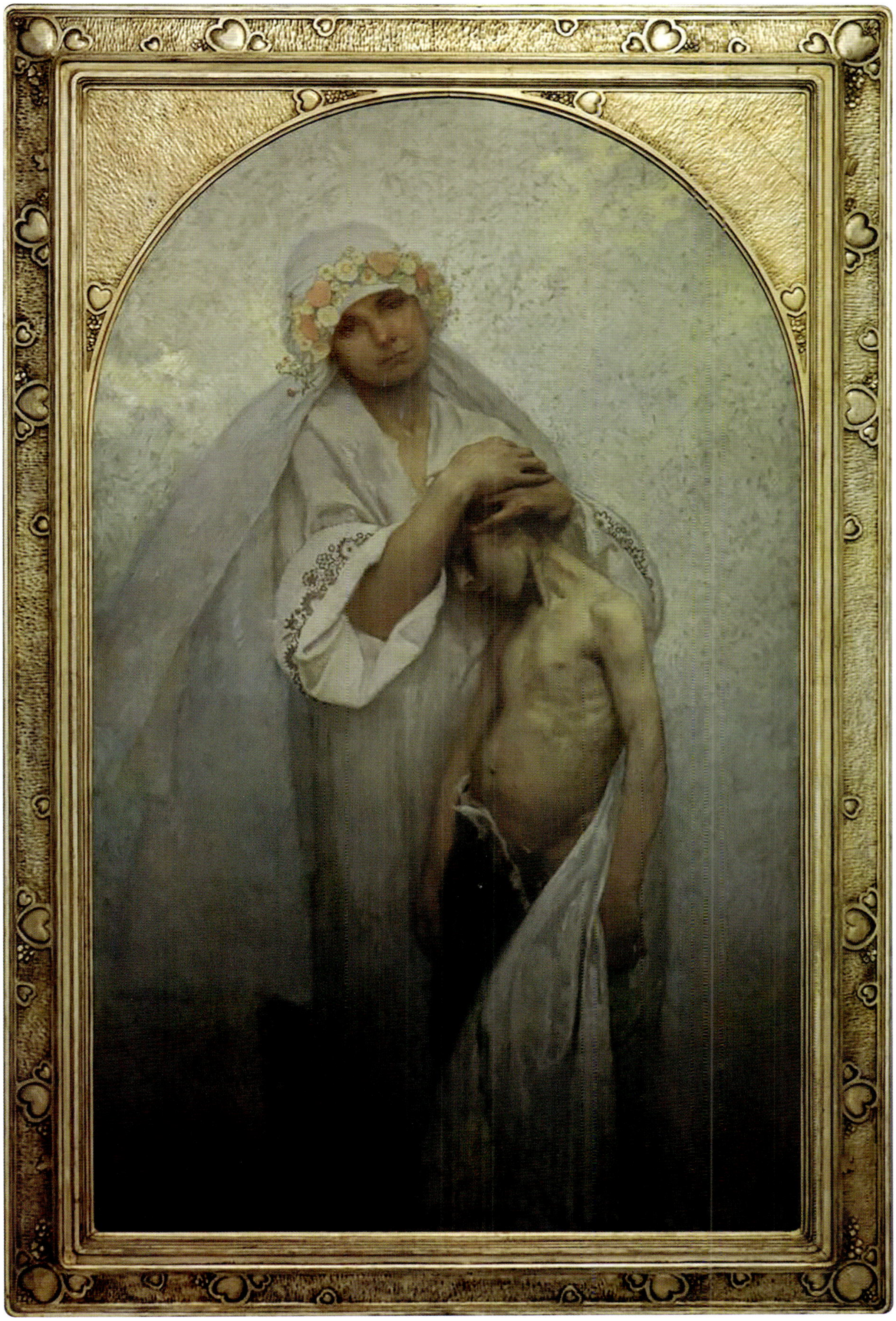

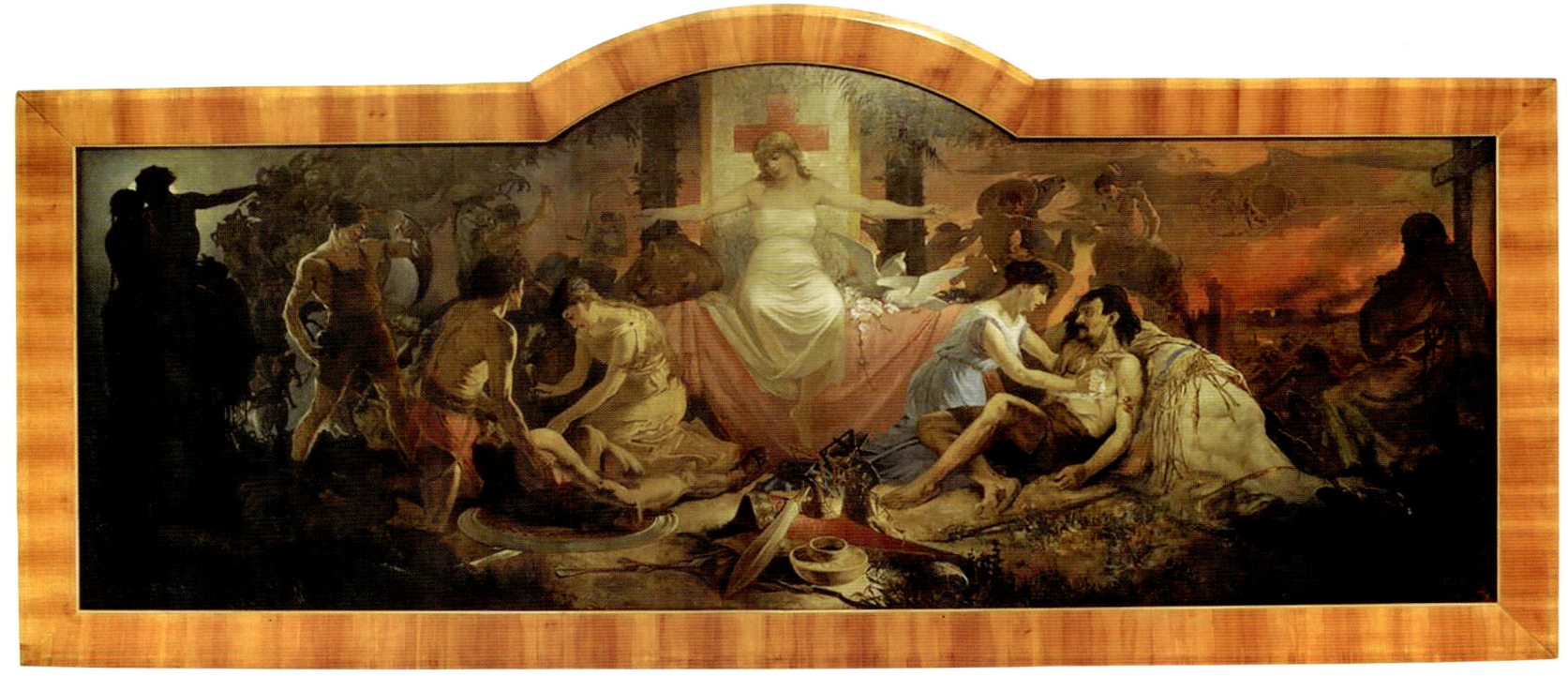

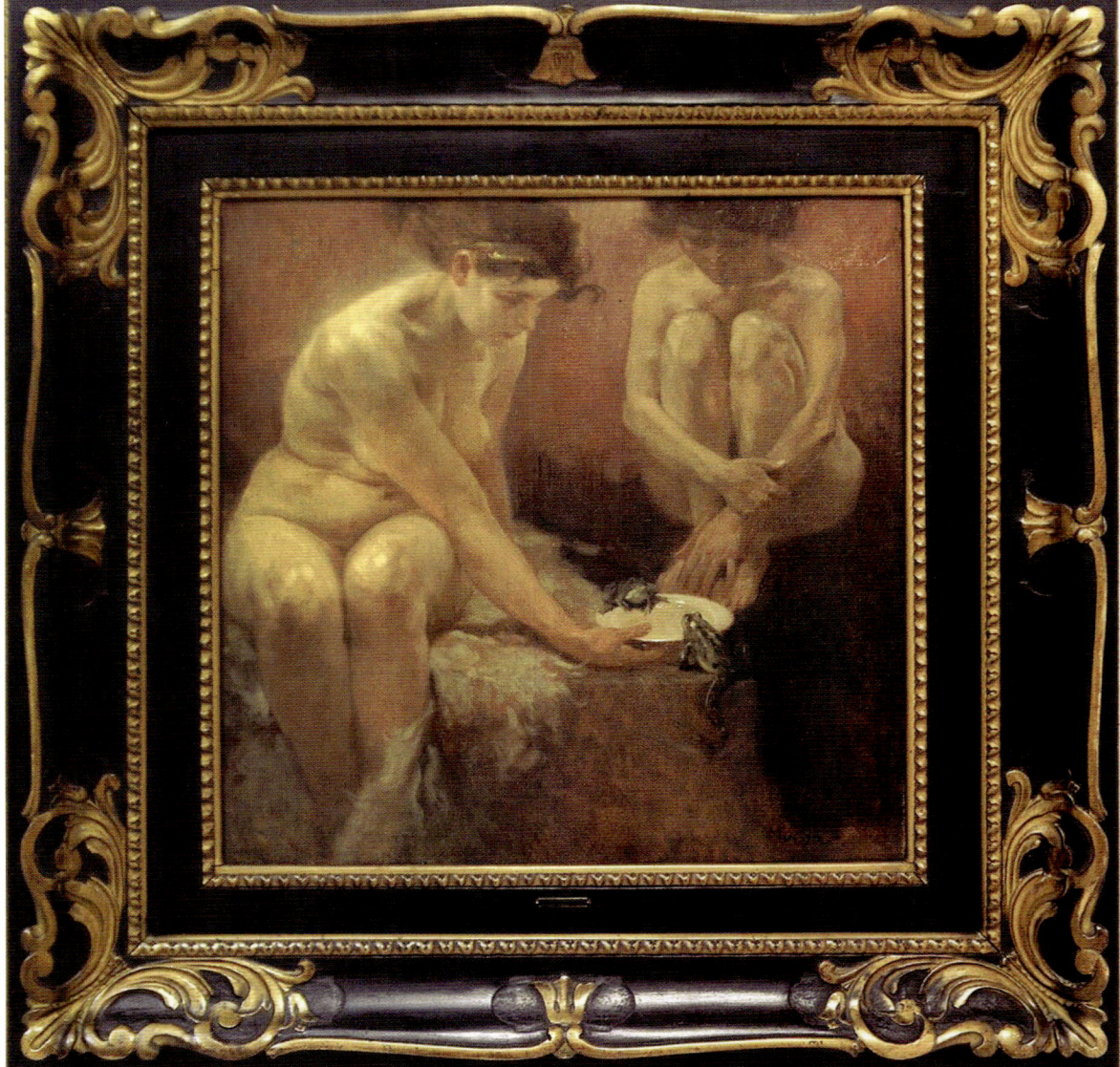

[ABOVE]
Charitas (1886).
Oil on canvas.
National Gallery Prague.

[LEFT]
Female Nudes and Frogs
(c. 1890). Oil on canvas.
National Gallery Prague.

[OPPOSITE PAGE]
Madonna of the Lilies
(1905). Tempera on canvas.

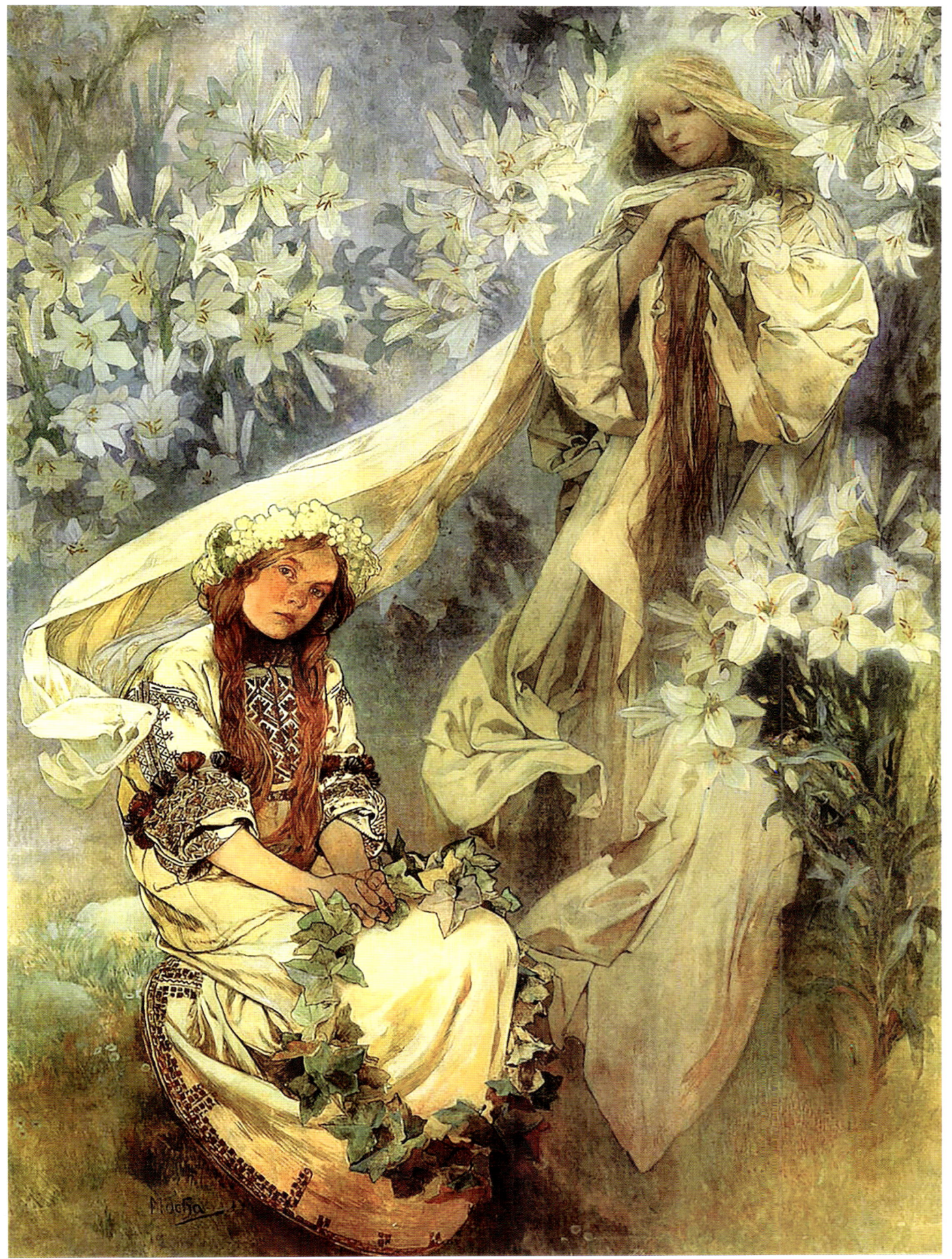

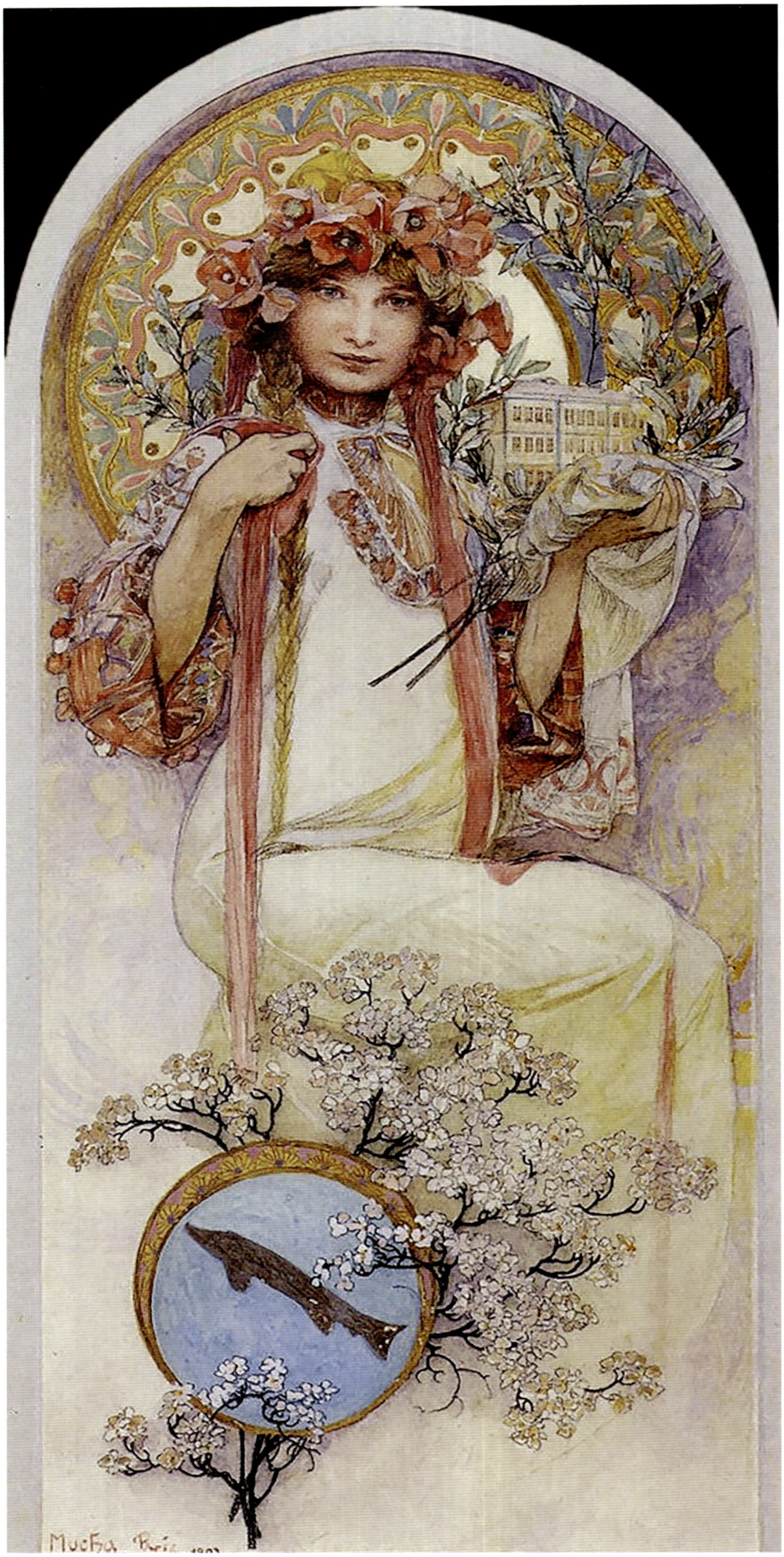

[LEFT]
The Girl of Ivančice
(1903). Oil and
tempera on canvas.

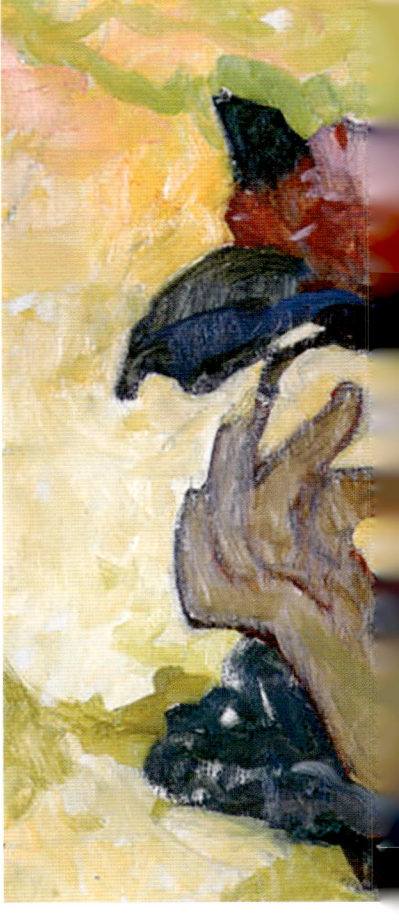

[TOP RIGHT]
Untitled
(c. 1880–1930).
Oil on canvas.

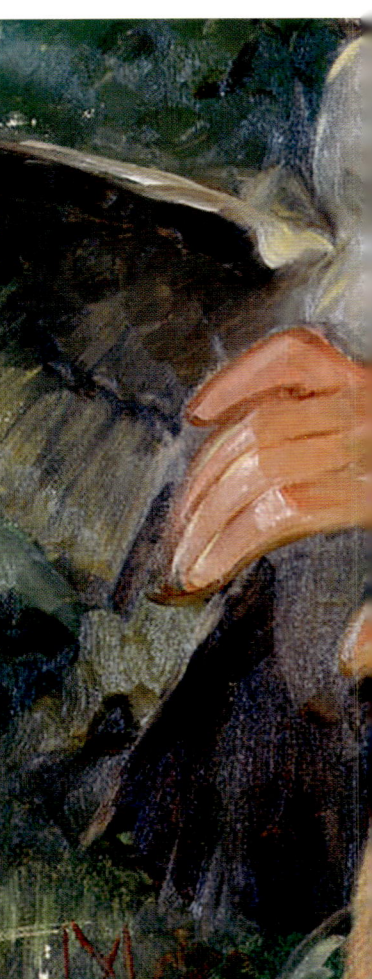

[BOTTOM
RIGHT]
Untitled
(c. 1880–1930).
Oil on canvas.

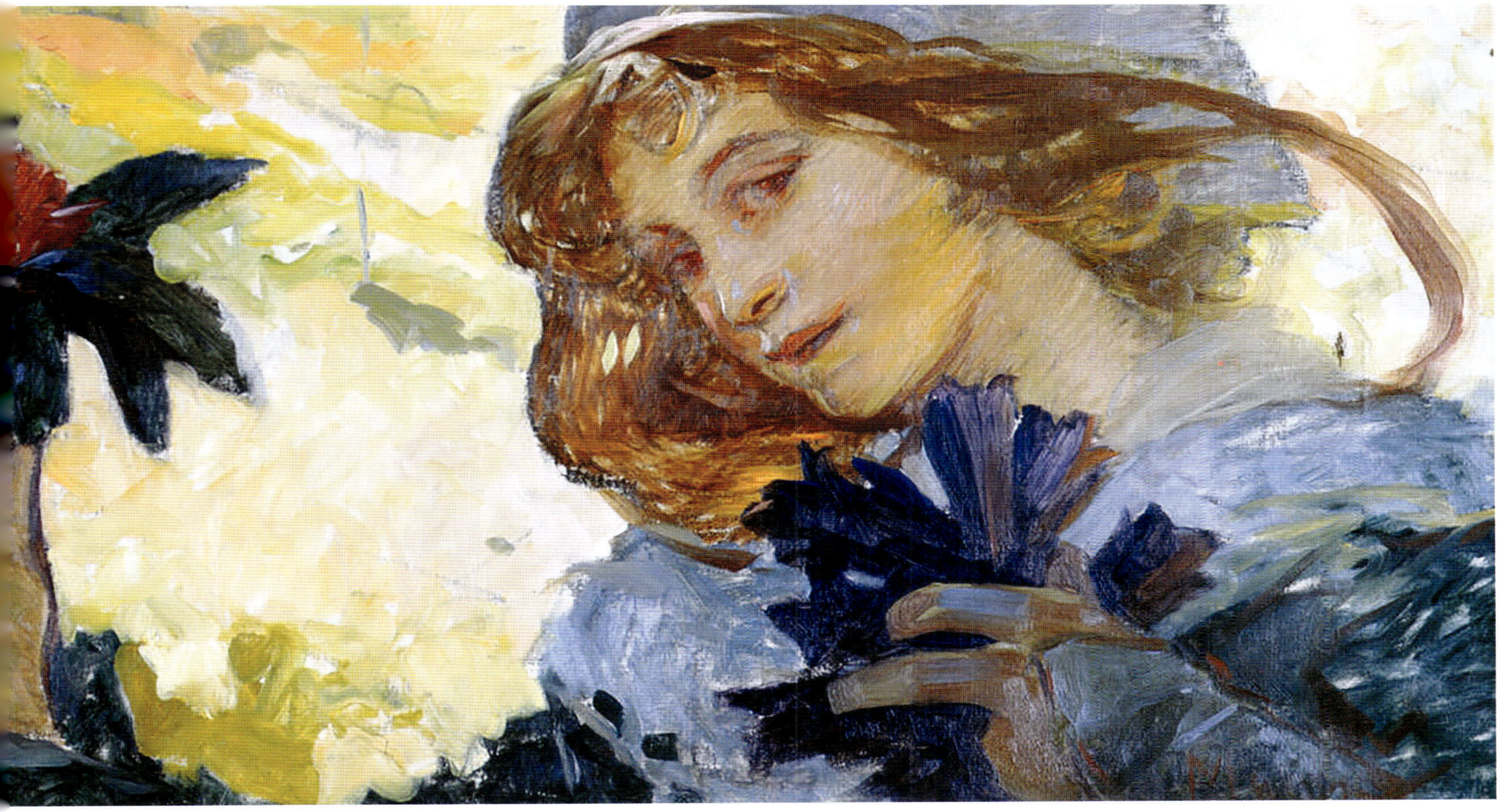

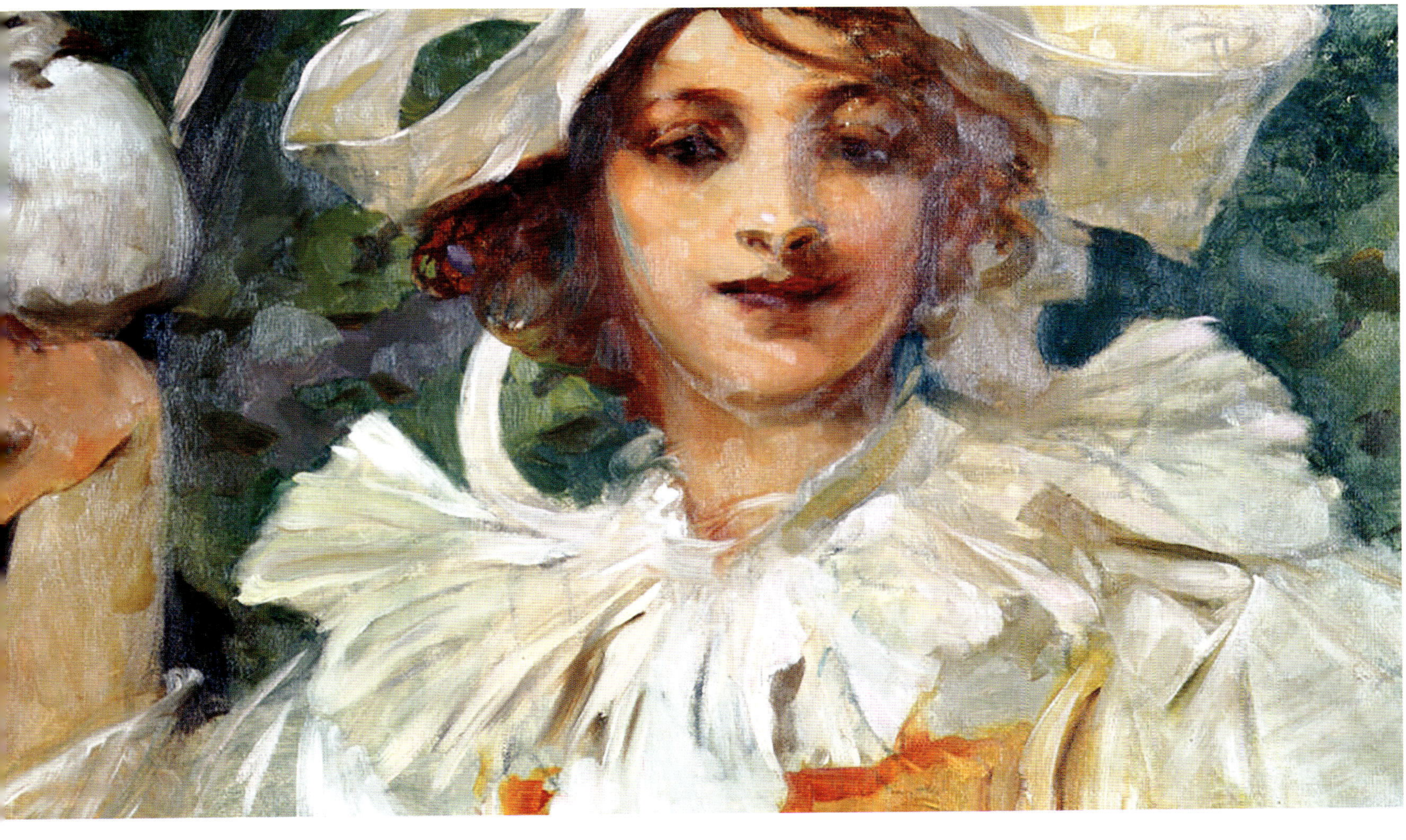

THE SLAV EPIC

A stark departure from the decorative Art Nouveau style that made Mucha famous, the Slav Epic (or *Slovanská Epopej*) is executed in a Romantic style that befits the solemnity of its subject matter. Between 1911 and 1926, Mucha devoted his artistic energy to producing a series of 20 monumental canvases that cover the key historical moments and mythology of the Slavic people. In order to complete such an ambitious project, he needed funding, and he secured it from Charles Richard Crane, a wealthy businessman and philanthropist in Chicago. Crane became the project's benefactor, supporting Mucha both financially and emotionally during the many years he worked on the paintings. Mucha completed the Slav Epic in 1928, the year of the 10th anniversary of the independence of Czechoslovakia. He and Crane then presented the series to the City of Prague as a gift to the nation.

[RIGHT]
The Slav Epic when it was on display in the Veletržní palác (Trade Fair Palace) in Prague. In this photo, the first painting of the series is in the foreground.

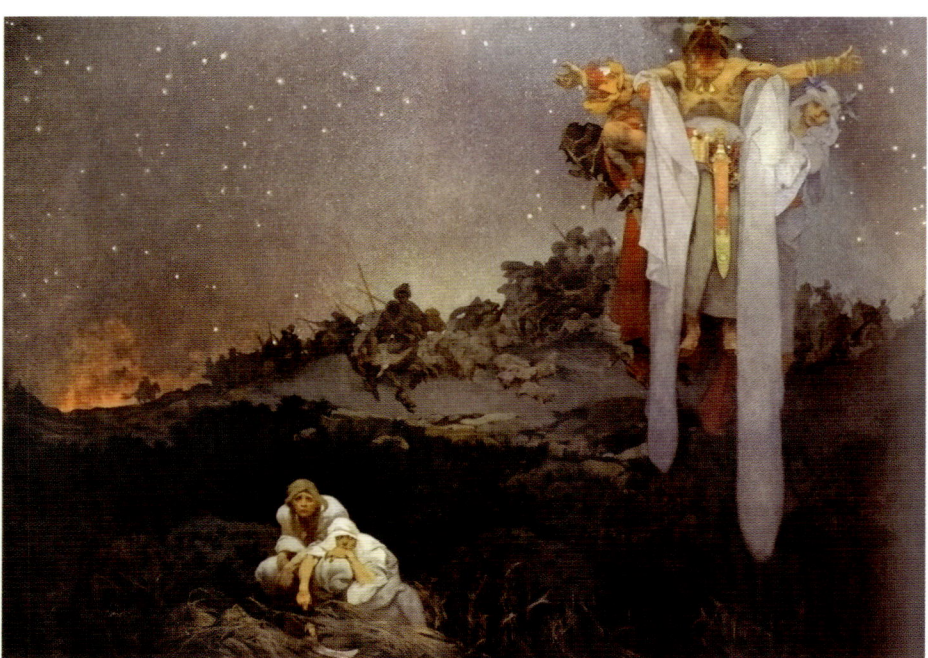

The Slav Epic: Cycle No. 1: The Slavs in Their Original Homeland. Between the Turanian Whip and the Sword of the Goths (between 3rd and 6th centuries) (1912).

The series begins in the 3rd to 6th centuries, when the Slavic people, who then lived an agricultural-based existence in the marshes between the Vistula River, the Dnieper River, the Baltic Sea, and the Black Sea, were under constant attack by Germanic tribes from the West. The figures floating in the right foreground—a pagan priest and the youthful figures of war and peace—symbolize the hope for coming peace and freedom.

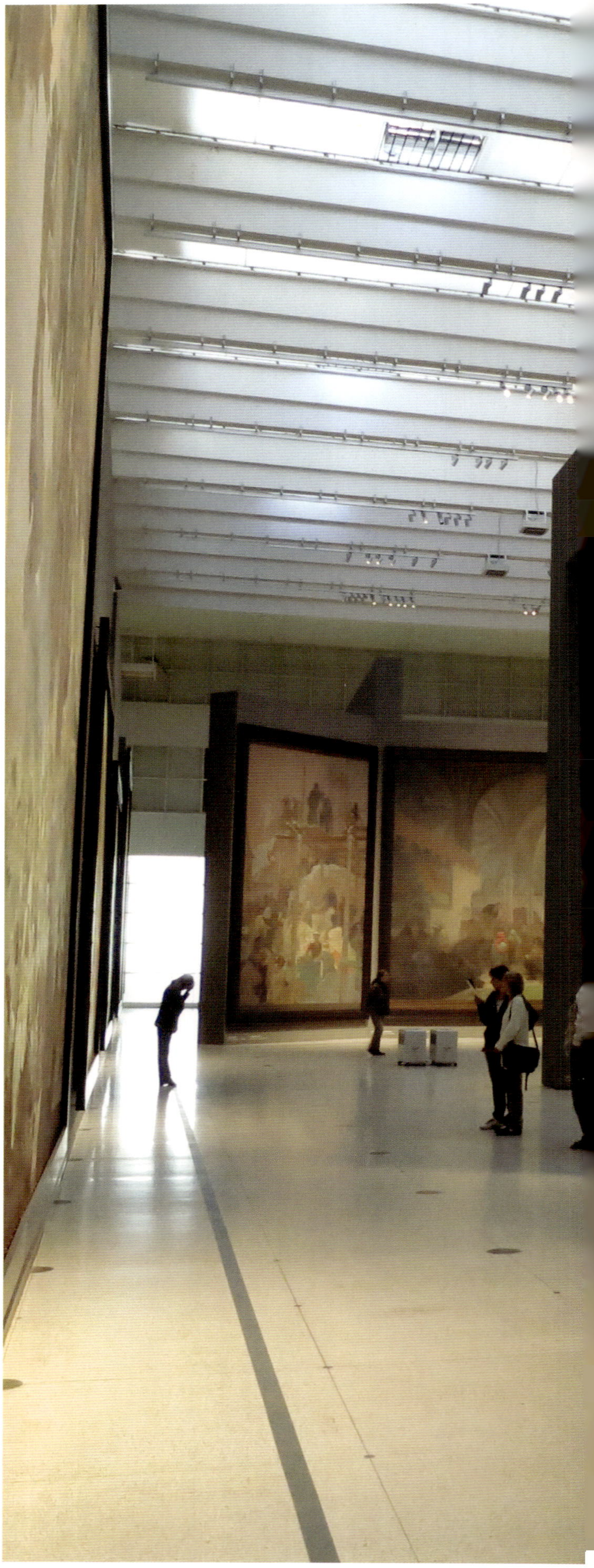

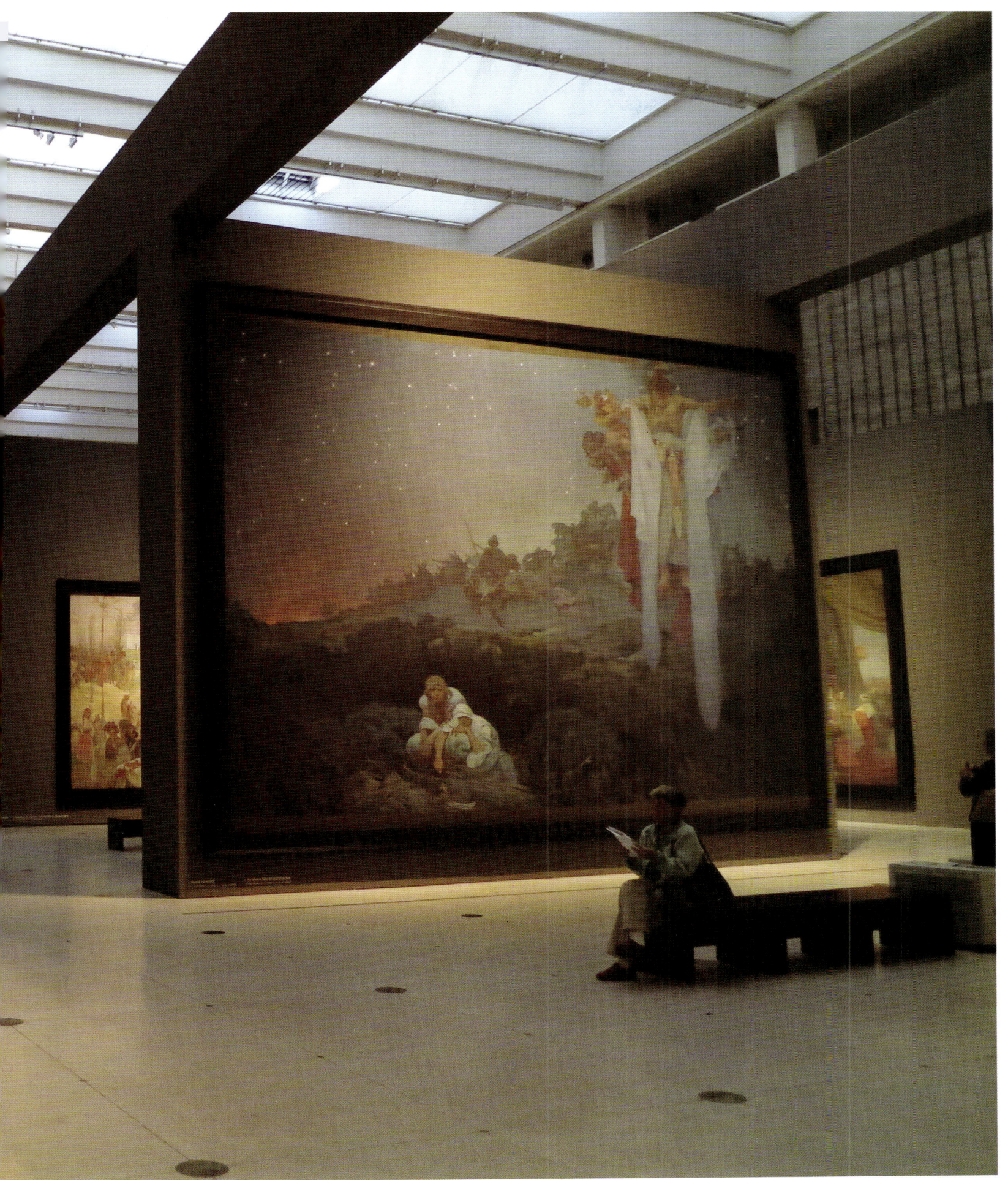

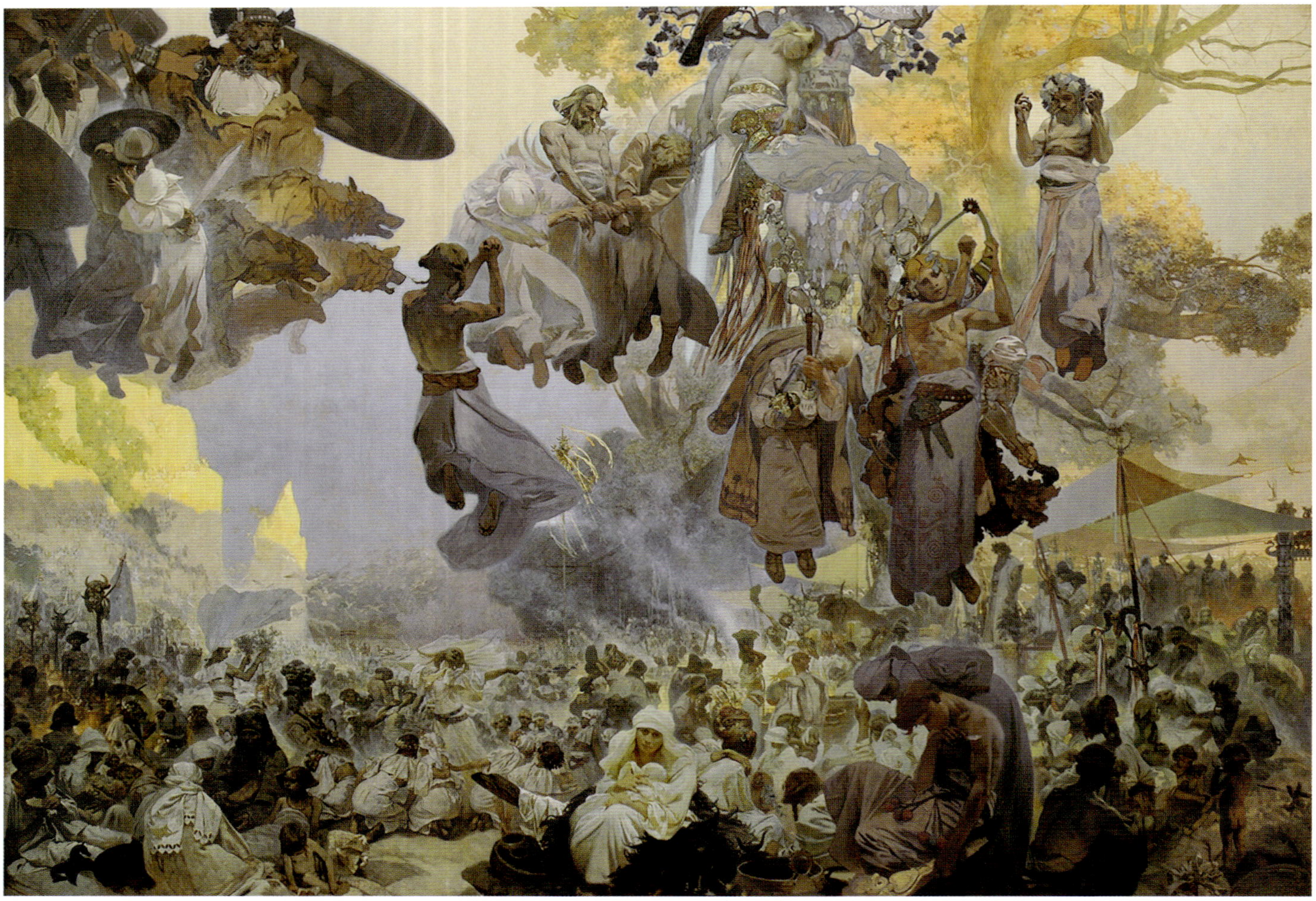

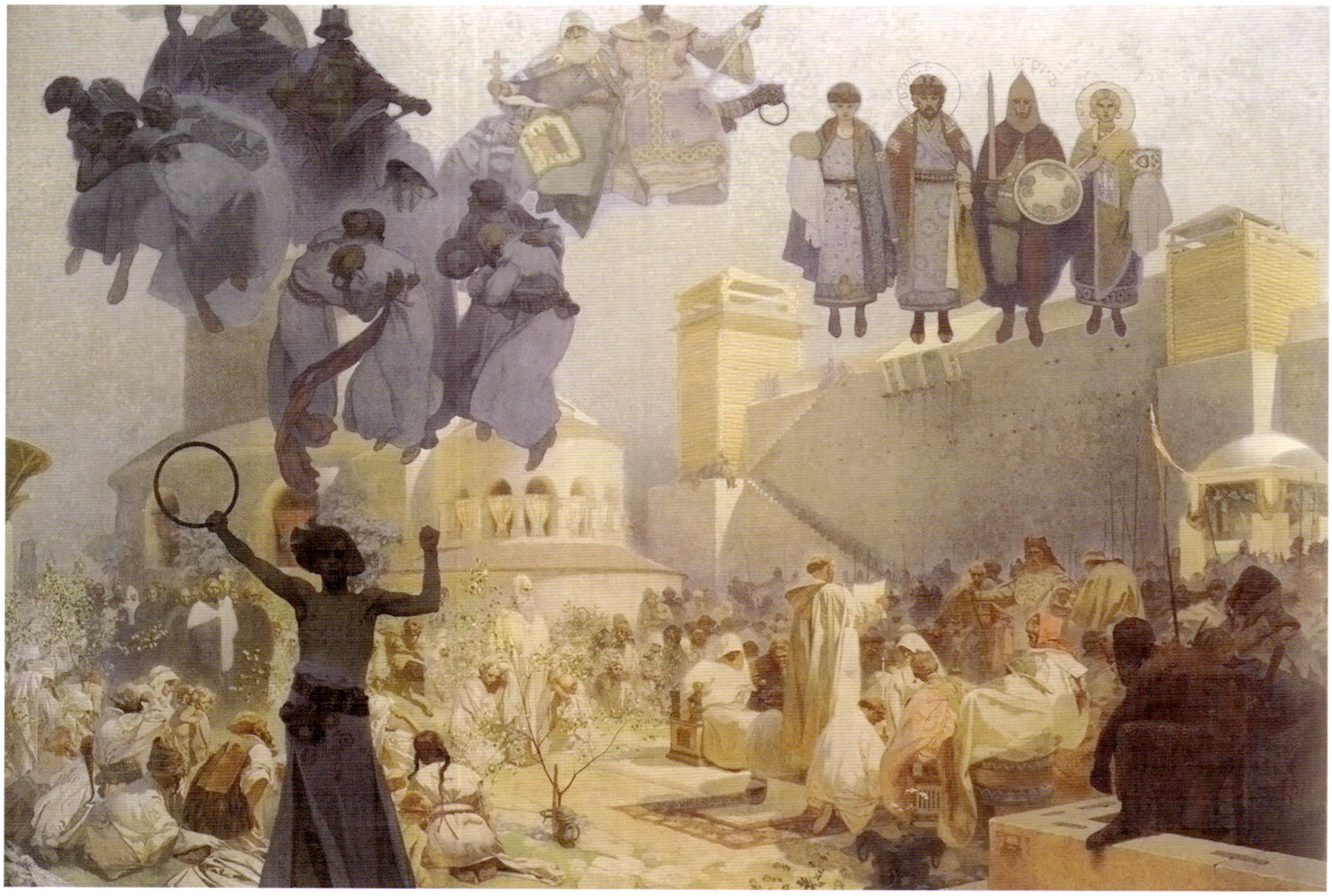

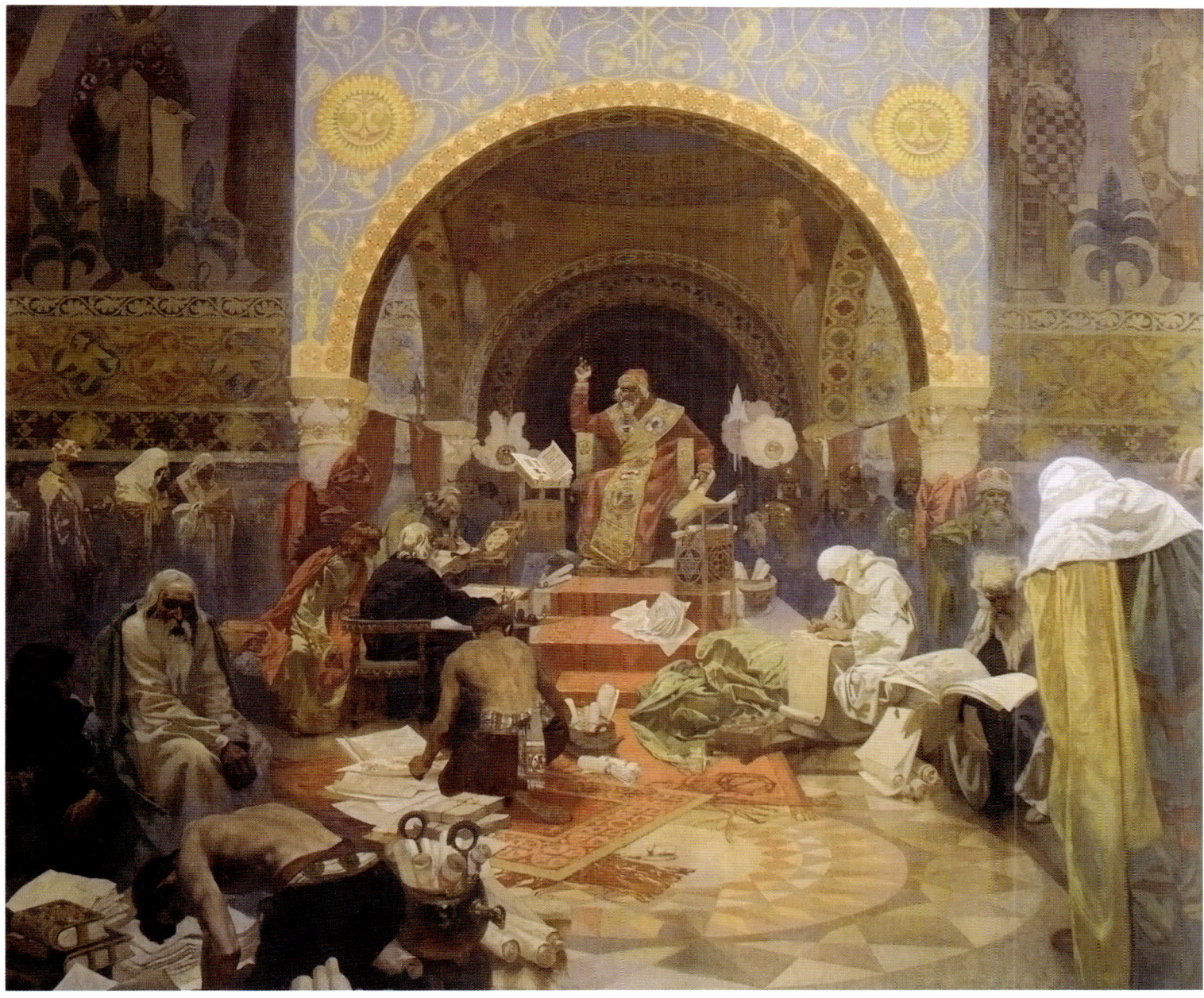

[ABOVE]
The Slav Epic: Cycle No. 4:
Tsar Simeon of Bulgaria.
The Dawn of Slav Literature
(10th century) (1923).

[OPPOSITE PAGE TOP]
The Slav Epic: Cycle:
No. 2: The Celebration of
Svantovít. When Gods Are at
War, Salvation Is in the Arts
(between the 8th and 10th
centuries) (1912).

[OPPOSITE PAGE BOTTOM]
The Slav Epic: Cycle No. 3:
Introduction of the Slavonic
Liturgy. Praise God in
Your Mother Tongue
(9th century) (1912).

"*To talk in my own way to the spirit of the nation, to its eyes which carry thoughts most quickly to the consciousness.*"

~ CHRISTINE VENDREDI-AUZANNEAU,

The number of canvases, as well as the colossal size of these works—the seven largest canvases are approximately 26 by 20 feet (8 by 6 meters)—calls for special housing so that art lovers can view these masterpieces all together. Prior to 2012, the Slav Epic was part of the permanent exhibition at the château in Moravský Krumlov in south Moravia. In 2012, the National Gallery Prague organized an exhibition of all 20 works on the ground floor of the Veletržní Palace that lasted until 2016. In 2018, nine of the canvases of the Slav Epic were shown in Brno during the RE:PUBLIKA Festival. After a restoration of the château, the paintings have been returned to Moravský Krumlov, where they will be on display until 2026.

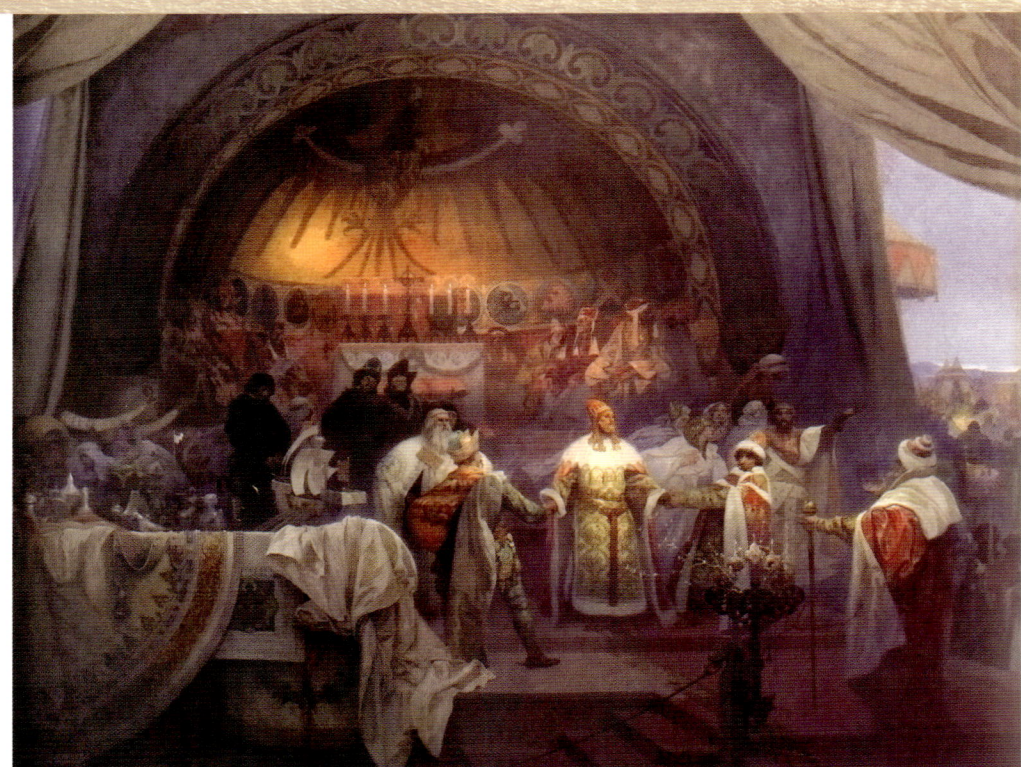

[OPPOSITE PAGE]
The Slav Epic: Cycle No. 7: Jan Milíč of Kroměříž. The Magic of the Word: A Brothel Converted into a Convent (14th century) (1916).

[BELOW]
The Slav Epic: Cycle No. 6: Tsar Štěpán Dušan. The Slavic Code of Law (14th century) (1923).

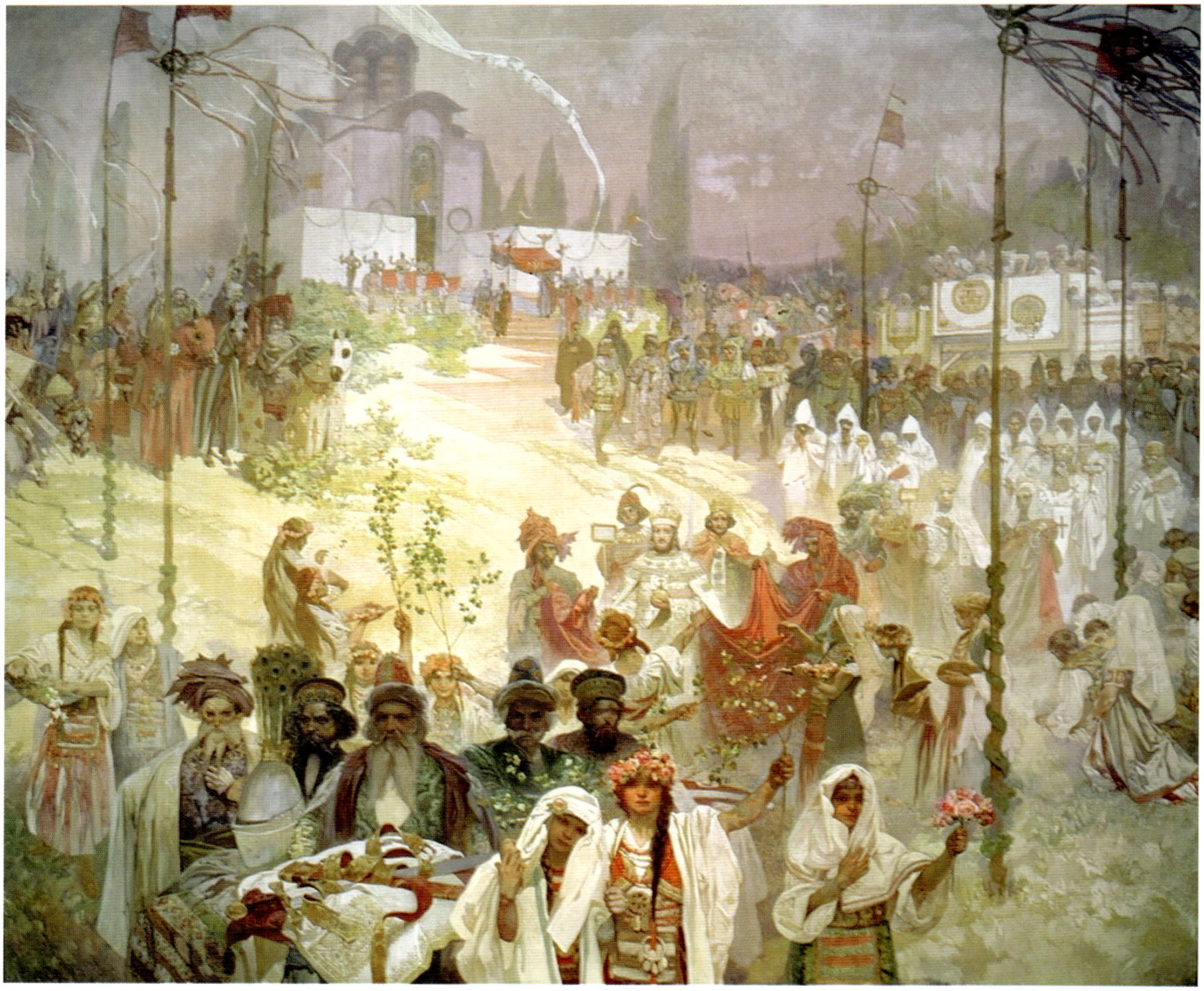

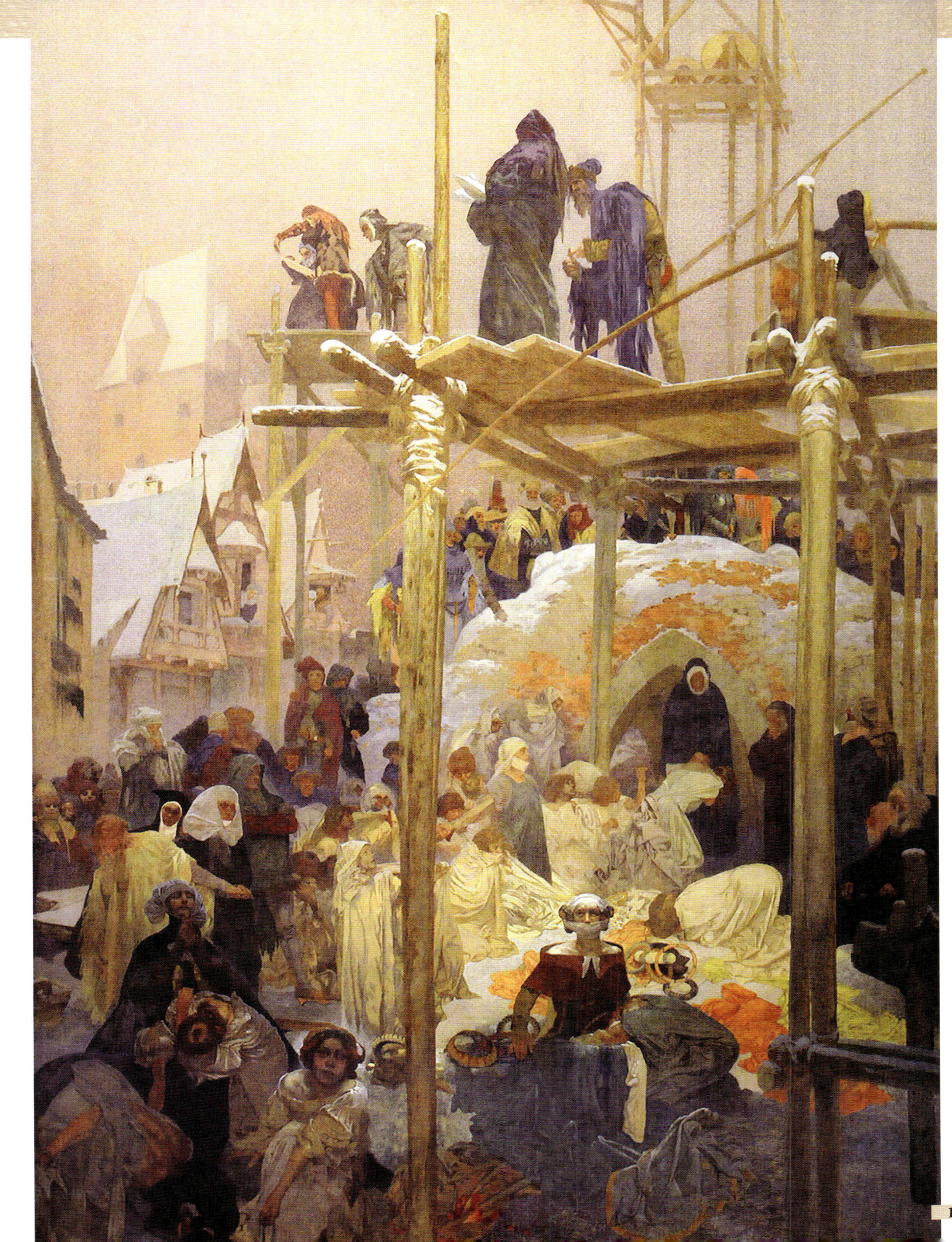

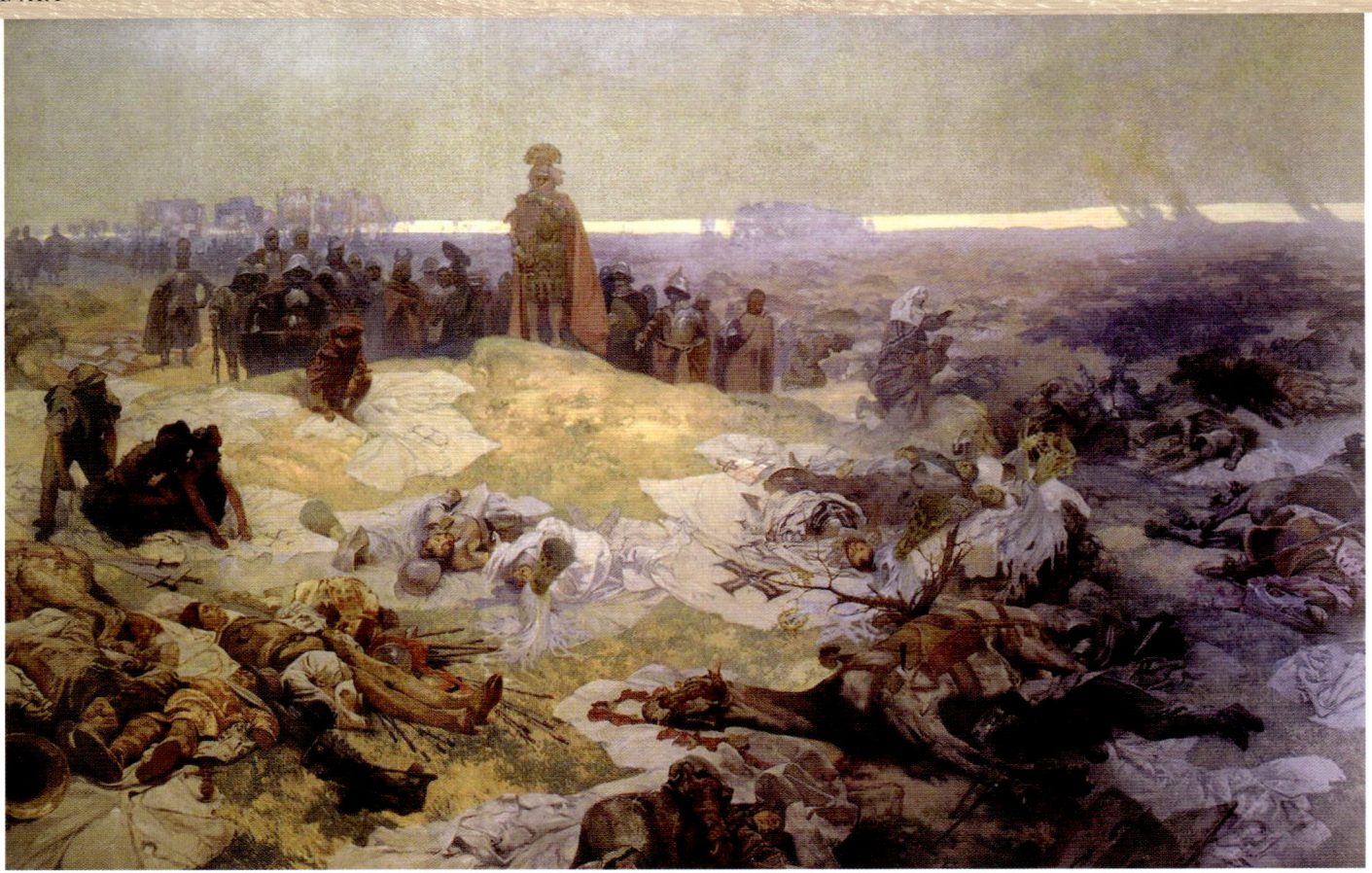

The Slav Epic: Cycle No. 8: After the Battle of Grunewald. The Solidarity of the Northern Slavs (1410) (1924).

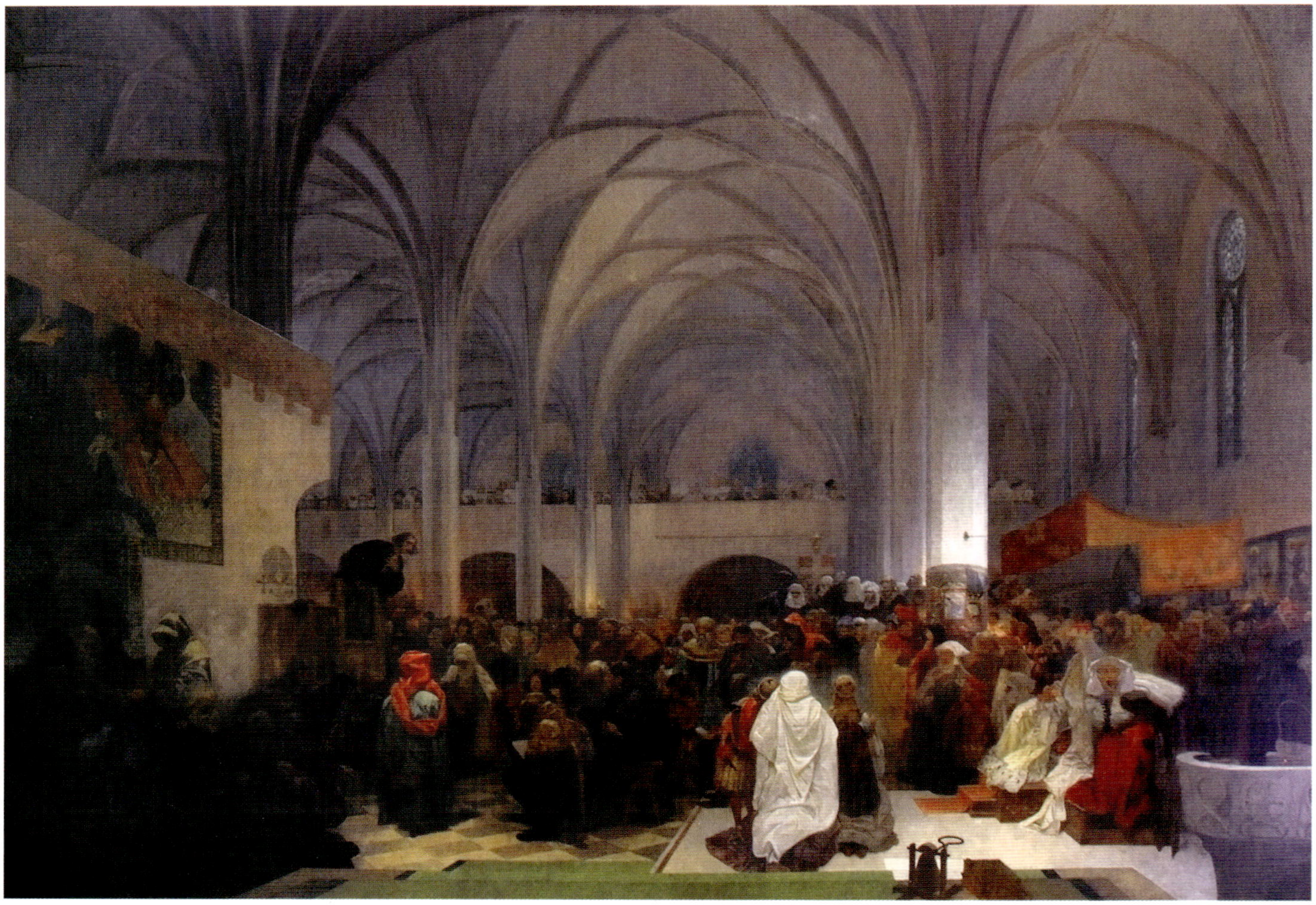

The Slav Epic: Cycle No. 9: Master Jan Hus Preaching at the Bethlehem Chapel. The Magic of the Word: Truth Prevails (1412) (1916).

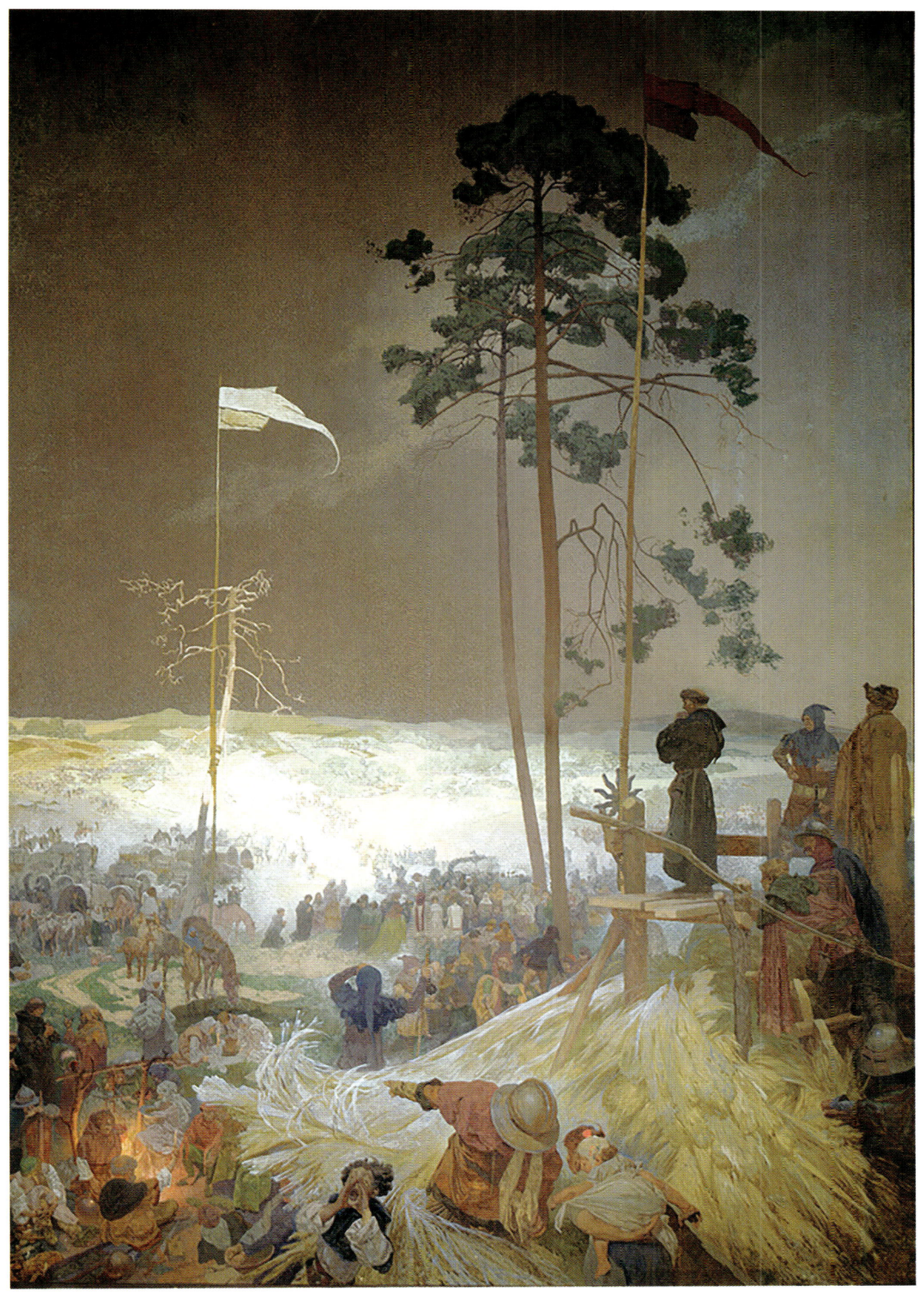

The Slav Epic:
Cycle No. 10:
The Meeting
at Křížky.
The Magic
of Words:
Sub utraque
(1419) (1916).

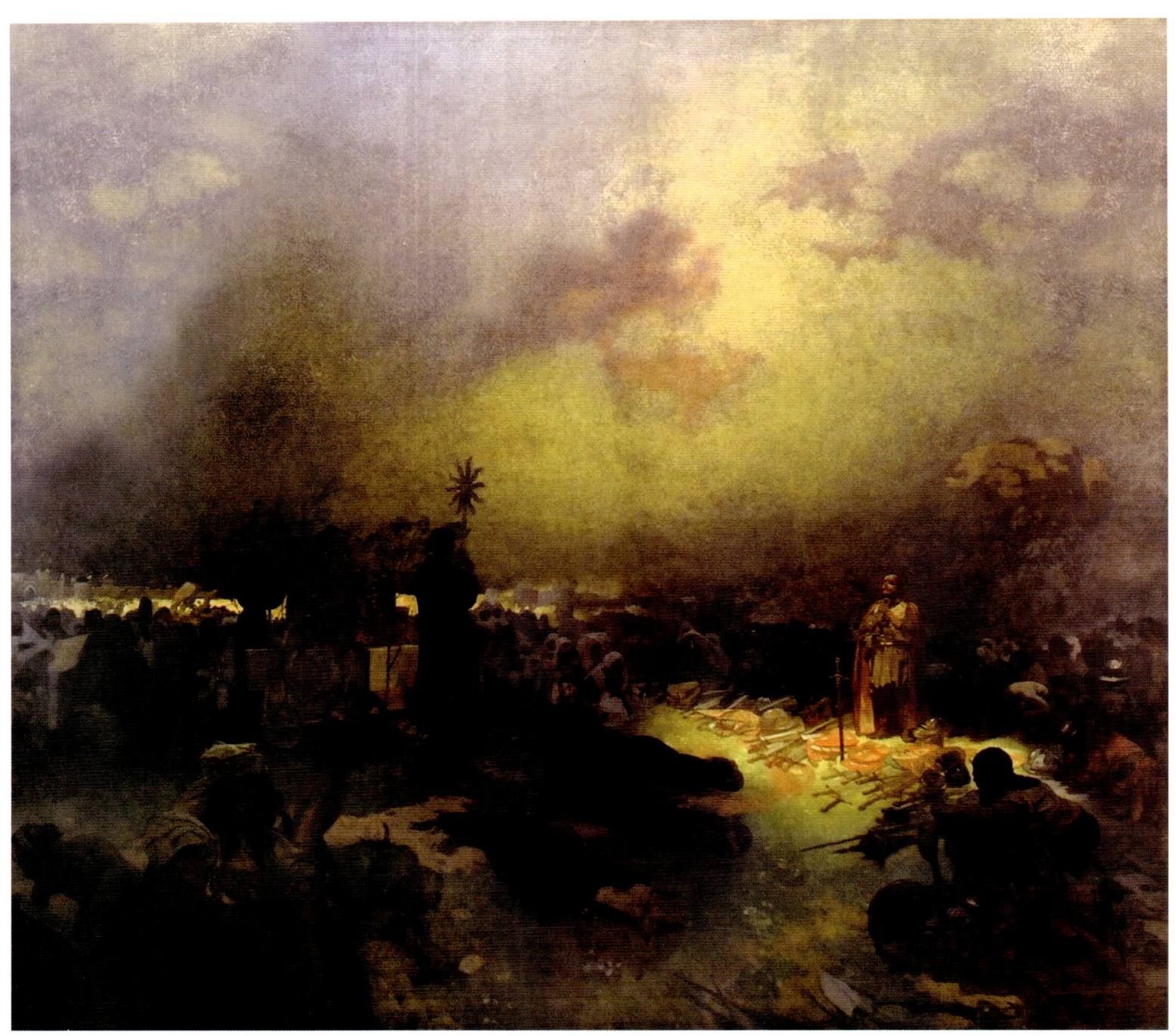

The Slav Epic: Cycle No. 11: After the Battle of Vítkov. God is Found in Truth, Not Force (1420) (1923).

"The purpose of my work was never to destroy but always to create, to construct bridges, because we must live in the hope that humankind will draw together and that the better we understand each other the easier this will become."

~ ALPHONSE MUCHA

The Slav Epic: Cycle No. 12: Petr Chelčický at Vodňany. Do Not Repay Evil with Evil (1433) (1918).

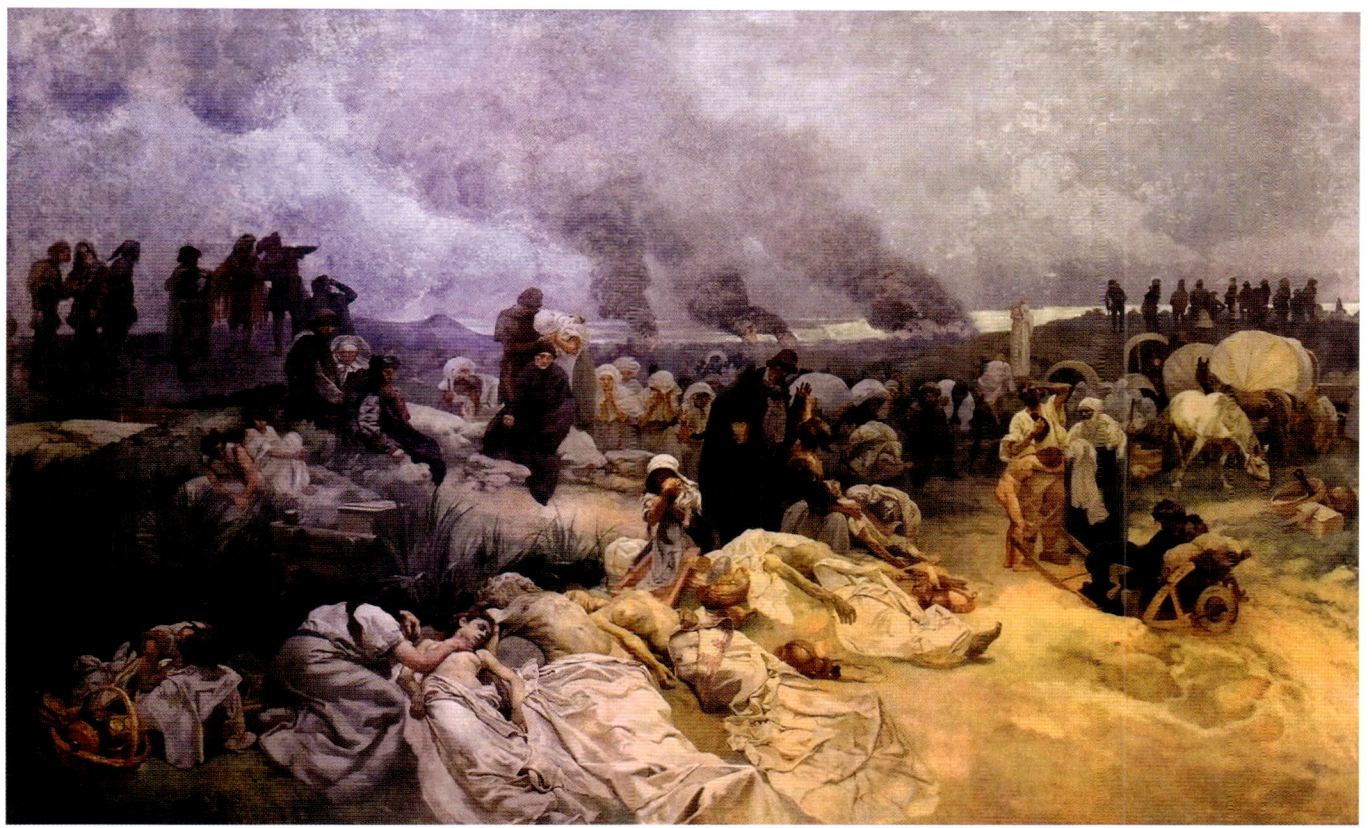

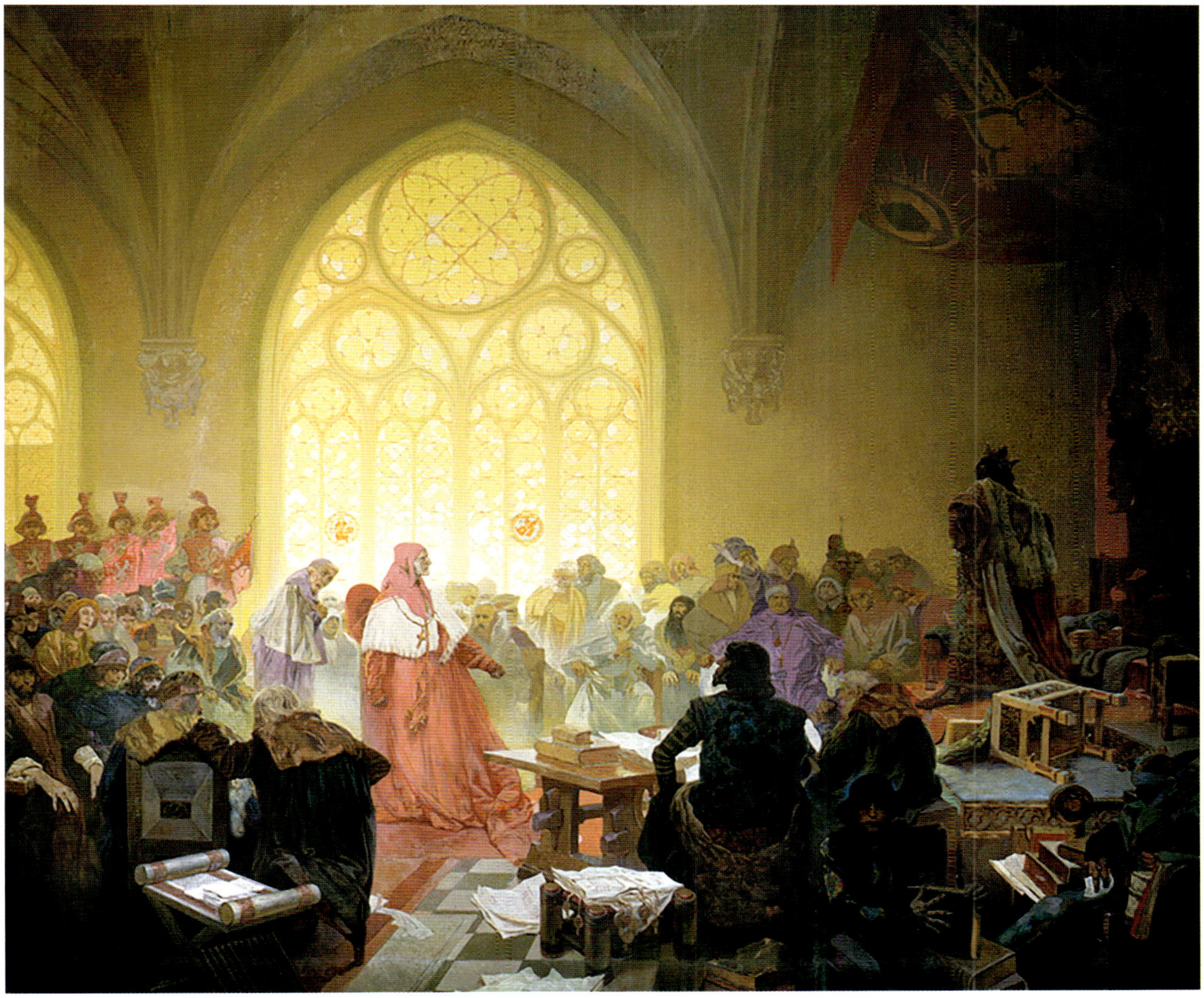

The Slav Epic: Cycle No. 13: The Hussite King Jiří of Poděbrady. Treaties Are To be Respected (1462) (1923).

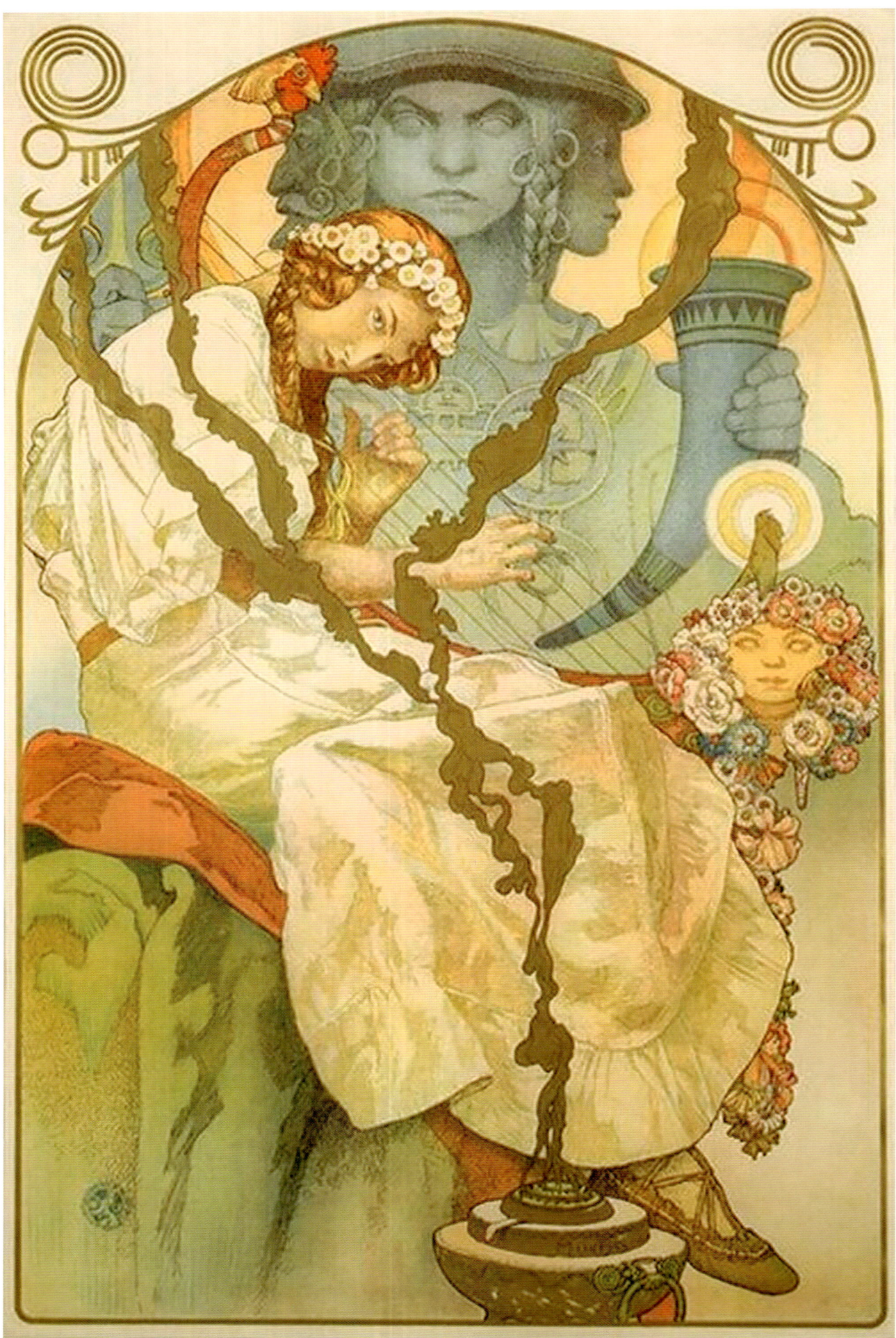

[LEFT]
Detail of **Slav Epic Exhibition, Brno, 1930** (1928–1930).

Mucha created this promotional poster for the Slav Epic exhibition in Brno in 1930. Mucha's first exhibition of the works was held at the Trade Fair Palace in Prague in the autumn of 1928.

[OPPOSITE PAGE TOP]
The Slav Epic: Cycle No. 14: The Sacrifice at Szigetvár by Nikola Zrinski. The Shield of Christendom (1566) (1914).

[OPPOSITE PAGE BOTTOM]
The Slav Epic: Cycle No. 15: The Brethren School in Ivančice, the Printing of the Czech Bible. God Gave Us the Gift of Language (1578) (1914).

[OVERLEAF]
The Slav Epic: Cycle No. 16: Jan Amos Komenský. A Glimmer of Hope (1670) (1918).

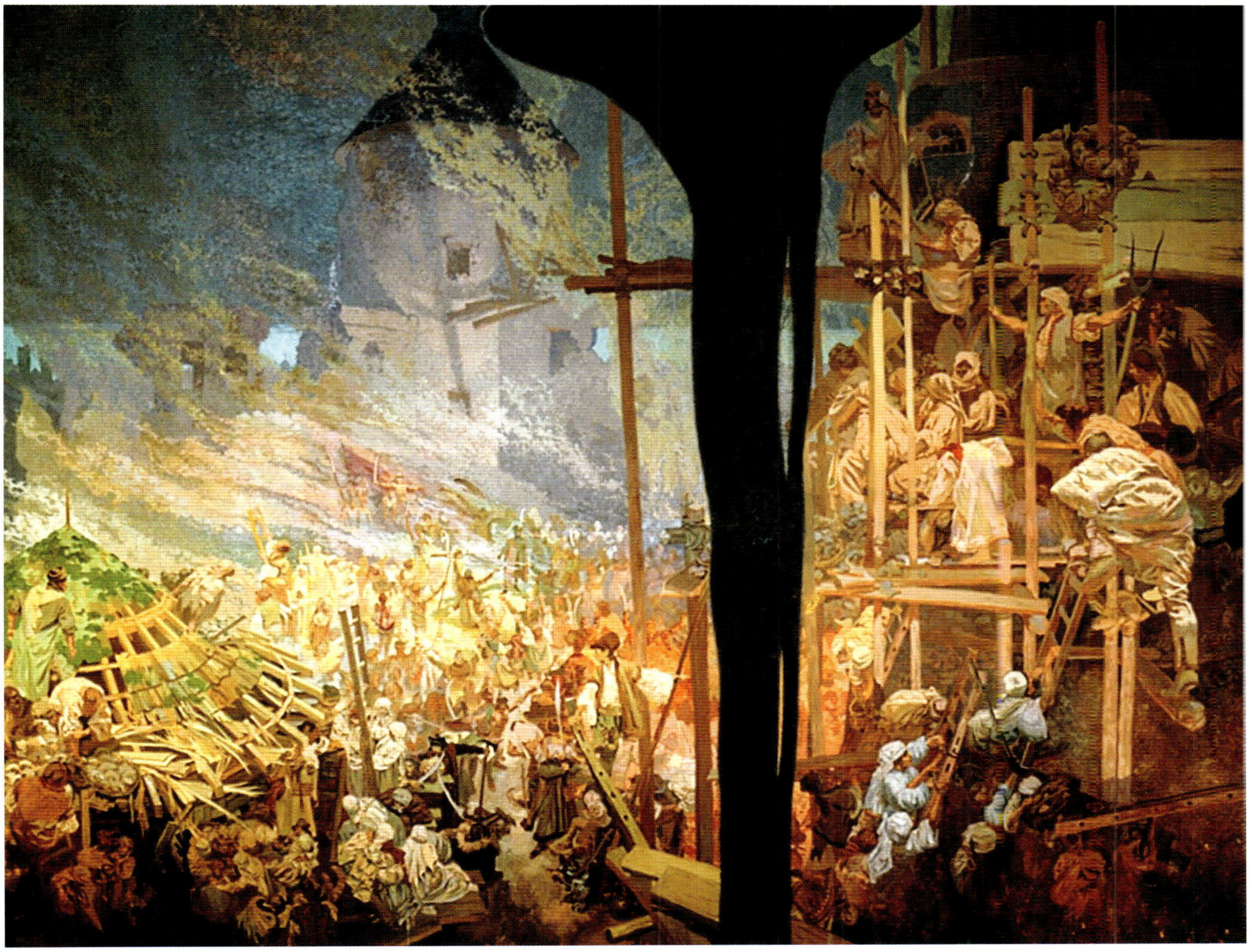

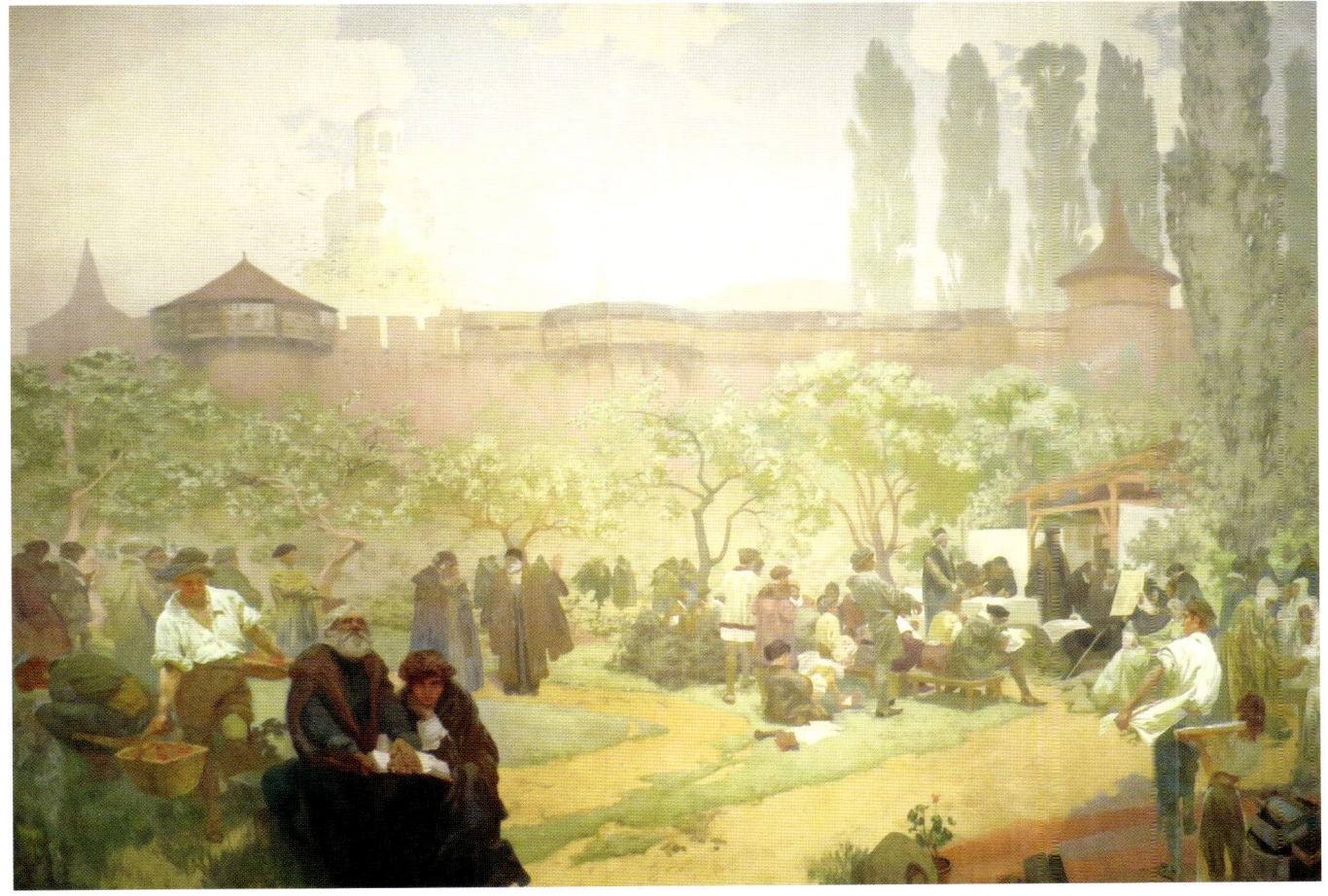

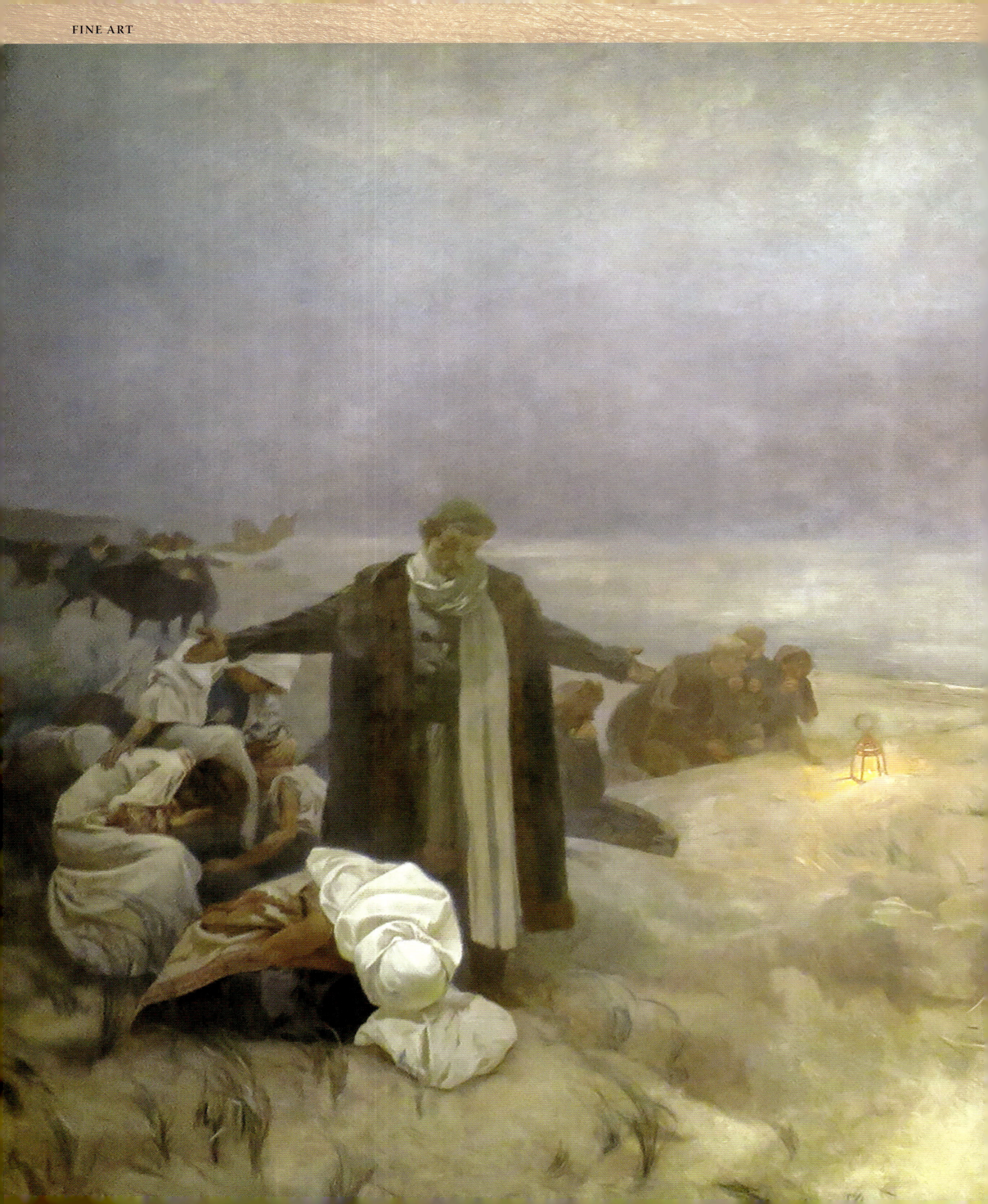

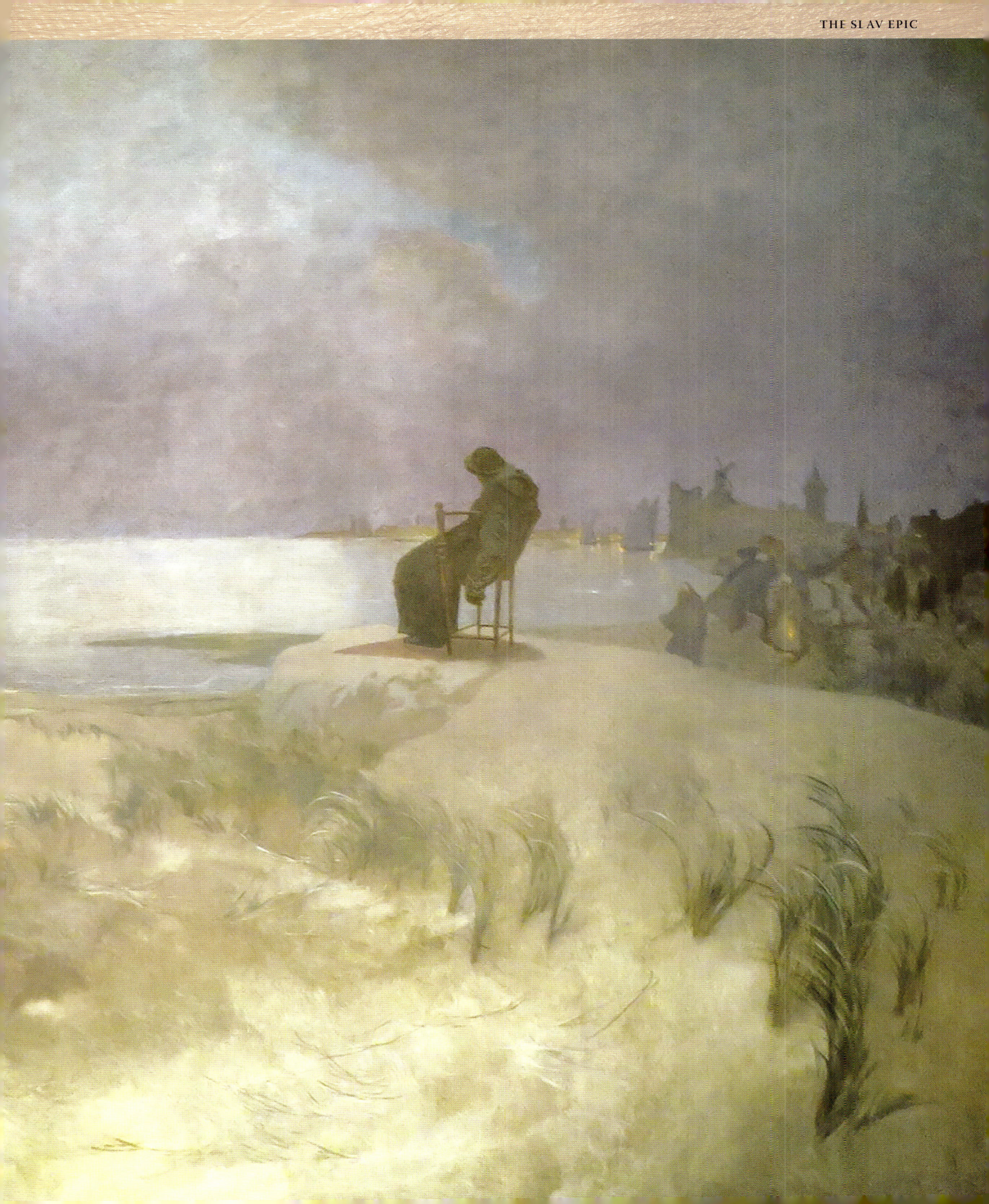

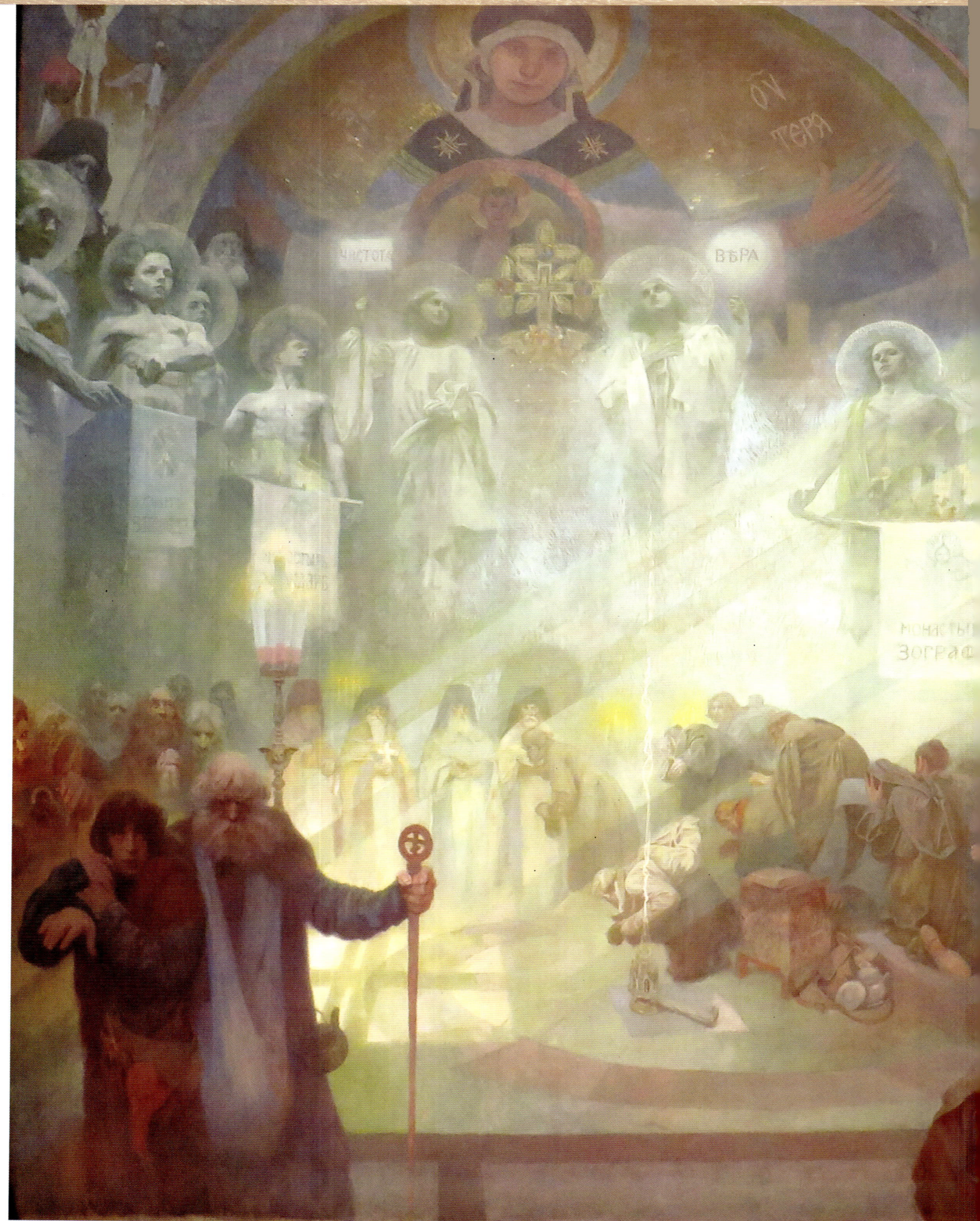

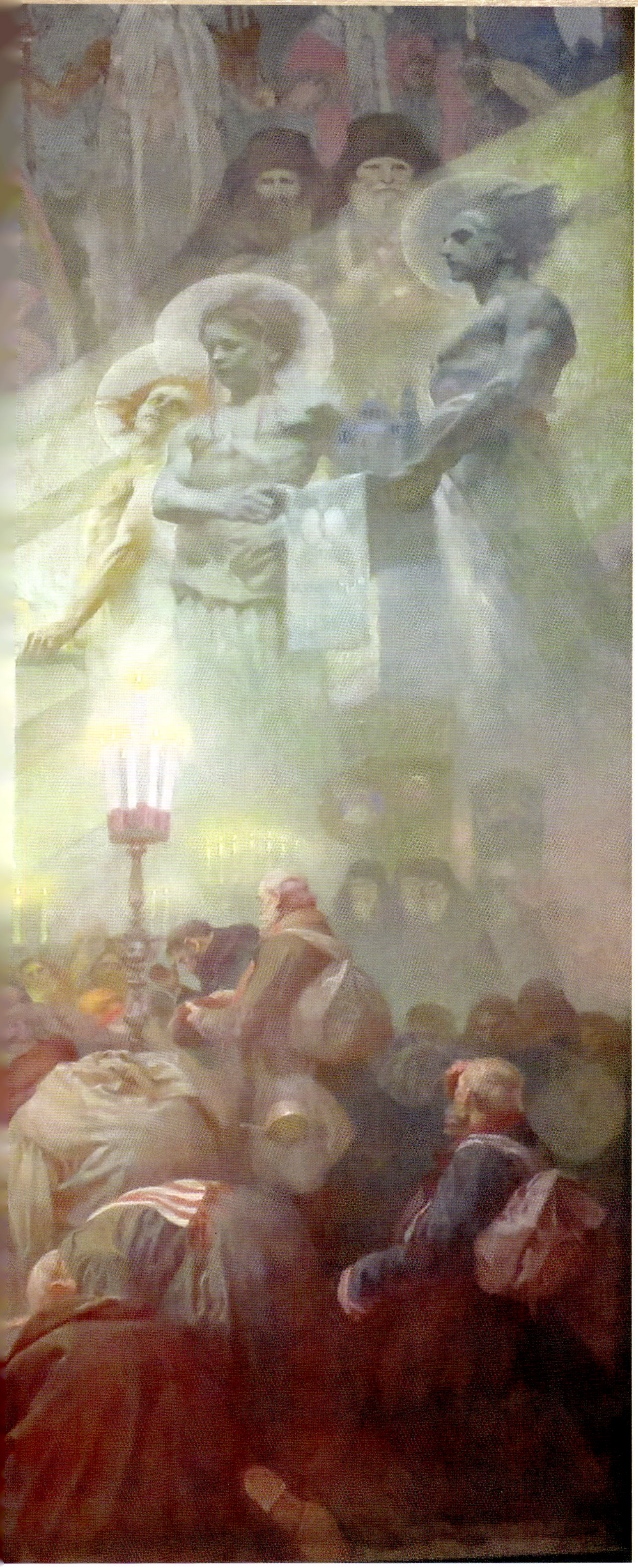

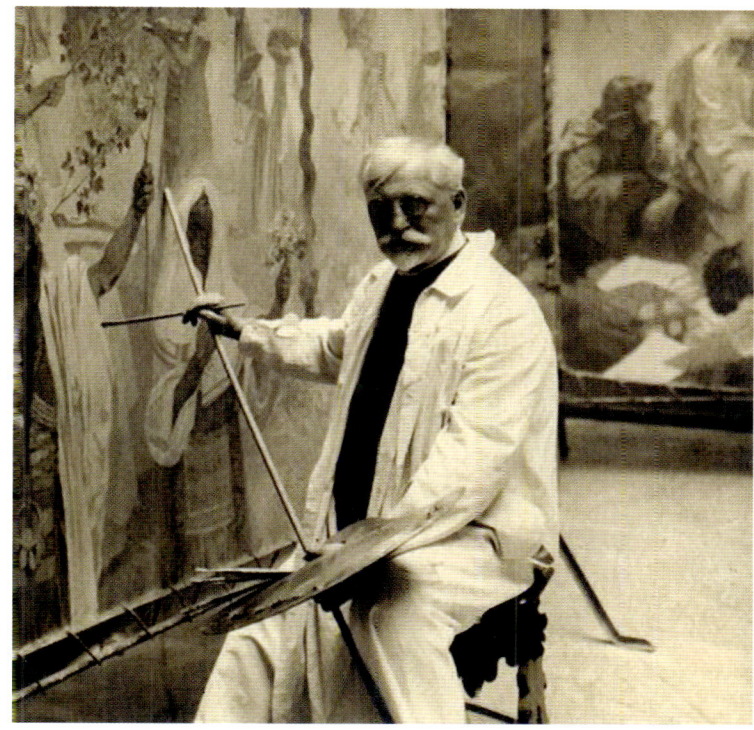

The artist at work on Cycle No. 6. In 1910, he had rented part of the Zbiroh château in Central Bohemia so that he could begin work on the Slav Epic. He spent 18 years painting the series there.

> " *I will be able to do something really good, not just for the art critic but for our Slav souls".*
>
> ~ ALPHONSE MUCHA

The Slav Epic: Cycle No.17: Holy Mount Athos. Vatican of Orthodox Christianity, Sheltering the Oldest Slav Literary Monuments (18th century) (1926).

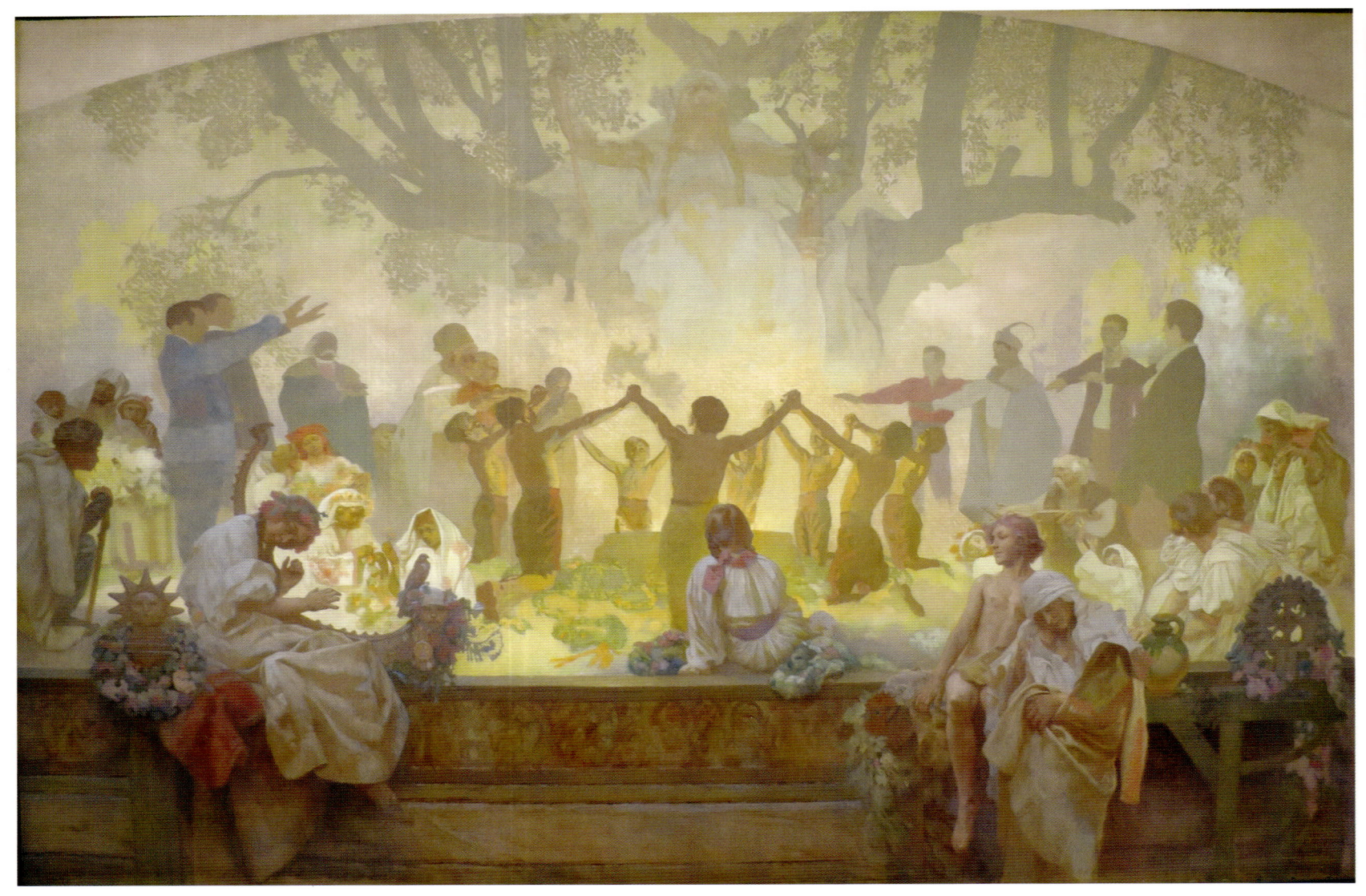

The Slav Epic: Cycle No.18: Oath of the "Youth" under the Slav Linden Tree. The Slav Revival (19th century) (1926).

Mucha never entirely completed this canvas, also known as The Oath of Omladina under the Slavic Linden Tree. *Several figures remain unfinished in egg tempera without an oil finish.*

" *The mission of the Epic is not completed. Let it announce to foreign friends – and even to enemies – who we were, who we are, and what we hope for. May the strength of the Slav spirit command their respect, because from respect, love is born."*

~ ALPHONSE MUCHA

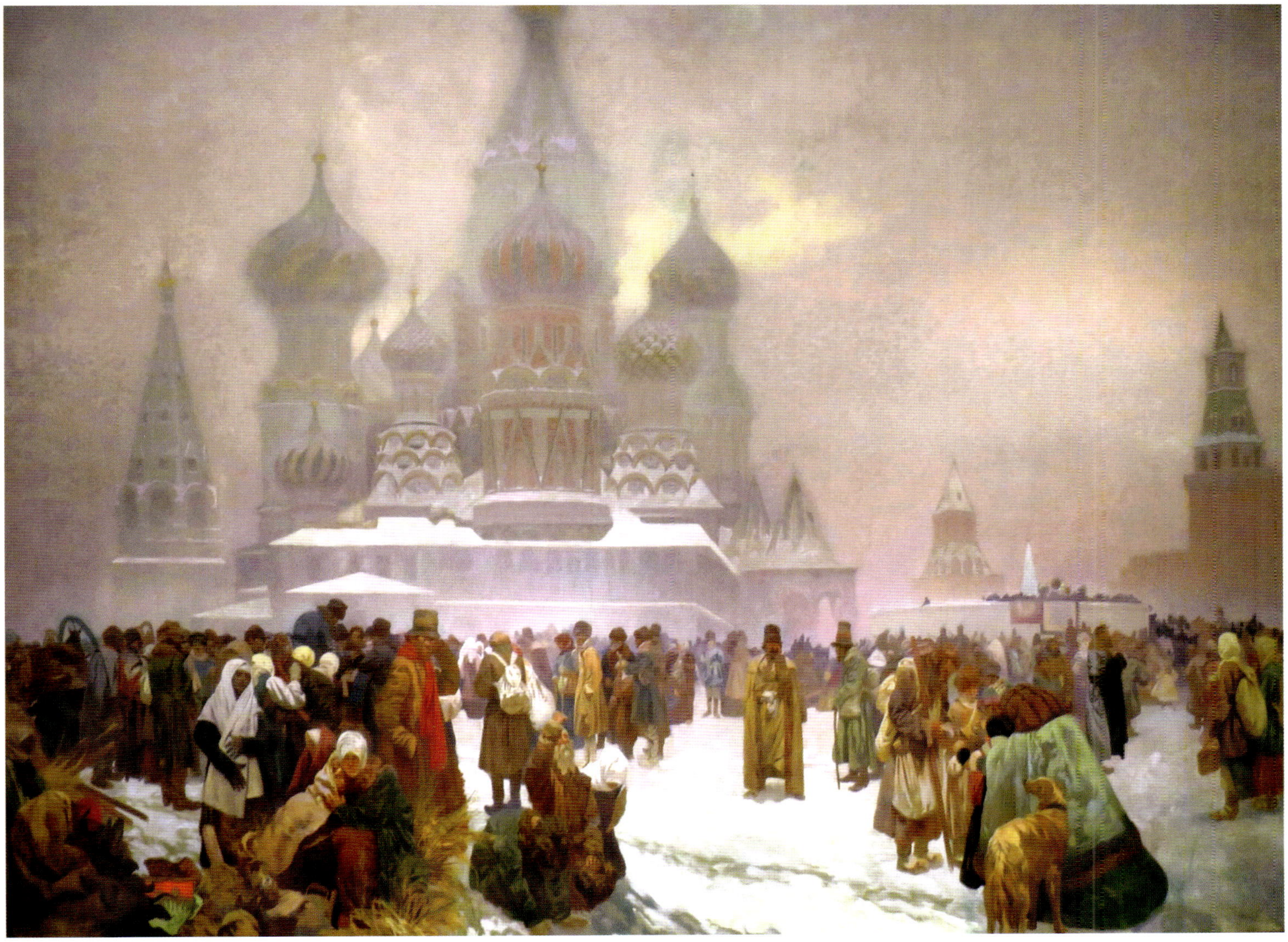

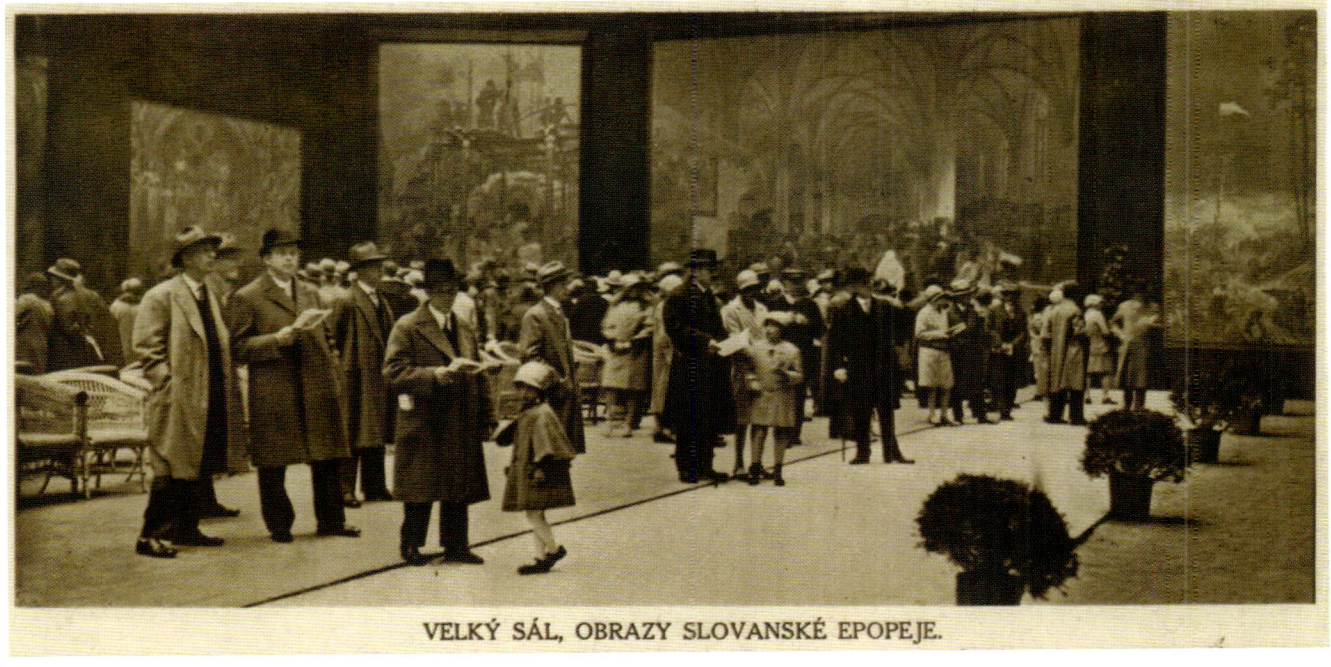

The Slav Epic: Cycle No. 19: The Abolition of Serfdom in Russia.
To Work in Freedom Is the Foundation of a State (1861) (1926).

VELKÝ SÁL, OBRAZY SLOVANSKÉ EPOPEJE.

A contemporary photo of visitors to the exhibition of the Slav Epic at the Trade Fair Palace in Prague in the autumn of 1928.

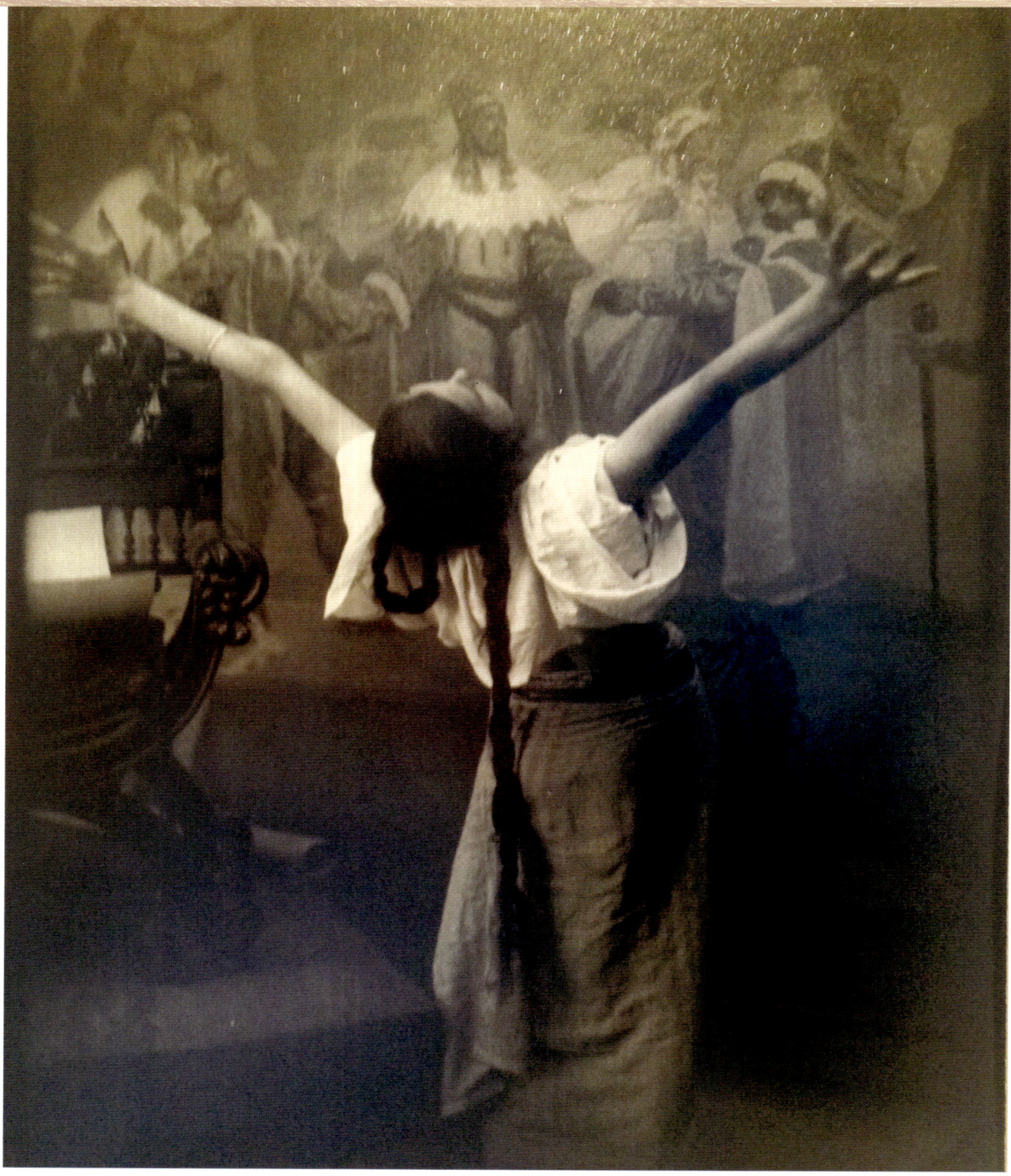

[ABOVE]
Photographic study
for *Apotheosis of
the Slavs* (1924).

This figure can be
seen in the center-
left foreground of the
completed painting.

[OPPOSITE PAGE]
**The Slav Epic: Cycle No. 20: Apotheosis: Slavs for Humanity.
Four Stages of Slav History in Four Colours (1918) (1926).**

A celebration of the long-awaited independence of the Slav nations, the final
painting unites the themes of all the previous ones. The way Mucha blocked areas
of the canvas with certain colors infuses the painting with meaning that relates
to the story of the Slavic people: The blue of the bottom right represents early
history; the red in the top right signifies the blood shed of the Middle Ages; the
dull tones of the shadowy figures in the background stand for all the enemies of
the Slavic tribes; and the brilliant yellow lighting up the center of the canvas not
only pays homage to the Czech and Slovak soldiers returning from World War I,
but also signifies the dawn of a new era. The exultant figure at the center, backed
by the protecting figure of Christ, embodies the strength of the new republic.

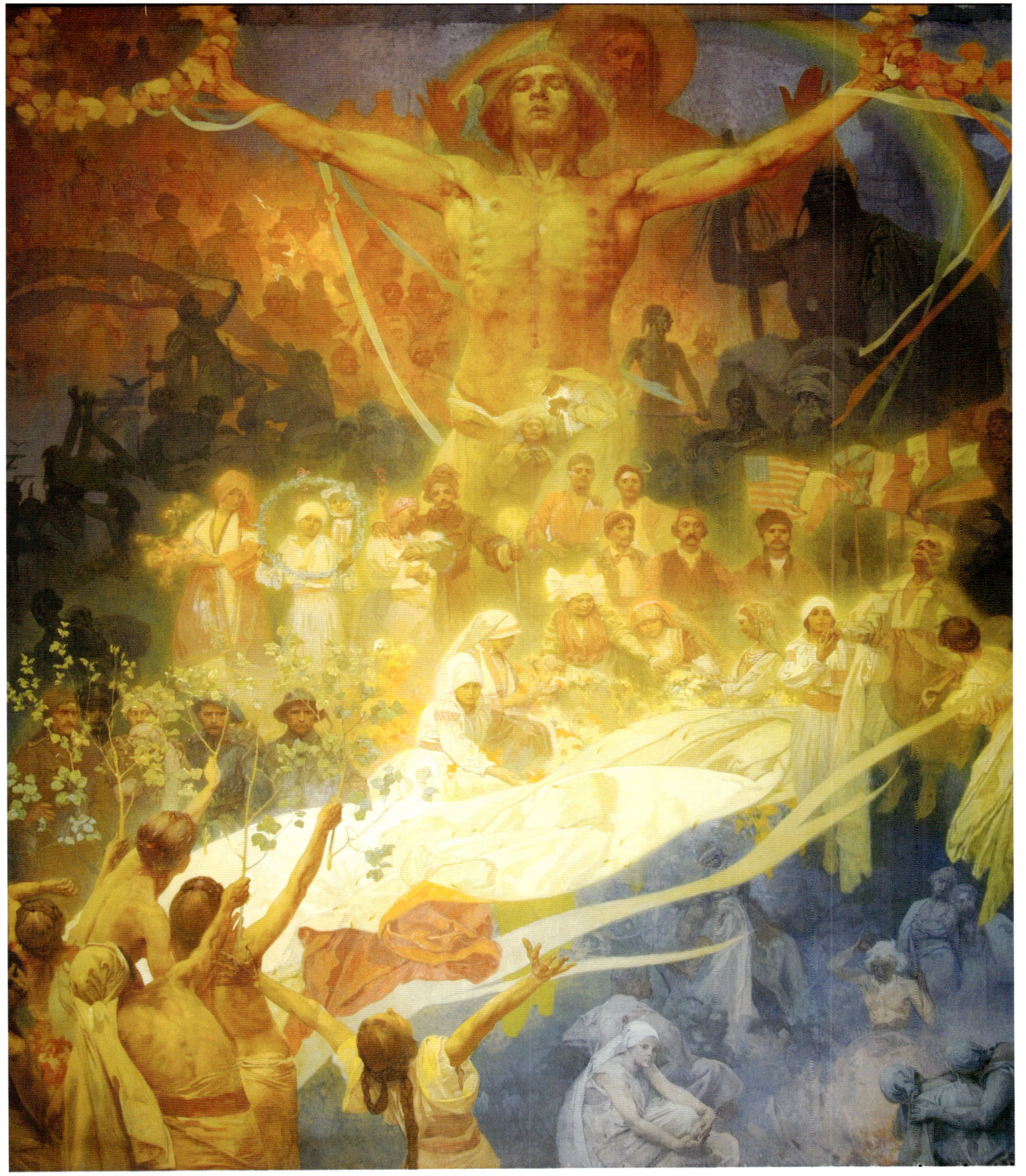

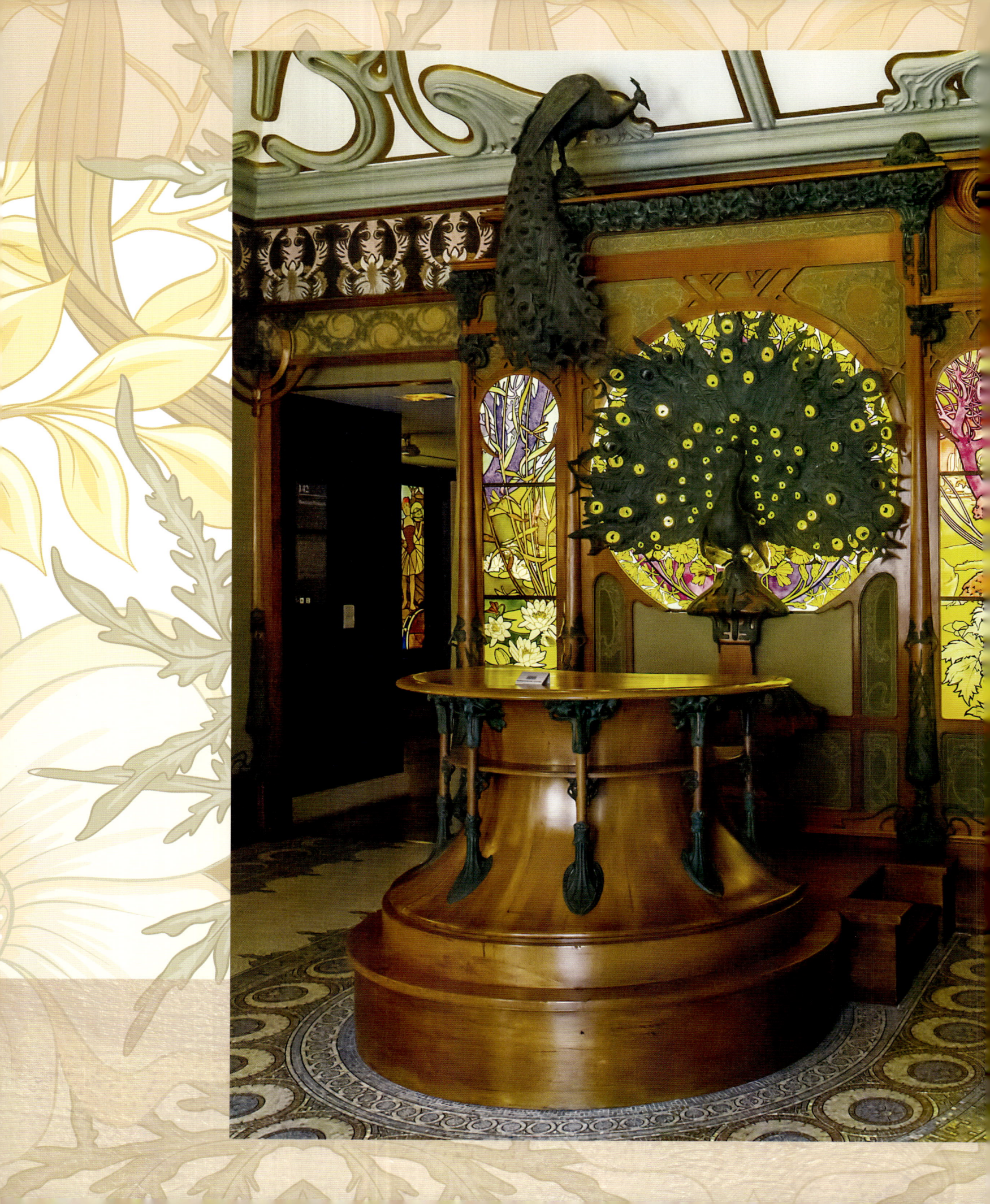

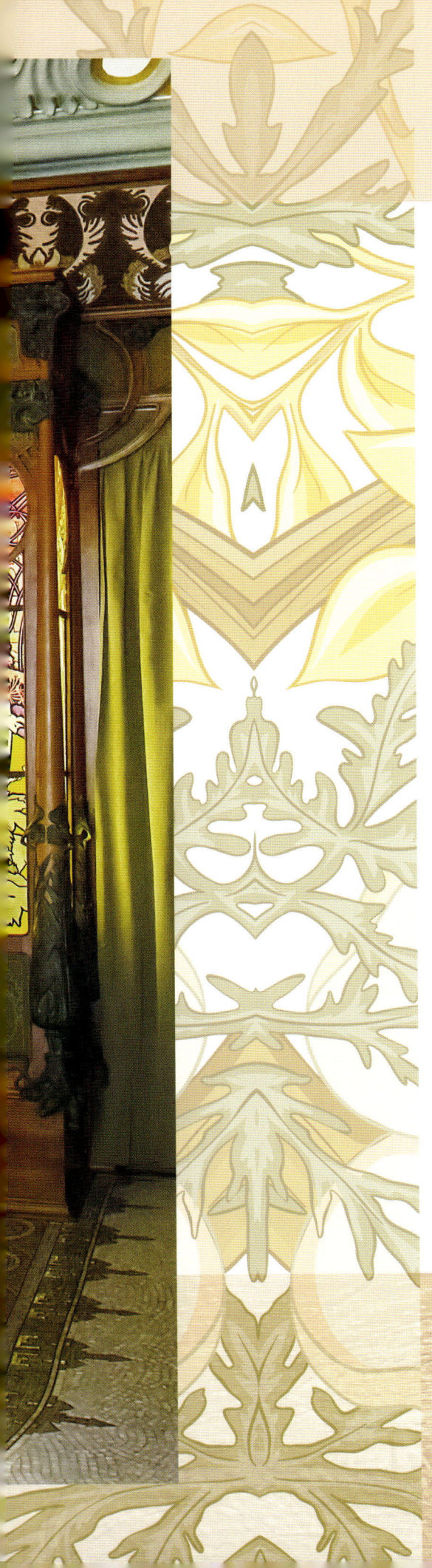

OTHER MEDIA

MUCHA'S INFLUENCE extended beyond painting and illustration into a variety of mediums. He designed exquisite stained glass windows, notably for Prague's St. Vitus Cathedral, integrating symbolic motifs with vibrant colors. In the realm of jewelry, his designs incorporated intricate metalwork, semi-precious stones, and enamel. His explorations into sculpture and photography further revealed his versatility, capturing the Art Nouveau aesthetic in three dimensions and through the lens. This broad artistic engagement underscores his profound impact on the decorative arts. He also designed Czechoslovakian banknotes and stamps following the nation's independence in 1918.

Reconstruction of the Boutique Georges Fouquet, decorated by Alphonse Mucha (c. 1900). **Musée Carnavalet, Paris.**

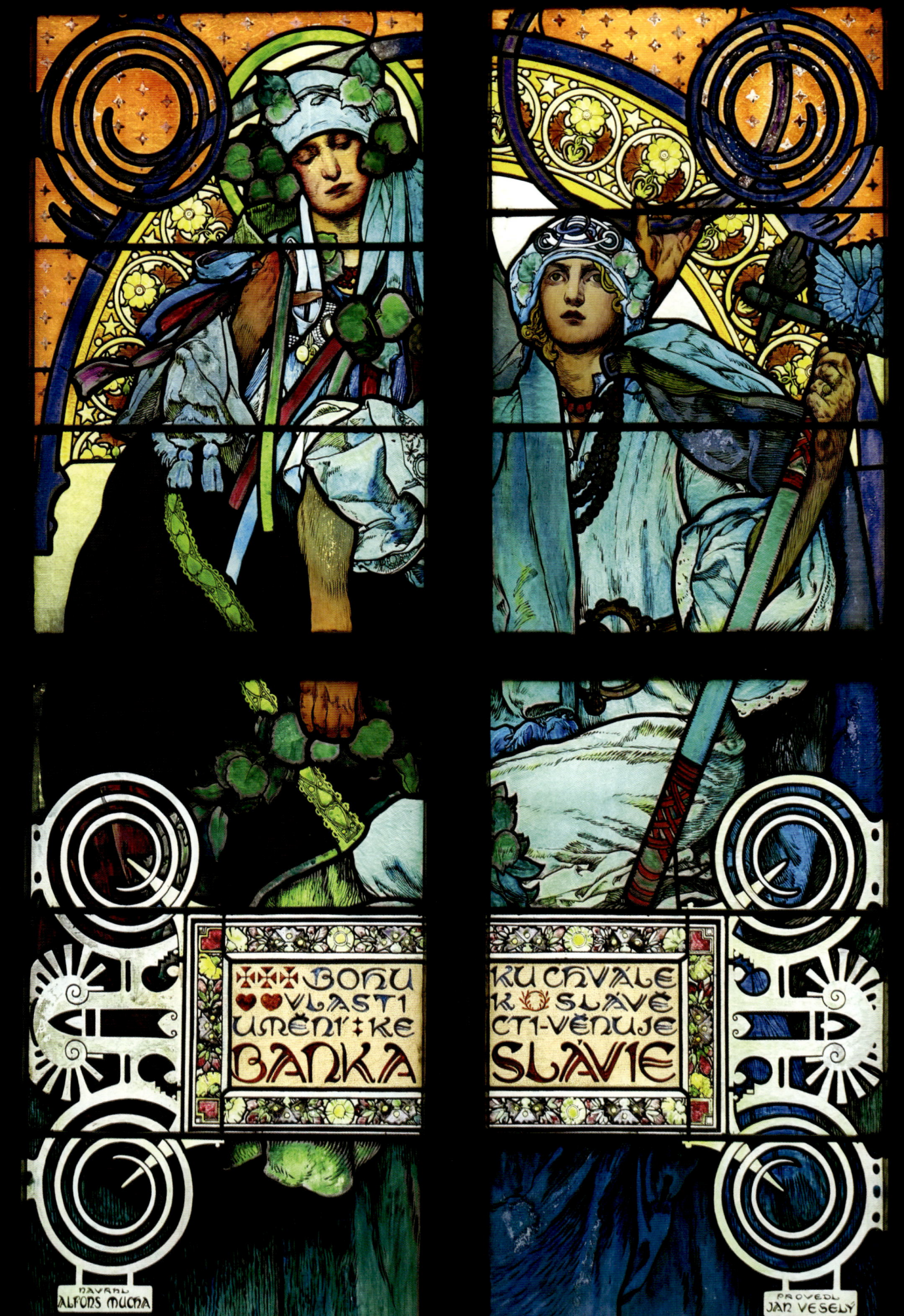

LUMINOUS STAINED GLASS

Prague's St. Vitus Cathedral (now called The Metropolitan Cathedral of Saints Vitus, Wenceslaus and Adalbert) is filled with incredible pieces of art. Mucha was among the artists commissioned to design its stained glass windows after the reconstruction of the Gothic building was completed in 1929 (the year that also celebrated the Millennium Jubilee of the Czech patron saint, Wenceslaus, Duke of Bohemia). His transcendent work, situated in the New Archbishop Chapel, is an allegory of Christ blessing the Slavic Nations. Installed in the north nave in 1931, its many panels portray the boy St. Wenceslaus with his grandmother St. Ludmila in the center. The two figures are surrounded by episodes from the lives of Saints Cyril and Methodius, who spread Christianity among the Slavs. Because it was funded by the Slavia Bank, Mucha included both an emblem of the bank in his design, as well as an image of Slavia below that of Christ.

[OPPOSITE PAGE]
Detail of center panel of window, which includes an homage to the Slavia Bank (1931). Stained glass. St. Vitus Cathedral, Prague.

[TOP RIGHT]
Detail of Jesus Christ at the top of the window. (1931). Stained glass. St. Vitus Cathedral, Prague.

[BOTTOM RIGHT]
Full window (1931). Stained glass. St. Vitus Cathedral, Prague.

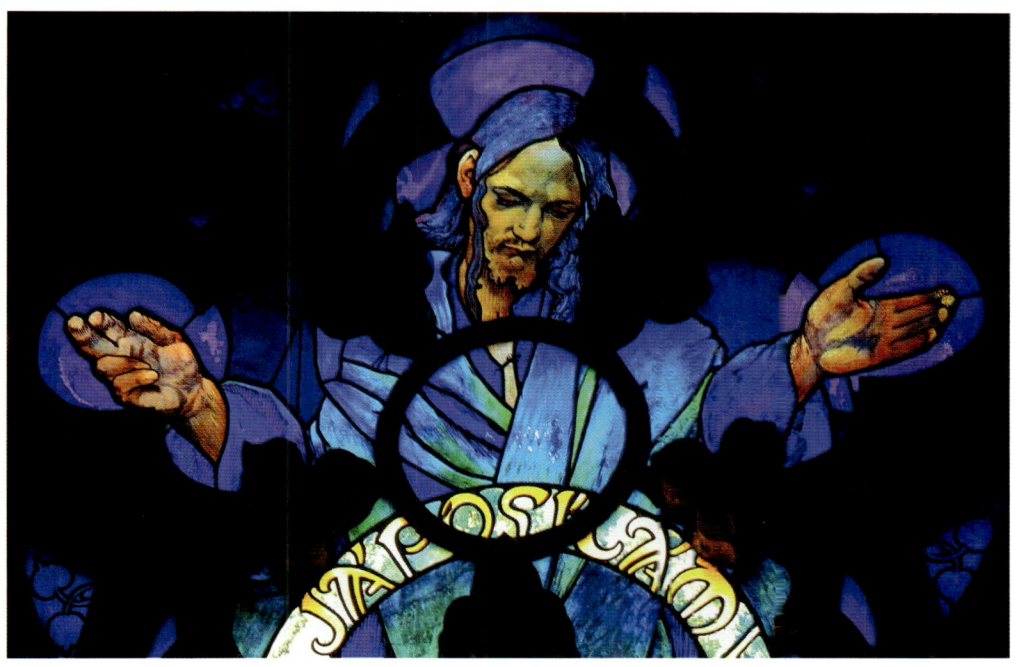

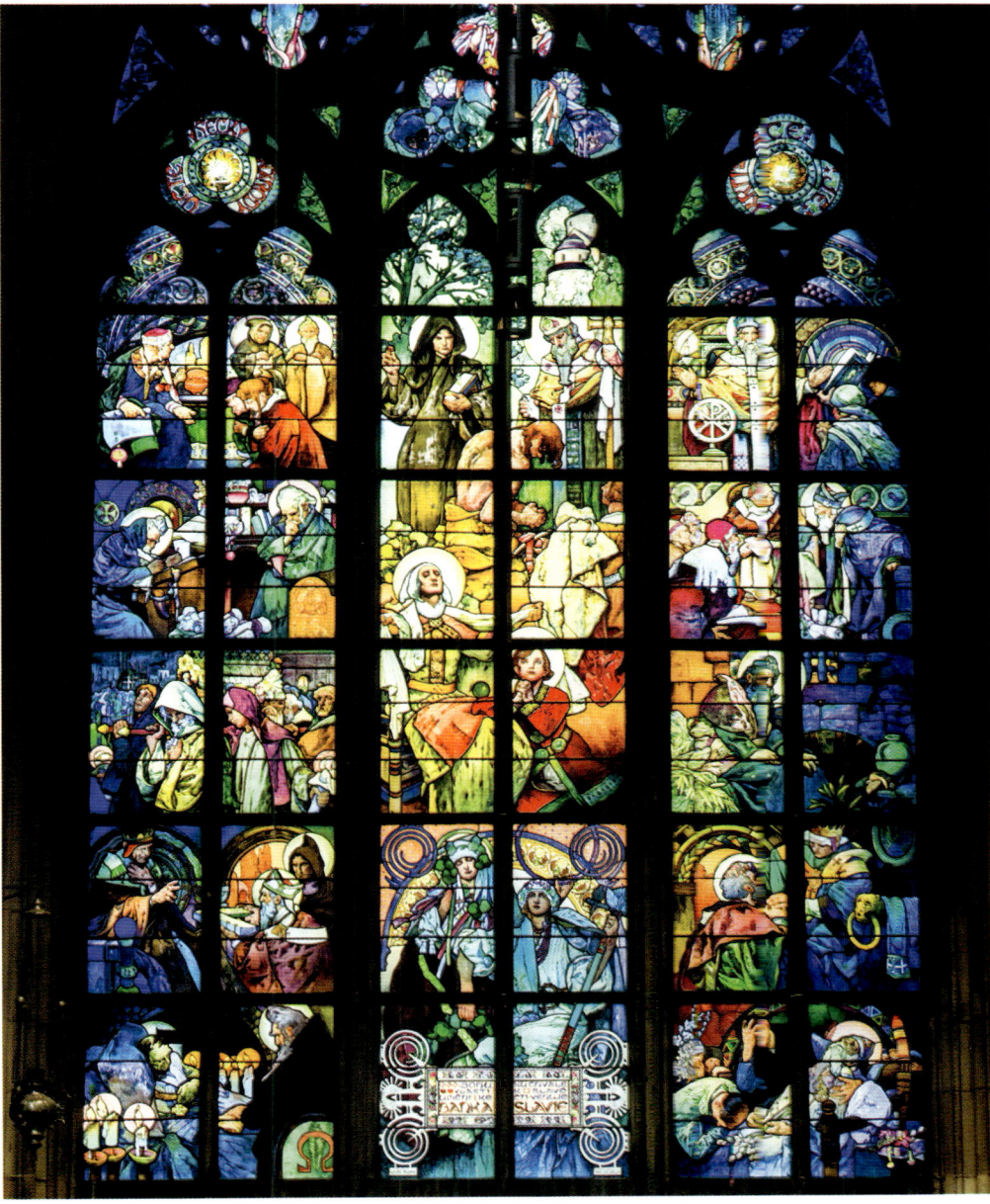

145

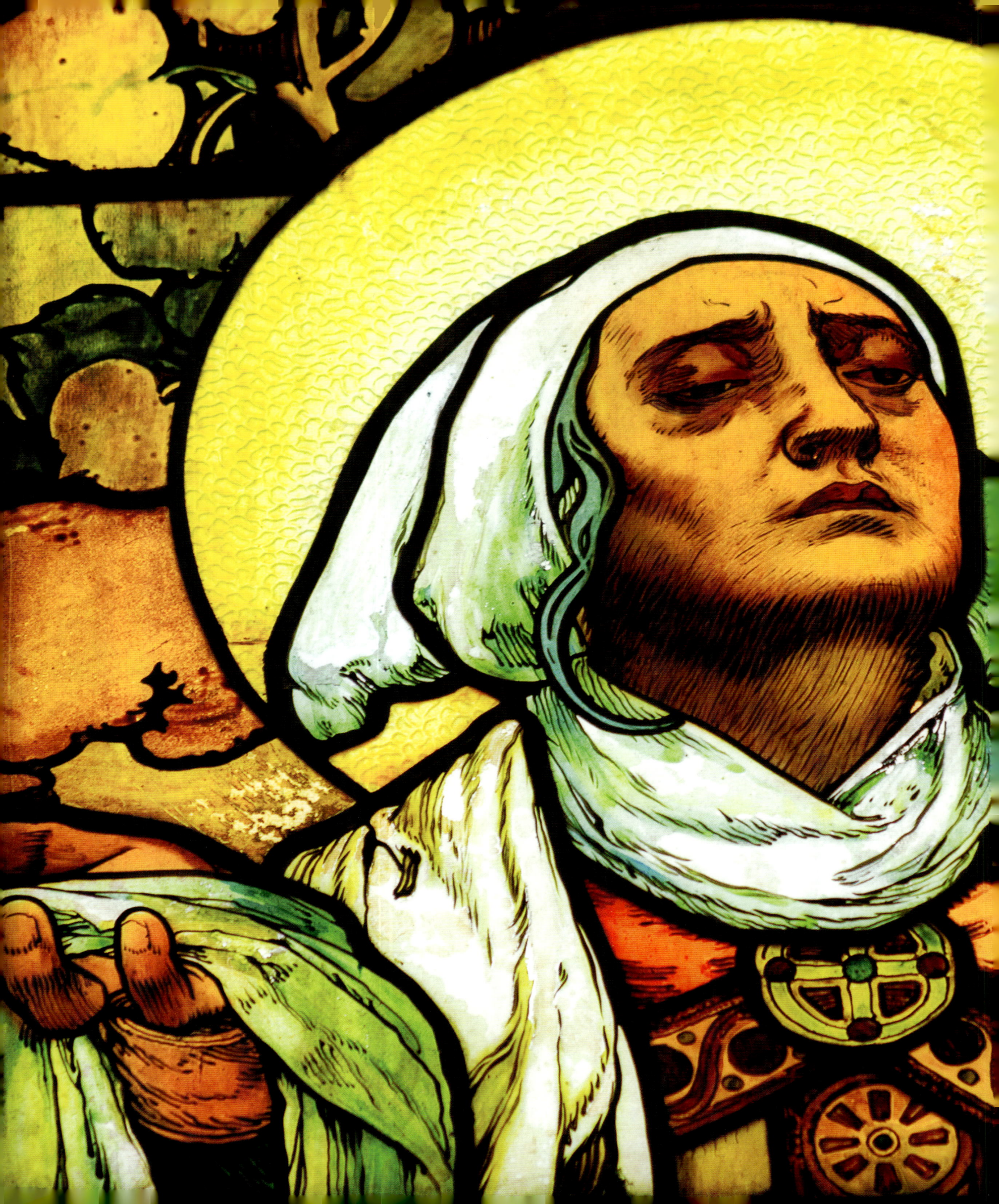

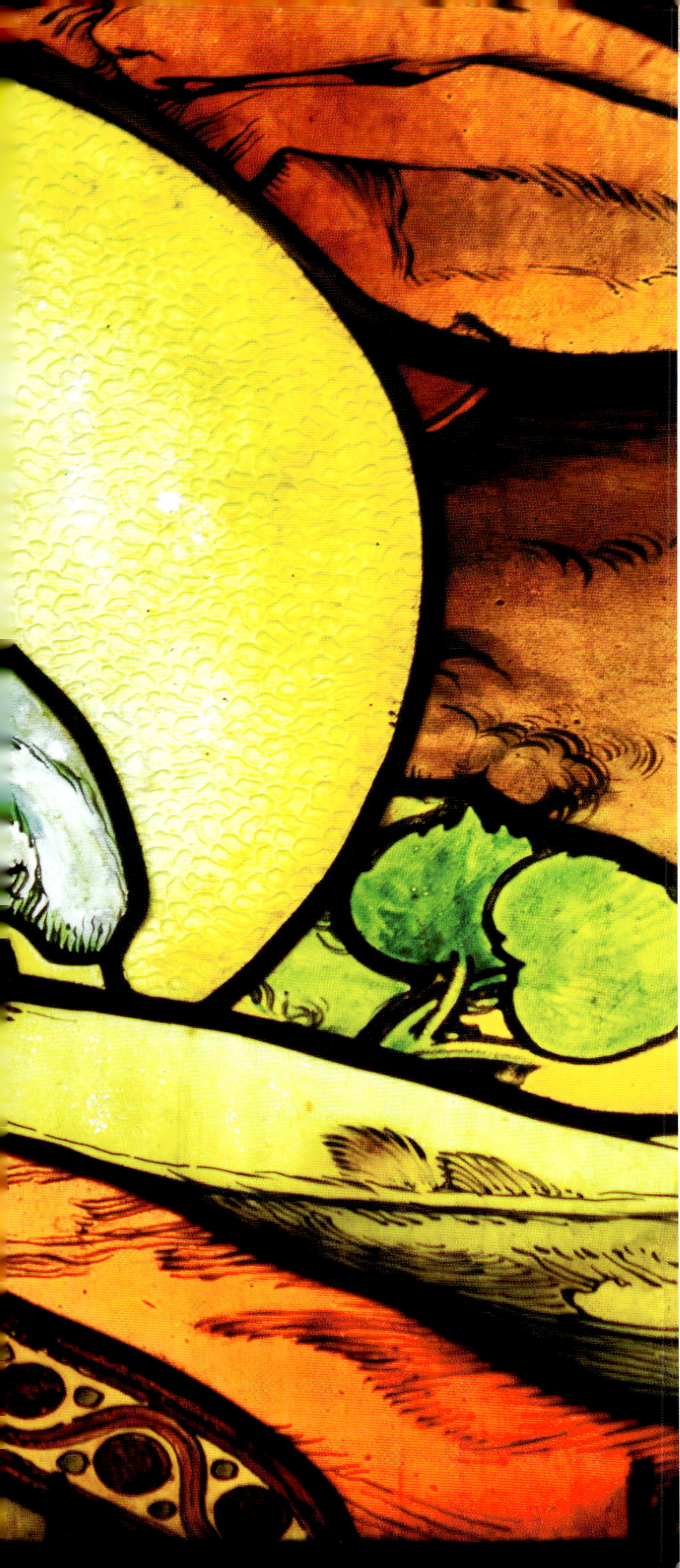

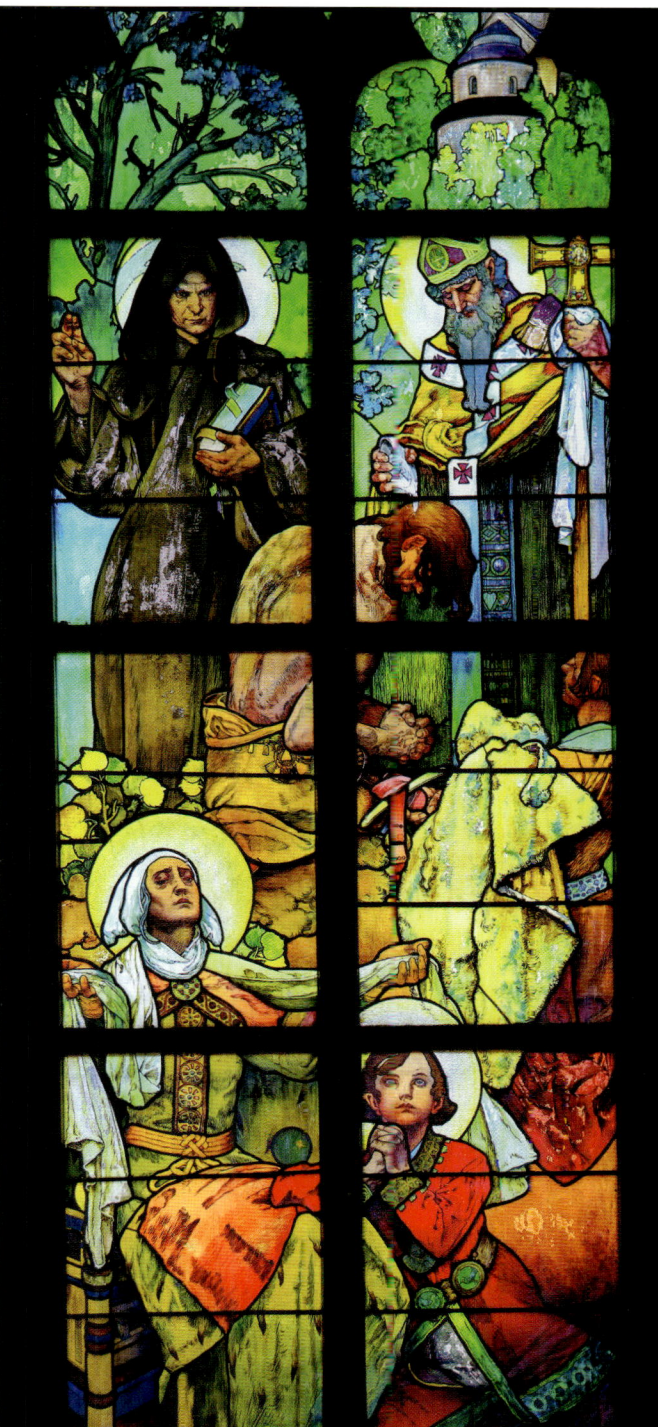

The top center panel shows a young St. Wenceslaus with his grandmother, St. Ludmila of Bohemia, surrounded by other saints. (1931). Stained glass. St. Vitus Cathedral, Prague.

[LEFT]
A closer detail of center panel showing St. Ludmila (1931). Stained glass. St. Vitus Cathedral, Prague.

[OVERLEAF]
Detail of lower center panel showing women personifying the Czech and Slovakian peoples (1931). Stained glass. St. Vitus Cathedral, Prague .

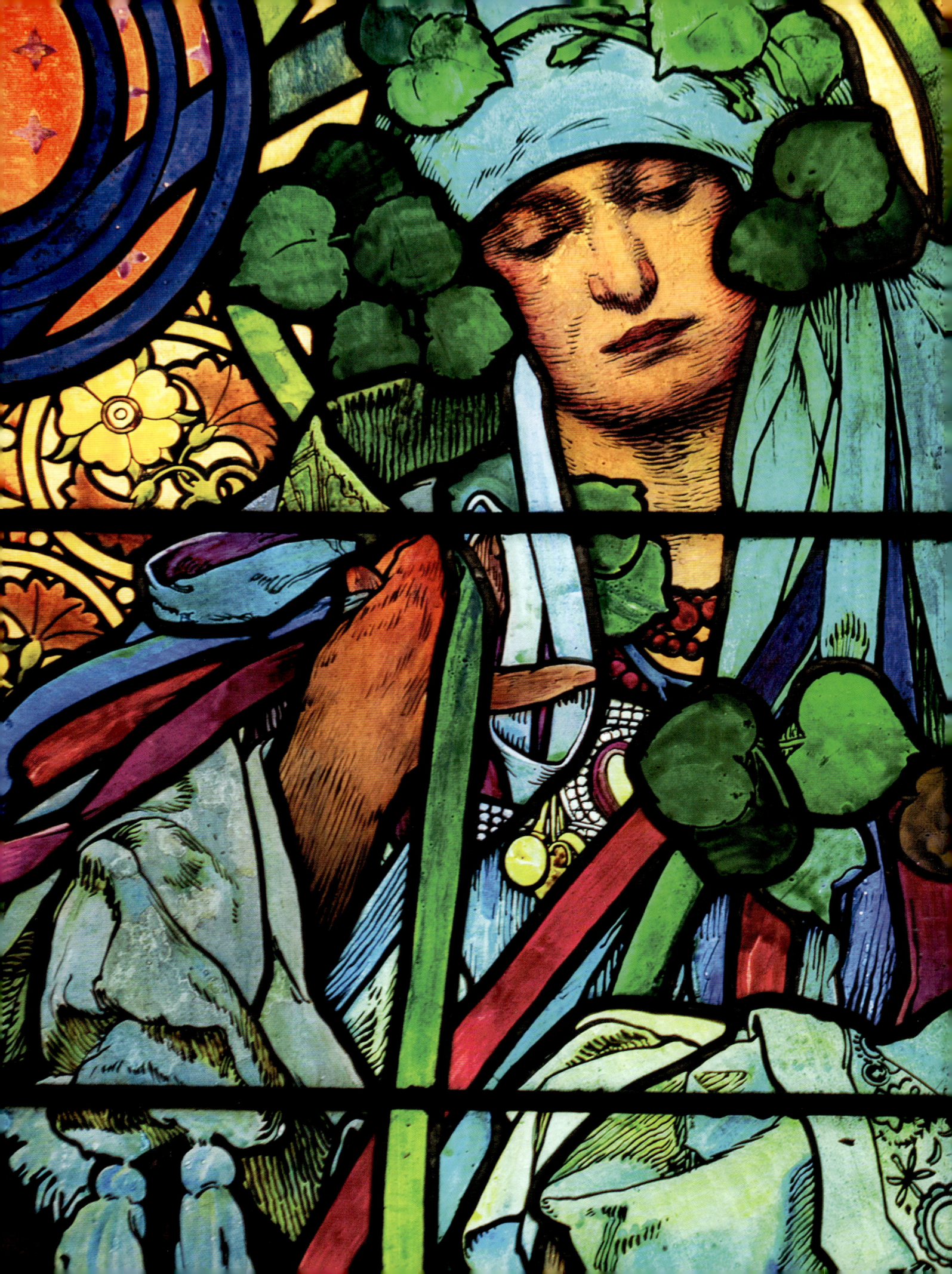

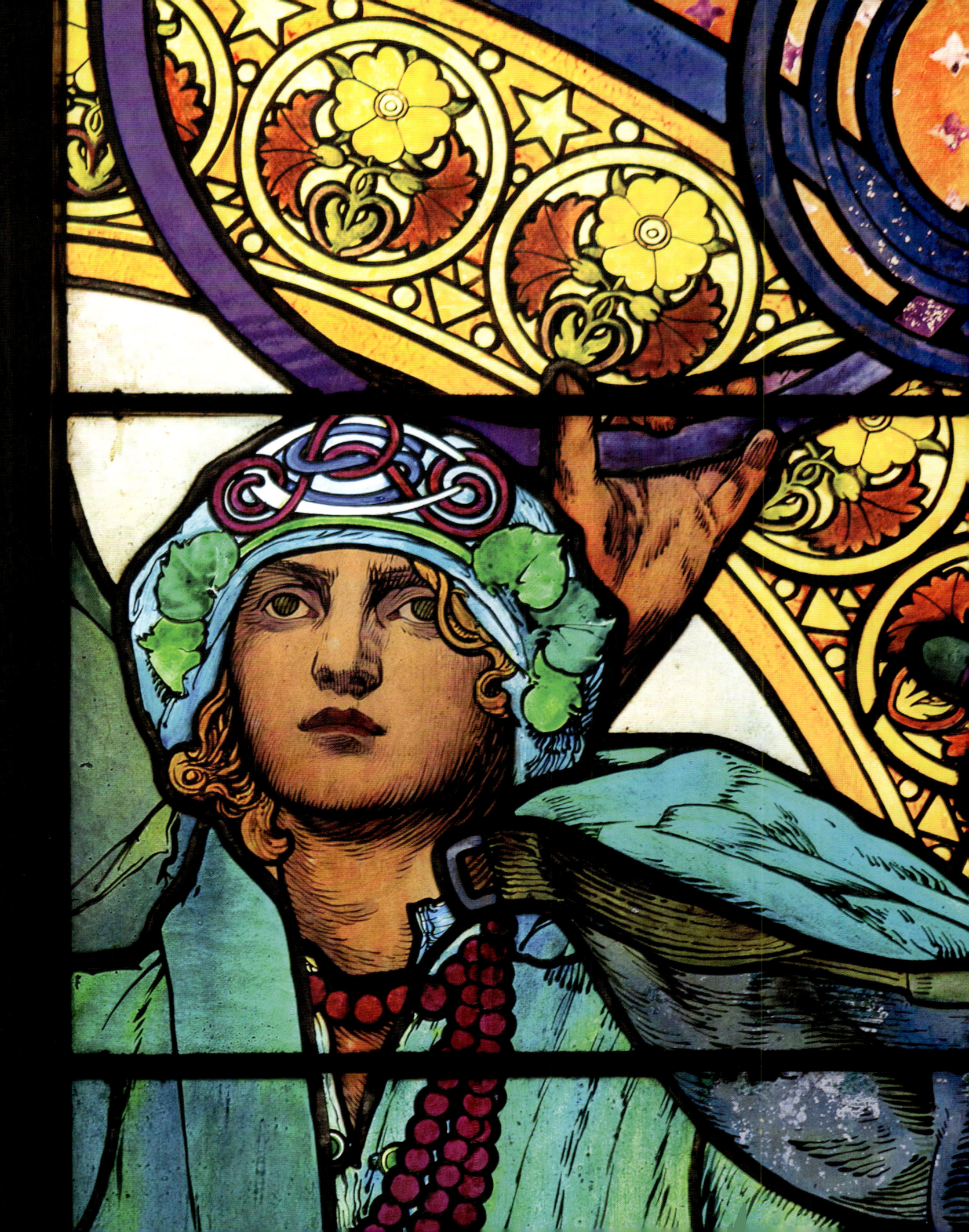

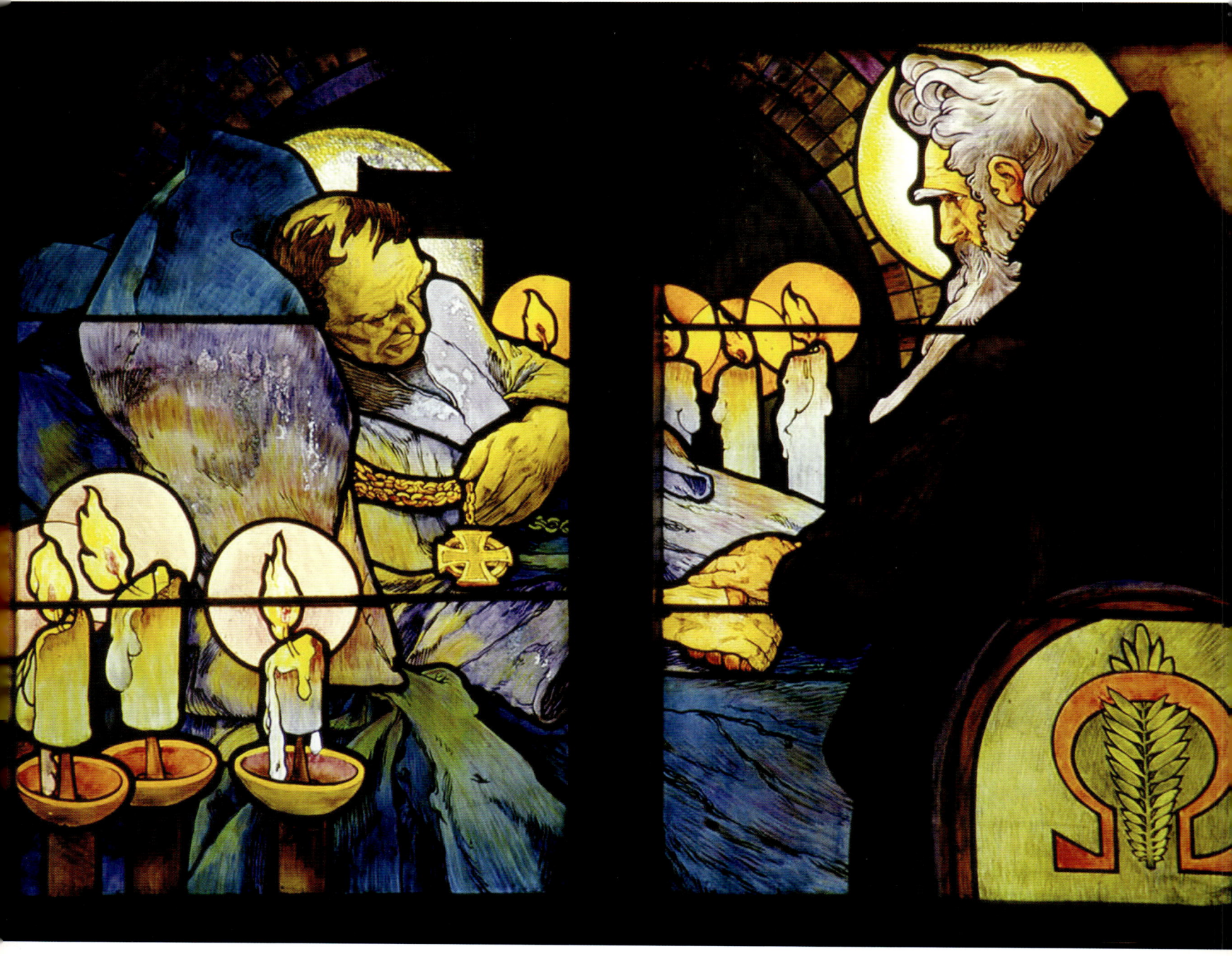

Detail of lower left panel showing Saints Cyril and Methodius (1931). St. Vitus Cathedral, Prague.

Mucha's stained glass features Saint Cyril and Saint Methodius, two brothers and Byzantine Christian theologians and missionaries, who became known as the "Apostles to the Slavs." During their missionary work, they are said to have devised the Glagolitic alphabet, the first alphabet used to transcribe Old Church Slavonic. This alphabet allowed the Slavic people to read the Bible.

[OVERLEAF]
Detail of a right panel, second from the bottom, showing Saints Cyril and Methodius (1931). St. Vitus Cathedral, Prague.

[OPPOSITE PAGE]
Detail of lower right panel showing Saints Cyril and Methodius (1931). St. Vitus Cathedral, Prague.

"*The new windows installed in St. Vitus's Cathedral in Prague in the first half of the twentieth century provide us with an example of the national sentiment that flourished in the Czech countries at that time.*"

~ CHRISTINE VENDREDI-AUZANNEAU,

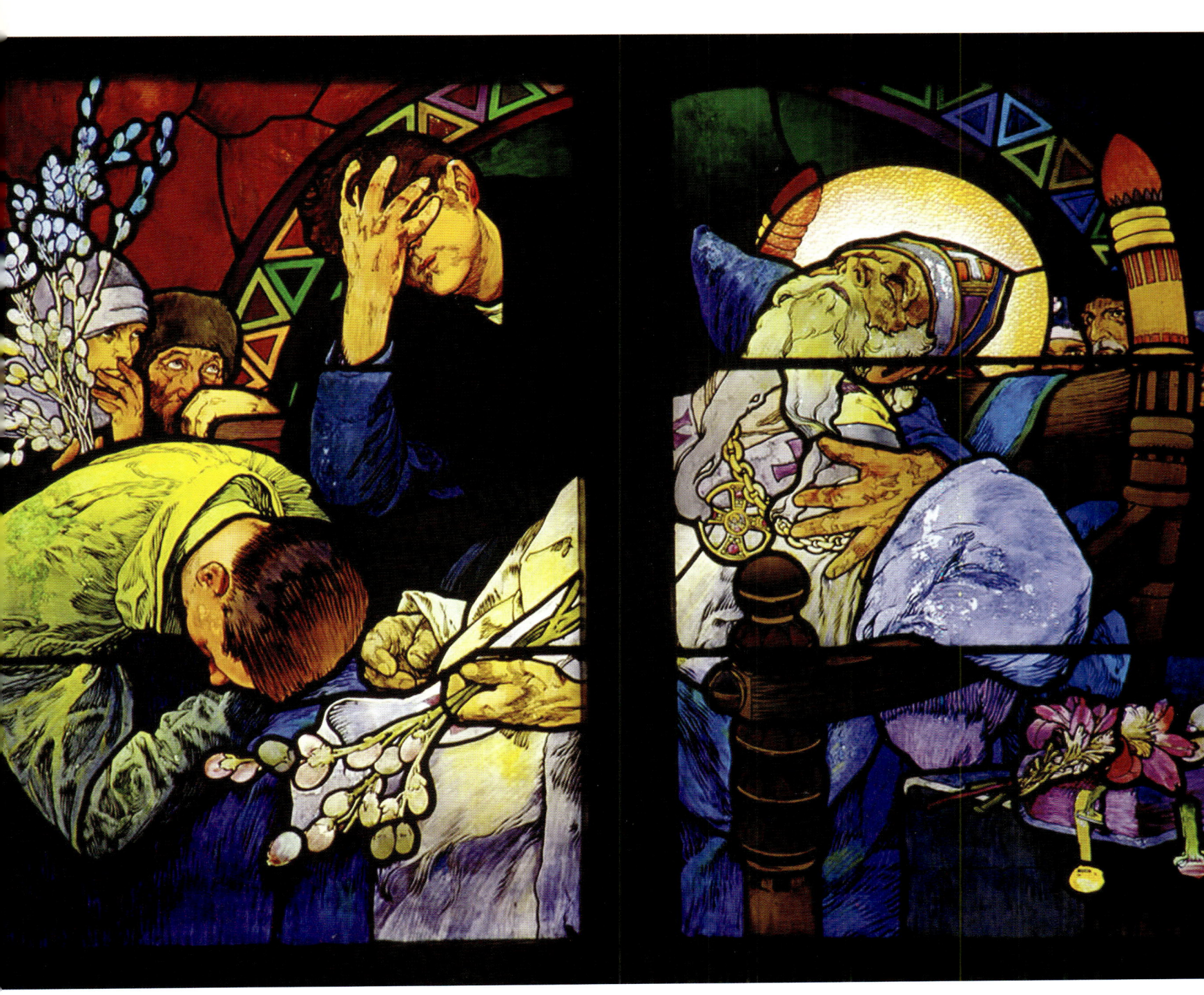

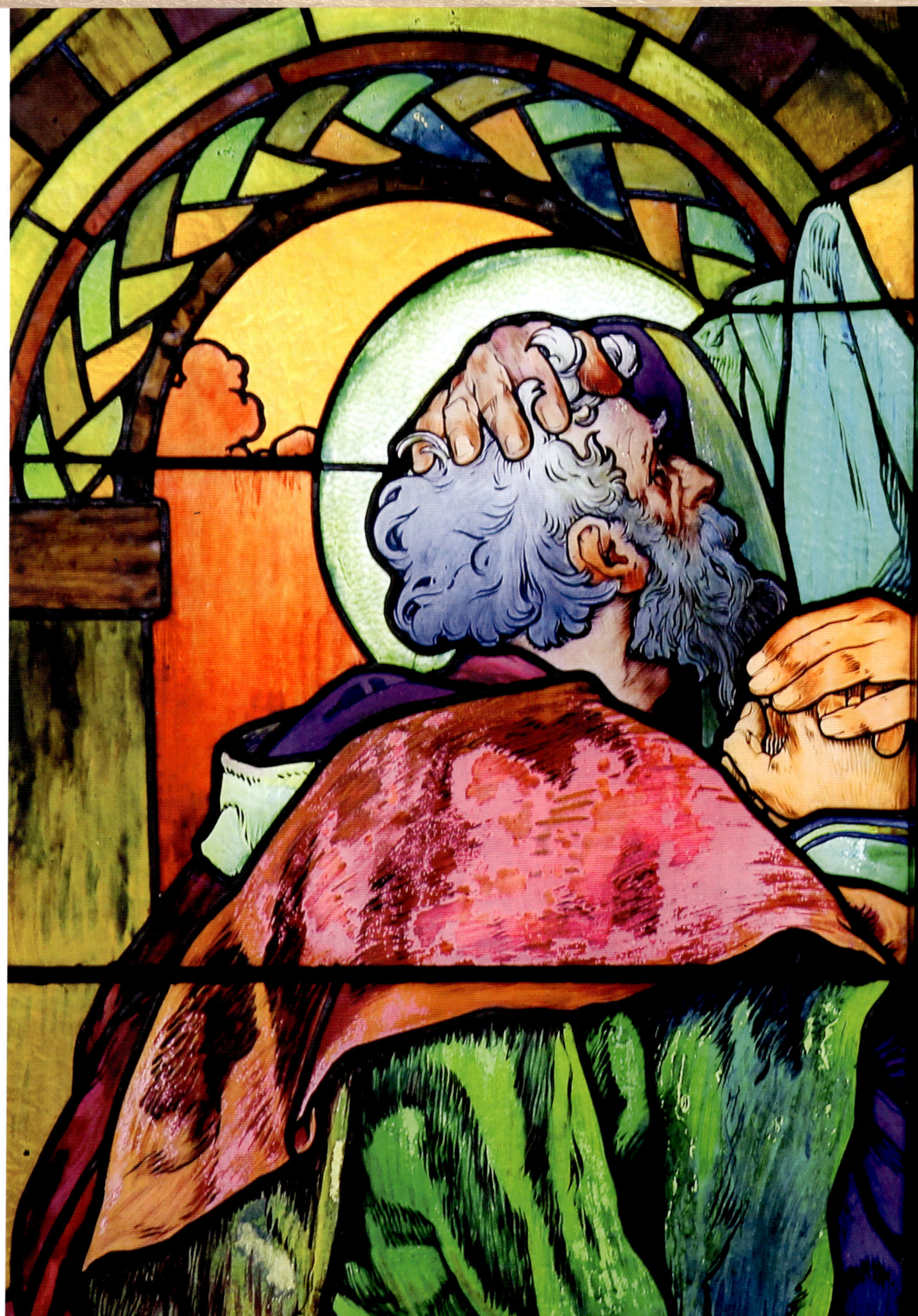

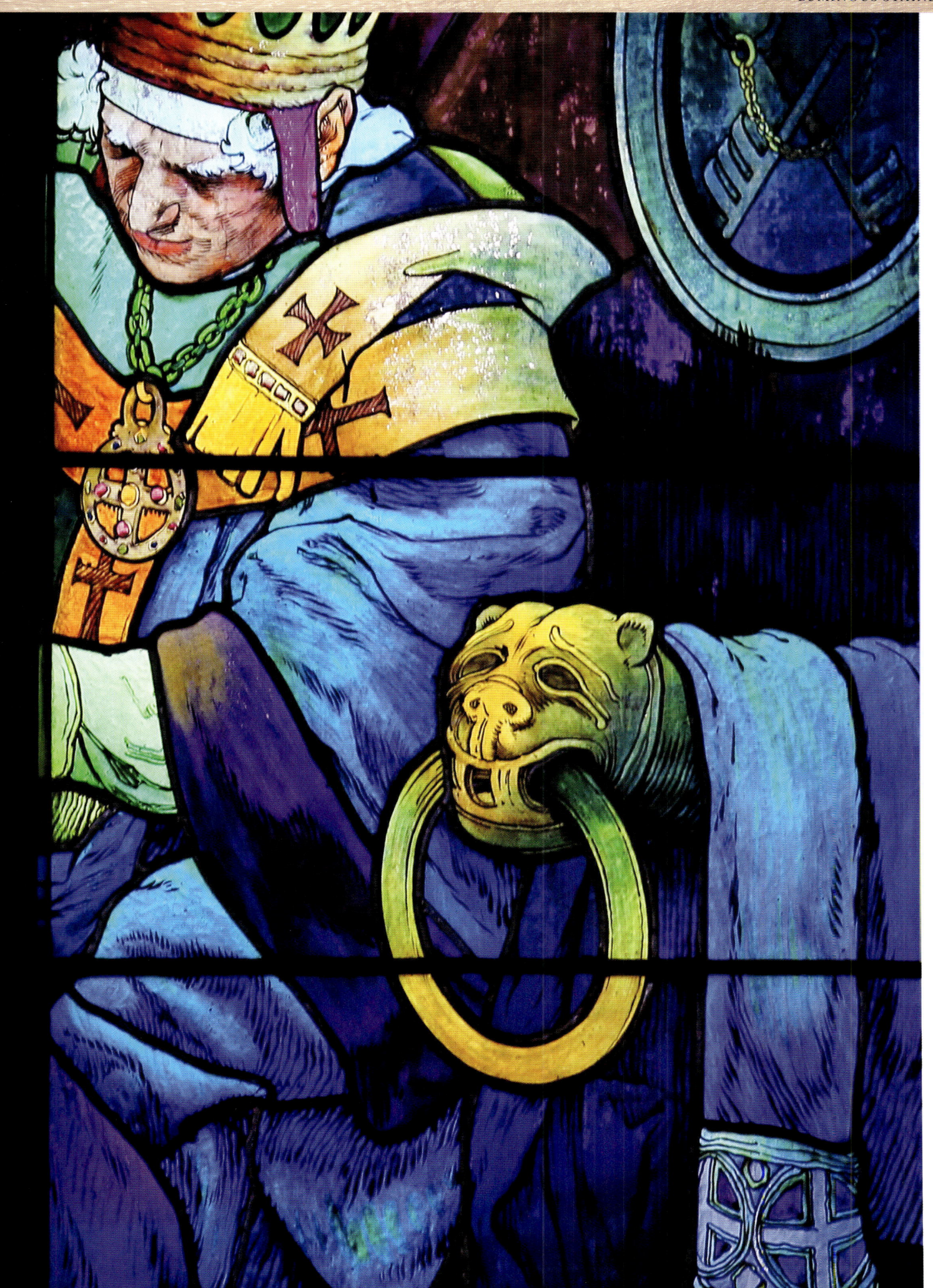

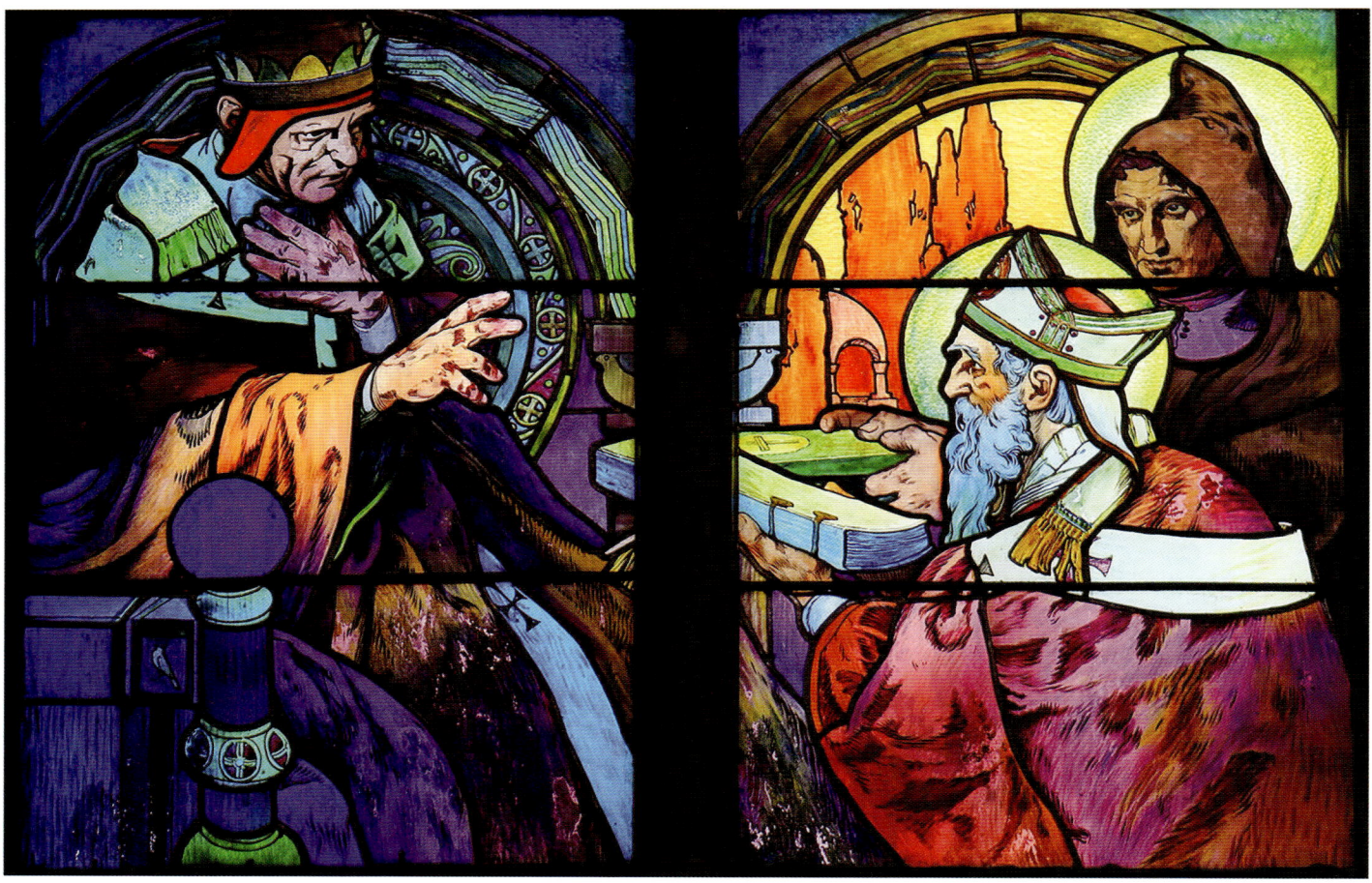

Lower-left panel, second from the bottom, showing Saints Cyril and Methodius (1931). St. Vitus Cathedral, Prague.

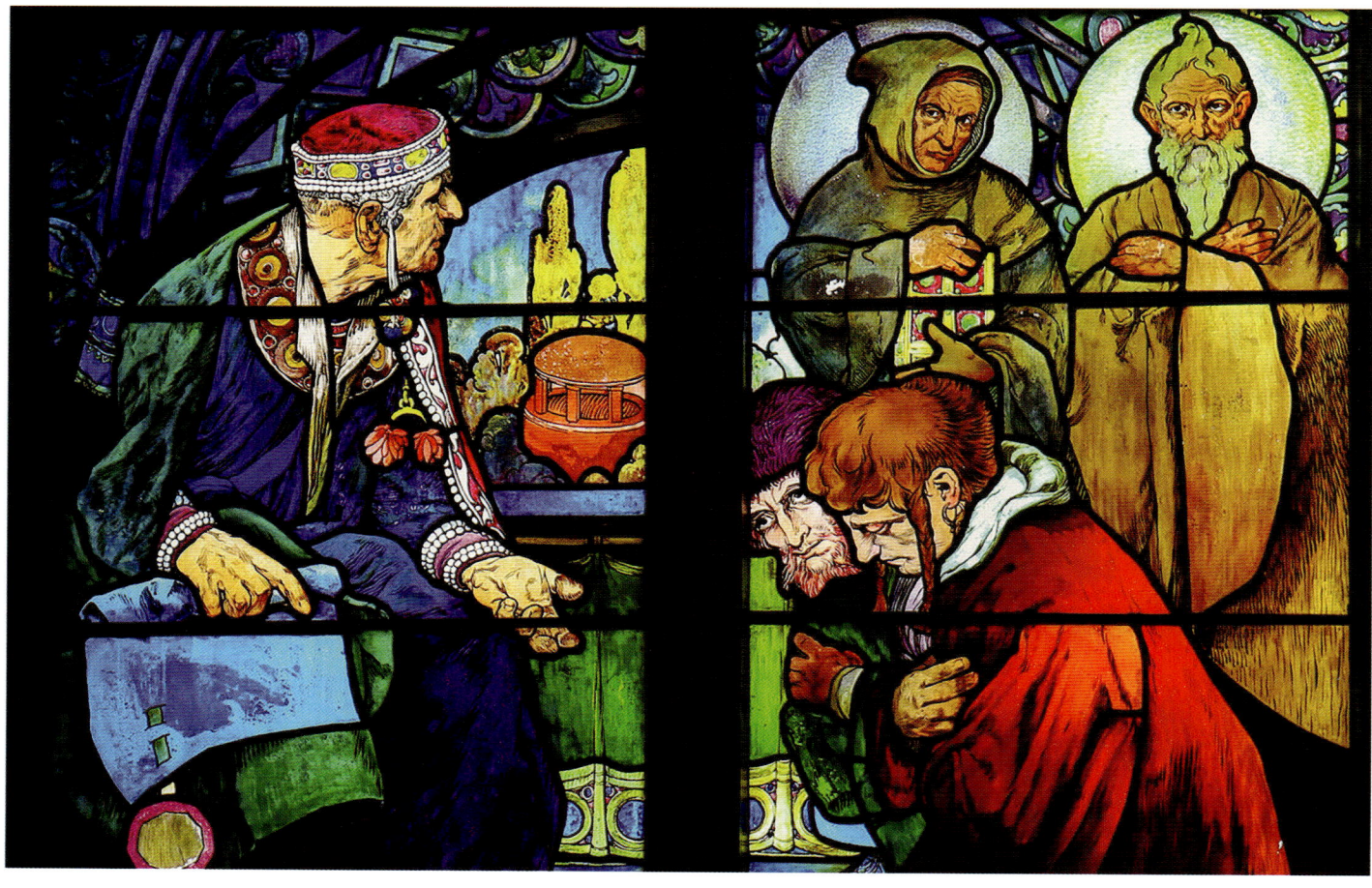

Top-left panel showing Saints Cyril and Methodius (1931). St. Vitus Cathedral, Prague.

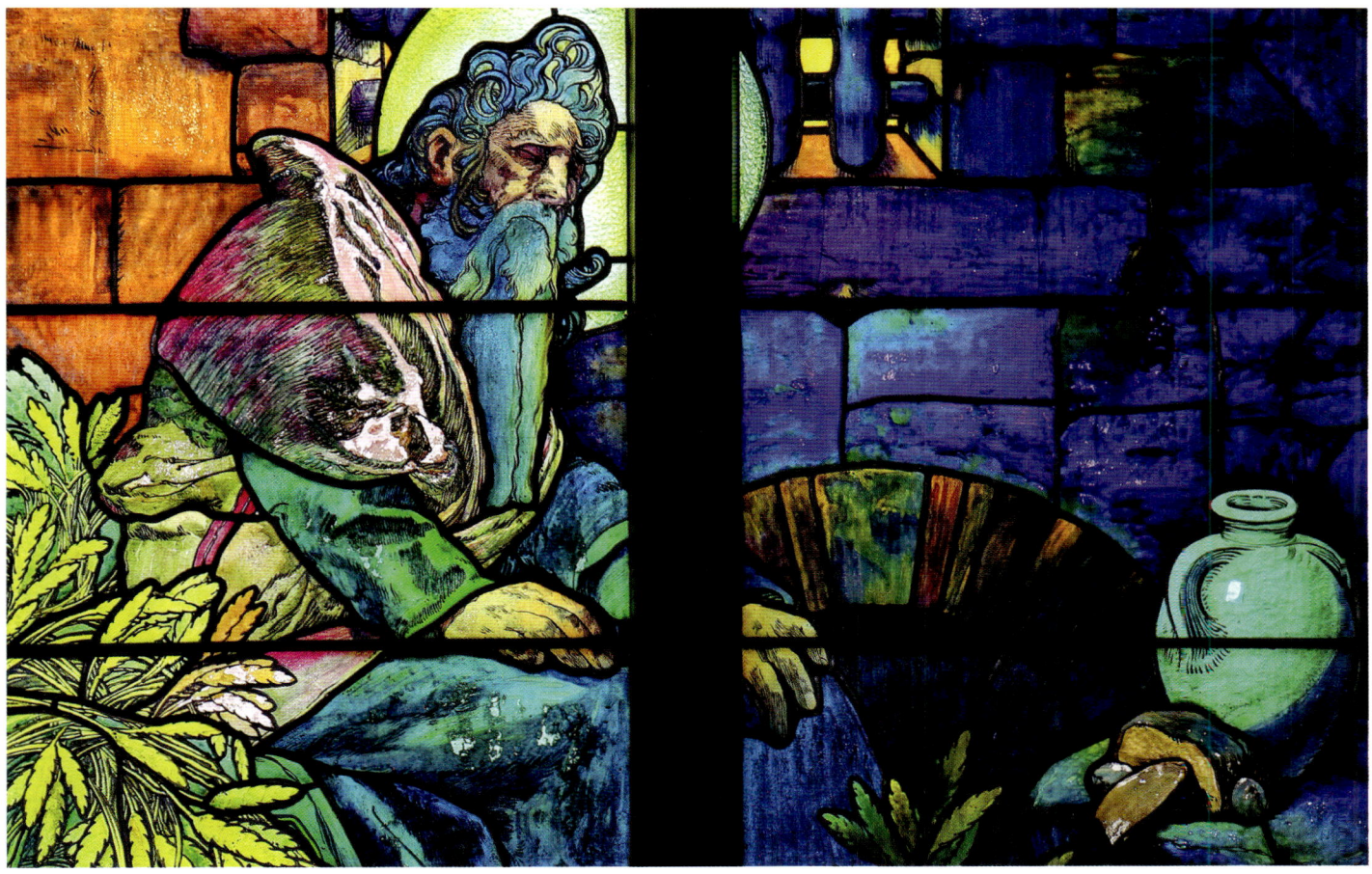

Right-middle panel showing Saint Methodius (1931). St. Vitus Cathedral, Prague.

[right]
Detail of center panel showing Saint Methodius baptizing a convert (1931). St. Vitus Cathedral, Prague.

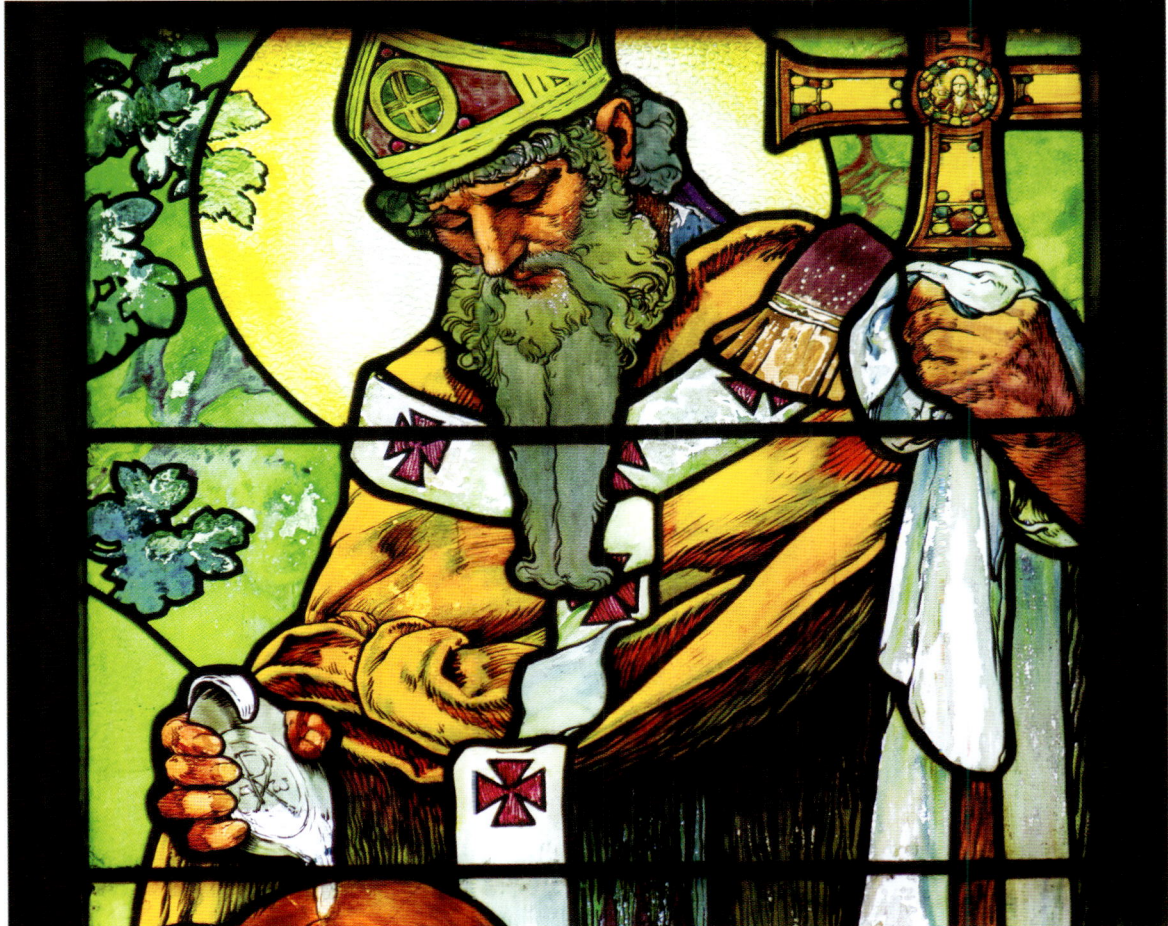

[OVERLEAF]
Left panel, second from the top, showing Saints Cyril and Methodius (1931). St. Vitus Cathedral, Prague.

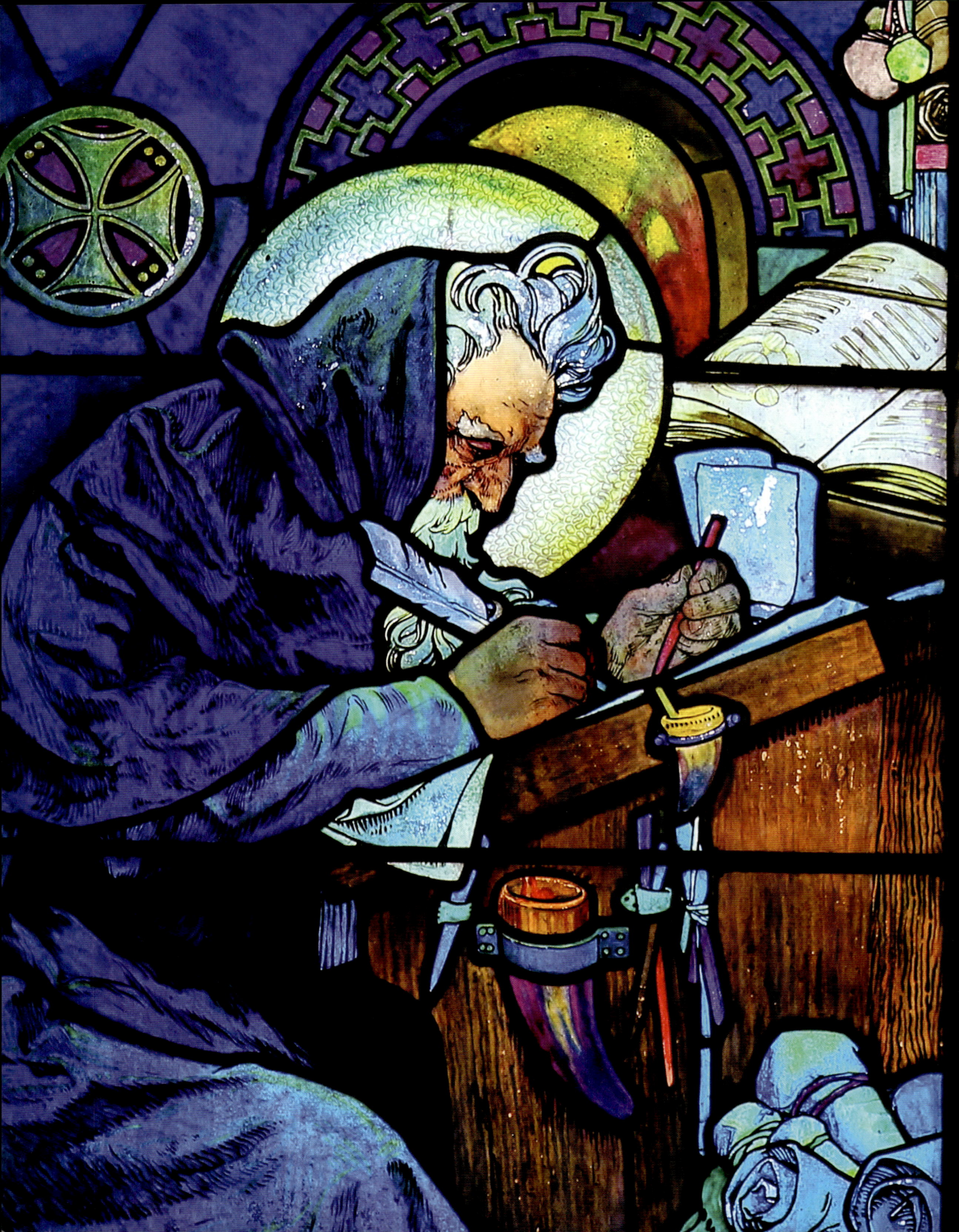

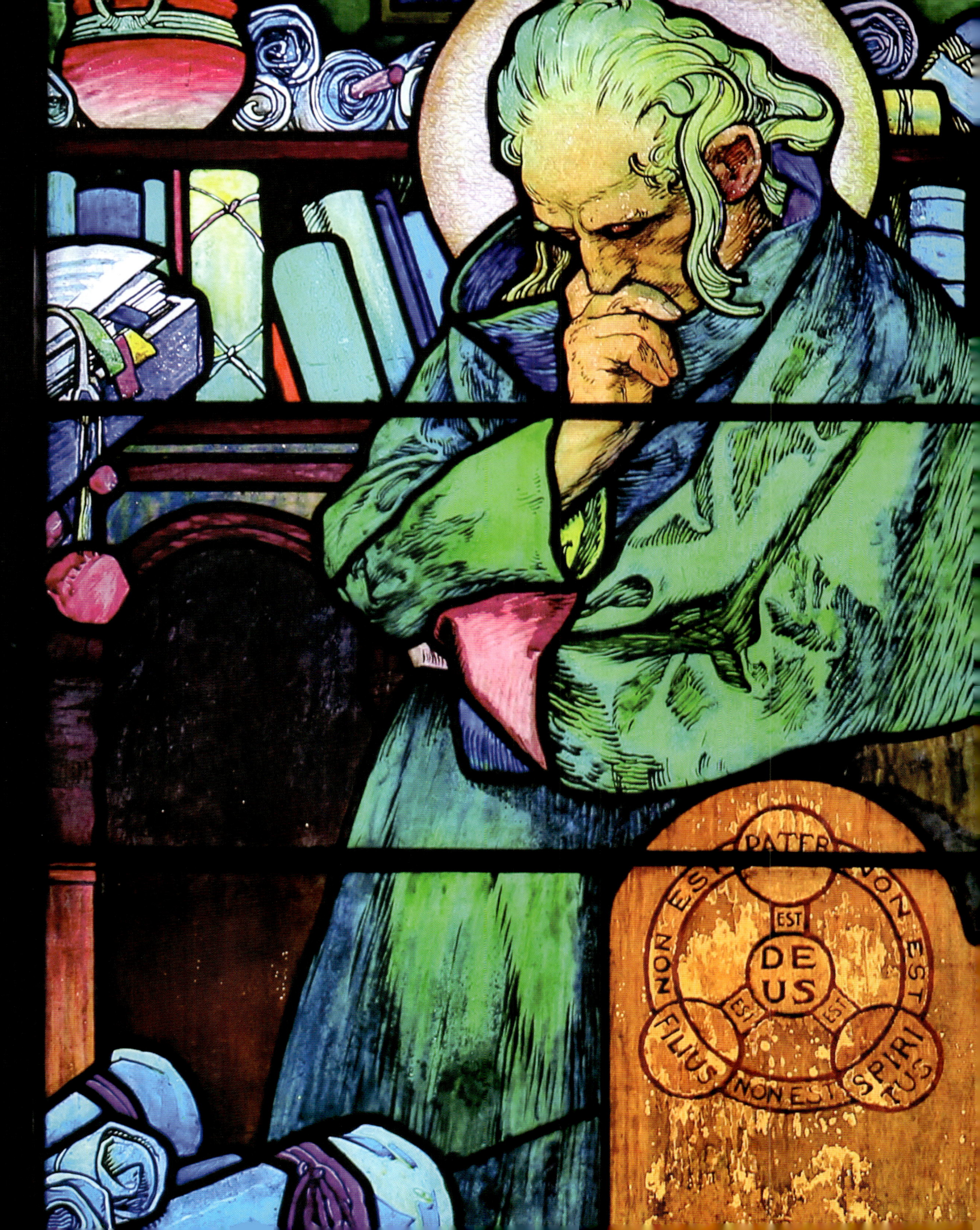

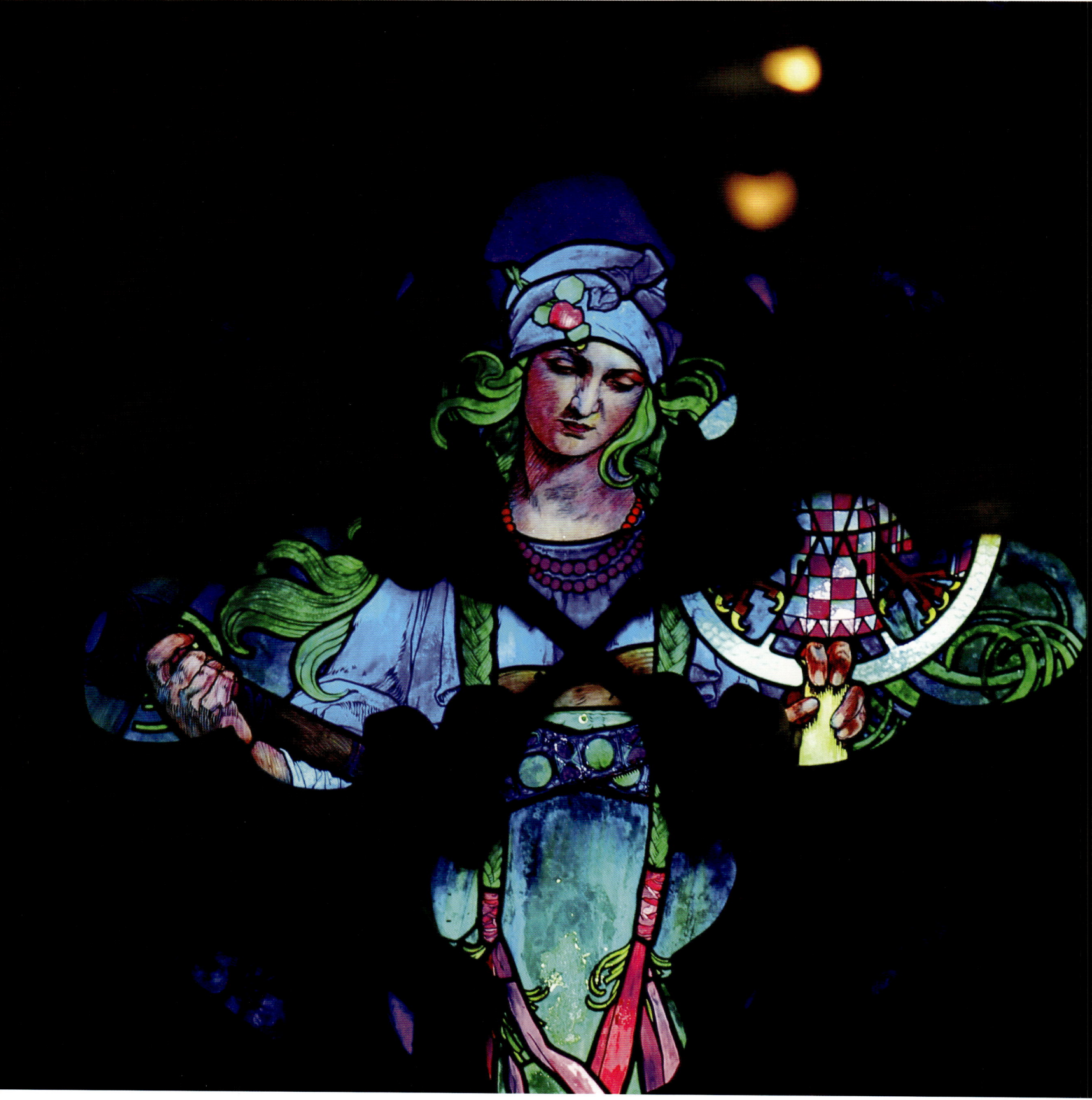

[OVERLEAF]
Left center panel, showing
Saints Cyril and Methodius (1931).
St. Vitus Cathedral, Prague.

[ABOVE]
Left rosette at top of panels
below Christ (1931). Stained glass.
St. Vitus Cathedral, Prague.

[OPPOSITE PAGE]
Right rosette at top of panels below
Christ (1931). Stained glass.
St. Vitus Cathedral, Prague.

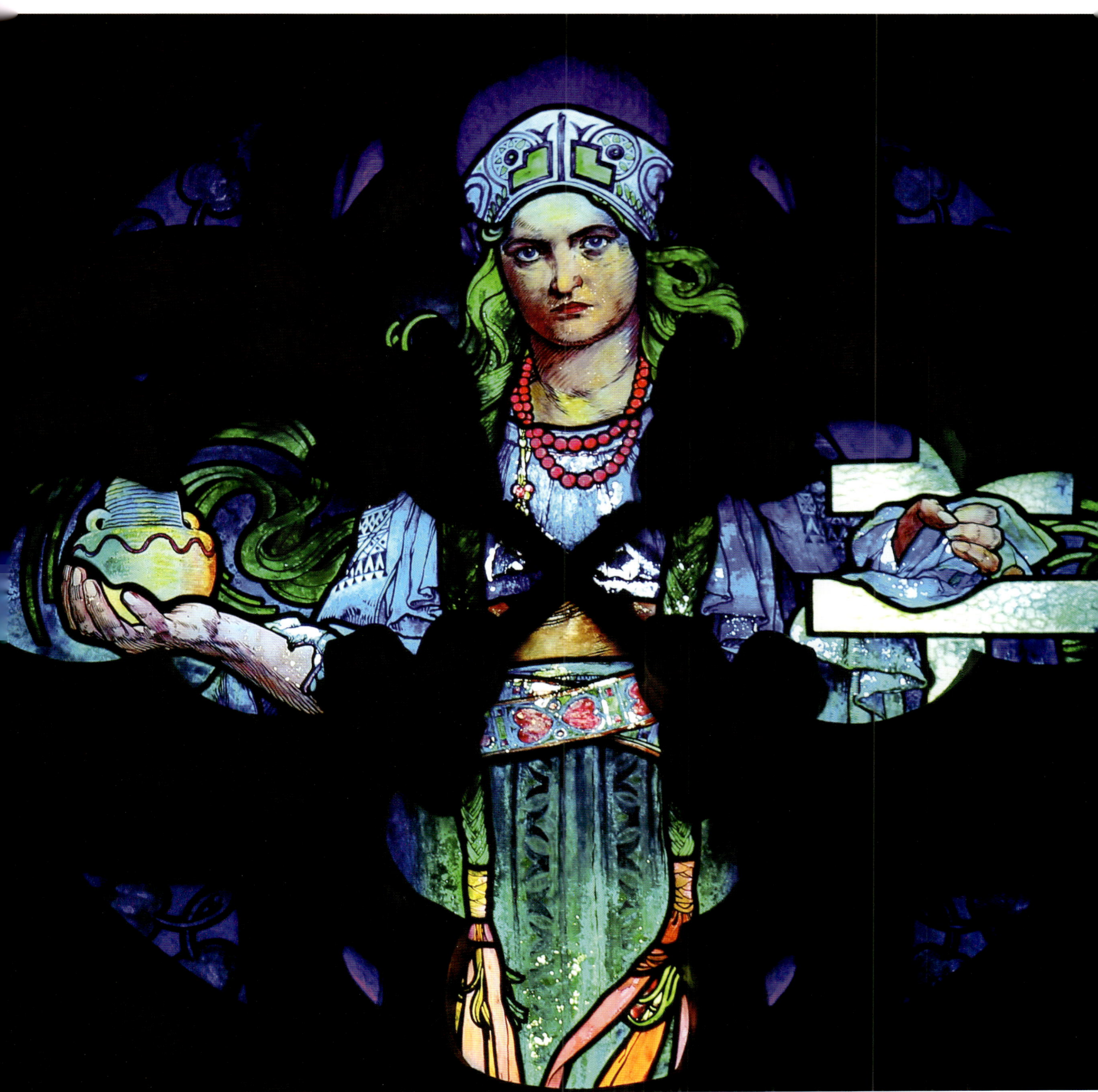

"*Art exists only to communicate a spiritual message.*"

~ ALPHONSE MUCHA

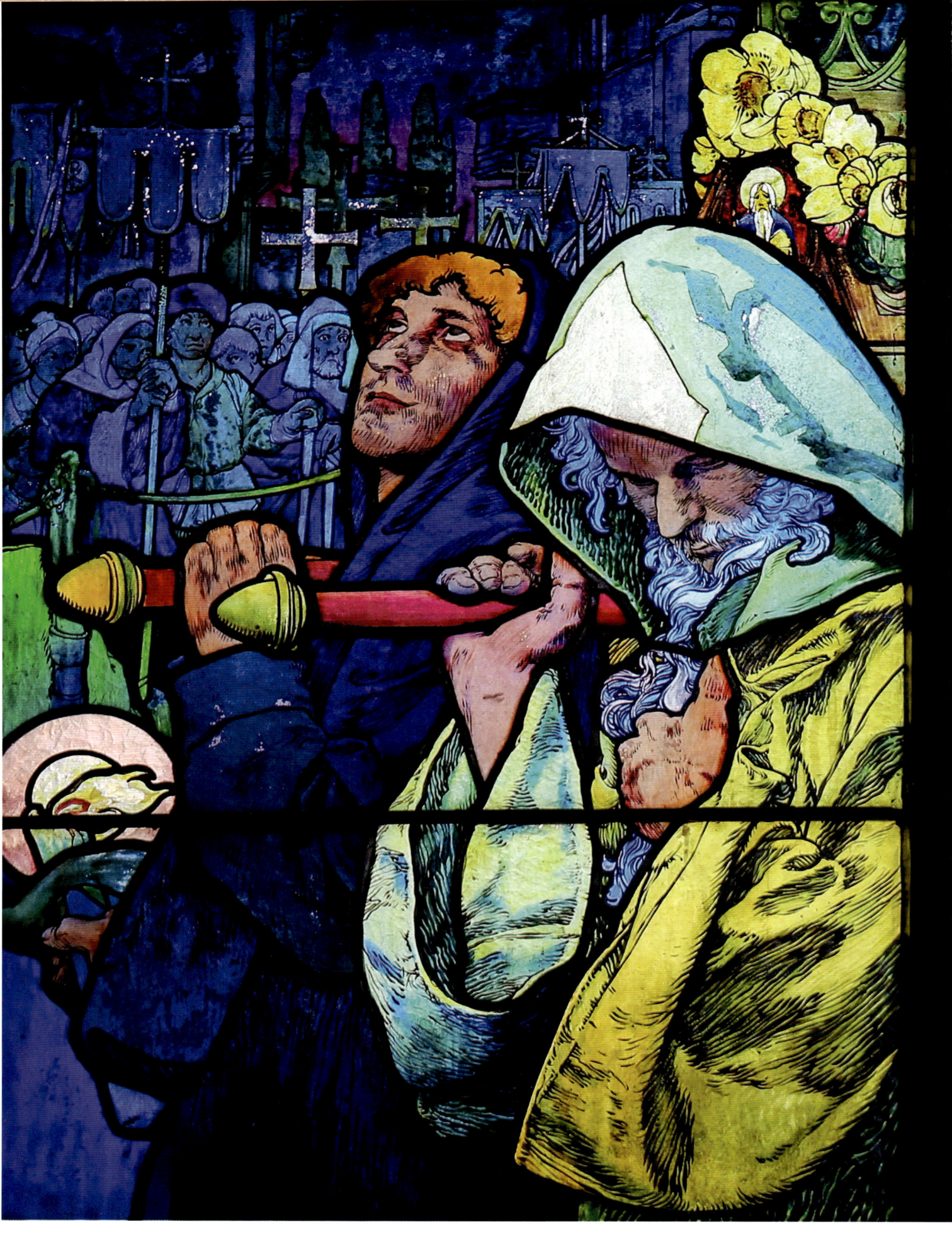

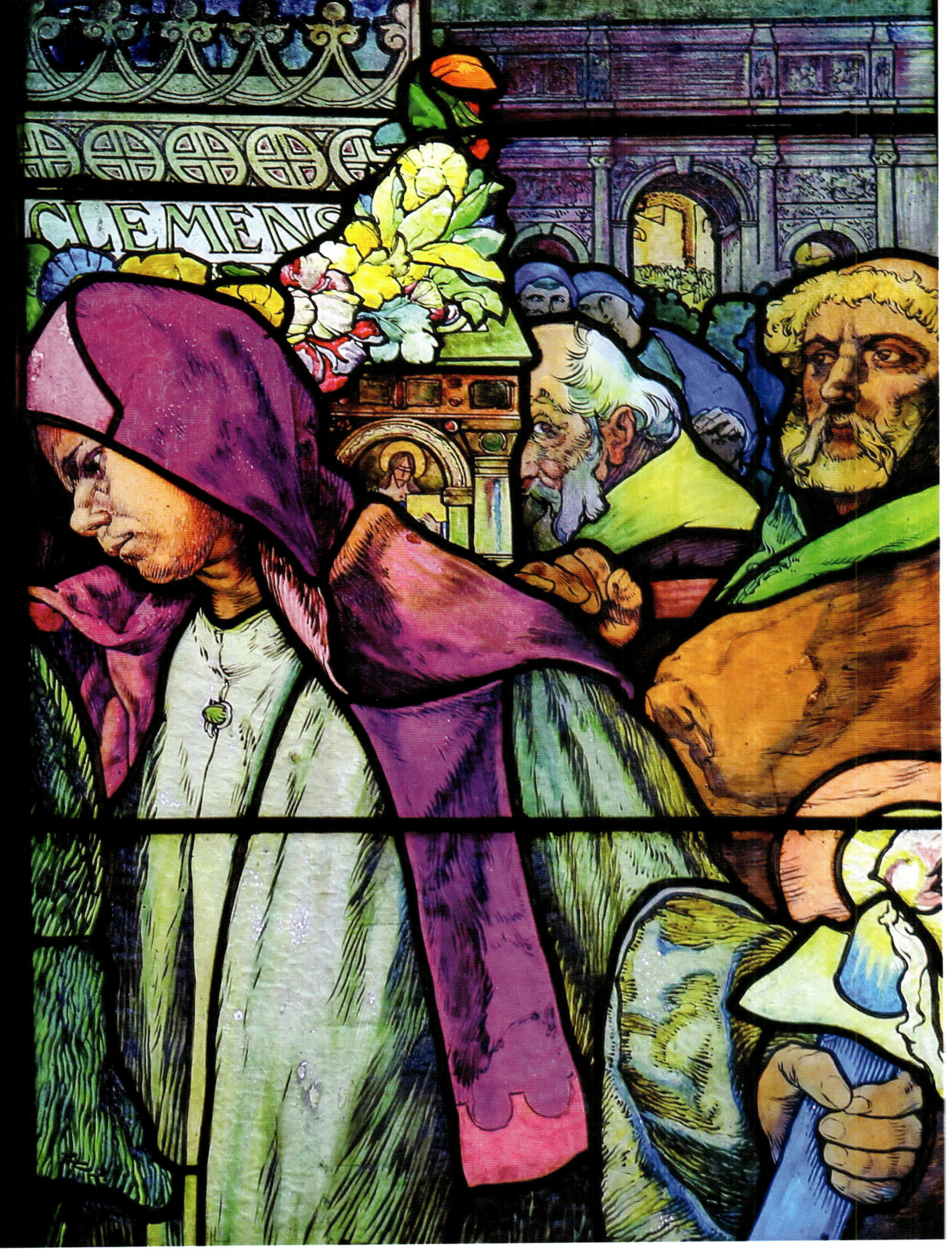

CRAFTING AN IMAGE FOR A NEW NATION

Mucha was a fierce patriot, and when the Republic of Czechoslovakia came into being on October 28, 1918, he wanted to do what he could to support its continuing existence. The government had need of a design for documents, which led Mucha to rush to complete the design of the new nation's postage stamps—a project he finished in just 24 hours. He chose for the first stamps a panorama of the eclectic Hradčany Castle (also known as the Prague Castle) enclosed within a frame of Art Nouveau–style borders.

"Every nation has a palladium of its own embodying past and future history. Ever since my boyhood I felt and saw in the architectural lines of St. Vitus Cathedral built so close to the castle, a powerful interpretation of our national symbol. I could, therefore, select no other subject for my design than Hradčany Castle and the surrounding architecture of the Middle Ages."

~ ALPHONSE MUCHA

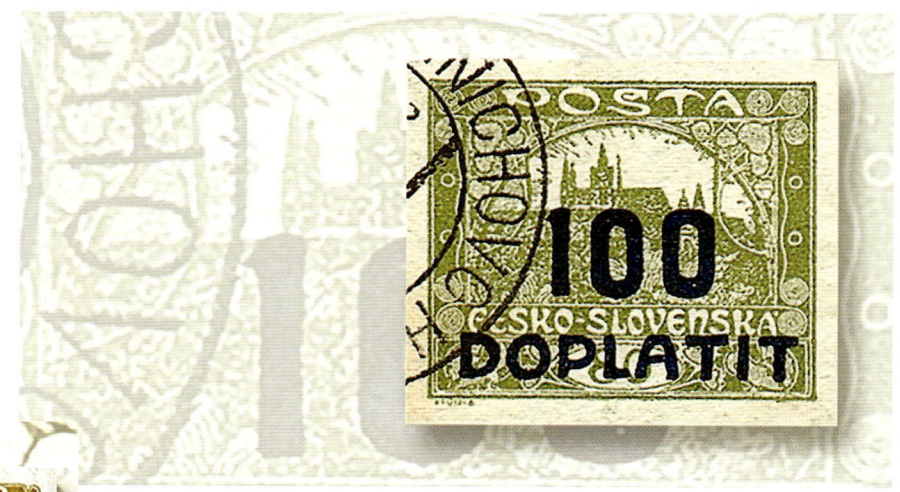

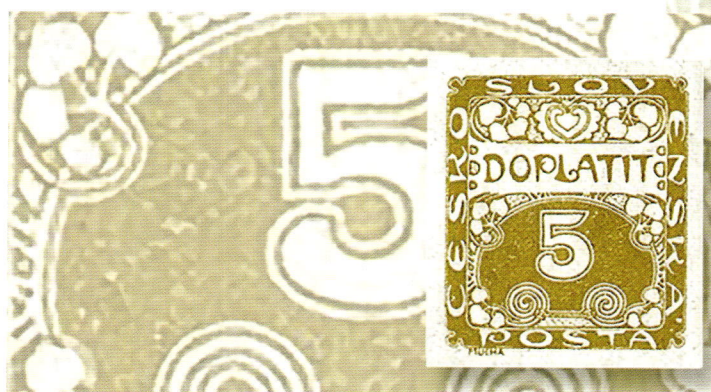

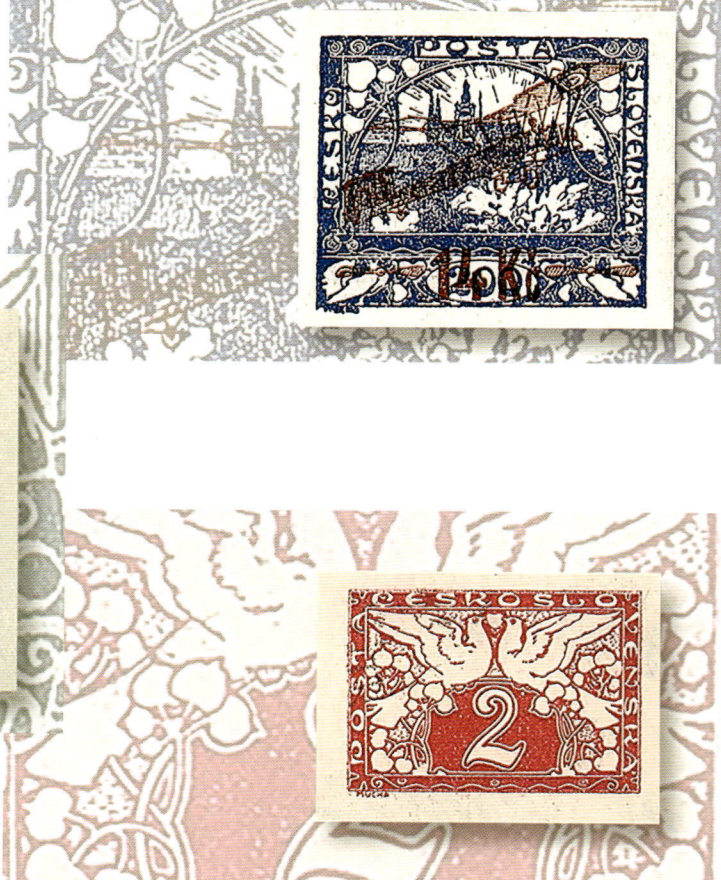

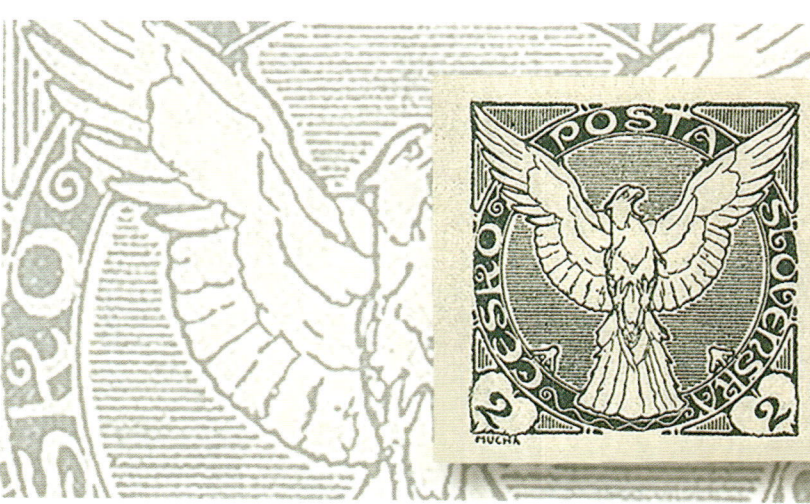

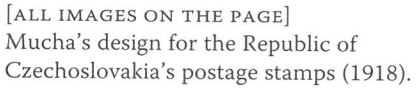

[ALL IMAGES ON THE PAGE]
Mucha's design for the Republic of Czechoslovakia's postage stamps (1918).

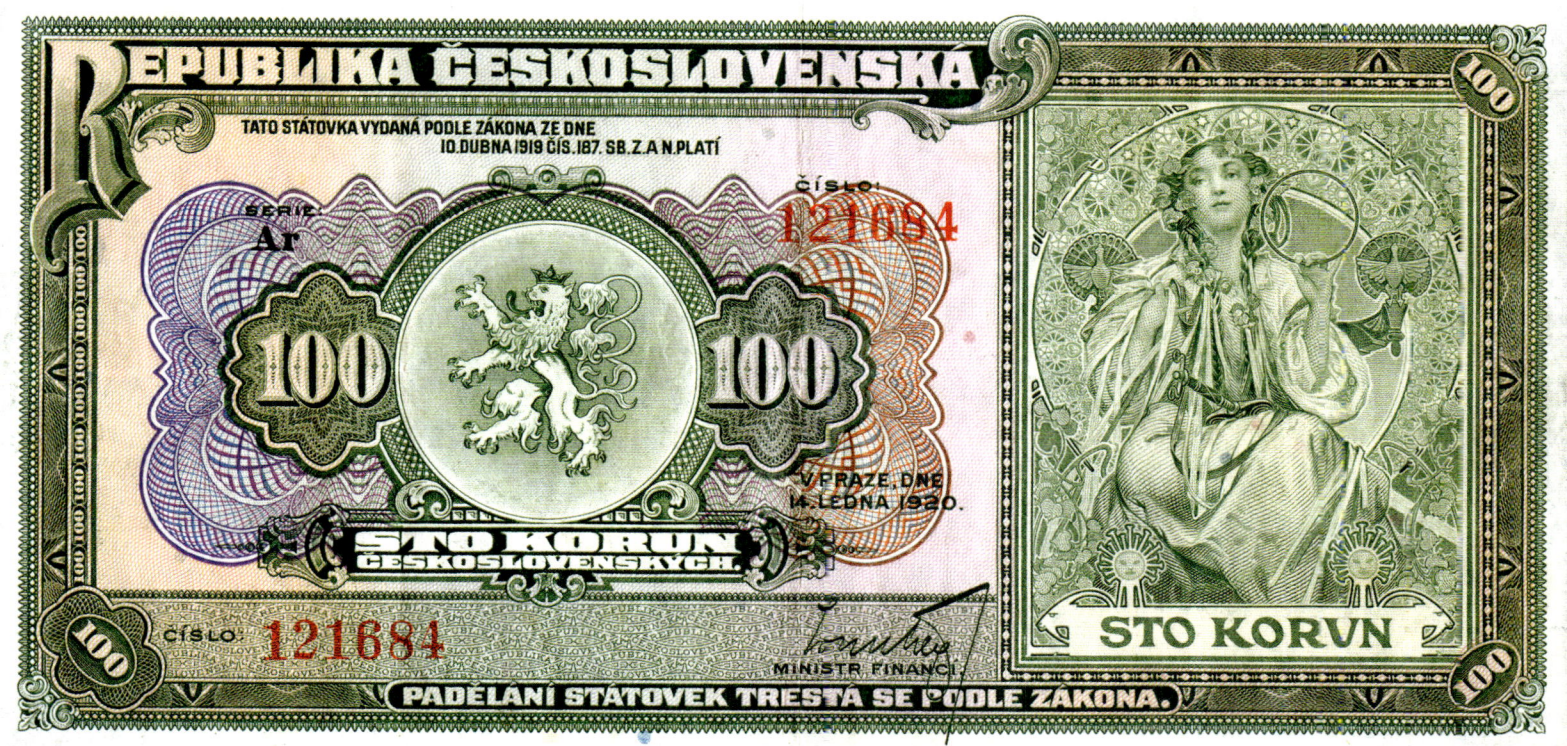

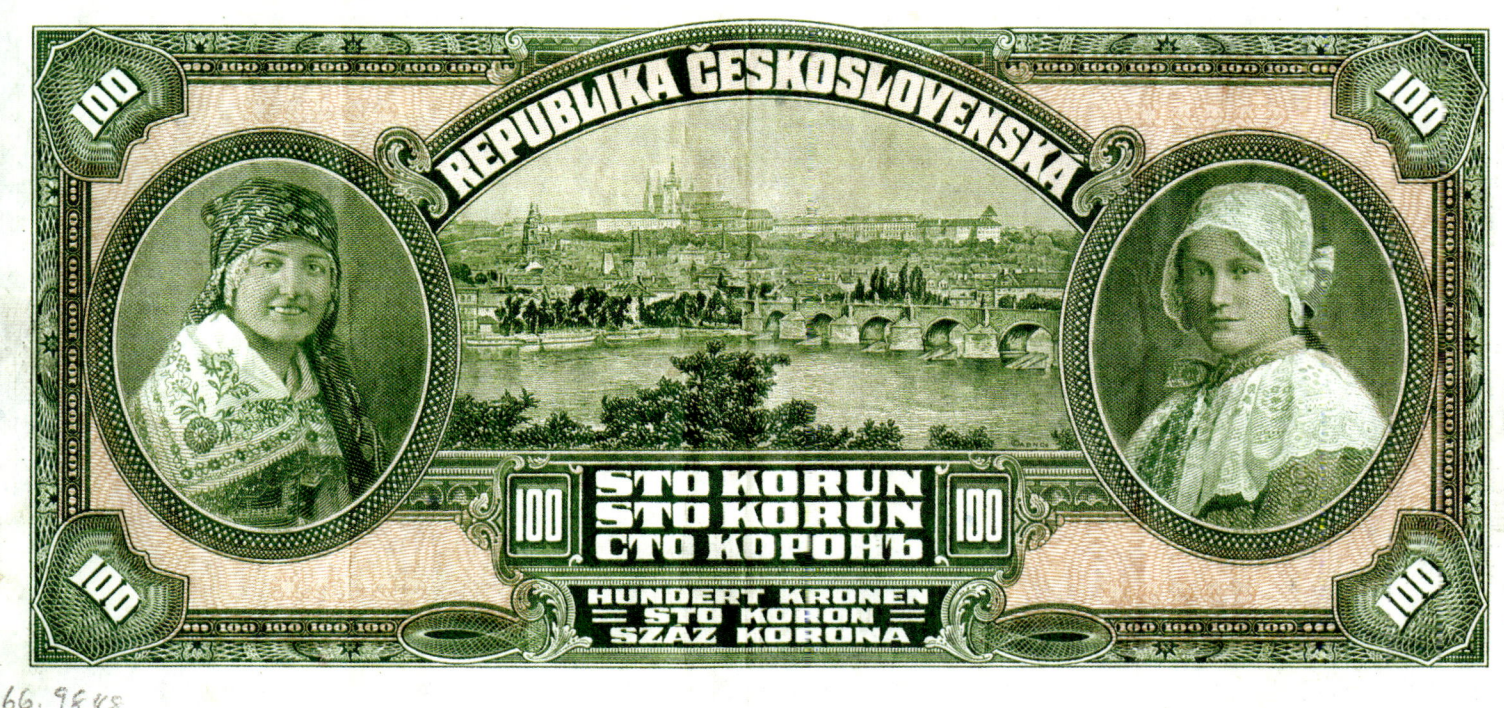

Back and front of **100 korun note**—artwork on the front right was originally designed by Alphonse Mucha for Slavia Insurance Company based on a portrait of Josephine Crane Bradley (1920). National Museum of American History, Washington, D.C.

In 1919, Mucha designed the Republic of Czechoslovakia's money, free of charge. The first design he completed was for the 100 korun note, and six additional notes followed over the next 10 years. To complete the urgent request, rather than come up with a completely new image for Slavia, the symbol of a unified Slavic state, Mucha reused his portrait of Josephine Crane Bradley.

"*Talk in my own way to the spirit of the nation, to its eyes which carry thoughts most quickly to the consciousness.*"

~ MUCHA TO HIS SON JIŘÍ, ON HIS JOY OF DESIGNING THE NEW MONEY

METAL WORK, SCULPTURE & PHOTOGRAPHY

Although Mucha was much more prolific an artist in the realms of graphic design, illustration, and painting, he also delved into sculpture, jewelry, and photography. His most notable sculpture is *La Nature,* a bronze bust of a woman wearing a tiara topped with a large ornamental stone. Mucha also developed several dozen photographs, mostly focusing on portraits and architectural subjects, as well as studies for his paintings and poster work.

[OPPOSITE PAGE]
La Nature (1900). Bronze, silver, gilding, and malachite. Royal Museums of Fine Arts in Brussels.

Mucha first displayed a cast of La Nature *in the Austrian section of the Paris Exposition in 1900. There are six casts of this gilded bronze statuette known to exist.*

[BELOW]
La Nature (1900). Bronze, silver, gilding, and marble. Virginia Museum of Fine Arts, Richmond (Sydney and Frances Lewis Art Nouveau Fund).

"*With her enigmatic expression, her closed eyes, focused on an inner world of reverie, the symbolist woman evokes chimeric images haunted by death, witchcraft and the widespread cult of the absorption of hallucinatory drugs.*"

~ PHILIPPE JULLIAN *ESTHÈTES ET MAGICIENS* (1969), ABOUT *LA NATURE*

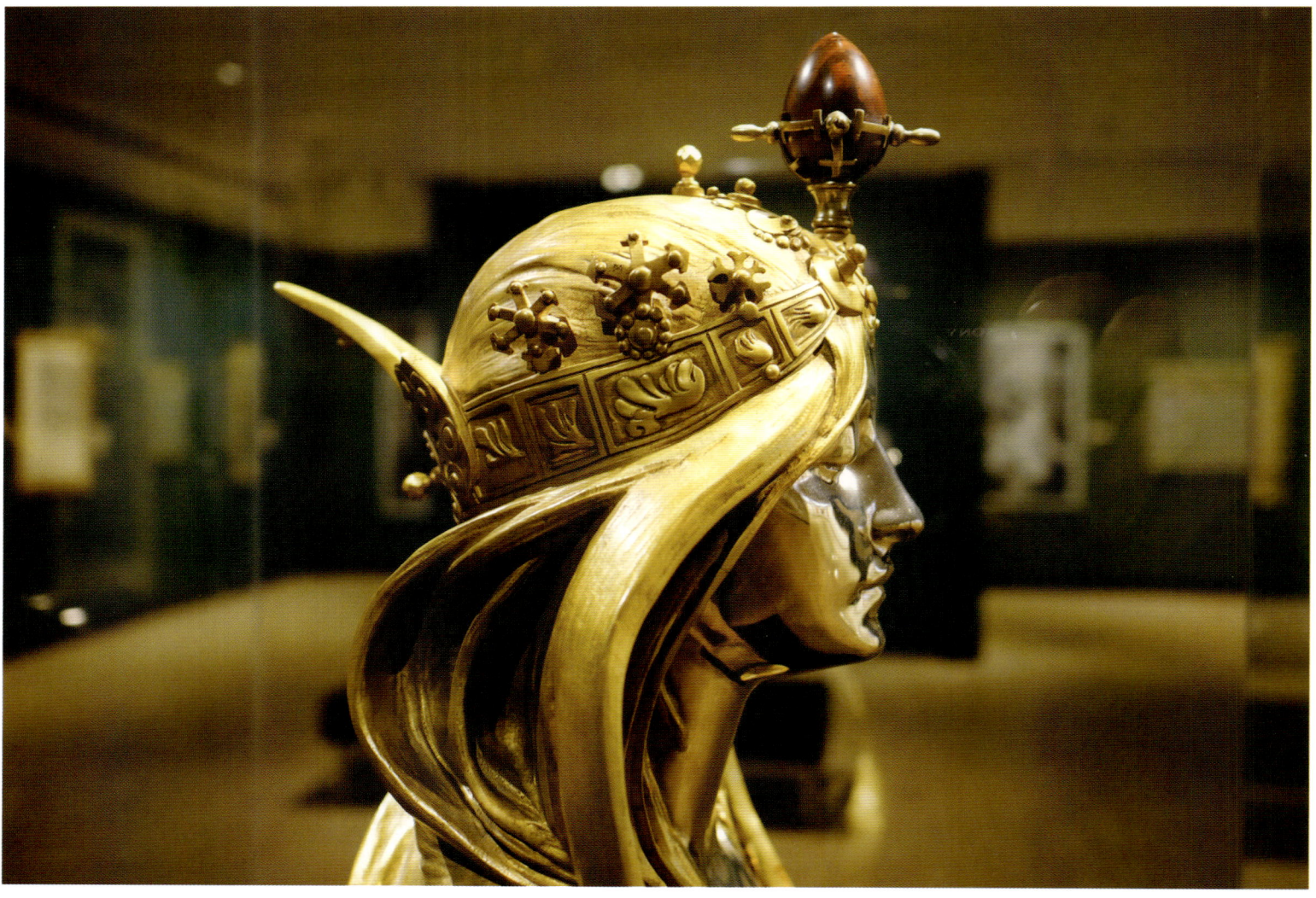

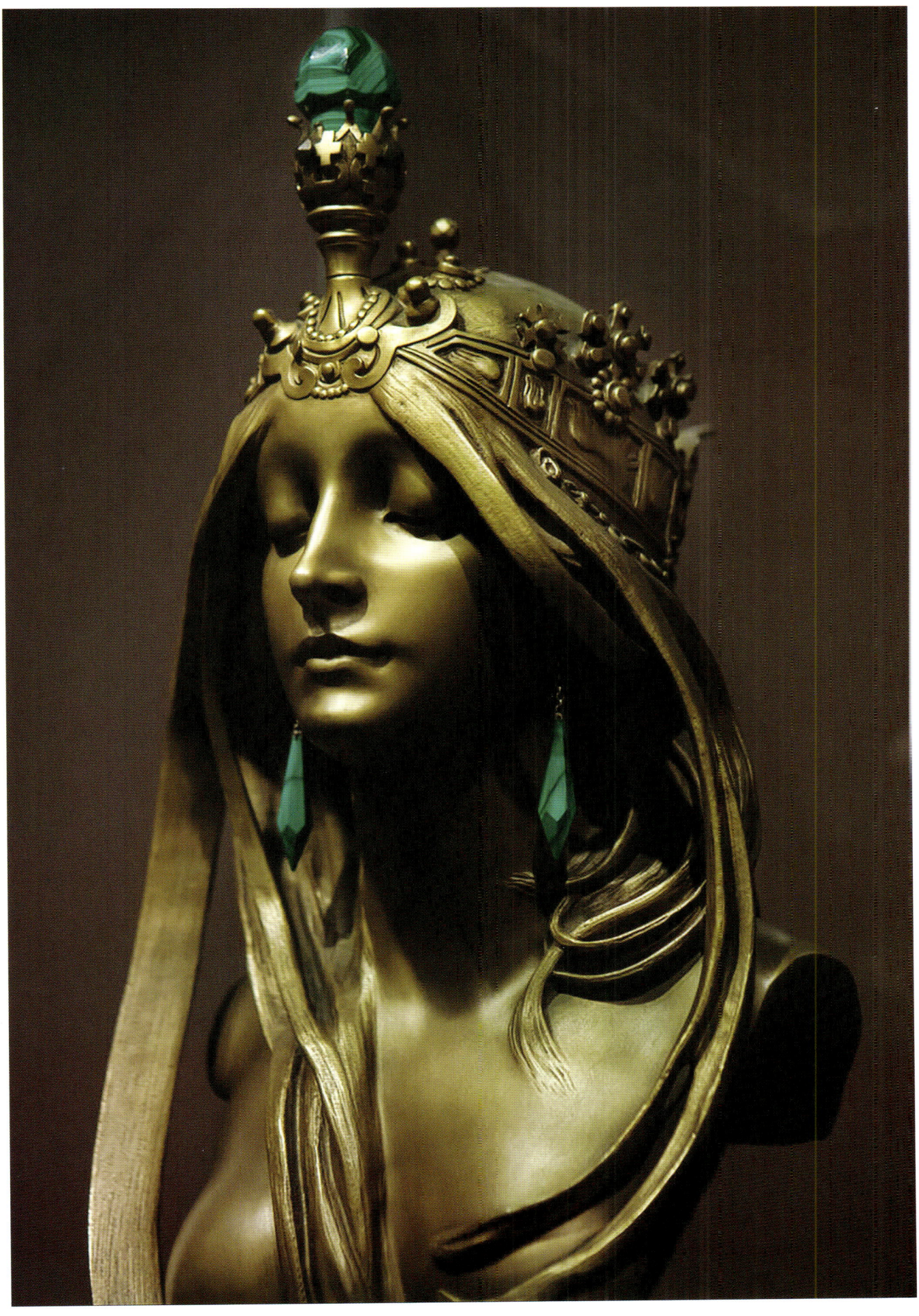

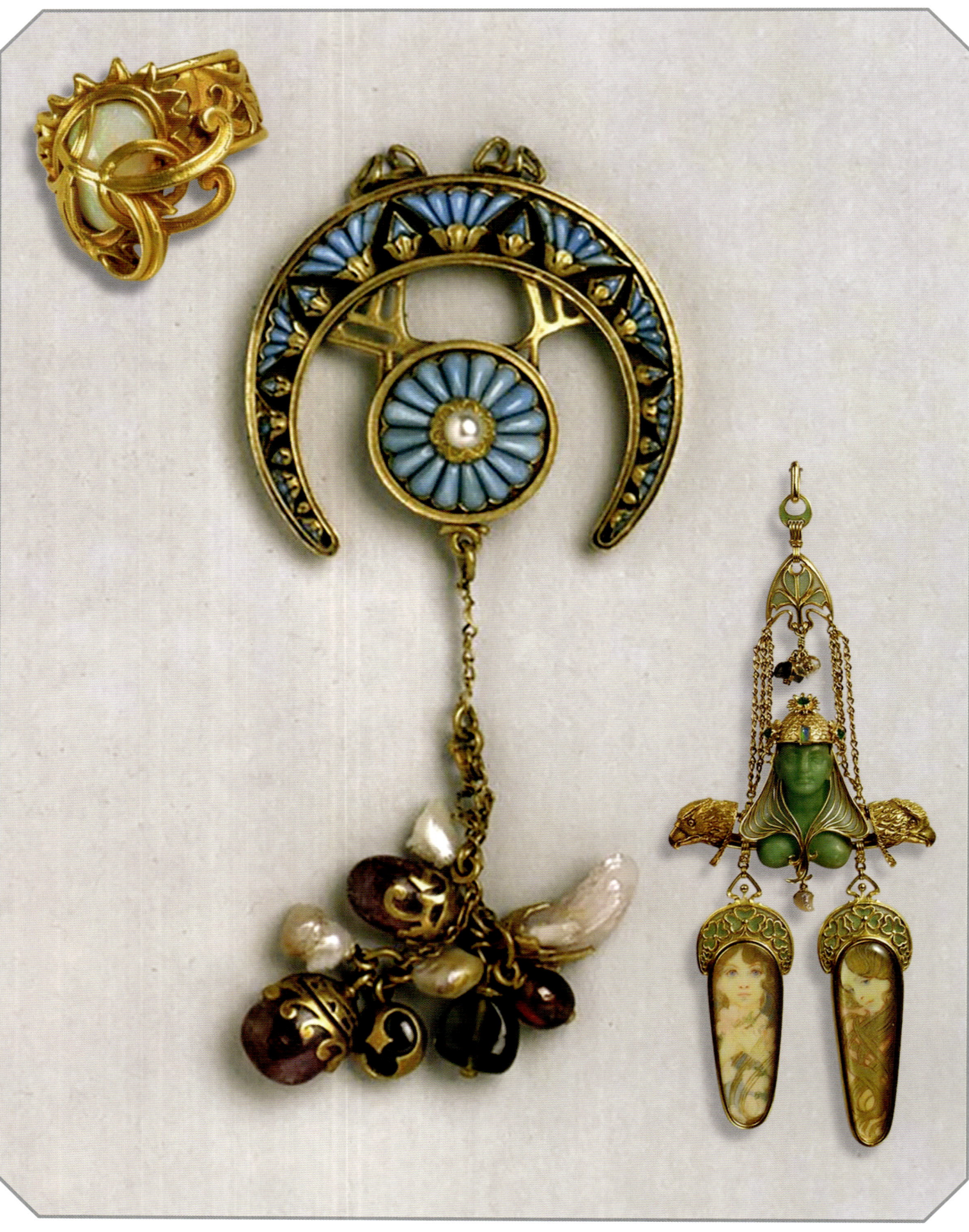

ART NOUVEAU JEWELRY

Jewelry lends itself to the sinuous forms and shapes of the Art Nouveau aesthetic. Mucha, who often depicted women wearing fantastical jewelry in his poster work, also had a hand in creating actual pieces. In a collaboration with the famed jeweler, he designed several pieces that Georges Fouquet executed into works of art. He also worked with other jewelry makers, and of note are the pieces René Lalique made for Sarah Bernhardt's stage performances.

[OPPOSITE PAGE TOP LEFT]
Georges Fouquet, designed by Alphonse Mucha. *"Peacock" ring made of gold and opal* (c. 1900). Mucha Trust Collection.

[OPPOSITE PAGE CENTER]
Georges Fouquet, designed by Alphonse Mucha. *Element of a hair ornament made of gold, enamel, turquoises, garnets, and baroque pearl* (c. 1900). Petit Palais, Paris.

[OPPOSITE BOTTOM RIGHT]
Georges Fouquet, designed by Alphonse Mucha. *Pendant made of gold, enamel, mother-of-pearl, opal, emerald, colored stones, and gold paint* (c. 1900). Metropolitan Museum of Art.

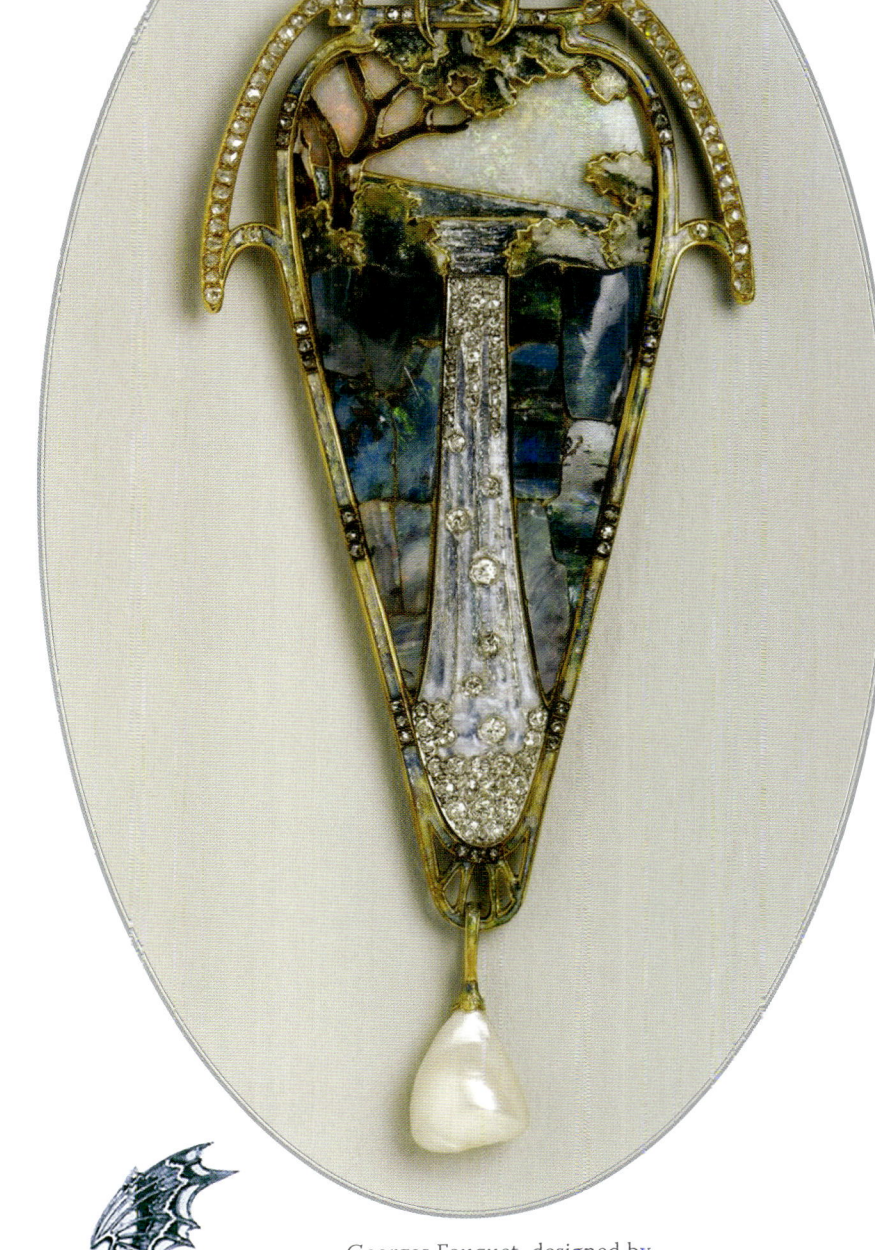

Georges Fouquet, designed by Alphonse Mucha. *Pendant waterfall in cloisonné enamel, pearl, opal, and diamonds* (c. 1900).

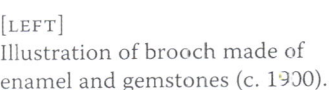

[LEFT]
Illustration of brooch made of enamel and gemstones (c. 1900).

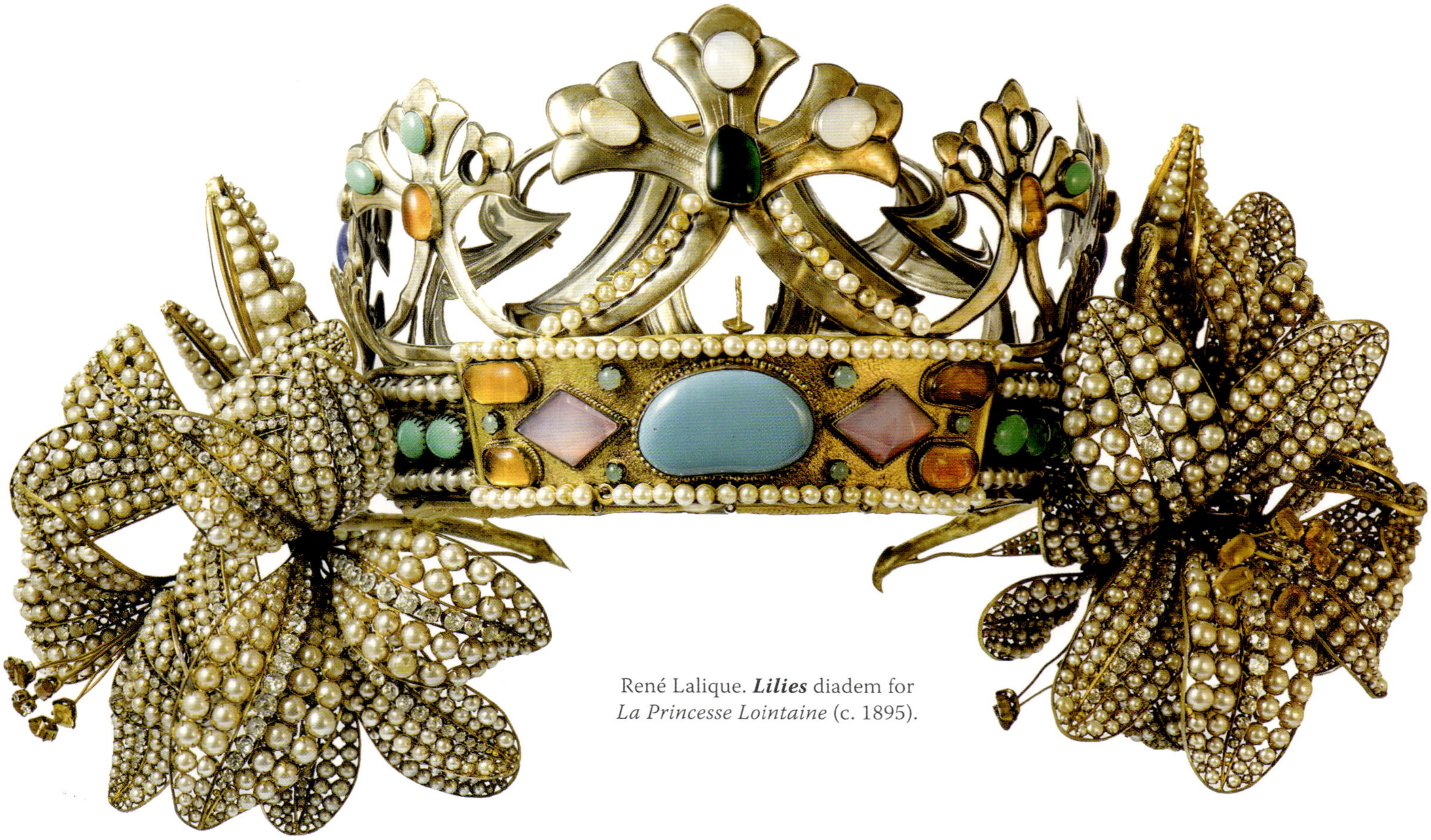

René Lalique. **Lilies** diadem for
La Princesse Lointaine (c. 1895).

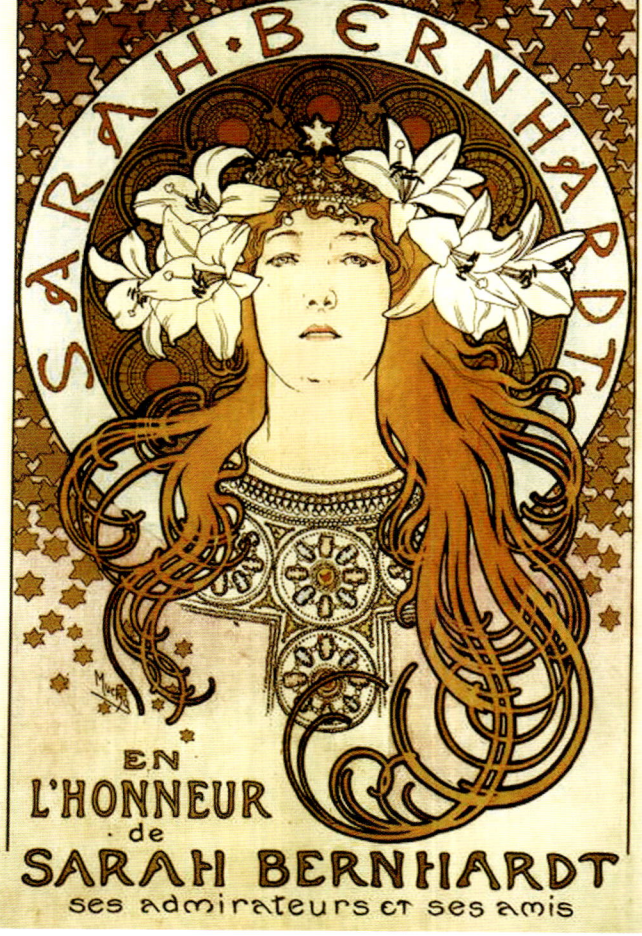

[LEFT]
Sarah Bernhardt as La Princesse Lointaine for *La Plume* magazine (1897). Color lithograph.

In 1895, Sarah Bernhardt had the starring role of Mélisande in Edmond Rostand's play La Princesse Lointaine *at the Théâtre de la Renaissance in Paris. Mucha designed her jewelry for the production, including a pendant and an ornate diadem with draping lilies crafted from pearls, which was made by French jeweler, metalworker, and glass designer René Lalique. Mucha later adorned Bernhardt's image with the iconic lily diadem in an illustration for* La Plume *magazine.*

[OPPOSITE PAGE]
Sarah Bernhardt as Mélisande in La Princesse Lointaine. Reutlinger, Paris (c. 1895–1897). Black-and-white-photograph.

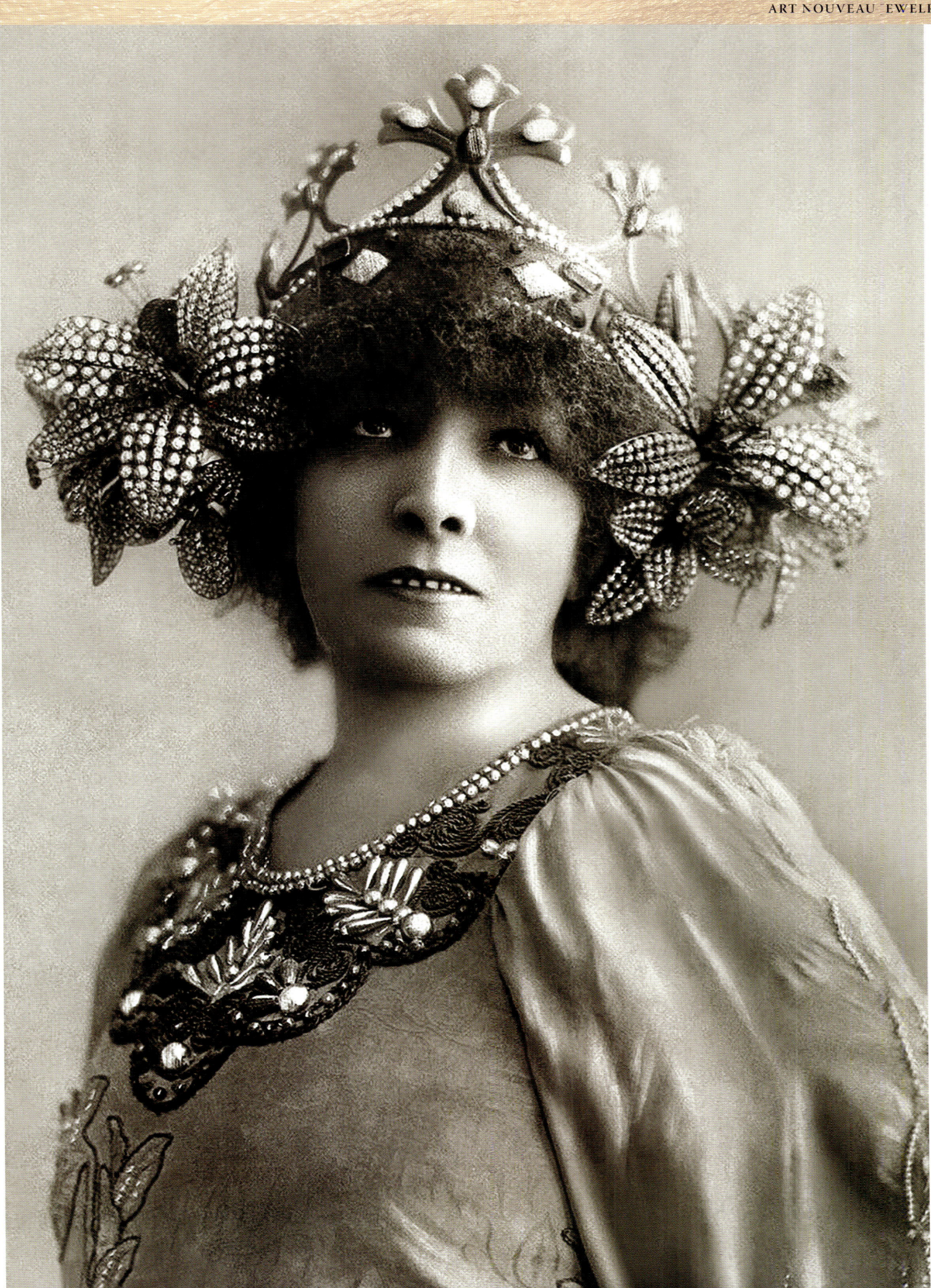

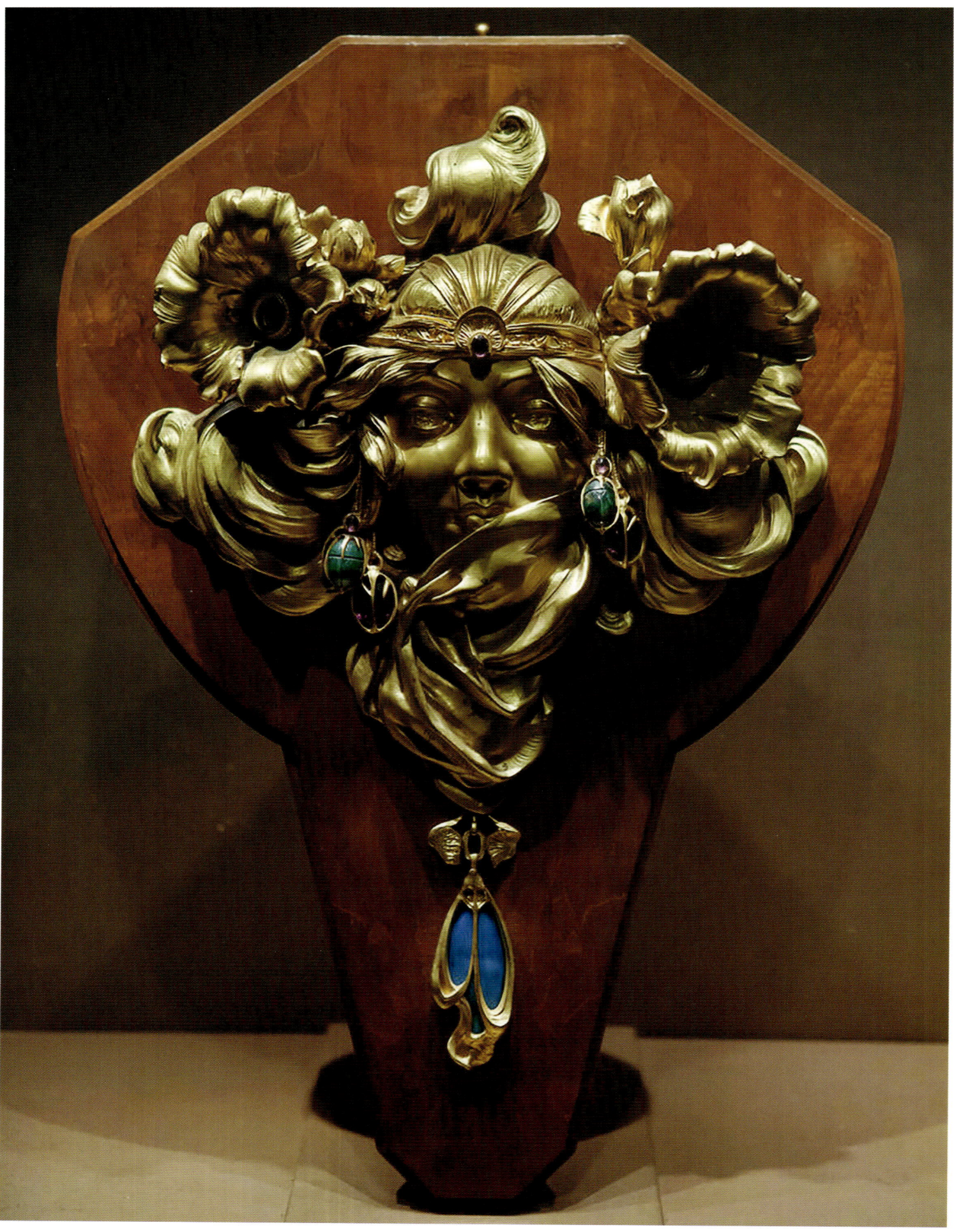

[OPPOSITE PAGE]
Adolphe Truffier, designed by Alphonse Mucha. *La Princesse Lointaine* (1900). Wall lamp, gilded and chiseled bronze, ornaments in semiprecious stone (cabochon), hard stone, and enamel plate.

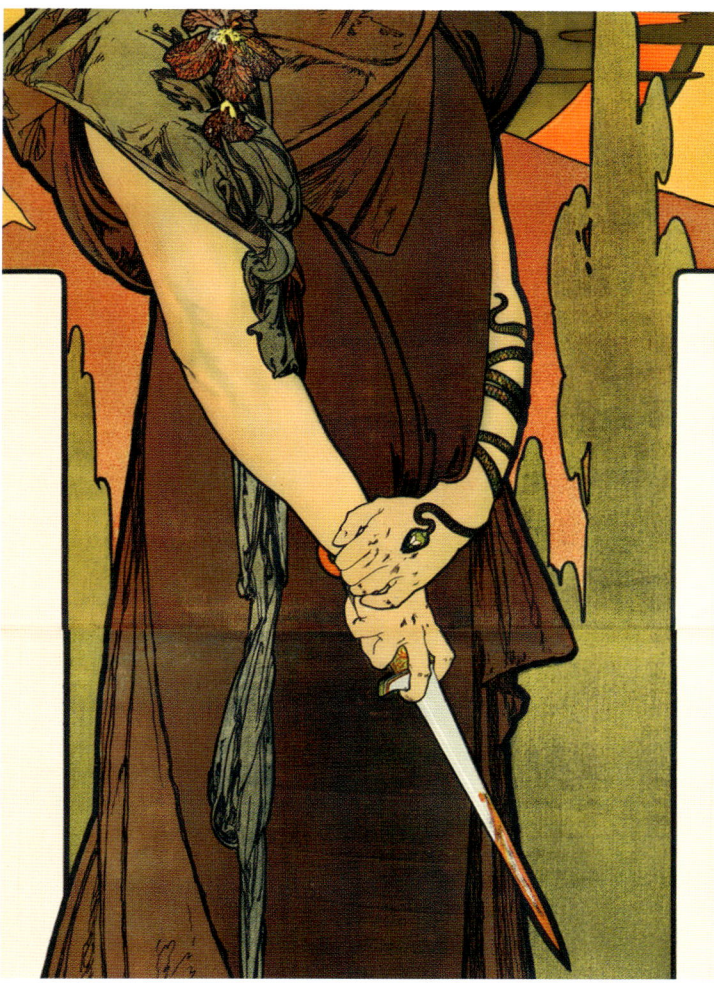

Detail of poster for *Médée* (1898). Color lithograph.

Bernhardt found the snake bracelet that Mucha illustrated entwining her arm in the Médée *poster so spectacular that she commissioned jeweler Georges Fouquet to copy the design for her to wear.*

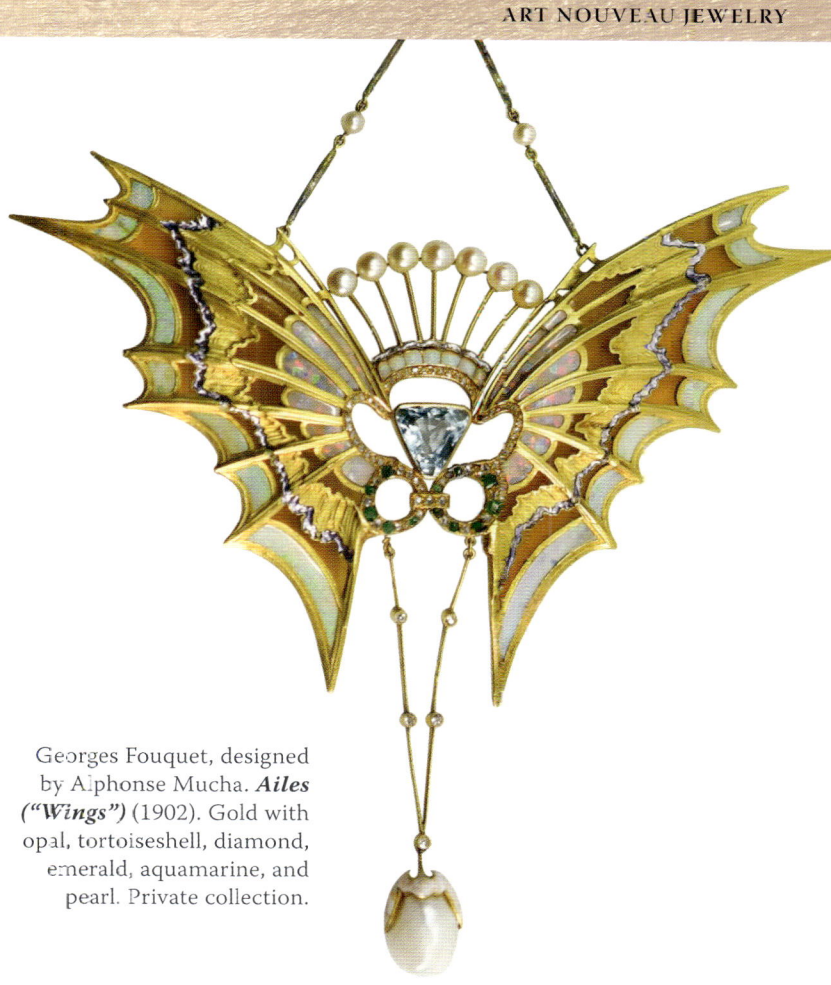

Georges Fouquet, designed by Alphonse Mucha. *Ailes ("Wings")* (1902). Gold with opal, tortoiseshell, diamond, emerald, aquamarine, and pearl. Private collection.

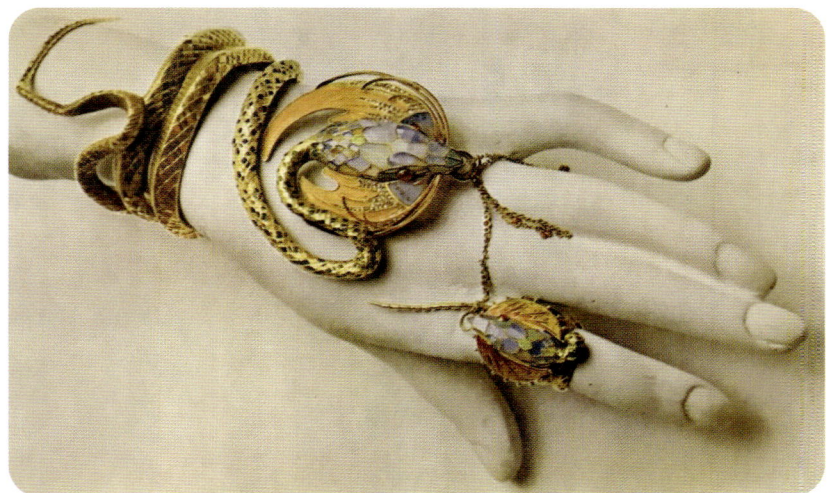

Georges Fouquet, designed by Alphonse Mucha. *Snake bracelet with a ring* (1899). Gold, enamel, opal, ruby, and diamond.

"*Here the snake coiled around the wrist, its tail extending up the arm, its winged head, set with a mosaic of enamel, opals, rubies and diamonds, resting on the back of the hand. It was linked by a series of chains to another 'snake,' this a finger ring, its head turned to face that of the bracelet. The piece was given extra flexibility by a discrete system of hinges which allowed movement of the hand.*"

~ DR. JEREMY HOWARD, LECTURER
IN ART HISTORY, UNIVERSITY OF ST. ANDREWS

A PHOTO ARCHIVE

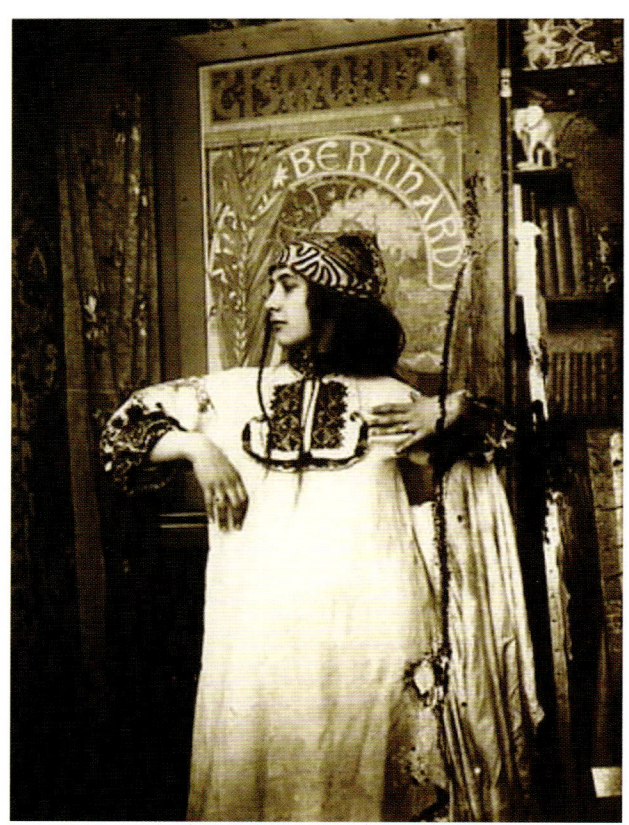

Mucha's first photos were snapped with a borrowed camera in the early 1880s, but when he had earned a bit of money and moved to a large studio in Paris in 1896, he had the opportunity to take more pictures. Most of the Parisian photos served as preliminary studies for his other work, but he often had his models improvise poses to amass an archive he could refer to when he had a new commission. In later years, such as when he planned out his Slav Epic paintings, he clearly directed his models—often his daughter, Jaroslava—into specific poses.

[OPPOSITE PAGE]
Self-Portrait with posters for Sarah Bernhardt at the studio in rue du Val-de-Grâce, Paris (c. 1901). Modern print from original glass plate negative. Mucha Trust Collection.

[LEFT]
Study for Figures Decoratives at the studio in rue du Val-de-Grâce, Paris (c. 1901).

[LEFT]
Mucha and Jaroslava posing for poster DeForest Phonofilm. Museum (c. 1920s). Mucha Museum.

[BELOW]
Jaroslava posing as Slavia for the Czech 50 korun banknote (c. 1929).

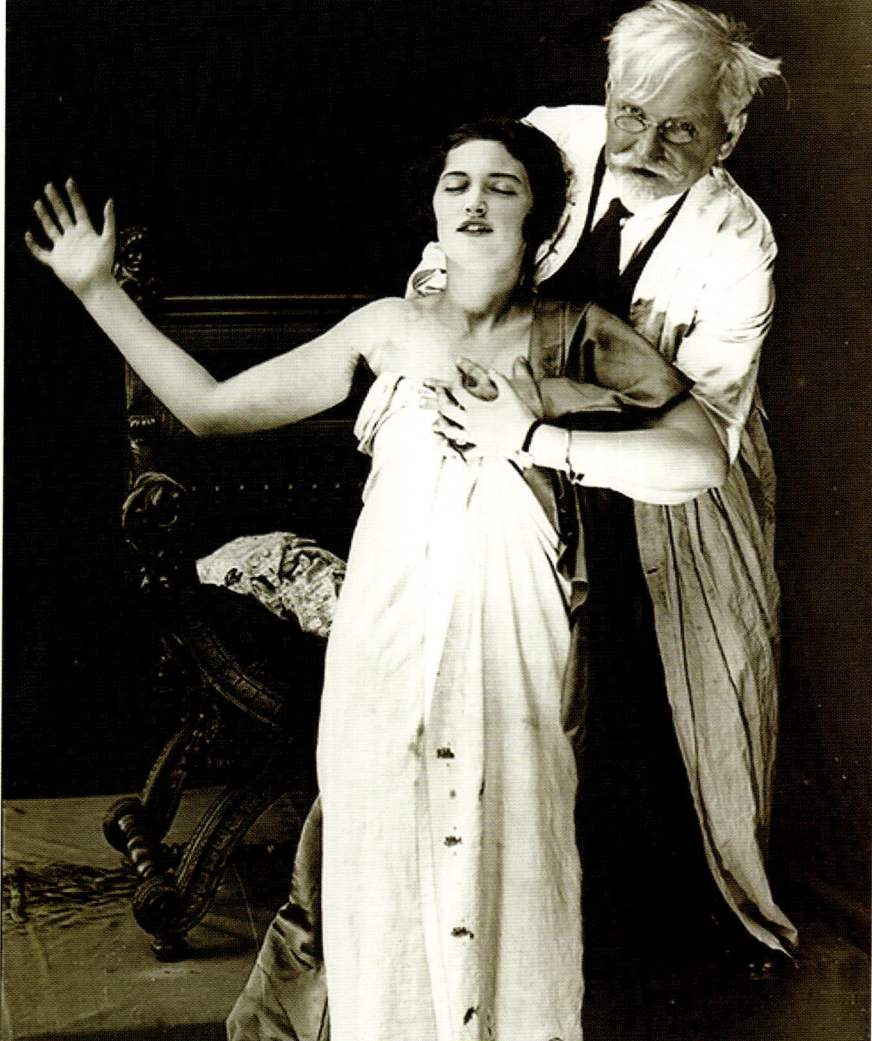

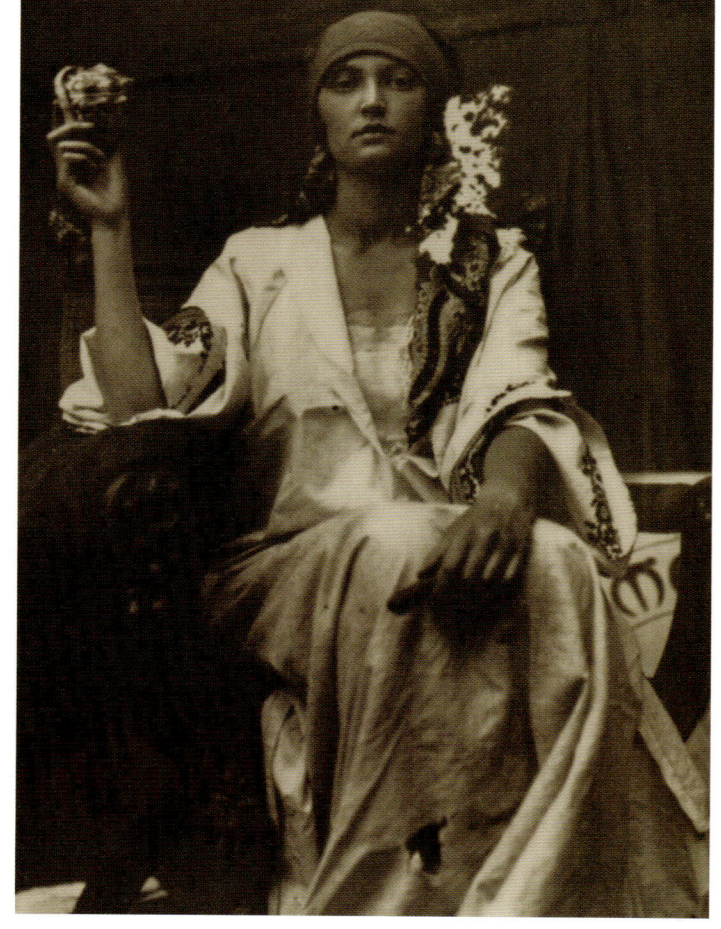

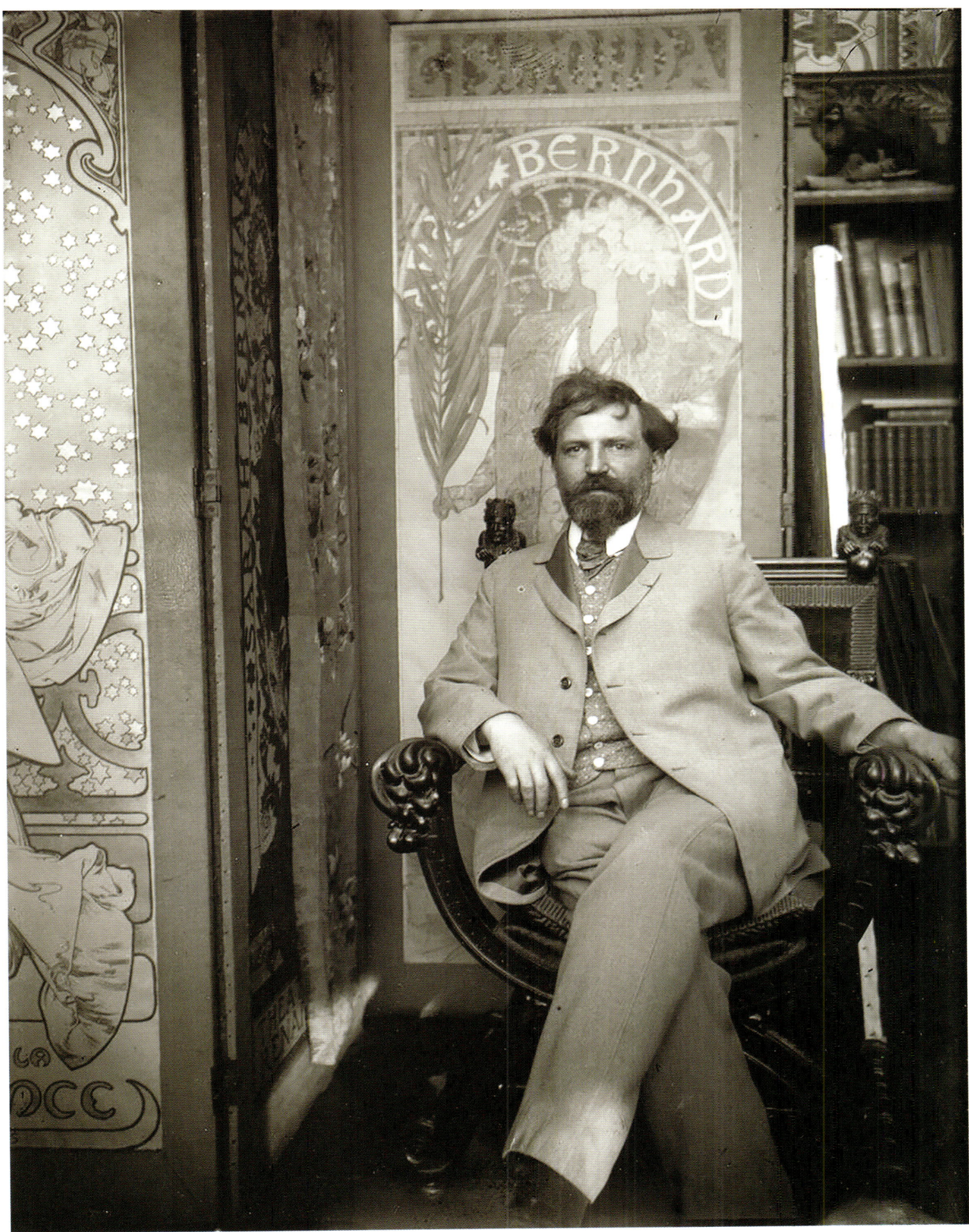

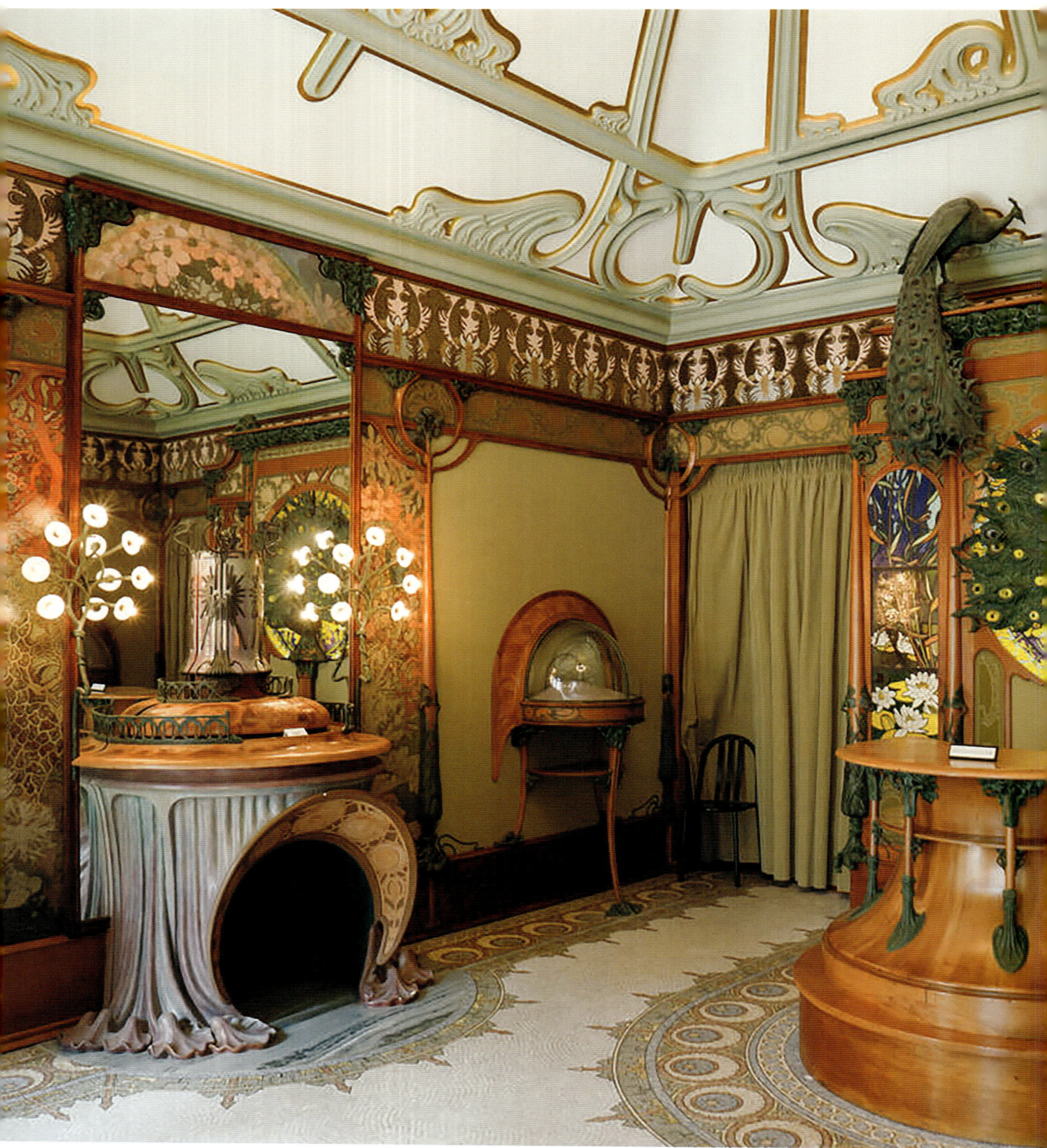

THE BOUTIQUE GEORGES FOUQUET

Mucha and Georges Fouquet, a French jewelry maker, shared a common interest in Art Nouveau aesthetics. Fouquet commissioned Mucha to design the interior of his Parisian boutique, which became a masterpiece of elaborate Art Nouveau architecture. Mucha transformed the interior into a comprehensive work of art that harmoniously showcased Fouquet's jewelry alongside elements inspired by nature, such as two magnificent peacocks set against a backdrop of stained glass. The boutique's interior was dismantled in 1923, but its architectural beauty was preserved and reconstructed in the Musée Carnavalet.

[LEFT]
Reconstruction of the Boutique Georges Fouquet, decorated by Alphonse Mucha. Musée Carnavalet, Paris.

[TOP RIGHT]
Sketch of the mosaic pattern for the flooring of the Boutique Georges Fouquet (c. 1900). Pencil, brush, wash, and watercolor on paper. Musée Carnavalet, Paris.

[BOTTOM RIGHT] The floor in the reconstructed shop.

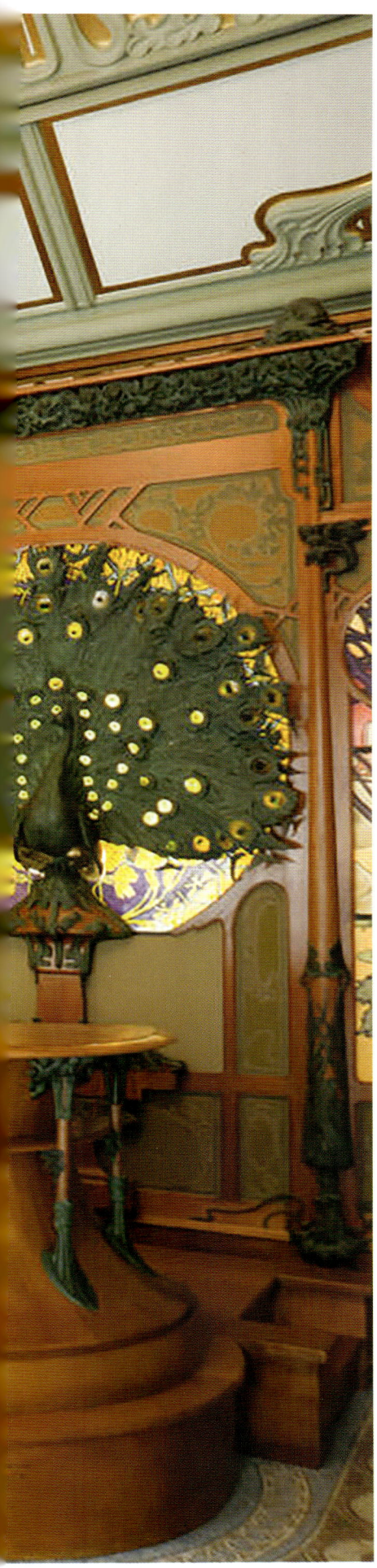

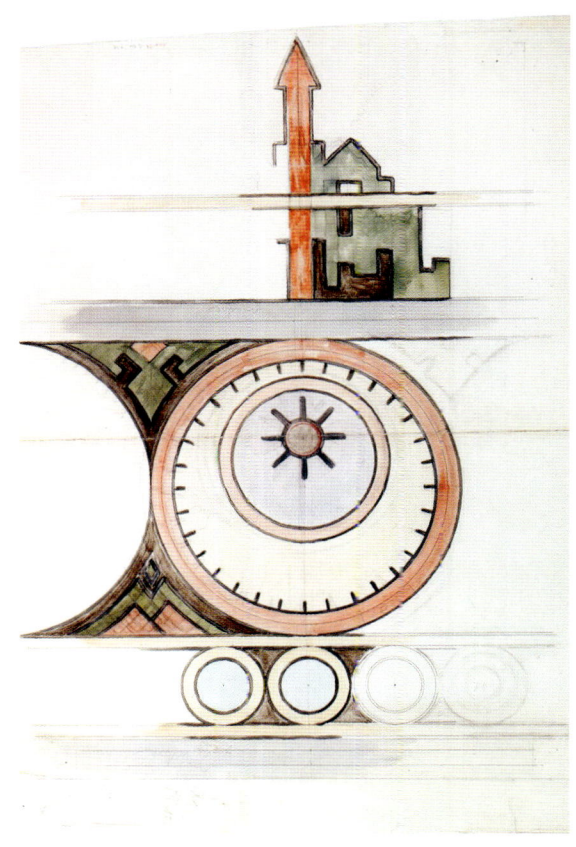

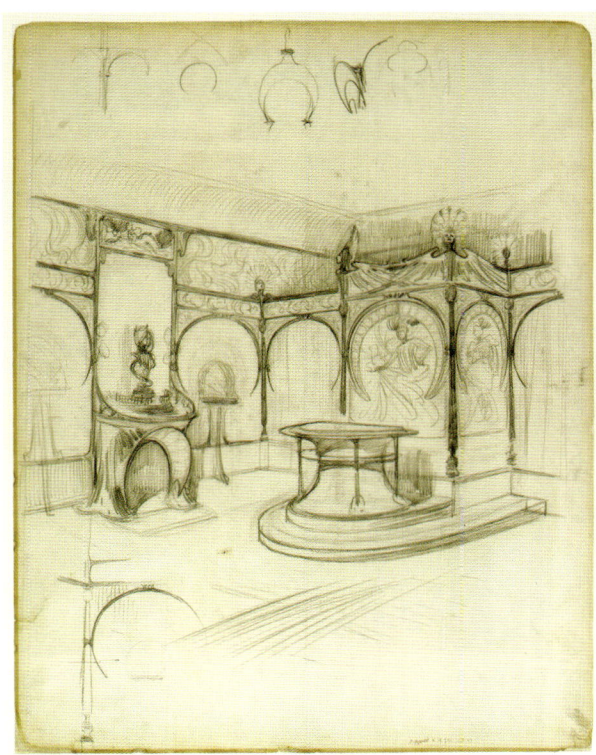

Sketch of the decor for the fireplace and interior of the Boutique Georges Fouquet (c. 1900). Pencil, pen, and Indian ink on paper. Musée Carnavalet, Paris.

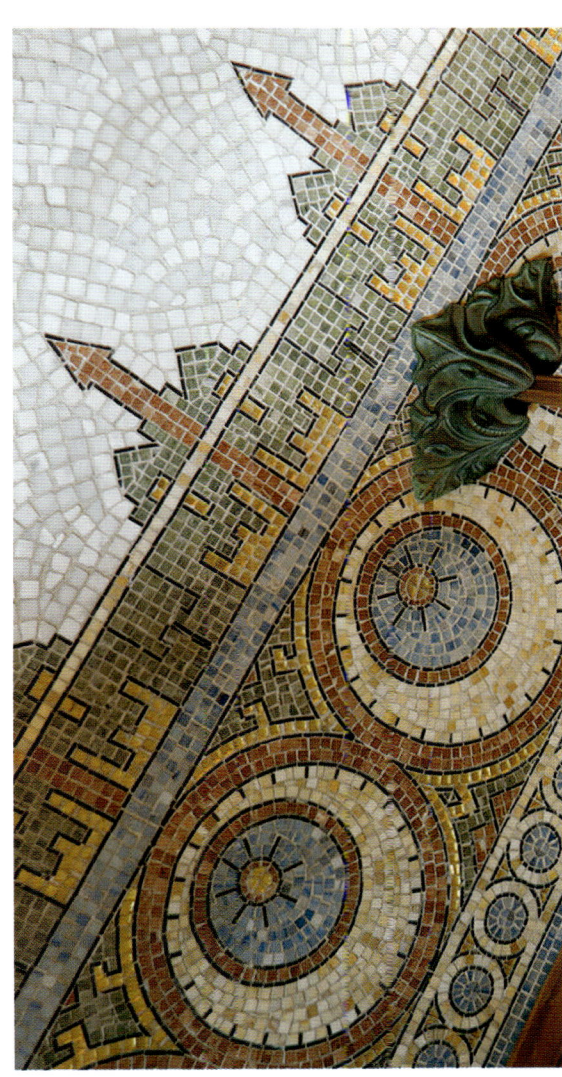

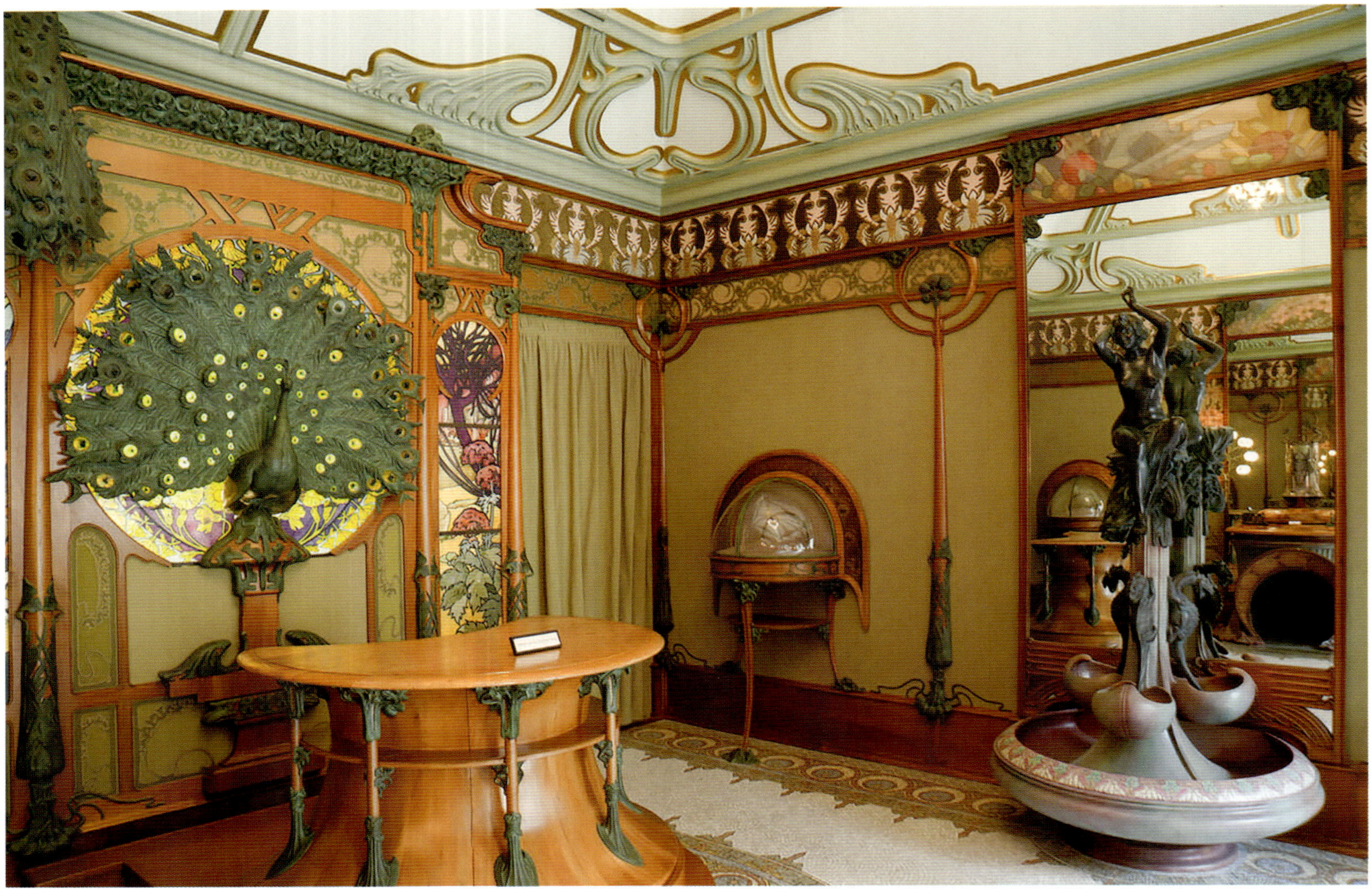

[ABOVE]
Reconstruction of the Boutique Georges Fouquet decorated by Alphonse Mucha
(c. 1900). Musée Carnavalet, Paris.

In the quintessential Art Nouveau style, the boutique is filled with images of nature. From blooming flower motifs to regal peacock statuary, nature abounds.

[RIGHT]
Studies for interior stained glass panels
(c. 1900). Pencil, brush, wash, and watercolor on paper.

[OPPOSITE PAGE]
Reconstruction of the Boutique Georges Fouquet decorated by Alphonse Mucha
(c. 1900). Musée Carnavalet, Paris.

A bronzed statuette of a smilingly demure woman with lowered gaze and long, flowing tresses perches at the center of the shop floor.

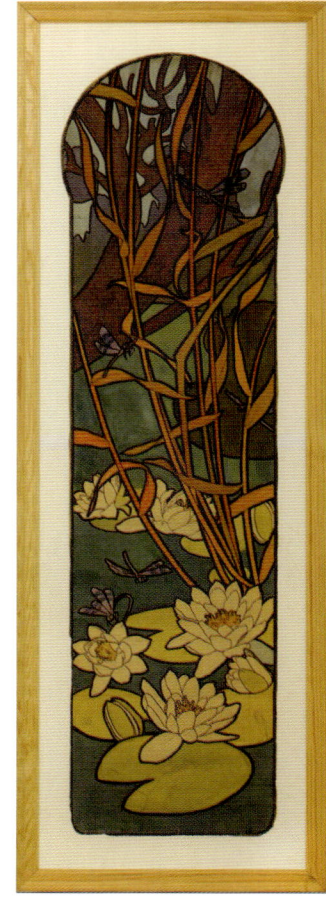
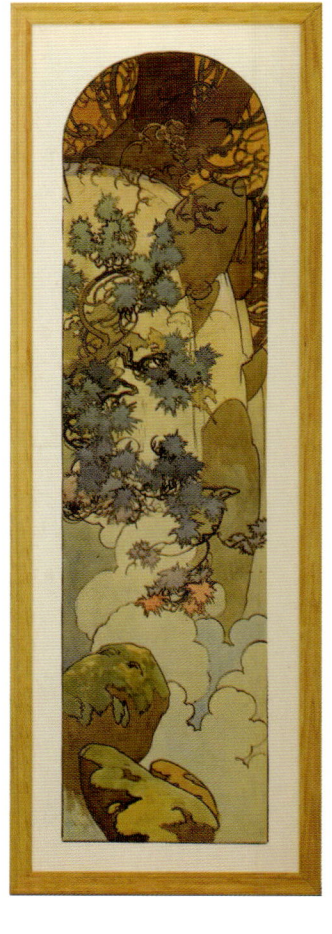

" *I always study nature. There is not a single plant, a flower, which would not have been full of suggestions and incarnations.*"

~ ALPHONSE MUCHA

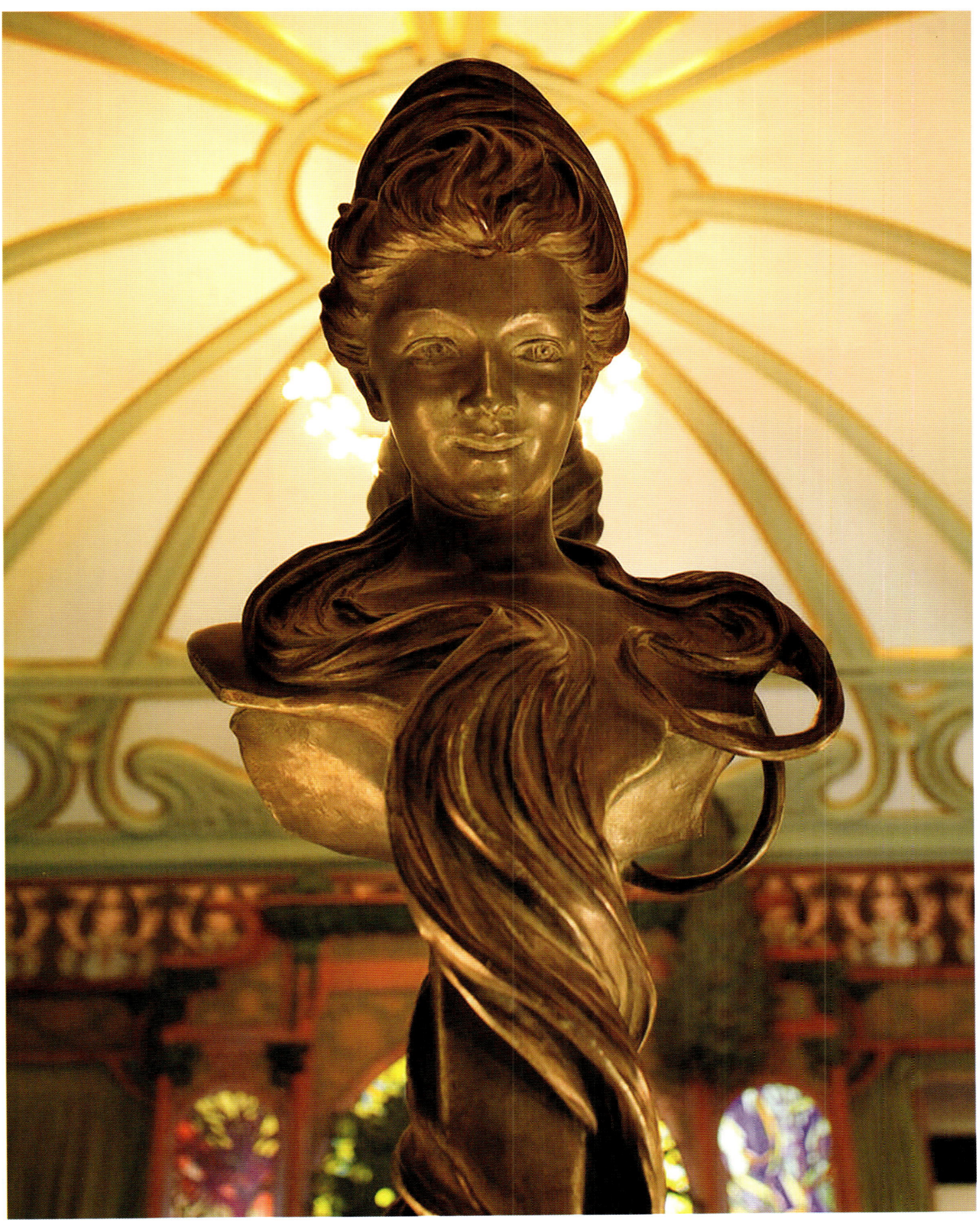

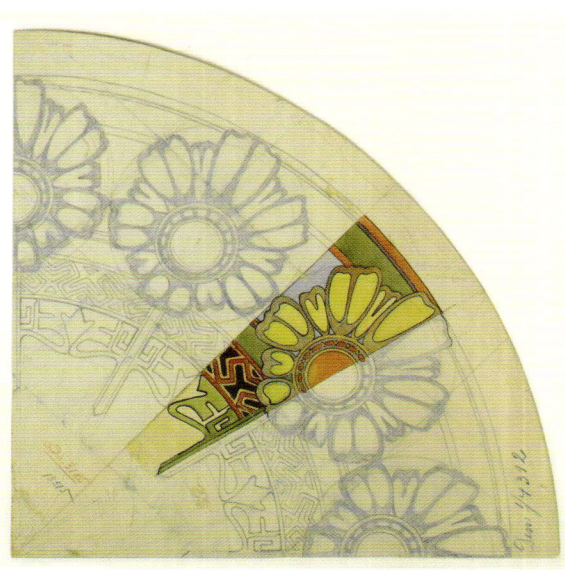

[LEFT]
Preparatory card for a
stained glass window.

[OPPOSITE PAGE]
The facade of the shop was adorned
with a central panel filled in with
a bronze relief depicting a woman
holding up draping necklaces while
her flowing hair swirls around the
arching curves of her body.

[BELOW]
A floor-to-ceiling mirror forms the backdrop of a fountain crested by a nude nymph.

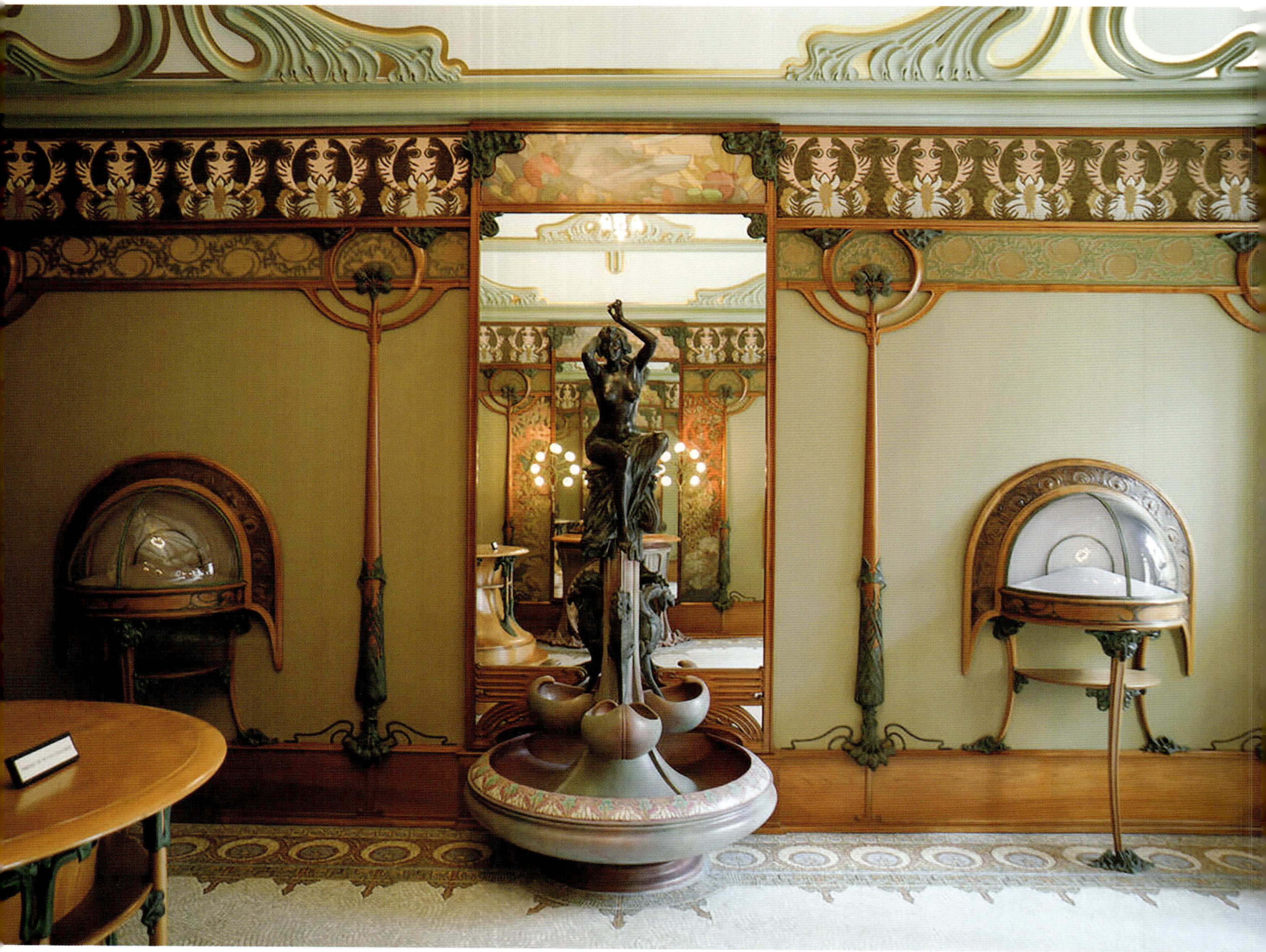

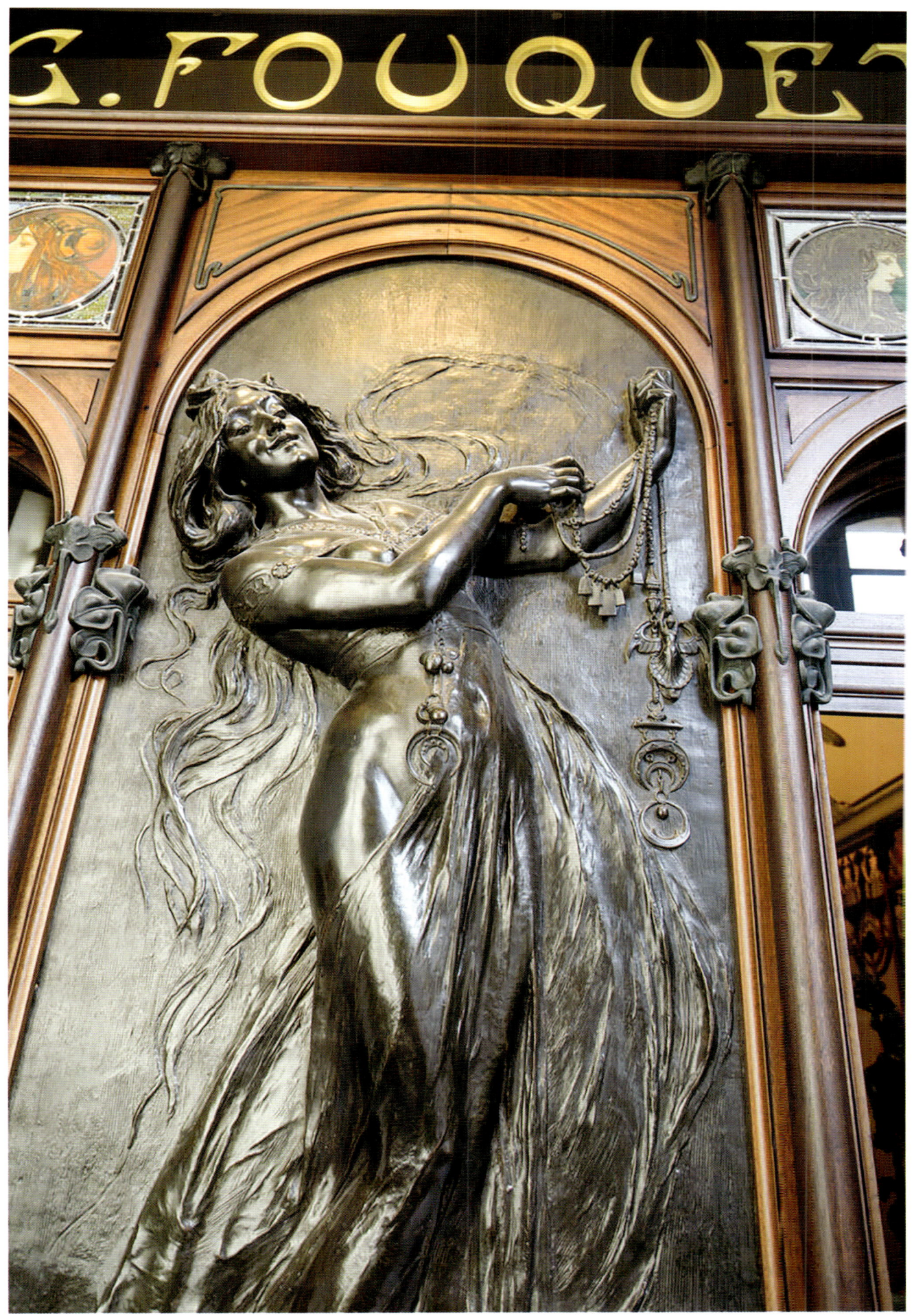

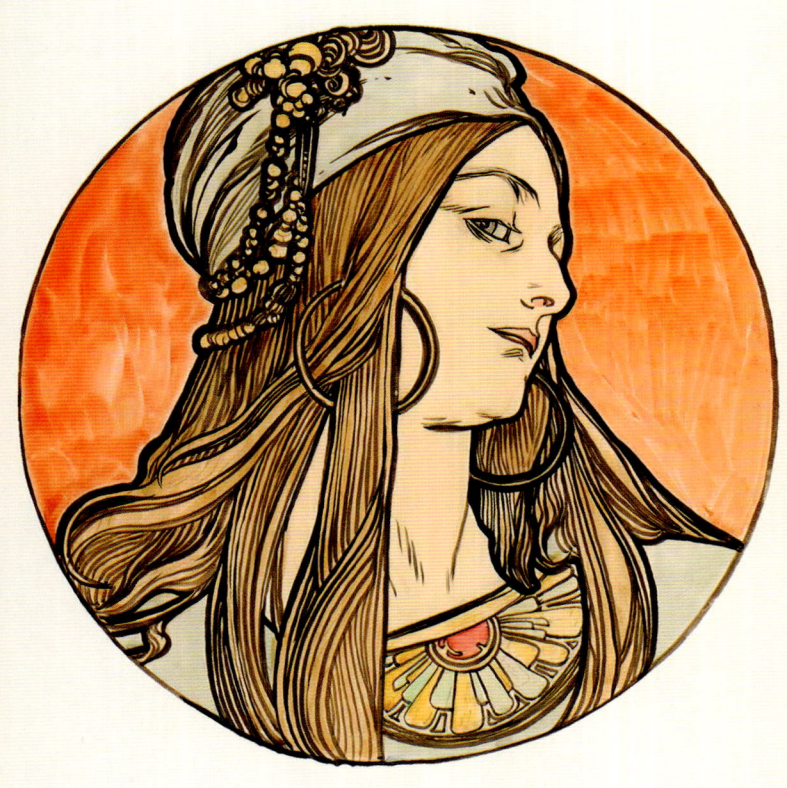

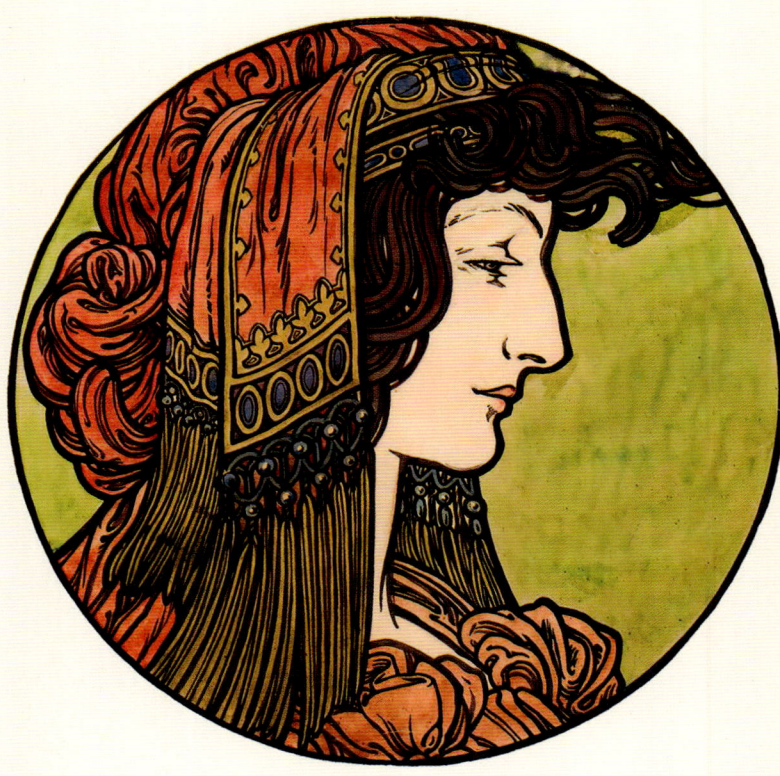

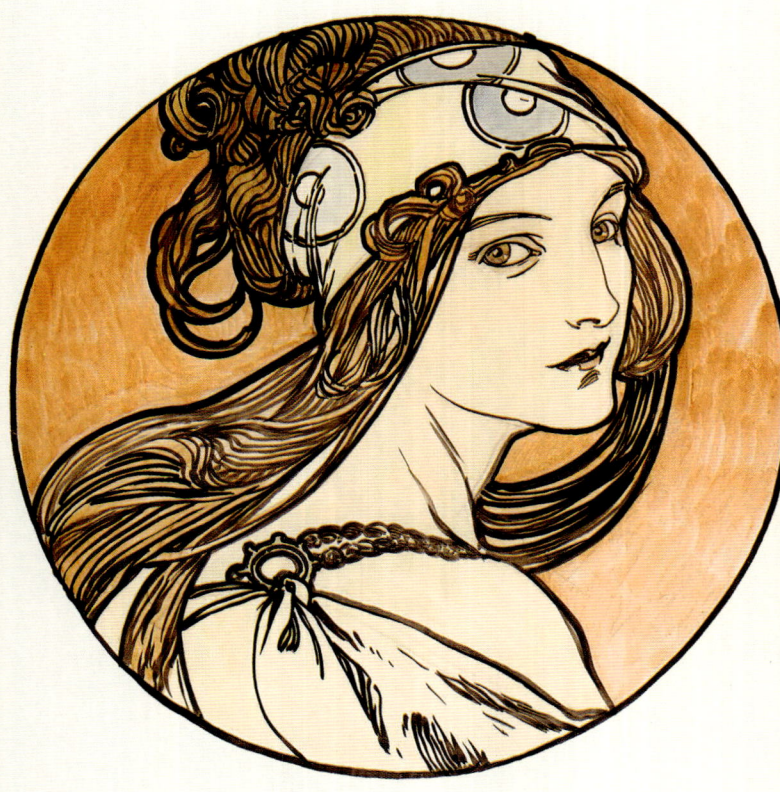

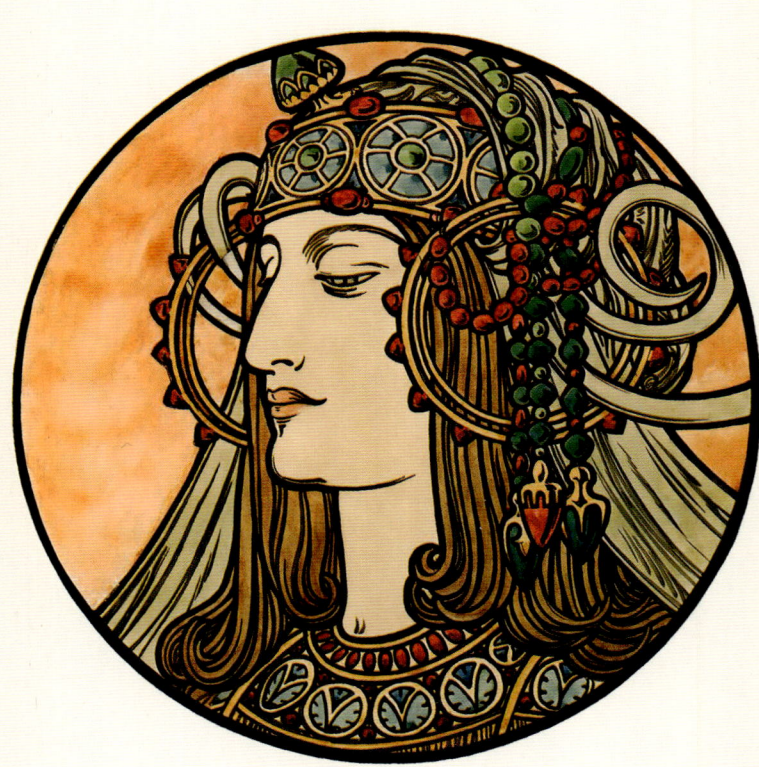

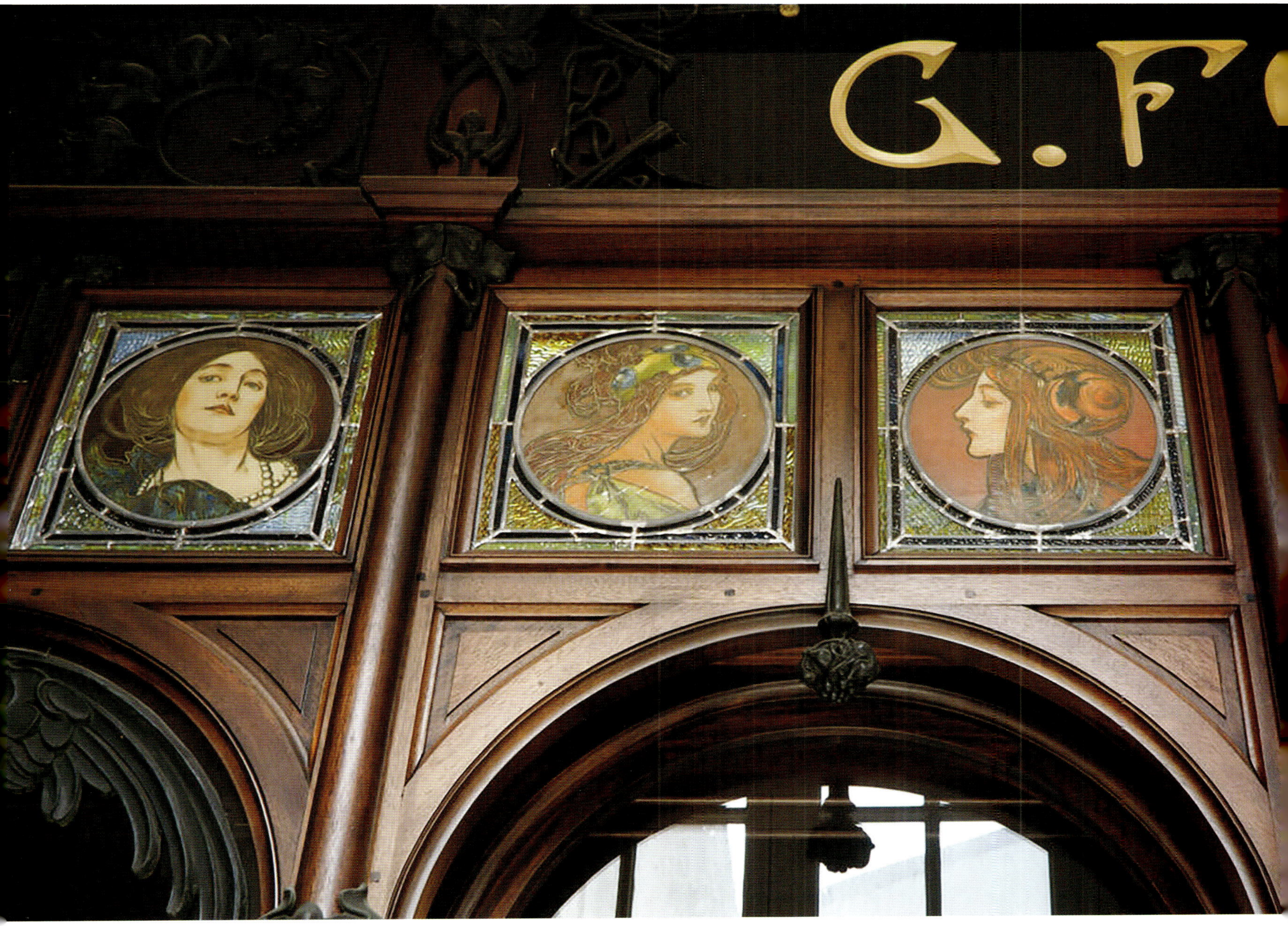

[ABOVE]
Trailing along the shop's facade was
a frieze composed of 10 stained glass
panels, each depicting a fashionable,
jewelry-bedecked woman.

[RIGHT]
*Sketch for exterior, showing
plan of stained glass frieze*
(c. 1900). Pencil, brush, wash,
and watercolor on paper.

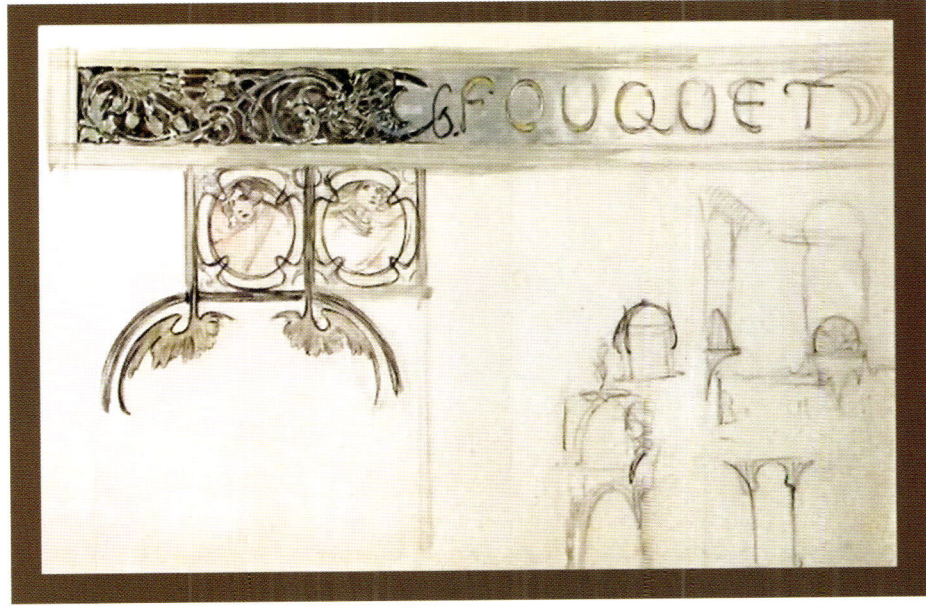

[OPPOSITE PAGE AND RIGHT]
*Studies for exterior stained glass
panels* (c. 1900). Pencil, brush,
wash, and watercolor on paper.

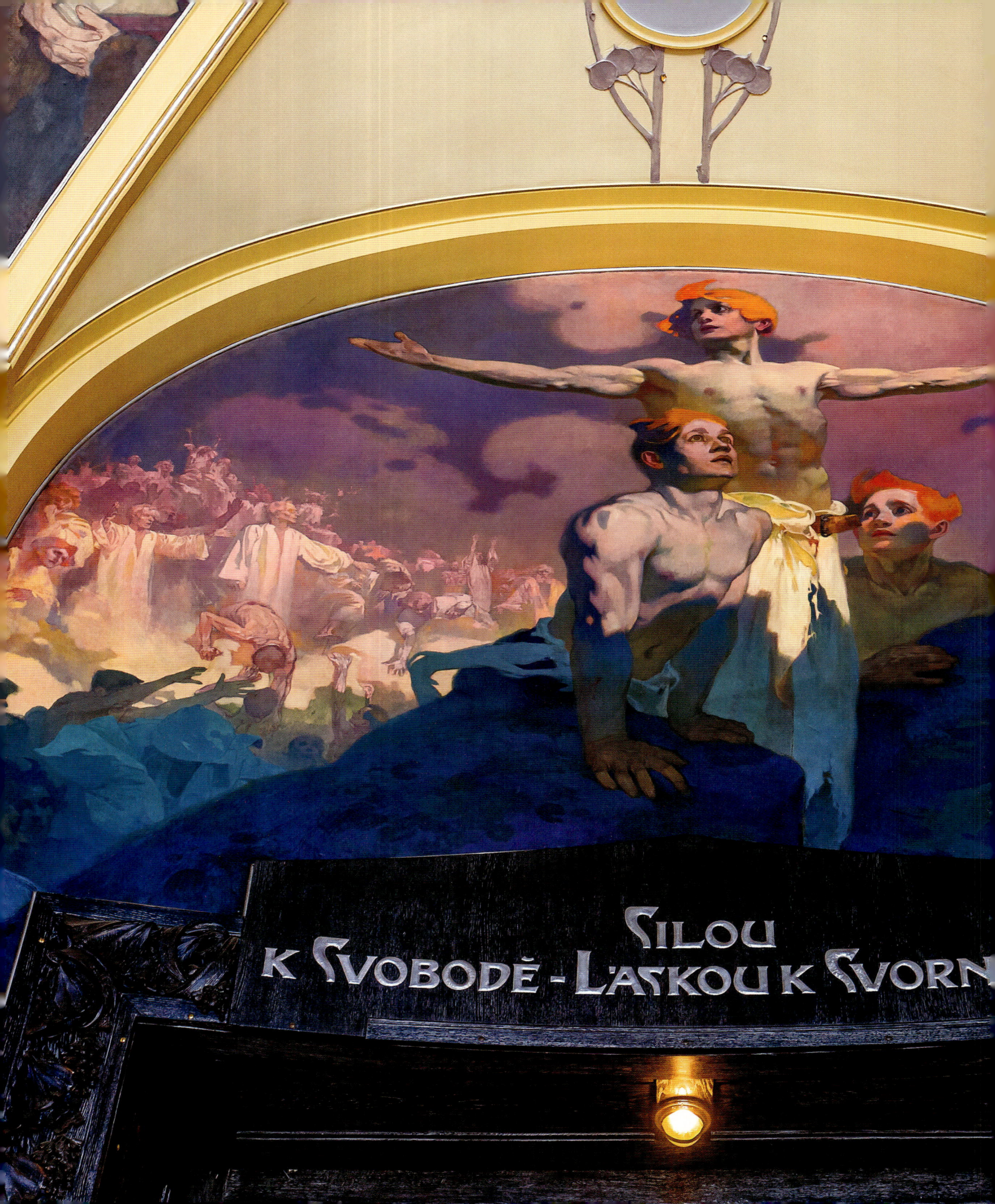

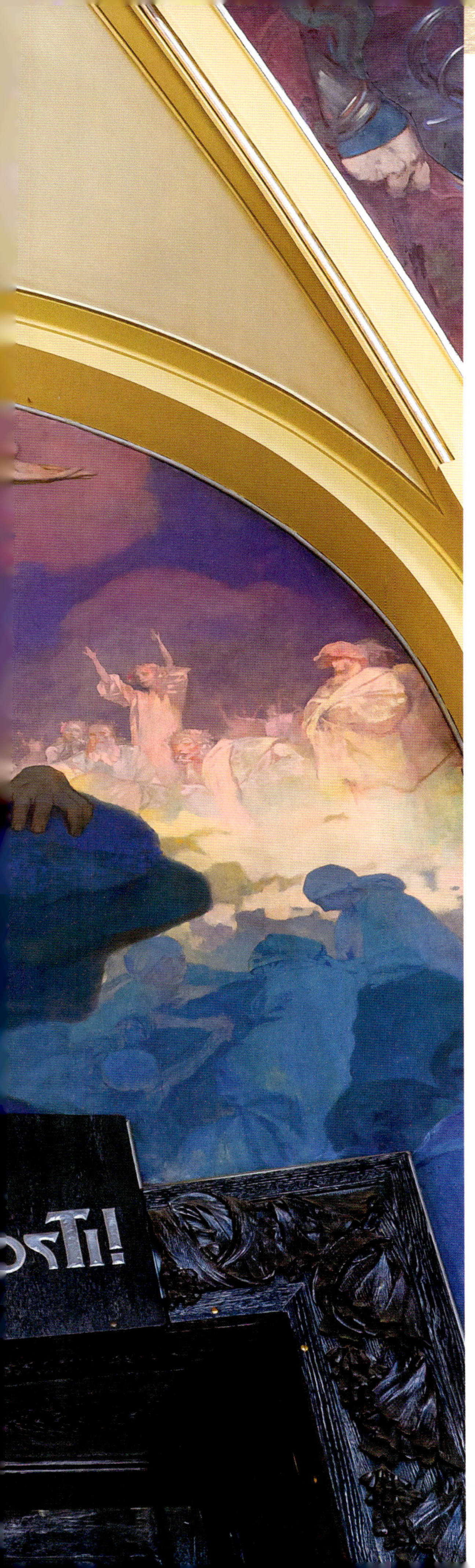

THE MUNICIPAL HOUSE

Mucha contributed significantly to the interior design of Obecní Dům, or the Municipal House, a historic building in Prague that exemplifies Art Nouveau architecture. A number of artists were commissioned to design separate interior spaces, and Mucha received the contract for the Lord Mayor's Hall. He painted the frescoes that adorn the walls and ceiling of the hall, as well as designing the stylistic details of the windows, drapery, and even the lighting. Mucha's designs incorporated many symbolic motifs, including scenes from Czech history and Slavic mythology.

[LEFT]
By Own Strength II: "By force towards freedom, with love towards unity!" (1910–1911). Mural. Lord Mayor's Hall, Obecní Dům, Prague.

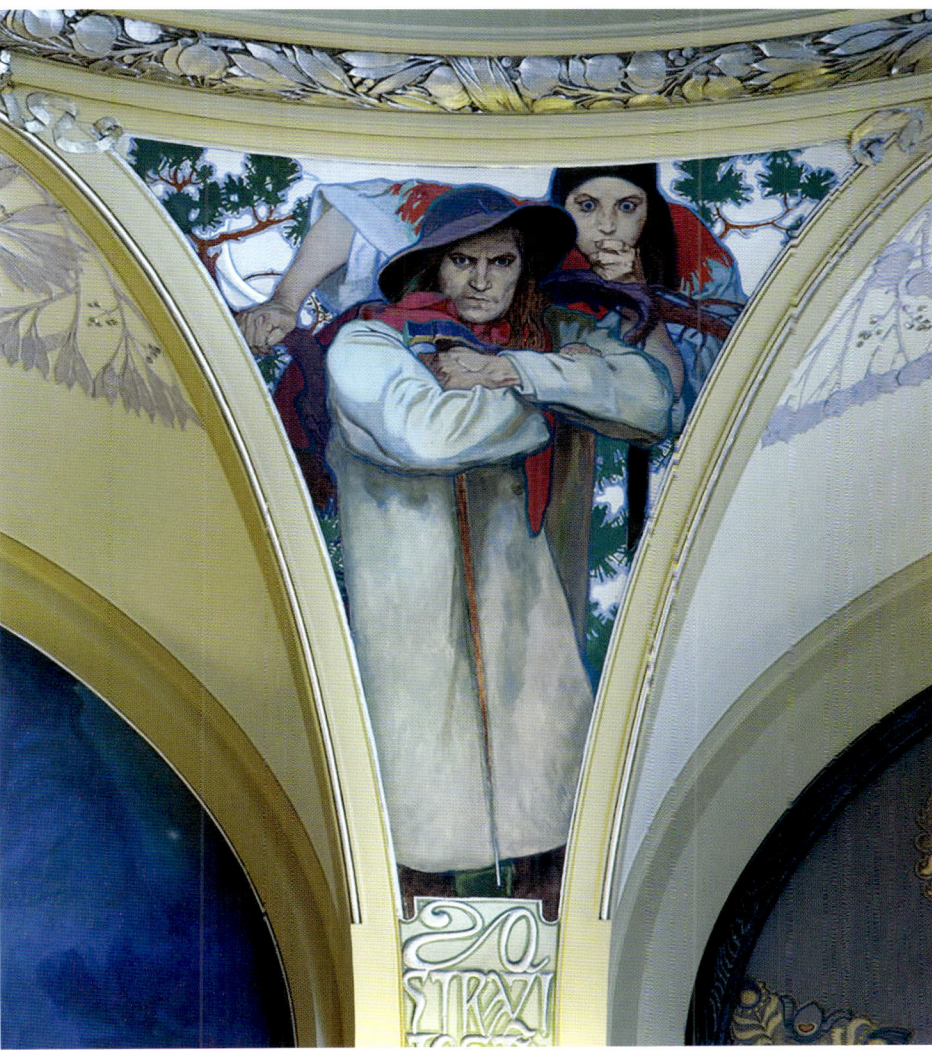

A closeup of one of the spandrels between the arches. These depict the personifications of virtues—Pugnacity, Fidelity, Independence, and Justice—through Czech historical figures.

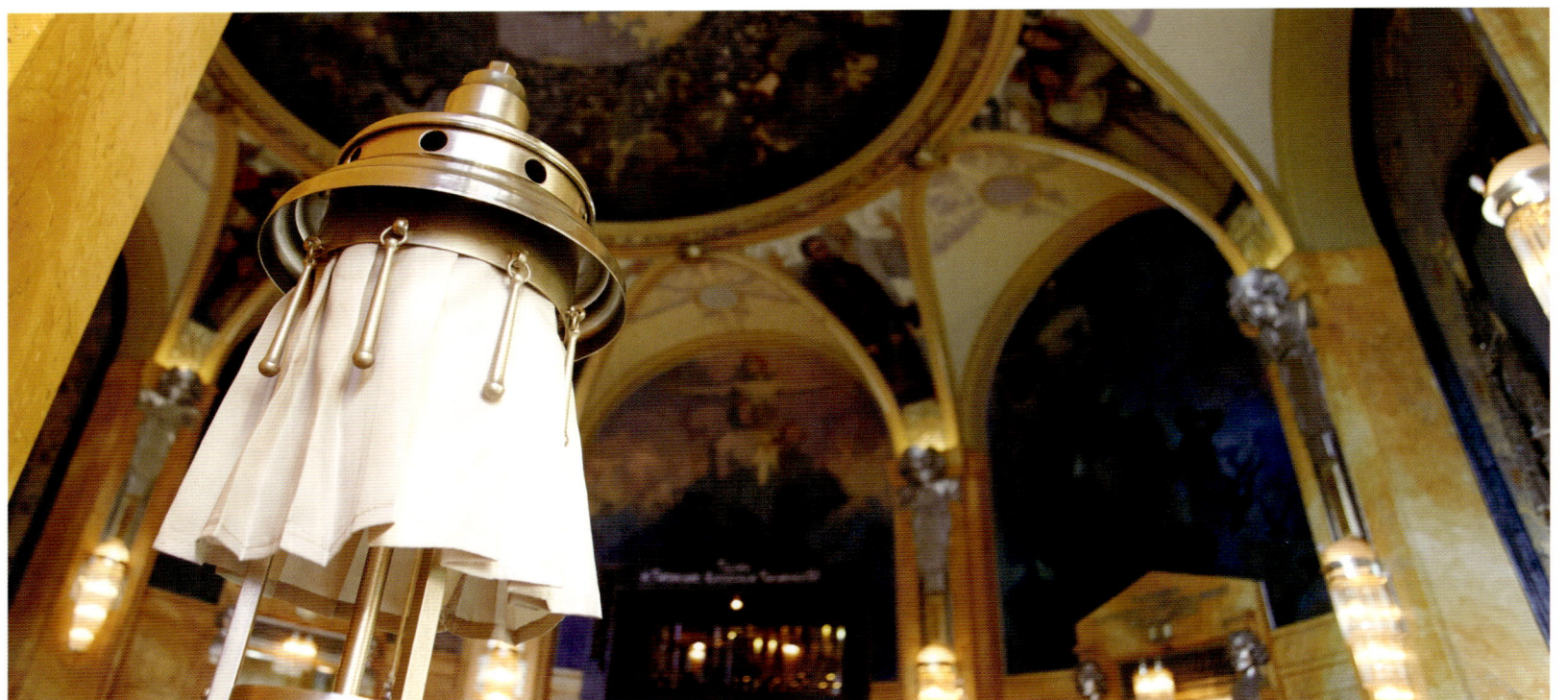

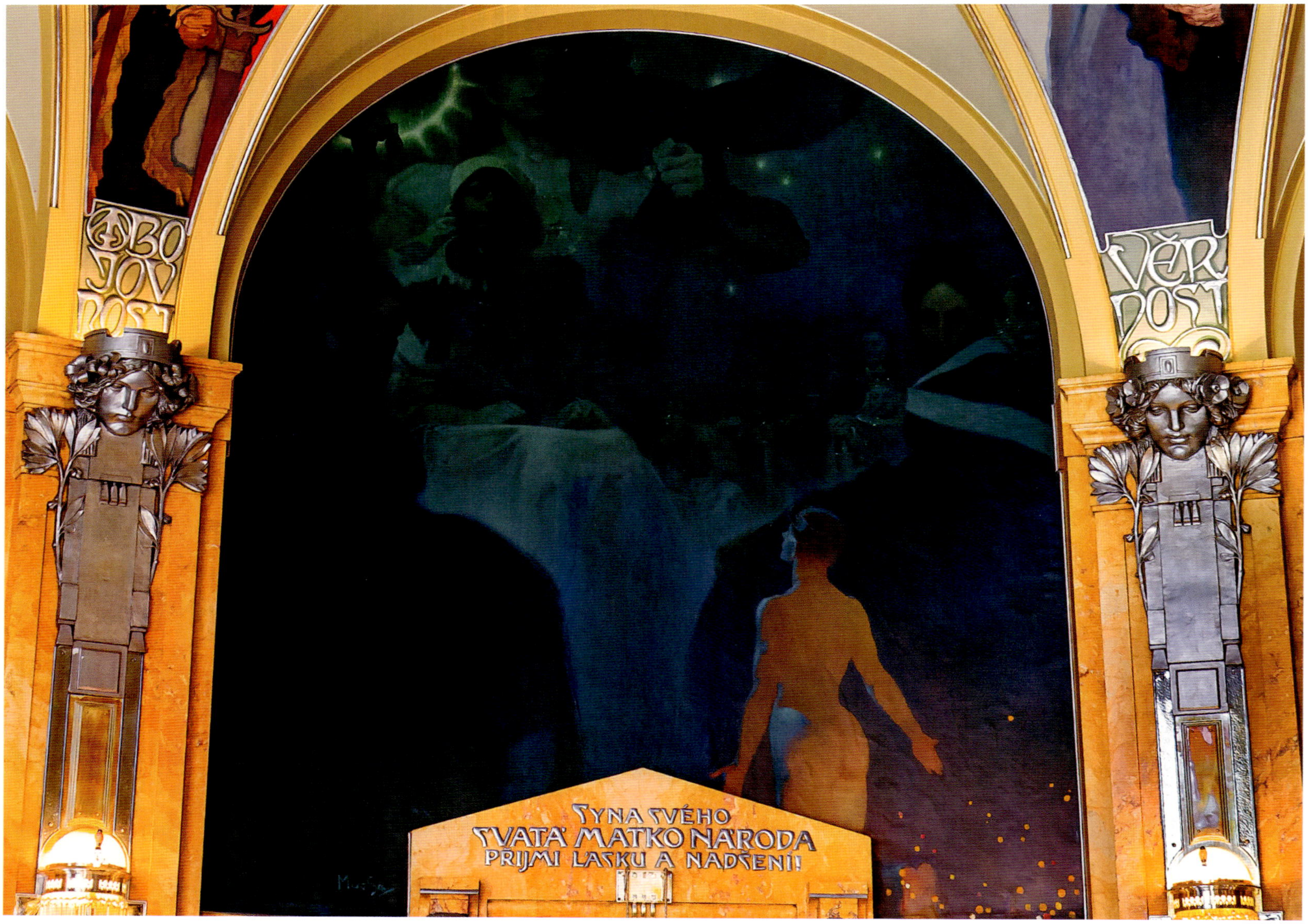

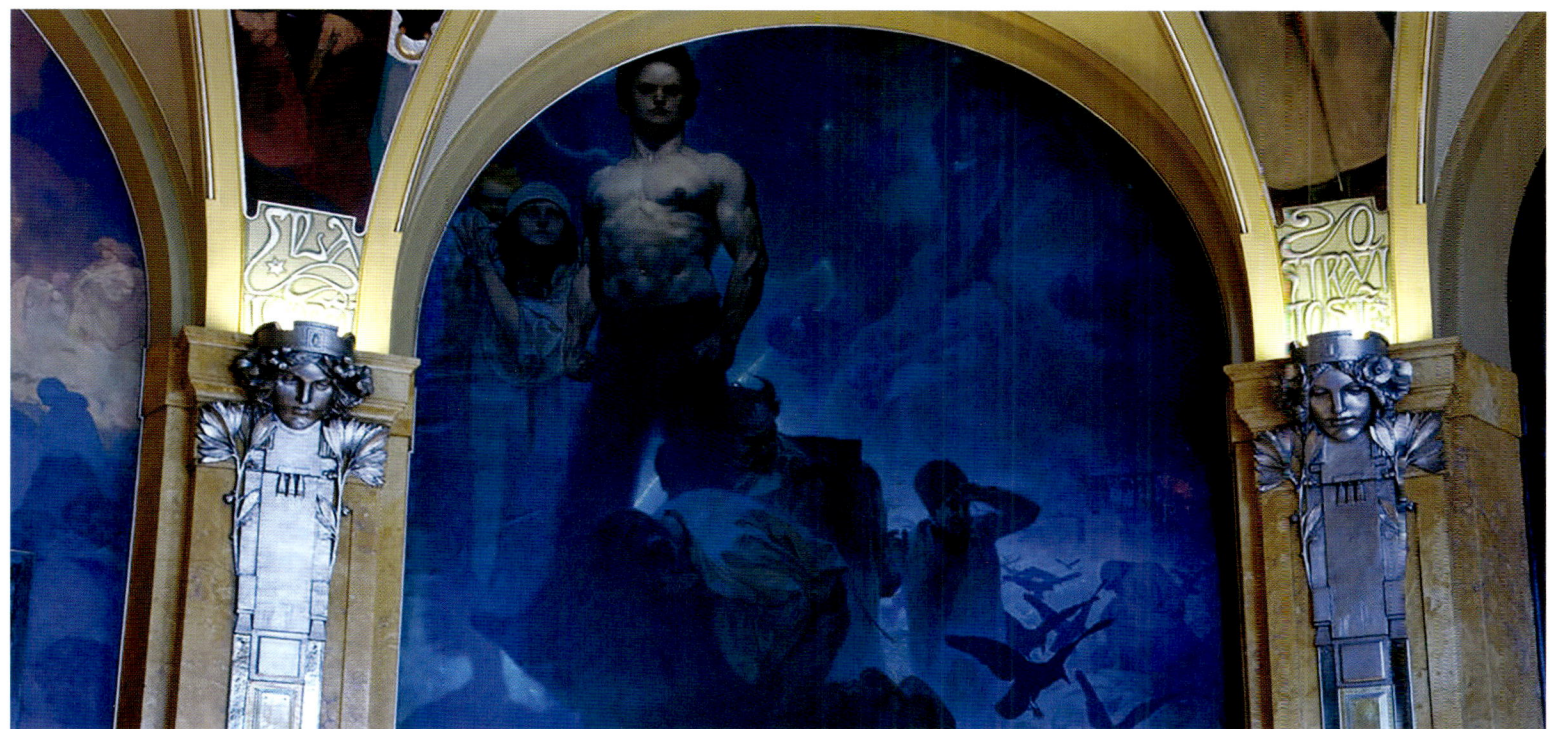

[ABOVE]
By Own Strength II: "Though humiliated and tortured, you will live again, my country!" (1910–1911). Fresco. Lord Mayor's Hall, Obecní Dům, Prague.

[OPPOSITE PAGE TOP]
Mucha designed all details of Lord Mayor's Hall, including the heating radiator grilles, windows, standing lighting, and drapes.

[OPPOSITE PAGE BOTTOM]
By Own Strength II: "Accept Love and Enthusiasm from Your Son, Mother of the Holy Nation" (1910–1911). Mural. Lord Mayor's Hall, Obecní Dům, Prague.

[RIGHT]
The center of Lord Mayor's Hall features paneled walls, stained glass windows, and a ring of chairs facing a desk.

[OVERLEAF]
"Slavic Concord" is the theme of the ceiling fresco. The composition is made up of figural motifs that form a circle with a view opening to the sky, shaded by the wings of an eagle in flight.

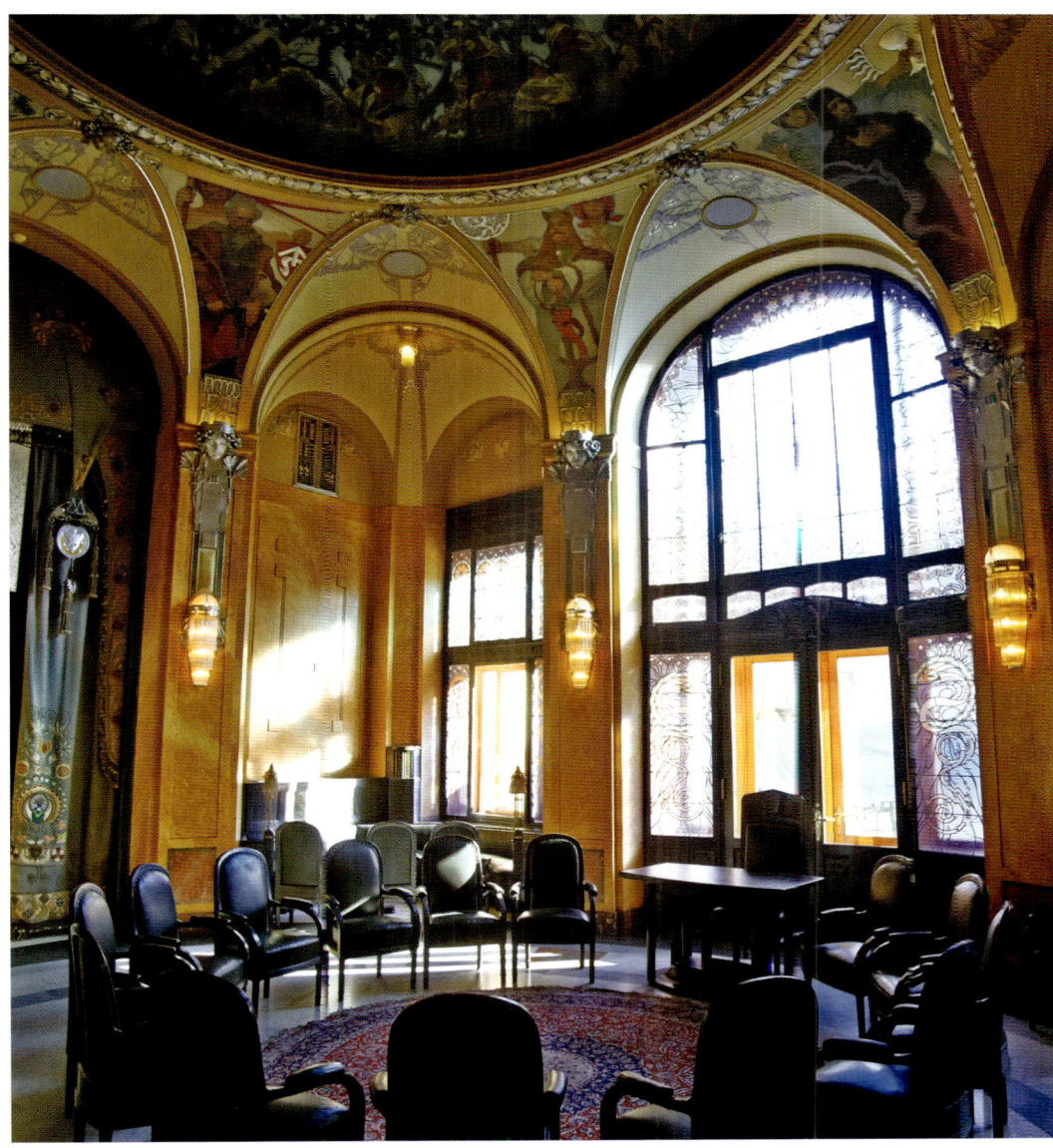

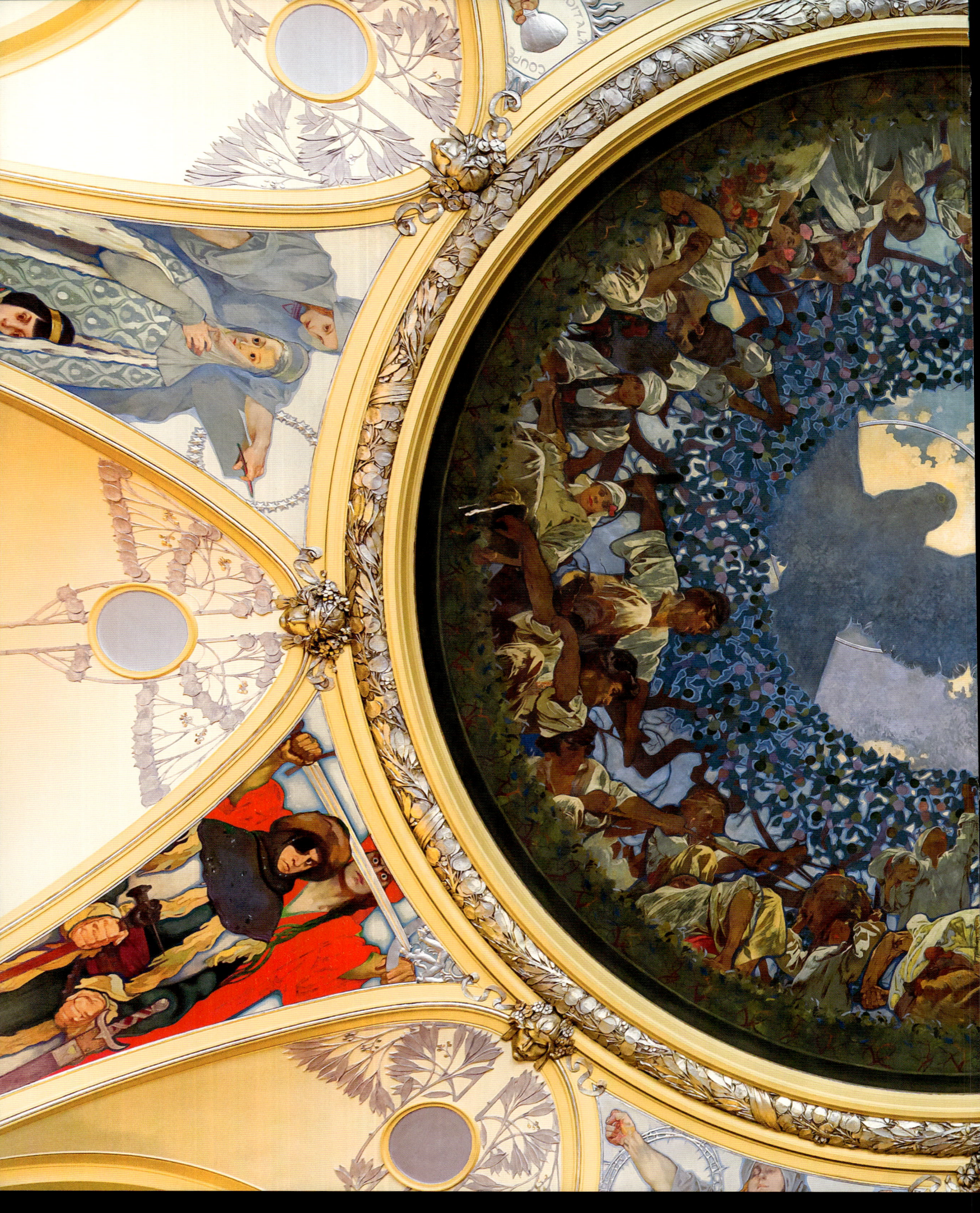

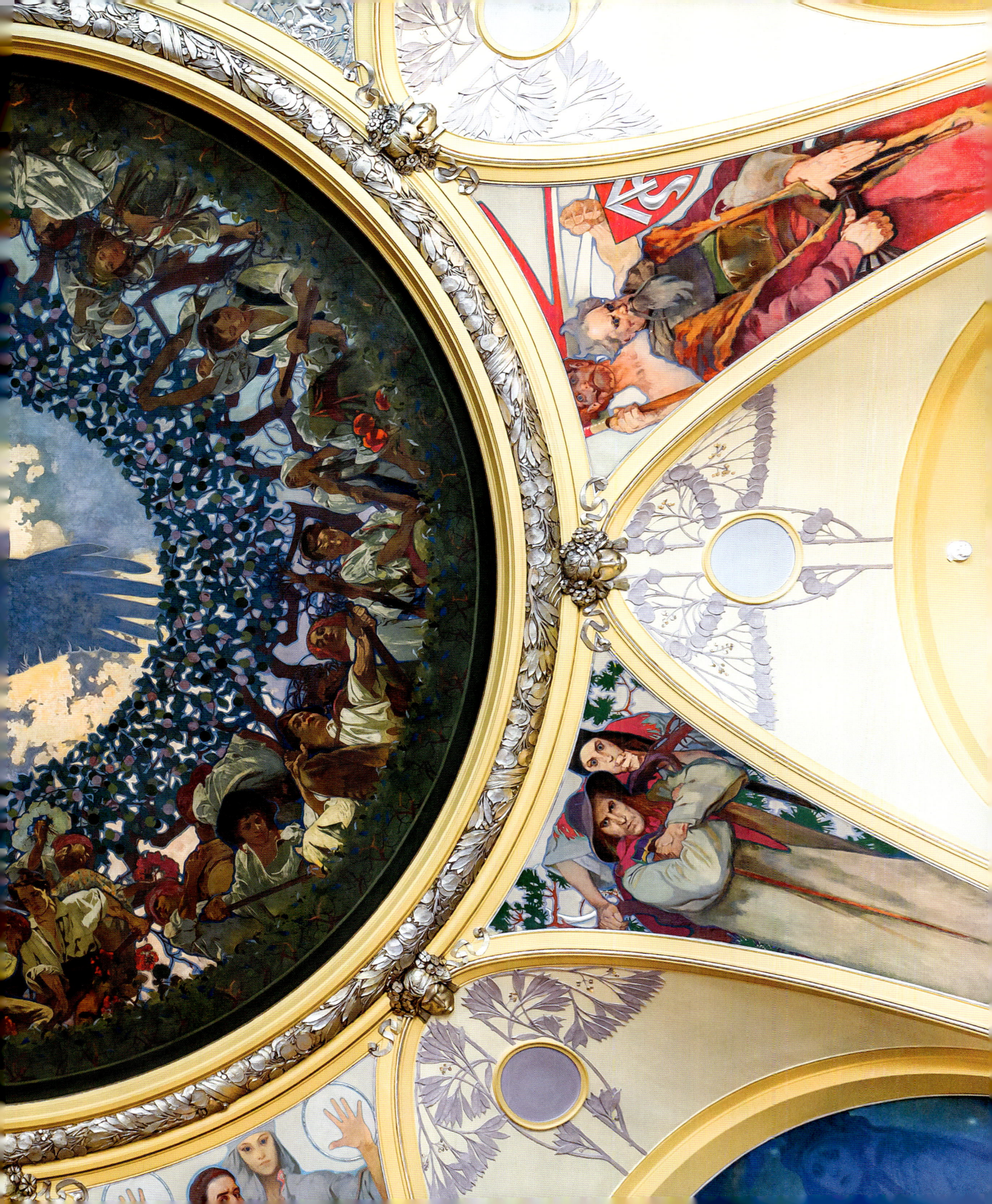

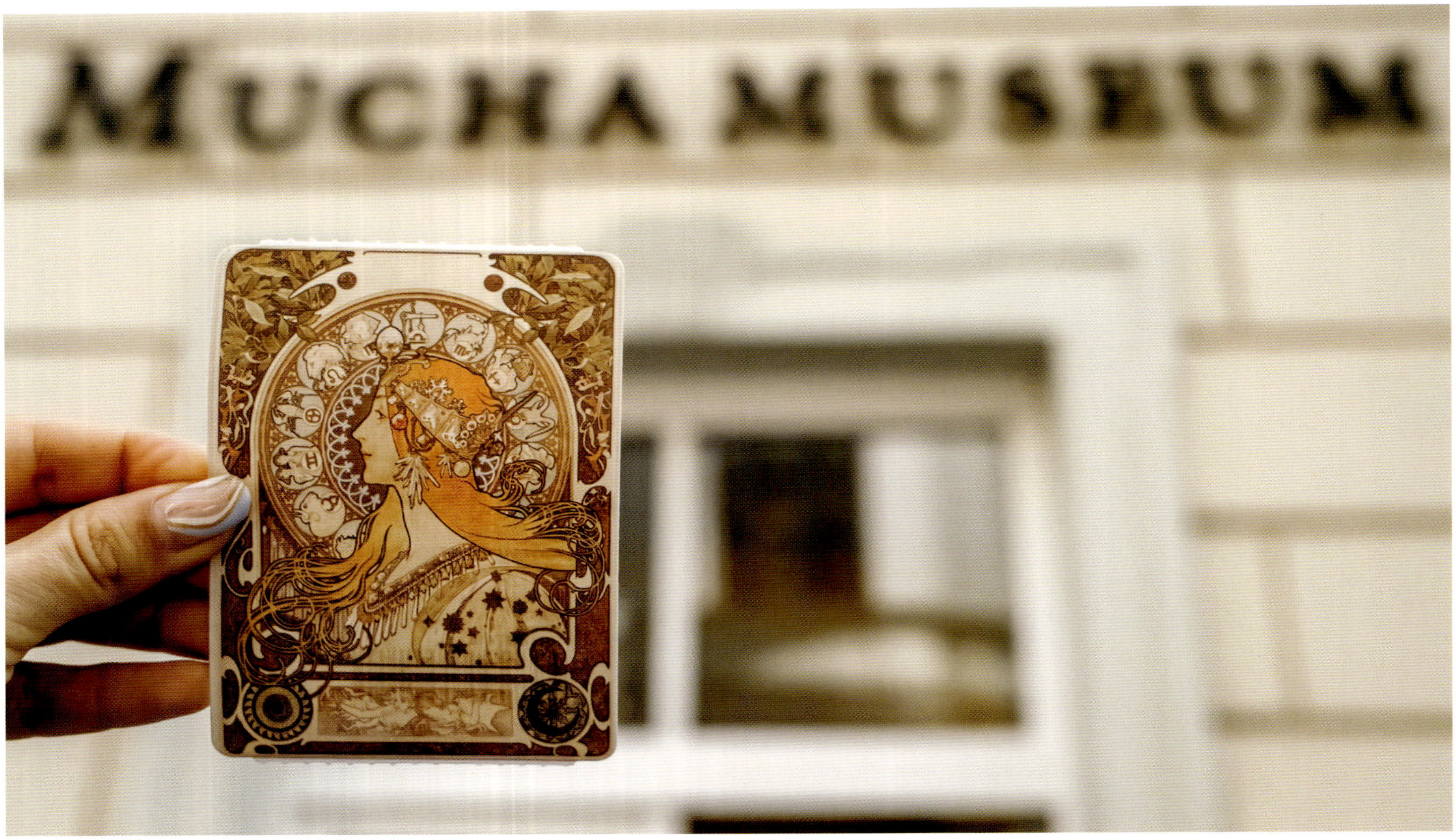

A museum entrance ticket with the Zodiac calendar image. The Mucha Museum is dedicated to the renowned painter, illustrator, and graphic artist.

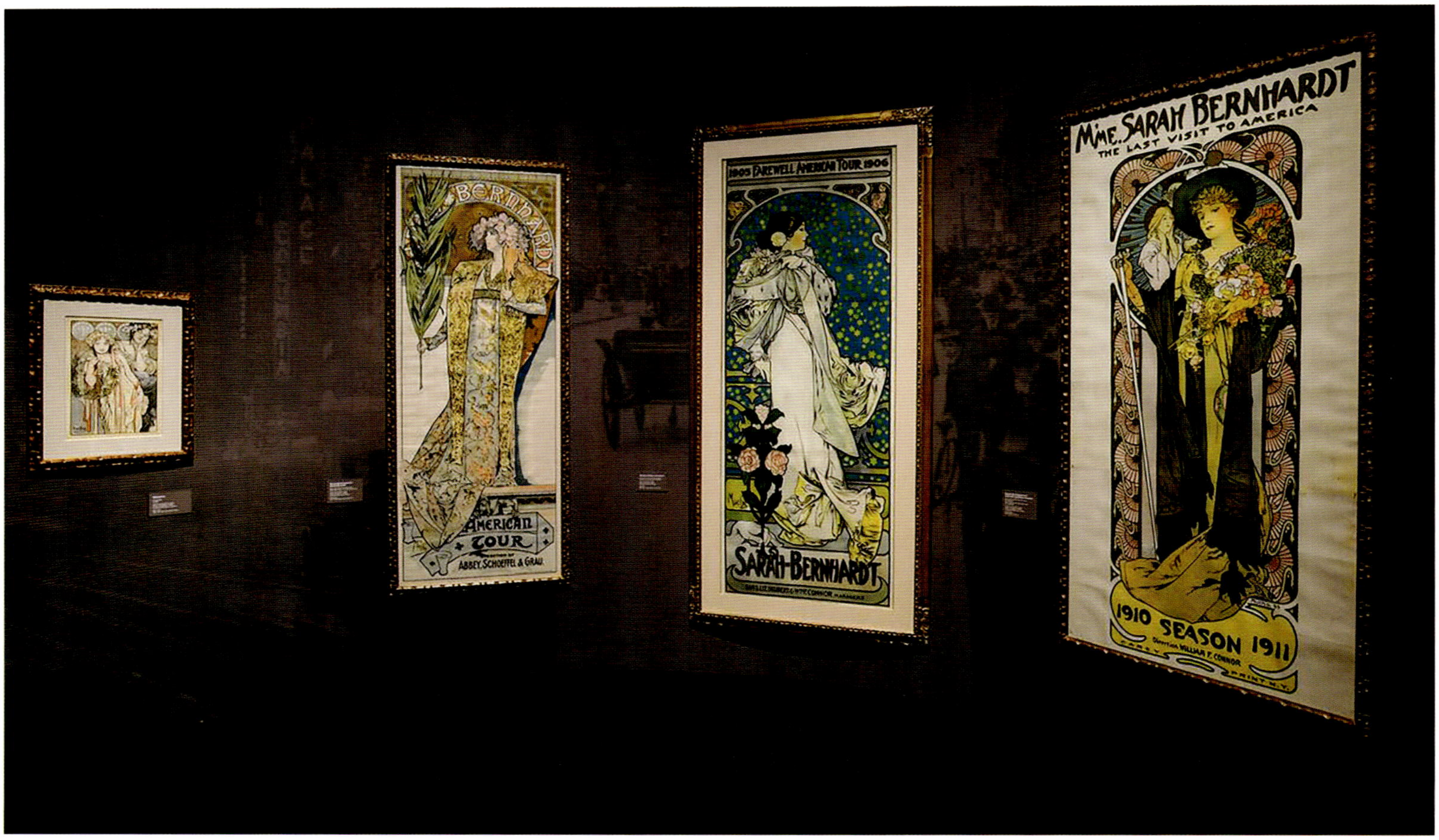

Gathered together on display in the museum are a collection of posters Mucha created to promote the plays of Sarah Bernhardt.

THE MUCHA MUSEUM

Dedicated to the life and work of Alphonse Mucha, the Mucha Museum in Prague holds an extraordinary collection of the artist's works. It was established in 1998 by the Mucha Foundation in partnership with COPA sro. All the works displayed in the museum are from the vast Mucha Trust Collection, which consists of approximately 3,000 works of art and approximately 4,000 photographs.

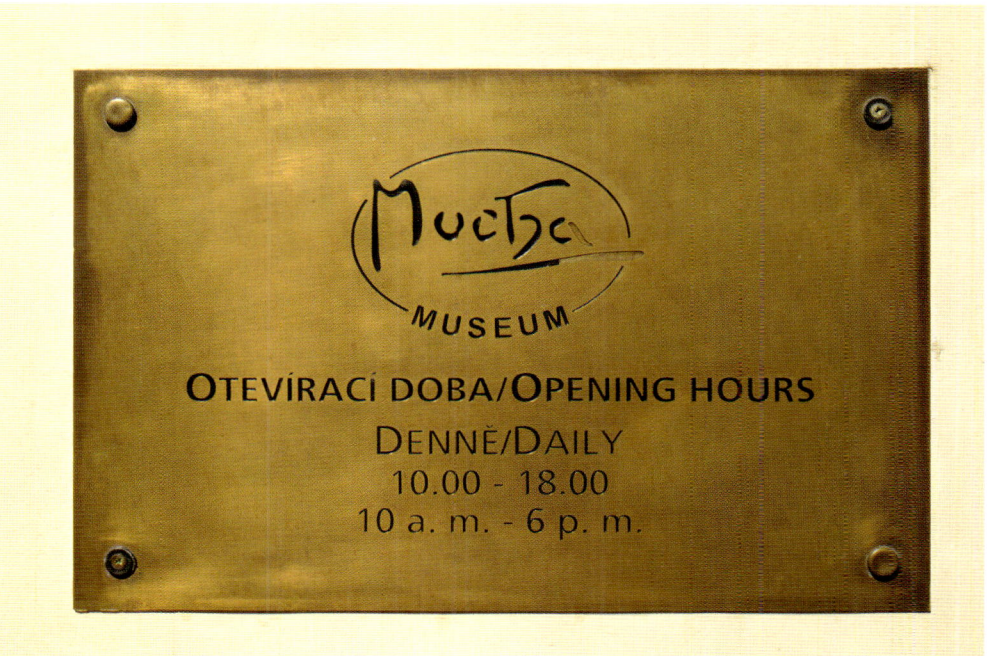

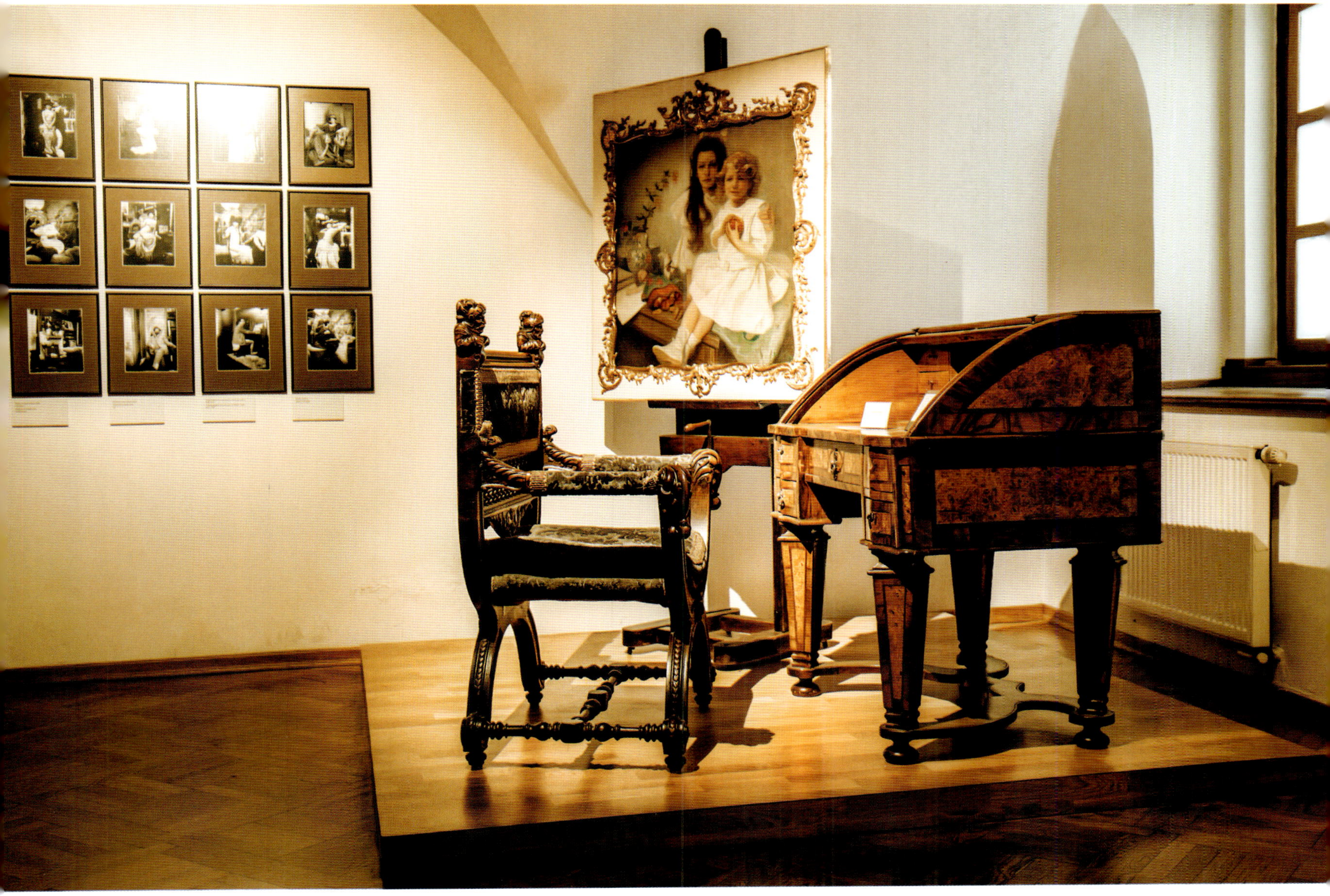

The artist's desk, chair, easel, and tools form a tableau.

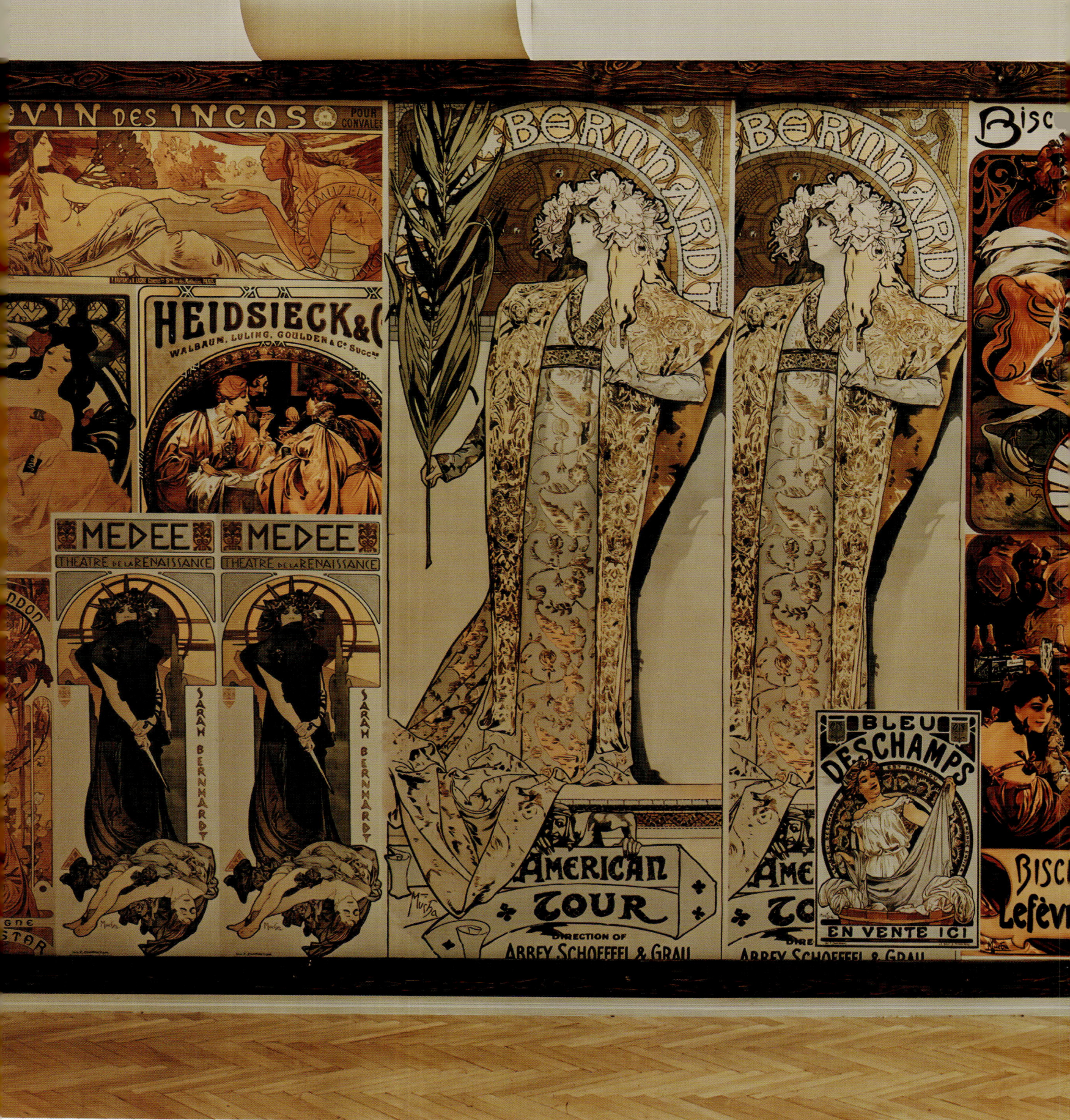

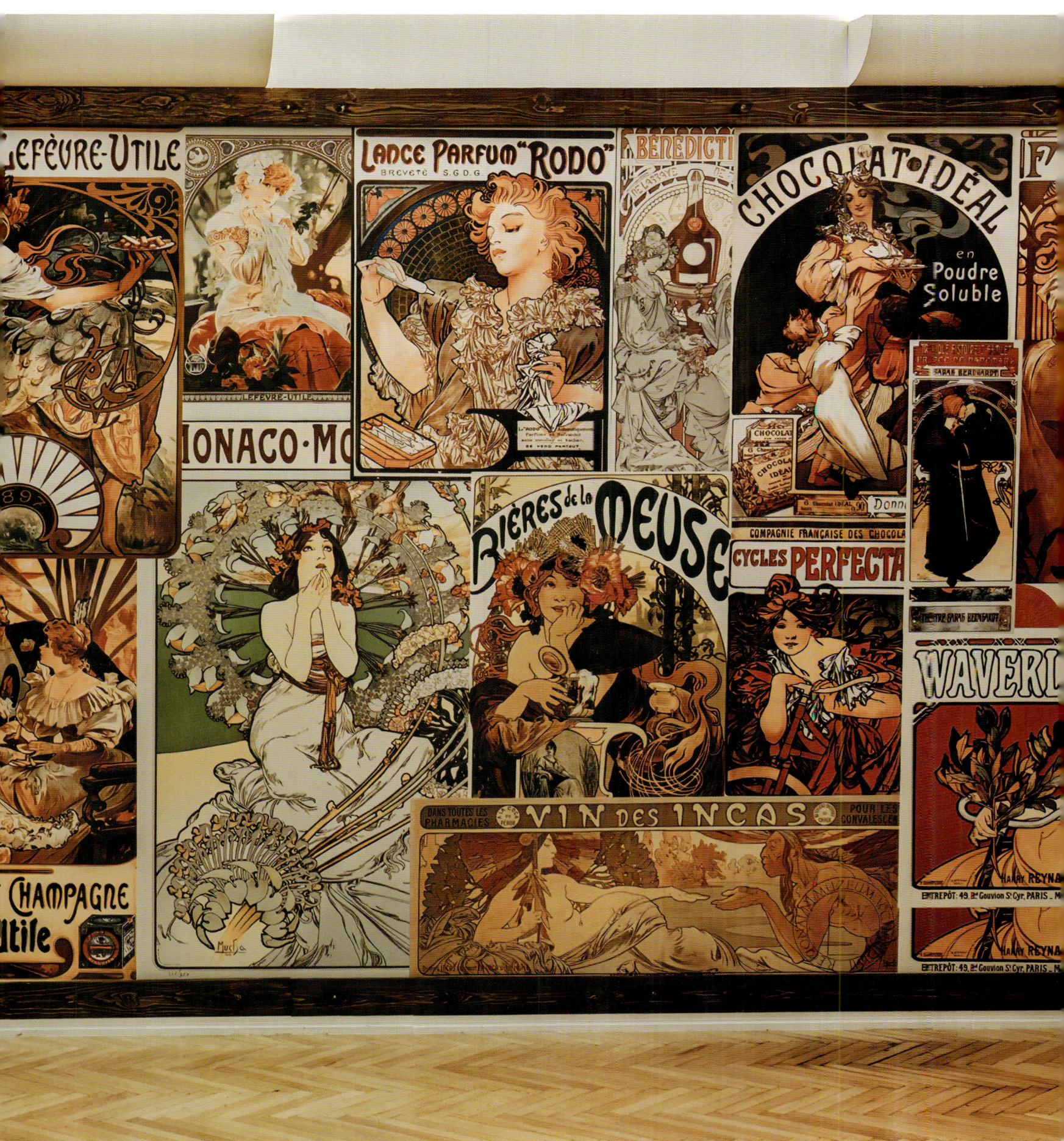

A gallery filled with Mucha posters pasted to a wall gives museum-goers a sense of how these large images appeared to Parisians on the street.

IMAGE CREDITS

All works are in the public domain, but the publisher and author would like to acknowledge the many museums that display the works of the artist. They would also like to acknowledge the following photographers for their photos of the artwork.

KEY

AL = Alamy Stock Photo
DT = Dreamstime.com
SS = Shutterstock.com

t = top   b = bottom   r = right   l = left

Cover: Bill Waterson/AL
Title page: Keith Corrigan/AL
Table of Contens: Keith Corrigan/AL
Introduction: 4 IanDagnall Computing/AL; 6–7 Historic Collection/AL
Background banner: Rjcvanhees/DT
Background: 8–9, 78–79, 102–103, 142–143 Helenlane/DT

POSTERS & PRINTS

8 Bill Waterson/AL; 10 RTRO/AL; 11l IanDagnall Computing/AL; 11r World History Archive/AL; 12l Bill Waterson/AL; 12r Archivart/AL; 13 Vintage Travel and Advertising Archive/AL; 14l Azoor Photo/AL; 14r Lordprice Collection/AL; 15l Archivart/AL; 15r Azoor Photo/AL; 16l Art Collection 2/AL; 16r incamerastock/AL; 17 The Protected Art Archive/AL; 18l Bill Waterson/AL; 18r Heritage Image Partnership Ltd /AL; 19t Archivart/AL; 19b Contraband Collection/AL; 20l Art Collection 2/AL; 20r Azoor Collection/AL; 21 Archivart/AL; 22l Realy Easy Star/AL; 22r JJs/AL; 23 Lordprice Collection/AL; 24 Pictorial Press Ltd/AL; 25l Archivart/AL; 25r IanDagnall Computing/AL; 26 IanDagnall Computing/AL; 27l JJs/AL; 27r Bill Waterson/AL; 28 Shawshots/AL; 29l incamerastock/AL; 29r Peter Horree/AL; 30 INTERFOTO /AL; 31 incamerastock/AL; 32 Painters/AL; 32–33 Neil Baylis/AL; 34 Archivart/AL; 35l incamerastock/AL; 35r Lordprice Collection/AL; 36l Painters/AL; 36r Bill Waterson/AL; 37 Archivart/AL; 38 World History Archive/AL; 39tl World History Archive/AL; 39tr World History Archive/AL; 39br World History Archive/AL; 40 Lordprice Collection/AL; 41l Lordprice Collection/AL; 41r steeve-x-art/AL; 42 Keith Corrigan/AL; 44 Azoor Photo/AL; 45 Heritage Image Partnership Ltd /AL; 46 JJs/AL; 47l Heritage Image Partnership Ltd /AL; 47r Artokoloro/AL; 48 Vintage Travel and Advertising Archive/AL; 49l Archivart/

AL; 49r Archivart/AL; 50 JJs/AL; 51 Heritage Image Partnership Ltd /AL; 52r Archivart/AL; 53l Bill Waterson/AL; 53r JJs/AL; 54 FineArt/AL; 55 Painters/AL; 56r Art Collection 3/AL; 57l Historic Collection/AL; 62 incamerastock/AL; 63 Photo 12/AL; 64 Vintage Images/AL; 65 Heritage Image Partnership Ltd /AL; 65 Klikk/DT; 66l Painters/AL; 66r Painters/AL; 67l Painters/AL; 67r Painters/AL; 68l History and Art Collection/AL; 68r Painters/AL; 69l Photo 12/AL; 69r History and Art Collection/AL; 70l Azoor Collection/AL; 70r Azoor Collection/AL; 71l Azoor Collection/AL; 71r Azoor Collection/AL; 72l The Artchives/AL; 72r The Artchives/AL; 73l The Artchives/AL; 73r The Artchives/AL; 74–75 Heritage Image Partnership Ltd /AL; 76–77 Heritage Image Partnership Ltd /AL

GRAPHIC DESIGN

78 Album/AL; 80t incamerastock/AL; 80b World History Archive/AL; 81 World History Archive/AL; 82bl Bill Waterson/AL; 83 JJs/AL; 85 Heritage Image Partnership Ltd /AL; 86 Peter Horree/AL; 87 Lordprice Collection/AL; 88t Heritage Image Partnership Ltd /AL; 88bl Peter Horree/AL; 88bm Peter Horree/AL; 88br Peter Horree/AL; 89 The Picture Art Collection/AL; 90 incamerastock/AL; 91tl IanDagnall Computing/AL; 91r Vintage Travel and Advertising Archive/AL; 93 Painters/AL; 94b Artokoloro/AL; 95 Album/AL; 96 JJs/AL; 99 Painters/AL; 100–101 Painters/AL; 101 Heritage Image Partnership Ltd /AL

FINE ART

102 Archivart/AL; 104 JJs/AL; 105tr Heritage Image Partnership Ltd /AL; 105b CTK/AL; 106tr Art Collection 4/AL; 106bl Keith Corrigan/AL; 107 Heritage Image Partnership Ltd /AL; 108 Painters/AL; 109l Artefact/AL; 109r Painters/AL; 110 Heritage Image Partnership Ltd /AL; 112 Heritage Image

Partnership Ltd /AL; 113tl Artefact/AL; 113tr The Picture Art Collection/AL; 113br Artefact/AL; 114 incamerastock/AL; 115 Heritage Image Partnership Ltd /AL; 116 Painters/AL; 117 Azoor Photo/AL; 118t PRISMA ARCHIVO/AL; 118b PRISMA ARCHIVO/AL; 119 Painters/AL; 120 Painters/AL; 121t The Print Collector /AL; 121b The Print Collector /AL; 122–123 Jiří Sedláček/Creative Commons: Attribution-ShareAlike 3.0 Unported; 132 Gainew Gallery/AL

OTHER MEDIA

142 Goga18128DT; 144 FulcanellliDT; 145t Jorisvo/DT; 145b Photofires/DT; 146–147 Alexanderxsmirnov/DT; 147 Jorisvo/DT; 148–149 Alexanderxsmirnov/DT; 150 Azoor Photo/AL; 151 Azoor Photo/AL; 152–153 Jorisvo/DT; 154t Aurelian Images/AL; 154b Aurelian Images/AL; 155t Jorisvo/DT; 155b Alexanderxsmirnov/DT; 156–157 Jorisvo/DT; 158 Jorisvo/DT; 159 Jorisvo/DT; 160–161 Jorisvo/DT; 164 Regan Vercruysse/Creative Commons: Attribution-NonCommercial-NoDerivs 2.0 Generic; 168bl The Picture Art Collection/AL; 169 Allstar Picture Library Limited./AL; 170 Azoor Photo Collection/AL; 171tl Azoor Photo/AL; 172tl PBarchive/AL; 172bl Album/AL; 173 The History Collection/AL; 174–175 Viennaslide/AL; 175bl PWB Images/AL; 175tr PWB Images/AL; 175br Viennaslide/AL; 176t Viennaslide/AL; 176bm PWB Images/AL; 176br PWB Images/AL; 177 Hemis/AL; 178tr PWB Images/AL; 178b Viennaslide/AL; 179 B.O'Kane/AL; 180 JJs/AL; 181t Viennaslide/AL; 182 Photogolfer/DT; 183 Jorge Royan/AL; 184t Petr Bonek/SS; 184 bPhotogolfer/DT; 185t Jorge Royan/AL; 185b Petr Bonek/SS; 186–187 Photogolfer/DT; 188t Csklyarova/DT; 188b CTK/AL; 189t Vodolej/DT; 189b Csklyarova/DT; 190–191 Csklyarova/DT; 192t Credit: Universal Images Group North America LLC/ AL, 192b JJs/AL

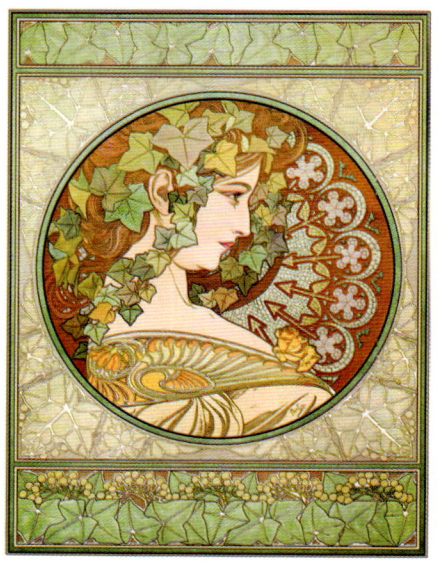

Laurel (1901). Color lithograph.

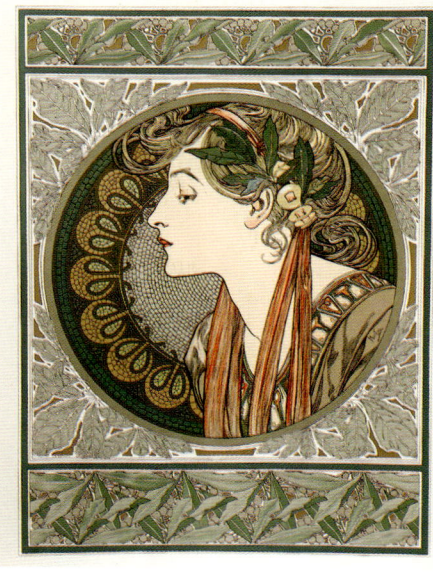

Laurel (1901). Color lithograph.